DECISION SUPPORT AND EXPERT SYSTEMS

William E. Leigh

Associate Professor
Computer Science
University of Southern Mississippi
Hattiesburg, Mississippi

Michael E. Doherty

Adjunct Assistant Professor
Quantitative Analysis
University of Cincinnati
Cincinnati, Ohio

Published by

J91 **SOUTH-WESTERN PUBLISHING CO.**

CINCINNATI   WEST CHICAGO, IL   DALLAS   PELHAM MANOR, NY   LIVERMORE, CA

ISBN: 0-538-10910-6

Library of Congress Catalog Card Number: 85-61785

1 2 3 4 5 6 7 8 D 9 8 7 6

Printed in the United States of America

CONTENTS

PREFACE

DECISION SUPPORT SYSTEMS: AN EMERGING DISCIPLINE

The wide availability of computers has affected the way people think, make decisions, and solve problems. For many years, the availability of computers was limited to large systems accessible only to technicians or to recipients of special technical assistance. With the flood of microcomputers, however, has come the opportunity to do elaborate computation for problems faced by managers at lower levels or even by individuals in their private lives. Businesspeople, other professionals, and problem solvers in general are assembling personal decision-aiding systems that are based on capabilities of personal computers.

These phenomena are related: Computers support human thinking processes and are also becoming more generally available. In turn, application of computers as decision making aids has led to an accelerating academic interest—through both research and course offerings—in a discipline that has come to be known as *Decision Support Systems (DSS)*.

DSS Implementation

Implementing a DSS requires an interdisciplinary endeavor. There is very little new in the specific set of factors or theories encompassed. The disciplines involved include behavioral, organizational, computational, and information processing. Creation and use of DSS cuts across all of these specialties as an underlying focus on an integrated process for decision making.

Building a DSS always involves an effort to synthesize what is known about decision making and to make that knowledge available to and effective in the hands of working decision makers. Usually, implementation of a DSS involves development of computer software (sometimes hardware as well) for application of appropriate knowledge and techniques. Software is also a convenient way to distribute (and derive income from) DSS techniques.

A typical definition sees a DSS as a "computer-based system that aids decision making." Although it is broad enough to be a catchall, this definition is essentially correct. Implied by this definition, however, is a series of activities that might be necessary to implement a DSS. These activities can include:

- Software development
- Programming
- Selection of software packages
- Application of decision theory
- Training of users.

Types of DSS

Deciding about the appropriateness of a DSS involves several dimensions of evaluation. For example, decision making can be empirical, or data based. If so, a good system would include a modern database management system (DBMS) and associated data collection and retrieval capabilities. Other requirements would include subsystems associated with the DBMS that provide capabilities for statistical analysis and graphics.

Decision making also can be analytical, or model based. Support for a model-based DSS would include operations research tools such as linear programming. In addition, the modeling tools would have to be subject to integration with data manipulation tools. This is because modeling can have an empirical dimension—as is present in setting parameters for a given situation.

Decision making also can be heuristic, or based upon rules of thumb. A module for a DBMS supporting a heuristically oriented DSS might be an expert system. An expert system has properties of artificial intelligence. That is, the system exhibits capabilities to respond to learning by users on the basis of experience.

In practice, a database management system (DBMS), analytic models, and expert system features might all be combined into a hybrid system providing decision assistance. This hybridization and integration of methods forms the area in which DSS research efforts are currently being concentrated. These relationships also account for a significant amount of content within this book that deals with expert systems.

User Requirements

Effective use of computer-aided decision making requires, in turn, an effective human-machine interface. Accordingly, major DSS concerns center around the interactions between decision makers and their computer-provided tools. Specific concerns include graphics packages, menus, command languages, and other aids. Therefore, as a discipline, DSS serves to form a link for research and application efforts by decision theorists, computer scientists, management scientists, and mathematicians. The role of the DSS specialist lies in the realm of engineering—engineering of computer-administered vehicles for decision making through use of the bodies of knowledge provided by established, more theoretical branches of study.

ABOUT THIS TEXT

This textbook supports the CIS-10 course of the Model Curriculum for Undergraduate Computer Information Systems Education of the Data Processing Management Association Education Foundation (DPMA-EF). The CIS-10 course of this curriculum is entitled *Decision Support Systems*. The course is designed as an upper-division elective for students who are presumed to have previous grounding in the principles of computer information systems. Beyond the obvious appeal to CIS majors, this course (and the text) are expected to have considerable appeal for general business majors who are prospective users of DSS and expert systems.

Learning Orientation

Two alternate approaches may be used in building student knowledge about decision support systems. These are bottom-up or top-down. Under the bottom-up approach, components are examined individually and accumulated gradually into full systems. Under the top-down method, an overall perspective is established first. Then, the total picture is dissected into parts for closer examination.

For a text and course aimed at undergraduates, the authors have elected to use the bottom-up approach for the main portion of the instruction. This makes it possible to understand and apply individual components one at a time. Examples include the DBMS, statistical packages, and so on. Comprehensible components can then be combined to support more complex, interrelated, decision requirements. However, the book does begin with a background briefing that indoctrinates students, establishing an understanding about what a DSS is and why a DSS is useful.

Following the background briefing, students are introduced to a specially designed, pedagogically oriented tool kit of fourth-generation software modules that can be used to construct decision support systems. This tool kit provides a simple, relatively easy basis for student understanding and success in building workable DSS elements. This modular approach is a major, unique feature of this book, one that helps assure comprehension and successful implementation of DSS programs within a single semester of instruction.

All of the BASIC source code students will need to implement the DSS tool kit is given in an appendix of this text. If further assistance is needed, the authors can provide tool kit modules on a single diskette for use on an IBM PC or compatible microcomputer.

ACKNOWLEDGMENTS

The practical, implementation-centered orientation and content of this book reflects contributions of two colleagues of the authors, Noemi Paz and Dr. John Gersting.

The experience from which much of the content of this book was derived resulted from support of Dr. David R. Adams, chairman of the CIS department at Northern Kentucky University. It was the support of Dr. Adams that made possible early establishment of a course required for all CIS and other business majors at Northern Kentucky. Three years of teaching experience in this course provided an opportunity for the research and development that led to creation of the DSS tool kit that complements the content of this book.

BACKGROUND I

This portion of the book has two chapters which introduce, first, the principles and needs for decision support systems (DSS) and, second, the elements of managerial decision making that lend themselves to computerized assistance.

Chapter 1 distinguishes between traditional information processing through computers and computerized decision support systems. Decision support systems are designed primarily for access to computer-stored information on a relatively unstructured basis that is determined by the needs and mental processes of the human decision maker. This is a different departure point than that which drives transaction-driven information systems. Most traditional information systems are designed to produce specific outputs to support transactions or to assist specific personnel in job performance.

An important capability of a DSS, it is stressed, lies in support of "what if . . . ?" speculations by managers and planners. The second chapter illustrates use of DSS principles by describing problems and decisions made by managers according to basic categories: structured, semi-structured, and unstructured. Simple case examples are presented to show how availability of a computerized database can provide support and guidance in managerial decision making.

1 DECISION SUPPORT SYSTEMS: INTRODUCTION AND OVERVIEW

Abstract

- DSS is oriented to decision making rather than to information processing.

- DSS is for semi-structured problems. The degree of structure in a problem is a function of the problem solver's knowledge and/or experience.

- A DSS can be thought of as a problem-solving "tool kit." Such a tool kit architecture might be called a "generic component" DSS.

- An important facility of any DSS is an ability to provide "what if . . . ?" analysis—that is, to simulate the effects of various alternative solutions.

- Problem solving is central to what managers do. Problem solving may be thought of as having the phases: problem identification and definition, generation and evaluation of alternatives, and implementation.

- A DSS is usually valuable only in the alternative evaluation part of the problem-solving process.

- A DSS is the product of knowledge, research, and skills derived from many disciplines. Computer science and computer engineering, along with management science, contribute to DSS, which is a recent focus of the applied field called "computer information systems."
- A DSS can be used for any type of decision making, but this book concentrates on its use in business organizations.

DEFINITION AND CHARACTERISTICS

A *decision support system (DSS)* is a set of computer-based tools used by a manager in connection with his or her problem-solving and decision-making duties. The manager, of course, makes the actual decisions and solves specific problems.

Within a management context, a *problem* is any situation or condition that requires change or adjustment to conform to the operating guidelines and/or goals of an organization. A problem may come to light through the mechanism of an organization's control system (such as the income statement that shows a loss for a division). A problem also may be found directly by the manager ("I think we need a new advertising slogan.").

Decisions are necessary steps in problem solving. Decision making within organizations is achieved through a process approach. There are many variations in decision-making process structures. However, there are also common elements that appear in the processes used within most organizations. Figure 1-1 is a schematic showing a decision-making process that will be used for the purposes of illustration in this book.

As indicated, the process of reaching a decision to solve a problem begins with identification of the problem itself. Once a problem is identified, it must be defined before it can be solved. A problem definition is a statement of a problem in operational terms. That is, the definition statement covers the aspects of the situation that must be corrected, or changed. To qualify for decision-making assistance from

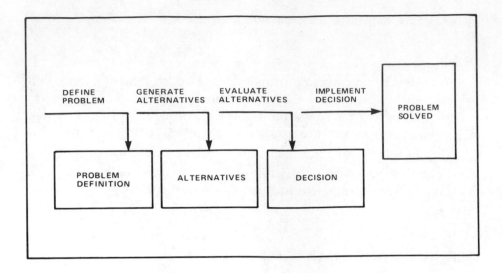

Figure 1-1. This diagram shows the steps in and outputs of the decision-making process. Outputs include a problem definition, a description of alternatives, and a final decision statement identifying the alternative or combination of alternatives to be implemented.

a computerized DSS, a problem should have a quantifiable dimension that can provide criteria for evaluation of alternative, candidate solutions.

When there is a problem definition, alternative solutions can be developed and evaluated using the evaluation criteria of the problem definition. The decision, then, is the choice of the one solution for implementation from among the alternative candidates.

THE ROLE OF COMPUTERS IN DECISION MAKING

Most of the steps in the decision-making process cannot be aided to any great extent by a DSS. This statement reflects a special meaning and role for decision support systems within overall, corporate computer information systems (CIS) programs. A DSS, as the term is used throughout this book, describes one of three types, or levels, of computer systems typically implemented under an overall CIS function. These three types of computer systems are:

- Data processing (DP) systems
- Management information systems (MIS)
- Decision support systems (DSS).

The relationships and organizational levels of these three types of systems are shown graphically in Figure 1-2.

Data Processing (DP) Systems

A *data processing (DP) system*, broadly, incorporates a set of procedures that handle one or more types of related business transactions. Examples of transactions processed under DP systems include payroll, billing, accounts receivable, accounts payable, inventory control, purchasing, and others. Each DP system, typically, is called an application.

Within the organization, as shown in Figure 1-2, DP systems support the broad base of operations. Any decisions required typically involve individual transactions: Should an order for an out-of-stock item be back ordered? Should a customer's credit be approved for purchase of ordered items? Has a given employee reached the cutoff point for social security deductions?

Data processing systems can be characterized as handlers of masses of transactions that, in turn, produce large volumes of data. As a matter of fact, data can take on avalanche proportions; storage peripherals that support many DP applications have capacities running into many megabytes, even gigabytes.

Herein lies a problem associated with possible use of files of DP systems in managerial decision making. That is, data volumes are too large. It is impossible to assess overall meaning because there is just too much detail. Accordingly, the power of computers has been used to summarize the data, reducing volumes and adding meaning to reports and inquiries.

Management Information Systems (MIS)

A *management information system (MIS)* summarizes and selects data from massive DP files so as to add meaning to system outputs. The process, overall, is often referred to as *exception reporting*, or *management by exception*.

In an MIS, managers implant data selection criteria based on content relevance within computer programs. A typical example can be seen in those systems that deal with inventory control and purchasing for stock replenishment. Each time that the DP order-processing

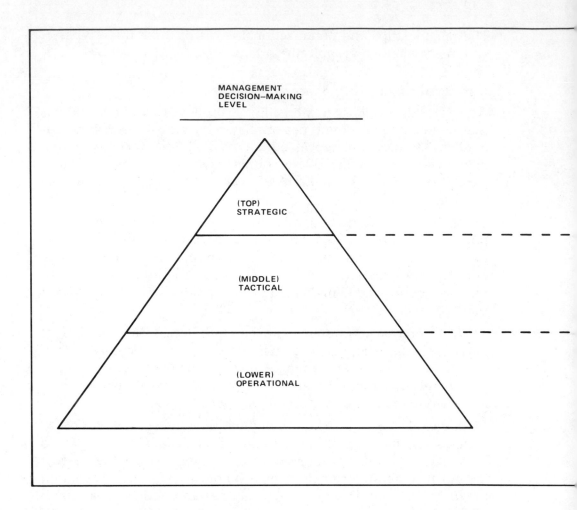

MANAGEMENT
DECISION–MAKING
LEVEL

(TOP)
STRATEGIC

(MIDDLE)
TACTICAL

(LOWER)
OPERATIONAL

Figure 1-2. Important information sources for decision support systems are derived from all levels of computer information systems. Operational and managerial information files are summarized or selected to produce data appropriate for management decisions.

application is run, the inventory stock levels for ordered items are reduced to reflect purchases and are increased to reflect replenishment orders or returns from customers. Thus, current inventory levels are reflected in item records.

INFORMATION REQUIRED FOR	TYPE OF CIS SUPPORT
PLANNING LONG–TERM POLICY DECISIONS AND PLANNING FOR FUTURE COMMITMENT OF A COMPANY'S RESOURCES	DECISION SUPPORT SYSTEM (DSS)
CONTROLLING COMPARING RESULTS OF OPERATIONS WITH PLANS AND ADJUSTING PLANS OR OPERATIONS ACCORDINGLY	MANAGEMENT INFORMATION SYSTEM (MIS)
OPERATING MAINTAINING BUSINESS RECORDS AND FACILITATING THE FLOW OF WORK IN A COMPANY	DATA PROCESSING SYSTEM (DP)

Following each transaction, stock levels for items can be evaluated by the program under a variety of exception-reporting techniques. One method is to incorporate minimum and maximum stock levels for each product into the item records. These stock level entries are provided by purchasing management. Another method is to apply an algorithm that computes usage history of the item and determines the length of time existing stocks will last. The algorithm would use a time factor in identifying exception items. For example, the program might identify all items with less than a 45-day supply on hand as exceptions. Under whatever method is used, exception items are flagged and are included in reports or displays provided for managers.

The exception-reporting feature of an MIS serves to focus management attention according to data relevance: If 90 percent of the items in inventory are within normal quantity levels, it is most profitable to focus management attention on the 10 percent of items that represent exceptions.

As this illustration indicates, MIS procedures are particularly helpful in dealing with problems that have known structures and are susceptible to solutions based on past experience. Problem solving of this type is often associated with the so-called tactical level of management. The term *tactical* implies ongoing operations within which decisions can be based on known quantities and/or standards. Within a DSS context, the identifying trait for this type of decision lies in its structured nature.

The inventory-ordering application is an example involving a continuing series of structured problems and decisions. That is, for the manager in this situation, there is a familiarity with the conditions and criteria encountered. There are reliable precedents that can be applied in making decisions. In effect, it is the knowledge and experience of the manager that identify a problem as structured and an area of management as tactical. For the same company's advertising manager, the same inventory problem might shape up as highly unstructured. Also, before the algorithm was developed and the MIS implemented, the problem was unstructured in the eyes of the managers responsible for inventory. At this juncture too, the planning involved might have been classified as strategic rather than tactical. Examples of how some basic, common problems might be viewed from structured, semi-structured, and unstructured perspectives are given in Figure 1-3.

The point: The nature of problems and the appropriate approach to their solution often depend on the situation, the experience, and the applicable knowledge of the problem solver.

Decision Support Systems (DSS)

The degree of structure present for the solution of a problem represents the key dividing criterion for applicability of DSS techniques. In this sense, the term *structure* is used inclusively. Structure includes the availability of appropriate data and standards. But

STRUCTURED	SEMI–STRUCTURED	UNSTRUCTURED
DETECT OUT–OF–BALANCE CHECKBOOK	FIND DEPOSIT NOT ENTERED IN CHECKBOOK	PREVENT CHECKBOOK ERRORS IN FUTURE
DRIVE CAR HOME	DIAGNOSE ENGINE NOT STARTING	DESIGN A CAR WHICH ALWAYS STARTS
CALCULATE PAYMENT ON CAR LOAN	FIND BANK TO LOAN MONEY	BECOME RICH ENOUGH NOT TO NEED LOAN
CALCULATE PRICE OF STOCK TRANSACTION	SELECT A GROUP OF STOCKS MEETING CERTAIN INVESTMENT CRITERIA	PREDICT ACCURATELY THE ACTION OF THE STOCK MARKET TOMORROW
FILL OUT SHORT FORM	DETERMINE DEPRECIATION POLICY FOR CORPORATION'S INCOME TAXES	REVAMP THE INCOME TAX CODE FOR THE U.S.

Figure 1-3. This table illustrates varying viewpoints for identification of problems and the formulation of decisions. Breakdowns are for structured, semi-structured, and unstructured approaches to decision making.

structure is also highly individual, dependent largely on the knowledge and experience of the individual problem solver.

A *decision support system (DSS)*, at this writing, is most appropriate to the range of problems that lie between the extremes of highly structured and highly unstructured solution patterns. An inventory reordering decision based on a long-established algorithm is a typical example of a structured problem—for the manager experienced in this area of operations. On the other hand, an unstructured problem-solving situation would probably exist if the same manager were assigned to select a new advertising agency for his or her company.

In between the extremes of structured and unstructured problems are a category of problem-solving situations that can be called *semi-structured*. Decision support systems lend themselves best to the selection of decision alternatives devised to deal with semi-structured problems.

DSS capabilities are generally applied to the managerial area classified as strategic planning. Unfortunately, tactical and strategic planning are often defined in terms of time frames, rather than in relation to their relative missions. Tactical planning, as described above, deals with ongoing situations involving application of known principles or standards. Strategic planning deals with situations that encompass some element of the unknown, that cannot be predicted with certainty. Strategic planning often does involve the future, but not necessarily the long-range future. Rather, the identifying characteristic lies in the semi-structured nature of the problem being faced.

Consider a not-unusual example: The chief executive of a company learns that there is an immediate opportunity to bid for purchase of a controlling interest of a leading competitor. This is no time to say that the decision is strategic and, therefore, cannot be dealt with for five years. The problem is both strategic and immediate. Another important distinction is that the problem is semi-structured. There are enough known elements to lend themselves to modeling under DSS techniques. For example, data can be assembled on the other company's marketing and financial performance. These data can be intermixed with data on the company's own operation.

Managers can then follow the dictates of their own intellects to establish comparative criteria or standards. The effect is a series of ''what if . . . ?'' simulations that regard the two separate entities as though they were being operated as a single, merged organization. There are no firm rules about what conditions would lead to either an affirmative or a negative decision. The manager must reach a subjective conclusion. But the burden is lessened by the availability of DSS-derived scenarios that could not be created through human capabilities alone.

The point is that the structure of a problem is defined by the person who perceives of and attempts to solve the problem. Thus, it is difficult to define problem structures in any absolute manner. This concept of problem-structure definition is especially important in understanding decision support systems. The computer is only a tool, albeit a powerful tool. People must define the structure of a problem and the criteria involved in evaluating the problem.

Decisions for semi-structured problems involve consideration of elements that are well known, partially known, and unknown. In such situations, a DSS can call upon existing data resources generated by DP and MIS applications. In addition, data or hypotheses that are completely external to existing CIS applications can be combined with existing information resources. The result is a picture that requires human judgment—and possibly further manipulation—as a basis for selection of alternatives.

In terms of the problem-solving model in Figure 1-1, a DSS establishes an environment in which problem identification can be aided by the organization's control system (the MIS). A tree-structured diagram showing a possible relationship of an MIS to a series of DSS packages devised for separate purposes is shown in Figure 1-4.

Generating alternative, candidate solutions is a task for human creativity. Implementation is beyond the scope of the DSS. Thus, the only aspect of problem solving that involves the DSS is the choosing of the "best" alternative.

To support the choice of an alternative, the DSS can aid the manager by providing several valuable tools, including:

- The DSS can search historical databases for the results of similar decisions in the past.
- Computational models can be applied to help predict the outcome of possible decisions.
- Graphic displays based upon past history can be generated to help detect trends that might affect the current decision.
- Quantified estimates can be developed to project the impact of each of the alternative solutions under consideration.

This problem-solving process of finding and defining the problem, generating alternatives and selecting one, and then implementing the chosen decision is present at all levels of business, and, indeed, in everything you do. This process is central to managing individual and organizational efforts in business, government, education, and the professions. The process may be implicit, as it is every time you solve the problem of getting to work or school in the morning. The process may also be highly explicit, with formal methods for each step.

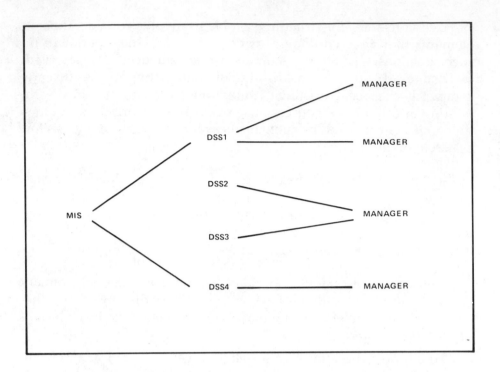

Figure 1-4. A DSS may or may not draw information from the corporate MIS, as shown in this diagram. There may be several DSS packages at work in an organization, but only one MIS. Several managers may use the same DSS. A manager may use more than one DSS.

No matter what the circumstances, the main purpose of the computer-based system is indicated by a key word in its title—*support*. A DSS can aid a manager in decision making and problem solving by improving the *quality* and *usefulness* of information resources. To be useful, these decision support resources, or tools, must be tailored to the specific needs of the manager and the organization. A particular decision support tool can be either a help or a hindrance, depending upon how well the tool fits in with the manager's personal style, the organization's purpose, and the characteristics of a specific decision.

Managers are problem solvers. The functional model of the manager as one who plans, organizes, and controls an enterprise may not be as adequate in portraying a manager as a product-type model that produces outputs in the form of ideas (problems found and defined as well as alternatives generated) and decisions. In this product model, the DSS can be a central aid in the manager's production (of ideas and decisions) system.

Incidentally, the term *manager* is used here in its universal sense. Everyone is a manager, whether or not he or she supervises others in an enterprise. You have a permanent responsibility to manage your own affairs through life. The principles of problem solving, decision making, and DSS are valuable in meeting this challenge, as well as within the ranks of business management.

In summary, decision support systems exist and are growing at all levels and within all segments of an organization where semi-structured problems are encountered. Application of a DSS requires some special tools and techniques. This book provides an opportunity for you to discover and apply such tools under realistic conditions.

DIMENSIONS OF DECISION SUPPORT

A computer-based DSS is implemented on an *interactive* basis. An interactive computer system is one that prompts (asks questions of) users for required inputs and also responds to user requests. Interactive systems provide *real-time* service, involving immediate response (in seconds) to service requests. Interactive service with real-time response is available with time-sharing systems and with many personal computers.

Because decision making often involves several unknown variables, users cannot anticipate the exact information that the decision support system will need to maintain. Thus, users should be able to adapt the system at any time to meet changing business situations. In this sense, a DSS is a framework for responding to new information processing needs rather than a finished system.

A decision support system can be a personal system for an individual manager or a shared system for a group of managers with similar jobs. The system may be custom built by or to the order of the manager or managers using it, or it may be assembled from commercially available components. In any case, the manager-users are the only people who can evaluate any decision support system. Managers know the business and its environment. Managers determine the course of the business. Managers are the only people—inside or outside of the organization—who know and understand the criteria for judging the effectiveness of a DSS.

There may be several decision support systems operating within an organization. These systems, of course, will gain much of their information by accessing the databases maintained within the MIS. However, such inquiries usually do not require any special processing capabilities to be built into the MIS. Rather, "bridging" programs extract desired information items from the MIS databases and transfer them to the decision support systems in their required formats.

DSS EVOLUTION

A DSS is an interdisciplinary endeavor. The evolution of DSS techniques extends the movement toward making a science of decision making and of mathematical decision theory. DSS draws on the work of the cognitive psychologists in understanding human decision-making processes. DSS is a later example of scientific management, a movement of the twentieth century to structure the problem of management. And, of course, DSS would not be possible without the products of computer science and computer engineering.

In many ways, DSS draws on the base built by MIS work. In some ways, as indicated graphically in Figure 1-5, an overlap exists in both technologies and in uses of data between MIS and DSS applications. MIS development was part of a movement in organizations in the 1960s to build large, global information systems to handle logistical management problems. MIS was an outgrowth of the computer technology of the sixties, which made feasible the accessing of large computer databases from geographically dispersed locations. MIS has been highly successful in manufacturing and distribution organizations where logistical problems were significant, but has been less successful in nonmanufacturing organizations or for nonlogistical problems.

DSS is a movement to extend computer-based decision aiding to those areas in which the global, general systems approach of MIS was

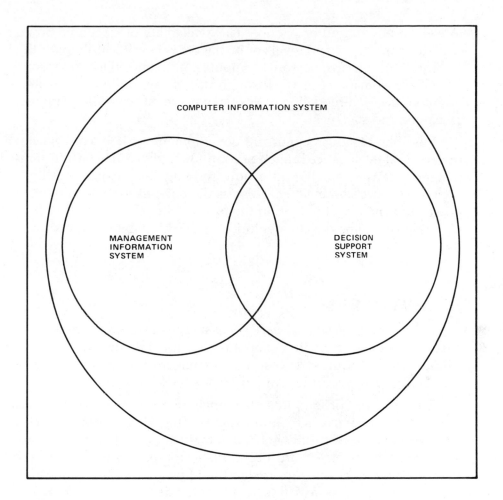

Figure 1-5. As indicated by this graphic, both MIS and DSS applications can exist concurrently within the sphere of overall CIS activities.

not successful. Accordingly, the DSS idea is to build flexible, quickly changed, tailored decision-aiding systems for very particular problem areas.

As MIS was an outgrowth of the available technology, so is DSS. This flexible approach to systems building has been made economically feasible by the efficient program-development tools recently introduced by computer science. The availability of DSS on a broad scale to many types and levels of managers is possible only with the advent of inexpensive personal computers and time-sharing systems. Also, DSS is made effective through use of the modern, manager-oriented, decision-modeling tools of management science, operations research, and statistics.

Possibly, the most significant development for DSS comes from the artificial intelligence branch of computer science. The artificial intelligence (AI) researchers are now refining the "expert system" approach to decision making. This has the potential of being the most powerful component of DSS in the future. The relationships of contributing disciplines to the evolution of DSS capabilities are shown in Figure 1-6.

EXAMPLE OF A DSS

A *Portfolio Management System (PMS)* is a type of DSS designed in the early 1970s to aid bank investment managers in the management of clients' trust accounts. Investment managers invest trust clients' money, often in securities traded on stock exchanges.

Through use of computer terminals, a PMS gives investment managers instant access to and display of the status and make-up of clients' accounts. Securities-related data, including historic-purchase and current stock prices, are also available for display through use of PMS software. The latest prices and holdings in a client's collection of securities, or *portfolio,* can be displayed side by side on a terminal screen. Other displays are possible. For example, an investment manager can call up information relating to growth rates or to price: earnings ratios for particular securities.

As described so far, a PMS appears to be only an information storage and retrieval system. Information storage and retrieval, usually through utilization of a *database management system (DBMS),* is a major function of most decision support systems. In some cases, information storage and retrieval are the sole functions of a DSS.

More often, however, other facilities are provided to supplement DBMS capabilities. A portfolio management system, for instance, presents the information retrieved from a DBMS in a form that can

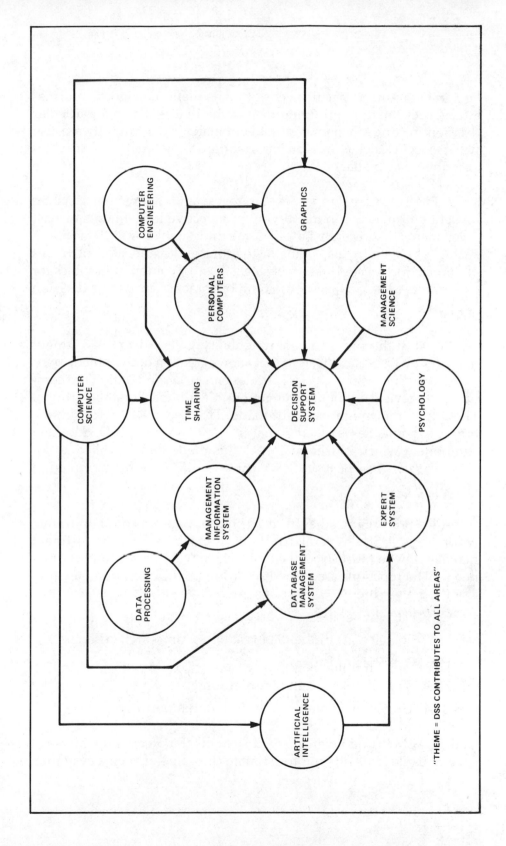

"THEME = DSS CONTRIBUTES TO ALL AREAS"

Figure 1-6. A viable DSS draws content and methodologies from a wide variety of sources and disciplines, identified in this illustration.

be applied to meet specific needs of investment managers. Information is presented by grouping data items that relate to a particular decision-making function of investment managers. PMS software also will perform calculations on information as needed to satisfy requirements of managers.

A PMS also can support exploratory examinations that assist an investment manager in identifying prospective investments or past investments that recently have become undesirable. A PMS facilitates such exploration by displaying histograms and scatterplots of values of interest for selected classes of stocks. Use of computer graphics for exploratory data analysis is a common practice in use of decision support systems.

Possibly the most valuable capability given to the investment manager by PMS is the feature that allows creation of hypothetic portfolios. This means that possible trades can be carried out on the computer to preview (without commitment) their impact on the portfolio. The actual trade might never be made. This use of a DSS for simulation of eventualities is called "what if . . . ?" analysis. A DSS or DSS component which is used mainly in this mode may be called a *decision simulator*. Information flows within a PMS are diagrammed in Figure 1-7.

A PMS is organized as a *tool kit* that provides a common framework for a DSS. Several functions are available to investment managers, who must select the tools which will best accomplish their needs. The functions are named according to the operation they perform. Some of the PMS functions are:

- CREATE: "what if . . . ?" analysis of portfolios.
- FILTER: select from the database based on search criteria.
- HISTO: display histogram graphic.
- SCATTER: display scattergram graphic.
- STATUS: show contents of an individual portfolio.

Versions of portfolio management systems (PMS) are now in use at several banks. It is difficult to estimate the value of such a system in

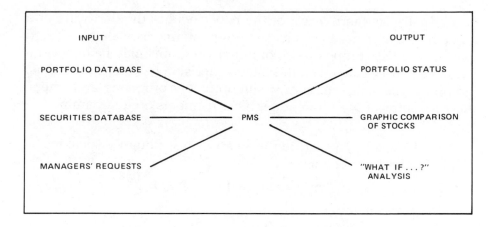

Figure 1-7. This diagram depicts information flows in the Portfolio Management System (PMS), an example of a DSS application.

dollars resulting from better investments. PMS is a success because its users have adopted it into their day-to-day work and regard it as an ally.

The expense incurred in developing and installing PMS was not offset by the displacement of many investment managers to new jobs. Perhaps the investment managers can service more accounts with PMS than they could without this tool. It is more likely that the system has justified itself in the minds of its users by the added assurance they feel during decision making, even though there is no way to quantify this benefit.

DSS ARCHITECTURE

Several elements of a DSS must be coordinated to create an effective, total tool. These elements include computer programs, databases, and the hardware and systems software of the base computer system. The manager who will use the DSS, and, possibly, an intermediary to help the manager work with the computer, are additional elements to be considered when structuring a DSS.

Usually, and in the rest of the book, neither the hardware and systems software nor the manager and/or intermediary are considered part of the DSS proper. The computer programs may be of several types: database management systems, decision modeling programs, graphics generating programs, communications programs, and others. Relationships of these integrated DSS elements are diagrammed in Figure 1-8.

A DSS may be structured in many ways. Roughly speaking, a DSS may be described as:

- General-purpose language based
- Generic component system
- Modeling system
- Special-purpose system.

These categories are not mutually exclusive; a single system might have attributes of all of these categories.

General-purpose language based.   A *general-purpose language-based* DSS, shown schematically in Figure 1-9, is one that runs within an environment of an interactive, general-purpose programming language. APL and BASIC are languages of this type and are commonly used for DSS development. Such a language-based environment can use the command structure of the language itself for programming and data manipulation. A DSS running in an interactive language environment is usually slower and less computationally efficient than one that is compiled into the language of the underlying machine. Also, there may be difficulties accessing large databases or interfacing with some types of standard graphics or database management programs from the interactive language environment. However, this type of DSS lends itself to quick and easy modification. Therefore, this may be the mode used to develop prototypes of a DSS which later may be reprogrammed for greater efficiency or for use with large databases.

Generic component system.   A *generic component system*, represented graphically in Figure 1-10, consists of a *tool kit* of general information processing and presentation functions. These functions may not apply

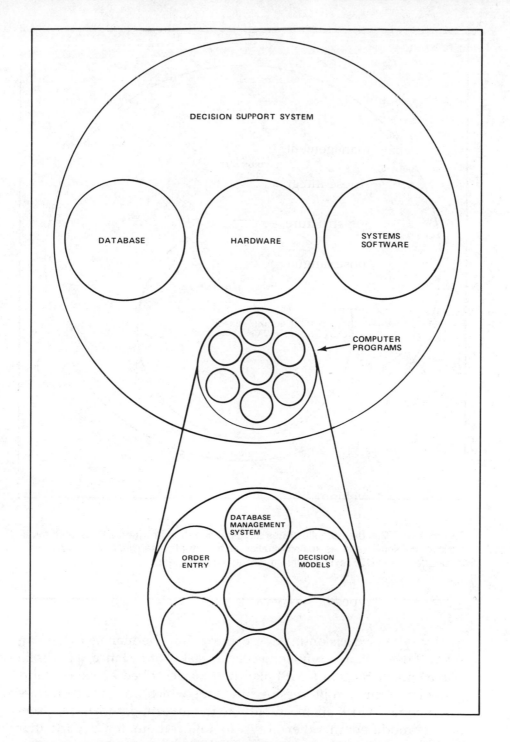

Figure 1-8. This Venn diagram illustrates the components and contributors to a DSS. Relationships among DSS parts are demonstrated.

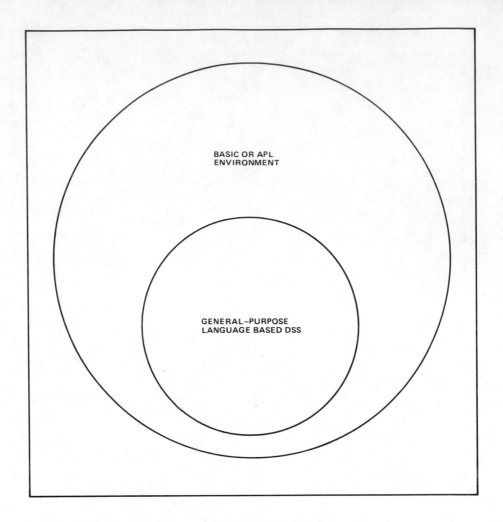

BASIC OR APL
ENVIRONMENT

GENERAL–PURPOSE
LANGUAGE BASED DSS

Figure 1-9. This diagram illustrates a typical situation in which a DSS uses multiple layers of software for its implementation. In the situation shown, a general-purpose, language-based DSS exists within a BASIC environment.

to any type of decision-making context, but the manager/user can select those that are useful for a specific task. For instance, a Portfolio Management System (PMS) like the one described above contains general information processing functions which, in some cases, are given names which are meaningful to the investment-manager users or are modified in other ways to tailor them for a particular investment-management function. FILTER, for example, is a function to search a database for certain information. This function would be

22

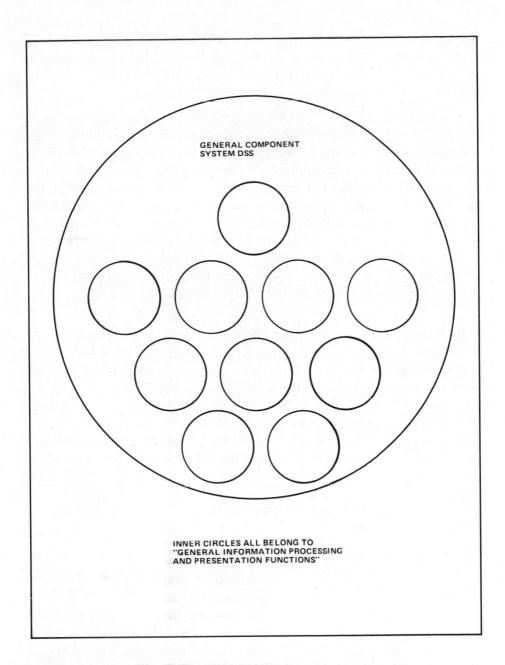

Figure 1-10. A DSS may consist of a series of generic software components, represented by the elements within the inner circle of this diagram. This generic DSS, then, exists within the overall information processing structure of the using organization.

needed, typically, in any DSS. In a PMS, the FILTER function is tailored to the PMS databases. HISTO and SCATTER are also general functions that would be useful in any DSS, but which are tailored in PMS to the investment management context.

There might be one general component in a generic component DSS which allows the user to put context-specific names on the functions or on combinations of the functions. This component might then show the selected components and composite components as entries on a special menu. A special-purpose DSS could be constructed in this way from the generic components. This type of organizing component is called a *user facility* in this book. This process of developing a DSS from generic components and amalgamating the derived components into a system which looks like a special-purpose DSS to the user is sometimes called *generating* a DSS. A generic component system that allows this is sometimes called a *DSS generator*.

Modeling system. A *modeling system* DSS provides features predominantly from a host modeling language. DYNAMO is a language used for modeling the economy and making macro-economic policy decisions through ''what if . . . ?'' analyses. GPSS is a modeling language used for logistical management. A modeling system is much like a general-purpose language-based system, except that the language used is suited primarily for building a type of model and may be difficult to adapt to data access or other kinds of processing which may not be required in the type of modeling supported by the specific language. Of course, a modeling language capability can be a component of a generic component DSS.

Special-purpose system. A *special-purpose system* DSS is tailored to the decision-making requirements of a particular manager or group of managers. PMS is a special-purpose DSS, as described previously.

PMS might have been developed from a generic component DSS generation system. PMS has a modeling component for developing hypothetic portfolios. PMS certainly could have been built using an interactive language such as BASIC or APL. Thus, PMS has attributes of all of these DSS types. These descriptors are not mutually exclusive, but they illustrate the diversity possible in DSS architectures.

Programs are available with this text for the reader to employ in a study DSS. These programs will be examples of generic components which may be used as is or tailored to special-purpose requirements. A user facility will be one of the supplied programs. Thus, the reader can experience several modes of DSS construction and use.

DSS IMPLEMENTATION

Implementing a DSS is an interdisciplinary endeavor that requires several skills. The DSS builder can be a manager-user working with a set of generic components or a computer information systems professional working directly with programming languages, operating systems, and database management systems at a technical level. In the case of the manager-user-builder, one person may possess the complete range of computer and decision-making knowledge to develop an effective DSS. In the case of the CIS professional builder, manager-users will probably have to be part of the design and implementation team.

Computer skills, decision-making skills, and knowledge of the problem area are the minimal prerequisites of a DSS-builder or DSS-building team. It also helps to have available appropriate interactive programming tools and DSS generation libraries.

This mix of required skills is characteristic of most information systems development work. The difference connected with the building of a DSS lies in considering the life cycle of a conventional information system. There are phases of feasibility study, analysis, design, implementation, and maintenance. The DSS life cycle is very different. The conventional phases are concurrent and never-ending. A DSS is a continual development project throughout its life. This is a result of the semi-structured nature of DSS problems. Their exact nature cannot be anticipated. The idea is to have a framework and tools available with which a system can be put together quickly when a particular problem arises.

A practice in information systems development is the building of a prototype, which is a full-scale model of the intended system. This prototype is used to verify the correctness of the design before the full-scale and more computationally efficient system is built. The DSS may be considered to exist continually in this prototype stage. It will constantly be changed and corrected.

Outlook

- A decision support system is a data handling application package that facilitates decision making. Typically, a database, an interface with other systems, and modeling techniques are associated with DSS capabilities.

- To understand, build, and use a DSS effectively, you will need some basic background on the decision processes to which these computer techniques can be applied. The chapter that follows, therefore, is an introduction to decision processes and for analytical processes for reaching decisions. These discussions are basic to the responsibilities and normal functions of human managers. Involvement of computers in the discussion of basic processes is minimal.

Assignments

1. Read Gerrity's article on PMS. (See Bibliography.) Prepare a scenario on how a particular investment manager might use PMS to make a particular investment decision.

2. Read the MIS articles listed in the Bibliography. Find other MIS articles or texts. Is DSS a successor to MIS in the research? Does DSS replace MIS? In your view, do MIS and DSS complement each other?

MAKING DECISIONS 2

Abstract

- This chapter reviews, in further depth, the decision-making process introduced in Chapter 1.

- Problem definitions are stated in terms of differences between existing and desired conditions. A problem description statement can begin: "Close the difference between . . ." and then identify the conditions involved.

- A number of group-participation and research techniques may be used as aids in identifying alternatives. Techniques discussed include brainstorming, the Delphi process, and technology transfer through research or use of consultants.

- The alternatives to be evaluated are often presented in the form of decision trees. Decision trees can show selection criteria and can also identify the alternatives under consideration. Decision criteria discussed include estimates of outcomes and probabilities of occurrence for alternatives. When quantified estimates and probabilities are provided, equations can be applied to develop quantitative ratings as a basis for selecting among decision alternatives. Cases are used to illustrate this technique.

THE PROBLEM-SOLVING PROCESS

Decision support systems are, as defined in the previous chapter, tools for problem solving. Within a management context, problems are solved by identifying alternative solutions and reaching a decision by selecting the most appropriate alternative. Chapter 1 presents an illustration that diagrams the decision-making process that underlies DSS applications. As a point of continuing reference, that diagram is reproduced as Figure 2-1.

As indicated in Figure 2-1, the basic steps in the decision-making model are:

- *Identify and define the problem.* Do this with a formal, written problem statement.

- *Identify alternatives.* This step is intuitive and judgmental. Alternatives are derived from the knowledge and experience of involved managers.

- *Select an alternative.* Problems that are highly structured can often be solved through application of data derived from existing MIS systems. Totally unstructured problems do not lend themselves to computer-assisted solution. Semi-structured problems represent the major area for current application of DSS techniques.

- *Implementation.* The selected alternative is carried out. In the process, resulting feedback may be applied to alter or modify the selected solution.

Problem-Solving Example

To illustrate application of this process, consider the decision-making required to transport a production lot of canned hams from Memphis, Tennessee, to New York City. A problem can be defined most usefully in terms of a difference to be closed. Thus, this ham transport problem might be defined as follows:

> Close the difference between the present physical location of the hams in Memphis and the desired location of the hams in New York City.

Alternative generation for the ham transport problem is relatively easy: rail, air, truck. Assuming that all three of these alternatives are available in Memphis, any of the three qualifies as a solution to the problem as stated.

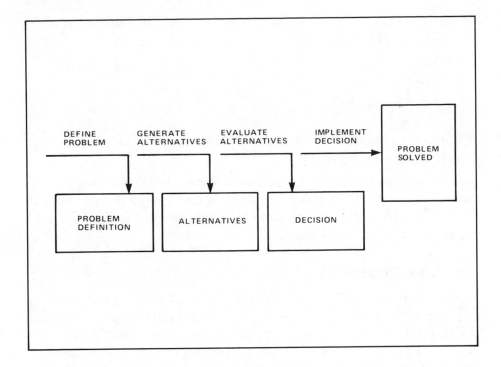

Figure 2-1. For convenience of reference, this is a repeat of the diagram of the decision-making process and its outputs.

To rank these alternatives as a basis for selection, some evaluation criteria must be added to the problem statement. The problem definition could be extended on the basis of management criteria. Two alternatives might be:

Close the difference between the present physical location of the hams in Memphis and the desired location of the hams in New York City as quickly as possible.

Close the difference between the present physical location of the hams in Memphis and the desired location of the hams in New York City at the lowest cost.

If quickness is to be the prime consideration, the ranking of alternatives would probably be:

1. Air
2. Truck
3. Rail.

On the other hand, if cost is the main consideration, the rankings could well be reversed.

The remainder of this chapter reviews the decision-making model to greater depth than has been done so far. Use of the model is illustrated with additional cases to highlight situations in which DSS application is appropriate.

DEFINING PROBLEMS

Notice how the problem definition focuses the subsequent problem-solving activity. A manager who lacked adequate criteria for a decision could concentrate on the methods of transportation and how to evaluate them. However, the extended problem definition demonstrates that relevance is introduced into the process readily. This is a desirable attribute of the problem-solving approach.

However, sometimes this focusing of the problem-solving work may be done prematurely. For example, a more creative approach to the ham transportation problem might not have assumed that the hams had to be moved physically. The problem might have been defined:

> Close the difference between the number of hams now in New York City and the desired number of hams (a production lot more).

This definition does not focus the process on the selection of a transportation mode—at least not yet. With this new problem statement, alternative solution generation might result in choices such as the following:

- Transport the hams in Memphis to NYC.
- Find a company in Memphis that has hams in NYC and needs hams in Memphis and trade.

- Find several companies with which to barter the Memphis hams so as to end up with hams in NYC.

- Sell the hams in Memphis and use the money to buy hams in NYC.

No matter what evaluation criteria were used, some of these other alternatives might be better than transporting the hams physically. Appropriate problem definition is critical to effective problem solving.

In summary, a problem definition can be expressed as a difference. The first phrase in the problem statement then should be: ''Close the difference between. . . .'' Then, the problem definition should list the evaluation criteria; in business, these criteria frequently involve such terms as ''quickest'' or ''lowest cost.'' The evaluation criteria should be measurable; in business, usually in ''dollars'' or ''hours.'' It is critical to the effectiveness of the process that the problem be defined specifically. Problem definition is an aspect of problem solving that cannot be computer-aided to any great extent. The work must be done by the problem solver.

GENERATING SOLUTION ALTERNATIVES

Like problem definition, the generation of solution alternatives is not easily delegated to a computer. This task, too, usually must be accomplished by the problem solver, aided mainly by personal creativity and knowledge. However, there are some general approaches to alternative selection, as discussed below.

Brainstorming

Brainstorming, one frequently used method, is a group process. In a brainstorming session, a group of people gathers specifically to stimulate one another in the contribution of alternative ideas. Agreement is obtained among all the group members before the session begins that no one's contribution will be discounted or belittled in any way. This leads to a free flow of ideas, without any premature evaluation. Remember, evaluation is not to occur until the alternative generation is completed.

Brainstorming is successful because ideas that can appear ridiculous when presented initially can later be modified and honed to lead to practical solutions. If no one is afraid of being ridiculed for offering a ridiculous idea, many really ridiculous ideas come out. But there will also be some that can be developed into valid alternatives, often by other members of the group.

Brainstorming is more effective when one person acts as a scribe to record the ideas on a chalkboard. It is also useful if the proceedings can be recorded verbatim. This record can be examined later for potentials that were overlooked under the tensions of the group session.

Another group process which can be employed for alternative generation uses a variation upon the brainstorming technique. This method, like brainstorming, uses group synergy. However, the level of discipline is greater. This method incorporates an evaluation activity within the alternative-generation procedure.

A moderator instructs each participant to write down the two, for example, alternative solutions that the member considers to be the best. After the group is allowed sufficient time for consideration, the moderator collects the contributions and writes all of the solutions on a chalkboard. At this point, anonymity may be maintained as the alternatives are discussed, or participants may be called on to defend their recommendations.

After discussion wanes (or after a preset time has elapsed), the participants are asked again to write down their two most favored solutions. This cycle can be continued until the same list of favored solutions repeats itself. If this process is allowed to converge on a single solution which is the favorite of the whole group, the alternative generation and evaluation phases are effectively merged.

Delphi Process

An alternative for securing multiple contributions without a central group meeting is the *Delphi* process. This approach gets its name from the Delphic Oracle in ancient Greece. Individuals with problems could write their questions and feed them into an opening in a stone idol. A fire within the idol mingled the ideas of participants. Solutions were pronounced by a wise person.

Under the modern version of the Delphi process, the functions of scribe, moderator, and recording secretary for group processes can be provided by a computer conferencing system. In such an arrangement, the members of the group would be remote from each other and would use computer terminals to communicate. A verbatim record of the session would be recorded automatically. In this format, brainstorming or other group processes need not be carried on in the same block of time by all participants. Group members could catch up on the transcribed proceedings at intervals of hours or days and make their contributions on an asynchronous basis. As an alternative, contributions of Delphi participants can be delivered to a coordinator through company mail.

Technology Transfer

The process of alternative generation can be accomplished by the many methods of *technology transfer*. Technology transfer makes known, in a new area, problem solutions developed and used in another, possibly nonrelated, area.

As applied by a single problem solver, technology transfer is the learning of the existence of possible solutions that were previously unknown or forgotten. Well-developed methods of technology transfer include literature and bibliographic database search and the use of consultants.

Technology transfer and alternative solution generation by literature search involves the reading of the many sources that might contribute to the problem solver's understanding of the problem or which might address the solution of the same or a related problem directly. These sources include technical and industry journals, as well as the books available in the library.

Technology transfer and alternative solution generation by bibliographic database search is one way the computer can help the problem solver. Hundreds of bibliographic databases are now available commercially. These systems are on-line and may be accessed over the telephone lines with computer terminals. These bibliographic databases have millions of citations, abstracts, and even the complete texts of articles from journals, magazines, books, and newspapers in computer-readable and searchable form. These entries are indexed by key words to facilitate searching. Any qualified librarian can make this powerful research tool available.

Technology transfer via consultants can be as informal as asking your friend for suggestions or as formal as engaging an accounting or consulting firm to conduct a study and deliver written recommendations. Asking someone else for an opinion gives the problem solver the benefit of a different point of view. If that consultant is expert in the problem area, the individual or firm may have previous experience in dealing with the same or similar problems.

In summary, the generation of alternative solutions is a creative task that may be aided through contributions of other people personally or through written suggestions. There are group processes which may be employed to get the most benefit from conferring with other people. Of course, conferring with others, especially groups, can be an expensive undertaking. Alternative solutions can be found in written sources in the library. Finding relevant sources can be aided by a subject index in a card catalog or by the indexing and search capabilities of on-line bibliographic databases.

EVALUATING ALTERNATIVES

The availability of solution alternatives can be diagrammed in tree form, as is done in Figure 2-2. In this diagram, the five alternative solutions to the PROBLEM are mutually exclusive. So, in solving the problem, one, and only one, of the branches of the tree must be chosen.

It is customary to calculate an "outcome" score for each of the branches. The alternative branch with the most desirable score is chosen as the solution. Some outcome scores are added to the decision tree, as illustrated in Figure 2-3. This tree shows three alternative solutions and their costs. In business, it is usual to minimize cost, so the rail alternative is the most desirable.

In many cases it is possible to determine these outcome costs directly and with certainty. In the ham transport problem, it might be possible to look up, or call commercial carriers for, published freight rates. This effort would yield exact costs of the alternatives. Thus, if cost is the dominant concern, the decision is relatively easy to make.

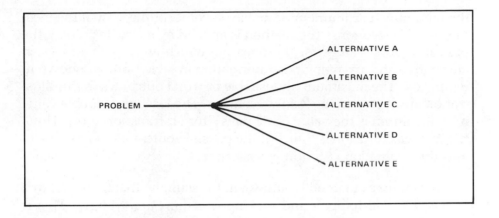

Figure 2-2. This is a tree-structure diagram showing the relationship of a problem to identified solution alternatives.

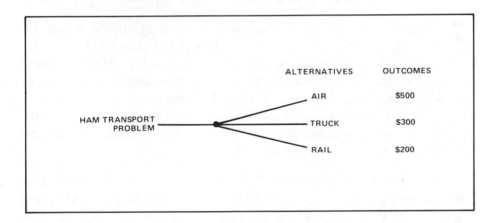

Figure 2-3. This is a tree-structure diagram in which alternative outcomes are weighted through calculations and listed as a basis for selection.

If minimum time is the evaluation criterion for this problem, it is probably not possible to determine the outcome values directly and with certainty for all the cases. This requires some methods for making decisions under conditions of uncertainty. A very conservative method is *minmax*. In this method, the alternative is chosen which has the minimum–maximum undesirable outcome, or the least of the most undesirable solutions. The method is applied by first determining the best and worst values for the outcome which are possible for each alternative and arranging this information in table form, as shown in Figure 2-4. The maximum undesirable or worst outcomes in this illustration are shown in the "slow" column. The least undesirable value in that column is the value of "2 days" for air transportation. Thus, the minmax decision is "air," if the possible outcomes are as above, and the evaluation criterion is least time.

The minmax method is equivalent to assuming that the worst that is possible will happen and making decisions accordingly. This is certainly a conservative decision-making strategy. An aggressive strategy might assume that the best will happen. This strategy is called *maxmax*. Following this method, the best alternative is either air or truck, since each has the same best value of one day.

Decision making under conditions of certainty implies that the decision maker can predict the exact outcome values accurately. Decision making under uncertainty implies that the decision maker cannot predict the outcomes accurately, but can establish a range of possible outcomes. A special type of decision making under uncertainty occurs when the decision maker cannot predict the exact outcome values, but can determine all of the possible outcome values and can estimate the probability of each occurring.

In the ham transport problem, it may be possible to determine that air requires one day 80 percent of the time and two days 20 percent of the time, while truck requires one day 30 percent of the time, two days 40 percent of the time, and three days 30 percent of the time. The outcomes and probabilities for rail are one day, three days, nine days; and 5, 30, and 65 percent. Notice that the probabilities on the possible outcomes total to 100 percent for each alternative solution. This information is conveniently presented in decision tree form in Figure 2-5.

If the possible outcome values and their probabilities are available, it is possible to make the decision using *expected value*. Expected value may be thought of as a weighted average. For example, if you make a bet under which you collect $10 if a six turns up on a single throw of a die but you lose $3 if one through five turns up, you can think

ALTERNATIVES	POSSIBLE OUTCOMES	
	FAST	SLOW
AIR	1 DAY	2 DAYS
TRUCK	1 DAY	3 DAYS
RAIL	2 DAYS	9 DAYS

Figure 2-4. This table presents the minmax solution for the ham transport problem.

---

about your average return on the bet from six throws. Since each outcome is equally likely, you can expect to lose $3 five times and to win $10 once. This is a loss of $15 and a win of $10, or a net loss of $5. This averages out to a loss of five-sixths of a dollar, or $0.166, per play of the bet. Thus, the expected value of a single play of this bet is −$0.166.

With the data in Figure 2-5, the best, or quickest, alternative method can be selected as a solution for the ham transport problem. The expected value of shipping by air can be calculated by thinking of the average time if the shipment was sent by air 10 times. On average, it would take 1 day twice (or 20 percent) and 2 days eight times (or 80 percent) for a total of 18 days for the 10 shipments. This is an average of 1.8 days per shipment, which is the expected value of the time needed for a single shipment. Notice that this same result can be derived by multiplying the probability for each outcome by the respective outcome value and summing the results for an alternative. In the case of air transportation, the method of calculation looks like:

$$(0.20 \times 1 \text{ day}) + (0.80 \times 2 \text{ days}) = 1.8 \text{ days.}$$

The expected value of transporting by truck is:

$$(0.30 \times 1 \text{ day}) + (0.40 \times 2 \text{ days}) + (0.30 \times 3 \text{ days}) = 2 \text{ days.}$$

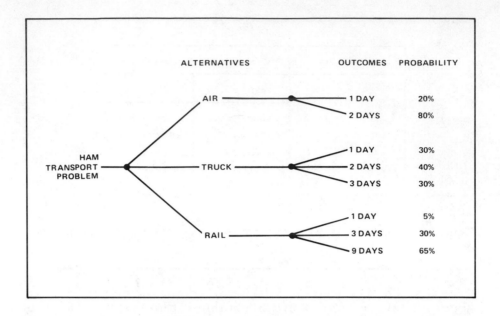

Figure 2-5. This is a tree-structure diagram for the ham transport problem. The diagram shows the probabilities for the identified outcomes. A graphic presentation of this type is known as a decision tree.

The expected value of transporting by rail is:

$$(0.05 \times 1 \text{ day}) + (0.30 \times 3 \text{ days}) + (0.65 \times 9 \text{ days}) = 6.8 \text{ days}.$$

So, the correct decision using this expected value formulation is air transportation, since this method is quickest.

In summary, there are three approaches to evaluating decision alternatives:

- Decision making under conditions of certainty
- Decision making under conditions of uncertainty without probabilities
- Decision making under conditions of uncertainty with probabilities.

Each of these alternatives, successively, requires more data on the decision situation.

Decision making under certainty requires only one value for the outcome of each alternative; but the decision maker must have confidence that that value is accurate. The values may then be compared directly and the "best" alternative selected.

Decision making under uncertainty without probabilities requires that the decision maker have a value for the best and worst possible outcomes for a given alternative. The minmax method then selects the alternative with the "least" worst outcome value (that is, it assumes the worst will happen). The maxmax method then selects the alternative with the "best" best outcome value (that is, it assumes the best will happen).

Decision making under uncertainty with probabilities requires that the decision maker list the possible outcomes for each alternative and their probabilities. The expected values of the outcomes for each alternative then may be compared to select the "best" alternative.

QUANTIFYING DECISION PARAMETERS

Much of the work in organizational decision making lies in determining the values for the parameters of the decision tree: outcomes and probabilities. In the certainty cases, the values for the outcomes often are fairly easily determined from tables, with calls to vendors, or with access to company historical records. Still, this may amount to some work.

The determination of best and worst outcome values might also result from table lookup, consultation with vendors, or accessing company records. However, many times the decision maker must rely on his own experience to make *subjective judgments*, also known as "educated guesses." These values might also be estimated through use of group participation methods discussed earlier.

Values for the probabilities of alternatives considered in connection with decisions under risk are seldom attainable without much effort. These probabilities can be estimated and used within the model on the basis of subjective judgments, but the best way to derive them is from company records regarding similar situations over a period of time. If data covering company experience are stored in a computer database, these values may be more readily extracted.

For example, in the case of the ham transport problem, the company might have a file of records of past shipments from Memphis to New York City by air. That information might be extracted from that file and placed in a list like the one shown in Figure 2-6. This list has 20 entries, one for each of the 20 times that the company has shipped hams by air from Memphis to New York City. Notice that four of the shipments took one day and the other 16 took two days. A logical estimate of the probability of this trip taking one day, assuming nothing has changed in the way this task is carried out since these records were begun, is four-twentieths. This reflects the data showing that the trip has taken one day four times out of the 20 it has been attempted. Four out of 20, or four-twentieths, is a probability of 20 percent. The probability of the trip taking two days is then sixteen-twentieths, or 80 percent. This might also be calculated by subtracting the 20 percent from 100 percent.

An important assumption in this process is that the historic data are sufficient in number to represent truly the possibilities that might occur. Another important assumption is that nothing has changed during the course of the collection of these data that might make another trip from Memphis to New York City substantially different from the "typical" trip represented by the data in Figure 2-6.

In summary, to use any of the alternative evaluation methods, the outcomes and, possibly, their probabilities must be evaluated. Often, this requires some educated guessing. The decision maker must judge what depth of research into this valuation is justified by a given problem. (This is a decision problem in its own right.) The more accessible this information is, such as availability via terminals linked into a computer system, the less expensive and more convenient the work will be. This is basically the rationale for decision support systems—that decision-making information be made available and accessible to decision makers to promote and make more informed decisions.

CASE STUDY: THE BANK LOAN DECISION

As an example of a decision problem, consider the process a bank loan officer goes through in deciding whether to grant a personal loan. As seen by the banker, the problem may be defined:

> Close the difference between the candidate borrower's current liquid assets and the liquid assets he would like to have with no risk to the bank.

Alternatives available to the banker include the various loan types granted by the bank, as well as the alternative of rejecting the application. Loan types include signature, or unsecured, loans and loans secured by different types of collateral, such as a house or automobile. The banker requires that his decision be made under certainty that there be no chance that the borrower cannot pay back the loan. Therefore, the banker requires as data for the decision the financial status of the borrower. What the banker is interested in is knowing what the borrower owns that can be pledged as collateral. (A so-called "unsecured" or signature loan is actually secured by the borrower's income, which can be attached in the courts to pay the loan.)

The outcomes for the banker's decision can be considered to be the difference between the value of the collateral and the amount borrowed. If the loan applicant wants to borrow $10,000, and the banker has determined that the values of the applicant's assets that might be pledged as collateral are: car, $5,000; house, $50,000; income (signature loan), $4,000; the banker's decision tree looks like the diagram in Figure 2-7.

This analysis makes it clear that the loan with the house pledged as collateral (a mortgage loan) is the best alternative for the banker. Notice that the second best alternative is "no loan." Remember that doing nothing is always an alternative.

In this bank loan analysis, the loan types are considered as separate alternative solutions. Of course, a type of alternative solution that is not investigated here is a mixed loan consisting of two or more separate loan types or collateral objects. For example, if the applicant owned a boat worth $5,000 and a car worth $5,000, those two articles could be considered together in a single alternative. The same could be done with two cars or other collateral combinations.

DATE	DAYS IN TRANSIT
09/12/82	1
10/01/82	2
10/20/82	2
11/13/82	2
12/15/82	1
12/17/82	2
12/27/82	2
01/12/83	2
02/22/83	2
02/23/83	1
03/20/83	2
04/11/83	1
05/22/83	2
05/24/83	2
06/12/83	2
08/03/83	2
10/11/83	2
12/14/83	2
12/26/83	2
01/17/84	2

Figure 2-6. This table presents historic data on past air shipments of hams from Memphis to New York City. Data are used as criteria for evaluating alternative solutions in the transport decision.

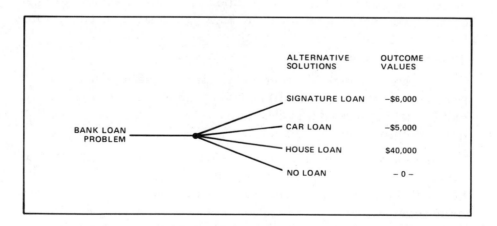

Figure 2-7. This decision tree shows the banker's decision on granting a loan.

CASE STUDY:
THE HAMBURGER FRANCHISE LOCATION DECISION

National fast-food restaurant chains are constantly opening stores in new locations. Placing those stores requires decision making, and these national chains have developed this process into a science. This problem can be approached as a decision to be made under conditions of uncertainty. The problem definition is:

> Close the gap between the profit we are making now and that which we would like to make by opening a new store.

It is common to set up a minimum profit target for a store. Assuming this is $100,000 per year, Figure 2-8 shows the way a list of possible locations for stores might be evaluated. Beside each address is an optimistic and a pessimistic profit estimate for a store in that location.

These figures have been prepared by the staff of the national chain. The 5 Front St. location is across the street from a planned new city sports arena. However, there is a possibility that the sports arena will not actually be built, in which case the location would not be profitable.

Under the minmax decision-making method, the selected alternative would be the one with the highest pessimistic profit value.

ADDRESS	OPTIMISTIC PROFIT	PESSIMISTIC PROFIT
99 WEST CHARLTON AVE.	$120,000	$110,000
8813 JONES ST.	$150,000	$ 80,000
5 FRONT ST.	$200,000	–$100,000

Figure 2-8. This table presents decision-relevant data that could be used in locating hamburger chain outlets.

Remember, the assumption under this method is that the worst that can happen will. The minmax decision is the 99 West Charlton Ave. location.

Using the maxmax decision-making method, the decision would be different. Remember that in this method the decision maker assumes that the best that can happen will. In this situation, the best that could happen would be that the sports arena would be built and that the 5 Front St. location would be very profitable.

The staff could be asked to forecast probabilities for the optimistic and pessimistic profit estimates. If this were done, an expected value for the profit for each location could be calculated. It is possible that these probabilities give equal expected profits for each of the locations. What should the decision be in that case?

Remember that the chain has a target that each store should have over $100,000 profit. Since two of the locations have the possibility of not making this target, no matter what the expected value is, those two locations could be eliminated from consideration.

A possibility that is very undesirable is called a *catastrophic outcome*. The presence of catastrophic outcomes may change the nature of the decision-making process from optimizing expected value to simply avoiding the possibility of a catastrophic outcome from occurring (a minmax strategy). A better example of a catastrophic outcome in business is bankruptcy. A company may have an opportunity to invest in a venture that, should it work out, would be very profitable. However, if the venture were to fail, the amount of money the company had invested would be enough to bankrupt the company. Therefore, the company might choose not to take this gamble, no matter how great the potential rewards.

CASE SCENARIO: PRESIDENT TRUMAN'S A-BOMB DECISION

A classic decision-making situation was President Truman's dilemma over whether to drop the A-bomb on Japan in 1945. The problem could have been defined in many ways. One way might have been:

Close the gap between our present rate of losing soldiers' lives and the desired rate of zero (0).

Another problem definition, perhaps equivalent, might have been:

> Close the gap between the present rate of winning/ending the war and the desired rate ("right now").

A third, more business-oriented problem definition could have been:

> Close the gap between the present rate of expenditure on the war and the desired rate of expenditure, zero (0).

The three problem definitions differ in the unit of measure for the outcomes: lives, time, money. President Truman's military advisors might have estimated the parameters of decision trees for all three of these ways of defining the problem. Figure 2-9 presents a decision tree showing alternatives based on lives. The time-based decision alternatives are shown in Figure 2-10, while Figure 2-11 is a decision tree based on money-related alternatives.

The expected values of "drop A-bomb" by any of the evaluation criteria are superior to the "do not drop" values. In this case, the "drop" decision is clearly superior to the alternatives. When multiple evaluation criteria must be considered, as is the case in many non-business situations, it is convenient for one alternative to be clearly superior to the others; that is, to be superior under all of the criteria. Otherwise, the decision maker is put in the position of deciding how to compare the criteria numerically. In this A-bomb decision, lives would have to be compared with dollars, for instance.

SUPPORTING DECISION MAKING WITH A COMPUTER

The purpose of this chapter is to put the use of the computer in supporting decision making into the broad context of problem solving through decisions involving selection of alternatives in a semi-structured environment. Problem solving is described as a phased process of problem definition, alternative generation, alternative evaluation, and implementation. It is pointed out that there are few ways to utilize the computer to aid the problem solver with the definition or alternative generation processes. Neither are computers much help with implementation of decisions. Rather, the chief usefulness of computers is in completing evaluations of alternatives.

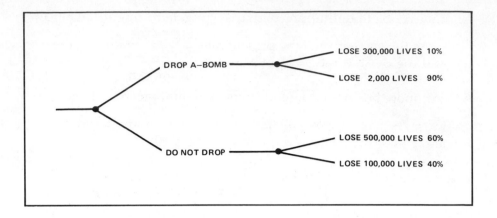

Figure 2-9. This is a decision tree for the A-bomb situation. Identified alternatives are based on lives to be expended.

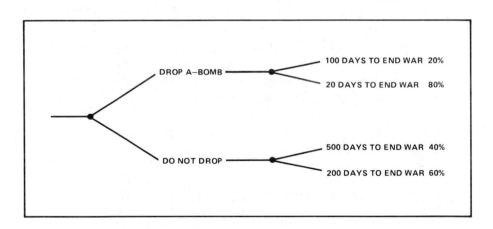

Figure 2-10. This decision tree shows A-bomb alternatives based on time periods until the end of the war.

It is in this third area—evaluation of alternatives—that the remainder of the content of this book is concentrated. Evaluating alternatives is a process of determining or estimating outcome values and also forecasting the probabilities for occurrence of each outcome.

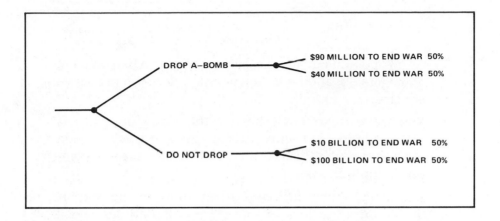

Figure 2-11. This decision tree views the A-bomb situation in terms of money-related alternatives.

Outcome estimating is appropriate to the decision-tree methodology for decision making. Computer databases can be repositories for detailed information about a business. If the type of information needed for decision making is available in a database, and if the decision maker knows how to use the retrieval capability of the database, decision making is much easier. This is a principle of DSS. Also, if a model is available that has been programmed into a computer, such as a program to calculate the expected values for the decision tree model of decision making, the computational phase of decision making can be easier. This is another principle of DSS.

Included at the end of this chapter is a description of a computer program that evaluates decision-tree information. This program, called DTREE, is an example of a *standalone* DSS tool. The program does not work directly with other DSS programs. Rather, DTREE receives input on an *interactive* basis directly from the user. This program is the first of several that, collectively, will make up a ''DSS Tool Kit.''

Outlook

- At this point, you have established a perspective on what managers do, and how, functionally, decision processes are structured.

- You are ready to move ahead to the acquisition of tools that will help you to support management-level decision making through the assembly and presentation of computer applications.

- The methodology introduced beginning in the chapter that follows involves use of processing modules (tools) with which you can assemble your own DSS applications.

- As you get into specifics of computer applications, be careful not to lose sight of the important lessons of this chapter: Decision making is a human process that requires major amounts of valuable management time. Your job will be to enhance the value of an organization's managerial resources. Computer techniques should support this mission—and should not be permitted to become an end unto themselves.

DTree Operation Summary

At the IBM-PC "A>" operating system prompt, type "DTREE" to invoke the decision tree calculation program. This assumes that you have placed a diskette with the DSS Tool Kit Program in drive A.

When invoked, the DTREE program will ask the user to supply decision tree information:

"How many alternatives are to be considered?"

For each alternative:

"What is the name of this alternative?"

"How many chance outcomes are to be defined?"

For each chance outcome:

''What is the name of this chance outcome (20 characters or less)?''

''What is the probability of this chance outcome (0.1 to 1.0)?''

''What is the outcome value for this chance outcome (−9999 to 9999)?''

When the information is entered completely, the DTREE program displays a summary of the results of the application of the expected value computation.

Example Session:

```
A>DTREE
This is DTREE, the DSS Tool Kit Decision Tree Computing Program

How many alternatives are to be considered?>2

1. What is the name of this alternative?>AIR
1. How many states of nature are to be defined?>2
1.1) What is the name of this chance outcome?>PLANE CRASH
1.1) What is the probability of this chance outcome?> 0.1
1.1) What is the outcome value for this chance outcome?>-9999
1.2) What is the name of this chance outcome?>SAFE ARRIVAL
1.2) What is the probability of this chance outcome?>0.9
1.2) What is the outcome value for this chance outcome?>1000

2. What is the name of this alternative?>TRAIN
2. How many states of nature are to be defined?>2
2.1) What is the name of this chance outcome?>TRAIN WRECK
2.1) What is the probability of this chance outcome?>0.1
2.1) What is the outcome value for this chance outcome?>-3000
2.2) What is the name of this chance outcome?>SAFE ARRIVAL
2.2) What is the probability of this chance outcome?>0.9
2.2) What is the outcome value for this chance outcome?>1000
```

The best alternative in this series of outputs of expected value computations is number 2. That is, the best alternative on the basis of safety criteria only is the train.

```
RESULTS OF EXPECTED VALUE COMPUTATIONS

ALTERNATIVE       CHANCE        PROBABILITY    OUTCOME     EXPECTED
                  OUTCOME                      VALUE       VALUE

1. AIR            1) PLANE CRASH   0.1          -9999       -999.9
                  2) SAFE ARRIVAL  0.9           1000        900
                                                           --------
                                                           - 99.9


2. TRAIN          1) TRAIN WRECK   0.1          -3000       -300
                  2) SAFE ARRIVAL  0.9           1000        900
                                                           --------
                                                             600


THE ALTERNATIVE WITH THE HIGHEST EXPECTED VALUE IS: 2. TRAIN
```

The best alternative in this series of outputs of expected value computations is number 2. That is, the best alternative on the basis of safety criteria only is the train.

Assignments

1. Calculate the expected values for the three decision trees of the A-bomb problem.

2. Apply minmax and maxmax to the decision trees of the A-bomb problem. Is the decision different?

3. Define the A-bomb problem to take into account possible deaths of noncombatants, both allied and nonallied. Are the decisions different?

4. Generate alternatives for President Truman that end the war without dropping the A-bomb. Use brain storming.

5. Is the approach to Truman's A-bomb problem valid? Is it an accurate representation of the decision-making process that actually occurred? How might ethical and public relations considerations have affected the solving of this problem?

A DSS TOOL KIT: COMPONENTS AND THEIR USES

II

One effective method for building a DSS is to assemble a series of modular components, or parts. Each part of such a system is relatively easy to explain, understand, and implement. When the parts are put together a flexible, effective DSS is formed. This methodology can be regarded as a "tool kit" approach to the building of a computerized DSS. Chapters within this section describe the discrete parts, or components, of a modular DSS. The section as a whole, then, presents the sum of the parts, a functional DSS.

The first component covered in this section is a *user facility* that establishes a gateway to the other components of a DSS.

The second major component is a database management system (DBMS). DBMS elements that figure in implementation of a DSS include a schema, programs for schema definition and maintenance, a query language, programs for implementing the query language, and capabilities for data entry.

The third element in the DSS tool kit consists of a set of models to aid decision making. These include a program used to calculate decision trees.

A fourth element within the DSS tool kit is a display capability that can present results graphically.

These elements are demonstrated as they are unfolded through use of a case scenario involving the decision-making tasks associated with management of a product line by a bicycle manufacturer.

3 A USER FACILITY

Abstract

- A DSS is regarded in this text as a personal problem-solving tool for an individual manager or management group.

- This means that managers themselves must be able to deal with computer systems and to derive information that they perceive as relevant to the problems they are trying to solve and the decisions they must make.

- This chapter presents a *tool kit* and accompanying methodologies that permit both development of the DSS structure by a computer information system (CIS) professional and direct interaction with the DSS by a manager. The software elements for tool kit assembly are reviewed.

- Also covered are the means that managers can use to interface with the systems developed through use of the specialized tools. The specific interface to be provided under the introduced methodology is the selection menu. Using the provided tools, the CIS professional can develop tailored menus that provide access to the resources within a DSS.

THE TOOL KIT APPROACH

As described in the previous chapter, application of a computerized DSS begins with an expressed management problem for which a decision is required. The decision requirement is then specified and parameterized through use of a decision tree. The computerized DSS is then used to estimate the parameters of the decision tree specification.

For example, in the case scenario involving a shipment of hams, parameters involve time and cost for alternate carriers, truck, rail, and air. The computer was used to search files containing data on past experiences. Reports from the file searches were then used to project probable future costs and delivery schedules. The manager in this semi-structured decision situation was supported directly in choosing the best shipping method.

Fourth-Generation Methods

The computer elements used for decision support, both in the Chapter 2 examples and in the management world at large, tend to consist of a series of major, in-place modules. These modules, in effect, are the tools that form a DSS kit. Assembling functional computer systems from generic, existing modules in this way characterizes what is known as the *fourth-generation* approach to computer software. Fourth-generation techniques, in effect, constitute an "erector set" methodolgy.

Fourth-generation methods have been likened to developments in the stereo field. There was a time when complete hi-fi sets were assembled and launched in their own furniture items or fixtures. As fans became more sophisticated, emphasis changed. People bought speakers, tuners, amplifiers, turntables, and tape decks according to dictates of individual tastes and pocketbooks. Home stereo systems were assembled from kits of components. The same analogy applies directly to the evolution of fourth-generation software tools. Instead of constructing separate, monolithic sets of program code to deal with individual problems, systems specialists can now shop the marketplace for components. Systems can be assembled rapidly and economically through this prefabricated approach.

By the time DSS became an identifiable discipline, fourth-generation software techniques were a known factor. DSS systems proved naturals for fourth-generation software methods because of both time and money constraints. The time constraints came from the fact that decisions are made under pressure. When help is requested, the next word spoken is usually "now!" A typical explanation is: "If I needed it tomorrow, I'd have called you tomorrow."

In the systems world, fourth-generation techniques for assembling systems are performed with the aid of special software tools. A common term used for such a software package is *user facility*. The same basic techniques are also referred to as *dialog management* and *menu generator* systems.

A common denominator of all user facility techniques is that they form an interface between a nontechnical user and a *hierarchical* software structure. That is, one underlying tool needed in constructing a DSS is a special purpose program that enables a user, in job-related terminology, to communicate with the multi-level set of software that constitutes a DSS tool kit.

Types of User Facilities

Several types of user facility, or interface, programs are available. These, typically, are identified by the type of interface used. Types of interfaces include:

- Command driven
- Menu driven
- Icon based
- Natural language.

As a basis for explaining these types of user facilities and their functions, the discussion that follows reviews the characteristics and components of a typical, tool-kit type of DSS. As a basis for this discussion, Figure 3-1 outlines the basic DSS components.

DSS COMPONENTS

Decision support systems, as described in Chapter 2, appear in virtually infinite varieties in response to decision situations and criteria.

1. UTILITIES FOR USER INTERACTION

    1.1 EDITORS FOR SCHEMA, DATA TABLE, AND DIALOG TABLE MAINTENANCE

        1.1.1 LINE–ORIENTED EDITOR (LED)
        1.1.2 SCREEN–ORIENTED EDITOR (SED)

    1.2 USER FACILITY

        1.2.1 MENU PROGRAM

2. DBMS

    2.1 TABLE MANIPULATION

        2.1.1 JOIN
        2.1.2 SELECT
        2.1.3 PROJECT
        2.1.4 COLUMN ARITHMETIC :
            ADD
            SUBTRACT
            MULTIPLY
            DIVIDE
        2.1.5 SUMMARIZE
        2.1.6 DISPLAY
        2.1.7 SORT
        2.1.8 DELETE
        2.1.9 UNION

3. MODELS

    3.1 DTREE (DECISION TREE)

    3.2 RLINE (RESISTANT LINE)

    3.3 ACCOUNTING MODELS

        3.3.1 INCO (INCOME STATEMENT)
        3.3.2 BALA (BALANCE SHEET)

    3.4 SPREAD (SPREADSHEET MODELING)

4. GRAPHIC DISPLAYS

    4.1 SCATTER (SCATTERGRAM)

    4.2 BANDW (BOX – AND – WHISKER DIAGRAM)

    4.3 HISTO (HISTOGRAM)

    4.4 PIE (PIE CHART)

5. EXPERT SYSTEMS

    5.1 ES

Figure 3-1.   This is a listing of the components of a generic DSS and the relationships among those components.

All of these individualized systems, however, require and use certain basic, fundamental, *primitive* software components. The general family of software components, identified by generic names and in typical hierarchical relationship patterns, are shown in Figure 3-1.

The remainder of this chapter deals with the first group of elements, utilities, identified in Figure 3-1. The specific topics are the line-oriented editor, the screen-oriented editor, and the MENU program. The succeeding portions of the hierarchical listing are covered in the remaining chapters of Part II.

To illustrate the content of this and succeeding chapters, a case scenario will be used. The case is built around the Olympic Bicycle Corporation and its decision making relating to product identification and selection. In preparation, the discussions that follow identify and describe briefly all of the software tools identified in Figure 3-1. As the case unfolds, individual tools, in order of description, will be described in relation to the illustrated decisions.

DSS Tool Kit Utilities for User Interaction

The first set of utilities to be used consists of the line-oriented and screen-oriented editors. The type of editor used will depend upon the computer available to the DSS designer. In general, line editors are used with time-sharing, mainframe systems. Screen editors are encountered more commonly with microcomputer systems. The functions and rules for editing, however, are similar for both types of editing utilities.

Use of editors in the implementation of a DSS under techniques described here can be likened to the process of program writing. That is, the editors are used to build tables of specifications that support the operations to be executed by the software packages to be called by the DSS. Typical of fourth-generation techniques, instructions entered in the Olympic Bicycle scenario will be declarative, rather than procedural. That is, the instructions will be closer to those written under database languages rather than in such procedure-oriented languages as COBOL, FORTRAN, and Pascal.

Four types of programs (declarative specifications) will be written through use of the line- and screen-oriented utilities:

- Data definition schema for the database management system (DBMS)
- Specification tables for the user facility (MENU program)
- Templates for the spreadsheet program
- Production rules for the expert system.

In addition, the utility editors will be used to key data into the database. This application is a matter of convenience. In a situation involving larger volumes of data, files could be shared with existing transaction processing and management information systems. However, for virtually any DSS, the potential is present for keying data through editing utilities.

Data definition schema for the DBMS.   A decision support system is based on selective use of data contained within a database. The database, in turn, has a specific structure for storing and managing data. In effect, a DBMS is a set of programs designed specifically to organize and handle data. For the purposes of this discussion, data for DSS use are organized in tables arranged in rows and columns. The data definition schema communicates the needs of the DSS to the DBMS by naming and describing the columns and rows of data to be used. The DSS designer establishes the needed definitions through use of the editing utilities.

Specification tables for the user facility.   In addition to defining the data tables to be used, the DSS designer must also create menus through which users will interact with the system. As identified above, a variety of interfaces is available, including command driven, icon based, and natural language. For the specific tool kit methodology to be applied in this and succeeding chapters, the authors have selected a menu-driven approach. This method, the authors feel, is both easy to explain and to implement. Under this approach, the DSS designer uses the editing utilities to enter specifications for the MENU program, a tool created for this purpose.

Templates for the spreadsheet program.   Spreadsheets, as described, are a standard, frequently used DSS tool. Thus, it is important to have underlying programs within the DSS tool kit that can be applied to create spreadsheet formats, accept data entries, and complete projections or forecasts usable as a basis for managerial decision making. The templates provided include settings of headings and formats for entry of computational operators to be applied within spreadsheets created by the user.

Production rules for the expert system.   Expert systems are outgrowths of work by scientists in the field of artificial intelligence. An expert system is a kind of DSS that applies rules to derive decision recommendations. The specific type of expert system incorporated in the tool kit under development in this discussion is known as a *production rule* expert system.

A production rule is expressed in a format such as: IF (condition) . . . THEN (action). That is, when the system senses a quantitative condition or the occurrence of a defined event, this causes a signal, or specified output. Typically, the system cannot get all of its answers from a database. Rather, on sensing a condition, the system asks a user to indicate whether the specific condition is TRUE or FALSE. As an alternative, the system might ask the user to input a value for the condition. In such situations, the expert system becomes a vehicle for "what if . . . ?" simulations.

The production rules for a specific problem situation or application are sometimes referred to as the system's *knowledge base.* Under this tool kit approach, editing utilities are used by the DSS designer to enter the rules that form the knowledge base.

The User Facility

Editing utilities support the designer's and builder's access to the system. The designer/builder specifies the details of the end user's interface with the system. The user facility software implements these specifications and forms the link between the end user (who is a manager) and the other software components that constitute a DSS.

The DSS software components, particularly those associated directly with a DBMS, have what amount to languages of their own. These database instructions are tools for navigating through masses of data and for finding specific data items.

The user facility serves, in effect, as an interpreter that communicates with the DSS operating languages on the basis of simple instructions easily mastered by a decision maker. The instructions included under a program such as MENU use terms native to the decision maker rather than to the DBMS. Thus, the decision maker is not burdened by having to learn DBMS command sets. Also, the user facility allows the designer to present a single communication path between the user and the DSS. Thus, as far as the user is concerned, the tool kit takes on the appearance of a uniform, responsive DSS, rather than of a collection of components.

To illustrate, a user can enter an instruction to SELECT delinquent bank loan accounts. The language used is foreign to the database package. But the MENU software will translate this instruction into a formal command that causes the DBMS to search for all accounts against which there have been no payments for 45 days or more. The commands actually executed are in the formal, structured terms of the appropriate DBMS languages.

Database Management System (DBMS)

A DBMS is a set of software that organizes and handles a collection of data. This may sound simple. But the software functions involved can be complex and massive. In building a DSS through the tool kit approach, attention focuses on the query capabilities of a DBMS.

The specific query functions to be used in your example DSS tool kit include JOIN, SELECT, PROJECT, column arithmetic (ADD, SUBTRACT, MULTIPLY, DIVIDE), SUMMARIZE, and DISPLAY.

JOIN is a command that causes the system to combine two data tables into one. SELECT is an operation that searches through and delivers rows within a table that conform to stated criteria. PROJECT identifies and delivers a subset of the columns of a table, also based upon application of stated criteria. Column arithmetic is a capability for performing basic arithmetic operations or combinations of operations upon entire sets of data elements within columns of a table.

SUMMARIZE combines data in multiple rows of a table on the basis of conditions or criteria. DISPLAY causes output of a table of processed, selected data to a display or printed document.

Models

Within a DSS context, the term *model* refers primarily to a set of mathematical formulas that represent, or emulate, the behavior of an organization or situation that is subject to investigation and decision making. The discipline of management science has developed many whole families of models. These include techniques such as linear programming, computer simulation, decision theory, regression analyses, and others, all of which are appropriate for inclusion within a DSS. Specific modeling techniques selected for inclusion in the tool kit under discussion include: decision tree, resistant line, accounting models (income statement and balance sheet), and spreadsheet models.

Decision trees are discussed and illustrated in Chapter 2. Resistant line is an exploratory data analysis technique for fitting a line to bivariate (two-dimensional) data. In other words, a linear model is able to represent table-type data sets for interpolations and projections. Accounting models represent the financial status of an entity at a given, stated point in time. Two common accounting models generate balance sheets and income statements. The balance sheet is cumulative, while the income statement reflects the results of transactions over a given time period. A spreadsheet program is a modeling system. That is, spreadsheet software makes possible the implementation of a number of user-specified, analytic models in the general format of an accounting spreadsheet. All of these terms and concepts are explained in subsequent chapters.

Graphic Displays

Graphic displays are techniques for representing sets of data in pictorial form. Within a DSS, graphic displays are convenient, natural techniques for presenting data from a system to a decision maker and also from a decision maker to a system. Within the DSS under discussion, interest centers around graphic outputs delivered to decision makers as an aid in visualizing the meaning and consequences of data to facilitate the process of selecting the most effective decision alternative. Techniques to be incorporated in the DSS tool kit under discussion include scattergrams, box-and-whisker diagrams, histograms, and pie charts.

A scattergram shows a series of points on a plane. The points are positioned to represent values of data pairs within a grid area. A box-and-whisker diagram is an exploratory data analysis technique for presenting a distribution of values for a single variable. Uses of box-and-whisker diagrams are similar to those for histograms. A histogram is a highly familiar graphic device often called a *bar chart*. Pie charts are circular presentations depicting relationships of parts of a whole entity.

Expert Systems

Expert systems are software packages credited with being the first commercial implementations of artificial intelligence principles. Programs that implement expert systems are designed to collect decision-relevant data for evaluation under imbedded rules and for consultation with human users regarding implications of findings.

Popular examples of expert systems include medical diagnosis programs. For example, if a diagnostic expert system is informed that a patient has three of four symptoms that could point to the presence of a given disease, the system might ask the using physician about the fourth symptom. On input, the system would then either report the possibility of the disease or rule it out. Should the system offer a diagnosis, the user can ask the system to outline the reasoning followed, providing an interactive double check. Many people regard expert systems as the wave of the future in the DSS field. A rudimentary DSS expert system is incorporated within the DSS tool kit discussed in this section of your text.

CASE SCENARIO: OLYMPIC BICYCLE COMPANY

Olympic Bicycle is a midwestern company founded late in the nineteenth century by two brothers who set up a shop in a garage behind their homes. The brothers eventually sold control of the business to a group of employees who became increasingly active as the business grew. Eventually, the company sold stock through a public underwriting and, as the fitness craze took hold, broadened the product line. During the 1960s, the company introduced a variety of small-wheeled and motocross bikes. These were added to an already extensive line of touring and road racing bicycles.

The company enjoys a quality reputation which is protected by exercising care in the choice of retail outlets. Select specialty stores are licensed to sell the company's line, as are limited numbers of sporting goods outlets. A few large department and mail order outlets also carry the Olympic line. All told, the company sells some 250,000 bicycles annually and has revenues of some $17 million. Profits have been averaging just below $1.5 million.

The bicycle business is extremely competitive. To keep ahead in this field, Olympic has built an image and a reputation as a company run under a shirtsleeve style of management. Key managers include the president, Roger Wheelwright, the vice president for manufacturing, John Gear, and the vice president for marketing, Sally Sellem. All three top managers depend heavily on the services and advice of the company's controller, Ian Sharp.

Manufacturing has a reputation for innovation and for embracing the latest fabrication techniques. In particular, model-year changes are used as opportunities to review and introduce improvements into fabrication methods. Gear is particularly interested in numerical control robotics techniques. For this reason, Gear is anxious, every year, to see market forecasts developed each July by Sellem. Gear looks continually for projected volumes that will support upgrading of capital equipment to produce and assemble product.

Under long-standing policies and practices, production and marketing commitments are brought into focus each year on July 15. On this date, Sellem is responsible for releasing a market forecast for products and units to be built and sold in the next model year. Model-year manufacturing in this business typically begins in September, reaches one peak for the Christmas season, then increases again the following spring. New, hand-made models for the next selling year are introduced at a series of shows that take place in April through mid-June.

Among other inconveniences, this schedule puts pressure on the July 4 holiday for Olympic managers. As the July 15 deadline approaches, Gear becomes a frequent visitor to Sellem's office. The two vice presidents regularly have lunch together to discuss the consequences and trade-offs of production costs and volumes.

These trade-offs represent important decision criteria in the formation of each year's product line. Sellem has to know the break points at which substantial production cost reductions can be realized. This knowledge helps her to pick the featured item in the product line, the item that will be the focus of advertising and dealer promotion. A break in manufacturing price that reduces costs can, obviously, make it possible to reduce price to the market. In selecting the product mix for each year, decision responsibility belongs entirely to Sellem.

The policy at Olympic is that product plans are market driven. The company responds to market demand rather than making manufacturing decisions and trying to press product upon the market based on production economies.

To reach product-line decisions, Sellem needs reliable historic information on sales for the previous years. The marketing department has a minicomputer system used to process customer invoices. Sales histories by product and customer are accumulated as by-products. This information is incorporated in a database. One of the tables in the database, named SLSFIG (for ''sales figures''), is organized to present the following data items in separate columns:

- Model year
- Wheel size
- Color
- Model type (motocross = MX, balloon tire = BT, racing = RA, touring = TO)
- Number of speeds (1, 3, 10, or 15)
- Boy or girl (B, G)
- Average unit sales price
- Average unit cost
- Total sales, in units, for model year.

Figure 3-2 shows this table in row-and-column format, with data included for illustrative purposes.

Model Year	Wheel Size	Color	Model Type	Speeds	Boy/ Girl	Price	Cost	Total Sales
83	20	R	BT	1	B	$85	$50	1,236
83	24	R	MX	1	G	$110	$55	8,921
86	24	B	MX	3	B	$120	$57	1,342
87	20	G	TO	10	B	$180	$88	8,132

Figure 3-2. This screen display devised for management at Olympic Bicycle identifies the company's product models and gives the major features of each.

Sellem's July 15 forecast is a preliminary plan. It is not necessary, at this time, to go into detail about color, wheel size, etc. Production is concerned mainly with tooling up to produce frames for the main models: MX, BT, RA, and TO. Thus, the first major query to the database will be aimed at discovering last year's total sales according to this model breakdown. That is, sales history will be derived to match the content of the decision to be made about production requirements. This involves summarizing all data in the table for the previous year into one record for each model type. The format of the data display sought by Sellem is shown in Figure 3-3. In this format, the entries showing groups of 9 values represent numeric fields. The number of 9 entries represents the number of digits that can be presented in the DSS display. The X entries represent alphanumeric fields.

Sellem could cause her minicomputer system to display this information through use of three simple database retrieval commands that act upon the SLSFIG data table: SELECT, SUMMARIZE, and DISPLAY. The SELECT command causes the system to choose only the data items that represent sales for the previous year. The SUMMARIZE command can cause all of the information on each model

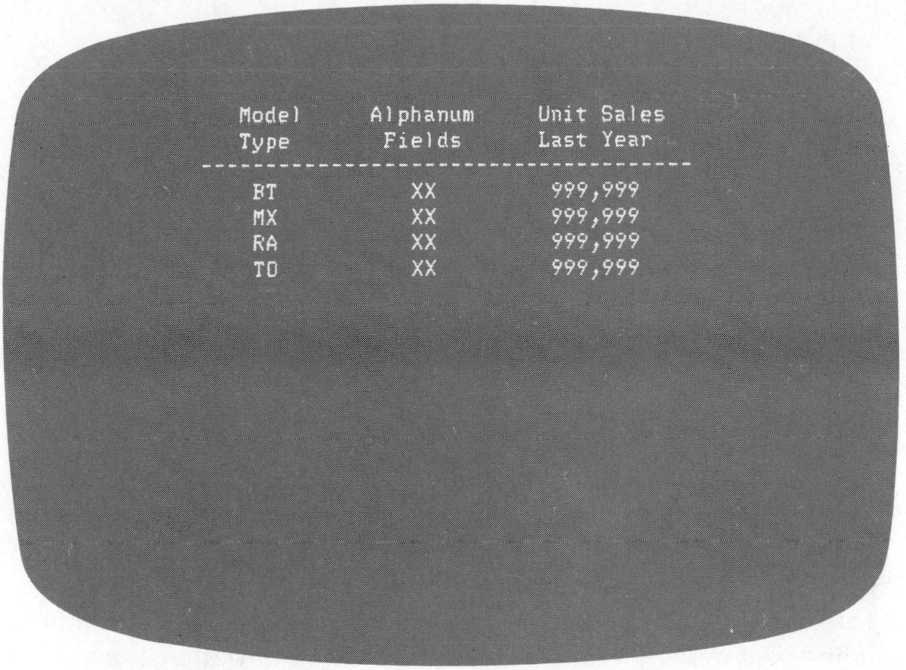

```
            Model      Alphanum      Unit Sales
            Type        Fields       Last Year
          ------------------------------------------
             BT          XX           999,999
             MX          XX           999,999
             RA          XX           999,999
             TD          XX           999,999
```

Figure 3-3. This screen display shows the format of the output summarizing sales histories of Olympic bicycles, by model, for a specific year.

type to be added, with the sum stored in another table. The DIS-PLAY command, then, can display the second table on Sellem's terminal screen.

The starting point for Sellem's July 15 forecast, then, is a report providing historic data on last year's sales for four product lines. Once this picture is in focus, Sellem would probably want to look at trends. To do this, Sellem could cause the DSS to present data plots on product sales for multiple years. Assume, for example, that she chooses five years as an adequate trend picture. Using the SLSFIG table, Sellem would command the system to SELECT five years of sales totals for the BT line. A PLOT command would then be used to cause the system to produce a scattergram graphic display on BT sales.

This same procedure could then be repeated for the MX, the RA, and the TO lines.

The trend information helps Sellem to decide which of the product lines is to be featured in next year's marketing program. The sales target for this product line would then be weighted to reflect the anticipated effect of advertising and marketing emphasis. This decision can be represented in a decision tree structure, as is done in Figure 3-4. This shows simply that Sellem must pick one of the product lines to be featured. Factors affecting this decision can include historic sales patterns and also a "gut feel" evaluation of trends or fads currently at work in the marketplace.

To forecast production quantities for all four lines, Sellem is guided by the trends indicated by the scattergrams on the individual products. She uses a rule of thumb for this purpose. If a product has experienced sales increases in the last three years, the quantity forecast is increased by 10 percent. If the increase was for the last year only, the increase is kept to 5 percent. Similar rules of thumb are applied if sales have been off. These are rules of thumb that have been in place at Olympic for many years. Figure 3-5 shows a decision tree representing application of this decision process for the BT model. Of course, decision trees for other products would be similar in appearance.

To interact with the DSS and its database for this kind of decision support, Sellem needs an interface capability. Popular interface techniques used in DSS software are reviewed within the context of the Olympic Bicycle case in the discussion that follows.

COMMAND-DRIVEN INTERFACES

Command-driven operations require an entry from the user without any benefit of format or choices presented by the system. In other words, the user must initiate an input in a form and format acceptable to the computer before anything can happen.

Typically, a computer displays a *prompt* to announce that the system is ready for a command to be selected by the user. In this context, a prompt is simply an indication or message from the system inviting entry of a command. On displaying a prompt, the computer waits passively for an instruction. If you have programmed in BASIC,

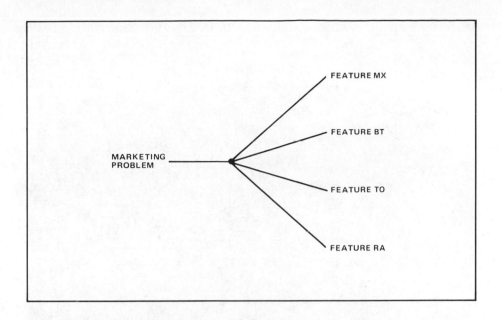

Figure 3-4. This diagram identifies the decision alternatives to be quantified in the Olympic Bicycle marketing decision. The product models are, in effect, the decision factors for which quantity values must be established.

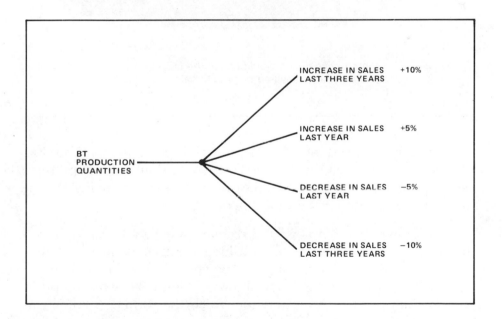

Figure 3-5. As an aid to selection of decision alternatives, the decision tree shows the percentage of production increase or decrease appropriate to given sales history conditions.

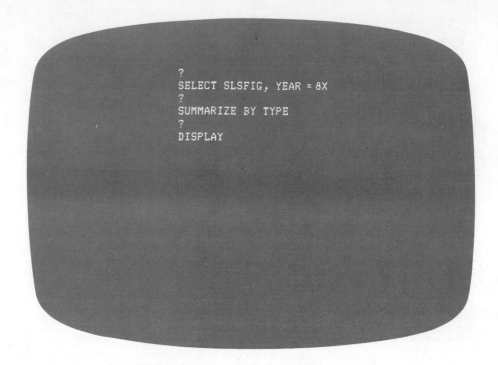

```
?
SELECT SLSFIG, YEAR = 8X
?
SUMMARIZE BY TYPE
?
DISPLAY
```

Figure 3-6. This interactive dialog would cause the DSS Tool Kit to display sales figures for the identified year, classified by type of sale.

you have experienced the READY prompt. If you have used an IBM PC, you have probably encountered the A> or simply the > prompt. These prompts tell the user that the system is ready for an instruction to be processed under the DOS operating system.

Assume that Olympic's DSS displays a question mark (?) as a prompt. In effect, the system is asking the user what is wanted. To generate the sales summary for last year's sales, Sellem and the computer engaged in the dialog shown in Figure 3-6. The computer would then display the report for which the format is shown in the illustration.

To plot five-year product histories, Sellem and her computer exchanged the dialog shown in Figure 3-7. This command set would

```
?
SELECT SLSFIG, YEAR > 8X, TYPE = BT
PLOT UNITS BY YEAR
```

Figure 3-7. A five-year product history would be generated in response to this interactive dialog.

cause display of a scattergram showing five-year sales figures for the BT line. The dialog would be repeated, of course, for the other product lines.

The command language illustrated above has been contrived specifically for this example. However, these instructions are typical of many command-driven DSS functions. As demonstrated, the use of a command-driven DSS requires previous knowledge from the user. Also, the user must be familiar with the content and makeup of the data structure being manipulated. The command vocabulary and the syntax for each command must be mastered before any results can be realized. True, the command set and the instructions are simple. However, the vocabulary of individual DSS packages can become extensive and complex. This represents a drawback for the use of pure command-driven interfaces.

On the other hand, command-driven interfaces are relatively easy to develop and implement. Further, simple command structures like those shown make efficient use of communication links to the computer. (Note on the sample dialogs that less than one line of data was transmitted to achieve an interaction between user and computer.) Until recently, the economies of the command-driven approach were extremely attractive to DSS designers. Because of this, many experienced computer users have become accustomed to and comfortable with command-driven interfaces. In effect, command-driven interfaces are, in some quarters, a habit that can be hard to break.

Another factor encouraging alternate design approaches has been the popularity of personal computers. As the computer-using population has grown into the millions, economies of scale have entered the picture. Even though other approaches may be more expensive to design and implement, the size of the user base, along with increased convenience for inexperienced users, has become a driving force in favor of the other approaches described below.

In evaluating any DSS interface, available user "help" facilities should be a considered factor. A help facility is a simplified request for assistance entered by the user that causes the system to respond with special directions or instructions. In a command-driven system, the initiating instruction might simply be HELP. This entry could, typically, cause the system to list its vocabulary of commands. The user could then specify a single command for which help is needed. A HELP entry accompanied by a specific command menu could trigger interactive presentation of what amounts to portions of a user manual.

MENU-DRIVEN INTERFACES

A *menu-driven* interface presents the user with a list of choices for available services. The user can be instructed to enter a number, letter, or name for a selected choice. This entry, in turn, causes the system to provide a service, to display a submenu for further selection, or to display an error or status message.

As an example, the sample menu in Figure 3-8 might be used in some portion of a DSS at Olympic Bicycle. Suppose Sellem had this

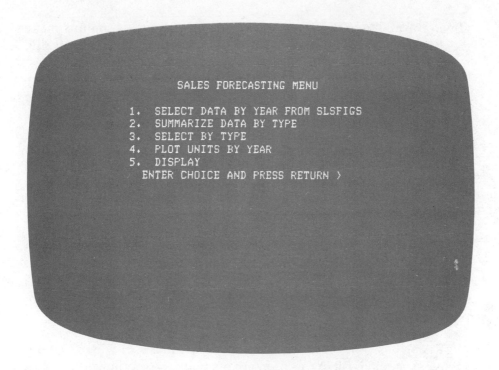

Figure 3-8. This is the SALES FORECASTING MENU for the Olympic Bicycle marketing DSS.

interface as a working basis for the developing data for her July 15 decision. This menu would provide a specialized tool that anticipates exactly the query pattern needed to derive her decision-supporting information for the specific forecasting problem. Bear in mind that this is a hypothetic case. The menu illustrates derivation of specific information for a special purpose. In reality, DSS menus rarely fit applications with such precision.

To derive a report on sales by product for last year, Sellem would simply step through selections 1, 2, and 5 on this menu. For the trend plots for each product type, she would select options 3 and 4 for each product to be evaluated.

A potential drawback to the menu approach is that the designer must anticipate, with full assurance, all of the possible uses for a DSS.

Given the ability of the designer to anticipate all needs, menus make it extremely easy for the user to interact with the system. Typically, menus are established in sequences, forming a hierarchy of choices. This is extremely convenient in helping an inexperienced user to step through the system in small increments. However, an experienced or expert user often finds it frustrating and wasteful to have to navigate through a series of menus when the destination is known in advance.

In comparison with a command-driven system, there can be disadvantages if a system has any serious communication constraints. It takes longer by far for a system to process menus in and out than it does to process prompts and commands.

Comparing the design efforts of command- and menu-driven systems, the need to anticipate every possible use of a system and coordinating selections within menus is far more difficult than design of a command-driven system. The menu system is simply more complex physically even though it is designed to be simple logically.

Regardless of technical design difficulties, however, menu systems remain easiest for interactive use by inexperienced or occasional users. Many top-level managers fall into this category. These individuals tend to prefer the simplicity of menu selection to a requirement for memorizing even a small set of control commands. Thus, menus are considered to be necessities for many decision support systems.

For situations in which there will be a mix of expert and inexperienced users, menu and command capabilities are often provided as alternate options within the same DSS. (This is feasible especially if a menu interface is added to or used to supplement a system that is basically command driven.) In such situations, a menu option makes it possible for an expert user to enter a command mode. In this mode, it becomes possible to navigate DSS functions far more efficiently than could be done through menu sequences.

''Help'' features can be incorporated through either of two approaches. First, a listed option on each menu gives the user a chance to ask for a help display. Second, there can be a designated key. Each time this key is pressed, the system enters the help mode.

ICON-BASED INTERFACES

An *icon-based* interface is a specialized menu system that uses pictures as a basis for user selection in place of descriptive phrases. Rather than keying in a number or letter as a basis for selection of services, the user operates a pointing mechanism. Pointer control can be manipulated through such devices as a mouse, a light pen, a track ball, a joy stick, or a touch screen.

In any case, an activating impulse is triggered after the pointer has been moved to the desired selection. In reality, a specific spot on the screen is selected to represent each offered function. Pictures identify the function for the user, who moves an arrow to a point of correspondence with an icon. Once the icon is selected, the computer performs the pictured function. Examples of icons in common use include pictures of file cabinets to indicate file processing and pictures of wastebaskets to represent a file erasure.

One drawback of an icon-based interface is that a much higher data transmission capacity is required to transmit images than to handle text. Thus, use of icon-based interfaces is considered impractical for remote work stations using telecommunications. Most icon-based systems are associated with a dedicated, stand-alone, microcomputer work station.

As another potential drawback, it can be difficult to devise original, unique icons for all functions that can be supported by a DSS. In practice, most icon-based systems also make extensive use of conventional text menus.

On the positive side, icon-based systems tend to be extremely attractive for inexperienced computer users. As a further advantage, icon-based interfaces can be convenient in graphics-oriented systems within which most input and service selection is through a pointing device. Users of such systems should not have to switch to a keyboard to enter routine commands.

Help systems can be implemented through use of especially developed icons. Help requests can be triggered through such icons as question marks.

NATURAL LANGUAGE INTERFACES

A *natural language* interface is one in which the user can enter commands in English statements composed of words or phrases of his or her own choosing. The idea is that the language used is natural to the job performance of the individual decision maker. Thus, commands entered by Sellem to derive data for her July 15 forecast might read:

> HOW MANY UNITS OF EACH PRODUCT DID WE SELL LAST YEAR?

> SHOW ME A FIVE-YEAR SALES TREND FOR EACH PRODUCT.

> PLOT FIVE-YEAR SALES HISTORY FOR BALLOON TIRE BIKES.

Natural language interfaces are, at this writing, largely in the domains of research and dreams for the future. That is, practical, workable, general-purpose natural language interfaces do not yet exist. However, the rate of research and development that'is taking place merits your awareness. During your working career, you may well have powerful tools of this type available.

One major, current problem inhibiting release of workable natural language interfaces lies in techniques for dealing with negative answers, situations in which a system has no answer for a user request. For example, suppose Sellem asked: WHAT WERE BT SALES IN CHICAGO LAST YEAR? If the system were loaded with the SLSFIG file at the time, this data would not be accessible. A poorly conceived interface might answer: NONE. This would be true based on data content within the system. However, such a response would be misleading at best, and probably highly frustrating for the user. The goal of designers is to produce natural language interfaces that are more cooperative with users. In this context, the term *cooperative* implies that the system would recognize its own potential shortcomings and would present hints for further attempts by the user.

For the purposes of this discussion, natural language interfaces are not a present factor except for a few, special situations involving extremely limited capabilities. Thus, natural language interfaces will not be considered further in your exposure to practical, working decision support and expert systems.

DSS TOOL KIT MENU INTERFACE

The DSS tool kit to which you are being introduced will, obviously, need a user interface. The particular interface tool chosen for your kit is menu driven.

Within the context of an overall DSS, a menu-driven interface is a program module that links to other program modules in executing instructions from the user. Instructions from the user, in turn, are in the form of selections of options presented by menu displays. These menu displays, obviously, must have been designed and encoded in advance by the DSS designer. These instructions, known as *menu specifications*, are stored in a data file that is created and modified through use of text editing software. Considerable latitude is possible in the formatting and writing of menu specifications. However, the menu-driven interface in your tool kit follows a particular philosophy and set of parameters that reflect an individual designer's preferences. These specifications are described and presented below.

A sample menu that could be used to meet the needs of decision makers at Olympic Bicycle is shown in Figure 3-9.

Coding for Menu-Driven Interface

To create and support the menu shown in Figure 3-9, the designer prepared the coding entries shown in Figure 3-10. These menu specifications were then keyed into the system with a line or screen editor and stored in a file named MSPEC. The tool kit MENU program expects to find this MSPEC file.

When a user initiates a DSS session, the first execution of the system is to initiate processing of the MENU program. The menu program then retrieves the menu specification file and displays the first menu encountered on the user terminal. The MENU program identifies menu content for displays through recognition of the alphabetic code shown in the leftmost column of Figure 3-10. In this instance, the letter ''A'' designates content for the first menu.

The second column in the program file in Figure 3-10 associates data items with specific menu options. A blank in Column 2 identifies a header, or title, line for the menu display.

Individual selection entries, contained in the third column of the program in Figure 3-10, can initiate different executions, depending

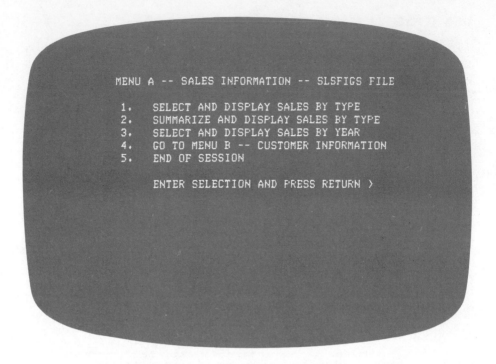

MENU A -- SALES INFORMATION -- SLSFIGS FILE

    1.   SELECT AND DISPLAY SALES BY TYPE
    2.   SUMMARIZE AND DISPLAY SALES BY TYPE
    3.   SELECT AND DISPLAY SALES BY YEAR
    4.   GO TO MENU B -- CUSTOMER INFORMATION
    5.   END OF SESSION

    ENTER SELECTION AND PRESS RETURN >

Figure 3-9. This menu would hold the key to user access to the files of sales figures within the Olympic Bicycle system.

---

on content. Statements enclosed entirely in quotation marks (''), without preceding key, command terms, represent message content to be displayed. The program in Figure 3-10 uses only two key, or command, terms: PROGRAM and GOTO.

The key term PROGRAM is followed by the name of the program module to be called and executed when the numbered option is selected by the user. Following the name of each called program is a set of data items in quotation marks. These data items are, in effect, transferred to the called program module for use in execution.

The key term GOTO is followed by a menu designator, such as the letter ''B,'' which identifies a target menu available for user selection. On execution, this command causes the system to display the designated menu.

```
A        "SALES INFORMATION -- SLSFIG FILE"
A    1   "SELECT AND DISPLAY SALES BY TYPE"
A    1   PROGRAM SELECT "SLSFIG, TYPE = ?TYPE?, WORK"
A    1   PROGRAM DISPLAY "WORK"
A    2   "SUMMARIZE AND DISPLAY SALES BY TYPE"
A    2   PROGRAM SUMMARIZE "SLSFIG, TYPE, WORK"
A    2   PROGRAM DISPLAY "WORK"
A    3   "SELECT AND DISPLAY SALES BY YEAR"
A    3   PROGRAM SELECT "SLSFIG, YEAR = ?YEAR?, WORK"
A    3   PROGRAM DISPLAY "WORK"
A    4   "GOTO MENU B -- CUSTOMER INFORMATION"
A    4   GOTO B
A    5   "END OF SESSION"
A    5   PROGRAM END
B        "CUSTOMER INFORMATION"
B    1   . . . and so forth . . .
```

Figure 3-10. This set of coding entries, using commands from within the DSS Tool Kit, would generate the menu shown in Figure 3-9.

In some situations, the designer may provide a capability for the user to insert variable instructions for a program module to be executed through an option selection. The MENU program permits the designer to designate such user entries through use of a word presented within two quotation marks to identify the stream of data being transferred to the called module. This feature is used in selections 1 and 3 in Figure 3-10.

When Selection 1 is executed, the system recognizes the question-mark-imbedded term TYPE. This condition causes the MENU program to display a message and wait for user entry of a value prior to execution of the user request. In response to Selection 1, the program asks: WHAT IS THE TYPE? The user then responds with an entry identifying the product line about which data are to be displayed.

The designer must be sure that the user's understanding of the message will be sufficiently specific to elicit a usable entry. Thus, a message might be expanded as follows: WHAT IS THE TYPE (PRODUCT LINE NAME)? If the designer wanted to expand the message in this way, coding in the program for this instruction would have to read: ?TYPE (PRODUCT LINE NAME)?

An important capability of this MENU program lies in the power of the PROGRAM command. All program modules within the tool kit to which you are being introduced are accessible through use of this PROGRAM command. Identification and explanation of these accessible modules will begin in this chapter and continue through several chapters that follow.

DSS TOOL KIT EDITOR PROGRAM MODULES

To create the menu specification program illustrated in Figure 3-10, the designer needs to choose a method for entering and saving the text that forms the menu specification. These entries require tool kit items for inputting and capturing text. These software utilities are known as *editors.*

In general, separate types of editors are used for work through on-line terminals to time-sharing systems and for microcomputers or work stations with separate, standalone intelligence.

Utilities used in conjunction with on-line systems are generally classified as *line editors.* That is, individual lines of text are entered and processed one at a time, with total content assembled in the main computer. The basic reason for this is that line editors were designed during an era of relatively slow data communication. It simply took too long to send texts of full documents to central computers for processing.

By contrast, microcomputers or terminals with distributed intelligence capabilities generally use *screen editor* software. This means, in effect, that an entire document can be entered, reviewed, and altered as an entity prior to transmission processing or compiling. In working terms, a line editor transmits all text on a given line each time a RETURN or ENTER key is pressed. By contrast, a screen editor captures coding for entire documents, including RETURN entries.

The result is essentially the same whether the designer works at a line editor or a screen editor. In general, screen editors are considered to be more effective methods because the user can command an overview of the entire document before committing the text to the computer. Your DSS tool kit includes both a line editor and a screen editor.

Tool Kit Line Editor—LED

The name of the line editor program module is LED. This module uses a command-driven interface that includes seven discrete commands. The prompt is a question mark. Figure 3-11 contains a table listing the LED commands and giving their meanings. Each of the commands listed can be called through entry of either the full term or just the first letter. Thus, an entry to get a file can begin with GET or just with G. The lower case indication of parameters asks for a literal entry of either a file name or a line number within the program. When a complete command has been keyed, the RETURN key is pressed and execution takes place.

Figure 3-12 represents a screen display for an LED session that could have led to creation of the first two lines of the menu specification program in Figure 3-10. In the first line of Figure 3-12, the program identifies itself as LED — DSS TOOLKIT LINE EDITOR. Then a question mark is displayed to indicate that the system is ready to accept commands. The first operator entry, NEW MSPEC, indicates that the operator wants the system to create a new file, called MSPEC. This name follows simple rules: All names must start with a letter. After the first character, any combination of letters or numbers may be used. The total length of the name cannot exceed six characters. Depending upon the computer and operating system used, there may be slightly different naming conventions. These rules apply specifically to the naming of files for your DSS tool kit.

In effect, the NEW command creates a new, empty file on the disk. The operator then must enter GET MSPEC. This command allows the operator to edit the file.

Returning to the session shown in Figure 3-12, once the computer accepts a valid name and the file is ready for editing, another question mark prompt is displayed. In response, the operator enters the command: I 1. This indicates an intent to INSERT line 1 into a file.

COMMAND	COMMAND PARAMETERS
GET	FILENAME
SAVE	FILENAME
DELETE	LINE#
INSERT	LINE#
REPLACE	LINE#
NEW	FILENAME
LIST	LINE# LINE#

Figure 3-11. This is a command summary for the DSS Tool Kit to be used in the remainder of this book.

```
<LED -- DSS TOOLKIT LINE EDITOR>
?  NEW MSPEC
?  GET MSPEC
?  I 1
A     "SALES INFORMATION -- SLSFIG FILE"
?  I 2
A  1  "SELECT AND DISPLAY SALES BY TYPE"
?  L
1: A     "SALES INFORMATION -- SLSFIG FILE"
2: A  1  "SELECT AND DISPLAY SALES BY TYPE"
?  S  MSPEC

<FILE MSPEC SAVED>
<LED ENDS>
```

Figure 3-12. This display shows an interactive session under the LED module of the DSS Tool Kit that could have led to generation of the instructions in the two opening lines of Figure 3-8.

The first line is keyed. Then, the operator enters a command to prepare the system to accept an INSERT for line 2. Line 2 is entered accordingly.

When the next question mark prompt appears, the operator enters an L command, indicating a LIST operation. When an L is entered without following line numbers, the system lists its entire file. Accordingly, the two lines entered to date are listed. In addition to the illustrated entry, two other uses of the LIST command are available. One entry is: LIST line#. This causes the system to list the single line at the specified location. The other entry option is: LIST line# line#. This causes a listing for all text from the first line number through to the second line number.

As the final entry in Figure 3-12, the user responds to the prompt with the entry: S. This causes the system to save the file under the designated name: MSPEC. If work is done on a file called through a G (GET) command, an S instruction will perpetuate the existing name. If no name is entered, following an S command, the system will terminate the session after saving the file. As another option, the user can enter a command under the format: S filename. This command format provides an opportunity to rename a file or to save the existing session separately from previous entries. If this optional format is used, the system saves the text entered during the session but does not terminate the line editing session.

Tool Kit Screen Editor—SED

The *screen editor* in your tool kit bears some resemblance to a word processor. However, there are restrictions that constrain the program module to its role as a programming tool.

Specifically, on initiating service, the user is confronted by a blank screen with which he or she can create any desired text. All entries are displayed on the screen without affecting computer files until a specific entry instruction is processed. Thus, in comparison with the LED program, there is no prompt and no need to interact on a line-by-line basis. The programmer simply enters instructions, one per line, until service is required.

In working with a screen editor, the user has full control over positioning of the cursor. Cursor movement can be to any position on the screen simply through manipulation of the cursor keys. This is an important element of distinction between line and screen editors. Screen editors are considered to be far more convenient and flexible because of this capability.

Keep in mind that these are properties and techniques for SED, an individual screen editor that has become a part of your own DSS tool kit. Other screen editors you encounter may present variations.

When a menu specification has been prepared through use of the LED or SED, programming for the entire DSS is effectively completed. This is literally true. No further programming is required. This capability, clearly, demonstrates the dramatic breakthroughs in system generation possible through fourth-generation software techniques.

To emphasize: Your training in programming for DSS development is complete. You are now ready to go ahead, in the ensuing chapter, with consideration of the DBMS component of a DSS.

Outlook

- A DSS is a hierarchical system that can be created through use of fourth-generation programming techniques. This chapter introduces the concept that will be carried forward through this section of the text. That is, a general-purpose software tool kit composed of fourth-generation software components will be introduced on a module-by-module basis over five chapters. This simplified software tool kit may be made available to you as a basis for completing class assignments.

- The first requirement in building a DSS is to select the technique to be used for establishing an interface between the user and the system. This chapter reviews four types of interfaces: command-driven, menu, icon, and natural language.

- The tool kit provided for your own DSS development utilizes a menu-driven interface approach. A program module, MENU, is used to develop the programs and displays that comprise the interface. A menu specification program that builds a menu-driven interface is introduced and demonstrated. Program writing tools, including a line editor and a screen editor, are introduced and their uses are described.

- The overall design of a DSS is, in effect, completed with the creation of a menu specification file. Once this menu specification is completed, no further programming is required. This type of capability demonstrates the power and potential of fourth-generation software techniques.

- In the chapters that follow, assembly of the tool kit continues.

Operation and Command Summary: LED

LED is a line-oriented text editor. It is used to create and maintain the various text files used in the DSS Tool Kit.

LED is invoked by keying "LED" and pressing ENTER at the "A>" prompt. Once invoked, the system will display a question mark prompt, "?." The question mark prompt is supplied by LED when it is waiting for the user to enter an editing command. Either the whole command or its first letter may be used.

LED allows editing to take place on files that have been brought into the computer's main memory with the GET command. Editing is accomplished through use of the IN-SERT, REPLACE, and LIST operations. When editing is complete, the file is rewritten to disk with the SAVE command. The DELETE command removes unwanted files from disk. The NEW command tells LED to create a new, empty file. The commands and their parameters are listed below.

GET filename

The GET command causes LED to read a previously created text file from diskette. The "filename" parameter tells LED which file to read. Filenames must be no longer than six characters and begin with a letter.

SAVE filename

The SAVE command causes LED to write an edited file to disk under the name specified in the "filename" parameter. If no filename is specified, the program will used the last name assigned to the file.

DELETE line#

The DELETE command causes LED to delete from the file the line number specified in the "line#" parameter.

INSERT line#
Lines of text are added to files with the INSERT command. The "line#" parameter specifies the number of the line that will precede inserted text. If the number given in the "line#" parameter does not exist in the file, LED will insert the text after the line previous to the "line#" asked for. To add text to the end of a file, use a "line#" parameter that is greater than any in the file.

REPLACE line#
The REPLACE command tells LED that the line indicated in the "line#" parameter is to be rekeyed. The specified line is deleted and the user is prompted for the replacement line. If the number given in the line# parameter is not present, LED displays an error message.

NEW filename
The NEW command creates a new text file. When this command is invoked, LED checks the disk to make sure that the file does not exist already. Then, an empty file is created on the disk. The GET command is used to read the new file into main memory and add text. The SAVE command is used to store the new file on diskette.

LIST line# line#
The LIST command allows users to reference or examine lines, or to call up lines that require editing. When invoked, LIST tells LED to list certain lines of text held in main memory. The "line#" parameters indicate which line(s). If only one "line#" parameter is supplied, LED lists only the line specified. Using both "line#" parameters causes LED to list all lines between and including those specified.

HELP
The HELP command lists the commands available.

Operation and Command Summary: SED

SED is a screen-oriented text editor used to create and maintain the various text files needed to build a DSS.

SED is invoked by keying "SED" and pressing ENTER at the "A>" prompt. Once invoked, SED presents a help menu that lists three options: create a new file, edit an existing file, or end the session.

Editing is accomplished by positioning the cursor where text is to be added or changed, and then keying the modification. The INSERT and DELETE control functions are supported. Pressing the ESC key ends the session.

Operation and Command Summary: MENU

The MENU program accesses the rest of the programs defined in the DSS tool kit. The program displays menus from which users select DSS functions. Menus consist of processing options that have been defined by the DSS designer and saved in a menu specification file.

The MENU program is executed by keying "MMENU" at the "A>" prompt. This command reads the menu specification file. Menu specifications are prepared using an editor and stored in a disk file called MENU. Menu specifications consist of individual lines of text. Columns are separated by one or more blank spaces.

The first column specifies the designation for the menu. The menu designation column can contain any combination of two letters and numbers. In this text, the use of a letter to designate the menu is followed as a convention.

The second column specifies the designation of a particular menu selection. The menu selection designation also can contain any combination of two letters and numbers. In this text, the use of a number to designate the menu selection is adhered to as a convention. Note that no entry is made in the second column for the line of descriptive text that will appear at the top of the menu when it is displayed for execution. The number of the description line is placed at the beginning of the lines for the menu selection entries.

The third column contains text that describes menu selection entries. This text is surrounded by double quote characters (''). The third column also may contain the substance of the menu selection entries, such as the set of operators and operands necessary to implement the menu selection. Each operator and its respective operands occupy one line in the menu specification file. Within a menu selection, these operator command lines are executed in the order in which they appear. (See Figure 3-10 for an example of a menu specification file.) Valid operators are:

PROGRAM

The PROGRAM operator requires two operands. The first operand is the name of the program to be invoked to implement the menu selection. Several programs may be invoked in this way in a single menu selection. The second operand is a list of control parameters for the designated program. This list of control parameters is surrounded by double quote characters ('').

The content of the control parameter list is dictated by the program designated. However, the MENU program scans this list before passing it to the designated program to identify any occurrences of question marks (?). Question marks cause the MENU program to prompt users with whatever appears between the two question marks, wait for a response, and pass the user response to the designated program in the control parameter list. The user response replaces the phrase bordered by question marks. If no question marks are present, the control parameter list is passed to the designated program as is.

A special program that can be designated as the operand of PROGRAM is the END program. The END program tells the MENU program to terminate and pass control back to the operating system.

GOTO

The GOTO operand requires only one parameter, the designation of the menu which is to be displayed next. Execution of GOTO causes the designated menu to be displayed for use by the operator.

Assignments

1. Design a menu for a DSS that would support a student's selection of courses for the next school term.

2. Design icons for the usual DSS functions of retrieving data items from a database, displaying a bar chart, signing on to a remote database system.

3. Devise four different ways to phrase the English language question, ''How many students took CIS-310 last semester?'' Consider specifying dates and the course name explicitly, as well as restructuring the grammar. Are multiple interpretations possible for any of your phrasings?

4. Compare the trade-offs between using a line-oriented editor and a screen-oriented editor in the environments: personal computer, time-sharing machine accessed by dial-up phone lines.

5. Design a menu for a DSS that would support an electronic mail subsystem. Make up program names for your functions. Code a menu specifications file for this subsystem and enter it with an editor. Execute this menu if you have access to a working version of the MENU program. Since your operators are probably not provided with the DSS tool kit, what does the MENU program do when you select a menu entry that uses one of your new program names?

6. Discuss the use of the tool kit editors in an electronic mail system. What are the trade-offs to be considered between the use of SED and LED? Compare SED with a commercial word processor. Would SED or the commercial word processor be better in the electronic mail system you have designed?

7. Teletext is a one-way communication system that uses TV technology to broadcast multiple screens of information simultaneously. In effect, users tune in, or choose, the screens they want to view. Simulate a teletext broadcast of several screens of information about sports scores. Use the MENU program. Multiple lines of menu description can be used to describe various sports news. The GOTO operator can be used to move among the screens. You should have several screens that contain only the information necessary to index the actual sports news screens.

4 A DATABASE MANAGEMENT SYSTEM

Abstract

- A database is a central resource for a decision support system.

- Given the presence of a database, a database management system (DBMS) is an effective tool for handling the stored data.

- DBMS packages represent a well-developed technology that provides methods for interacting with a variety of models that can be used as schemes for the storage of data.

- Of the models available for organizing a database, the tool kit used in this text is based upon the relational model.

- A relational model incorporates methodologies for both structuring and retrieving data.

ROLE OF A DBMS IN A DSS

A database is a prerequisite for the development of any decision support system. The term *database* has accumulated many connotations. Therefore, it is appropriate at the outset to identify the meaning of the term within the context of this discussion.

A database is a computer-stored collection of data that incorporates a specialized set of data to identify the content and structure of all other units of data. The identifying, or descriptor, data set within a database is known as a *schema*. A schema, then, is an internal set of data that defines and keeps track of a larger collection of data.

A database is described, created, accessed, updated, and otherwise controlled through use of a special software package known as a *database management system (DBMS)*. DBMS packages are general-purpose software tools that permit user programs to access and update a database even though the user programs themselves contain no specifications for the database. This is because the DBMS is designed to interact with the data through an integral schema. Thus, even if the size, content, or elements of data structures are changed, a DBMS can still retain its usefulness, as long as the schema is kept current to reflect changes.

In most corporate or governmental entities considering a DSS, a database will usually exist already. Thus, development of a DSS involves incorporating parts, or even all, of existing data resources within the DSS. Even though the DSS may be relatively simple in structure and intent, any operational DSS will probably incorporate a database, a schema, and a DBMS. Thus, the role of a DBMS within a DSS is as a ready-made access and control mechanism available to a DSS designer.

DATA MODELS

A DBMS must support one or more ways of structuring and handling data. These separate methods of treating data are called *data models*. A data model, then, provides a logical system for representing collections of data and data relationships. Many techniques have been devised for representing data through models. However, three methods are widely used and are felt to be representative of modeling techniques:

- Hierarchical
- Network
- Relational.

Hierarchical and network models are organized to follow tree structures or modified tree structures. These methods have been extremely popular for large operational databases, possibly because these methods organize data efficiently for purposes of repetitive transaction processing systems.

A relational model differs from tree-structured modeling approaches in methods of organizing and using data. Hierarchical and network models are oriented especially toward accessing and reading individual data records, such as a person's payroll records. In effect, operations in these models involve proceeding step-wise from one specific data unit to another. Users seldom perform operations over a large collection of records and, when they must, have to write a special program to do so. By contrast, a relational model is oriented to operating on the entire aggregate of data that are represented within a table consisting of defined rows and columns of data items. Relational DBMS packages provide simple-to-use query languages so that aggregate operations can be stated without writing programs.

The data table that serves as the basis of a relational model is called a *relation*. Under the technical terminology of the database field, data columns are called *attributes*. Rows of data, each containing two or more attributes, are called *tuples*. The association of attributes constitutes, within tuples, a relation that gives this type of database its name.

Relational databases are natural support facilities for DSS purposes. A relational database is considered to be the easiest type of model for a management decision maker to understand. This is because the structure of a two-dimensional table consisting of rows and columns is easier to grasp than tree-structured models.

A simplified relation, or table, containing part of the data from the SLSFIG table used in the Olympic Bicycle case is shown in Figure 4-1. This table presents columns used for entries of product TYPE, UNITS sold, and YEAR. Rows within the table include information about bicycle models for individual years. Note that this table has been named BSALES (bicycle sales).

DATA MODELING FOR DSS DESIGN

A corporate database, if it exists, represents a starting point for developing the collection of data needed to support a typical DSS. Corporate databases tend to be inclusive, encompassing multiple facets of an organization and the data generated in the course of the transactions needed to operate the business. The manager requiring support of a DSS, on the other hand, tends to want to focus upon

UNIT SALES TABLE		
TYPE	UNITS	YEAR
BT	13,786	8X
BT	14,584	8X
MX	23,128	8X
MX	25,321	8X
MX	24,985	8X
MX	29,435	8X

Figure 4-1. This simplified relation is drawn from the SLSFIG file at Olympic Bicycle. Columns show type of bicycle, units sold, and year. Each row in the table represents a different bicycle model.

some subset of a large mass of data. It is entirely possible that the problem being addressed by the decision results, at least in part, from a surfeit of data generated by computer systems.

With some DBMS packages, it is possible for a DSS to *view* only part of a large database. In this context, a view is a selective subset of an overall database from the viewpoint of, or need to be met by, a specific user. If an existing DBMS provides this capability, the DSS designer may be able to tap directly into the in-place database mechanisms. To accomplish this, the DSS designer must be able to define his or her specific view to the DBMS. This, in turn, requires a knowledge of data modeling.

More typically, an existing DBMS does not support view-type usage. In such situations, representing a majority of cases, the DSS designer must assemble a database specifically for support of the application under development. Usually, some subset of data can be derived from the corporate database and incorporated within the database that supports the DSS under development.

Still another situation that might be encountered is a corporate database built upon a model that is incompatible with the requirements of the proposed DSS. For example, a large, corporate database may be built upon a hierarchical model. Even if the DBMS supports views, the DSS designer may determine that it is preferable, for the reasons cited above, to create a relational database for the DSS.

To create a database to support a DSS, the designer should have prior experience with the principles of data modeling. Within this context, data modeling is a process used to define *templates* for data storage. A template, generically, is a holding fixture, or pattern. In the database area, a template is a pattern under which data will be stored to support a specific application. The template, in turn, conforms to the conventions of the data model selected for the database—hierarchical, network, or relational. To illustrate, the template for a relational data model to support the Olympic Bicycle application would include a list of headings for the columns of the data tables to be constructed. The set of templates for a given database is its schema.

To build a data model for a DSS, the designer must meet a knowledge prerequisite: The DSS designer must be thoroughly immersed in and familiar with the problems to be solved and decisions to be supported.

This requirement represents a major difference between the challenges of DSS design and the traditional approaches and levels of familiarity typically described in conjunction with systems analysis for transaction applications. In developing a transaction processing system, it is possible, through detailed study and conferences with users, to define a finite list of capabilities to be encompassed. As a matter of fact, it is a basic tenet of application systems development that a cutoff point be fixed beyond which any afterthoughts or changes will have to wait until after implementation.

A DSS simply doesn't work this way. A prospective user is rarely able to define exactly what data will be needed, at what times, for which purposes. Thus, if a DSS is to function effectively, it is necessary that the DSS designer be steeped sufficiently in the decision-making situations to evaluate and forecast management needs for data and reports. In the course of requirements analysis, the designer recognizes that it is impossible to anticipate every need that will arise.

However, it is possible to anticipate more requirements than are typically stated by users. Beyond that, flexibility is the key. The designer, conscious that the system will almost definitely have to be expanded, keeps as many doors open as possible.

This is another reason for the popularity of relational models for DSS implementation: The relational model is the most flexible of the three models that are most commonly used to support database systems.

ELEMENTS OF A DATA MODEL

The process of data modeling itself begins with identification of the *data elements* that will be required. A data element is a basic, individual unit of data that identifies a person, place, thing, concept, or event. Another term with the same general meaning is *data item*.

Examples of data elements include hair color, first name, middle initial, part number, make of car, model of car, license plate number, sex, height, weight, social security number, and an infinity of others. For decision support systems, data elements tend to center around the manager's sphere of concern. For example, in the Olympic Bicycle situation, Sellem's area of concern encompasses products, sales, and trends. Within this context, specific data entities required for the DSS include:

- TYPE (of model)
- YEAR
- UNITS (sold)
- WEIGHT (of bicycle)
- PRICE (of bicycle).

After the data elements are identified, the designer must establish the relationships among them. Relationships are highly dependent on the way the data items will be used within the application under development. For example, the item YEAR above may relate differently to UNITS and TYPE.

Once elements have been identified, *data dependencies* must be defined. Although an experienced designer can usually establish dependencies through mental efforts, it is easier to explain this concept if sample data sets are available. Figure 4-2 shows a table of data that might have been collected to represent the decision-making domain at Olympic Bicycle. A table of this type could be used within a DSS in the form shown in Figure 4-2. However, an examination of data dependencies can help to develop a structure that is both more efficient and more flexible.

Look at the data items listed in Figure 4-2. Note that the weight elements are the same for all BT units (40) and for all MX units (28). Given that these data represent the universe involved, the WEIGHT element appears to be dependent only on the TYPE element. PRICE shows a similar dependency upon TYPE. However, the UNITS field is not uniquely identifiable by TYPE alone. Rather, the UNITS element depends on both TYPE and YEAR.

These dependencies can be used as a basis for organizing data into two separate, smaller tables, as has been done in Figure 4-3. Note that Figures 4-2 and 4-3 contain exactly the same information. However, the two tables in Figure 4-3, together, contain a total of only 27 data items, compared with 30 in Figure 4-2. (Within tables, these data positions may be referred to as *cells*.) This difference is small for the amount of data used for illustrative purposes. Note, though, that the difference is 10 percent. Further, the reduction in number of cells would be more dramatic if the data sampling were more extensive. Thus, in a full-scale database for a DSS, efficiency improvements could be significant.

More important than the compression of size is the improvement in file-updating characteristics. By eliminating duplications, this approach does away with repetitions in changes to data elements. Thus, if the price of the BT model changes, only one correction would be needed in Figure 4-3, three in Figure 4-2 and many more in a real situation.

The comparatively formal process followed in identifying dependencies, eliminating duplicated data items, and improving table structures is known as *normalization* of data. The subject of normalization is treated extensively in texts dealing with systems analysis and database design. Normalization procedures, however, are beyond the scope of this book.

DATA SAMPLING TABLE

TYPE	YEAR	UNITS	WEIGHT	PRICE
BT	X1	12	40	80
BT	X2	18	40	80
BT	X3	7	40	80
MX	X3	63	28	150
MX	X4	42	28	150
TO	X2	7	33	180

Figure 4-2. The data sample in this display establishes parameters for the decision-making domain at Olympic Bicycle. Note redundancies in these source data items.

SALES HISTORY TABLE

TYPE	YEAR	UNITS
BT	X1	12
BT	X2	18
BT	X3	7
MX	X3	63
MX	X4	42
TO	X2	7

TYPE MASTER TABLE

TYPE	PRICE	WEIGHT
BT	80	40
MX	150	28
TO	180	33

Figure 4-3. Normalization of data to support Olympic Bicycle product decisions produces these separate tables in which duplications of items have been eliminated and updating has been simplified.

Identification of dependencies and elimination of duplications through normalization represent important elements of the process of data modeling for the design of a DSS. These requirements become particularly important if the DSS development program is to derive its data from a massive corporate database. By contrast, if the designer is working on a relatively simple DSS intended for personal use by one or a few managers, these requirements are far less important—and may not apply at all.

DEFINING THE SCHEMA FOR THE DSS TOOL KIT

Your evolving DSS tool kit includes a relational DBMS. The DBMS, in turn, requires a schema for its database relations, or data tables. This presentation develops coding for a schema associated with the Olympic Bicycle case. As a basis for determining design requirements for a schema, consider the structure of the two tables in Figure 4-4.

These tables are labeled PRODS (types of products) and SHIST (sales history). The PRODS table contains four rows, one for each model of Olympic Bicycle. The columns of the table identify the TYPE of bicycle, a description (DESC) of each type, as well as WEIGHT and PRICE for each type. Cells in this table can be searched for data relating to any attribute and type of bicycle. For example, WEIGHT data items could be used to calculate shipping requirements. PRICE items might be helpful in projecting cash flow, and so on.

The second table in Figure 4-4, SHIST , gives sales in units, by TYPE of bicycle, and by YEAR. This relation contains only one row, or *record,* for each bicycle type, for each year.

The point of presenting two data tables is to demonstrate how a single schema can be used to direct access to both sets of data, or to additional tables that may be added as the DSS grows. A schema that does this job is shown in Figure 4-5.

The illustrated schema has three columns. The first column identifies the name of the relation to be accessed. The second column gives the number of the first column within the identified table. Thus, the second column in the first row of the schema establishes an access path to the TYPE column in the PRODS table. Succeeding rows of the schema correspond with the left-to-right ordering of the columns of the identified table. The third column of the schema contains the

PRODUCT INFORMATION TABLE

TYPE	DESC	WEIGHT	PRICE
BT	BALLOON–TIRE	40	85
MX	MOTO–CROSS	35	120
TO	TOURING	38	140
RA	RACING	35	180

SALES HISTORY TABLE

YEAR	TYPE	UNITS
X1	BT	84
X2	BT	68
X3	BT	73
X2	MX	105
X3	MX	145

Figure 4-4. These tables provide the basis for construction of a schema that can direct access to data in relations dealing with product information and sales histories.

column name that corresponds with the designated column number. For the first table in Figure 4-4, the first column is named TYPE. Note the corresponding entry in the first row of the schema.

The convention used in constructing the tool kit schema requires that the columns for relation name and column (attribute) name match the convention for assigning file names within the DSS. That is, these table and column names must have a maximum of six characters, may not use blank spaces or punctuation, and must start with a letter.

Note the open-ended design of the schema in Figure 4-5. This specific schema covers two tables. However, when a dynamic DSS requires additional data content, the schema then could be expanded routinely, simply by adding a row of entries for each column in every table.

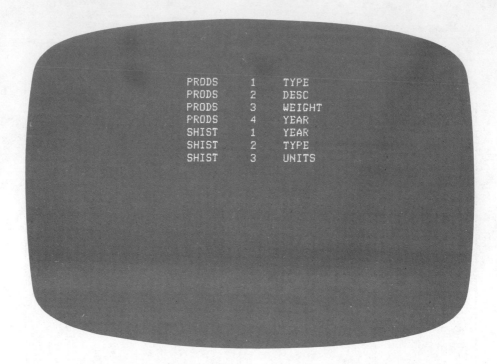

Figure 4-5. This is the schema that will support access to the two relations illustrated in Figure 4-4. Note the open-ended nature of this schema design. As new tables are constructed, entries can be made to the schema to identify the name of the new relation and the identifiers of its columns.

The schema shown would be created (or modified) through use of either a line or a screen editor. The convention established for your DSS tool kit requires that the name SCHEMA be assigned to the schema file.

CREATING DATA TABLES

Any workable DBMS software package must provide a capability for loading data into the database. Most commercial packages provide interactive software tools for this purpose. These present users with a series of prompt screens for entry and immediate acceptance of data elements or, at most, individual records. These methods represent an effective and productive approach. However, for small collections of data or for demonstration purposes such as your general-purpose tool

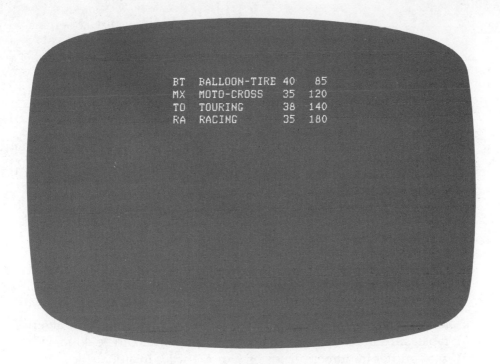

```
BT   BALLOON-TIRE  40    85
MX   MOTO-CROSS    35   120
TO   TOURING       38   140
RA   RACING        35   180
```

Figure 4-6.   This display contains the source data entries for the PRODS table illustrated in Figure 4-4.

kit, editing tools can also be used. The method to be demonstrated in this presentation uses a screen editor to capture the content of individual tables.

Use of a screen editor, in addition to being convenient, helps a student to picture the makeup and structure of the data content of a DSS. The point: reduced to basics, all data collected and accessed within a DSS are simple data files. An understanding of the structure of files, in turn, provides a valuable knowledge basis for building and using a DSS.

A screen display for entry of the PRODS table (shown originally in Figure 4-4) is presented in Figure 4-6. Refer to this illustration to help recognize application of rules for entry of data tables:

- Each data table must be named according to conventions cited earlier. The name is recorded in the system directory and is used in the schema.

- Each row of a table is typed on a single line entered under the screen editor. Items are separated by one or more blank spaces, or a comma (,). As a convenient practice, columns may be spaced for alignment as has been done in Figure 4-6. However, this alignment is not a requirement. The system will recognize and position individual cells within the table.

- Normally, no blank spaces are permitted within data entries. Thus, if an entry contained the first and last names of a person, a hyphen or other filler would have to be used. In this way, the system cannot encounter gaps that will be treated as separate columns. If you need to use blanks, surround the entire data value with double quotes ('').

- Entries must be made for all fields. In building data records, no field blanks are permitted. Thus, if data are missing for a given table, substitute characters must be entered. This can be done with zero entries in numeric fields or A or X entries in alphabetic fields.

- The simplified system provided for your tool kit does not accept decimal points. Most commercial systems do require decimal entries where appropriate. But the illustrated system and its accompanying software do not.

SEARCH AND INQUIRY COMMANDS

A DBMS, remember, is a software package that manages data resources. Part of the role of a DBMS lies in searching for and delivering user-requested data. In a DSS context, these search and delivery functions represent the main user expectations from a DBMS.

Search and data delivery functions of a DBMS are performed in response to commands in a *query language.* There are many types of and approaches to development of query languages. Some alternatives include command-driven, menu-driven, icon, and screen oriented.

As you know, your tool kit is designed to function through menu-driven interfaces with users. You also know that these menus are created through use of a program called MENU. The MENU program, in effect, is a special design tool that is not apparent to the user. This program is used to enter commands that cause the display and interactive functioning of the menu. To support user queries into the database, MENU specifications may include search and inquiry commands. The DSS designer uses these commands in composing alternatives presented to users on menus. The specific structures or wording of these commands are not necessarily significant to users. However, precise use of the query commands is essential to the providing of workable menus.

The query language vocabulary usable with your tool kit is presented and defined in Figure 4-7. The query language within your tool kit uses principles and formats of a technique known as *relational algebra*. Sets of query commands using relational algebra are used, traditionally, with relational databases and are considered a standard component for a relational DBMS.

The discussion below presents a series of generic commands that can exist within virtually any relational DBMS. However, the specific implementations of the commands described below are particular to the DSS tool kit under development. As with other explanations relating to the tool kit, the presentation that follows is a mixture of generalized knowledge that applies to any work you will do with a DSS and of particularized applications of knowledge to support a given DSS implementation, such as the tool kit.

The sections that follow explain both the generic implications of the commands and their functions within the DSS tool kit.

DISPLAY

The DISPLAY command refers to the schema to develop a format for a data presentation. The command operates upon one table at a time; one execution of the command formats one data table.

Each command in the relational algebra query language presented here is implemented as a separate program module. Therefore, each command is invoked through use of the PROGRAM statement of the MENU language. The format for the program command is as follows:

PROGRAM name ''parameters''

This generic format indicates that the PROGRAM command calls a named query language command program module, such as DISPLAY. The parameters required by the command format displayed

DISPLAY	COMPOSES DATA TABLES AND SHOWS ON VDT SCREEN
SELECT	CREATES NEW DATA TABLE FROM SELECTED ROWS OF EXISTING DATA TABLE
PROJECT	CREATES NEW DATA TABLE FROM SELECTED COLUMNS OF EXISTING DATA TABLE
ADD	ADDS NUMERIC CONTENT OF EXISTING COLUMNS AND ENTERS RESULT IN NEWLY CREATED COLUMN
SUBTRACT	SUBTRACTS NUMERIC CONTENT OF EXISTING COLUMNS AND ENTERS RESULT IN NEWLY CREATED COLUMN
MULTIPLY	MULTIPLIES NUMERIC CONTENT OF EXISTING COLUMNS AND ENTERS RESULT IN NEWLY CREATED COLUMN
DIVIDE	DIVIDES NUMERIC CONTENT OF EXISTING COLUMNS AND ENTERS RESULT IN NEWLY CREATED COLUMN
SORT	REORDERS ROWS WITHIN A TABLE ACCORDING TO VALUES IN DESIGNATED COLUMN, ACCORDING TO ASCENDING OR DESCENDING ORDER
SUMMARIZE	ADDS NUMERIC VALUES FOR IDENTIFIED CELLS AND GENERATES SUBTOTALS
UNION	COMBINES TWO RELATIONS TO CREATE A THIRD RELATION THAT HAS ALL THE ROWS OF BOTH ORIGINAL TABLES
JOIN	COMBINES TWO RELATIONS TO CREATE A THIRD RELATION WITH ATTRIBUTES OF THE FIRST TWO BUT WITH ADDITIONS OR DIFFERENCES IN DATA CONTENT RESULTING FROM THE COMBINATION OF ATTRIBUTES
DELETE	DELETES A TABLE

Figure 4-7. This listing presents some basic commands for the DSS Tool Kit, along with corresponding definitions.

above are identified by a set of quotation marks. The named parameters, in turn, provide information to be passed to the called command. To DISPLAY a table, the parameter portion of the command structure presents the name of the table to be shown. Thus, to implement a display of the PRODS table, the following line would be included in the MENU specifications:

PROGRAM DISPLAY ''PRODS''

As an option, the DISPLAY command can be instructed to output to the printer, rather than to a terminal screen. To choose this alternative, the entry is modified through addition of a comma after the file name, followed by a "P." To cause a printout of the PRODS file, the following command would be used:

PROGRAM DISPLAY "PRODS, P"

SELECT

The SELECT command causes the program to search for required records and insert them into a new table. The data objects of the search are defined within a Boolean search statement incorporated in a SELECT command. The generic format of a SELECT command is as follows:

SELECT input table name, Boolean search statement,
output table name

Using the MENU language, a SELECT command would be coded as follows:

PROGRAM SELECT "input table, search statement,
output table"

As a specific example, the following statement will cause the program to select all records with prices greater than $100 from the PRODS table (Figure 4-4).

PROGRAM SELECT "PRODS, PRICE > 100, WORK"

This instruction would create a table called WORK that contains the bottom three rows of the PRODS table shown in Figure 4-4—all records with a PRICE value greater than 100. Boolean search statements can become highly complex as new functional dimensions are added through the use of AND and OR operators. For example, consider the following instruction, which would cause the system to search for all rows representing products with a price greater than $100 and a weight of less than 38 pounds.

PROGRAM SELECT "PRODS,
PRICE >100 AND WEIGHT <38, WORK"

As another example, the statement below will trigger a search for any records that include a price greater than $100, and a weight of less than or equal to 38 pounds, or a BT type. This command exercises all of the major capabilities of Boolean statements: compare, AND, OR, and equal to.

PROGRAM SELECT "PRODS,
(PRICE >100 AND WEIGHT < =38) OR TYPE=BT, WORK"

PROJECT

A PROJECT command extracts specific columns from an input table and creates a new table that consists of these selected columns. The generic format for a PROJECT command is:

PROJECT input table name, columns to be included,
output table name

The typical tool kit instruction using this command, shown below, causes the system to extract the first two columns from the PRODS table and write them into a new table named WORK.

PROGRAM PROJECT "PRODS, TYPE; DESC, WORK"

The instruction above names the table to be used, then the columns. The multiple columns are separated by a semicolon. If three columns were to be used, there would be an additional semicolon in this instruction. Again, the newly created table is named WORK.

References to columns at any point in the relational DBMS tool kit can be identified alternatively by their assigned names within the schema, as is done above, or by column number. Use of column number designations for the same command shown above is illustrated in the statement below.

PROGRAM PROJECT "PRODS, 1; 2, WORK"

The ability to use column numbers as designators makes it possible to work with relations that have not previously been established within the schema. To process queries within a DSS, you will come across many situations in which it is convenient to establish "working," or temporary, data tables that hold intermediate results.

Column Arithmetic
(ADD, SUBTRACT, MULTIPLY, DIVIDE)

The four *column arithmetic* commands cause mathematical operations to take place on cells in two columns for any given operation. The answers, then, are written into a newly created column. The conventions of the tool kit call for creation of a new table to receive the outputs of column arithmetic functions. Other implementations of these functions may add columns to existing tables, or even write over existing columns. In a learning environment, however, experience has shown that it is best to separate sources and results.

The generic format of a column arithmetic command can be expressed as follows:

arithmetic operator input table name, first column,
second column, output table name

To demonstrate this operation, consider the table shown in Figure 4-8. This table has columns that show sales in units and dollar volume for two quarters, by type, by year. A column arithmetic command applied to this table could read:

ADD SLSVOL, QTR1, QTR2, WORK1

This command would generate a table like the one shown in Figure 4-9. The content of this second table is the same as for the one in

SALES HISTORY TABLE

YEAR	TYPE	QTR1	VOL1	QTR2	VOL2
X1	BT	23	2345	35	4893
X2	BT	27	3187	41	5373
X1	MX	56	6589	78	9234

Figure 4-8. The table in this display shows cumulative entries of data into a sales history table.

Figure 4-8, except that a new column has been added to record the results of the ADD operations. For execution under the tool kit, this command would be stated as follows:

PROGRAM ADD "SLSVOL, QTR1, QTR2, WORK1"

The commands for SUBTRACT, MULTIPLY, and DIVIDE follow the same principles. SUBTRACT takes the value in the second column from the value in the first column. MULTIPLY uses the values in both columns as factors. DIVIDE causes the value in the second column to be divided into the value in the first column. All of the commands enter results in an answer column in a newly created table.

SORT

The SORT command reorders, in sequence according to value, the data elements in one or more columns. Sequencing by the sort function is in either ascending or descending order. The generic structure for the SORT command is as follows:

SORT input table name, list of columns, ascending or descending, output table name

In using the SORT command, attention focuses on the list of columns to be included. Any number of columns can be listed. The first column

108

YEAR–TO–DATE SALES TABLE

YEAR	TYPE	QTR1	VOL1	QTR2	VOL2	YTDSLS
X1	BT	23	2345	35	4893	58
X2	BT	27	3187	41	5373	68
X1	MX	56	6589	78	9234	134

Figure 4-9. This table demonstrates the application of calculation commands to data in existing tables. In this instance, the system has added sales quantities for the first two quarters to derive year-to-date sales tallies for each product, for every year.

is known as the *major* sort field. Succeeding columns are *minor* sort fields. Sort routines are applied to the major field first. Then, if two or more major field items match, the minor fields are used to determine sequencing. Possibly the most typical example occurs in the sorting of names for directory listings. The last name is the major sort field. The first name is the first minor sort field; and the middle initial can be a second minor sort field.

To apply the SORT command to the DSS tool kit, the following instruction sorts the SHIST table in Figure 4-4:

PROGRAM SORT "SHIST, YEAR; UNITS, A, WORK"

This instruction will cause the existing file to be reordered, with year as the major field and units as the minor field. The results would be the table shown in Figure 4-10, which represents an output generated under the DISPLAY command after a sort had been executed.

SUMMARIZE

The SUMMARIZE command causes the system to develop the same kinds of subtotals used in producing control break reports under conventional programming techniques. That is, the command causes the

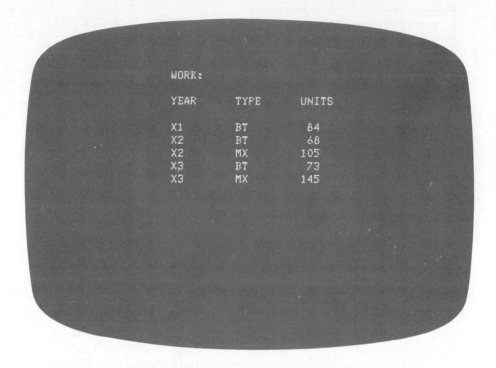

```
WORK:

YEAR        TYPE        UNITS

X1          BT          84
X2          BT          68
X2          MX          105
X3          BT          73
X3          MX          145
```

Figure 4-10.   This table results from the application of a SORT command to the content of the table in Figure 4-4. Rows of data have been placed in ascending order according to the values in the YEAR column.

---

system to total values according to selected field values. The generic format for the SUMMARIZE command is as follows:

SUMMARIZE report table name, list of control fields,
output table name

To illustrate the operation of this command, consider the content of the SLSVOL file in Figure 4-8. Suppose a manager wanted to total sales units and volumes by year. The following tool kit command would be applied to Figure 4-8.

PROGRAM SUMMARIZE "SLSVOL, YEAR, WORK9"

The output is written into a new file, WORK9, shown in Figure 4-11. Note that this output of SUMMARIZE has one more column than the input file. The extra column contains a count of the number of rows summarized into one row of the report. Data in an unneeded column, TYPE, is blanked out because the data are not meaningful. In Figure 4-11, there is a row for each unique value in the specified control field column. The control field was YEAR. The input file had two unique values, X1 and X2. Thus, the output file has two rows. For every unique value in the input file, the amounts were summed and entered into the output file.

UNION

The UNION command *concatenates,* or forms a composite from, the content of two tables. The term *concatenate* implies a sequential grouping of stated values or terms. The number of rows in an output table is equal to the sum of the number of rows in both the input tables. The generic format of the UNION command is as follows:

UNION first input table name, second input table name,
output table name

A tool kit implementation of the UNION command is illustrated through the three tables in Figure 4-12. The concatenation of TABLEA and TABLEB into TABLEC results from the following command.

PROGRAM UNION "TABLEA, TABLEB, TABLEC"

As explained above, the new table, TABLEC, contains a combination of the data items in both input tables, TABLEA and TABLEB.

JOIN

The JOIN function matches input rows from two tables and produces a coordinated output in a third table. The newly created table, then, is a composite of the first two tables. The generic format of the JOIN command is as follows:

JOIN first input table name, second input table name,
list of control field pairs, output table name

GROSS SALES TABLE

YEAR	TYPE	QTR1	VOL1	QTR2	VOL2	COLUMNS
X1		79	8944	113	14127	1
X2		27	3187	41	5373	2

Figure 4-11. This table is generated through use of the SUMMARIZE command. Data in Figure 4-8 are summarized according to year, showing gross sales in units and dollars. Product breakdowns are eliminated.

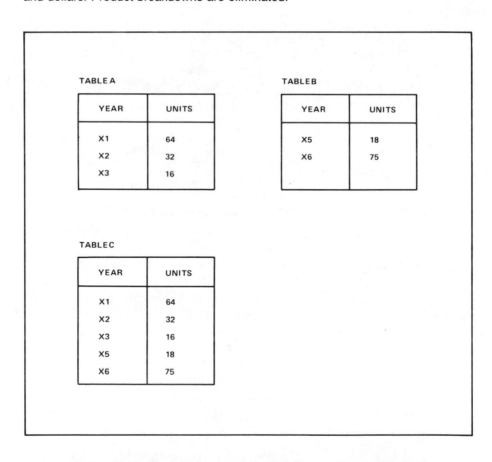

TABLE A

YEAR	UNITS
X1	64
X2	32
X3	16

TABLE B

YEAR	UNITS
X5	18
X6	75

TABLE C

YEAR	UNITS
X1	64
X2	32
X3	16
X5	18
X6	75

Figure 4-12. The results of the UNION command are illustrated in this set of tables. TABLEA and TABLEB are concatenated to form the composite structure in TABLEC.

A tool kit implementation of the JOIN command is illustrated through the three tables in Figure 4-13. The composite of the two input tables is created in response to the following command:

PROGRAM JOIN "TABLEX, TABLEY, TYPE:TYPE, TABLEZ"

In Figure 4-13, TABLEZ is a composite formed from elements contained in TABLEX and TABLEY.

Two special, or exception, conditions may be encountered in applying the JOIN command:

1. If there are two or more rows in the second input table that can be paired with a row in the first table, the output table will contain a record for each of the rows in the second input table.

2. If there are no rows in the second input table that can be paired with corresponding rows in the first table, no rows are written to the output table.

Application of both these exceptions is illustrated with the three tables in Figure 4-14. This illustration contains three tables. Two, TABLEM and TABLEN, are input tables. The third, TABLEO, is the output. The tool kit command to process the inputs and produce the illustrated output is as follows:

PROGRAM JOIN "TABLEM, TABLEN, TYPE:TYPE, TABLEO"

DELETE

The main use for the DELETE command is to eliminate the temporary work files created for special inquiry situations. After their purpose has been served, these files are no longer needed. Deleting these tables helps to free up disk space for future inquiries. The generic form of the DELETE command is as follows:

DELETE table name

A tool kit command that would delete the working table created in the previous example of the JOIN command would be:

PROGRAM DELETE "TABLEO"

TABLEX

TYPE	UNITS
BT	43
MX	27
BT	17

TABLEY

TYPE	DESC
BT	BALLOON–TIRE
MX	MOTO–CROSS

TABLEZ

TYPE	UNITS	DESC
BT	43	BALLOON–TIRE
MX	27	MOTO–CROSS
BT	17	BALLOON–TIRE

Figure 4-13. The results of the JOIN command are illustrated in this set of tables. TABLEX and TABLEY are joined to form the composite structure in TABLEZ.

CONSTRUCTING QUERIES

To process an inquiry, the designer begins by laying out the required output—the display or report to be produced. Once the content of the output is known, the designer examines the database and identifies all relations that contain needed data items.

Given this starting point, the designer has a number of options open for producing the required results. As a rule of thumb, however, it is practical to work through the job in the following sequence:

- JOIN the identified source tables.

114

TABLEM

TYPE	LOC
BT	AZ
MX	TN
BT	KY

TABLEN

TYPE	PRICE	YEAR
BT	83	X1
BT	88	X2

TABLEO

TYPE	LOC	PRICE	YEAR
BT	AZ	83	X1
BT	AZ	88	X2
BT	KY	83	X1
BT	KY	88	X2

Figure 4-14. Exceptions applied in the execution of the JOIN command are demonstrated in this set of tables. The JOIN function combines TABLEM and TABLEN to form TABLEO. Note that the MX row in TABLEM is not copied to the new table because there is no counterpart in TABLEN. Note also that the outputs in TABLEO show a separate row for each record because the combining of data creates records with dissimilar values in some of the columns.

- SELECT the required rows.
- SORT or SUMMARIZE, as necessary.
- PROJECT the needed columns.
- DISPLAY the results.

Returning to the DSS that is so valuable for Olympic Bike, assume that Sellem wants to relate the size of the field sales force to the number of BT bikes sold. The situation to which this information is to be applied involves a decision on whether to increase the number of representatives in the field. This specific query is aimed at relating the size of the field sales staff to the number of BT bikes sold. Thus, Sellem asks for a report containing information on BT bikes only. Data in the report are to be categorized under the following headings: DESC, YEAR, UNITS, and NUMSLS. The final item refers to the number of salespeople handling BT bikes.

The database from which the report is to be derived is illustrated in Figure 4-15. Three tables—TABLEF, TABLEG, and TABLEH—are to be used. TABLEF contains data on TYPE and DESC. TABLEG shows sales, by year. TABLEH shows number of salespersons, by year. The tool kit instruction to produce the desired report is as follows:

```
PROGRAM JOIN "TABLEF, TABLEG, TYPE:TYPE, WORK1"
PROGRAM JOIN "WORK, TABLEH, 3:YEAR, WORK2"
PROGRAM SELECT "WORK2, 1=BT, WORK3"
PROGRAM PROJECT "WORK3, 2; 3; 4; 5, WORK4"
PROGRAM DISPLAY "WORK4"
```

A NEW OLYMPIC BICYCLE CASE: DSS DESIGN

You are ready, now, to consider how all of the elements covered in this chapter go together to develop a complete DSS. As a basis for your next set of experiences, prepare to follow a new managerial decision situation at Olympic Bicycle:

This time you will be looking over the shoulder of John Gear. Remember, he is vice president, manufacturing, at Olympic. It seems that Sally Sellem has interested the company president, Roger Wheelwright, in a new product. Sellem thinks Olympic should enter the moped market. In case you haven't been previously curious, a moped is a combine term derived from MOtor and PEDal. In effect, a moped is a bicycle with a motor. The motor is minimal. The general idea is that the rider starts out pedaling. When speed is sufficient, the motor cuts in, starting in its one gear. The motor then maintains the pedaling speed the rider has attained; a moped cannot accelerate beyond the rate achieved through the rider's foot power.

TABLEF

TYPE	DESC
BT	BALLOON–TIRE
TO	TOURING

TABLEG

TYPE	YEAR	UNITS
BT	X1	83
BT	X3	22
BT	X4	34
TO	X3	64

TABLEH

YEAR	NUMSLS
X1	6
X2	8
X3	7
X4	8
X5	11

Figure 4-15. The source data in these three tables are to be combined to produce an output detailing information on BT bicycles according to DESC, YEAR, UNITS, and NUMSLS (number of sales representatives).

Wheelwright has expressed an interest in the moped project. Ian Sharp, the controller, has asked for some numbers to help determine whether the moped line might be profitable. As it turns out, Wheelwright has some property out in Arizona, purchased with an eye toward future retirement. By coincidence, he has located a nearby site zoned for manufacturing. Based on Wheelwright's strong "recommendation," the other executives decide to base the study on the prospective costs of constructing a new facility in Arizona.

Gear is working from scratch. His first step, beginning from a mid-winter start-up, is to travel to Arizona to inspect the site personally. In the course of his visit, he invites proposals from several local firms of architects and engineers. These are expressed back to the home office. On the basis of phone conversations, it is decided to deal with the local firm of Lloyd Bildum and Associates. Gear explains that the Bildum firm will be engaged if Olympic decides to go ahead with construction. At the outset, however, the architects are to provide only minimal advisory services on construction feasibility and on estimates of costs per square foot for building needed structures.

Building Blocks

Gear's labors are documented in a set of accompanying illustrations, Figures 4-16 through 4-22. These illustrations are organized to provide meaning from your present perspective. For this reason, Figure 4-16 is a schema for the database to support Gear's DSS. Figure 4-17, then, is the DSS menu specification. Continuing with the presentation sequence, Figure 4-18 is the menu that results from execution of the menu specifications in Figure 4-17. The remaining illustrations in the set then present the results of Gear's data gathering efforts.

Figure 4-19 is a set of construction-cost notes provided by a member of the staff of the architectural firm. Figure 4-20 shows a beginning step toward preparation of a worksheet that Gear himself will have to develop from his knowledge of the manufacturing requirements supplemented by the architect's input. Eventually, the worksheet will have hundreds of lines of data. Data entries on the worksheet in Figure 4-20 include classification for type of use for structures, the type of equipment to be installed, the number of square feet required, overall cost estimate for the facility, and special requirements (such as electric power needs).

As he begins to compile the data worksheet, Gear realizes that he won't be able to model his decision situations with manual documents. It will be necessary to use his company's tool kit to build a DSS for his specific situation. Continuing, he designs input formats to be used for entry of cost and requirements specifications through use of a screen editor. Figure 4-21 shows input of cost data provided by the architect (Figure 4-19). Figure 4-22 captures specification inputs from

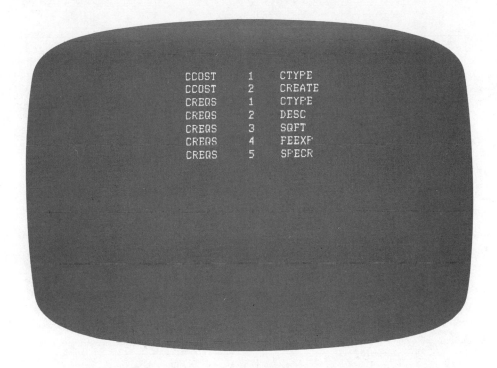

```
CCOST     1     CTYPE
CCOST     2     CREATE
CREQS     1     CTYPE
CREQS     2     DESC
CREQS     3     SQFT
CREQS     4     FEEXP
CREQS     5     SPECR
```

Figure 4-16. This is the database schema for the Arizona plant construction DSS to be used by John Gear.

Gear's worksheet (Figure 4-20). Note that the data formats in Figures 4-21 and 4-22 are consistent with the schema designed by Gear, shown in Figure 4-16.

Design Approach

The underlying design criteria for any DSS lie in the expectations of the using manager. These, in turn, are expressed in the items listed on the main menu for the system and incorporated into the menu specs within the DSS program. The menu items listed in Figure 4-18 reflect the requirements for Gear's decisions:

Gear determined that it would be necessary to isolate and identify major purchases of manufacturing equipment. Selection of the

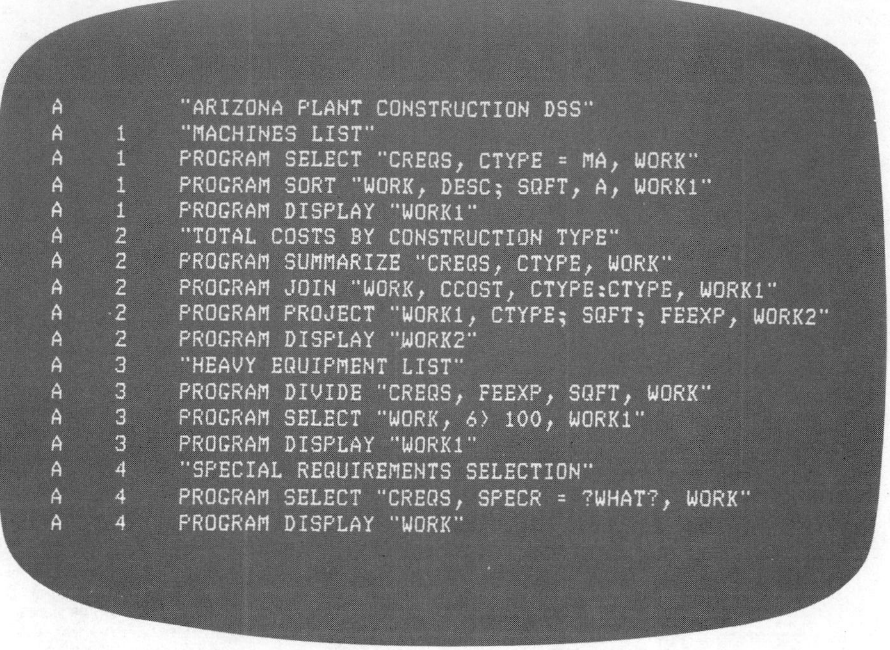

```
A               "ARIZONA PLANT CONSTRUCTION DSS"
A        1      "MACHINES LIST"
A        1      PROGRAM SELECT "CREQS, CTYPE = MA, WORK"
A        1      PROGRAM SORT "WORK, DESC; SQFT, A, WORK1"
A        1      PROGRAM DISPLAY "WORK1"
A        2      "TOTAL COSTS BY CONSTRUCTION TYPE"
A        2      PROGRAM SUMMARIZE "CREQS, CTYPE, WORK"
A        2      PROGRAM JOIN "WORK, CCOST, CTYPE:CTYPE, WORK1"
A        2      PROGRAM PROJECT "WORK1, CTYPE; SQFT; FEEXP, WORK2"
A        2      PROGRAM DISPLAY "WORK2"
A        3      "HEAVY EQUIPMENT LIST"
A        3      PROGRAM DIVIDE "CREQS, FEEXP, SQFT, WORK"
A        3      PROGRAM SELECT "WORK, 6> 100, WORK1"
A        3      PROGRAM DISPLAY "WORK1"
A        4      "SPECIAL REQUIREMENTS SELECTION"
A        4      PROGRAM SELECT "CREQS, SPECR = ?WHAT?, WORK"
A        4      PROGRAM DISPLAY "WORK"
```

Figure 4-17. This is the set of commands used to establish the menu specification for the Arizona plant construction DSS.

first menu item, MACHINES LIST, will initiate access to the CREQS table, which contains records for all equipment and facilities that will be needed to complete the proposed plant. The instructions that support this menu item carry "1" codes in the second column of Figure 4-17. The first instruction establishes the menu name. The second "1" instruction controls the selection of data; the CREQS file and the CTYPE column within that file are designated as data sources. Data selection, then, is to be based upon the presence of the coding "MA," which is Gear's designation for machines. Selected items are to be placed in a temporary file, WORK. The third instruction is to sort the selected file, with the DESC field as the major key and the SQFT field as the minor key. The fourth, and final, instruction for the first command is to display the menu item.

Figure 4-18. This is the menu to be displayed for access to the Arizona plant construction DSS.

CONSTRUCTION TYPE	COST PER SQ. FOOT
MACHINERY	200
WAREHOUSE	40
WALKWAY	60
OFFICE	60

Figure 4-19. Handwritten notes on construction costs for the Arizona plant.

CONSTRUCTION TYPE	DESCRIPTION	SQ. FT.	FIXTURES + EQUIPMENT COSTS	SPECIAL REQUIREMENTS
MACHINERY	FRAME-WELDER	300	120,000	440V
MACHINERY	SPRAY PAINTER	500	190,000	440V 4 INCH DRAIN
OFFICE	GENERAL	3,000	200,000	220V
WAREHOUSE	FINISHED GDS.	10,000	100,000	
WAREHOUSE	RECEIVING	3,000	40,000	

Figure 4-20. These are John Gear's preliminary notes on requirements for construction of the Arizona plant.

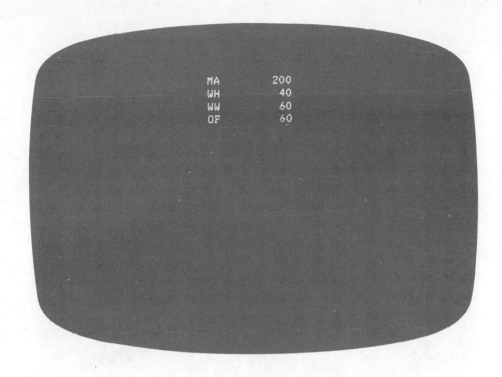

```
                    MA          200
                    WH           40
                    WW           60
                    OF           60
```

Figure 4-21. This display shows the capture of cost data provided by the architect. The source data for this set of entries appears in Figure 4-19.

As shown in Figure 4-18, the remaining menu items are for TOTAL COSTS BY CONSTRUCTION TYPE, HEAVY EQUIPMENT LIST, and SPECIAL REQUIREMENTS SELECTION. Menu specs for these items are identified, respectively, by the codes 2, 3, and 4, in the second column of Figure 4-17. Note the PROGRAM SELECT coding line for item 4. This instruction contains an item set off by question marks: ?WHAT?. The menu program within the DSS tool kit responds to this use of question marks by pausing during execution and requesting the appropriate value from the user. In this instance, the menu item supports a search of SPECIAL REQUIREMENTS listed in the rightmost column of the display in Figure 4-22. The user can then control the data search through a series of alternatives:

- The user can enter a specific value. In response, the system will select only the entered literals. As an example, an entry of 440V would call up only the first line in the display in Figure 4-22.

123

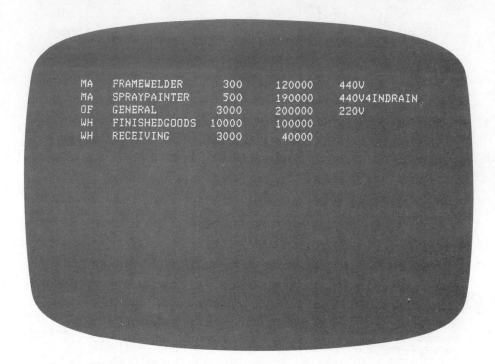

```
MA    FRAMEWELDER      300    120000    440V
MA    SPRAYPAINTER     500    190000    440V4INDRAIN
OF    GENERAL         3000    200000    220V
WH    FINISHEDGOODS  10000    100000
WH    RECEIVING       3000     40000
```

Figure 4-22.   This input screen display is used to capture the source data on plant requirements from Figure 4-20.

Although the table shows two items with 440V entries, one of the lines contains other data items and would thus not be selected.

- The user can append an asterisk to the entry, initiating what is known as a "wild card search." In response to a 440V* entry, the system would select all data items beginning with the designation 440V.

- A third option would enclose the data value in asterisks: *440V*. This entry also initiates a "wild card" search. This format would cause retrieval of any data which had "440V" embedded in the SPECIAL REQUIREMENTS data field.

Outlook

- Within an application context, and within a set of activities natural to everyday business situations, this chapter introduces and applies the basic principles of relational algebra.

- Relational algebra, simply, is a language subset that can be used to retrieve and manipulate data within a relational database system. Operators featured in this chapter include PROJECT, SELECT, JOIN, DISPLAY, SORT, and SUMMARIZE.

- You also have witnessed application of a relational DBMS and other specialized tool kit items to construct a small DSS. Thus, you have become acquainted with two of the three main parts of a DSS: dialog management (menu program) and data management (DBMS).

- In the next chapter, you take hold of the third, and final, element of a DSS, model management.

Operation Summary: DBMS

The DBMS of a DSS tool kit consists of a series of programs that access a database schema and data tables to perform data manipulation operations. DBMS programs receive control information from the MENU program. Control information is set up by the DSS designer as a list of control parameter operands for the MENU PROGRAM operator.

The database schema for the DBMS in a DSS tool kit is created with an editor and stored in a file called SCHEMA. An example schema is shown in Figure 4-5.

Schema files have one line for each data item in the file. Each line consists of 3 columns. The first column is the data table name. The second column holds the index for the data item within the data table. For example, the first data item, left to right, is indexed as ''1,'' the second data item is indexed as ''2,'' and so forth. The third column contains the data item name. Decimal numbers are not allowed. Columns are separated by one or more blanks in the schema file.

Data files are created and maintained with an editor. The name of the data file must be the same name as that used in the schema. Data are entered into data files in lines that correspond with the rows of the data table. Individual data elements in the rows are separated by commas (,), or by one or more blank spaces. When data are entered, it often is convenient to maintain column format. However, it is not necessary that the columns line up correctly for the operation of the programs.

The list below notes the control parameters that must be present in the control parameter lists for the respective programs. In coding the control parameter list for the PROGRAM operator of the MENU program, remember to surround the complete list with double quotes ('') and to separate the individual control parameters with commas (,).

The commands and their respective parameters are:

DISPLAY data table name
The DISPLAY command refers to the schema to develop a format for a data presentation. The ''data table name'' parameter instructs the DBMS which data table to output.

SELECT input data table name,
Boolean search statement, output data table name
The SELECT command causes the program to search for required records and insert them into another data table. The ''input data table name'' parameter tells the system which data table to search. The ''Boolean search statement'' parameter defines selection criteria. Selection criteria are specified as the data item name or index to be searched for, followed by the arithmetic operator to be used during

selection, $>$, $<$, $=$, or $<>$, followed by the appropriate comparison values. Comparison values can be, but do not have to be, surrounded by single quotes ('). However, comparison values must be surrounded by single quotes if a blank space is embedded in the parameter. The "output data table name" parameter names the file in which data items that meet selection criteria are to be placed.

PROJECT input data table name,
columns to be included, output data table name
The PROJECT command extracts specific columns from a data table and creates a new table that consists of these columns. The "input data table name" parameter tells the system which data table to search. The "columns to be included" parameter informs the system which data columns, or fields, to extract. Field names or indexes are separated by semicolons (;). The "output data table name" parameter defines the data table in which extracted data are to be placed.

ADD input data table name, first column,
second column, output data table name
The ADD command causes addition to be performed on cells in two columns. Answers are written in a newly created column. The "input data table name" parameter tells the system which data table to input. The "first column" and "second column" parameters give the system the names or indexes of the columns to be totalled. The "output data table name" parameter, of course, instructs the system in which data table to place outputs.

SUBTRACT input data table name, first column,
second column, output data table name
The SUBTRACT command follows the same basic principles as the ADD command. However, the SUBTRACT command causes the cells in the column identified by the

"second column" parameter to be subtracted from the cells in the column identified by the "first column" parameter.

MULTIPLY input data table name, first column, second column, output data table name

The MULTIPLY command also follows the same basic principles as the ADD and SUBTRACT commands. However, the MULTIPLY command causes the cells in the columns identified by the "first column" and "second column" parameters to be used as factors.

DIVIDE input data table name, first column, second column, output data table name

The DIVIDE command also follows the same basic principles as the ADD, SUBTRACT, and MULTIPLY commands. However, the DIVIDE command causes the cells in the columns identified by the "first column" parameter to be divided by the cells identified by the "second column" parameter. In effect, the "first column" parameter defines the dividend, and the "second column" parameter defines the divisor.

SORT input data table name, list of columns, ascending or descending, output data table name

The SORT command reorders, in sequence, the data elements in one or more columns. The "input data table name" parameter instructs the system which data table to sort. The "list of columns" parameter tells the system which columns are to be used as sort criteria. The first column identified is the major sort field. The second column identified represents the minor sort field. The "ascending or descending" parameter instructs the system in which order to sort items. The "output data table name" parameter, of course, names the file to which the newly sorted file is to be written.

SUMMARIZE input data table name,
list of control fields, output data table name
The SUMMARIZE command causes the system to develop
the same kinds of subtotals as control break reports. The
"input data table name" parameter identifies the table from
which the report is to be generated. The "list of control
fields" parameter defines the major and minor break fields.
The first control field listed represents the major break field,
and so on. Control fields are separated by semicolons (;).
The "output data table name" parameter identifies the file
that will receive outputs.

UNION first input table name,
second input table name, output table name
The UNION command concatenates two data tables. The
"first input table name" and "second input table name"
parameters define the data tables to be concatenated. The
"output data table name" parameter tells the system where
to save the new file.

JOIN first input data table name, second input data table
name, list of control field pairs, output data table name
The JOIN command matches input rows from two data
tables and produces a third, coordinated table. The "first input data table name" and "second input data table name"
parameters define the files to be joined. The "list of control
field pairs" parameter tells the system the name of the field
that occurs in both data tables. The field name is given twice
and the two names are separated by a colon (:). The "output data table name" parameter identifies the data table to
which outputs are to be written.

DELETE data table name
The DELETE command eliminates the data table given in
the "data table name" parameter. This command also can
be used to eliminate other unwanted files.

Assignments

1. Define data tables for college class registration. Have a table for student information and a table for class information. Have a third table that contains columns for student number and class number as a registration record. Define the MENU specifications to allow a decision maker to produce reports showing which students are in a specified class. Also, define MENU specification entries to allow a decision maker to list the schedules of individual students, along with the textbooks that the students will need.

2. If you have access to working versions of MENU and the tool kit DBMS, construct the database described in Question 1, enter sample data, and carry out the operations requested.

3. The manager of a string of gas stations must track information about the sales of different types of gasoline. Design a database and a DSS to support this situation. Start with a decision tree describing one decision this manager will need to make, and structure the database around this decision.

4. If you have access to working versions of MENU and the tool kit DBMS, implement the gas station manager DSS.

5. Implement a grade book database for high school teachers. Is this a DSS? Is a decision tree an appropriate or useful way to organize this problem?

6. Is every database supported by a DBMS or a DSS? Why or why not? Does it matter? Is a DSS only a function of how a DBMS is used?

DESCRIPTIVE MODELS AND GRAPHIC DISPLAYS 5

Abstract

- Chapter 4 establishes that a database is a requirement for a DSS. This chapter indicates that a capability for modeling is also a DSS requirement.

- Possibly the most common type of business modeling takes place through accounting systems. An accounting system is a descriptive model; that is, it describes the status of the business at a given point in time that corresponds with the report date.

- One computerized tool used in modeling is the electronic spreadsheet, which is reviewed in this chapter.

- Another tool used in descriptive modeling is computer graphics. These tools describe their object through pictures, rather than through use of numbers or words.

- DSS tool kit techniques for presenting accounting, spreadsheet, and graphic models are presented in this chapter.

DEFINITIONS AND TERMS

A *model* is a representation of some actual person, place, thing, event, or idea with an identified substitute. Thus, tabletop sets of electric trains are called model railroad equipment.

Representations can also be carried out through use of data. When data are used to represent an entity, the result is a *data model*. In this sense, all of the files and/or databases covering an organization constitute models of that entity. Data models can be segmented: There can be data models that represent the performances of individual employees or departments. Data models can also replicate entire, large corporate entities.

Equations can be used as the basis for models that represent the performance of an entity. In effect, sets of equations are used as shorthand notations to abbreviate the massive content that can accumulate in a data model. Equations open the opportunity to use models to analyze the behavior of a represented entity. Therefore, models built around use of equations are known as *analytic models*.

Still another modeling technique for representing an entity involves use of *graphic displays*. A graphic display, in this context, is any two-dimensional, pictorial presentation that carries the meaning of data and permits presentations about or analysis of an entity.

Together, data, analytic, and graphic display techniques constitute a class of modeling. These techniques, cumulatively, are known as *descriptive modeling*.

RELATIONS AS MODELS

Since a relation is a collection of data in table, or array, form, it follows that a relation can be a data model. To cite a common, everyday form, accounting statements model the financial condition of a company as of a given date. As a relation, financial statements are both specific and restrictive. Note that accounting statements model financial condition. Financial condition, in turn, consists of factors that are money or can be represented in monetary terms. Thus, if a company were able to lure a topflight executive whose presence promised growth and progress, this condition would not be reflected in the relation that is an accounting report. The point is that models have defined boundaries and purposes. The validity and usefulness of a model, in turn, is limited by these boundaries and purposes.

Models can be as simple as is appropriate to represent a situation under study. As an illustration, return to the stylized world of Olympic Bicycle to look at a set of data tables (in Figure 5-1) that represent the bicycles built by the company. Recognize, first, that the two tables are independent of one another. The table labeled BIKEM refers

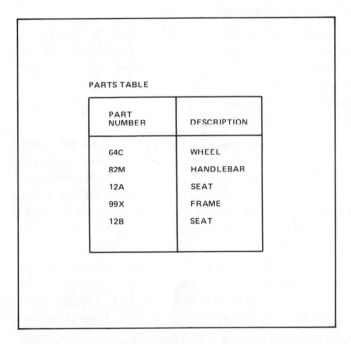

BIKEM TABLE

PRODUCT NUMBER	PART NUMBER	QUANITY
MX3	64C	2
MX3	82M	1
MX3	12A	1
TO3	64C	2
TO3	82M	1
TO3	12B	1

PARTS TABLE

PART NUMBER	DESCRIPTION
64C	WHEEL
82M	HANDLEBAR
12A	SEAT
99X	FRAME
12B	SEAT

Figure 5-1. The tables in this illustration present models for two Olympic Bicycle products, the MX3 and the TO3.

to two specific bicycle models, motocross, model 3 (MX3) and tour-ing, model 3 (TO3). The company makes other models of types of bicycles and even has other models of the MX and TO types. Thus, this model is specific and restricted. The BIKEM table identifies specific parts used to build each of the two models.

The PARTS table identifies the numbers and names of the parts called out in the BIKEM table. By itself, the PARTS table could be con-sidered as a model of certain portions of Olympic's inventory. Together, the tables contain a greater dimension than either presents by itself. The composite picture identifies and describes parts for two bicycle models.

The Role of the Schema

Figure 5-1 establishes that there can be different models that relate to the same entity. It is also possible to model an entity at different levels. Thus, the tables in Figure 5-1 represent two bicycles through data models. At another level, the data models can be represented by a schema. Thus, a schema is a model of a model.

A model that models another model is known as a *metamodel*. Database and decision support systems can have multiple levels of models of models, or metamodels. Extending this principle, the models that underlie database organization—hierarchical, network, and relational—implement a next level of metamodel. The DBMS itself is another level of metamodel.

The purpose of these explanations involves more than exercises in DBMS semantics. (Database professionals have been accused, with some apparent justification, of focusing on terminology at the expense of substance.) At stake in this discussion, is a bedrock understanding of the nature and makeup of databases. Databases are built upon models. Models, in turn, determine the generality and the breadth of usefulness of collections of data. Files, remember, are application specific. Databases are application independent. Data independence comes from modeling at a level above applications, or independent of applications. Thus, the skill in DBMS design and DSS application lies in choosing an effective level at which to construct models.

Figure 5-2 is the schema that models the tables in Figure 5-1. This schema, note, follows the format of the tool kit schema introduced in Chapter 4. The schema establishes a row for each column in both

```
SCHEMA MODEL TABLE

    BIKEM        1        PROD

    BIKEM        2        PART

    BIKEM        3        QTY

    PARTS        1        PART

    PARTS        2        DESC
```

Figure 5-2. This is a schema that models and supports access to the tables in Figure 5-1. Thus, a schema acts as a model of a model.

tables. Thus, the schema provides an overall model of data on bicycle models and parts. This schema could be used within a DSS to project parts requirements on the basis of product sales forecasts. Extended versions of models like the one in Figure 5-2 find frequent use in general bills of materials for manufacturing companies.

In another dimension, the schema in Figure 5-2 can be seen as a subset of larger collections of data. Thus, parts requirements derived from such a model could be projected upward within a data hierarchy to model costs and operations of the entire company. Thus, a bill of materials model can relate sales information to project manufacturing needs. The process is referred to as "exploding" a bill of materials. Parts requirements, in turn, generate needs for information on subassemblies. Subassembly data lead to forecasts of raw materials requirements. Thus, a series of models, metamodels, and submodels is linked to generate entire production operating plans on the basis of sales estimates. Overall, these procedures constitute a system known as *manufacturing requirements planning*.

In a sense, this type of systemic hierarchy is typical for the DSS area. A DSS uses models representing small parts of an overall entity. At the other end of the spectrum, models represent the entire company. For example, an accounting system or a management in-formation system (MIS) models aspects of the company as a whole. The discussion that follows uses accounting statements, which are models in their own right, to illustrate techniques for and relationships among descriptive models.

DESCRIPTIVE MODELS: ACCOUNTING

At the overall business level, management emphasis is on results. In a business, the main measure of results, inevitably, is in profits. Profits, in turn, are identified by their position on financial statements, referred to as *the bottom line*.

Accounting statements, in an overall sense, are models of the financial results and status of a business. Financial models can con-tain virtual mountains of data items. There can be so much detail in accounting systems that this area is cited frequently as an ideal instance in which equations provide more effective models than col-lections of data.

Income Statements

The financial statement that leads to development of a profit figure is the *income statement*. Income statements are models that include breakdowns to show sources of revenue and also of expense. Revenues and expenses are accumulated separately. Then, expenses are subtracted from revenues. A positive difference means the busi-ness had a profit. If the resulting figure has a minus value, a loss is indicated. Even this brief description serves to illustrate the value of a modeling equation:

$$P = I - E$$
$$P = \text{profit}$$
$$I = \text{income}$$
$$E = \text{expense}$$

This single, simple equation provides an ideal demonstration of the power implicit in this type of modeling. The *profitability model* can be applied to a single work center or machine within a factory. That is, profitability can be determined for a machine tool, for a welding group, for the entire factory, for a product line, or for the company as a whole. The same model can be applied at each level according to time increments: week, month, quarter, half-year, year, or multiple years. The point: This single equation, used as a model, has the power to encompass any entity for which managers face decisions involving measurement of financial results. Ultimately, almost any business-related decision involving financial results will require application of this single model.

A DSS may not actually produce an income statement. However, if the decision has financial dimensions, the profitability model will still have to be applied implicitly. For example, the sales forecast case in Chapter 4, though it does not produce a corporate profit figure, does connect implicitly through decisions that will bear upon the income of the corporation.

When actual profitability determinations have to be made, an explicit development of financial statements may be necessary. If this becomes necessary, your DSS tool kit has a command that can be used to trigger development of an income statement. Another command causes output of the other major type of financial statement, the balance sheet. A balance sheet is a statement of financial condition for an entity, based upon assets owned, liabilities owed, and equity retained in the business.

Balance Sheet

The equation that models the balance sheet is:

$$A = L + E$$
$$A = \text{assets}$$
$$L = \text{liabilities}$$
$$E = \text{equity}$$

For financial statement purposes, the terms *assets*, *liabilities*, and *equity* have special shades of meaning. Assets are items of value owned by the reporting organization. In effect, assets consist of money or items that have a monetary value. Thus, one balance sheet item is Cash. Inventory items that have been paid for represent important asset values for many companies. Also shown are amounts owed to the company, accounts receivable. Together, cash, inventory, and accounts receivable generally represent the bulk of an organization's *current assets.* Current assets, cumulatively, are seen as representing cash value that is available or can be realized in a short time.

Another class of assets is, typically, established for items that would take longer to convert to cash. Examples are plant and equipment. A company pays money for buildings and machinery. These remain as assets of the company. Such *long-term assets* are usually valued according to accounting formulas because their worth can be hard to determine. For example, a company might have bought a factory building 40 years ago. Certainly, the value of the property is greater today than it was then. But, rules for the accounting model might assign zero worth to this property. Such conditions, which prevent the reflection of reality in models, are sometimes called *modeling errors.*

Liabilities are amounts owed by a business. As with assets, there are current and long-term liabilities. Current liabilities can be amounts owed for taxes or for payment of bills to other entities. Long-term liabilities can be loans to be repaid over multiple years.

Equity is a strict accounting term that reflects the difference between assets and liabilities. In common speech, the term is often used differently, as a reflection of ownership position. It might be acceptable, for example, for an individual to describe equity in terms of potential yield from the sale of a home. Business executives may also indicate worth of a business in terms of market value for buildings, inventory, or other assets. However, the term *equity* is reserved and limited to its meaning within the *balance sheet equation.*

Based on these definitions, the equation for the balance sheet can be expanded to read:

$$AC + AL = LC + LL + E$$

AC = current assets
AL = long-term assets
LC = current liabilities
LL = long-term liabilities
E   = equity

FINANCIAL MODELING TOOLS

Your DSS tool kit has operators designated specifically for modeling of income statements and balance sheets. In both instances, the operators are descriptive models. From the definitions at the beginning of this chapter, remember that descriptive models describe and relate the data elements. You have tools available that can create two separate types, or levels, of financial modeling tools.

One type of model can be used for random entry of data items for inclusion in statements. Your tool kit has separate program modules that can be used to capture sets of data items for inclusion in income statements and in balance sheets. The program for income statements is called INCO, for balance sheets BALA. Both these programs represent a first level of modeling involving the capture and validation of data. For the second level, the programs can be used to generate actual financial statements.

Income Statement Modeling

At the first level in using the INCO program, you have a relation that serves as input to the DSS program. This models the financial statements through a two-dimensional table like the one in Figure 5-3. This exhibit has three columns that describe a series of income and expense fields for INCO. The INCO program actually performs a relatively simple set of functions. It sorts and formats input statements, transposing them from entry fields to output formats.

```
IN     12    "Sale of MX bicycles"
IN     36    "Sale of TO bicycles"
IN    114    "Sale of BT bicycles"
EX    117    "Production Expense"
IN     36    "Sale of RA bicycles"
EX    104    "Sales Expense"
```

Figure 5-3.   This is a listing of inputs that provide a series of income and expense items and values for the INCO program.

The second modeling tool is the report generated by INCO, shown in Figure 5-4. This is a straightforward rearrangement of the data in Figure 5-3. However, in this form, the model is clearly more meaningful to human users than the input specification because there is a standard format with which people are readily familiar. Familiar makes for comfort, which, in turn, makes the income statement more useful as a descriptive model. The Tool Kit Command Summary at the end of this chapter lists all of the functions performed by the operator and details their coding.

Balance Sheet Modeling

The table containing input entries for the BALA program that will produce a balance sheet is shown in Figure 5-5. Coding designations are the same as those used in the balance sheet equation above. Each row in Figure 5-5 represents a balance sheet entry.

An example of a balance sheet output report produced from the BALA input is shown in Figure 5-6. Again, the Tool Kit Command Summary at the end of the chapter lists all of the functions performed by the operator and details their coding.

CASE STUDY: FINANCIAL PROJECTIONS FOR OLYMPIC BICYCLE'S ARIZONA PLANT

On the basis of John Gear's preliminary study, reviewed in Chapter 4, management at Olympic Bicycle has decided to take a further look at the prospects for the moped plant in Arizona. Gear's part in the study centered around determining what facilities would be needed and what the proposed plant would cost. Gear's work, in turn, becomes input for more detailed financial analyses to be performed by the company's controller, Ian Sharp.

The standard financial projections prepared to cover situations of this type are known as *pro forma* statements. The purpose of these statements is straightforward: Pro forma means ''provided in advance.'' Pro forma financial statements, therefore, show predictions of income, expense, and projected profits for some designated future periods. When they apply to existing, operational entities, pro forma statements often include the current year's actual figures, then proceed into the future. Pro forma statements showing multiple years of results are often prepared with spreadsheet-type software. Your

```
                                    INCOME STATEMENT

        INCOME
                Sale of MX bicycles            12
                Sale of TO bicycles            36
                Sale of BT bicycles           114
                Sale of RA bicycles            36

                                              198


        EXPENSE
                Production Expense            117
                Sales Expense                 104

                                              221


        PROFIT (LOSS)                         (23)
```

Figure 5-4. This income statement is produced under control of the INCO function in the DSS Tool Kit. The INCO function sorts and formats items in the income statement, transposing them from item to output formats.

```
        AC    230         "ACCOUNTS RECEIVABLE"
        AC    140         "CASH"
        AL    446         "PLANT"
        EQ    119         "STOCK"
        LC     43         "ACCOUNTS PAYABLE"
        LC     12         "NOTES TO OFFICERS"
        LL     27         "BONDS"
        AC     50         "INVENTORY"
```

Figure 5-5. This is a listing of inputs that provide a series of assets, liabilities, and equity items and values for the BALA program that will generate a balance sheet.

```
                    BALANCE SHEET

ASSETS
     CURRENT
             Accounts Receivable         230
             Cash                        140
             Inventory                    50

        LONG-TERM
             Plant                       446

   TOTAL ASSETS                          866

   LIABILITIES
        CURRENT
             Accounts Payable             43
             Notes to Officers            12

        LONG-TERM
             Bonds                        27

   EQUITY
             Stock                       119
             Net Worth                   665

   TOTAL LIABILITIES AND EQUITY          866
```

Figure 5-6. This balance sheet is produced under control of the BALA function in the DSS Tool Kit. The BALA function sorts and formats items in the balance sheet, transposing them from item to output formats.

DSS tool kit uses the INCO program and relational algebra instructions to support preparation of pro forma statements.

To establish a perspective for his work, Sharp begins by specifying the menu display for the DSS he will develop for the Arizona plant study. This menu is shown in Figure 5-7. The items in this menu relate

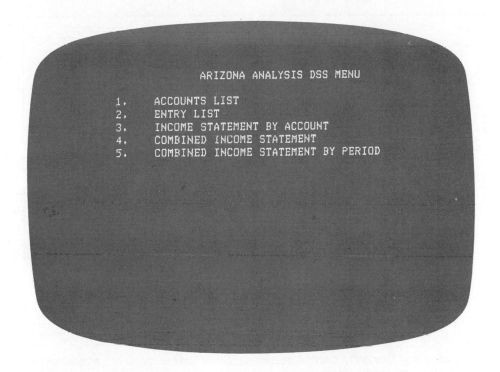

```
                    ARIZONA ANALYSIS DSS MENU

         1.     ACCOUNTS LIST
         2.     ENTRY LIST
         3.     INCOME STATEMENT BY ACCOUNT
         4.     COMBINED INCOME STATEMENT
         5.     COMBINED INCOME STATEMENT BY PERIOD
```

Figure 5-7. This is the menu to be used for access to the DSS for pro forma projections for Olympic Bicycle's Arizona plant.

clearly to the needs of an accounting-oriented system. To illustrate, the first menu item is an ACCOUNTS LIST. The cumulative entries called up on selection of this menu item would correspond with a chart of accounts within a typical accounting system.

The ACCOUNTS LIST itself is shown in Figure 5-8. Its structure shows all of the characteristics of a chart of accounts. Each item has a major and a minor account number, as is done in traditional accounting practices. In this instance, the product number serves as a natural identifier for the minor account code. Each item also has an identifying description that will correspond with financial report entries. Finally, each account is classified as income (IN) and expense (EX). Classification could be achieved by using the major account

```
        CHART OF ACCOUNTS -- ARIZONA PLANT PROJECTIONS

    ACCT        PROD        DESC                              TYPE

     10          1          SALES OF MP1                       IN
     10          2          SALES OF MP2                       IN
     10          3          SALES OF MP3                       IN
     20          1          COST OF MP1 MATERIALS              EX
     20          2          COST OF MP2 MATERIALS              EX
     20          3          COST OF MP3 MATERIALS              EX
     30          1          DEPRECIATION ALLOCATED FOR MP1     EX
     30          2          DEPRECIATION ALLOCATED FOR MP2     EX
     30          3          DEPRECIATION ALLOCATED FOR MP3     EX
     40          1          LABOR FOR MP1                      EX
     40          2          LABOR FOR MP2                      EX
     40          3          LABOR FOR MP3                      EX
```

Figure 5-8. This is the chart of accounts called from the menu to be used for pro forma projects for the Arizona plant.

number to identify income and expense items. However, in this case, there is an overriding requirement: The classification code identifies each account for processing under the INCO program.

Note the accounts with primary keys of 30. These are set up to handle depreciation of the plant and equipment to be used in moped manufacturing. The numbers to be entered under these account designations will be derived from inputs provided by Gear. The values will be derived by Gear from the construction requirements database described in Chapter 4.

Once the menu format and the charts of accounts were in place, Sharp was able to begin to collect data items that fit his formats. In doing this, Sharp followed Olympic Bicycle guidelines requiring that the Arizona facility be brought to a profitable level of productivity within 18 months. That is, once the plant is built and available, management requires that it go into production immediately. By the sixth accounting period (quarter) after start-up, management wants to generate enough cash flow to cover the carrying costs (depreciation expense) on the new facility.

Within this framework, Sharp developed the series of data entries shown in Figure 5-9. Note that there is an entry for each major account for each of six periods. Note also that the amounts for income items (sales) increase in successive calendar periods while depreciation accounts are constant. Note also that expenses for inventories are higher initially than in later quarters. This reflects the need to establish initial levels of inventories. Parts and materials costs then level off and begin to decline as normal operational levels are attained. Conversely, labor costs start low and increase as the plant moves into full staffing.

For illustrative purposes, Figure 5-9 includes data items for one product only. The income and expense trend figures are derived from past experience of the company and from Sharp's past work on product-line start-ups. Naturally, an actual pro forma analysis would require more data and greater breadth of coverage.

Figure 5-10 is the schema that models the database within Sharp's Arizona analysis DSS. The coding used needs no elaboration at this point. The same is true for the menu specifications in Figure 5-11. These entries follow conventions of the DSS tool kit. All of the operators used have been identified and demonstrated previously.

SPREADSHEETS AS DESCRIPTIVE MODELS

Today, the term *spreadsheet* presumes the presence of a software package that runs on a personal or larger computer. The spreadsheet program has either finite or user-definable formats that create spaces for columns and rows of data and provide a means for inserting specific data values into the *cells*, or points of intersection. The spreadsheet gets its name from an age-old accounting document in which entry areas were provided through the ruling and printing of columns and rows on wide forms. The width of the forms led to the spreadsheet designation.

Physically, the appearance of a spreadsheet suggests a table of columns and rows—a typical relational model. In this sense also, a spreadsheet is a prototypical descriptive model.

ACCT	PROD	AMT	PERIOD
10	1	0	1
10	1	0	2
10	1	10	3
10	1	11	4
10	1	13	5
10	1	25	6
20	1	20	1
20	1	20	2
20	1	20	3
20	1	20	4
20	1	20	5
20	1	20	6
30	1	3	1
30	1	3	2
30	1	3	3
30	1	3	4
30	1	3	5
30	1	3	6
40	1	8	1
40	1	8	2
40	1	10	3
40	1	10	4
40	1	10	5
40	1	12	6

Figure 5-9.   These are the journal entries prepared as inputs to produce pro forma projections for the Arizona plant.

However, most spreadsheet programs have features that can change these characteristics. Specifically, spreadsheet software provides for entry of equations that will act upon content of the cells. Thus, entry and application of an equation can serve to alter the entire content of the spreadsheet. In this respect, a spreadsheet program

```
ACCTS      1      ACCT
ACCTS      2      PROD
ACCTS      3      DESC
ACCTS      4      TYPE
ENTRY      1      ACCT
ENTRY      2      PROD
ENTRY      3      AMT
ENTRY      4      PERIOD
```

Figure 5-10. This is the schema that models the data tables within the Arizona plant projection database.

---

functions as an equation-driven descriptive model. Considering overall capabilities, a spreadsheet program can be said to implement a hybrid between a data descriptive and an equation-driven modeling method.

Possibly the most common use of spreadsheet software packages and their outputs is for financial forecasts like those described earlier in this chapter. To illustrate, consider a typical market forecast of the type that might be prepared for top management and owners at Olympic Bicycle. Using projections from reports on past results, Sellem and Sharp confer and predict that the touring line of bicycles will have sales growths of 10 percent annually for the next three years. They estimate that this growth will be matched by increases of only 5 percent in advertising, materials, and labor costs. As input to top-level planning, these projections are to be captured in a spreadsheet report.

Using the spreadsheet operator of the tool kit, SPREAD, an analyst reflects the present figures and growth projections in a table like the one shown in Figure 5-12. This instruction set, or *template*, incorporates actual sales and expense data for the current period. For each cell with a value to be computed, the formula to be applied is

```
A        "ARIZONA ANALYSIS DSS"
A   1    "ACCTS LIST"
A   1    PROGRAM DISPLAY "ACCTS"
A   2    "ENTRY LIST"
A   2    PROGRAM DISPLAY "ENTRY"
A   3    "INCOME STATEMENT BY PRODUCT"
A   3    PROGRAM SELECT "ENTRY, PROD=?PROD?, WORK"
A   3    PROGRAM JOIN "WORK, ACCTS, ACCT:ACCT; PROD:PROD, WORK1"
A   3    PROGRAM PROJECT "WORK1, 3; 5; 6, WORK2"
A   3    PROGRAM INCO "WORK2"
A   4    "COMBINED INCOME STATEMENT"
A   4    PROGRAM JOIN "WORK, ACCTS, ACCT:ACCT; PROD:PROD, WORK1"
A   4    PROGRAM PROJECT "WORK1, 3; 5; 6, WORK2"
A   4    PROGRAM INCO "WORK2"
A   5    "COMBINED INCOME STATEMENT BY PERIOD"
A   5    PROGRAM SELECT "ENTRY, PERIOD=?PER?, WORK"
A   5    PROGRAM JOIN "WORK, ACCTS, ACCT:ACCT; PROD:PROD, WORK1"
A   5    PROGRAM PROJECT "WORK1, 3; 5; 6, WORK2"
A   5    PROGRAM INCO "WORK2"
```

Figure 5-11. This is the list of coding used to generate the menu that will control access to the Arizona plant projection database.

```
SALES            PERIOD 1        PERIOD 2        PERIOD 3
   TO1              10          {B2*1.1}        {C2*1.1}
   TO2              13          {B3*1.1}        {C3*1.1}
   TO3               9          {B4*1.1}        {C4*1.1}
TOTAL SALES     {B2+B3+B4}      {C2+C3+C4}      {D2+D3+D4}
EXPENSE
   MATERIALS         2          {B7*1.05}       {C7*1.05}
   LABOR             1          {B8*1.05}       {C8*1.05}
   ADVERTISING       3          {B9*1.05}       {C9*1.09}
TOTAL EXPENSE   {B7+B8+B9}      {C7+C8+C9}      {D7+D8+D9}
GROSS PROFIT    {B5(-)B11}      {C5(-)C11}      {D5(-)D11}
```

Figure 5-12. This display shows a template used by the SPREAD operator of the DSS Tool Kit to generate a financial projection.

contained within the appropriate field and enclosed in braces { }. The addressing scheme for this table designates columns by letters (left to right starting with A) and rows by numbers (top to bottom starting with 1). The SPREAD operator establishes spreadsheet values a full column at a time, going from left to right, top to bottom. This is necessary because the values to be derived are cumulative and successive.

The result derived from applying the SPREAD operator to the template in Figure 5-12 is shown in Figure 5-13. Bear in mind that the results shown in Figure 5-13 are principally derived. When spreadsheets were developed manually, each cell required individual computation and notation. The ability to designate templates as shown in this demonstration opens a virtual infinity for experimentation with projections and planning documents. This potential for looking at decision alternatives is covered in Chapter 6.

GRAPHIC DISPLAYS

Graphic displays are descriptive models that represent data values pictorially. As with all descriptive models, the function of graphic displays is to present data to promote ready understanding and to facilitate communication.

Your DSS tool kit has several commands that can be used to produce graphic outputs. Two of the most commonly used and well known methods are covered first in the discussion that follows. These are pie charts and histograms.

Pie Charts

A *pie chart* is a graphic method of comparing a whole entity with the size or magnitude of its constituent parts. The basic structure is a circle, the outline of a pie. Individual parts are represented by portions of the circle, slices of the pie. This display technique is sufficiently common that it needs no elaboration. Figure 5-14 is a pie chart showing the elements of cost for the product, MP1, the first moped to be built in the new plant. The values in the pie chart represent costs from Ian Sharp's figures for Period 6. This pie chart, or others of similar design, can be generated through use of the PIE command in your DSS tool kit. The format and operations for this

```
SALES            PERIOD 1        PERIOD 2        PERIOD 3
   TO1               10              11              12
   TO2               13              14              15
   TO3                9               9              10
TOTAL SALES          32              34              37
EXPENSE
   MATERIALS          2               2               2
   LABOR              1               1               1
   ADVERTISING        3               3               3
TOTAL EXPENSE         6               6               6
GROSS PROFIT         26              28              31
```

Figure 5-13. This is the spreadsheet generated from use of the SPREAD operator, as illustrated in Figure 5-12.

command are described at the end of this chapter in the Tool Kit Command Summary.

Histograms

A *histogram*, also known as a *bar chart*, compares multiple items by representing their values as varying line lengths. Again, this is a highly familiar technique for presenting data graphically. To illustrate, Figure 5-15 is a histogram comparing MP1 sales figures for the six reported periods. This chart is generated through use of the HISTO command in your tool kit. The format and operations of this command are presented in the Tool Kit Command Summary section at the end of this chapter.

Histograms can also be used to represent component values of a single entity. To illustrate, Figure 5-16 is a bar chart built from the same data as the pie chart in Figure 5-14.

Because the represented data items on a bar chart are ordered along a straight line, time relationships among items can be established. The natural tendency is to read the values of a bar chart from left to right or from top to bottom if the bars are horizontal. Thus, in

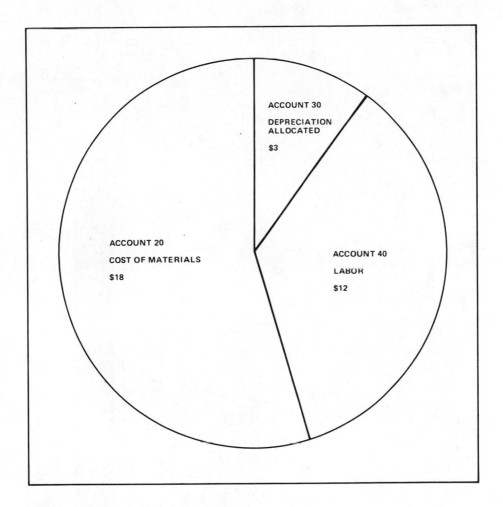

Figure 5-14. This pie chart provides graphic representation for the data for Period 6 represented in Figure 5-9.

Figure 5-15, the bars are presented in left-to-right order corresponding with the natural time sequence of the data from periods 1 through 6. This type of data is called *time series* data.

Because bar charts can order data items sequences, they can be used to present *distribution* data. For example, in preparing production estimates for MP1, John Gear might ask a group of experienced

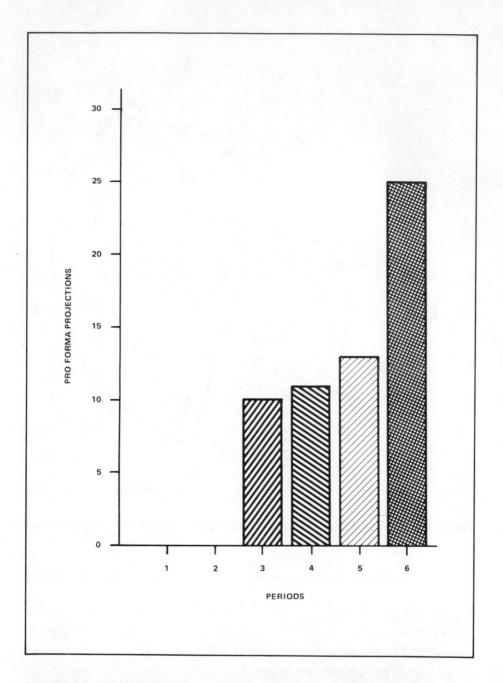

Figure 5-15. This graphic output represents the data in Figure 5-9 as a histogram, or bar chart. The bars in this diagram identify the periods for which data are reported.

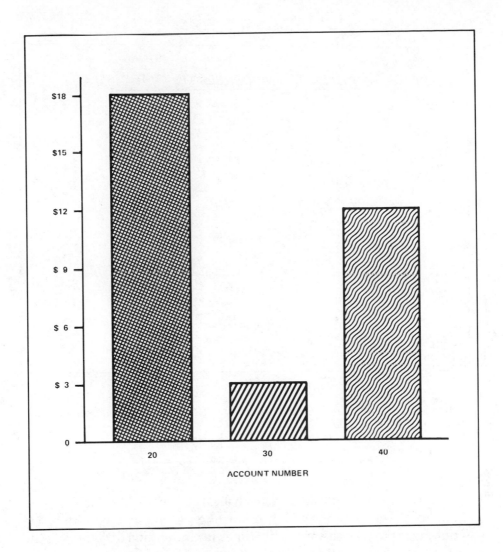

Figure 5-16. This histogram corresponds with the pie chart in Figure 5-14 and with the data for Period 6 in Figure 5-9.

production workers to assemble and mount engines on unit frames. Each iteration of this task would be timed. Data would be entered on an informal table like the one shown in Figure 5-17. The average time then could be computed and used as a basis for an estimate.

# MIN	INCIDENCE AT TIMES
4	3
5	3
6	4
7	6
8	14
9	12
10	7
11	4
12	2
13	0
14	0
15	3
16	2

Figure 5-17.   This table of source data covers distribution data on assembly operations at Olympic Bicycle.

However, an experienced industrial engineer like Gear would want to be more thorough in analyzing assembly operations. He would want to take the assembly times for individual iterations of the assembly job and group them according to time consumed, as is shown in Figure 5-18. The length of the bars in this display indicate the number of times the job was done in a specific time interval. Ideally, the high point on such a chart would be centered to reflect a tight distribution of assembly experience values. But, note that Figure 5-18 has a "tail" to the right. This indicates that, in some instances, the assembly task took a lot longer than the average time.

Noting data of this type, Gear would investigate. He might find the aberration due to an inexperienced worker. However, he might

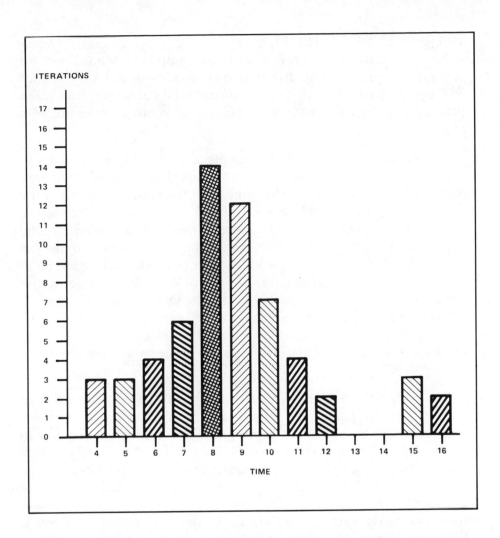

Figure 5-18. This histogram represents time values for the performance of a specific production job, with items grouped according to time-interval values. The "tail" at the right in this chart identifies exception situations in which the operation took considerably longer than the normal duration.

also discover a correctable problem, such as defective parts that had to be set aside. Inspection procedures might then be instituted to eliminate the particular problem.

Box-and-Whisker Diagram

A *box-and-whisker* diagram is a relatively simple, powerful tool for presenting and analyzing distribution-type, analytical data. Box-and-whisker diagrams are applied to *univariate* data analyses, indicating that data are arrayed within a single dimension, or column, of a relation.

To illustrate, Figure 5-19 represents a first step toward developing a box-and-whisker diagram for a single column within a relation. Note that the data used are the same as in the second column of the relation in Figure 5-17. However, in Figure 5-19, the data have been sorted into ascending order. Notations in this illustration indicate the *median*, or middle point, in the data array. Also identified are the upper and lower *hinges*. Statistically, hinges mark quarter-points in data arrays. In other words, one-quarter of the values are above the upper hinge and one-quarter are below the lower hinge. This leaves about one-half of the values in the range between the hinges. This group of values is the *midspread* interval. The midspread value is determined, as shown, by subtracting the lower hinge value from the upper hinge value.

In creating a box-and-whisker diagram like the one shown in Figure 5-20, the midspread interval establishes the length of a box on a scale. The box, in effect, is presented as containing the points in the midspread range. The whiskers, then, are determined through calculations using the hinge and midspread values. To illustrate, the upper hinge value in Figure 5-19 is 6. The midspread value, 4, is added, to produce a sum of 10. This new, derived value is then positioned in the data array. Then, the next value at or below this derived value establishes the point of the upper *whisker*. A corresponding procedure is applied to establish the point of the lower whisker.

The derived whisker points are identified by ''X'' marks in Figure 5-20. The values not included within the whisker intervals are identified by ''O'' marks in Figure 5-20. In analyses, the ''O'' marks are treated as exception values. Central tendency, statistically, is represented by the box, which contains a vertical line marking the median point.

Box-and-whisker diagrams can be prepared through use of the BANDW command available in your DSS tool kit. Descriptions of the

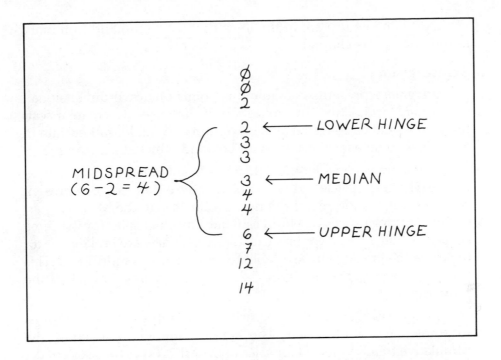

Figure 5-19. This manually prepared set of data are organized for use in preparation of a box-and-whisker diagram. Identifications include the median, hinges, and midspread of distribution to be used in the diagram.

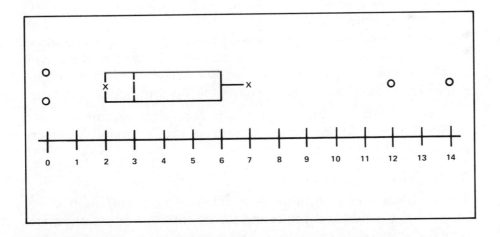

Figure 5-20. This box-and-whisker diagram is the graphic output derived from the processing of data in Figure 5-17.

command and its use are in the DSS Tool Kit Command Summary at the end of this chapter.

Scattergram

A *scattergram* represents data items as points on a two-dimensional, or *bivariate*, grid. Thus, the collection of data used to create a scattergram would be collected as two columns in a table, rather than in a single column as is the case with box-and-whisker diagrams.

To illustrate, consider the data items listed in Figure 5-21. Thinking of Olympic Bicycle's Arizona plant, these data could represent sales projections for one of the new products, say the MP2. As part of the planning process, Sellum estimates product sales for the same six periods being used for financial forecasts. Sales are broken out for the three sales regions to be established for the new product line. This explains the presence in Figure 5-21 of three entries for each of the six periods.

In Figure 5-22, the sales forecast data are represented as a series of points on a scattergram. The scattergram serves to show the cumulative trend projected for sales of the MP2. Over the six periods, sales increases are reflected for each of the regions, and for the product line as a whole.

In Figure 5-23, additional depth of meaning is added to the data by marking the scattergram points with distinguishing symbols representing individual sales regions. In Figure 5-22, the same symbol is used for all scattergram points. In Figure 5-23, use of the letters A, B, and C serves to identify individual performance data items with specific regions. Thus, the single graphic makes it possible to track sales in individual regions, as well as for the company as a whole.

The tool kit operator used to produce scattergrams is called SGRAM. Details for its use are in the Tool Kit Command Summary at the end of this chapter.

Resistant Line Diagram

The *resistant line* technique is a relatively simple method for establishing trends and projecting future results from scattergram-type, bivariate, data collections. The effect is as though a trend line were superimposed over a scattergram and extended beyond the bounds of existing point entries to show the effect of continuation of

SALES REGION	YEAR	SALES
A	1	16
B	1	15
C	1	14
A	2	17
B	2	19
C	2	18
A	3	21
B	3	22
C	3	20
A	4	18
B	4	24
C	4	26
A	5	28
B	5	27
C	5	30
A	6	22
B	6	33
C	6	30

Figure 5-21. This is a set of source data to be represented in a scattergram.

an established performance pattern. The technique illustrated here is characterized as ''resistant'' because the resulting line resists the effects of errors in establishing individual data points. That is, the data can be varied, as might occur with measurement error, without any significant effect upon the line.

A resistant line presentation of the data on the first region from Figure 5-21 is shown in Figure 5-24. To achieve this presentation, the analyst divides the time frame of the diagram into three vertical bands with an equal number of data points in each. Within the left and right

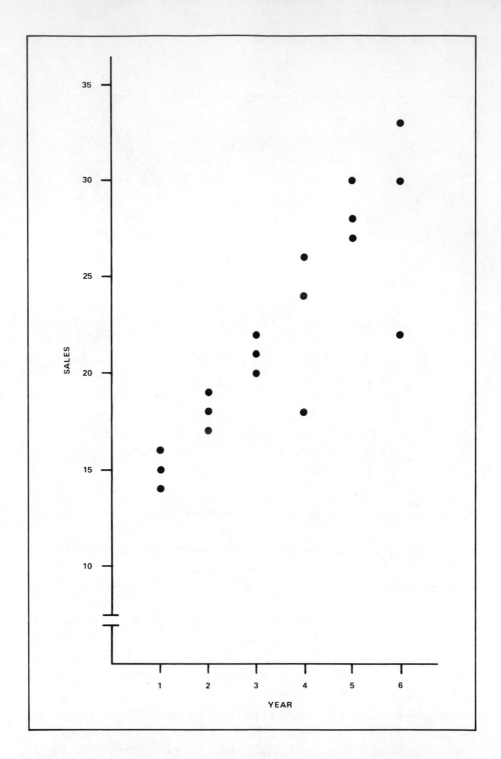

Figure 5-22. This is the scattergram derived from the source data in Figure 5-21.

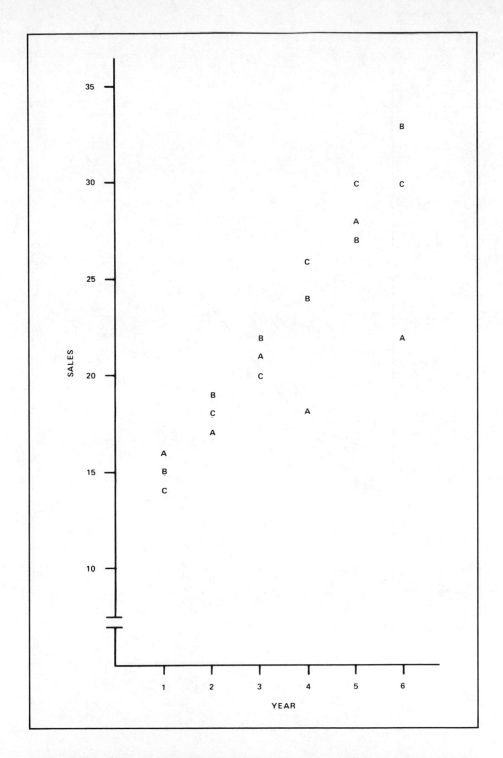

Figure 5-23. This is another version of the scattergram using data from Figure 5-21. In this graphic, data are identified according to region through use of letters to represent regional identifications.

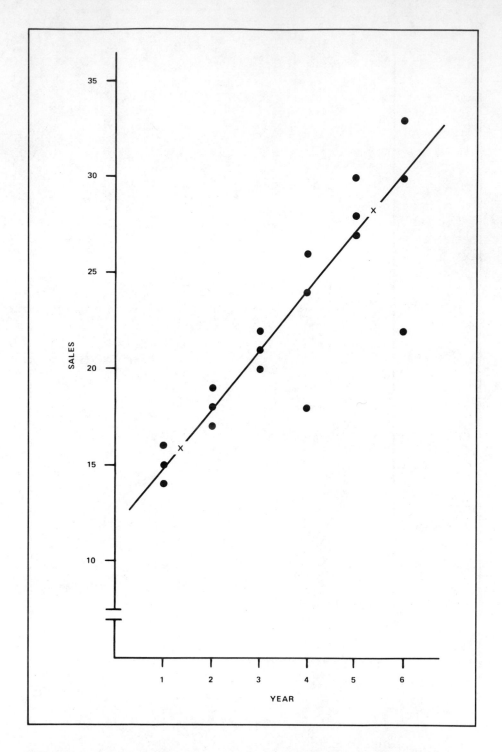

Figure 5-24. This is a resistant line diagram for the data represented in Figure 5-21.

bands, a point is positioned centrally to the data representations. That is, the selected point should have an equal number of data points to its left and right and also above and below. A line drawn through these points is a resistant line, getting its name from the fact that this technique resists aberrations in the data due to extreme variations of individual points. (This line might be adjusted on the vertical axis without affecting its slope. In this way, there would be an equal number of points above and below the line.)

To demonstrate the value of resistant line methods to project, or *extrapolate,* trends, see the graphic in Figure 5-25. This is based on the same initial data as the diagram in Figure 5-24. However, the time-line dimension of the chart has been extended over 18 periods. The resistant line, then, has been extended over this time frame as a means of forecasting sales for the same district if the established trend continues. Note this implied assumption: Virtually all forecasting algorithms based on historic data assume that past, established trends will continue into the indefinite future.

Resistant line methods can also be used to *interpolate* results from data that may not be appropriate to the exact situation of a forecast. For example, assume that John Gear has extensive data on the painting of bicycle frames in Olympic's current plant. At the existing facility, painting is done in batches of 100, 110, and 120. As a basis for start-up of the new plant, he has data from test runs on batches of 10, 20, and 30. Now, Gear is asked to project costs for a future situation involving batches of 60 and 70 frames. The interpolation could be handled through a resistant line presentation like the one in Figure 5-26. Gear has simply shown a resistant line relationship encompassing available data. The linear value of the intermediate batches has been assumed to be part of a continuous trend.

The Tool Kit Command Summary at the end of this chapter contains a command, RLINE, that can be used to generate resistant line diagrams.

Median Trace Diagram

Median trace methods are designed to show *nonlinear* trend patterns. The methodology is similar to that of resistant line diagramming, except that multiple points are used. In resistant line presentations, remember, only two key points are established. These are connected

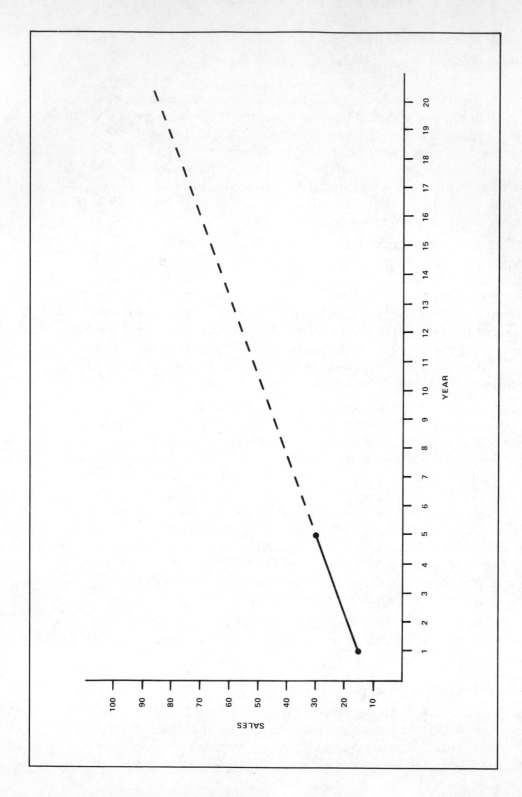

Figure 5-25. This is an extended resistant line diagram. Again, the data are derived from Figure 5-21.

with a straight line. In a median trace presentation, usually six points are established. When these points are connected, the resulting diagram is apt to be a curve, rather than a line.

To illustrate, Figure 5-27 presents a median trace of the same data introduced in Figure 5-21. Again, the data selected represent the first sales region. In preparing Figure 5-27, six vertical bands were created, each with approximately the same number of data points. Within each band, points were identified that reflect a median position. Connecting the six points generated the curved line. Lines in median trace diagrams can be used for extrapolation and interpolation in the same manner as resistant line graphics.

The tool kit operator for a median trace, included in the Tool Kit Command Summary at the end of this chapter, is MTRACE.

GRAPHICS IN THE OLYMPIC BICYCLE DSS

The Arizona plant turns out to be a major commitment that will affect the entire history of Olympic Bicycle. Ian Sharp receives word from Roger Wheelwright that formal presentations will have to be made for both the company's commercial bankers and also for a group of investment bankers. The rationale is that, if the venture is successful, Olympic Bicycle will need to increase either debt or equity funding sources to underwrite the greatly increased investments in product inventory and promotion.

Sharp decides that the kind of presentation he will have to make can benefit from graphic representations of his data. The prospect becomes attractive when he learns that the graphics he needs can be derived from the same DSS he has already created. All that will be needed is a submenu display and an extension of the menu specification that has already been prepared.

The menu to be used in calling up graphics is shown in Figure 5-28. Note that Sharp plans to develop graphics much like those you encountered in the previous presentation:

- Pie charts will be used to display information on product expenses. When the first menu item is selected, the program asks the user which period is to be covered.

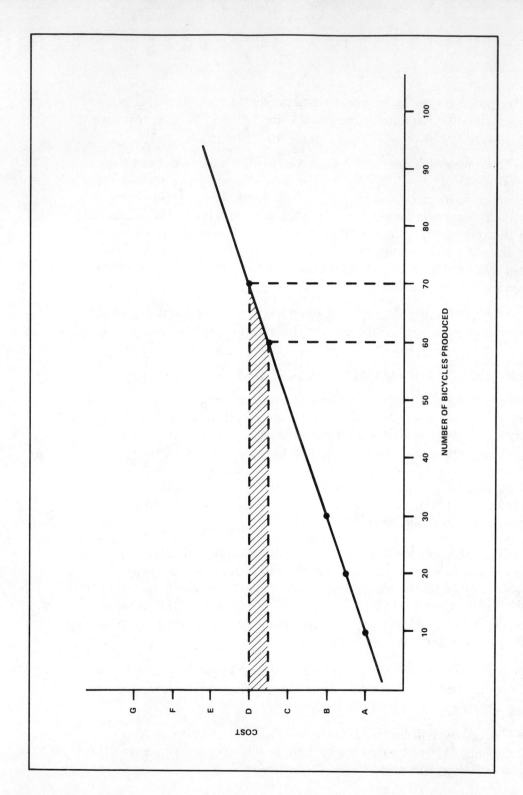

Figure 5-26. This resistant line diagram is designed specifically to support interpolation of data.

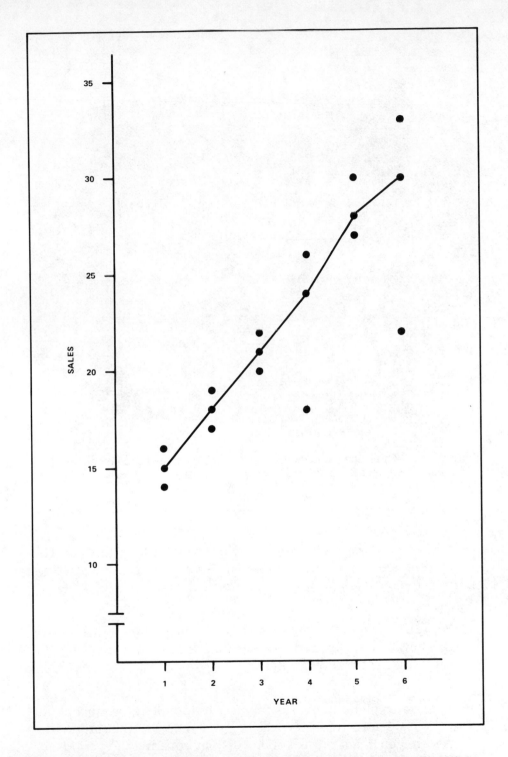

Figure 5-27. This is a median trace diagram based upon the data in Figure 5-21.

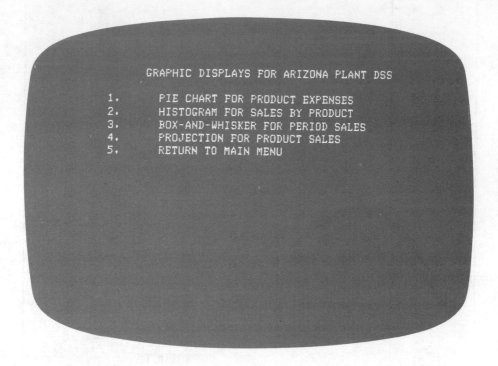

Figure 5-28. This is the menu for the graphics DSS to be used to present displays interpreting data on the Arizona plant study.

- Histograms will be used to display data on sales, by product. The system is set up to present a separate bar representing sales for the covered period for a single product.

- For presentations on sales by period for the entire product line of the new plant, box-and-whisker diagrams can be activated by selecting the third menu item.

- The fourth menu item asks the user to identify a product about which a sales projection will be shown. From this input, the system generates a resistant line display covering the periods for which the system has data on file.

Note that a menu selection is provided that returns control to the main menu. As explained above, this menu and its accompanying specifications are additions to the DSS described earlier in this chapter.

The menu specification that implements the graphics subsystem is shown in Figure 5-29. By this point in your learning experience, no further explanations are necessary. Remember, however, that further study is possible through reference to the tool kit specifications at the end of this chapter.

```
A    6    "GRAPHIC DISPLAYS"
A    6    GOTO B
B         "GRAPHIC DISPLAYS FOR ARIZONA PLANT DSS"
B    1    "PIE CHART FOR PRODUCT EXPENSES"
B    1    PROGRAM SELECT "ENTRY, PERIOD=?PER?, WORK"
B    1    PROGRAM SELECT "WORK, ACCT>10, WORK1"
B    1    PROGRAM PIE "WORK1, ACCT, AMT"
B    2    "HISTOGRAM FOR SALES BY PRODUCT"
B    2    PROGRAM SELECT "ENTRY, ACCT=10, WORK"
B    2    PROGRAM HISTO "WORK, PROD, AMT"
B    3    "BOX-AND-WHISKER FOR PERIOD SALES"
B    3    PROGRAM SELECT "ENTRY, ACCT=10, WORK"
B    3    PROGRAM SELECT "WORK, PROD=?PROD?, WORK1"
B    3    PROGRAM BANDW "WORK1, AMT"
B    4    "PROJECTION FOR PRODUCT SALES"
B    4    PROGRAM SELECT "ENTRY, ACCT=10, WORK"
B    4    PROGRAM SELECT "WORK, PROD=?PROD?, WORK1"
B    4    PROGRAM RLINE "WORK1, PERIOD, AMT"
B    5    "RETURN TO MAIN MENU"
B    5    GOTO A
```

Figure 5-29.   This is the menu specification input for the graphics package to support the Arizona plant DSS.

Outlook

- This chapter presents some tools and techniques with which you can perform descriptive modeling. It is established that descriptive modeling tends to represent an organization on the basis of past activities or developments.

- Descriptive models, though they are past-oriented, are important foundations for decision-making programs or activities. Current status, in a sense, is a base upon which to construct plans and from which to choose future courses of action.

- However, a full tool kit for decision support also requires modeling techniques that are more forward looking. These are known as prescriptive models, which provide the subject matter for the next chapter.

Operation Summary: The SPREAD Operator

The SPREAD operator implements an elementary spreadsheet capability for the DSS tool kit. SPREAD will impart to you the concept of a spreadsheet, but do not judge the power of modern commercial spreadsheet programs from your exposure to SPREAD. Commercial spreadsheet packages exhibit the best of interactive, personal computer programming achievement and are routinely offered with capabilities rivaling database management systems for data storage and manipulation, and rivaling general-purpose programming languages for computation. SPREAD is much more modest.

The spreadsheet specification for SPREAD is prepared with one of the editors. The cells in this specification are addressed A to E, and the rows are addressed 1 to 99. Thus, the cell in the upper left-hand corner is referenced as A1, and the cell in the lower right-hand corner of a 24 line CRT screen is referenced as E24. The columns are fixed-format, each allowing for use of, at most, 16 characters.

The DSS designer can place headings, formulas, or constants in any of the cells. Constants can be with or without decimal points. Headings may include any characters printable on your computer. Headings may extend across the 16 character cell boundaries. Formulas must be placed within brackets, ({ }). If brackets are not placed around formulas, the computation references will appear on your spreadsheet as headings. Cells also can include user prompts. User prompts must be surrounded by question marks (?). Prompts are displayed when a cell is calculated, allowing users to enter correct values.

Formulas can include constants (such as 1.23 or 37), legal cell references (such as A1 or C5), and arithmetic operators (such as + for addition, − for subtraction, * for multiplication, and / for division). Formulas cannot use parentheses to establish the order of computation. All formulas are calculated from left to right, regardless of the arithmetic operators involved. If a formula consists of more than 16 character positions (the maximum allowed in a cell), the master formula can be broken down into auxiliary formulas. Auxiliary formulas perform a specific part of the calculation. Auxiliary formulas can be placed in other cells. Cell addresses of auxiliary formulas are placed within square brackets ([ ]) in master formulas. During computation, auxiliary formulas are called and calculated, and the result is passed to the master formula. Any characters other than valid cell references, the arithmetic operators, constants, parentheses, or the square brackets are ignored during computation.

Computational references to noncomputational cells are regarded as references to constants. Nonnumeric characters are disregarded in the evaluation of constants. Thus, a reference to a heading in a computational cell can result in a reference to the value zero.

The evaluation of the spreadsheet is done by columns, left to right. Within the column, evaluation proceeds top to bottom.

Note that you can manipulate spreadsheet specifications with the DBMS operators (and DBMS files with the SPREAD operator) if the file is defined with 16-character-wide columns.

Operation Summary:
Descriptive Models and Graphic Displays

Descriptive models and graphic displays are implemented as individual programs accessible from the PROGRAM operator of MENU. The discussion that follows lists and explains the control parameters that must be coded to use the programs. Remember that the control parameter list must be surrounded by double quotes (''), and the individual control parameters separated by commas (,) when the list is supplied as an operand to the PROGRAM operator. The commands and parameters are:

INCO data table name
The INCO command generates an income statement. The ''data table name'' parameter instructs the system from which data table to develop the income statement. Note that the input data table must consist of three columns: account type (EX for expense or IN for income), amount, and account description.

BALA data table name
The BALA command causes output of a balance sheet. The ''data table name'' parameter instructs the system which

data table to use in building the balance sheet. Note that the data table must consist of three columns: account type (AC for current assets, AL for long-term assets, LC for current liabilities, LL for long-term liabilities, and EQ for equity), amount, and account description.

PIE data table name, x-coordinate data item name or index, y-coordinate data item name or index
The PIE command generates a pie chart from two columns in a data table. The ''data table name'' parameter tells the system which data table to input. The ''x-coordinate'' and ''y-coordinate'' parameters name the columns of data that will be used to generate the graphic display.

HISTO data table name, x-coordinate data item name or index, y-coordinate data item name or index
The HISTO command generates a histogram, or bar chart, from two columns in a data table. The HISTO command functions like the PIE command. The ''data table name'' parameter tells the system which data table to input. The ''x-coordinate'' and ''y-coordinate'' parameters name the columns of data that will be used to generate the graphic display.

BANDW data table name, data item name or index
The BANDW command generates a box-and-whisker diagram from one column, or field, in a data table. The ''data table name'' parameter tells the system which data table to input. The ''data item name or index'' parameter instructs the system which field to use in generating the graphic display.

RLINE data table name, x-coordinate data item name or index, y-coordinate data item name or index
The RLINE command produces a resistant line diagram from two fields in a data table. The ''data table name'' parameter tells the system which table to input. The ''x-coordinate'' and ''y-coordinate'' parameters define the fields to be used in generating the graphic display.

SGRAM data table name, x-coordinate data item name or index, y-coordinate data item name or index
The SGRAM command produces a scattergram from two columns of data in a data table. The ''data table name'' parameter tells the system which table to input. The ''x-coordinate'' and ''y-coordinate'' parameters name the columns of data to be used in generating the graphic display.

MTRACE data table name, x-coordinate data item name or index, y-coordinate data item name or index
The MTRACE command generates a median trace diagram from two columns of data in a data table. The ''data table name'' parameter tells the system which table to input. The ''x-coordinate'' and ''y-coordinate'' parameters name the columns of data to be used to produce the graphic display.

SPREAD template file name
The SPREAD command generates a spreadsheet. The ''template file name'' parameter tells the system which file contains the template to be used in generating the spreadsheet. Note that the template file contains all data and formulas to be used in generating the spreadsheet.

Assignments

1. Develop a spreadsheet template that can print a report similar to the income statement shown in Figure 5-4. The spreadsheet template should specify the automatic generation of totals.

2. Compare the utility and economy of using a spreadsheet to generate income statements with using DBMS operators, the INCO command, and data tables to generate income statements. Consider volumes of and availability of data captured during normal transaction-oriented operations of a company.

3. Use RLINE, MTRACE, and historical data from the past three months to forecast next month's daily temperatures. Perform the same operations and calculations using historical data from the past six months and the past nine months. Are your forecasts different? Why?

4. Locate books or manuals describing commercially available statistical analysis computer programs. Do they support resistant line, median trace, histogram, or scattergram analyses? What other capabilities do they offer? How are data stored and manipulated within these packages?

5. Imagine that you have hardware components that can produce color graphics and are reprogramming your DSS tool kit to take advantage of color. How could you use color to enhance graphics capabilities? Would the functions be more effective with color? How?

6. Use the SPREAD command to develop a spreadsheet analysis of your own personal wealth projections for six years. Have one column for the present year and five columns for future years. Enter your percentage of expected wealth increase for each year and have the spreadsheet program calculate the yearly values. Use several categories of wealth such as savings, interest, income, and investments.

7. Consult the appendix on DSS tool kit operation to determine how you could make spreadsheets accessible with menu entries. You will want to invoke a text editor from a menu. What types of DSS users should be allowed this capability? Is it limiting not to allow this capability? Discuss.

8. Devise a scheme by which an operator like SPREAD might accept input from a data table. How might this be used? Show examples in which the values for a balance sheet are read from a data table and the spreadsheet operator formats, totals, and prints the report.

6 PRESCRIPTIVE MODELS AND EXPERT SYSTEMS

Abstract

- Models that project outcomes of future decision alternatives as a basis for decision recommendations are called prescriptive.

- The basis for a prescriptive model is a set of assumptions about future conditions.

- Also considered within a prescriptive model are statements about anticipated consequences for considered alternatives.

- Prescriptive models relate more directly to the choice of alternatives to implement decisions than do descriptive models. This is because a prescriptive model presents, tests, and effectively recommends the choice to be made while a descriptive model is passive, providing an information base only.

- Descriptive models can be used prescriptively under a method that tests consequences of multiple alternatives. This method is known as "what if . . . ?" analysis.

- Decision support systems, whether they use descriptive or prescriptive models, are based on application of data. Techniques that apply existing bodies of *knowledge* to support operations or decisions are called expert systems. Expert systems, which support decision making and can be considered as a type of DSS, are also described in this chapter.

PRESCRIPTIVE MODELS: PRINCIPLES AND CONTRASTS

In most uses of data models, the data are collected first, and uses or decisions follow content. *Prescriptive models,* however, are a special case. A prescriptive model preconceives a situation that should exist and that may not yet have come to pass. In such situations, a prescriptive model can create a monitoring and control mechanism. Model content is monitored as data are collected. When prescribed conditions are recognized, the control mechanism is triggered.

The models described and applied so far within this book have all been descriptive. A *descriptive model* is one in which data are gathered inclusively to reflect a situation under study or subject to management. Thus, a descriptive model of a manufacturing inventory would contain data covering all items in stock and on order. Usage histories might also be part of such a model.

These characteristics of descriptive models help to establish another common feature of prescriptive models. That is, prescriptive models can often be built upon or use the data of a descriptive model. Continue to think about the inventory data model. A descriptive model would be inclusive in its data content. By contrast, a prescriptive model might concentrate upon determining and enforcing purchasing practices that use economic order quantity (EOQ) values as their basis. An EOQ, basically, is a purchasing volume that controls ordering practices to assure that purchasing will be carried out at minimum overall cost.

Thus, prescriptive models are designed to assure presence of predetermined conditions as a basis for defined actions. The idea is to get the best results in every instance for the conditions being modeled. Examples of prescriptive targets might be lowest cost, highest profit, maximum stock turnover, fastest deliveries, and so on.

The main mechanism of a prescriptive model is a factor known as a *control variable.* This, simply, is what a prescriptive model is about: Management establishes criteria for actions. Determinations then are made about the best methods for satisfying the criteria. In some instances, control values may reflect product pricing. Quantities to be purchased are based on a combination of discounts and promotional allowances.

On the other hand, another controlling philosophy may be the "just in time" model for inventory management. Under this approach, it is felt that handling and stocking costs for any inventory are too high. The idea, rather, is to set up collaboration programs with vendors under which newly purchased stocks go right to the factory floor. The principle: Management sets policies. Prescriptive models can establish control mechanisms to help implement those policies. To summarize:

- A descriptive model is a function of collected data values. The data values, in turn, represent the entity being modeled. The descriptive model, then, provides an effective way to represent that collection of facts and relationships. Thus, a descriptive model may be a drawing, a three-dimensional sculpture, a tabular report, or a histogram.

- A prescriptive model is selective, centering on a particular value or choice identified as the best among an available group or selection. The control variable is one or a range from among a complete set of data values that may comprise a desciptive model. A control value can also be identified as a specific management selection or specification.

PRESCRIPTIVE USE OF DESCRIPTIVE MODELS

All modeling starts from a descriptive base. Thus, a prescriptive model represents a kind of use for a descriptive model rather than being a distinct entity in its own right.

This principle is true universally, applying beyond the realm of collections of data or equations. For example, consider a physical model. In developing new automobiles, manufacturers typically build physical (plastic) models to a scale of 40 percent of full size. The miniature structures model the bodies of future cars. Overall, these models are used to evaluate appearance. In terms of performance, the models are often placed in wind tunnels to test aerodynamic properties. At this point, the descriptive model is put to prescriptive uses.

The model, for example, may be fitted with variable tail or fender foils to derive varying performance control values, such as the height or shape of the foils. The value that comes closest to meeting design and production criteria is adopted. Such prescriptive use of descriptive models is also common for equation models.

To demonstrate prescriptive use of a descriptive data model, consider the median trace diagram in Figure 6-1. The vertical axis of this diagram represents corporate profit. The horizontal axis identifies advertising expense. This is a classic use of graphic outputs from data models. The diagram shows that a relationship apparently exists between advertising expenditures and corporate profits.

The illustrated prescriptive use of this model is to pick the level of advertising expenditure that serves to optimize profits. This is done by drawing a vertical line that passes through the highest point of the profit curve and reading the point on the bottom axis representing the corresponding level of advertising expenditure. In effect, this procedure serves to prescribe the company's most advantageous level of advertising expenditure.

Figure 6-1 illustrates conversion of a descriptive model for prescriptive use through procedural techniques. Prescriptive models can also be derived by applying analytic techniques to descriptive models.

Analysis of Descriptive Models

To demonstrate analytic conversion of a descriptive model into a prescriptive model, consider the following, simple equation that models total inventory stocking costs for a product (inventory item):

$$TC = OC + CC$$

TC = Total Cost
OC = Ordering Cost
CC = Carrying Cost

This is a simple mathematical model indicating that total cost of inventory is equal to the cost of ordering and carrying stock items. To

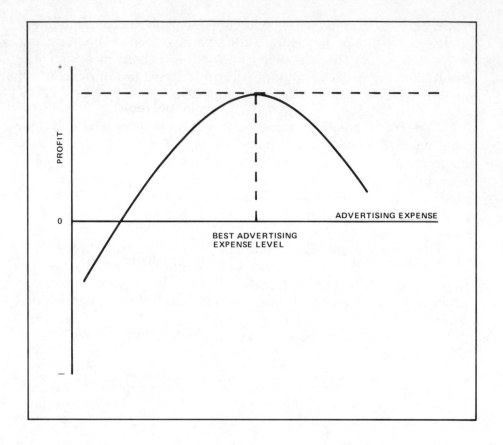

Figure 6-1. This diagram presents a median trace diagram that relates advertising expenditures to profits.

complete the model, it is necessary to establish the equations used to determine ordering cost and carrying cost. The submodel for ordering cost is as follows:

$$OC = C \, (\, D \, / \, Q \,)$$

C = Cost of processing a single order
D = Demand for the product for the
     accounting period (such as annual)
Q = Quantity of a single order

This indicates that ordering cost includes the cost of processing an order multiplied by the number of times orders are placed in an accounting period. The number of orders is determined by dividing the standard order quantity (Q) into the total usage for the period (D).

The submodel for carrying cost can be represented by this equation:

$$CC = i\,(\,Q\,/\,2\,)$$

i = the cost rate for carrying a single unit of inventory

To determine carrying charge under this formula, the cost rate is established for carrying a single item of inventory through the accounting period being used. This cost is usually based on the time value of the money tied up, with a factor added for the staff time and space required. This factor is then multiplied by a value equal to half the quantity ordered value. This factor assumes that orders are placed when stock runs out and that replenishment is immediate. Thus, half of this quantity becomes the average stock level.

This set of equations represents a descriptive model of the value of inventory stocking cost for a single item. A prescriptive use would apply this descriptive model to determine the value of Q that minimizes TC. This is done by using a mathematical procedure that optimizes ordering levels. This set of procedures leads to development of an equation to derive economic order quantity (EOQ). The EOQ formula for inventory stocking costs, as described in the model, is:

$$EOQ = \sqrt{2CD/i}$$

To illustrate, assume:

$$C = 2$$
$$D = 25$$
$$i = 1$$

In this instance, CD over i is equal to 50. Using the value 2 as a multiplier produces a result of 100. The square root of 100, then, is 10. This is the prescribed ordering quantity.

Alternative-Selection Models

Descriptive models are also used prescriptively in problem-solving and decision-making situations. Modeling techniques in this category include decision trees, spreadsheets, and scoring models.

Decision trees.   Decision trees are introduced and described in Chapter 2. A decision tree, within the context of the present discussion, can be regarded as a descriptive model that represents results of courses of action. Prescriptive use of a decision tree occurs when the model is used to evaluate alternatives and choose the best as the course of action to be followed.

Spreadsheets.   Spreadsheets, as described in Chapter 5, are usually prepared under special software that makes it possible to apply equation modeling techniques to data descriptive models. For this reason, spreadsheets prepared under special software are often used as analytic tools. The user enters a factor or equation that embodies his or her assumption about conditions that will prevail, during a future planning period for example. The formula is then applied to all data in the spreadsheet table, projecting an entirely different set of results. These procedures can be iterated indefinitely until all assumptions or forecast conditions have been reflected in outputs. In effect, the user poses a question about the future: "What if these specific conditions prevail?" The answer lies in a newly generated spreadsheet report. This method, because it is responsive to such questions, is often called "what if . . . ?" analysis.

To illustrate, recall the market/profit forecasting done with the SPREAD operator in the examples shown in Chapter 5. The forecast derived in the earlier example and presented as Figure 5-13 is reproduced as a present illustration in Figure 6-2. To carry the demonstration further, assume that the results projected in Figure 6-2 arouse management curiosity:

- A 5 percent increase in costs apparently returns a 10 percent increase in sales and an even greater increase in profits. What if advertising were increased 7.5 percent and overall sales increased by 13 percent?

- What if advertising were increased 10 percent and sales growth was 16 percent?

```
SALES           PERIOD 1        PERIOD 2        PERIOD 3
   T01             10              11              12
   T02             13              14              15
   T03              9               9              10
TOTAL SALES        32              34              37
EXPENSE
   MATERIALS        2               2               2
   LABOR            1               1               1
   ADVERTISING      3               3               3
TOTAL EXPENSE       6               6               6
GROSS PROFIT       26              28              31
```

Figure 6-2. This illustration repeats, for reference convenience, the spreadsheet developed as a forecasting tool in the last chapter and used previously as Figure 5-13.

The second "what if . . . ?" question above is addressed in the SPREAD template shown in Figure 6-3. The resulting spreadsheet printout is shown in Figure 6-4.

Scoring models. Scoring models are used to select among alternatives identified as potential solutions for problems or as decision selections. Two-dimensional tables are used. One dimension covers the alternatives while the other lists the decision factors under consideration.

To illustrate, consider what might happen when Olympic Bicycle is determining which moped model to produce first in its new Arizona plant. Assume four models have been developed. The company plans to introduce and market all four models eventually. All models are expected ultimately to become equally profitable. But, production is to be phased in one model at a time. The obvious idea is to begin production with the model that is expected to enjoy the greatest initial success. The trick, then, lies in determining which model this will be.

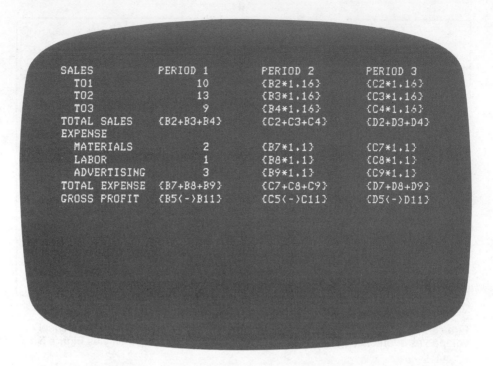

```
SALES           PERIOD 1        PERIOD 2          PERIOD 3
   TO1             10           {B2*1.16}         {C2*1.16}
   TO2             13           {B3*1.16}         {C3*1.16}
   TO3              9           {B4*1.16}         {C4*1.16}
TOTAL SALES     {B2+B3+B4}      {C2+C3+C4}        {D2+D3+D4}
EXPENSE
   MATERIALS        2           {B7*1.1}          {C7*1.1}
   LABOR            1           {B8*1.1}          {C8*1.1}
   ADVERTISING      3           {B9*1.1}          {C9*1.1}
TOTAL EXPENSE   {B7+B8+B9}      {C7+C8+C9}        {D7+D8+D9}
GROSS PROFIT    {B5<->B11}      {C5<->C11}        {D5<->D11}
```

Figure 6-3. ''What if . . . ?'' simulations of potential future conditions can be implemented with spreadsheet software simply by introducing new mathematical operators to derive values for occurrences under different scenarios.

As a basis for this decision, top managers hold a brainstorming session and select a series of criteria to apply in making the decision. These criteria are listed in the left column of Figure 6-5. Along the top of Figure 6-5 are column designations for the products under consideration. In each cell, managers have entered rating values for each criterion as it applies to every product. Ratings are from 1 through 5, with 5 best. Under the rules applied in completing the scoring model in Figure 6-5, MP1 is a clear winner.

However, it is also possible to weight the criteria. That is, management decides that certain of the criteria are more important than others. Weights are assigned, as has been done in Figure 6-6. In this instance, it was decided that financial decision criteria are three times

```
SALES              PERIOD 1      PERIOD 2      PERIOD 3
   TO1                10            11            12
   TO2                13            15            17
   TO3                 9            10            11
TOTAL SALES           32            36            40
EXPENSE
   MATERIALS           2             2             2
   LABOR               1             1             1
   ADVERTISING         3             3             3
TOTAL EXPENSE          6             6             6
GROSS PROFIT          26            30            34
```

Figure 6-4. This is a printout, with values in place in all spreadsheet cells, of the "what if . . . ?" simulation established in Figure 6-3.

more important than nonfinancial factors. Accordingly, the ratings for the first two criteria in Figure 6-6 were multiplied by three. On this basis, MP4 achieves the highest score.

The tables in Figures 6-5 and 6-6 can be regarded as descriptive models to which prescriptive analysis has been applied. The totaling of ratings as a basis for selection is the prescriptive part of the process.

PRESCRIPTIVE MODELS: DECISION TABLES

It is also possible to devise data models that are prescriptive and are suitable for providing direct support to *expert systems*. Expert systems are discussed in some depth in succeeding sections of this chapter. For the purposes of this discussion, consider an expert system to be one which provides management support through application of prescriptive models. Because of this characteristic, a prescriptive model applies selectivity in establishing data criteria for execution of commands or actions that are management supportive. The most common data model of this type is the *decision table*.

	PRODUCTS			
	MP1	MP2	MP3	MP4
EASE OF STARTUP	4	3	1	5
TOOLING COST	3	2	3	4
MARKET APPEAL	5	3	3	1
PARTS COMPATIBILITY	3	4	4	2
DEALER ACCEPTANCE	4	2	2	4
PROSPECTIVE MARKET SIZE	3	2	2	3
TOTALS	22	16	15	19

Figure 6-5. This is a scoring model to be used as a basis for selection of decision alternatives for the product mix of the Arizona plant of Olympic Bicycle.

Typically, a decision table is two dimensional. One set of conditions is listed along a side of the table, the other set is at the top and bottom. One set of entries is a series of questions while the other is a response or action to be implemented on the basis of answer combinations. In the cells where these columns and rows meet, simple yes (Y) or no (N) entries are made. A Y entry indicates a positive response to a question. A Y can also indicate that a statement at the head of the column is true. An N, then, indicates the statement is false. Because of these true-false assigned meanings, decision tables are sometimes called *truth tables*.

Truth tables are able to provide directly prescriptive selectors to control responses or actions of expert systems. To illustrate how a decision table might provide the basis for an expert system, consider the table in Figure 6-7. This type of truth table could be used at Olympic Bicycle's new plant to screen the personnel to be hired and

	WEIGHT	PRODUCTS			
		MP1	MP2	MP3	MP4
EASE OF START–UP	3	12	9	3	15
TOOLING COST	3	9	6	9	12
MARKET APPEAL	1	5	3	3	1
PARTS COMPATIBILITY	1	3	4	4	2
DEALER ACCEPTANCE	1	4	2	2	4
PROSPECTIVE MARKET SIZE	1	3	2	2	3
TOTALS	10	36	26	23	37

Figure 6-6. In this scoring model for selection of a product mix, weighted values have been added.

trained. In Figure 6-7, the screening criteria are personnel qualifications. Criteria include qualifications of union membership, high school graduation, and a physical condition that qualifies a person to lift heavy loads. Along the side of the table are categories for which combinations of Y and N entries might qualify individuals. Included are jobs requiring physical stamina (such as the loading dock), high school graduation (office), and union membership (assembler, forklift driver).

A table of this type would be used as a screening device by a personnel receptionist in the new plant. Incoming applicants would be asked questions about level of education, union membership, and physical capabilities. The receptionist could then use the table to advise individuals about the kinds of work for which they are apparently qualified. Candidates who expressed an interest would be given a

UNION MEMBER?	HIGH SCHOOL GRADUATE?	LIFT HEAVY WEIGHTS?	
Y	Y	Y	FORK LIFT – DRIVER; ASSEMBLER
Y	Y	N	TOOL CRIB CLERK
Y	N	Y	LOADING DOCK; ASSEMBLER
Y	N	N	DON'T HIRE
N	Y	Y	OFFICE
N	Y	N	OFFICE
N	N	Y	DON'T HIRE
N	N	N	DON'T HIRE

Figure 6-7. This is a truth table that could be used within an expert system aimed at screening and hiring personnel for Olympic Bicycle's Arizona plant.

formal application and directed to an interview with an appropriate personnel consultant or department supervisor.

EXPERT SYSTEMS

The entire field of *expert systems* is new enough so that the experts themselves are still divided about its definition. If a person did happen to be looking for a definition, he or she could simply shop around. Each inquiry would almost surely uncover variations. You could then quit when you found a pleasing definition. Putting it another way, the term *expert system* still holds many meanings for many different people. Within the context of a book directed primarily toward decision support systems, it is impossible to attempt to treat the entire spectrum that the expert systems area encompasses. For instance, there are many branches of expert systems that deal primarily with areas of science and/or medicine. These have no direct bearing upon the management decision support and planning scope of this book.

Given this preamble, the coverage of expert systems within this book is specific and limited: Expert systems designed for business managers are designed to consider possibilities and to find the best choice among them in a given situation. In computer application terms, the expert systems to be described in this book are directed specifically at IF . . . THEN analyses.

Role of Expert Systems in Business

The first point to be stressed in describing the use of expert systems in business is that the word *expert* has to be handled with care. People seem to want to put a special connotation on the use of expert systems. The term seems to imply that people can delegate control or decision responsibility to a computer and some sophisticated, mystique-shrouded software package. *This simply isn't so.* The first requirement in dealing with expert systems in business is to establish a realistic perspective.

In using a DSS, managers tend to think that the emphasis is on the word *support*. Throughout this book, the parts of an available DSS have been referred to as a tool kit. This is natural: A DSS is a tool for use by relatively sophisticated managers in solving problems or making decisions. There is no question of responsibility when a DSS is used. Most emphatically, the manager is in charge and retains full responsibility for all commitments or actions.

Different assumptions have been made within many statements involving the use of expert systems. It is true that certain aspects of decision making can be delegated for automatic execution by an expert system. It is also true that expert systems can and do select courses of action on the basis of processing results. But it is NOT true that an expert system can relieve human managers of any responsibilities for the consequences of decisions. A computer cannot accept authority, nor can a machine exercise responsibility. Therefore, an expert system remains a tool for responsible, sophisticated managers faced with decisions involving multiple, complex facets.

As is true for a DSS, an expert system requires and relies on availability of a database and of a DBMS for its control and operation. Managers have learned, too often from regretful experiences, that they must approach the use of a DBMS with a healthy skepticism. The fact that data items come out of a database under DBMS control does not automatically make them accurate, reliable, and applicable to any given situation. The astute manager has to challenge presented data and satisfy himself or herself that the proper tools are indeed at hand.

The same mind set is needed in dealing with expert systems which are, in effect, extensions of DBMS and DSS methodologies.

A SIMPLE EXPERT SYSTEM

As is true in establishing any computer-inclusive system, a decision to use an expert system should hinge around applicability to identified user needs. Computers and their software support are problem solvers. Thus, understanding the need for and configuration of a system begins with a description and understanding of a specific problem.

Needs and potential for expert systems can exist in virtually any company, including the ubiquitous Olympic Bicycle. From a user standpoint, the main qualifiers are the presence of multiple criteria for a management commitment and relatively complex relationships among the data to be gathered and evaluated. Sally Sellem has posed just such a problem to the company's information resources group.

Based on positive experience with DSS, Sellem has come looking for help with the company's advertising program. Like many manufacturers of recreational equipment, Olympic Bicycle supports a cooperative advertising program for participating dealers. The rules are simple: If a local dealer secures approval, Olympic will pay 75 percent of the cost of advertising charged by local newspapers, magazines, TV stations, or radio stations. The condition is that each ad for which cooperative funds are paid must feature Olympic products only.

Sellum reports that the program has been moderately successful to date. However, she thinks Olympic can increase effectiveness in reaching audiences and in selling products if the company can do a better job of screening the media in which cooperative advertising is placed. Accordingly, Sellem and her staff have set up a series of criteria for matching Olympic's advertising messages with the audiences of media available to dealers. For example, the MX, or motocross, line made by Olympic is designed for appeal to a market of males from 12 to 15. Sellem feels that logical media for ads on this product might include comic sections of local newspapers and possibly sports sections. The MP1 moped, on the other hand, has its greatest appeal to males from 15 to 18, and the MP2 is designed to appeal to females between 16 and 20. High school and college newspapers are seen as potentially valuable media for ads on these products.

In the past, Sellem feels Olympic dealers have lacked the sophistication and the direction from the factory that is needed to enhance the effectiveness of advertising investments. As her computer sophistication increases, Sellem recognizes that all of the media in which she advertises publish audience data. She reasons that, if media information could be added to her working database, she could help her dealers and her company to improve advertising coverage. On discussing this possibility with her information resources staff, Sellem learns that her application is ideal for use of newly acquired expert system tools. She learns that these tools are similar to and can be considered as extensions of the DSS tool kit with which she is already familiar.

Working with an analyst in information resources, Sellem captures the set of IF . . . THEN rules roughed out in Figure 6-8. Note that the rules are specific and selective. Sellem intended to match individual products with identified audiences. To do this, she has identified specific, high-profit products, the MX and the new moped line, for which advertising budget allocations are heaviest. Dealers would be advised that their cooperative advertising allocation has been tied to the purchase and promotion of these specific products. Media programs would then have to qualify under the stated rules by submitting statistical data on audience makeup (demographics). These data would be incorporated in the Olympic database for expert system analysis.

The analyst in information resources proceeds to capture data on a few prospective media and to prepare a program that permits Sellem to evaluate cooperative advertising proposals. Sellem provides, and the analyst enters, demographic data on the comic section of the first test newspaper, *The Smithtown Eagle*. Sellem can then exercise the expert system by applying the questions noted in Figure 6-8. The dialog between Sellem and the expert system is shown in Figure 6-9.

As shown, the system qualifies the comic section as having a readership consisting primarily of 12- to 16-year-old males. Cost and

IF 60% or more of audience 12 to 16 years old THEN BIKEAGE.
IF 60% or more of audience 15 to 17 years old THEN MOPEDAGE.
IF 60% or more of audience male THEN MALEAUDIENCE.
IF cost per 1000 audience less than $19 THEN PRICEOK.
IF medium has promotional tie-ins THEN PROMOTION.
IF PRICEOK and PROMOTION THEN BOTHOK.
IF BIKEAGE and MALEAUDIENCE and BOTHOK THEN MX.
IF MOPEDAGE and MALEAUDIENCE and BOTHOK THEN MP1.
IF MOPEDAGE and NOT MALEAUDIENCE and BOTHOK
        THEN MP2.
IF BOTHOK and MALEAUDIENCE and NOT BIKEAGE
        THEN MP3.
IF BOTHOK and NOT MALEAUDIENCE and NOT BIKEAGE
        THEN MP4.

Figure 6-8. These are the source notes that would be used as the basis for creating an expert system to be applied in the selection of advertising media for Olympic Bicycle products.

---

promotional qualifications are met, and the medium is qualified for advertising of the MX and the MP3.

For another demonstration, the analyst codes in data on the Young Adults section of the same newspaper. The dialog for this application of the expert system is shown in Figure 6-10. In this instance, the questions lead to qualification of the section for advertising of the MP4 and the MP2.

The coding that supports the expert system inquiries in Figures 6-9 and 6-10 is shown in Figure 6-11. The coding applies the format and command set for the DSS tool kit. (The tool kit operator for the expert system is ES.) The entries in Figure 6-11 are captured under

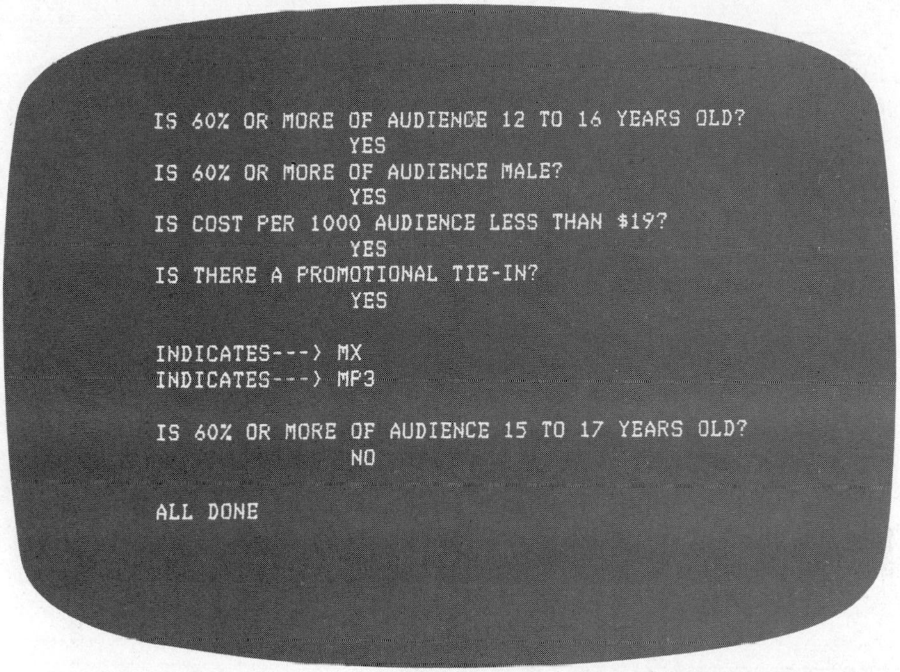

```
IS 60% OR MORE OF AUDIENCE 12 TO 16 YEARS OLD?
              YES
IS 60% OR MORE OF AUDIENCE MALE?
              YES
IS COST PER 1000 AUDIENCE LESS THAN $19?
              YES
IS THERE A PROMOTIONAL TIE-IN?
              YES


INDICATES---> MX
INDICATES---> MP3


IS 60% OR MORE OF AUDIENCE 15 TO 17 YEARS OLD?
              NO


ALL DONE
```

Figure 6-9. This screen display presents the first dialog that might be created in the evaluation of newspaper comic sections for advertising of Olympic Bicycle products.

---

the screen editor available with the DSS tool kit. Specific entries and techniques worth noting about the coding in Figure 6-11 include:

- Statements set off in quotation marks are questions to the user, to be displayed on the screen by the system.

- The semicolon (;) stands for the operator AND.

- Square brackets ([ ]) around a phrase indicate a NOT notation, giving the statement a negative meaning.

- The prescriptions of the system are noted in the rightmost column. Conditions about which the user should be notified contain the notation (GOAL).

```
    IS 60% OR MORE OF AUDIENCE 12 TO 16 YEARS OLD?
           NO
    IS COST PER 1000 AUDIENCE LESS THAN $19?
           YES
    IS THERE A PROMOTIONAL TIE-IN?
           YES
    IS 60% OR MORE OF AUDIENCE MALE?
           NO

    INDICATES ---> MP4

    IS 60% OR MORE OF AUDIENCE 15 TO 17 YEARS OLD?
           YES

    INDICATES ---> MP2

    ALL DONE
```

Figure 6-10.   This interactive dialog would be generated in the course of evaluating young adult sections of newspapers under the Olympic Bicycle media selection expert system.

One characteristic that helps to identify the program in Figure 6-11 as an expert system is the isolation of the program from the set of decision rules (or knowledge base). The program, in this instance, is the ES operator from the DSS tool kit. The decision rules are imbedded in the listing in Figure 6-11, which also can be regarded as the knowledge base for the expert system. The final element of an expert system is the data upon which the program and knowledge base will act. The data, as described above, are provided by the user and are entered interactively through the terminal. However, it is easy to imagine an expert system that accesses a database to apply its rules.

Another characteristic of an expert system is that, on entry of an inquiry by the user, the system will announce what it is doing and

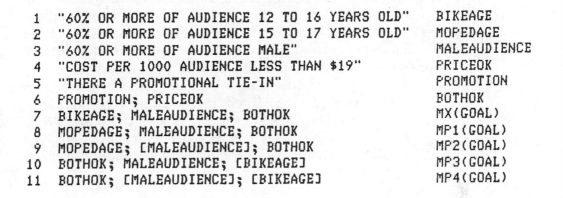

```
 1   "60% OR MORE OF AUDIENCE 12 TO 16 YEARS OLD"    BIKEAGE
 2   "60% OR MORE OF AUDIENCE 15 TO 17 YEARS OLD"    MOPEDAGE
 3   "60% OR MORE OF AUDIENCE MALE"                  MALEAUDIENCE
 4   "COST PER 1000 AUDIENCE LESS THAN $19"          PRICEOK
 5   "THERE A PROMOTIONAL TIE-IN"                    PROMOTION
 6   PROMOTION; PRICEOK                              BOTHOK
 7   BIKEAGE; MALEAUDIENCE; BOTHOK                   MX(GOAL)
 8   MOPEDAGE; MALEAUDIENCE; BOTHOK                  MP1(GOAL)
 9   MOPEDAGE; [MALEAUDIENCE]; BOTHOK                MP2(GOAL)
10   BOTHOK; MALEAUDIENCE; [BIKEAGE]                 MP3(GOAL)
11   BOTHOK; [MALEAUDIENCE]; [BIKEAGE]               MP4(GOAL)
```

Figure 6-11.   This is the coding that establishes the expert system for selection of advertising media that supports dialogs like those in Figures 6-9 and 6-10.

what rules it is applying. Within the advertising analysis system, the ES operator has a trace facility that can be activated from the terminal. On entry of a trace command, the system will output listings of the commands it has executed.

All of the provisions of the advertising analysis system could have been incorporated within decision tables. However, the demonstrated system uses the preferred, more flexible IF . . . THEN form of prescriptive statement. One advantage of the approach used is that IF . . . THEN statements can reflect a confidence factor assigned by the user. Some expert system packages permit users to assign numeric confidence ratings to statements. The rudimentary tool kit commands detailed at the end of this chapter do not support confidence-rating capabilities. However, this capability is worth knowing about and considering.

The order in which rules are stated within the knowledge base can affect the operation of the system. In particular, one of the available options instructs the system to close itself down when the first stated goal is achieved. In turn, the goal that is achieved first depends, in a major sense, upon the sequence in which the rules are stated. To avoid biasing the system, the example program contains instructions that all achieved goals are to be listed. However, in some situations, the user may want to bias the system to search for certain criteria first. In such an instance, the rules would be stated in order of perceived importance and the system would be instructed to shut itself down when the first requirement was realized.

The details required to operate the ES expert system supplied in the tool kit are included in the command summary at the end of the chapter.

Outlook

- This chapter completes the assembly of a tool kit that can be used to construct decision support systems. Note that no claim is made that this is the only method or the best technique. Rather, the tools are here. They are yours to use as you see fit.

- Now that the tools exist, the chapters that follow deal with methods for using the tool kit.

- The methods applied in the coming chapters are generic. That is, even though you now have a tool kit of your own, the techniques demonstrated will help build decision support systems through use of any commercial or other techniques you may have available.

Operation Summary: ES Expert System Operator

The ES Expert System Operator adds fundamental expert system facilities of the IF . . . THEN rule type to the DSS tool kit. The ES Expert System Operator is invoked with the MENU program command. The only control parameter passed to ES is the name of a rule specification file.

The rule specification file is created with one of the editors. The rule specification file has one row for each rule. Each row, or rule, contains three fields. Fields are separated by at least one blank space.

The first field is the rule number. The second field is the IF part of the rule. The IF part may be a question to the user, which is surrounded with double quote characters (''). Or the IF part may consist of one or more references to THEN rule part names. Questions to the user must be phrased so that they begin with "IS" and are answerable with a "YES" or a "NO." The references to the THEN rule part names can be surrounded in square brackets ([ ]) to denote negation. If multiple THEN rule part names are referenced in the IF part of one rule, they must be separated by semicolons (;). Multiple THEN rule references are regarded as containing a logical AND connector.

Finally, the third field of each rule, or the "THEN rule part," contains the name to be applied to a positive condition for the rule. Some of the THEN rule part names must be followed by "(GOAL)" to denote that they represent terminal, or goal, states. Unlike the second field, the THEN rule part reference in the third field may not be surrounded by square brackets for negation. Only one reference may be in this third field.

Assignments

1. Design a line of sunglasses. Include models for the young-at-heart as well as for the geriatric set. Prepare expert system rules for selecting the type of stores (boutiques, specialty shops, department stores, and so forth) that you will want to carry your product line.

2. Find an issue of *Consumer Reports* magazine. Convert the magazine's recommendations on some type of product into expert system rules.

3. Develop expert system rules to be used in a computer store to help prospective customers to select their personal computers.

4. Propose some ways to tie together the expert system and the DBMS. Consider how rules that reference values in the database might be evaluated automatically, rather than by querying the user.

5. Use the SPREAD operator in the DSS tool kit to aid the use of the scoring models referenced in Figure 6-5 and Figure 6-6.

6. Use the ES expert system operator to implement an interactive version of the decision table for personnel selection referenced in Figure 6-7.

DSS IMPLEMENTATION **III**

The chapters that follow conclude this book with a look at the way things are and the way they are apt to be in the near future in the overall environment for practical computer applications. To this point, discussions have covered the principles of decision making, the value of computers as decision-making tools, and the use of a specific, generic set of tools usable for implementation of a workable DSS. Within the larger world, tool kits such as the one you have used may not be available. So, the chapters that follow introduce the concepts and tools with which you may actually find yourself working.

Chapter 7 covers the kinds of situations in which DSS development may take place within a business organization. That is, DSS development might involve: 1) a major systems development project that builds a custom system, 2) creation of DSS capabilities through maintenance projects applied to existing systems, and 3) "entrepreneurial" approaches under which individuals or small groups create systems (usually on personal computers) through use of off-the-shelf tools.

Chapter 8 follows through by showing how systems are developed through use of commercially available, off-the-shelf tools. It is explained that the tools may be applied to any of the three types of situations identified in Chapter 7.

Chapter 9 relates DSS applications to the principles and methods of management science, a major factor in development of DSS applications in large organizations.

Chapter 10 extends your background with a look toward future DSS-related techniques. The chapter includes a survey of the field of artificial intelligence and its impact on DSS.

7 DSS DEVELOPMENT

Abstract

- All decision support systems share a few common denominators. These include dialog management, data management, and model management capabilities.

- DSS development needs to be managed. This chapter presents a series of techniques appropriate for determining the need for and managing development of a DSS.

- This chapter identifies and illustrates three separate DSS development techniques: life cycle methods, maintenance of existing management information systems, and an entrepreneurial approach that uses off-the-shelf hardware and software and is user driven.

DEVELOPMENT ALTERNATIVES

Where does a DSS come from?

All of the examples presented thus far assume the presence or creation of a suitable database. You have acquired a set of tools that includes a DBMS for management of database resources and a set of commands that makes it possible to implement a DSS. The tools also include appropriate models and a user facility that manages interactive dialog for the processing of user inquiries. This tool kit, in effect, replicates most of the conceptual and functional elements of a "real" DSS like those you might buy in a friendly computer store—or be given when you go to work for a large organization.

The sad truth, however, is that a DSS doesn't just happen. The last name of a DSS is "system." Systems, by definition, are collections of procedures, equipment, data, people, and support resources. Systems are complex; they require development. A DSS as a system has some special developmental requirements and options on its own. This chapter deals with three major operations or alternatives that might be followed in developing a DSS:

- A DSS can be developed as an integral part of a major computer-inclusive system or as a set of systems involving managerial or technical processing and data handling (or both).

- A DSS may be appended to an existing database-inclusive system as a maintenance project.

- A DSS may be created on an *ad hoc* basis by a manager or operating group that faces a specific problem. In these instances, a central information resources function may not even know of the existence of the DSS. It may even be possible that the independent effort generates and manipulates its own data within an independent, entrepreneurial-type activity.

Although the approaches identified above are distinct and reflect some important differences in DSS development, there are also some common denominators. That is, each DSS has some common denominator parts that must be available in the finished product, no matter what developmental methodology is followed. There are, however, a number of options and alternatives that can be applied in selecting and assigning properties to DSS components. These options do vary with developmental conditions and situations. For these reasons, the discussion that follows reviews the functional components of a DSS. The generic systems development methodologies are then covered as implementations of these basic ingredients.

DSS COMMON DENOMINATORS

The DSS itself is a subsystem that presents all of the implications and requirements associated with design and development of computerized capabilities. These aspects of a DSS environment have been effectively masked through most of this book by the presence of the implementation tool kit. The tool kit, in effect, elevates the assembly of a DSS to a high-level plane above the concerns with consideration and selection of technical alternatives and concerns over program design and coding.

The creators of the tool kit made most of the developmental decisions. These decisions were motivated by special, selective requirements. The tool kit has been designed as a teaching, as well as a system-building, aid. It was felt to be more important that students understand the underlying problem-solution relationships behind DSS creation than that they become involved in the technical trade-offs that the developers made without consulting them.

It is felt to be more valuable that you have had a chance to experience building of actual, workable decision support systems than it would have been to involve you in evaluations of all of the methods available for technical implementation. However, now that you have worked with DSS programs, you should be aware of the elements behind a DSS and the trade-offs involved in their selection.

A computerized decision support system encompasses three broad, logical components:

- Dialog management
- Data management
- Model management.

Dialog Management

This is the component that enables the system to meet and serve its users. Within your tool kit, end user dialog management is handled as a separate, identifiable component, called MENU. This is known as a *user facility* approach because this module is dedicated specifically to linking the data and modeling resources to keyboard and display operations. Dialog management with the designer/builder user is handled with line and screen editors.

A designed user facility represents only one approach to dialog management. This method was chosen because of the generic nature of the package provided. If a system were to be machine-specific, the probability for selection of a general-purpose dialog manager would diminish greatly. For example, suppose a DSS is to be implemented on a personal computer with a menu driven operating system or a unit with an incorporated icon selection system. These facilities could have been used as dialog managers. As still another option, dialog capabilities incorporated within commercial database or statistical packages could be used for the DSS.

There is no intent within this discussion to identify the "best" approach or to justify the selection made for the tool kit. The method chosen seems best for the situation for which it was designed. Other methods are available. You should be familiar with both the overall availabilities and the specific operations of the individual system you may be using at any given time.

Data Management

In your tool kit, a conscious, specific choice was made to use a DBMS approach to data management. Accordingly, a DBMS capability has been provided. These facilities create relational databases that share a central set of schema through which data are assembled and retrieved.

The authors regard a database and a DBMS as prerequisites for a modern DSS. It is actually possible to build a DSS without either having or creating a database. But such a process would produce a system that was more difficult to use and less effective. Thus, the decision to assume a DBMS represents a choice of alternatives in itself.

Given the scope and purpose of the tool kit, relational database capabilities were felt to be most appropriate. It is certainly possible to build a DSS with a hierarchical or network database. However, relational databases generally are easier for managers to understand and use. Therefore, many DSS systems interact with relational databases.

Model Management

A model is the hub of a computerized DSS. Think of it this way: The dialog manager interacts between user and model. The model, in turn, interacts with the data. Thus, the model is in the middle—positioned directly between the user and the needed data. A clear example of how this happens can be seen in considering the graphic display capabilities described in Chapter 5. When the user wants a pie chart, the dialog manager is instructed to call the PIE operator. The operator, in turn, gathers needed data without involving the user. The user's responsibilities end with a clear statement of need.

For the purposes of this book, model management has been less critical a concern than it is for systems used by large organizations. This is because, for instructional purposes, databases tend to be relatively small, designed for demonstration rather than bleak realism. Within database or DSS systems you may encounter in actual job situations, the modeling technique used may reflect upon the size and capacities of the computer upon which the job runs. Bear in mind, always, that operations in memory typically run thousands of times faster than data transfer from high-speed disk devices. Thus, if the data to support a DSS can be contained in memory at execution time, the finesse of data structuring or modeling becomes virtually irrelevant. No matter what search command is given, the result will be at hand in a few milliseconds. Thus, the capabilities of the computing machine become a determining factor in model selection and management.

For the purposes of the tool kit you have been using, it has been assumed that students would be working on personal computers. Models have been limited accordingly. Designers have provided just enough capabilities to demonstrate functional and logical diversity.

The three components described above will be factors in the development of any DSS, regardless of the environment within which the DSS is created. Therefore, an understanding of these three components provides a natural framework for the discussions that follow dealing with systems development considerations that affect DSS activities.

THE DSS WITHIN A MAJOR NEW SYSTEM

Formal methodologies in place for major computer systems development are rooted largely in a crisis-prevention mentality that has been a major factor in the computer field since the late 1960s. The building of major, integrated computer systems got off to a running start in the early 1960s, just a few years after introduction of random access disk files that made integrated systems possible. Psychologically, particularly with the benefit of hindsight, the events that took place appear to have resembled a gold rush. Enthusiasm to a level of hysteria was rampant. One industry after another and one leading company after another within the leading industries rushed toward promised panaceas involving an on-line world wired for automated success.

Just as a gold rush leads to more broken than fulfilled dreams, the stampede of the 1960s into major computer systems floundered, financially, in huge seas of red ink. In one case, an airline reservation system with a developmental budget of $10 million cost more than $40 million. And, by the time the $40 million had been spent, the system was obsolete and ready to be redone. The first computerized banking systems overran their budgets even more dramatically.

In retrospect, the discoveries of the 1960s can be simplified this way: Projects of any type don't run themselves. They need to be managed. Development of a major computer system is a specialized project undertaking. Therefore, computer system development requires specialized management. The industry then cast around for a ready, quick dose of project management expertise. Close at hand, fortunately, were a series of tools that had been developed just a few years before by military and other governmental agencies in managing projects ranging from the atomic bomb, to the building of aircraft to break the sound barrier, to the construction of radar networks designed to protect the entire North American continent.

The principles applied to computer systems development during the late 1960s and early 1970s are, for the most part, still in place. These principles themselves are simple and logical:

- When an overall job is big enough so that all requirements and potential problems cannot be known and anticipated in advance, break the project into a series of identifiable management steps. To illustrate, the project aimed at putting a man on the moon in the 1960s was fraught with unknowns. Attempting to deal with all elements of this job simultaneously would have led to chaos. Instead, the overall job was broken into a series of manageable units such as propulsion, navigation, vehicle structure, life support, capsule recovery, etc. Similarly, computer systems development was broken into a series of logical, manageable components.

- Set strict, incremental budgets. Then check performance against those budgets at frequent intervals. If there are serious overruns or unforeseen problems, reserve the right to abort the project rather than continuing to throw money at it.

- Place control of projects in the hands of their owners—managers or system users. User needs must be the driving force. Technology serves the needs. These priorities must not be reversed.

PROJECT STRUCTURES—THE LIFE CYCLE

The management structure established for monitoring and control of computer systems development, typically, is referred to as a *life cycle*. This term reflects the fact that a computer system is expected to go through a developmental/decline pattern resembling an animal or human life. That is, a system has an inception, is created, functions, becomes obsolete, and is replaced. Customarily, this cycle is broken into a number of major phases, or stages. The phases, in turn, are subdivided into activities, assignments suitable for small teams. The activities, for their part, are broken into tasks, or units of work for one person to complete in two weeks or less.

The series of books that includes this text uses a life-cycle structure with five major phases. These phases are structured in a straightforward, linear pattern with interspersed decision points, as shown in Figure 7-1. The life-cycle activities and the time relationships among them are indicated on the Gantt chart in Figure 7-2.

Bear in mind that a life cycle methodology is designed to deal with the problems of and to produce a system of major proportions. Therefore, the content of the life cycle itself is too extensive for complete review in this book. Instead, continue to refer to the identified phases and activities as they relate to DSS considerations within an overall information system context.

THE OLYMPIC BICYCLE PLANT MANAGEMENT SYSTEM

Olympic Bicycle is faced with a typical, modern-day information system decision in conjunction with the commitment to open the Arizona plant. The company has an in-place information system facility at the home office. It would seem tempting to equip the new facility with a satellite computer that runs the same programs and transmits files for consolidation back home.

However, the very idea of moving to a remote location mitigates against the straightforward, bodily transfer of old techniques and methods. Remember that management has determined to start production in Arizona with an entirely new product line. Thus, a

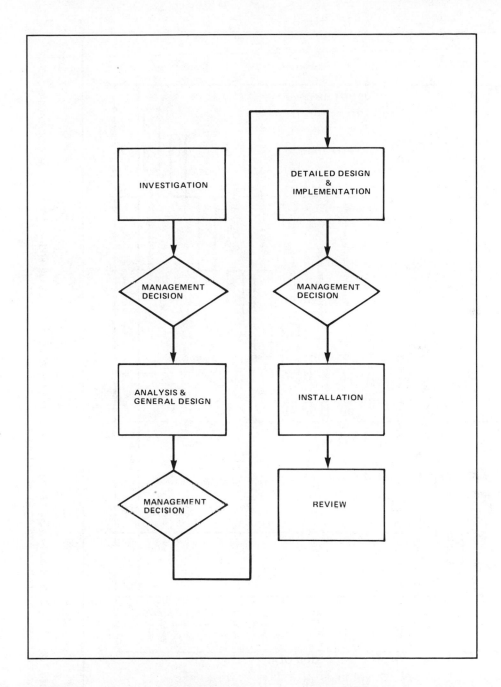

Figure 7-1. This flow chart identifies the phases and major go/no-go decision points within a typical structure of a systems development life cycle.

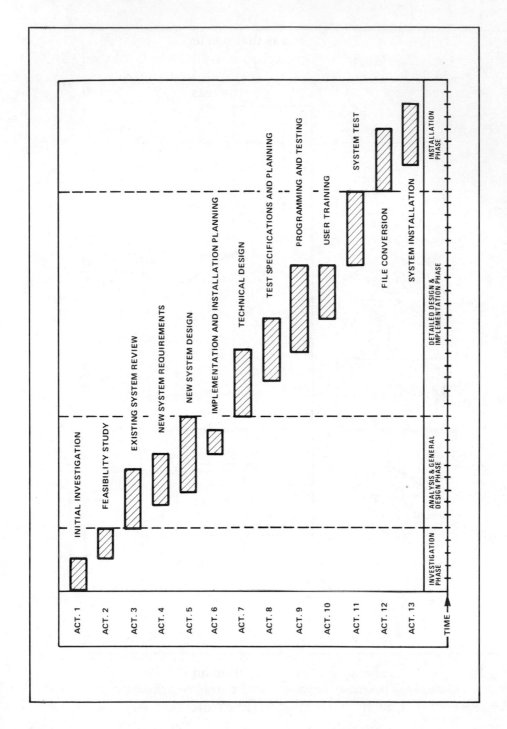

Figure 7-2. This illustration is a Gantt chart that identifies the major activities within the systems development life cycle and shows the time relationships among those activities.

premium is being placed upon new ideas that will lead to expansion and a modern image. Further, the mopeds to be made in Arizona are far more complex than the bicycles produced in the home plant. It seems logical, therefore, at least to look into the feasibility of a new, improved system.

Upon consultation, Olympic's CPA firm recommends strongly that a new system be developed. One of the areas of agreement between the accountants and top management is that it is time to update or replace existing financial processing and reporting procedures. The present methods, management recalls with shock, have been in place for almost nine years. The methods and equipment introduced since the present system was implemented promise to make possible far greater efficiencies and lower incremental operating costs. Olympic bicycle is considered to be in an excellent position to undertake systems life cycle development. The time required to build and outfit the new plant is about the same as the lead time needed to select and implement advanced computer systems.

Investigation phase. The consultations among managers and with the accounting firm correspond roughly with the first phase of the life cycle, Investigation. Out of the discussions, managers develop a "want list" to be implemented by the systems development project. Among the listed items are:

- On-line attendance and production reporting to eliminate manual timekeeping and to incorporate current data on production status so that inventory and production scheduling data will be available for dealing with both vendors and customers.

- Cost and profitability reporting on a monthly basis as a by-product of the separate transaction processing and financial reporting system to be established for the new plant. When the new system is operational, it will be implemented as the corporate accounting system, an integrated approach that will provide operational and historic reporting capabilities from a single system.

- The production reporting and control system would include a capability for automatic low-stock notification and reorder initiation procedures. This is felt to be a requirement to minimize inventory investments through "just in time" ordering policies.

• The new system is to have an integrated database. Data management capabilities are to include a broad, general inquiry capability that will support decision making by all managers whose departments are served by the system. Top management realizes that the inventory management system specifications they have established border on the area of expert systems. Management is interested in moving to and maintaining a position on the leading edge of database utilization technology.

Thus, database and decision support concerns are among the reasons that management gives for its willingness to make a six-figure investment in a new information system. Management's impact, typically, is strongest at the front end of a project, when specifications and objectives are established. From this point on, the next big impact by top management will come when budgets and plans are presented for review. Given approval of the budget, the work of systems development falls onto the shoulders of computer professionals.

To demonstrate the level and type of interaction that takes place at this early stage of a major project, Figure 7-3 shows a master menu that could have been developed to communicate overall system makeup to managers and prospective users. Note that one of the menu items calls up a DSS submenu. That submenu is illustrated in Figure 7-4.

Analysis and general design phase.   During the second phase of systems development, close coordination is established between the information resources group and prospective users of the system. At the DSS level, menus and displays are developed once general content of the database becomes predictable. For example, one of the scheduled outputs might be a spreadsheet comparing costs, by product, over several periods and also with standard costs being set up as management targets. Variations would be highlighted on this report as a guide to inquiries, under an expert system, into data that could identify sources for nonstandard performance.

Another, major end product of this phase would be a complete plan, a schema, for the data resources to be accumulated. An important first step toward developing a database lies in identifying all of the data elements that will be needed. These items are listed and

```
                OLYMPIC BICYCLE CO. ARIZONA
                       SYSTEMS MENU


                 MANUFACTURING APPLICATIONS
            1.   ATTENDANCE REPORTING
            2.   PRODUCTION REPORTING
            3.   PROFITABILITY REPORTING
            4.   LOW-STOCK REPORTING
            5.   DECISION SUPPORT FACILITIES
            6.   TRANSACTION ENTRY
```

Figure 7-3. This is the master menu that could provide management at Olympic Bicycle an access path to all of the decision support and expert systems developed in the case scenarios reviewed to date.

related in a *data dictionary* like the one shown in Figure 7-5. Establishing a database approach to information resources facilitates the implementation of DSS and expert systems later in the project or after the basic system is in operation. In the past, there has been a tendency to put off consideration of inquiry programs and DSS concerns until after the basic system has been built. Increasingly, however, managers are gaining the sophistication to make their needs felt at early stages in systems projects. Planning for DSS capabilities through provision for attachment of specialized modeling and inquiry tools, increasingly is being incorporated into the mainstream of systems development efforts.

Once the menus, display formats, and data dictionary are approved, management effectively turns the project over to the computer professionals.

Detailed design and implementation phase. At this point, systems designers and programs build the actual systems. Emphasis is on

```
                    OLYMPIC BICYCLE CO. ARIZONA
                       DSS FACILITIES MENU

    1.  EDIT COST FORECAST SPREADSHEET
    2.  EXECUTE COST FORECAST SPREADSHEET
    3.  EDIT RULES FOR COST VARIANCE DIAGNOSIS EXPERT SYSTEM
    4.  EXECUTE EXPERT SYSTEM FOR COST VARIANCE DIAGNOSIS
    5.  LIST MONTHLY PRODUCTION STATISTICS
    6.  LIST MONTHLY COST SUMMARY STATISTICS
```

Figure 7-4. This is a submenu within the Olympic Bicycle system that permits active use of the DSS routines associated with the Arizona plant situation.

technical specifications that establish modules for the transaction processing and other volume segments of the system. DSS and expert system involvement during these extensive activities is limited largely to a review of the names assigned to the DSS and expert system operators to be sure that the designations are meaningful and natural for operating and top managers.

The DSS modules are programmed along with the rest of the system and are encompassed within the overall testing and acceptance procedures. Major technical decisions center around whether commerical program packages can be used to implement portions of the system or even the entire set of procedures. Since Olympic Bicycle already has some DSS and expert system procedures in place, these are evaluated to determine whether they should be carried over or discarded in favor of either commercial or newly designed elements.

Before this phase is complete, managers should have used and evaluated the DSS and expert system capabilities of the new system. At the conclusion of this phase, the system should be ready for conversion to day-to-day operational status.

Installation.   This is an intensive phase in which the new system begins its routine, operational life. Files and the overall database are assembled and made available for use. Routine applications are implemented and used on a regular basis. During the early days of system availability managers are apt to make heavy use of inquiry capabilities, leading to concern that they may regard the new system as something of an expensive toy. After some months, the system settles down and finds routine use as a source of data on which to base decisions or to deal with problems.

Review.   Any effort as extensive as a system development project is bound to have some experience-related lessons for its participants. The review phase of the life cycle is established to be sure that these opportunities for learning are not overlooked. Two reviews are recommended, one shortly after the installation phase is complete and the other perhaps six months later, when perspective and hindsight have had a chance to set in.

Ongoing maintenance.   Although not an established phase, a notation about ongoing system maintenance almost always accompanies any description of the systems development life cycle. In most cases, maintenance actually begins before installation is complete. That is, as a system becomes operational, users and technicians invariably uncover new opportunities. These are listed and scheduled for later consideration as modifications, or enhancements, of a system. To remain viable, any information system needs continuing maintenance. The addition of DSS capabilities is, increasingly, being considered as a logical, valuable addition to many operational information systems.

IMPLEMENTING A DSS THROUGH SYSTEM MAINTENANCE

The maintenance of an ongoing information system can be likened to the experience of living in a house. A house might look perfect for a family before it is occupied. The act of use, however, creates needs for modification. Changes range from cup hooks in the kitchen to adapting a basement as a family playroom. Growing families often add to their homes.

An information system, similarly, becomes part of the facility within which an organization exists. Individual members of the

FILES

```
A/R-SUMMARY-FILE          = (A/R-SUMMARY-RECORD)
A/R-SUMMARY-RECORD        = ACCOUNT-NUMBER +
                            ORDER-NUMBER +
                            ORDER-DATE +
                            INVOICE-TOTAL


BACKORDER-DETAIL-FILE     = (BACKORDER-DETAIL-RECORD)
BACKORDER-DETAIL-RECORD   = ORDER-NUMBER +
                            PRODUCT-NUMBER +
                            BACKORDER-QUANTITY


DISCREPANCY-FILE          = (DISCREPANCY-RECORD)
DISCREPANCY-RECORD        = ORDER-NUMBER +
                            INVALID-PRODUCT-NUMBER


CUSTOMER-FILE             = (CUSTOMER-RECORD)
CUSTOMER-RECORD           = ACCOUNT-NUMBER +
                            CUSTOMER-NAME +
                            STREET-ADDRESS +
                            CITY-STATE-ZIP +
                            CREDIT-LIMIT +
                            ACCOUNT-BALANCE
```

Figure 7-5.   This is a data dictionary of the type that would be used to identify data elements with the Olympic Bicycle multisystem.

<u>FILES</u>

```
ORDER-DETAIL-FILE      = (ORDER-DETAIL-RECORD)
ORDER-DETAIL-RECORD    = ORDER-NUMBER +
                         PRODUCT-NUMBER +
                         QUANTITY-ORDERED +
                         QUANTITY-SHIPPED +
                         QUANTITY-BACKORDERED


ORDER-HEADER-FILE      = (ORDER-HEADER-RECORD)
ORDER-HEADER-RECORD    = ORDER-NUMBER +
                         ORDER-DATE +
                         ACCOUNT-NUMBER +
                         SHIP-TO-CUSTOMER-NAME +
                         SHIP-TO-STREET-ADDRESS +
                         SHIP-TO-CITY-STATE-ZIP


PRODUCT-FILE           = (PRODUCT-RECORD)
PRODUCT-RECORD         = PRODUCT-NUMBER +
                         LOCATION-CODE +
                         PRODUCT-DESCRIPTION +
                         UNIT-OF-MEASURE +
                         UNIT-PRICE +
                         QUANTITY-ON-HAND +
                         REORDER-POINT +
                         REORDER-QUANTITY
```

organization continually discover methods to use the system to make themselves more efficient or comfortable. In part, the stimuli for information system change come from the computer community in the same way that ideas for home modifications come from news and entertainment media. A TV commercial might convince home owners to install electronic garage door openers. An article in a professional journal about DSS might trigger a request for system expansion.

Assume, as an illustration, that Olympic Bicycle's management opted for a different approach in developing the accounting/production management system described earlier in this chapter. Top and middle managers simply couldn't take hold of all of the details to be encompassed by the new system. Accordingly, information resources specialists were asked how else the situation could be handled. Managers were told that the technical team could go ahead and build a database to support basic accounting, inventory, and production management functions. Special reporting and analysis functions, including DSS, could then be added after the basic system was operational. Managers were told that such practices are becoming commonplace and have been recognized with the coining of a term that applies just to such techniques, *adaptive design.*

Now assume that the underlying system is up and running. Managers who have used individual DSS packages at the home office now want more of the same in Arizona. Even at the initial set of conferences called to discuss DSS implementation, it is agreed that this is a good time to examine the company's entire decision-making structure and apparatus. The idea, at this time, would be to anticipate as many benefits as possible and to provide a mechanism for implementing appropriate DSS capabilities. For this phase of the project, the computer professionals recommend a developmental approach that is different from the life cycle. A technique called *prototyping* is suggested.

Reduced to basics, prototyping is a little more formal version of the developmental techniques described in connection with Olympic Bicycle cases in earlier chapters. The essence of prototyping lies in postponing the extensive, expensive design and programming steps encountered when systems are developed from scratch. Prototyping is also called a *fourth generation* systems development and software technique. Users apply powerful, *macro* commands like those demonstrated in the DSS tool kit. These procedures serve to develop files and outputs that give users a chance to examine realistic-looking results. Prototyping results then can be evaluated for application suitability. Should they be desirable, modifications can be made easily.

In effect, an entire system can be prototyped through use of macro tools. Once the system is proven, management has a new set of options. One option, which can be selected if volumes are relatively low for the new system, is simply to keep the prototype and use it as is. However, if large volumes are to be handled, it may be desirable to buy more powerful program packages or to prepare more efficient coding from scratch.

In prototyping the DSS for the Arizona system, Olympic Bicycle specialists decide to use the tool kit system that already has been implemented on the home office computer. The same tools are to be used to interact with the Arizona system. The first concern is to identify and establish data sources for the DSS applications. One choice is to tie right into the database set up for the Arizona system. The other option is to select data to meet specific DSS needs and to build a separate database through use of the DBMS module in the tool kit. The second option is selected, largely because of an identified need to add data for DSS use that are not already included in the existing database.

Within the present scenario, management would be shown the schema in Figure 7-6 and the menus resulting from the menu specification in Figure 7-7. Sample data could be developed easily and the use of the DSS for general decision-making scenarios could be illustrated.

SYSTEMS FOR ENTREPRENEURS

The personal computer has brought a new dimension to information systems. This was to be expected. Today, the amount of computing power installed on the desk of a secretary or executive is greater than the largest systems available in the world of the early 1960s. Literally, it used to require massive rooms with special air conditioning to house systems equivalent to many of today's personal computers.

The personal computer trend, in turn, has been built upon important new concepts in systems development and software. Through

```
            PRODS     1     TYPE      A      2
            PRODS     2     DESC      A     15
            PRODS     3     WEIGHT    N      3
            PRODS     4     YEAR      N      2
            PRODS     5     COST      N      4
            PRODS     6     UNITS     N      7
            SHIST     1     YEAR      N      2
            SHIST     2     QTR       N      1
            SHIST     3     TYPE      A      2
            SHIST     4     COLOR     A      2
            SHIST     5     UNITS     N      7
            OVHD      1     YEAR      N      2
            OVHD      2     QTR       N      1
            OVHD      3     COST      N      8
```

Figure 7-6.   This is the schema, created through use of DSS Tool Kit commands, for the prototype system developed for the Olympic Bicycle study dealing with the Arizona location.

---

the 1960s and 1970s, systems and programs were predominantly built to order. This changed gradually. The concept of prepackaged software and the microcomputer arrived on the scene almost concurrently. Certainly, the personal computer and packaged software have become mutually interdependent. It would have been unthinkable to go through the extensive, expensive procedures of special software development for $2,000 to $3,000 computers. At the same time, the computers themselves would have been useless unless they were backed by shelves full of software packages with competition-depressed prices.

In this environment, information-system decision making takes on entirely new dimensions. The time and effort of a life cycle clearly cannot be justified. The life cycle itself is a decision-making,

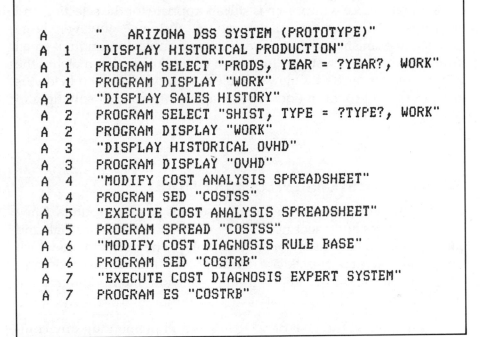

```
A           "    ARIZONA DSS SYSTEM (PROTOTYPE)"
A    1    "DISPLAY HISTORICAL PRODUCTION"
A    1    PROGRAM SELECT "PRODS, YEAR = ?YEAR?, WORK"
A    1    PROGRAM DISPLAY "WORK"
A    2    "DISPLAY SALES HISTORY"
A    2    PROGRAM SELECT "SHIST, TYPE = ?TYPE?, WORK"
A    2    PROGRAM DISPLAY "WORK"
A    3    "DISPLAY HISTORICAL OVHD"
A    3    PROGRAM DISPLAY "OVHD"
A    4    "MODIFY COST ANALYSIS SPREADSHEET"
A    4    PROGRAM SED "COSTSS"
A    5    "EXECUTE COST ANALYSIS SPREADSHEET"
A    5    PROGRAM SPREAD "COSTSS"
A    6    "MODIFY COST DIAGNOSIS RULE BASE"
A    6    PROGRAM SED "COSTRB"
A    7    "EXECUTE COST DIAGNOSIS EXPERT SYSTEM"
A    7    PROGRAM ES "COSTRB"
```

Figure 7-7. This is the menu specification that would support access to the Olympic Bicycle DSS for study of the Arizona location.

risk-averting apparatus. This mechanism is unneeded when the entire decision may involve expenditures of under $5,000. Within large organizations, there are probably hundreds of executives and managers who can authorize this level of expenditure on the basis of their signatures alone, without benefit of committees, project teams, or the budgets to support them.

At the same time, even though they are inexpensive, computers are not toys. Even small computers deserve the dignity of treatment due to a major tool for business management. Even at $4,000 or $5,000 for equipment and software, nobody wants to be sloppy in the selection process. Further, since many personal computers are used by executives, the value of the time that goes into selecting, installing, and using personal computers has become nontrivial. This is by way of saying that a process approach is still appropriate for the selection and implementation of even small computer systems. However, large project mechanisms are not appropriate for implementation of small computer-inclusive systems. Instead, a methodology that matches the requirement is needed. One workable approach, described below, is based upon a proven model for management problem solving and decision making.

THE SMALL-SYSTEM DEVELOPMENT MODEL

Small computers exist for the same reasons as large computers: They solve problems and meet needs. The difference between small and large problems lies chiefly in relative scales. The problems to which small computers are applied are of lesser scope and narrower concern. Thus, personal, rather than group, selection methodologies are appropriate.

Nonetheless, the task of selecting and implementing any computerized system warrants some formality of process. In reaching any significant managerial decision, a series of steps, or the process approach, can be valuable. The steps involved, illustrated in Figure 7-8, are:

- Decision statement
- Definition of needs
- Identification of alternatives
- Evaluation of alternatives
- Selection of the best alternative
- Implementation
- Evaluation of results.

Note that Figure 7-8 presents the process steps themselves in linear order but also provides for feedback from each succeeding step to all of its predecessors. Thus, the process and its parts may be used iteratively if the complexity of an individual situation warrants.

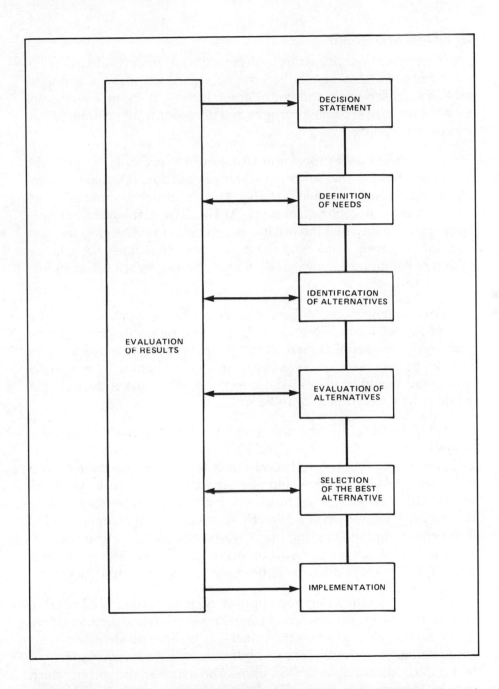

Figure 7-8. This is a schematic diagram identifying the steps within a universal model appropriate for managerial problem solving and decision making.

Decision Statement

The first process decision lies in deciding what to decide. This is not intended to be facetious. Rather, the point is to stress that it is important to establish goals and boundaries. Putting it another way, care must be taken to separate problems and decisions from symptoms that can be misleading.

In a typical data processing situation, for example, it might be tempting to state that an organization is out to: "Develop a computerized accounts payable system." This, however, is more of a conclusion than a decision statement. At the outset, it would be more appropriate to say that the organization wants to: "Develop the best method for paying vendors, at the lowest cost, on a timely basis, while taking maximum advantage of discounts and other cash management opportunities."

This statement would then be qualified further with some definition of its key terms. For example, it would be necessary to define "timely." One set of criteria would be involved if accounts payable were to be processed on a weekly or semi-weekly basis. Another requirement would be identified if it were necessary to produce checks while trucks were lined up to be unloaded.

Within a DSS, the situation would be similar. Consider the decision about entry into the moped business. One way of stating the decision might follow a technical mind set: "What hardware, software, and data resources would be needed, and what costs would be involved, in building a computerized decision support system to determine whether Olympic Bicycle should enter the moped field?" A more appropriate starting point would be: "What is the best approach, and what support will be needed, in determining whether entry into the moped field will be profitable for Olympic Bicycle?"

In dealing with a decision support system, further qualification may be necessary. For example, elaborations of the statement might indicate an outside budget for the project, guidelines on whether an existing database was available or whether outside data resources would be needed, identification of DSS users, and a time frame within which the decision must be made. These, in effect, are the boundaries, or constraints, within which the decision-making process must function.

In summary, the decision statement must identify needs and values associated with a DSS decision. The questions to be answered by the statement include:

- What is to be decided?
- By whom?
- At what cost?
- Within what time frame?
- What resources are to be available?

Definition of Needs

Bear in mind that this process is designed for relatively small, comparatively low-cost situations. Major systems tend to be developed under formal management projects, or life cycles. However, modern microcomputer systems viable for management use may cost anywhere from $2,500 to $8,500. The higher end of this range might involve a system with a hard disk, a set of packaged software, and extensive graphics capabilities. Realistically, the microcomputer or mainframe equipment and resources needed to support a decision might already exist. The executive making the decision may already command enough resources to proceed without formalities or permissions, simply by requesting service from people whose job it is to respond to his or her requests.

The point is that, by business and governmental standards, the money involved in implementing a typical DSS is not a problem. Today, there might be thousands of executives in large corporations who can make purchases in this range on the basis of their signatures alone. Thus, the decision itself may be trivial.

The need for a process to guide decision making, therefore, is not financially motivated. Rather, attention and emphasis focus on the effects, or results, of a decision. Even if the support system doesn't cost much, a commitment to bring out a new product line can involve multimillion-dollar expenditures.

Thus, definition of needs for a DSS need not be hung up on hardware and software costs. Rather, the decision structure itself becomes the focal point. Having defined the decision to be made, a logical next step is to identify and specify needs by preparing decision trees. Sets of decision trees, in effect, define the uses to which decision support systems will be put. Further, the decision trees establish the requirements and the working steps involved in creating a viable DSS. The decision trees, in effect, define the models, the database, and the dialog capabilities that a DSS will require.

Bear in mind that needs are defined as an early step in the DSS development process. By definition, a DSS tends to be open-ended; it is virtually impossible to foresee and to predefine all decision situations and requirements. Thus, the decision trees developed at this stage are representative and general in nature. Decision trees are general guidelines rather than road maps. Thus, even though a set of graphic diagrams might exist, the decision-making process should remain flexible while the decision makers keep themselves open-minded.

Development of typical decision trees and methods for identifying, evaluating, and selecting alternatives to implement them are discussed and illustrated within a case situation in the succeeding chapter.

Identification of Alternatives

Alternative tools available for implementation of a DSS, quite literally, approach infinity in their number. Thus far, this book has stressed a single, simplified tool kit with which DSS capabilities can be developed. Even in a single tool kit, a variety of alternatives can be identified: The spreadsheet package, by itself, might support the decisions to be made. Other alternatives already demonstrated would include database development and management, graphics capabilities, an expert system, and combinations of these.

These are alternatives out of a single simplified set of tools. Now, if you will, wander into your friendly, neighborhood software store or look into any voluminous microcomputer magazine. Alternatives, literally, can run into the thousands. This, however, is not to say that you have to look at thousands of alternatives to develop a DSS. Rather, the idea is to develop a conceptual framework of DSS tools within which you feel comfortable and effective. The software and hardware tools that meet these tests become your alternatives, as reviewed and illustrated in the chapter that follows.

Evaluation of Alternatives

Each of the alternatives identified for consideration can be evaluated against a simple series of criteria:

- How well does each of the tools, or combined sets of tools, considered meet the goals of the system, as defined in the decision trees that define needs?

- How well does each potential tool or set of tools fit within the constraints established by the decision statement?

- In meeting a universal requirement for every decision support system, how flexible and extensible is each considered alternative?

Selection of the Best Alternative

As alternatives are evaluated, they are rated. Procedures for evaluation can use numeric values for considered DSS alternatives. One method might be to assign ratings. That is, based on how well a system meets goals, deals with constraints, and retains flexibility, a rating of 0 through 9 might be assigned. These ratings could then be used to establish a numeric ranking for the alternatives.

Given a set of rankings, the selection process, finally, centers around a challenging of the apparent winner under conditions simulating use. That is, the evaluator should look for and consider all of the adverse consequences that can be identified for a top-ranked alternative. The process is similar to desk checking or debugging a program. Think of everything that can go wrong; then assume that it will go wrong, at the worst possible moment. In other words, you anticipate and apply the precepts of Murphy's law. As a result, you have a good idea about how "robust" a performance your top-ranked alternative might deliver.

Should the top-ranked alternative fail the adverse-consequences test, the next choice is put through the same process. Ultimately, a single choice should prove best. However, there is a chance that all of the considered alternatives might fail. If so, the feedback loop in the process is followed back to the point at which new alternatives are identified and put through the same gauntlet.

Implementation

In areas such as DSS or microcomputer applications, the implementation activity tends to be relatively trivial. The term, relatively, in this instance, envisions a comparison between DSS-sized undertakings and major, mainframe applications that can involve months of testing and training of hundreds of workers. With a DSS, the designer and user both function at the package or tool kit level.

Thus, even though a system may call upon a massive database, it may be implemented, as shown in earlier chapters, with less than a page of instructions. Similarly, a purchased DSS package may be implemented with a few hours of study and initialization entries. This, basically, is the look of the world of fourth-generation software. The time has come when a few, easily applied tools produce results that formerly required multiple working years of effort.

Evaluation of Results

After a computer system has been developed through traditional, life-cycle methods, evaluation is a past-tense activity. That is, the idea is to look back and learn from experience. In the world of DSS, there is no such luxury. Nor, is there a past tense.

Users and DSS capabilities challenge one another continually. Once an appropriate result is achieved, users will find other, different uses for the capabilities they have mastered. Users push the system continually. Users also have the tools to change the system virtually at a whim. Users, in this world, become self-sufficient almost from the day a system is activated.

Even if a specialized designer was involved at the outset, the user takes hold of his or her own destiny, quickly and firmly. Change becomes a way of life. Change is also relatively easy, since there are no massive documentation changes to worry about in a world that includes one or a few people making personal use of a system.

A DSS is dynamic, changing continually. In a conventional data processing situation, this would be a negative condition, indicating shortcomings in design or implementation. A DSS, however, is supposed to change with newly perceived opportunities. When a DSS stops changing, it usually falls into disuse and, effectively, disappears.

Outlook

- The relatively simple framework presented in this chapter is all that is needed in the way of systems development structures for DSS. This relative simplicity is among the reasons for the rapid growth and acceptance of DSS approaches and tools.

- Tracing the content of this book to date, it can be said that Chapter 7 provides a kind of workbench for the DSS tool kit. In addition, the same framework is appropriate for the selection and application of commercial DSS packages that abound in increasing numbers.

- The chapter that follows identifies families of commercial tools, presenting the major characteristics and showing how they can be used as the basis for assembling active DSS capabilities.

Assignments

1. Why is a full life cycle development project not justified for DSS applications?

2. What are the alternatives to a full life cycle development project? Are any of the life cycle steps really skipped? Or are they merely abbreviated?

3. What part of the traditional life cycle does the "small system development model" emphasize?

4. What does a traditional programmer do in each of the three DSS implementation models discussed in this chapter?

5. What do "fourth-generation methods" mean to traditional programming? How much or how little programming as we know it now do you expect to be going on in 1999?

6. How much or how little programming was expected to be needed after the development of the first high-level programming languages, such as FORTRAN and COBOL?

8 USING COMMERCIAL PACKAGES TO BUILD DSS

Abstract

- This chapter describes the feasibility of and methods for building decision support systems from off-the-shelf, commercially available software packages, particularly those developed for use on personal computers.

- Three types of packages are identified and discussed: data management, model management, and dialog management.

- The potential for use of programming languages as DSS development tools also is discussed.

THE ROLE OF COMMERCIAL PACKAGES

DSS development is a macro-oriented activity. The term *macro* implies use of *macroinstructions*, powerful commands that initiate extensive sets of processing. Also implied is a modular, building-block capability for constructing programs or systems by combining or linking software components. Another description refers to a tool kit approach, such as that discussed in earlier chapters. Overall, DSS approaches are part of a massive trend in software implementation that fall under the heading of *fourth-generation techniques*. The term *end user programming* covers the same developments and methods.

The previous chapter identifies a number of approaches to DSS development, including life cycle projects and the adding of DSS capabilities through maintenance projects. In addition, there is the entrepreneurial, or *ad hoc*, approach under which users decide what they need and make it happen, with or without assistance from computer professionals.

Any of these approaches can make use of existing commercial packages that can provide some or all of the capabilities needed to implement a DSS. Since most DSS programs are developed through macro techniques on a user-controlled, entrepreneurial basis, this chapter deals with the use of commercial packages from that point of view. However, application packages can be incorporated into any systems or program development methodology.

Modern corporations often delegate selection of personal computers and software to information centers. The information centers then make these tools available to internal users. DSS components certainly can be offered in this way, along with more commonplace items such as word processing and file management packages.

At this writing, it still takes some special understanding of needs to build a DSS from existing packages. This statement is intended to show a contrast between the decision support requirements and the needs of operational applications such as invoicing, accounts receivable, or accounts payable.

It is possible to find a number of off-the-shelf, ready-to-use alternatives for transaction processing systems that issue, collect, and pay bills. These are high-volume, homogeneous applications with many prospective users. Software developers have been willing to invest in the development of such products.

By contrast, demands for decision support systems are more limited. Most decision support systems created from commercial packages involve some level of selectivity or compromise. In general, software packages applicable to a DSS fall into three broad categories:

- Data management

- Model management

- Dialog management.

DATA MANAGEMENT

Data management packages perform a number of specific functions connected with the collection and maintenance of data within a computer. These functions, introduced and reviewed in Chapter 4, include:

- Data entry
- Data maintenance
- Select
- Project
- Join
- Sort
- Display
- Print.

Commercial programs that perform these functions fall into two broad categories:

- File managers
- Database managers.

File Managers

File management programs are, typically, likened to index card or document files that have been converted to electronic media. In computer science terminology, a file manager is said to implement an *implicit schema*. This means, simply, that the schema for a file's data structure is inaccessible, or *transparent*, to the user. The user communicates with the software by placing a layout of a single record display on a terminal screen. The process, referred to as *painting a screen*, is illustrated in Figure 8-1. The software then establishes an internal structure that corresponds with the user's picture.

In general, file managers operate upon only one file at a time, with no capability for combining data elements from multiple sources on a dynamic basis. However, these packages do provide extensive single-file capabilities, including sort, search, list, display, and print.

```
FILE: B:1099        EOF       KEY: SEQ     DIR: +     SCREEN: 1
RECORD: 46 ( 46 )             DEL:N        TYPE:A
 1  Payer's Name Carrol Smith_____
 2  Payer's Address 10801 Kurt Street_____
 3  Payer's C,S,Z Lake Terrace, CA  91342_____
 4  Payer's Fed# FD2440293_
 5  Rec Name    _____
 6  Rec Address _____
 7  Rec C,S,Z   _____
 8  Rec Iden No _____
 9  Rents       _____
10  Royalties   _____
11  Prizes      _____
12  Fish Proc   _____
13  NonEmp Comp _____
14  Fed Tax With _____
15  Medical Pay _____
16  Sub Payment _____
17  Recip Acc#  _____



    1=Lft   2=Rt   3=Up   4=Dwn   5=Insert  6=C dlt  7=Last   8=Date  9=F dlt  10=Exit
```

Figure 8-1. This display shows a series of typical entries that would be used to create a format used to input records to a computer-maintained file under a standard software package.

Database Managers

A *database management system (DBMS)* has more powerful capabilities than a file manager. Among these are:

- A DBMS has an explicit schema. This means that the user can become aware of the design and content of computer-maintained files. To illustrate, the screen editor of the DSS tool kit presented in this book can be used to edit and maintain the schema. Remember that the schema resided in a data file that could be called up, reviewed, and, as necessary, modified through use of the screen editor.

- A DBMS has multi-table and large-file capabilities. Data items can be searched at the element level and joined as necessary to create coherent outputs.

- A DBMS has an explicit query language. This type of capability has been cited and demonstrated earlier in this book as part of the presentations covering the DSS tool kit. In effect, an explicit query language consists of a finite set of commands that cause the DBMS to search its database.

- A DBMS provides a capability for establishing and optimizing data access paths. Use of these access paths is referred to as *navigation* of the database. Through application of this capability, frequently used inquiries can be optimized so that they execute more rapidly than would normally be the case.

- A DBMS has a host language interface that opens access to data content by instructions written in an application programming language such as COBOL or FORTRAN.

- A DBMS supports a data model. Within that data model, it is possible to specify access keys. Key integrity (uniqueness for reference purposes) is maintained automatically by the DBMS. Within the model, it is also possible to specify constraints upon references that can be processed. For example, if a value is entered as a key to be used in placing or using data elements from multiple tables, the key value must be the same in all instances. If the user attempts to enter a different value, the transaction will be rejected.

- A DBMS supports the building and maintenance of audit trails and the creation of checkpoint backup files.

Most DBMS packages do not have all of the capabilities mentioned above. In evaluating a DBMS for implementation of a DSS, the most important requirements include an explicit schema, the data model, and the query language.

MODEL MANAGEMENT

Recall that the term *model* refers to methods for organizing information. Two general approaches to modeling have been identified in earlier chapters:

- *Descriptive models* are representations of real entities. The models are created as a means of dealing with a massive, complex reality that cannot be comprehended readily in its actual state. Reality often is so massive or so complex that it is easier to access and deal with a representation than with the actuality. To illustrate, a database is one type of descriptive model. The data themselves form a model representing an organization, a group of people, or other entities. A schema, in turn, is a model describing organization of data within a database. Other types of descriptive models might be mathematical equations, blueprints of buildings, etc.

- *Prescriptive models* project reality into a preconceived idea of some future entity. In many instances, users of prescriptive models seek to optimize facilities or entities. Examples include productivity plans to optimize factory outputs, feed blending to maximize animal development, and spreadsheet projections of future financial performance.

In the DSS area, model management implies, descriptively, the devising of effective methods for data presentation. An example might be graphics outputs to show trends or performance comparisons. Prescriptive modeling in a DSS situation involves superimposing a set of objectives upon a collection of data. The model, then, shapes the selection and output of data to deal with the assumptions being tested by users.

Types of model management packages appropriate for implementation of decision support systems include:

- Statistical analysis
- Graphics
- Spreadsheets
- Financial modeling
- Project management
- Mathematical programming
- Expert systems.

Statistical Analysis

The design emphasis of commercial packages within this category is on computation and manipulation of data under control of statistical algorithms. Application examples include hypothesis testing, regression analysis, cross-tabulation reports, and others. The common denominator of these techniques is that they accept and reduce masses of data for meaningful presentation and/or display. Thus, one common feature of many packages is graphics output. Also, to achieve data reduction and graphics representation, some data management capability is usually essential.

Most *statistical analysis* packages are applied through use of a line-oriented command language. Typical uses within a DSS environment involve batch processing of masses of existing data.

Statistical analysis was one of the early mathematical application demands for which computers were created at the end of World War II. Thus, statistical analysis was an available tool at the birth of today's DSS concepts. Given this history, it follows that initial application packages were developed for mainframe computers. Many of these proven standby systems are now being converted for use on microcomputers.

Graphics

Development of *graphics output* packages have paralleled the introduction and acceptance of microcomputers. As with statistical analysis, graphics tools have been available on mainframe systems for decades. However, initial approaches involved large, expensive plotters or special display or recording techniques, including microfilm and xerographic outputs.

Video game technologies, over time, have led to incorporation of image generation and display packages for microcomputers. In addition, plotter manufacturers have brought the price of hard-copy graphics output devices down from many thousands of dollars to less than $1,000. Concurrently, laser-driven printers that create xerographic images have come down in price from hundreds of thousands of dollars, to tens of thousands, to a few thousand. A histogram, or bar chart, created under control of a graphics program is illustrated in Figure 8-2.

Graphics capabilities tend to be included in many commercial packages. For example, statistical packages usually have some capability for graphics outputs, as do spreadsheet processors. Graphics capabilities are even being added to word processors to produce outputs that simulate typesetting, line drawing, or musical scoring.

Standalone graphics packages also exist. As a rule, these products have extremely limited data manipulation capabilities, but rely instead on interfacing with data or file management application packages.

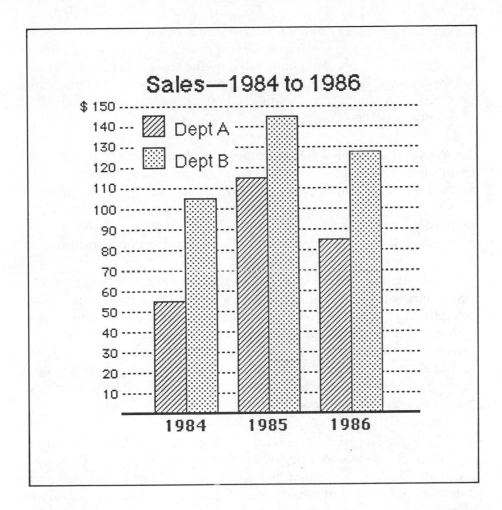

Figure 8-2. This is a histogram output under control of a graphics program and recorded on an ordinary dot-matrix printer.

Spreadsheets

Spreadsheets have been among the most popular packages introduced into the microcomputer market, following only behind word processors. Popularity apparently stems from the fact that these packages meet a need of many managers to prepare budgets and financial projections. In general, available packages are easy to understand and to apply. In effect, users can enter data into cells of a spreadsheet display with the same ease as writing figures on columnar pads. The simplicity of spreadsheet use is demonstrated by the screen display in Figure 8-3. Because of their popularity, the spreadsheet package market has become highly competitive, leading to low costs and wide availabilities of quality packages.

Whether used on a microcomputer or mainframe (a number of mainframe versions of personal computer programs have been introduced), spreadsheet packages offer advantages of ease of use. Packages are self-contained, providing all capabilities for dealing with relatively simple information modeling. Even a relatively unsophisticated user can create files, reports, and graphics outputs.

There are also offsetting disadvantages. In particular, it can be difficult to interface spreadsheet packages with other data manipulation or modeling programs. To overcome this problem, many vendors are now offering integrated programs in which spreadsheet software can interact with accounting, transaction processing, database, and even word processing programs. As another enhancement, most spreadsheet packages can interface with a number of standard graphics programs, as indicated above.

Many DSS applications lend themselves to solution through spreadsheets. However, be aware that spreadsheets are not appropriate for all management decision making. Complex problems or data manipulation requirements can overtax spreadsheet capabilities in a short time.

Financial Modeling

These packages are used for the same general purpose as spreadsheets. That is, the main purpose is to project financial performance of some entity, ranging from a department, to a government, to a simulation of a portion of the economy. The primary difference is that *financial modeling* programs provide a vocabulary of programming commands tailored to this application area. Included may be subroutines that have special value for accountants or financial officials, such as present value calculation algorithms. Implementation of a

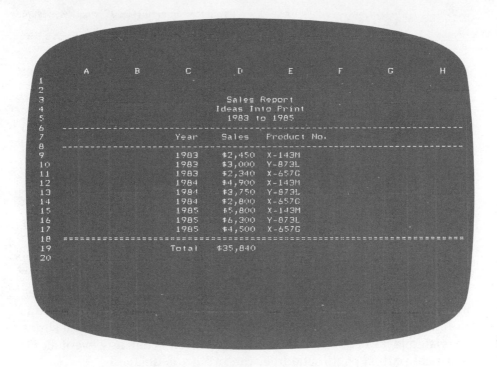

```
        A        B        C        D        E        F        G        H
 1
 2
 3                              Sales Report
 4                             Ideas Into Print
 5                              1983 to 1985
 6      -------------------------------------------------------------------
 7                        Year    Sales    Product No.
 8      -------------------------------------------------------------------
 9                        1983   $2,450    X-143M
10                        1983   $3,000    Y-873L
11                        1983   $2,340    X-657G
12                        1984   $4,900    X-143M
13                        1984   $3,750    Y-873L
14                        1984   $2,800    X-657G
15                        1985   $5,800    X-143M
16                        1985   $6,300    Y-873L
17                        1985   $4,500    X-657G
18      ===================================================================
19                        Total  $35,840
20
```

Figure 8-3. This is a typical input format for creation of a spreadsheet under control of a commercial software package.

---

financial modeling package is through lists of code that look like conventional, high-level source programs rather than resembling spreadsheets.

Financial modeling packages can be used for both descriptive and prescriptive modeling, such as mathematical programming. A difference from spreadsheet techniques is that the user must build a program from scratch rather than having a framework available. Some financial modeling packages come with integrated graphics capabilities. Financial modeling programs are usually weak in data management capabilities; they also can be difficult to integrate with other information modeling packages.

In summary, applictions for financial modeling packages are similar to those for spreadsheets, except that the problems addressed are usually larger and more complex.

Project Management

Packages of this type apply descriptive modeling to project outcomes, in terms of completion dates, for major projects. *Project management,* in general, is an established, staple area of computer application. The U.S. Navy pioneered computerized project management techniques in the late 1950s and 1960s for development of major weapon systems. Packages are now available for use on microcomputers, as well as many that still require mainframe capabilities.

All project management application packages have some type of special graphics output capabilities, generally for the formation of networks or Gantt charts. A network is a graphic, descriptive model presented as an interconnected series of events along a time line. Events are linked in performance sequences, with the connecting lines showing elapsed time for their completion. Some network presentation techniques identify a *critical path* that represents the longest series of related tasks needed to complete the project. When any event along a critical path slips its schedule, the project is delayed.

Popular methods for project management through network graphics techniques include PERT (Project Evaluation and Review Technique) and CPM (Critical Path Method). CPM tends to be used for construction and other types of projects within which durations for completion of key events can be predicted with some reliability. PERT, on the other hand, is more generalized, functioning with ranges of times for tasks and permitting schedule adjustments with greater flexibility. A typical network printout for a project is shown in Figure 8-4.

Gantt charts are named after their developer, Henry Gantt, a pioneering industrial engineer. These charts present a series of time lines to represent overlapping or related functions within an overall process or project. Gantt charts are still used widely to depict manufacturing or production situations. A Gantt chart produced on a microcomputer is shown in Figure 8-5.

Project management software packages are the only tools among those discussed that provide complete, though specialized, DSS capabilities. Capabilities include data management, modeling, graphics outputs, and dialog management capabilities tailored specifically to decisions related to management of project development or manufacturing-type processes.

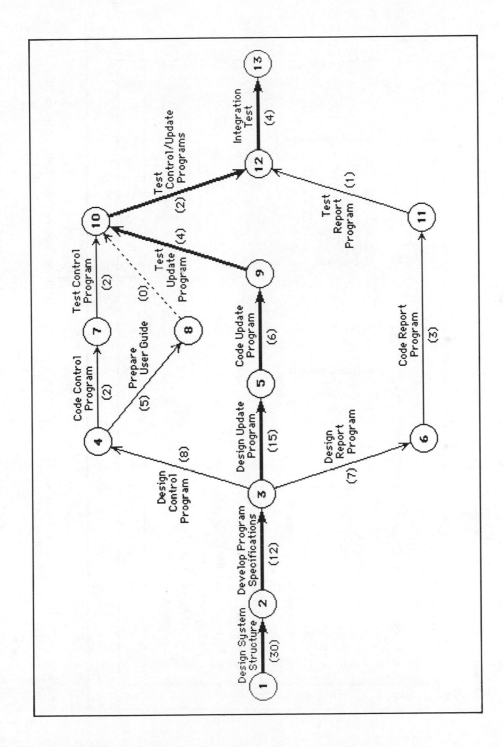

Figure 8-4. A commercial software package produced this project control/scheduling network diagram.

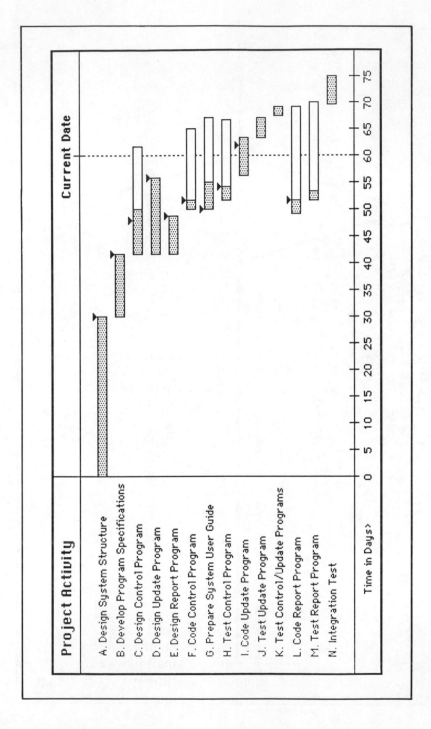

Figure 8-5. This is an example of a Gantt chart appropriate for project scheduling that has been produced on a dot-matrix printer controlled by a microcomputer.

Mathematical Programming

The term *mathematical programming* refers to techniques for establishing complex sets of equations that represent objectives and constraints. The equations constitute a mathematical model of the behavior of an entity. The model is manipulated to project results to be delivered under represented conditions or assumptions. The models created through mathematical programming are prescriptive in that they establish conditions that match results developed through application of the sets of equations. The execution of the equations ultimately identifies the best, or optimal, decision for the situation being modeled.

Packages that apply mathematical programming capabilities require highly skilled technical specialists with training in such areas as management science or operations research. Some of the better-known techniques in this category include linear programming and integer programming, a variation of linear techniques.

The extent of computation involved tends to prohibit interactive use and dictate execution under batch methods. These methods require capacities that can be delivered only by large minicomputers or mainframes (at least at this writing). Because of the level of sophistication involved, data management and graphics tools are minimal. Rather, results are interpreted by the technical specialists required to apply these advanced methods.

Expert Systems

As described earlier, *expert systems* are application program packages that seek input and guidance from a user in the course of execution. Another qualification for an expert system is that it can trace and identify the logic it applied in reaching a recommendation.

Expert systems represent, at this writing, a leading-edge technology. These packages derive from work done in the area of artificial intelligence. At this time, expert systems tend to be designed for specific, relatively narrow application areas. In other words, an expert system can be expected to do a relatively small job well. However, there is virtually no integration between existing expert systems and other data management or modeling techniques.

As with mathematical programming techniques, expert systems can be powerful tools in the hands of highly trained specialists. But expert systems have not yet been qualified as general-purpose management tools. There is not yet the promise that they will catch on as spreadsheet software has done.

DIALOG MANAGEMENT

Dialog managers are keys for unlocking, or accessing, resources maintained under data management or model management techniques. A key, current term in this area is *user friendly*. Marketers of virtually all database and DSS products assure prospective customers, one more loudly than the other, that theirs is the most friendly package of all. Reassurances aside, software designers have discovered, comparatively recently, that separate, easily integrated software tools are needed if users are truly to gain ready access to data resources for decision making purposes. Thus, dialog managers are now being recognized as packages in their own right. To achieve this status, dialog management software requires interfaces for linkage with data management and model management packages. The most common types of dialog management software packages include:

- Keyboard macros
- Windowing
- Shell programs
- QBE (Query By Example)
- Desktop metaphor
- Natural language
- Communications programs.

Keyboard Macros

A *keyboard macro* is a software tool that is positioned between the user and the operating system of a computer. Normally, an operating system has a limited number of prompts that are presented to the user. A user response can then call up macros available within the operating system. As an example, an IBM PC prompts the user to indicate which disk drive is active. At startup, or "boot," the designated system drive is active and holds the diskette with the operating system. The user can then command use of any of the routines on the operating system disk.

Keyboard macros permit addition of additional program vocabulary and accompanying routines. In a typical DSS application of keyboard macros, a sequence of commands is loaded into a macro and associated with a specific function key. When the user, in response to an operating system prompt, enters one of these function keys, the prerecorded sequence of commands is called up and executed automatically. Thus, a user who identifies a need for complex, or compound, functions can record these and call them up for execution through use of individual function keys.

Windowing

A *windowing* program makes it possible for a microcomputer user to deal with and integrate use of two or more programs concurrently. The windowing software, under user command, automatically partitions main memory to accommodate the multiple programs. The software also sets up a frame, or window, on the terminal screen for each program in memory. The window displays have the same content as though the programs they represent are in normal use. A multi-window screen display is shown in Figure 8-6.

A windowing superstructure then makes it possible for the user, through manually entered controls, to cause interfacing among otherwise incompatible programs. For instance, a window-program user building a spreadsheet could call up a data manager, find a needed unit of data, and enter that data into the spreadsheet. Although not elegant or sophisticated, the windowing approach does hold the potential for quick, inexpensive, and effective implementation of a rudimentary DSS.

Shell Programs

The MENU facility in the DSS tool kit is an example of a *shell program*. This type of software package, in effect, superimposes menus or other command structures over an established operating system. The idea is that the commands within the MENU-type program form a shell around the operating system and resident application programs, creating an integrated DSS capability.

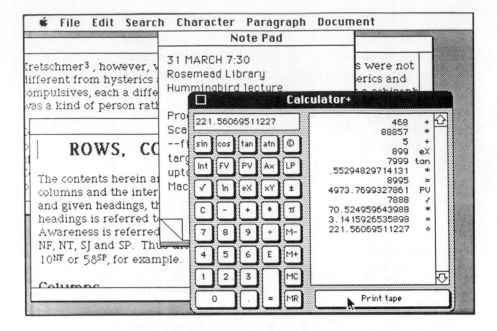

Figure 8-6. This is an example of a windowing display that permits access to multiple software packages stored by a microcomputer.

QBE (Query By Example)

QBE, an IBM software product, is a graphically oriented database query language. The QBE entries, in effect, serve as translators to activate query commands native to a DBMS. In a typical example, the user creates a report or document format on a terminal screen. The user enters descriptors and data elements he or she already knows. QBE then enters this simulated document, searches the database, and fills in the blank spaces with extracted data.

Desktop Metaphor

The name *desktop metaphor* derives from the fact that this type of dialog manager uses pictures, or *icons,* representing devices found on a desk or in an office. As examples, an icon picturing a file cabinet is used to initiate a file access operation while a picture of a wastebasket initiates erasing of a record or file. In most instances, icons are arrayed around the perimeter of a screen. The cursor is moved to the icon for the instruction to be executed, typically through use of a desktop *mouse*. A command key serves to select and activate the command represented by the icon. Figure 8-7 depicts a screen display of icons used for function selection.

Natural Language

Dialog management through use of *natural language* commands is a hope for the future. Artificial intelligence specialists are studying this possibility intensively. At present, however, there is no workable product suitable for quick, inexpensive application to a DSS.

The theory of natural language interfacing is easily understood and desirable. A user would enter a query instruction in everyday language. The system would respond to indicate the words it had decoded and to indicate its interpretation of the command. The user could then accept or modify the representation of the computer. Interaction would continue until the query need was satisfied.

This approach is worth mentioning because products purporting to provide convenient, natural language query capabilities are beginning to appear in the marketplace.

Communications Programs

So-called *smart modems* hold the potential for increasing the scope and depth of data available to a DSS. *Communications programs* of this type combine hardware and software features to make it possible for computers to call one another and for their users to exchange information. The information can exist in computer-maintained databases or in human minds. Both are potential resources available through computer communication techniques.

A typical smart modem package includes a circuit board mounted in or attached to a computer. Telephone network connections are wired into this board. The hardware is then controlled by a diskette-loaded program that provides window-type capabilities to establish connections with and access to files within distant computers. The communications software permits the computer to dial telephone numbers of other computers. This establishes contact, enabling the computer to transmit data into a remote computer's files, and to access and retrieve data from another computer.

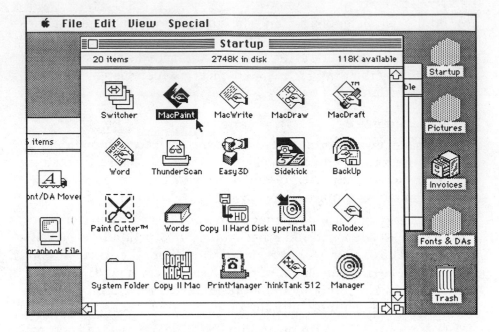

Figure 8-7. This illustration shows an icon screen used for the selection of software applications.

Communications programs can function either under direct keyboard control or by executing instructions initiated through a shell-type feature or as keyboard macros. A user, for example, can imbed instructions that permit a computer to answer and respond to calls from other users. Messages or files can be left for access. Callers can also leave messages. This type of operation is sometimes called *bulletin board* or *electronic mail* service.

The significance of communications programs within a DSS context is that a manager can share ideas and/or responsibilities with others. An individual can collect data from widespread sources.

Systems can also be set up under which groups of qualified persons conduct *teleconferences* and *computer conferences* to examine problems and seek solutions. The computer thus becomes a tool for the sharing of ideas under such established techniques as *brainstorming* or the *Delphi process*. Brainstorming is a participative session in which individuals contribute suggestions for later evaluation. Multiple sessions may be held.

The Delphi process draws its name from the Delphic Oracle in ancient Greece. Citizens used to ask questions in writing to be answered through signs by the Oracle. Under the modern Delphi process, written suggestions are collected, evaluated, and reported in several iterations that attempt to come closer to a solution.

The breadth available from communications programs applies to the sizes of the systems involved as well as to their geographic dispersion. Microcomputers can interact with mainframes and, as appropriate, *download* information from a corporate database into a personal DSS. Similarly, data collected by an individual microcomputer user can be *uploaded* to corporate systems and shared with other decision makers.

STANDARDS

Throughout the brief history of computing, standardization has been a mark of progress. Without standardization, effective use of high-level programming languages would have been virtually impossible. The development of software and hardware standards has made possible some of the major applications that are now part of everyday life. For example, the adoption of MICR character sets for checks and OCR character sets for credit cards has made possible systems that now process billions of documents daily. Supermarkets have come up with a standard bar-code for labels, called *universal product code (UPC)*, that makes possible additional billions of transactions every day.

The applicability of standards to the DSS field traces from the introduction and universal acceptance of such high-level languages as FORTRAN and COBOL. With these introductions, the American National Standards Institute (ANSI) formed working groups responsible for developing drafts of standards, circulating the drafts for professional comment, then releasing working documents.

During the 1970s, ANSI advanced its work into the database area, forming working groups to evolve standards in a number of areas affecting the design and use of databases. At this writing, no formal standards have been published. However, draft documents in wide circulation have begun to assume the stature of standards. Obviously, standardization of the development and use of databases will affect the creation of decision support systems.

Of particular interest to DSS builders are standards-development programs that will relate to a number of database areas, including:

- Application development tools

- Database design tools

- Decision support tools

- Data entry software

- Download/upload utilities

- Support for multiple data models.

Standards, as they emerge, will encourage and support the trend toward creating building blocks for the construction of decision support systems. The main areas affected will be the designs and functions of interfaces between a DSS and its database.

PROGRAMMING LANGUAGES FOR DSS IMPLEMENTATION

Within the computer field at large, application-development progress has been related directly to the evolution of appropriate programming tools. Scientific and engineering programming grew rapidly following introduction of FORTRAN. Business applications moved into dominance in computer utilization following introduction of COBOL. As the use of computers for decision making has become commonplace, special-purpose programming languages have evolved to support these applications. Some of these specialized programming tools, described briefly in the discussions that follow, are:

- APL (A Programming Language)

- SIMSCRIPT

- MUMPS

- PROLOG.

APL (A Programming Language)

If specialized support is available, or if the decision maker happens to be a skilled management scientist or operations researcher, *APL (A Programming Language)* can be a valuable, readily available tool for building and implementing a DSS. APL is a standalone language particularly well suited for mathematical modeling. The reference to a standalone language derives from the fact that APL programs tend to build their own little worlds. APL creates its own, separate workspace within computer memory. Its program interpreter and files exist outside those created under control of and monitored by the standard operating system.

For persons with the requisite mathematical qualifications, these features of APL tend to be seen as advantages. For others, these same features are limiting, as is the lack of interfacing capability with other files, programming languages, or DBMS software. Any interfaces that are created require modifications at the systems programming level.

The writing of programs in APL can be classed as an esoteric skill—a domain for specialists (who support it enthusiastically). The command structure is highly symbolic and imbedded in principles of advanced mathematics.

SIMSCRIPT

The *sim* in *SIMSCRIPT* stands for "simulation." The language is used to create mathematical models of systems characterized by discrete events. Thus, SIMSCRIPT would be a viable tool for simulation operation of a factory or a military battle.

SIMSCRIPT is written in a code structure that bears a close resemblance to the PL/1 language. PL/1, as you probably know, is a general-purpose language designed to implement both business- and quantitative-type systems. The resemblance is close enough so that SIMSCRIPT routines can be integrated into PL/1 programs. SIMSCRIPT also has an excellent facility for integrating with a number of commercial DBMS packages. That is, SIMSCRIPT can call upon the facilities of a number of DBMS programs.

With these characteristics, SIMSCRIPT can be implemented by experienced programmers who have worked on simulations. Advanced skills in mathematics, management science, and operations research are not prerequisites.

MUMPS

The *MUMPS* language was developed in the medical field, as a cure, not as a disease. The language was initiated as a means of implementing a medical information system. From this starting point, MUMPS has spread into other disciplines and information system areas.

This language can be an excellent DSS development tool if management requirements lead to extensive data management demands. Data management is a special strength of MUMPS. Another special feature is the language's extensive report-generation capabilities.

PROLOG (PROgramming in LOGic)

A major difference in orientation in comparison with traditional programming languages is perhaps the major characteristic that holds the key to understanding and using *PROLOG (PROgramming in LOGic)*. Traditional programming is *procedural*, oriented toward implementation of step-by-step algorithms. In simple terms, traditional programming starts at a defined beginning and proceeds to a predicted result.

PROLOG, on the other hand, is *declarative*. The PROLOG user begins by establishing and loading a knowledge base into the system. This knowledge base is a PROLOG program. Execution of a PROLOG program, then, consists of querying the knowledge base. PROLOG manipulates and relates elements of the knowledge base to devise responses.

PROLOG is one of the first commercially available, general-purpose software products to emerge from work in expert systems. The language implements principles of predicate calculus logic and automatic theorem-proving developed by researchers in artificial intelligence. Many computer scientists believe that the ability of PROLOG to integrate functions of data management and inferential reasoning holds great promise for development of sophisticated future DSS techniques.

CASE SCENARIO: ATV INTERNATIONAL

Sally Sellem's research and planning experience with Olympic's moped line—coupled with a marked success with product introductions that she supervised—drew attention to her skills as a marketer of recreational products. This visibility, in turn, led to an offer involving considerably more money, a greatly expanded responsibility, from ATV International. This company is a division of a major foreign manufacturer of motor vehicles, including automobiles, trucks, buses, forklifts, and movable cranes.

Sellem has defined her first task as including a responsibility to "establish respectability and identity" for a three-year-old line of ATVs (all terrain vehicles). These are three-wheeled units with balloon tires that appeal to off-road enthusiasts. ATVs are noisy and have not been popular among conservationists and traditional campers. Sellem has plans to coordinate industry programs for special areas where ATVs can be used. She also has ambitious plans to recruit, train, and stock a group of dealers to handle her ATVI line. All of her plans for the product line must now be coordinated to come up with a marketing projection for the coming year.

Back at Olympic Bicycle, Sellem had become comfortable with the DSS tool kit approach. However, at ATVI, a division of a much bigger company, tools and methods are a lot more formal. Computer professionals lean toward use of commercially available packages. Executives at Sellem's level can have personal computers installed in their offices. However, company policy insists that these be equipped with "smart" modems. Executives are required to upload data files for any budgets or forecasts they prepare to the company's large mainframe system. Similarly, executives at Sellem's level can access all corporate databases and can download information usable on their own systems. Sellem has purchasing authority to buy an approved model of a personal computer, procured at a special price through the ATVI purchasing department. The company's Information Resources Manager also has a list of commercial software packages authorized for use on personal computers of executives. These policies and rules, Sellem learns, are designed to assure compatibility with the corporation's mainframe system.

In building her staff, Sellem recruits a young systems analyst from the information resources group. This individual, Hector Peres, has been working as a software maintenance specialist. Sellem believes he has the qualifications needed both to put corporate resources at her disposal and to adapt available packages to create the DSS she is about to define. In launching her DSS program, one of Sellem's first requirements is to establish a developmental framework. She determines that a decision-based approach is best. The methodology is established quickly in a staff memo and is followed in creating a DSS to support the ongoing use of decision support systems within her department. From past readings and training, Sellem hits upon and installs the methodology introduced in Chapter 7. The steps to be followed include:

- Decision statement
- Definition of needs
- Identification of alternatives
- Evaluation of alternatives
- Selection of the best alternative
- Implementation
- Evaluation of results.

Decision Statement

Sellem's decision statement has two parts, to reflect that she has both immediate and long-range DSS needs:

- Develop data to support a realistic projection by the marketing department, to be made within 60 days, of dealer sales of ATVs for the next fiscal year.
- Design the DSS to support next year's projections so that data can be developed as models or supports for ongoing marketing operations.

To round out the statement, Sellem prepares a budget projection that calls for purchase of a personal computer with 30 megabytes of hard-disk storage, two diskette drives, and 512K of main memory. In addition, she budgets salaries for Peres and one administrative assistant and arranges for internal charges to cover use of the corporate mainframe system.

Definition of Needs

To define needs, Sellem begins with a decision tree that depicts selection of a sales target from among a range of alternatives. This simplified decision tree, illustrated in Figure 8-8, sets targets of $40, $45, and $50 million. Remember an earlier reference to the nature of this methodology. The technique is a tool for making decisions about decisions.

In this case, the range of decisions would be pretty well prescribed for a marketing executive like Sellem. To go into and support a business, the company must realize certain minimum levels of revenues. Acceptable minimum and maximum levels are set in consultations between the chief financial officer and the head of production. These executives decide the level of sales needed for minimal profitability and the maximum production that can be achieved in available facilities. In the case of an international company, import quotas may be a factor in setting the requirements and ranges.

Identification of Alternatives

In this situation, the alternatives identified are the software packages and data resources that exist or can be purchased. These resources are available on the corporate mainframe computer, from a corporate information center with software packages available on a library basis, and from local computer stores that can provide commercial packages not available within the company. Sellem assigns Peres to come up with a list of available tools from which the departmental DSS will be assembled. Peres identifies the following potential tools:

- Programs can be written from scratch. Peres is a highly qualified COBOL programmer. COBOL is supported on an all-day basis by the corporate mainframe.

- Data resources exist within an extensive, corporate database maintained on the mainframe. This database has both regional and individual dealer sales histories for the past three years, on a monthly basis. Product sales can be segregated for ATVs.

- The corporate database is maintained by a hierarchical data model DBMS with query language capabilities. The DBMS is transaction-processing oriented, meaning that considerable manipulation is needed to derive selective data for use in a DSS.

- The mainframe supports a large, batch-oriented statistics package. Current uses are for quality control analysis in production and for marketing penetration studies.

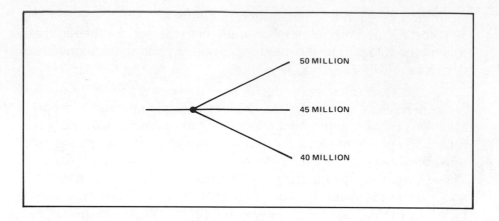

Figure 8-8. This decision tree would be the starting point for an effort aimed at setting a marketing target for Olympic Bicycle.

- The mainframe supports a batch-oriented project management system. This capability has been used to control construction of new plants and to schedule movement of products from overseas on a fleet of freighters.

- The corporate information center has available a graphics package for the personal computer. Strengths of this package include abilities to generate pie charts and histograms.

- A standard "smart" modem is available through the information center. This package is in use in other departments. Users can upload to and download from the mainframe.

- The corporate information center can furnish a microcomputer spreadsheet program. This is a commercial package in wide use.

- A microcomputer file manager is available. This package permits the user to paint an index card on the screen and to select file building and file access operations from a menu.

- A local computer store can furnish an APL package for the computer to be installed in the marketing department.

Evaluation of Alternatives

The alternatives, in effect, are used as a shopping list. Sellem and Peres spend three separate half-day meetings studying the capabilities of the available items. It is determined that some needed capabilities will involve combining two or more packages. Others have value on their own. Sellem and Peres identify these requirements and possibilities:

- The finished DSS will need capabilities for projections. From identified resources, projections can be accomplished by combining capabilities from the spreadsheet package, the statistical program, the graphics capability, and APL.

- Data storage and retrieval will be required. These can be achieved through the corporate DBMS, a microcomputer file manager, and the spreadsheet program.

- Historic sales data will be required. This, as indicated, is available through the corporate database. To access the database, the communications package will be needed.

- Management presentations will require a graphics capability.

Selection of the Best Alternative

Obvious selection requirements, given the deliberations outlined above, include selection of the communications program to acquire sales history data and the graphics program to prepare presentations.

To store and retrieve historic data on ATVs, Sellem and Peres reject the corporate mainframe DBMS as being too much work and too cumbersome a job. APL and COBOL are turned down because they would involve too much effort for the job at hand. This leaves the file management package which, on initial study, appears to be adequate for the DSS under development.

To handle the projections their DSS will require, Sellem and Peres are faced with either compromise or a continuing search requirement. Some statistical computation will be necessary to project sales for the coming year. However, it is impossible to tell, at the outset, just how complex or difficult these computations will be. At this point, there is a choice between uploading back to the corporate mainframe and using the existing statistical program or applying the rudimentary computational capabilities of the graphics package. They decide to try the graphics package, recognizing that, as a stopgap, they can make occasional use of the mainframe statistical system. In the meantime, they will shop for a suitable statistical package that can run on the microcomputer. It is decided that it would be better to handle these computations on the personal computer because a decision has already been made to house the DSS files on the small system.

Based on this line of thinking, it is determined that the ATVI marketing DSS will have the following components:

- Corporate database for marketing history
- Personal computer with communications program for access to corporate database
- File manager on personal computer to be used for storing and manipulating marketing data
- Graphics package on the personal computer for preparation of management presentations
- Interim statistical capabilities through use of graphics package, with corporate program as backup.

Sellem and Peres decide to start with these components and to continue shopping for an appropriate statistical package for the personal computer.

These components provide for implementation of a full-feature DSS. Sellem and Peres have provided for the acquisition of data, maintenance of resource files, outputs, and some degree of manipulation. Thus, the three basic requirements of a DSS—data management, dialog management, and model management—have been accommodated.

Implementation

As is typically the case when planning is done effectively, implementation is almost an anticlimax. Peres has become familiar with the tools and their capabilities during the study phases of the project. He also knows the makeup of the files needed to produce the projections. Therefore, implementation is simply a matter of connecting the components, plugging in the computer, and loading the software.

Evaluation of Results

As with most actual application situations, evaluation results from experience. Sellem and Peres will know as they prepare their reports whether their system needs modification and/or enhancement. Since their whole system is modular, feedback need not be a problem; if they find themselves needing additional software or hardware elements, they can simply be purchased and attached.

In summary, this case helps to make the point that development and implementation of a DSS centers around understanding and solving problems. With the fourth-generation tools that are available readily, DSS capabilities can be assembled on an off-the-shelf basis. The skills needed in today's marketplace lie more in decision making and decision analysis than in computing equipment and programming skills.

Outlook

- This chapter ends the discussions of how to build and use DSS.

- The chapters that follow deal with the significance and future of decision support and related systems.

Assignments

1. Go through a recent issue of *Computerworld* and list all of the software packages you see written about or advertised. How many of these packages are applicable to DSS? Categorize them. In which articles or advertisements is reference made to DSS uses?

2. Pick one commercially offered, DSS-useful package to analyze in depth. Summarize its features and uses. Determine how it might be integrated with other packages. Compare it with the DSS tool kit developed in this text. Look back through this book and identify some scenarios in which this tool might have been appropriate. What types of computer equipment and software does this package require? What does the package cost? How much study and training will it take to use this tool effectively?

3. Identify three commercially-offered database management systems. Be a consultant to the Olympic Bicycle Company and recommend one of these packages for DSS implementation. Prepare a cover letter summarizing your recommendation and attach a detailed definition of Olympic's problems and an analysis of how the different DBMS packages offer solutions.

MANAGEMENT SCIENCE AND DSS 9

Abstract

- The specialty of *management science* is concerned with application of quantitative, mathematically oriented principles and methods applicable to the guidance of and planning for organizations.

- Close relationships have evolved between the still-developing discipline of management science and the body of knowledge that has helped to build DSS.

- Management scientists are among the primary users of DSS tools and techniques. Further, management scientists are key people in helping executives to create the models and devise the forecasts that evolve from use of DSS tools.

- Since management science represents a major focus for DSS development and application, the related topics are brought together in this chapter as a single continuity.

ROLE OF MANAGEMENT SCIENTISTS IN DSS

Who is a management scientist and what does he or she do?

In one important sense, management scientists have a lot in common with computer scientists and CIS professionals: Management science is a computer-dependent, computer-using discipline. The major difference lies in chosen areas of specialization. Management scientists come upon the computer scene from a background of practical, applied mathematics. This base of knowledge, in turn, is used

259

to direct computers into the modeling of problems and behavior patterns of organizations, projecting results that can be anticipated under stated, assumed situations.

Earlier presentations overview the DSS field as encompassing three areas: data management, model management, and dialog management. The management scientist focuses on just one segment of this area, model management. Traditionally, management scientists have concentrated upon one type, or branch, of computer modeling: mathematical modeling. More recently, however, the emerging area of expert systems has drawn management science attention. This interest, in turn, has required acquisition of skills in data modeling as well. Within this overall scope, this chapter concentrates upon the traditional, mathematical areas of management science. The chapter that follows traces other developmental areas, including artificial intelligence and expert systems.

In the overall development of DSS technologies, management scientists and CIS professionals can look forward to working as teammates. For DSS techniques to reach anything approaching their full potential, the skills of both types of specialists, along with others from computer technologies and business administration, will be required.

MODELING IN MANAGEMENT SCIENCE

All models are caricatures of parts of the real world. Models never fully represent every aspect of a system; but good models capture the important characteristics of the subject. Some models are *iconic*, bearing a physical resemblance to the subject. Examples include scale models, such as those prepared in reviewing designs of buildings or aircraft. Other models are abstract representations of their real-world counterparts, such as mathematical models of atomic behavior characteristics or a computer model of the national economy.

In any case, models are developed as an attempt to gain a better understanding of the behavior of an actual system. A common denominator leading to preparation of all types of models lies in the controlled risk and cost made possible—models cost only fractions of the actualities they represent. Also, modeling makes it possible to represent a future situation that does not currently exist.

The modeling method of special interest to management scientists is through computer programs. These models are frequently examples of one or more techniques from the areas of operations research, management sciences, or statistics. The study of those quantitative techniques is outside the scope of this text. However, anyone with an interest in DSS can benefit from an understanding of what these techniques are and how they are used. The discussions that follow are positioned at this type of overview level.

From the highest and simplest perspective, a model is just a *black box* that has inputs and outputs. Inside, there is some method that reads the inputs and calculates the outputs. If the same inputs are given a second time and under identical conditions, the same outputs will be produced. A systematic study, methodically changing the inputs while controlling processing conditions and observing the change in the outputs, could lead to "understanding" what goes on inside. This means the user would be a reliable forecaster of the outputs for a set of new, untried inputs. This describes the abstract notion of a "general systems model."

At the most fundamental level, a model is a single computational step. To qualify as a model, the computation must be specified completely and must be understood fully by those who will use the results. A simple example of a mathematical model might be an equation that develops the square root of a number. Such fundamental models can be connected (like toy blocks) to make a large, complex whole. Some of the large complexes are viewed as "prefabricated" units by model builders who are engineering even larger systems. For instance, a model builder may assemble a queuing simulation model and an economic payoff model in building a decision model for studying how many cash registers to install at a fast-food restaurant.

MODELS IN A DSS

Within a DSS model are the facilities directed by the user, through a language, that perform computation on data selected from a database. See Figure 9-1. Models are mechanisms for creating the data that are not directly stored in the DSS databases. As appropriate, the DSS

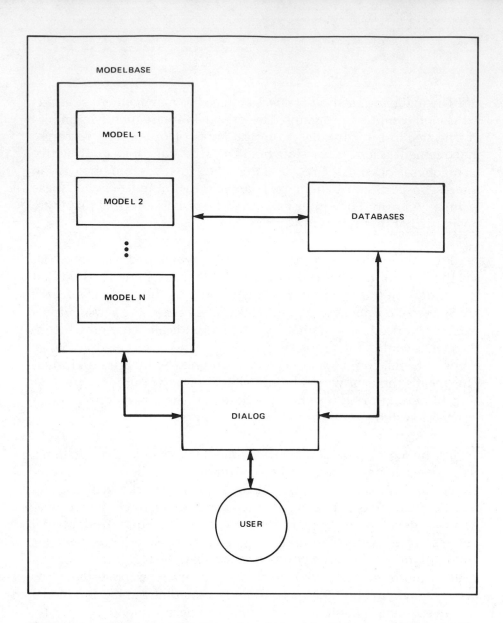

Figure 9-1. This diagram illustrates the relationships between models and databases within a DSS.

user selects what models to employ and orchestrates their execution, often in an exploratory fashion. As described earlier in this text, models can be methods either for testing hypotheses or for performing "what if . . . ?" simulations.

Model Inputs

Models usually have several input values. Those which can be controlled in the real world are decision variables. These inputs can be controlled by the user. For example, a user can specify the size of a plant, the number of shifts it will operate, rail or truck access, etc. Variables that are controlled systematically in exercising the model (whether or not they can be controlled in the real world) are called *parameters.* Examples of parameters include assumptions about future economic conditions, assumed delivery times for supplies, etc. Other inputs might be termed *exogenous variables* because they are imposed on the system from the outside world.

The number of inputs to a model may be small or large. For example, an investment model may have daily commodity prices for the past six months as input. In some cases, large amounts of input use statistical *data reduction* techniques to minimize the number of values input (such as average, variance, etc.). Also, detailed historical data may be entered to represent future operational situations.

Model Outputs

A good model outputs more than you need to know. This is desirable for two reasons:

- First, what you need to know is not clear at the start.
- Second, many outputs are required to confirm that the model is actually working correctly, at the required level of detail. During development, a model may have 10 to 100 times more output than the finished product will show.

One absolutely mandatory output of a model is complete self-identification. This might be done in a very brief title and version statement.

Verification and Validation

Two crucial requirements for models are verification and validation. Verification confirms that a model operates as it was designed to do. That is, all the logic and mathematics are correct: there are no implementation mistakes. This is also called *debugging* in the case of general computer programming.

The second requirement, validation, refers to the confirmation that the model actually represents the real world in the required respects. This, of course, is much more difficult and requires intimate familiarity with the real-world system. Also required is substantial exercising of the model. A verified model may be no good because it implements a design that does not capture the real-world system accurately.

TYPES OF MODELS

As described earlier, models can be identified according to broad categories, or types:

- Prescriptive
- Descriptive
- Optimizing
- Satisficing
- Ad hoc
- Formal
- Macro/micro
- Predictive.

Prescriptive Models

A prescriptive model produces outputs that direct activities of a business. For example, a fast-food restaurant might use a prescriptive model to learn that more counter personnel are needed over lunch hour than at other times. The model might help to pinpoint the number of personnel needed.

Descriptive Models

Instead of pointing to a solution, as is done by a prescriptive model, a descriptive model concentrates on identifying the problem. Thus, a descriptive model of a fast-food operation would let management know that there is a shortage of help over lunch hours. The model would make no attempt to solve the problem by indicating that more people were needed. Nor, would it estimate how many additional people were required.

Optimizing Models

An *optimizing model* establishes performance criteria, then attempts to identify the best set of conditions and/or actions that will come as close as possible to meeting those criteria.

Satisficing Models

A *satisficing model* deals with constraints rather than optimizing criteria. The idea is to do as well as possible within given, quantified constraints. The decisions that result are often called "least worst" solutions. An example would be a model devised for scheduling student classes. It is a given that each student cannot be assigned to every class that he or she requests. Thus, the objective of the model is to do as well as feasible under circumstances that are, in total, impossible.

Ad Hoc Models

The term *ad hoc* implies selectivity of purpose and application. Thus, in legislatures, ad hoc committees are formed to deal with specific problems. When their reports are submitted, the committees are usually disbanded. An ad hoc model, similarly, deals with a specific, identified problem. When the cause of the problem is identified, the model may be of no further use. In effect, ad hoc groups are seen as wearing blinders so that they look at one narrow topical area only. An example of an ad hoc model would be one set up to consider a response to an unusual request for quotation on a procurement that is outside a company's normal operating field. Ad hoc approaches also imply a lack of formality and/or organization.

Formal Models

When enough precedent for a given type of decision exists, a *formal model* may exist to deal with this need. A formal model, in this context, is one with established theoretical principles and application potentials that are general. Mathematical structures should also be known and proven. Examples include consideration of capital budgeting, production planning, site selection, and transportation routing.

Macro/Micro Models

The amount of detail, or relative complexity, required to reach a decision or solve a problem determines whether a *macro* or a *micro* model will be needed. These terms mean the same in modeling as in other areas of management, in economics, or in computer utilization. That is, a macro model has comparatively little detail while a micro model is highly detailed. Thus, a macroeconomic study would be at an overview level while a microeconomic study would delve into great detail.

Predictive Models

A model that attempts to extrapolate past data to derive future meaning is called a *predictive model*. In addition to historic data, of course, it is necessary to include assumptions in a predictive model. Thus, the results of a predictive model tend to say: "If you have guessed correctly, these are the conditions you will experience."

MODELING TOOLS

To this point, models have been identified in terms of their inputs, outputs, and functions. It is also relevant to remember that a model is a basis for organizing an effort or a set of resources to generate specific results. In management science, models are mathematical methodologies for dealing with specific situations. Previous discussions in this chapter have been aimed at establishing an understanding of what models are and what they do for management scientists. The discussions that follow, then, identify some specific modeling tools and demonstrate their usefulness. The models described are commonly used, proven tools. These include:

- Mathematical programming models
- Simulation models
- Statistical models
- Financial models
- Decision analysis models
- Project planning models.

MATHEMATICAL PROGRAMMING MODELS

Mathematical programs are formal models with mathematical functions (formulas) that combine input variables. Such functions are used to represent constraints and objectives. A constraint might be the total amount of raw materials available for the next production cycle. An objective might be the minimizing of the unit cost of a finished product. Through mathematical, formal procedures called algorithms, such models can be "solved," producing a set of values for the decision variables. This set of values must obey all the constraints and maximize (or minimize) the objective function.

One of the most common types of these models exists when all the mathematical functions are linear combinations of the variables. The resulting model is called a *linear program (LP)*. Problems with thousands of variables and thousands of constraints can be solved routinely. Other real life conditions sometimes require that some of the answers (decision variables) have to be integers. For instance, if one of the questions is how many warehouses to build, the answer 2.6 is not meaningful. Furthermore, rounding such an answer up or down is not valid and can lead to unsatisfactory answers.

The need, in this situation, is for a type of model called an *integer program (IP)*. IP models are also common for business applications. However, IP models can be much harder for the computer to solve than LP models. Actually, the difficulty may be great enough to disqualify IP techniques and recommend other approaches.

Commercial software packages are available to solve many types of these models once they have been stated in an appropriate form. However, the task of generating the precise description of such a model can be an extremely detailed and logically tedious computer programming exercise. Also, the choice of the particular mathematical representation that captures the requirements and is suitable for computer solution can involve artistic and creative talents.

Case Example

Sportsco Corporation makes plastic balls, bats, and frisbees. Profit on a bat-and-ball set is $2.00, while for frisbees it is $1.50. A bat-and-ball set requires 14 oz. of plastic and four minutes of packing time. Each frisbee takes 6 oz. of plastic and six minutes of packing time. Assume a production shift has 200 lb. of plastic and three packers available for eight hours. The molding equipment cannot make more than 200 frisbees in one shift. What number of bat-and-ball sets and how many frisbees should be produced to maximize profit?

Model:
There are two decision variables (number of frisbees, number of bat-and-ball sets) and three constraints (plastic available, packing hours, frisbee limit). The objective function is to maximize total profit.

The decision variables are nonnegative.

$$\text{Maximize} \quad 2.00x + 1.50y$$
$$\text{subject to} \quad 14x + 6y <= 200 * 16$$
$$4x + 6y <= 8 * 60 * 3$$
$$y <= 200$$

$x >= 0$ the number of bat-and-ball sets
$y >= 0$ the number of frisbees

Solution:
$$x = 176$$
$$y = 122$$

$$\text{Profit} = 536$$

Method:
The technique used most commonly for solving a linear program is the simplex method algorithm programmed on a computer. However, for illustration purposes, a graphic method can be used that is suitable for analyzing problems in just two variables. The x axis is the number of bat-and-ball sets, and the y axis is the number of frisbees. Each point on the graph has an x value and a y value and, hence, represents a potential answer.

Not all points are allowable. For instance, since x and y may not be negative, only points in the first quadrant are allowed. If a vertical line is drawn at $x = 200$, only points to the left of that line will be allowed. Each constraint leads to a line that separates the graph area into two parts: On one side are allowable points and on the other side are forbidden points. For the plastic constraint and the packing constraint, straight lines have been plotted. These straight lines correspond with the mathematical statements in the above model. For plotting purposes, these statements are treated as though they were equations, rather than as statements of inequality, as indicated above.

Figure 9-2 shows the graph and the allowed region, called the *feasible region*. The mathematical theory shows that the optimal solution to a linear program always is located at an *extreme point*, or corner, of the feasible region. (The optimal solution never is located inside the region.) The objective function determines which of the extreme points is the best.

To determine the optimal solution, a line is plotted that corresponds with any one value of the objective function. For instance, it is possible to plot the line, $2.00x + 1.50y = 200$, as shown. If you mentally "slide" this line parallel to itself, you can derive new lines corresponding with higher or lower objective function values. All the points on an objective line yield the same objective function value. So, you must slide the line in a direction that increases that value more and more (because you are maximizing). Ultimately, you will reach a point at which any further increase will move the line completely outside of the feasible region. At that time, the line will touch the region at a vertex (the optimal solution) whose coordinates can be read graphically.

SIMULATION MODELS

The primary use of a *simulation model* is to respond to "what if . . . ?" questions. These descriptive models can produce large amounts of detailed output because they work by mimicking many parts of the real-world system. One major weakness is that no automatic searching or optimizing is done by the model. (Any such features must be built on top of the simulation model and must be used as a submodel.) In such cases, the simulation may have to be performed many, many times while a search for the best decision parameters is under way. This can be quite expensive if the simulation is complex.

Two major issues in simulation modeling are how long a simulation run must proceed to achieve *steady state* (typical behavior) and how many different runs must be performed to achieve statistical significance. Inside most simulation models is a pseudo random-number generator. This is a mathematical subroutine that produces numbers that appear to be random. These random numbers are manipulated further to represent parts of the model that are not deterministic. Examples might include the arrival of customers at a ticket counter or the time of failure of an electronic circuit component. These

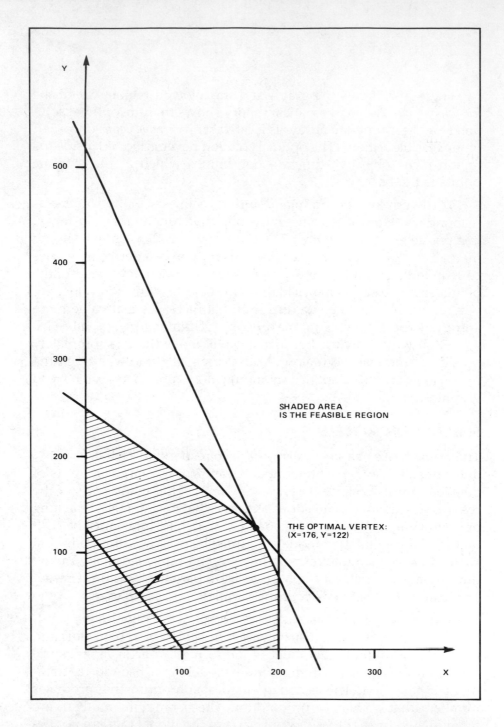

Figure 9-2. This graphic output would serve to identify the optimal solution to a linear program aimed at establishing production targets. The optimal solution is represented by the vertex point in the feasible area of the graphic display.

random number generators can be "seeded" with special input parameters to make them produce different streams of random values. Repeating runs with different seed values provides a set of outputs that has a statistical distribution to be analyzed.

Many commercial software packages are available that can be used to build simulation models. Some of these are general-purpose simulation languages that have general-but-powerful features, such as waiting lines and resource pools that ease the modeling task. At the other extreme are tailored simulation models (such as oil refinery models) that are already built but afford the user the ability to specify input parameters to describe the precise configuration under study. In between these extremes are simulation languages that are suited for a large class of models, such as networks, that are a formalism in which many problems can be represented.

Case Example

During lunch hour, customers arrive at a fast-food restaurant at a rate of three per minute. They require 1.5 minutes to place an order and pay the bill before going to pick up the food. How many cash register stations are needed to ensure that the number of customers waiting in line does not exceed six and that this waiting time does not occur more than 30 percent of the time during the lunch hour rush?

Model:

Figure 9-3 shows a simulation model for this problem as expressed in the SLAM II simulation language. The language consists of symbols that can be composed on a computer terminal screen into a diagram like the one shown. The first circle represents customer arrivals. The second circle represents the queue, or waiting line. The last circle represents departures from the system. The number in the small circle specifies the number of servers. This item was set to different values for each computer simulation run.

A random normal probability distribution was chosen to model the customer arrivals. The mean, or average, time between arrivals is set at 20 seconds, and the standard deviation is set to 5 seconds. The simulation model was run for 3,600 seconds for each experiment. The number of servers was changed between runs.

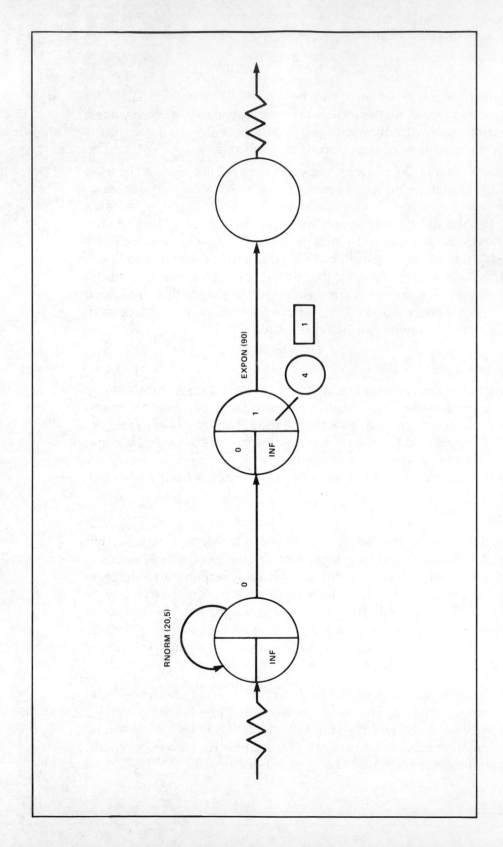

Figure 9-3. This SLAM II simulation model reflects customer arrivals, a waiting queue, and departures from a fast-food restaurant.

The service time was represented by an exponential distribution with a mean of 90 seconds.

Solution:
Statistics describing the queue are produced automatically by the simulation software package. The table in Figure 9-4 shows that five servers are needed to ensure that the queue will be no longer than six persons for 70 percent of the time. A thorough analysis would involve making more runs to confirm that the above statistics still hold true when different random numbers are used and longer periods of simulation are tried.

Method:
The simulation software generates random numbers using mathematical formulas and then computes when customers arrive, how long they require for service, and so forth. A clock is simulated to keep track of what should happen next. These performance statistics are collected and reported.

STATISTICAL MODELS

Statistics is a broad area of quantitative analysis and is often employed in conjunction with other techniques as well as by itself. *Statistical models* are used primarily for descriptive applications. In this context, the main value of statistical models is to establish understandings of the relationships among data items within a model.

One extremely common type of statistical model is *regression.* Regression analysis works backward from data observations to compute the parameters of a mathematical function that best describes that data. For instance, you might compute the best straight line that "fits" a set of points giving sales volume and commission rate. The results of the regression are the slope and intercept numbers for that straight line. Also produced are indicators of how well that straight line actually represents the observed data. Fitting curved lines or even surfaces to more complicated data can also be done statistically.

Another major statistical technique is hypothesis testing, in which a statement is judged quantitatively for acceptance or rejection on the basis of observed evidence. For example, the statement may be "Fertilizer A gets grass greener than Fertilizer B." The data may

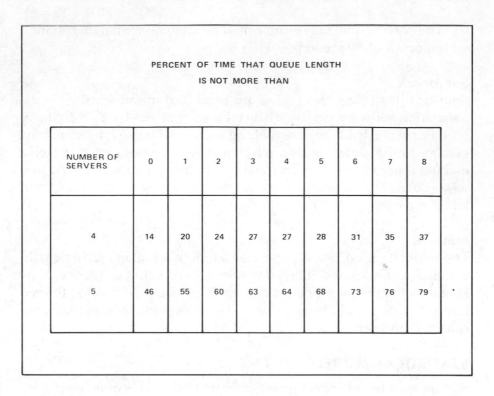

PERCENT OF TIME THAT QUEUE LENGTH
IS NOT MORE THAN

NUMBER OF SERVERS	0	1	2	3	4	5	6	7	8
4	14	20	24	27	27	28	31	35	37
5	46	55	60	63	64	68	73	76	79

Figure 9-4. This table would serve as a tool for establishing optimal staffing levels for a fast-food restaurant. The data show that a staff of five servers would ensure that the waiting queue would have no more than six patrons for 70 percent of the time.

be greenhouse measurements taken with colorimeters to determine the extent of greenness for different plots of grass. For each product, there is a distribution of measurements. The question is whether the means (averages) of those distributions are really different and which one is higher.

In hypothesis testing, there are two kinds of errors: accepting a false hypothesis and rejecting a true hypothesis. Each of these errors may have different consequences. Depending on the quality and volume of data, a statistical analysis will show the probability of occurrence for each error, leaving selection of decision alternatives to managerial judgment.

Case Example

A sales manager wants to estimate the potential sales volume for a new product that is being considered for introduction into a district. It is believed that the volume will be related to the total category volume in that district. The manager has data for other districts in which the new product has already been introduced. These data include the new product's volume and the total category volume for each district.

Model:

$$y = a x + b$$

Where:

y = new product volume
x = total category volume.

The values of a and b should be determined by finding which values best describe the historical data; a linear regression will be used. The historical data are plotted in Figure 9-5.

Solution:

The regression model output indicated that the best straight line through the data has the values:

$a = 0.062$
$b = -700.$

Results also show a "good fit" to the data by the straight line. Since the new district has a category volume known to be $x = 120,000$ cases, the projected volume for the new product is expected to be:

$$y = (0.062) \times (120,000) - 700 = 6,740 \text{ cases.}$$

Method:

The regression model searches for the a and b values that make the line do the best job of going through or staying near the data points. The derived values minimize the sum of the squares of the distances of the points from the line.

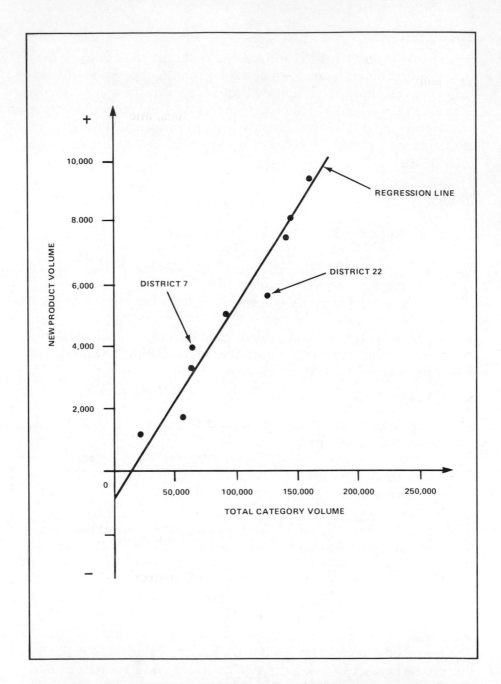

Figure 9-5. This graphic output would be used to document regression analysis of sales volumes in a situation involving new product introductions.

FINANCIAL MODELS

Consequences of decisions involving money can be tested through use of *financial models*. A primary concern is the dynamics of cash flows and interest rates. These models, for instance, combine data representing capital investments, expenses, revenues, and tax items occurring at different times into integrated measurements such as net present value and rate of return. These latter parameters serve as candidate objective functions (or payoffs) for comparing the relative merits of alternative investment strategies. It is important that these models be tailored to the particular financial policies of the user, such as depreciation methods, discount rates, tax rates, expected life, salvage values, inventory methods, and so forth.

As an example, consider a decision for funding research and development projects. Total capital is a constraint, as is human resource availability. Scenarios detailing investments and revenues over time can be analyzed through cash flow models to clarify the relative value of the alternatives. Often, detailed cost models are needed to provide the major inputs to such analyses, as are marketing projections.

Case Example

A research and development facility needs a special instrument that can be purchased for $350,000 or leased for $100,000 annually on a four-year contract. After the fourth year, the major project will be complete and the instrument will not be needed. Which alternative is more attractive?

Model:

Since both choices satisfy the need, the one with the best net present value will be chosen. The interest rate for discounting future payments is set at 15 percent. The salvage value of the instrument is estimated at $60,000.

Solution:

The net present values are:

NPV(purchase) = −$316,000

NPV(lease)   = −$328,000.

Purchase is preferred, since the cost is lower and, conversely, net present value is higher.

Method:

$$\text{NPV(purchase)} = -350,000 + 60,000/(1.15)[sp]4$$
$$= \$-315,695$$

$$\text{NPV(lease)} = -100,000 - 100,000/(1.15)$$
$$-100,000/(1.15)[sp]2$$
$$-100,000/(1.15)[sp]3$$
$$= \$-328,322.$$

Other cash flow details, such as taxes, insurance, depreciation, and investment tax credits should be included for a complete analysis.

DECISION ANALYSIS MODELS

There are several quantitative models for assessing the relative merits of decision alternatives. These models derive considerable value for evaluation of alternatives. This richness of value comes from considering probabilities associated with outcomes which are uncertain. If those probabilities are not addressed, it becomes necessary to compute best and worst cases and to elect whether to be aggressive (maximizing the best possible outcome) or conservative (minimizing the worst possible outcome).

However, if the probabilities of uncertain events can be estimated, the mathematical notion of an "expected value," or weighted average result, can be computed and incorporated in a decision tree. Figure 9-6 presents a decision tree that has square boxes representing choices management can make and circles representing uncertain events. Branches coming out of the circles are labeled with the probabilities that the particular event will occur. At the ends of the branches in the tree are triangles, each of which represents a complete scenario.

The value, or payoff, of the scenario must come from some model, perhaps a financial model that computes the net present value for that set of decisions and chance outcomes. The tree provides a systematic way to compute, at each circle, the expected value, or weighted average, of the payoffs at that point. At each square, the value on the

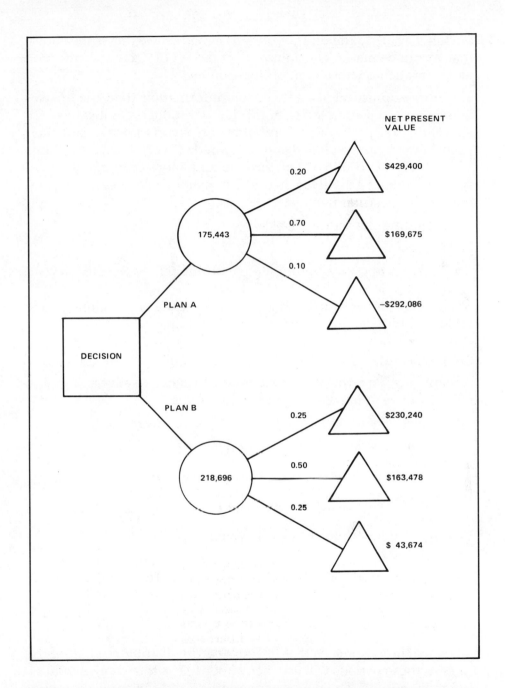

NET PRESENT VALUE

0.20 — $429,400

0.70 — $169,675

0.10 — −$292,086

175,443

PLAN A

DECISION

PLAN B

218,696

0.25 — $230,240

0.50 — $163,478

0.25 — $ 43,674

Figure 9-6. This is a decision tree that would be used in establishing values to be used in formulating an advertising plan.

branch leading to the best payoff is assigned, since that is the choice that would be made. The "answer" is the set of decisions indicated by the branches chosen out of the squares.

More sophisticated and valuable information than the answer illustrated can be derived from this kind of model. For instance, for alternative decisions, the distribution of payoffs (values and their probabilities) can be plotted and compared. This clarifies the notions of risk and payoff into one picture, doing a more thorough job than simply producing expected values. The major challenges in developing a good decision tree are:

- Including the right variables
- Assessing the probabilities
- Constructing the appropriate payoff model.

Some decision trees can be drawn on the back of an envelope, while others require detailed computer programming.

Case Example
A marketing department is considering which of two advertising campaigns to use in launching a new snack food:

- Plan A: Spend $800,000 on TV and radio advertising.
- Plan B: Spend $300,000 on TV and radio advertising and $200,000 on coupon distribution.

Which is the better plan?

Model:
Net present value is chosen as the payoff criterion for a pilot analysis. The unit profit is $0.50 without a coupon. The coupon is for 10 cents off and the grocer gets 7 cents for handling each one. Figure 9-7 shows the expected shares determined during the market research study.

The study estimates that, if coupons are distributed, half of the sales in these periods will use the coupons. The total market volume is 3 million units. The periods are quarters and the annual discount rate is 16 percent.

Solution:
Plan B is preferred because its expected NPV is higher:

- Plan A: Expected Value of NPV = $175,000.

- Plan B: Expected Value of NPV = $218,000.

Method:
For each triangle in the decision tree, a cash flow had to be computed. For example, for node (triangle) 4 the cash flow is:

$$-\$300,000 \text{ advertising expense}$$
$$-\$200,000 \text{ coupon distribution}$$

Revenue Period:
1 = [$0.50 × 0.5 + $0.33 × 0.5] × (2,000,000) × (0.25)

2 = [$0.50 × 0.5 + $0.33 × 0.5] × (2,000,000) × (0.20) / (1.04)

3 = [$0.50 × 0.5 + $0.33 × 0.5] × (2,000,000) × (0.15) / (1.05)[sp]2

Total Revenue   = $ 230,240.

After this is done for each triangle node, the values of the two circle nodes are computed by using the probabilities of each arc as weights. Since the resulting "expected" NPV is higher for the bottom circle, Plan B is the preferred choice.

PROJECT PLANNING MODELS

A common business model responds to the need for planning and managing complex projects with many interdependent activities. PERT (Program Evaluation and Review Technique) and CPM (Critical Path Method) are methods that express a project as a network diagram, as described in an earlier chapter. The network diagrams indicate which activities must be completed before others start and show estimates of the ranges of time each activity might take.

Mathematical algorithms trace through a network to find the critical path. If any activity on the critical path is not completed on time,

| | PROBABILITY | SHARE | | |
		PERIOD 1	PERIOD 2	PERIOD 3
PLAN A	0.20	0.30	0.30	0.25
	0.70	0.25	0.22	0.20
	0.10	0.15	0.10	0.10
PLAN B	0.25	0.25	0.20	0.15
	0.50	0.25	0.15	0.15
	0.25	0.20	0.15	0.10

Figure 9-7. This table is used to project market shares that would result from alternate plans for evaluating returns on the basis of net present value criteria.

---

the entire schedule will slip and the completion will be delayed. If the deadline for the project must be moved up, the PERT method can be used with linear programming to find out what critical path activities need to be "crashed"—done faster at increased cost, in the most economical way. Of course, if some activities are accelerated, others may be moved to the critical path. Thus, the solution is not always easy to see.

Case Example

The table in Figure 9-8 shows a list of activities and their required completion times, as well as those that must be completed before others begin. What is the minimum amount of time to complete all the

ACTIVITY	TIME (WEEKS)	PREREQUISITE COMPLETIONS
A	10	NONE
B	10	NONE
C	5	NONE
D	7	A
E	5	B, C
F	7	B, C
G	2	B, C
H	5	C
I	8	G, H
J	4	D, E

Figure 9-8. This is the table of input data from which CPM or PERT network diagrams could be constructed for project planning and control.

activities? Which activities must be completed on time to avoid delaying project completion?

Model:

The network in Figure 9-9 shows the relationships of the activities. The model finds the path of critical activities that must be completed in sequence and on schedule to assure on-time project completion. All the activities on that path are "critical" because a delay in any one of them will lengthen the completion time of the project.

Solution:

The project will require 21 weeks. Activities A, D, and J are on the critical path. If any of them are delayed, the project will not be on time.

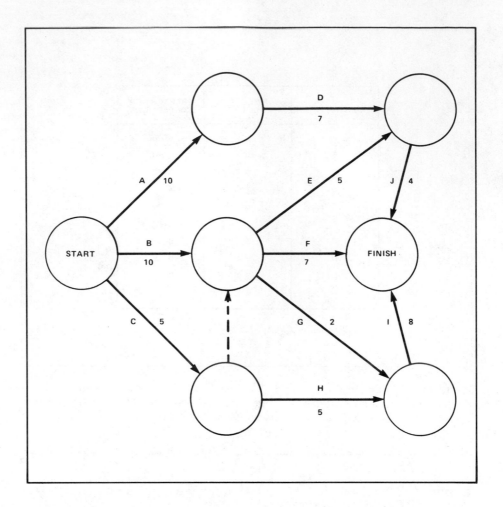

Figure 9-9. This is an activity network derived from use of the data in Figure 9-8.

Method:

Since only single values are given for the length of time for each activity (as opposed to best, worst, and average time values), the CPM technique is used. This method calculates the earliest and latest start times and finish times for every activity by tracing forward and backward through the network, ensuring that no activity can be started until all of its prerequisite jobs are completed.

Outlook

- Models are approximations of the real world and involve many assumptions.

- Models are exercised through systematic changes of their inputs, observing the outputs, and developing insights about how the system behaves.

- To be useful, models must be verified technically and validated with real-world data.

- Many quantitative techniques are employed in models. Frequently, special or complex situations require application of combinations of two or more mathematical modeling methods.

- The frontiers of modeling and management science have been expanded in recent years by the growing field of artificial intelligence. These trends are covered in the chapter that follows.

Assignments

1. Discuss how historical monthly sales data might be used with a regression model to estimate future sales. How might such a model be validated?

2. Describe some business criteria—aside from profit and cost—that might be optimized in a business model.

3. What problems are caused when more than one criterion must be optimized? Suggest some alternatives for overcoming these difficulties.

4. Rework the decision tree for the advertising example: Assume that, under Plan B, 90 percent of the sales use coupons. Does the best strategy switch to Plan A?

10 ARTIFICIAL INTELLIGENCE AND DSS

Abstract

- This chapter provides a look at the special roles, values, and applications of artificial intelligence and DSS.

- Decision support and expert systems are, largely, offshoots of research and development efforts in artificial intelligence.

- You may well find that your existing knowledge and experience lead to new opportunities in the area of artificial intelligence.

AI AND DSS: THE RELATIONSHIPS

Artificial intelligence is a branch of computer science that is studying how to cause computers to perform functions considered to be high-level human activities. Examples of such activities include reasoning, seeing, hearing, planning, and manipulation. One of the striking characteristics of these activities is that they involve symbol processing. Symbols may be phonemes (sound units), lines or surfaces (vision units), words (language units), or propositions (logic units).

Historically, the computer was applied to problems in which its speed and accuracy at arithmetic were exploited to solve large and complex scientific and engineering problems. The first commercial appeal was in managing large volumes of data, primarily numbers, but without performing complex operations on that data. Artificial intelligence is pioneering the frontier of performing complex operations on symbolic data.

The following areas of artificial intelligence have the greatest potential for integration with decision support system technologies:

- Natural language processing
- Knowledge systems/expert systems
- Computer languages in AI
- Commercial tools
- Commercial application systems
- Expert decision support systems
- Knowledge systems within DSS.

NATURAL LANGUAGE PROCESSING

This area is concerned with the analysis of communications in a language such as English. It does understand speech or handwriting, but assumes that the words have been expressed and captured accurately through such measures as entry into a computer terminal keyboard. The processing challenge is to "interpret," or conclude the meaning of, the expression entered. Within this context, the meaning of the term "correct meaning" depends on the task at hand. For instance, correct interpretation may mean that the natural language processor generates a correct database query (in a database query language). A correct database query, in turn, can be taken to mean that the retrieval function corresponds with the user's request.

Natural language interpretation is difficult because use of a language such as English produces many ambiguities of meaning. To illustrate, at least four different sets of spellings and meanings can be attributed to words with the pronunciation "there." People have the interpretive skills to resolve these problems as they are encountered. Computers do not. Therefore, computer researchers are continually searching for ground rules and principles that can be applied by computers to resolve such ambiguities.

A natural language processing component of a DSS can be part of a dialog management facility. A natural language processor, for example, might permit queries for data to be expressed in English as spoken or written by people rather than a special computer language.

Speech Recognition

In AI terms, *speech recognition* is a pattern recognition and interpretation process. A stream of sounds must be broken up into units that are grouped symbolically into words. Identification of words and their meaning is a key to breaking up the sounds. Thus, the problem is circular. Many types of analysis must be applied and coordinated to achieve speech recognition. An additional challenge is to perform this analysis in real time.

HEARSAY-II was one of the first systems able to perform speech understanding on discourse from a 1,000-word vocabulary. However, this was a research project; commercial products are still to come.

KNOWLEDGE SYSTEMS/EXPERT SYSTEMS

Expert systems are described and discussed briefly in Chapter 6. As indicated, an expert system performs logical analysis of a specialized, limited body of information to reach suggestions or recommendations, often through interaction with a human user. It is also true, in a larger sense, that an expert system is a type of *knowledge system.*

A knowledge system applies logic in an area bounded by stated, formal rules. However, a knowledge system applies AI capabilities to the level of judgmental selection. In computer science terms, knowledge systems are said to apply stated rules of thumb, known as *heuristics.*

Thus, the main difference between knowledge systems and expert systems lies in level of performance: Expert systems are narrower in scope but greater in their depth of application for AI techniques. Knowledge systems, on the other hand, are broader in scope and less sophisticated.

To illustrate, consider a petroleum exploration and refining environment. A consultation with one of the industry's top geophysicists about evaluation of substrata soil samples would contribute to design of an expert system. On the other hand, observations and interviews with console operators at a refinery would contribute to the building of a base for a knowledge system.

Functionally, knowledge systems are computer programs and data that solve problems by applying logic systematically. Schematically, knowledge systems can be represented by a simple flow diagram like the one in Figure 10-1. At the center of the illustration in Figure 10-1 is a *logic machine,* or *inference engine,* that is capable of combining facts and rules to conclude new facts. For example:

Data Fact: Smith's balance is 95 days past due.

Rule: IF X's account balance is more than 90 days past due, THEN X's account is delinquent.

Conclusion: Smith's account is delinquent.

Further facts and rules can be used to "compute" more results, often through use of the results of earlier steps. The inference engine automatically searches for rules and facts that can help it draw a conclusion to satisfy a request. Although it appears to be clever, the construction of an inference engine is rather easy. The difficult part is to establish the set of rules, called the *knowledge base.*

Knowledge Engineering

Knowledge engineering is a style of systems analysis that develops rule-based models of problem solving by interviewing human knowledge sources and iteratively prototyping models on a computer. This is more like scientific research than traditional MIS analysis because experimentation must be intertwined with design. The expert is usually not aware of the model he or she is following to solve problems. Hence, a discovery/invention activity takes place. Currently, knowledge engineers are scarce, come from academia, and can be found in highly specialized consulting firms.

One of the benefits of the knowledge engineering process is that the resulting knowledge base is mostly a set of "IF . . . THEN" format rules using a consistent set of English words and phrases. Further, these rules are NOT intertwined in the form of a complex algorithm, as is true for FORTRAN program statements. Each rule can be understood independently and applied in any context. The inference engine then will seek out and apply appropriate rules to fit given situations. The addition of new or updated rules to a knowledge base can be implemented easily once the initial system has been validated.

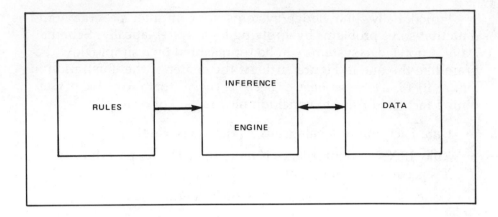

Figure 10-1.   This is a schematic diagram of a knowledge system.

Consultations

The user of a typical knowledge system initiates a dialog in which he or she is asked questions about the specifics of the problem and receives advice in the form of conclusions or recommendations. This procedure is known as a *consultation*.

It is possible for uncertain information to be input during user-system interaction. If so, the inference process will keep track of which evidence is applied and how each item is weighted in devising the answer. During a consultation, a user can ask for an explanation at any point and the system can display its line of reasoning and cite the rules that provoke its questions or determine its conclusions. Depending on the level of detail of the model (how deep the knowledge base is), systems responses may be suitable for instructional purposes, such as training. Even an expert may use such a system to check for completeness or for suggestion of alternatives.

Figure 10-2 presents a consultation from EMERGE, an expert system for emergency room use with chest pain patients. This consultation incorporates interrogation and advice exchanged with an expert system on medical diagnosis. The human user is an emergency-room doctor examining a 53-year-old male patient who has come in with chest pains. The system prompts the physician for data required for

Figure 10-2. This display presents a consultation dialog generated under EMERGE, a medical diagnostic program, for evaluation of an emergency room patient complaining of chest pains. (This illustration is reprinted from the *IEEE Transactions on Pattern Analysis and Machine Intelligence,* Vol. PAMI-6, Jan. 1984.)

```
ENTER THE NAME OF THE PATIENT
?A
PATIENT AGE
?53
PATIENT SEX (M OR F)
?M
DO YOU HAVE CLINICAL INFORMATION TO ENTER ON THIS PATIENT
?N
ECG INTERPRETATION
?N
BP < 100/60
?N
CHEST X-RAY INTERPRETATION
?N
SYNCOPE
?N
NEW NEUROLOGICAL DEFECT
?N
PAIN EXCRUCIATING
?N
PAIN ANTERIOR
?Y
PAIN REPRODUCED AT ONE OR MORE LOCI IN CHEST
?N
HISTORY OF TRAUMA
?N
REFERRED PAIN OR ANTERIOR-POSTERIOR OR SIDE TO SIDE
?N
HISTORY OF PREVIOUS MI
?N
PAIN ANGINA
?Y
HX OF PREVIOUS EPISODES
??
ONSET < 48 HOURS PRIOR TO ER VISIT
?Y
INCREASED IN SEVERITY OR INTENSITY
?N
DURATION > 20 MINUTES
?N
```

```
PAIN DIFFUSE AND PRECORDIAL
?Y
>45 YEARS OLD
Y
SX > 20 MINUTES
?N
SWEATING
?Y
ASSOCIATED WITH ONSET
?Y
DEPENDENT RALES
?N
RALES > 50% OF CHEST
?N
BRONCHOSPASM
?N
S3 GALLOP, NEW OR INCREASED
?N
PEDAL EDEMA, NEW OR INCREASED
?Y


THE FOLLOWING TREATMENT IS RECOMMENDED

OXYGEN
IV LINE

ADMIT
```

Figure 10-2. Concluded.

---

analysis. Following the interactive consultation, the system recommends initial treatment and hospital admission for the patient.

An example rule from the knowledge base used to produce this consultation is:

IF dependent rales
    NOT proved old
    currently taking furosemide 200 mg

THEN furosemide, 150 mg IV
      oxygen
      admit.

COMPUTER LANGUAGES IN AI

Two of the most prevalent computer languages used in artificial intelligence are PROLOG and LISP. AI researchers have built many systems in these languages. Often, a specialized tool or "higher language" is built on top of PROLOG or LISP. These higher languages resemble the macro routines or tool kit items demonstrated in earlier chapters. In general, high-level languages contain powerful commands and are part of fourth-generation software techniques. But PROLOG, combined with supercomputers, offers such an extension to present computing capabilities that it sometimes is considered to be the basis for a fifth generation.

Unlike conventional languages such as FORTRAN, COBOL, BASIC, or PASCAL, LISP and PROLOG are not procedural. Rather than expressing a sequence of steps to be performed one after another, programs in these languages are declarative, stating relationships in terms of other relationships.

PROLOG Example

The following is a simple PROLOG program. Note that the use of upper and lowercase in the expressions below is different from styles in conventional languages. Use of upper and lowercase is highly significant in PROLOG. Specifically, uppercase strings are treated as variables that have to be pattern-matched.

```
owns(bill,car).
owns(bill,radio).
owns(mike,radio).
knows(mike,bill).
mayborrow(X,Y)   :- owns(Z,Y), knows(X,Z), needs(X,Y).
needs(X,Y)       :- not(owns(X,Y)).
```

This program can accept "questions" such as:

```
mayborrow(mike,radio)
```

For the above question, the answer is "false." Another question might be:

```
mayborrow(mike, X)
```

The answer to the second question is "car."

LISP Example

The following is a simple LISP program. The use of upper and lower-case notation styles is not critical in LISP.

```
(DEFUN PALINDROME (L)
        (EQUAL L (REVERSE L) ))
(DEFUN REVERSE (X)
        (COND ((NULL X) NIL)
                (T (APPEND (REVERSE (CDR X)) (CAR X) ))))
```

This strange looking program checks whether a list reads the same forward as backward. For instance:

```
(PALINDROME (A, B, C, B, A))
```

The statement above evaluates as ''true.'' (LISP programmers are famous for their ability to keep track of parentheses!)

COMMERCIAL TOOLS

Commercial software tools for building knowledge systems have appeared recently. These programs provide the inference engine, the dialog management, and the development utilities for building and testing the knowledge base. The first notion of such a generalized facility came as the outgrowth of a medical diagnosis expert system, called MYCIN, built at Stanford University by Dr. Edward Shortliffe, a medical doctor who also holds a doctorate in computer science. The approach to evolution of a commercial tool was to take Shortliffe's computer program, extract all the particular medical information, and retain the shell. This shell was called EMYCIN, for ''Essential'' (or ''Empty'') MYCIN.

A detailed discussion of AI software packages is beyond the scope of this book. However, as AI tools become more widely available, computer professionals at all levels may benefit from a basis of questions that can be used to learn about and discuss these offerings. The following are some key questions that can be asked in considering the appropriateness of software packages in this area:

- What computers does the tool run on? In part because of their academic origins, tools may be based on such languages as LISP or

PROLOG, which have been shunned by some major commercial computer vendors until recently.

- How many rules can the tool accommodate? This parameter determines the complexity of the problems that can be addressed. Demonstration systems may require a couple of hundred rules, whereas a production knowledge base may have several thousand rules.

- How elaborate is the "explanation facility"? This can range from simple restatement of the current rule to a more elaborate system of inference path tracing and text substitution.

- What integration facilities are available to outside data sources, such as database management systems or user-supplied software?

- Are the tool facilities at the fundamental level or the prefabricated construct level? This represents a spectrum of capabilities. In theory, BASIC can do everything a database management system can do. But it takes a lot more work! So it is important to find how many prebuilt facilities are provided.

COMMERCIAL APPLICATION SYSTEMS

In the AI area, the differences between commercial tools and commercial application systems center around the inclusion of a knowledge base. A commercial tool consists of software that can exercise a knowledge base. But the user must provide the base. By comparison, a commercial application system has both software tools and a knowledge base.

For example, an investment advisor expert system would come with a valuable knowledge base of rules about investment strategies, risk assessment, and portfolio evaluation. Of course, success for such systems requires a market base that is broad enough to support a profitable level of sales and still narrow enough to build high performance problem-solving models.

Whether technology can provide future, "generic" knowledge base systems—more tailored than tools but not as finished as an application system—poses an exciting but difficult question. Such facilities would be analogous to spreadsheet software such as VisiCalc or

Lotus 1-2-3. The user would be able to generate, express, and exercise knowledge models without the help of the intermediary analyst—knowledge engineer in this case.

EXPERT DECISION SUPPORT SYSTEMS

Despite the excitement around the subject of artificial intelligence, a toolbuilder should view knowledge systems as one more kind of model. AI provides an important new kind of model because it does symbolic calculation, a void left by mathematical models and data models. DSS and expert systems also focus the attention of management on a major and key business resource: knowledge. A mantra of the artificial intelligence community is: "In the knowledge lies the power." Mining that corporate resource and organizing it into knowledge bases is a bottleneck. But it is important to realize that bringing that codified knowledge to bear on business problems will also be a challenge, for it is there that the integration of technologies is the key problem.

The phrase *expert decision support systems* is ambiguous. The term definitely refers to a DSS that involves a knowledge subsystem. That knowledge base may be derived from an expert's special knowledge, giving rise to the description, "expert decision support system." Also, it is possible that such a system would be used by an expert and hence support him or her, making it truly an "expert decision support system." For the purposes of this discussion, the critical characteristic is that a knowledge subsystem be integrated into the DSS.

KNOWLEDGE SYSTEMS WITHIN DSS

What roles might knowledge subsystems play within a DSS?

Such systems could serve as technical experts, invoked when a particular problem needs to be addressed—such as performing an investment strategy consultation through a "what if . . . ?" scenario. In this sense, a knowledge system is a special kind of model, but nonetheless just a model.

A knowledge system might operate at a higher plane in the DSS by suggesting scenarios to probe, given high-level objectives and the outcomes of previous scenarios. For instance, a system might advise that a rough econometric analysis be performed to screen variables for possible inclusion in a more elaborate optimization model.

At a much more detailed level, knowledge systems may be incorporated to guide and critique the use of quantitative models. For instance, a knowledge base on how to use a statistical model for clustering analysis and how to interpret its outputs could help a user who is a novice in that technique.

Outlook

- Artificial intelligence includes several technologies, such as robotics, vision systems, speech recognition, natural language understanding, and knowledge systems.

- Natural language systems are a kind of dialog component within a DSS that translate English-like commands into formal queries for data or models.

- Knowledge systems are symbolic processing models that solve nonmathematical problems by using ''IF . . . THEN'' rules stored in a knowledge base. Expert systems are high-performance knowledge systems.

- In terms of DSS development, knowledge systems are special kinds of models.

- This chapter concludes your introduction to DSS, but not your total exposure. This is a growing field that will impact the working lives of millions of executives and CIS professionals in years to come.

Assignments

1. How are the computer languages used in artificial intelligence different from conventional data processing computer languages?

2. Are the rules in a knowledge base input data or program logic? Discuss.

3. Give examples of three kinds of problem solving that are based on knowledge rather than mathematics or data retrieval.

APPENDIX A

INTRODUCTION

This appendix presents case studies that can be used as the basis for project assignments that parallel materials covered in the text. Assignments require that students perform activities related to DSS development, implementation, and use. Students learn methods for determining data requirements and also gain experience in designing new and different applications of basic DSS principles.

This appendix contains seven case studies that correspond with development of the DSS Tool Kit, DSS operations and commands, DBMS applications, and the use of expert systems. Each case study concentrates on specific aspects of DSS design and implementation. The case studies are:

1. Mayflower Bank
2. Central High School Advising
3. Jill January for Mayor
4. Soft Soap Company
5. The DSS Analyst
6. The DRIVER Interface
7. Break-even Analysis.

CASE STUDY 1: Mayflower Bank

Mayflower Bank is a commercial banking institution located in a small, midwestern town in the United States. The commercial loan officers at Mayflower receive loan applications throughout the year from local retail and trade establishments. Applications usually are for short-term loans. Local businesspeople use loans to generate enough working capital to survive busy seasons. For example, many local retailers borrow money during the summer months to build inventories in preparation for the holiday shopping season. In the winter, farm and ranch suppliers use short-term loans to stock up on planting supplies, hay, and other types of feed.

Over the years, loan officers have compiled a history of all loan applications received. Whenever a local business submits a new application, the loan officers refer to similar proposals by the same and like businesses in years past. The officers have found that such historical references are useful in determining both the reasonableness of the figures and trends in the local business climate. Mayflower's loan application asks for the following information:

- Last three years' sales figures by quarter
- Last three years' product- and material-expense figures by quarter
- Last three years' miscellaneous expense figures by quarter
- Last three years' total short-term debt by quarter
- Last three years' total long-term debt by quarter
- Next year's debt service coming due by quarter
- Amount of working capital loan applied for to be repaid within six months.

Mayflower's working capital loans are short-term. Officers expect loans to be repaid within six months. The officers review figures submitted by applicants to estimate whether applicants will be able to repay loans within the allotted time period.

Assignment

Design a DSS for Mayflower that supports the collection, review, and maintenance of application data, and aids the loan officers in determining whether to grant loans. Include capabilities to:

- Compare new loan proposals with old ones made by the same applicant. The purpose is to examine consistency.

- Project the profitability of individual businesses.

- Project the profitability of collective types of businesses.

- Project the profitability of the local area (to be used for setting general lending policies).

- Project the profitability of individual and collective types of businesses, assuming different rates of inflation and their effects on expenses and different rate increases and their effects on income.

- Project the bank's overall cash need for the next five years.

Make sure to describe and document any extra information that Mayflower should require on its commercial loan application form.

CASE STUDY 2: Central High School Advising

Central High School has a very progressive guidance counselor, Bobby Wenders. Mr. Wenders is tireless in his efforts to guide students toward greater success in school and in their lives. One of Mr. Wenders' pet projects is designing a DSS for advising seniors about which colleges they should attend.

Mr. Wenders has a complete library of publications concerning the choice of institutions of higher education, including the usual "college guides" and bulletins describing new areas of study and achievement at various colleges and universities.

In addition, Mr. Wenders has tracked the careers, adventures, and misadventures of many of his past students for 10 years. About 25 percent of the students graduating from Central High have cooperated with his data-gathering activities.

The information Mr. Wenders has gathered for individual students includes:

- High school grades for all subjects
- College entrance examination scores
- College attended
- College major
- College grade point average, by semester
- Total college expenses, by year.

Mr. Wenders wants to install a personal computer to implement his DSS. He envisions this DSS as a system that he can use to help prospective graduates to choose the college at which they will be most likely to succeed.

Assignment

Design the DSS for Mr. Wenders. Once the system is operating, answer the following questions:

1. How did you define "college success" for this situation?
2. How much data do you think Mr. Wenders needs for his system to be valid from a statistical standpoint?
3. How much data does he need for the system to be useful?
4. Can Mr. Wenders' sample data be considered altogether representative of the graduates of Central High?
5. What additional data might be useful in Mr. Wenders' data bank?
6. How might a DBMS be used in this DSS?
7. How might an expert system be used?
8. Is there any place for forecasting or graphics?
9. Can this DSS also be used for evaluating and managing the overall instruction performance of Central High School?
10. Do you think an expert system developed from Mr. Wenders' experience and ideas about this problem might be as useful as a data-based DSS?

CASE STUDY 3: Jill January for Mayor

Jill January has made a name for herself in Mayberry through a successful and prosperous career in the insurance business. Jill is 42 and has decided to pursue a second career in politics. Her first goal is to be elected Mayor of Mayberry.

Ms. January wants to construct her election campaign on sound, quantitative decision-making principles. Ms. January is employing her computer and DSS software to support decision-making for the election campaign.

The main issue of the campaign involves a tax increase for the city of Mayberry. The reality of an impending insolvency is necessitating an increase in municipal revenues or a decrease in spending. The public supports a tax increase. Income tax is one alternative. Others include property and sales taxes.

Ms. January wants to win the election. She plans to use her DSS to choose the tax alternative that is most likely to get her elected. She believes that the increase that costs the majority of the public the least amount of money will be the winning ticket.

Assignment

Design a DSS for Ms. January that will help her choose a taxation policy for Mayberry. Assume an increase in income of 5 percent per year, per person, and an increase in assessed property values of 4 percent per year for the next 10 years, with an increase in city revenue needs of 5 percent per year. The city has budgeted $636,000 for this year. Income data are listed in the table below.

Household Income Group	Population (households)	Average Household Size (persons)	Average Assessed Property Values
$0–10,000	576	1.7	$22,000
$10,001–20,000	1,324	2.1	$29,000
$20,001–30,000	896	2.3	$42,000
$30,001–?	421	2.2	$89,000

Once the DSS is designed and built, answer the following questions:

1. What policy should she choose if Mayberry needs an increase in revenue of $0.2 million for the first year?

2. Can you assume that people will vote to maximize their financial well-being?

3. What other data would you like to have available to help Ms. January?

4. What is the effect of the alternate tax strategies after 10 years?

5. What other useful data would probably be available to Ms. January in city hall?

CASE STUDY 4: Soft Soap Company

The Soft Soap Company manufactures a line of liquid hand soaps for use in garages. The liquid soaps are especially formulated to deal with the heavy grime and grease that must be removed from the hands of mechanics and other workers in commercial garages. The Soft Soap Company is not large by chemical industry standards. The entity consists of two plants, a small research and development facility and a central administration office.

Soft Soap has had a central data processing capability for 20 years. This capability has been updated periodically and now consists of on-line order entry, accounts receivable, billing, sales analysis, and payroll systems, all interacting with a central database management system.

Corporate management at Soft Soap has decided that decision support capabilities should be provided for the two plant managers and their plant controllers, the head of research, both vice presidents (marketing and production), the corporate controller, and three staff planners. Furthermore, management has decided to provide this decision support capability via commercial software packages and personal computers.

Assignment

Select commercial packages and specify personal computer requirements for the Soft Soap Company's DSS installation. Develop a training and installation plan. Consider the individual needs of different DSS users. Once the system is designed, answer the following questions:

1. How do you propose to interface with the corporate data processing systems?

2. How much will implementation of your plan cost?

3. How long will implementation take?

4. Who will implement the plan?

5. What cooperation will you need from the current data processing staff for your plan to succeed?

6. Prepare examples of typical uses of the DSS you have designed.

CASE STUDY 5: The DSS Analyst

Ms. Ramirez is a DSS analyst for the manufacturing division of a large corporation. Several managers whom she supports have notified her of information needs that could be met through application of the DSS Tool Kit that accompanies this text. However, the equipment Ms. Ramirez has available supports the COBOL programming language.

Assignment

Prepare an estimate of the time it will take to convert the DSS Tool Kit to COBOL and have it functioning. In the estimate, include the cost of a programmer, the programming time required (in hours), and the cost of computer time required to convert and test the COBOL version.

Many of the files with which Ms. Ramirez will be working contain several thousand records. Design changes to the DSS Tool Kit that will support these large files as part of an estimate of the cost of implementing changes into the COBOL version.

Finally, design a DSS operator that performs bivariate statistical regression analysis using two fields from a user-specified data table. Design the syntax for invoking this operator from the MENU program. Then estimate the time needed and cost of implementing this operator for the COBOL version. (You will need to review other texts to learn how to perform regression analysis.)

CASE STUDY 6: The DRIVER Interface

Included in the DSS Tool Kit is a program called DRIVER. The DRIVER program allows DSS users to access tool-kit functions without using the MENU interface. Use your knowledge of the DRIVER program to answer the questions that follow. (See Appendix C for source code.)

1. In what situations would the DRIVER program be more convenient or more effective than the MENU interface?

2. For what types of users is the DRIVER interface appropriate? Consider managerial personnel as well as CIS personnel who use a DSS for personal decision making.

3. How might the error-checking facility of the DRIVER program be improved?

4. Discuss how the MENU interface could be used to provide a generalized interface to database or graphics programs. Include use of the MENU program's user-prompting facilities (''?prompt?''). Then determine if there is a better way to provide user prompts through use of the DRIVER program. As an example, consider having prompts for each of the command-string parameters required to implement a tool-kit program.

5. Use the MENU program and user-prompting facilities to develop generalized interfaces to database and graphics programs. What types of decision-making situations would require generalized interfaces instead of those designed for specific decision-making situations? Who designs an interface for a specific decision-making situation? When is this done? Is there a place for both interfaces in a routine DSS? Why?

6. Discuss the feasibility of building a natural language interpreter for the generalized interfaces designed in Question 5 and for interfaces that must be designed for specific decision-making situations. Include economic considerations. When is a natural language interpreter justified? For what types of users? Do generalized natural language interface packages exist that can be used in a DSS?

7. Icon-based interfaces have been described as ''user friendly.'' Prepare an external design specification for an icon-based interface to the DSS Tool Kit. Is the interface you have designed generalized? Or is it tailored to specific decision-making situations? How is your interface more ''user friendly'' than the MENU or DRIVER interfaces within the DSS Tool Kit? Describe the special hardware/software requirements needed for implementing such an interface and prepare a development project timetable and budget for the external design.

CASE STUDY 7: Break-even Analysis

Break-even analysis refers to the use of descriptive models to represent graphically and to measure relationships among sales revenue for a product, the cost of making the product, and profit. Sales revenues usually increase in direct proportion to the quantity of an item sold. Sales revenues also are zero (0) when no units are sold. Total production costs also generally increase in direct proportion to the number of items sold. However, production costs are not zero (0) when no products are sold. Certain fixed costs, such as buildings, tooling, and design, are required before the first unit can be made. In addition, as the number of products made increases, the unit cost for making a single product often decreases.

These relationships can be expressed through spreadsheets or graphic displays. The horizontal axis of either form of presentation represents the quantity of items sold or the number of items produced. The vertical axis represents production costs or sales revenues, in dollars.

For example, a graphic display of break-even analyses results in two curved lines. One line plots the relationship between the amount of revenue received for sales of a certain number of items. That is, the horizontal axis represents number of items sold and the vertical axis represents sales revenue. The plotted line begins at the intersection of the horizontal and vertical axes, (0,0), and forms an upward-sloping curve to the highest sales-revenue/items-sold value in the upper right corner of the chart, or grid.

The second line plots the relationship between production costs and number of items produced. The horizontal axis represents production costs and the vertical axis represents the number of items produced. The plotted line begins at the point, (0,F), where F equals the fixed-cost value. The line rises and curves at a slower rate than the revenue line, causing the two lines to intersect. The intersection is the break-even point, or the production/sales level at which a business venture turns a profit.

A graphic display shows the continuous relationships (two curved lines) among revenues, costs, and profits. A spreadsheet, on the other hand, must make these relationships discrete so that they can be represented in rows and columns of data. A break-even spreadsheet has columns for the different production quantities, beginning with zero (0) in the left column. Each column contains values that represent sales revenue, the cost of making the number of products represented by the column, and a cell that calculates the difference between revenues and costs, or profit. The column in which profit becomes positive represents the break-even point.

   Using this information, answer the questions that follow:

1. Devise a spreadsheet template that can be used for break-even analysis. In addition, define one spreadsheet cell to represent the slope of the cost line, or the unit cost. Define a second cell to represent the slope of the revenue line, or the unit selling price. Also define a cell in which the fixed-cost amount can be placed.

2. Design an operator that will present the spreadsheet as a graphic display. Generalize this operator so that it might be used for simultaneous display of multiple linear relationships.

3. In general, can you expect the total revenue and the total cost curves to be linear? How could you handle nonlinear curves in the spreadsheet you have devised?

APPENDIX B

INTRODUCTION

This appendix presents a summary of the programs, commands, and parameters that you will need to apply the DSS tool kit that accompanies this text. (Note: If an interpreted implementation of the tool kit is used, the user will not see the ''A>'' prompt.)

The summary parallels the development of the DSS tool kit as presented in the text:

- The DTREE program
- LED
- SED
- The MENU program
- DBMS programs
- The SPREAD operator
- Descriptive models and graphic displays
- ES expert system operator
- The DRIVER program.

OPERATION SUMMARY: The DTREE Program

The DTREE program generates and calculates decision trees. At the IBM PC ''A>'' operating system prompt, type ''DTREE'' to invoke the program. This assumes that you have placed a diskette with the DSS Tool Kit Program in drive A.

When invoked, the DTREE program will ask the user to supply decision tree information:

"How many alternatives are to be considered?"

For each alternative, the program asks two questions:

"What is the name of this alternative?"

"How many chance outcomes are to be defined?"

For each chance outcome, the program asks three questions:

"What is the name of this chance outcome (20 characters or less)?"

"What is the probability of this chance outcome (0.1 to 1.0)?"

"What is the outcome value for this chance outcome (-9999 to 9999)?"

When the information is entered completely, the DTREE program displays a summary of the results of the application of the expected value computation.

EXAMPLE SESSION:

```
A>DTREE
This is DTREE, the DSS Tool Kit Decision Tree Computing Program

How many alternatives are to be considered?>2

1. What is the name of this alternative?>AIR
1. How many states of nature are to be defined?>2
1.1) What is the name of this chance outcome?>PLANE CRASH
1.1) What is the probability of this chance outcome?>0.1
1.1) What is the outcome value for this chance outcome?>-9999
1.2) What is the name of this chance outcome?>SAFE ARRIVAL
1.2) What is the probability of this chance outcome?>0.9
1.2) What is the outcome value for this chance outcome?>1000

2. What is the name of this alternative?>TRAIN
2. How many states of nature are to be defined?>2
```

```
2.1) What is the name of this chance outcome?)TRAIN WRECK
2.1) What is the probability of this chance outcome?).1
2.1) What is the outcome value for this chance outcome?)-3000
2.2) What is the name of this chance outcome?)SAFE ARRIVAL
2.2) What is the probability of this chance outcome?).9
2.2) What is the outcome value for this chance outcome?)1000
```

```
RESULTS OF EXPECTED VALUE COMPUTATIONS

ALTERNATIVE         CHANCE        PROBABILITY    OUTCOME     EXPECTED
                    OUTCOME                      VALUE       VALUE

1. AIR              1) PLANE CRASH   0.1          -9999       -999.9
                    2) SAFE ARRIVAL  0.9           1000        900
                                                            --------
                                                             - 99.9


2. TRAIN            1) TRAIN WRECK   0.1          -3000       -300
                    2) SAFE ARRIVAL  0.9           1000        900
                                                            --------
                                                              600
```

```
THE ALTERNATIVE WITH THE HIGHEST EXPECTED VALUE IS: 2. TRAIN
```

OPERATION SUMMARY: LED

LED is a line-oriented text editor. It is used to create and maintain the various text files used in the DSS Tool Kit.

LED is invoked by keying "LED" and pressing ENTER at the "A>" prompt. Once invoked, the system will display a question mark prompt, "?." The question mark prompt is supplied by LED when it is waiting for the user to enter an editing command. Either the whole command or its first letter may be used.

LED allows editing to take place on files that have been brought into the computer's main memory with the GET command. Editing is accomplished through use of the INSERT, REPLACE, and LIST operations. When editing is complete, the file is rewritten to disk with the SAVE command. The DELETE command removes unwanted files from disk. The NEW command tells LED to create a new, empty file. The commands and their parameters are listed below.

GET filename

The GET command causes LED to read a previously created text file from diskette. The "filename" parameter tells LED which file to read. Filenames must be no longer than six characters and begin with a letter.

SAVE filename

The SAVE command causes LED to write an edited file to disk under the name specified in the "filename" parameter. If no filename is specified, the program will use the last name assigned to the file.

DELETE line#

The DELETE command causes LED to delete from the file the line number specified in the "line#" parameter.

INSERT line#

Lines of text are added to files with the INSERT command. The "line#" parameter specifies the number of the line that will precede inserted text. If the number given in the "line#" parameter does not exist in the file, LED will insert the text after the line previous to the "line#" asked for. To add text to the end of a file, use a "line#" parameter that is greater than any in the file.

REPLACE line#

The REPLACE command tells LED that the line indicated in the "line#" parameter is to be rekeyed. The specified line is deleted and the user is prompted for the replacement line. If the number given in the line# parameter is not present, LED displays an error message.

NEW filename

The NEW command creates a new text file. When this command is invoked, LED checks the disk to make sure that the file does not exist already. Then, an empty file is created on the disk. The GET command is used to read the new file into main memory and add text. The SAVE command is used to store the new file on diskette.

LIST line# line#

The LIST command allows users to reference or examine lines, or to call up lines that require editing. When invoked, LIST tells LED to list certain lines of text held in main memory. The "line#" parameters indicate which line(s). If only one "line#" parameter is supplied, LED lists only the line specified. Using both "line#" parameters causes LED to list all lines between and including those specified.

HELP
The HELP command lists the commands available.

OPERATION SUMMARY: SED

SED is a screen-oriented text editor that can be used to create and maintain the various text files needed to build a DSS.

SED is invoked by keying "SED" and pressing ENTER at the "A>" prompt. Once invoked, SED presents a help menu that describes the operating options.

Editing is accomplished by positioning the cursor at the place where text is to be added or changed. The cursor keys, INSERT and DELETE, are supported. Pressing the ESC key ends the session and saves the edited file.

OPERATION SUMMARY: The MENU Program

The MENU program accesses the rest of the programs defined in the DSS tool kit. The program displays menus from which users select DSS functions. Menus consist of processing options that have been defined by the DSS designer and saved in a menu specification file.

The MENU program is executed by keying "MMENU" at the "A>" prompt. This command reads the menu specification file. Menu specifications are prepared using an editor and stored in a disk file called MENU. Menu specifications consist of individual lines of text. Columns are separated by one or more blank spaces.

The first column specifies the designation for the menu. The menu designation column can contain any combination of two letters and numbers. In this text, the use of a letter to designate the menu is followed as a convention.

The second column specifies the designation of a particular menu selection. The menu selection designation also can contain any combination of two letters and numbers. In this text, the use of a number to designate the menu selection is adhered to as a convention. No entry is made in the second column for the line of descriptive text that will appear at the top of the menu when it is displayed for execution. The number of the description line is placed at the beginning of the lines for the menu selection entries.

The third column contains text that describes menu selection entries. This text is surrounded by double quote characters (''). The third column also may contain the substance of the menu selection entries, such as the set of operators and operands necessary to implement the menu selection. Each operator and its respective operands occupies one line in the menu specification file. Within a menu selection, these operator command lines are executed in the order in which they appear. (See Figure 3-8 for an example of a menu specification file.) Valid operators are:

PROGRAM

The PROGRAM operator requires two operands. The first operand is the name of the program to be invoked to implement the menu selection. Several programs may be involved in this way in a single menu selection. The second operand is a list of control parameters for the designated program. This list of control parameters is surrounded by double quote characters ('').

The content of the control parameter list is dictated by the program designated. However, the MENU program scans this list before passing it to the designated program to identify any occurrences of question marks (?). Question marks cause the MENU program to prompt users with whatever appears between the two question marks, wait for a response, and pass the user response to the designated program in the control parameter list. The user response relaces the phrase bordered by question marks. If no question marks are present, the control parameter list is passed to the designated program as is.

A special program that can be designated as the operand of PROGRAM is the END program. The END program tells the MENU program to terminate and pass control back to the operating system.

GOTO

The GOTO operand requires only one parameter, the designation of the menu which is to be displayed next. Execution of GOTO causes the designated menu to be displayed for use by the operator.

OPERATION SUMMARY: Invoking DTREE, SED, and LED from the MENU Program

DTREE, SED, and LED also can be invoked by using the PROGRAM command in the MENU program. The commands and their respective operators are:

DTREE text file name

The DTREE command causes the DTREE program to be invoked from the MENU program. The text file specified in the "text file name" parameter contains answers to DTREE prompts. In effect, this file is a list of the user responses required to invoke the DTREE program. Each line of text in the text file should be a response to DTREE prompts. In addition, the text file can contain questions that prompt users for important values. User prompts should be placed in the proper location in the text file and surrounded by question marks (?).

Example: A 1 PROGRAM DTREE "ANSWER"

SED input file name

The SED command invokes the screen-oriented text editor from the MENU program and allows editing of the file specified in the "input file name" parameter.

Example: A 1 PROGRAM SED "AFILE"

LED input file name

The LED command invokes the line-oriented text editor from the MENU program and allows editing on the file specified in the "input file name" parameter.

Example: A 1 PROGRAM LED "ATABLE"

OPERATION SUMMARY: DBMS Programs

The DBMS of a DSS tool kit consists of a series of programs that accesses a database schema and data tables to perform data manipulation operations. DBMS programs receive control information from the MENU program. Control information is set up by the DSS designer as a list of control parameter operands for the MENU PROGRAM operator.

The database schema for the DBMS in a DSS tool kit is created with an editor and stored in a file called SCHEMA. An example schema is shown in Figure 4-5.

Schema files have one line for each data item in the file. Each line consists of 3 columns. The first column is the data table name. The second column holds the index for the data item within the data table. For example, the first data item, left to right, is indexed as ''1,'' the second data item is indexed as ''2,'' and so forth. The third column contains the data item name. Decimal numbers are not allowed. Columns are separated by one or more blanks in the schema file.

Data files are created and maintained with an editor. The name of the data file must be the same name as that used in the schema. Data are entered into data files in lines that correspond with the rows of the data table. Individual data elements in the rows are separated by commas, or by one or more blank spaces. When data are entered, it often is convenient to maintain column format. However, it is not necessary that the columns line up correctly for the operation of the programs.

The list below notes the control parameters that must be present in the control parameter lists for the respective programs. In coding the control parameter list for the PROGRAM operator of the MENU program, remember to surround the complete list with double quotes ('') and to separate the individual control parameters with commas (,). The commands and their respective parameters are:

DISPLAY data table name
The DISPLAY command refers to the schema to develop a format for a data presentation. The ''data table name'' parameter instructs the DBMS which data table to output.

Example: A 1 PROGRAM DISPLAY ''TTABLE''

SELECT input data table name,
Boolean search statement, output data table name
The SELECT command causes the program to search for required records and insert them into another data table. The ''input data table

name" parameter tells the system which data table to search. The "Boolean search statement" parameter defines selection criteria. Selection criteria are specified as the data item name or index to be searched for, followed by the comparison operator to be used during selection, $>$, $<$, $=$, or $<>$, followed by the appropriate comparison values. Comparison values can be, but do not have to be, surrounded by single quotes ('). However, comparison values must be surrounded by single quotes if a blank space is embedded in the parameter. The "output data table name" parameter names the file in which data items that meet selection criteria are to be placed.

Example: A 1 PROGRAM SELECT "ATABLE,1='A',WORK"

PROJECT input data table name, columns to be included, output data table name

The PROJECT command extracts specific columns from a data table and creates a new table that consists of these columns. The "input data table name" parameter tells the system which data table to search. The "columns to be included" parameter informs the system which data columns, or fields, to extract. Field names or indices are separated by semicolons (;). The "output data table name" parameter defines the data table in which extracted data are to be placed.

Example: A 1 PROGRAM PROJECT "TABLEA,1;2;3,TABLEB"

ADD input data table name, first column, second column, output data table name

The ADD command causes addition to be performed on cells in two columns. Answers are written in a newly created column. The "input data table name" parameter tells the system which data table to input. The "first column" and "second column" parameters give the system the names or indexes of the columns to be totalled. The "output data table name" parameter, of course, instructs the system in which data table to place outputs.

Example: A 6 PROGRAM ADD "WORKA,4,5,WORKB"

SUBTRACT input data table name, first column, second column, output data table name

The SUBTRACT command follows the same basic principles as the ADD command. However, the SUBTRACT command causes the cells in the column identified by the "second column" parameter to be sub-tracted from the cells in the column identified by the "first column" parameter.

Example: A 1 PROGRAM SUBTRACT "WORKA,4,5,WORKB"

**MULTIPLY input data table name,
first column, second column, output data table name**
The MULTIPLY command also follows the same basic principles as the ADD and SUBTRACT commands. However, the MULTIPLY command causes the cells in the columns identified by the "first column" and "second column" parameters to be used as factors.

Example: A 1 PROGRAM MULTIPLY "WORK1,1,2,WORK2"

**DIVIDE input data table name,
first column, second column, output data table name**
The DIVIDE command also follows the same basic principles as the ADD, SUBTRACT, and MULTIPLY commands. However, the DIVIDE command causes the cells in the columns identified by the "first column" parameter to be divided by the cells identified by the "second column" parameter. In effect, the "first column" parameter defines the dividend, and the "second column" parameter defines the divisor.

Example: A 1 PROGRAM DIVIDE "WORK1,3,4,OUTPUT"

**SORT input data table name, list of columns,
ascending or descending, output data table name**
The SORT command reorders, in sequence, the data elements in one or more columns. The "input data table name" parameter instructs the system on which data table to sort. The "list of columns" parameter tells the system which columns are to be used as sort criteria. The first column identified is the major sort field. The second column identified represents the minor sort field. The "ascending or descending" parameter instructs the system in which order to sort items. The "output data table name" parameter, of course, names the file to which the newly sorted file is to be written.

Example: PROGRAM SORT "WORK1,1;2;3,A,WORK2"

SUMMARIZE input data table name,
list of control fields, output data table name
The SUMMARIZE command causes the system to develop the same kinds of subtotals as control break reports. The "input data table name" parameter identifies the table from which the report is to be generated. The "list of control fields" parameter defines the major and minor break fields. The first control field listed represents the major break field, and so on. Control fields are separated by semicolons (;). The "output data table name" parameter identifies the file to receive outputs. An additional column is appended to the output table that contains a count of the number of rows summarized for each total.

Example: C 3 PROGRAM SUMMARIZE "IN,3;2,OUT"

UNION first input table name,
second input table name, output table name
The UNION command concatenates two data tables. The "first input table name" and "second input table name" parameters define the data tables to be concantenated. The "output data table name" parameter tells the system where to save the new file.

Example: D 4 PROGRAM UNION "AFILE,BFILE,OUT"

JOIN first input data table name, second input data table name,
list of control field pairs, output data table name
The JOIN command matches input rows from two data tables and produces a third, coordinated table. The "first input data table name" and "second input data table name" parameters define the files to be joined. The "list of control field pairs" parameter tells the system the name of the field that occurs in both data tables. The field name is given twice and the two names are separated by a colon (:). The "output data table name" parameter identifies the data table to which outputs are to be written.

Example: A 3 PROGRAM JOIN "A,B,1:1;3:2,CTABLE"

DELETE data table name
The DELETE command eliminates the data table given in the "data table name" parameter. This command also can be used to delete other unwanted files.

Example: A 3 PROGRAM DELETE "ATABLE"

OPERATION SUMMARY: The SPREAD Operator

The SPREAD operator implements an elementary spreadsheet capability for the DSS tool kit. SPREAD will impart to you the concept of a spreadsheet, but do not judge the power of modern commercial spreadsheet programs from your exposure to SPREAD. Commercial spreadsheet packages exhibit the best of interactive, personal computer programming achievement and are routinely offered with capabilities rivaling database management systems for data storage and manipulation, and rivaling general-purpose programming languages for computation. SPREAD is much more modest.

The spreadsheet specification for SPREAD is prepared with one of the editors. The cells in this specification are addressed A to E, and the rows are addressed 1 to 99. Thus, the cell in the upper left-hand corner is referenced as A1, and the cell in the lower right-hand corner of a 24 line CRT screen is referenced as E24. The columns are fixed-format, each allowing for use of, at most, 16 characters.

The DSS designer can place headings, formulas, or constants in any of the cells. Constants can be with or without decimal points. Headings may include any characters that are printable on your computer. Headings may extend across the 16 character cell boundaries. Formulas must be placed within brackets, ({ }). If brackets are not placed around formulas, the computation references will appear on your spreadsheet as headings. Cells also can include user prompts. User prompts must be surrounded by question marks (?). Prompts are displayed when a cell is calculated, allowing users to enter correct values.

Formulas can include constants (such as 1.23 or 37), legal cell references (such as A1 or C5), and arithmetic operators (such as + for addition, − for subtraction, * for multiplication, and / for division). Formulas cannot use parentheses to establish the order of computation. All formulas are calculated from left to right, regardless of the arithmetic operators involved. If a formula consists of more than 16 character positions (the maximum allowed in a cell), the master formula can be broken down into auxiliary formulas. Auxiliary formulas perform a specific part of the calculation. Auxiliary formulas can be placed in other cells. Cell addresses of auxiliary formulas are placed within square brackets ([ ]) in master formulas. During computation, auxiliary formulas are called and calculated, and the result is passed to the master formula. Any characters other than valid cell references, the arithmetic operators, constants, parentheses, or the square brackets are ignored during computation.

Computational references to noncomputational cells are regarded as references to constants. Nonnumeric characters are disregarded in the evaluation of constants. Thus, a reference to a heading in a computational cell can result in a reference to the value zero.

The evaluation of the spreadsheet is done by columns, left to right. Within the column, evaluation proceeds top to bottom.

Note that you can manipulate spreadsheet specifications with the DBMS operators (and DBMS files with the SPREAD operator).

Example: A 1 PROGRAM SPREAD ''TMPLAT''

OPERATION SUMMARY:
Descriptive Models and Graphic Displays

Descriptive models and graphic displays are implemented as individual programs accessible from the PROGRAM operator of MENU. The discussion that follows lists and explains the control parameters that must be coded to use the programs. Remember that the control parameter list must be surrounded by double quotes ('') and the individual control parameters separated by commas (,) when the list is supplied as an operand to the PROGRAM operator. The commands and parameters are:

INCO data table name
The INCO command generates an income statement. The ''data table name'' parameter instructs the system which data table to use in developing the income statement. Note that the input data table must consist of three columns: account type (EX for expense or IN for income), amount, and account description.

Example: PROGRAM INCO ''TABLEA''

BALA data table name

The BALA command causes output of a balance sheet. The "data table name" parameter instructs the system which data table to use in building the balance sheet. Note that the data table must consist of three columns: account type (AC for current assets, AL for long-term assets, LC for current liabilities, LL for long-term liabilities, and EQ for equity), amount, and account description.

Example: PROGRAM BALA "TABLEB"

PIE data table name, x-coordinate data item name or index, y-coordinate data item name or index

The PIE command generates a pie chart from two columns in a data table. The "data table name" parameter tells the system which data table to input. The "x-coordinate" and "y-coordinate" parameters name the columns of data that will be used to generate the graphic display.

Example: B 2 PROGRAM PIE "A,1,2"

HISTO data table name, x-coordinate data item name or index, y-coordinate data item name or index

The HISTO command generates a histogram, or bar chart, from two columns in a data table. The HISTO command functions like the PIE command. The "data table name" parameter tells the system which data table to input. The "x-coordinate" and "y-coordinate" parameters name the columns of data that will be used to generate the graphic display.

Example: A 1 PROGRAM HISTO "TABLEX,X,Y"

BANDW data table name, data item name or index

The BANDW command generates a box-and-whisker diagram from one column, or field, in a data table. The "data table name" parameter tells the system which data table to input. The "data item name or index" parameter instructs the system which field to use in generating the graphic display.

Example: B 2 PROGRAM BANDW "DATA,3"

RLINE data table name, x-coordinate data item name or index, y-coordinate data item name or index
The RLINE command produces a resistant line diagram from two fields in a data table. The "data table name" parameter tells the system which table to input. The "x-coordinate" and "y-coordinate" parameters define the fields to be used in generating the graphic display.

Example: A 3 PROGRAM RLINE "DATA,2,3"

SGRAM data table name, x-coordinate data item name or index, y-coordinate data item name or index
The SGRAM command produces a scattergram from two columns of data in a data table. The "data table name" parameter tells the system which table to input. The "x-coordinate" and "y-coordinate" parameters name the columns of data to be used in generating the graphic display.

Example: A 5 PROGRAM SGRAM "DATA,1,2"

MTRACE data table name, x-coordinate data item name or index, y-coordinate data item name or index
The MTRACE command generates a median trace diagram from two columns of data in a data table. The "data table name" parameter tells the system which table to input. The "x-coordinate" and "y-coordinate" parameters name the columns of data to be used to produce the graphic display.

Example: B 6 PROGRAM MTRACE "DATA,1,2"

SPREAD template file name
The SPREAD command generates a spreadsheet. The "template file name" parameter tells the system which file contains the template to be used in generating the spreadsheet. Note that the template file contains all data and formulas to be used in generating the spreadsheet.

Example: B 3 PROGRAM SPREAD "TEMP1"

OPERATION SUMMARY: ES Expert System Operator

The ES Expert System Operator adds fundamental expert system facilities of the IF . . . THEN rule type to the DSS tool kit. The ES Expert System Operator is invoked with the MENU program command. The only control parameter passed to ES is the name of a rule specification file.

The rule specification file is created with one of the editors. The rule specification file has one row for each rule. Each row, or rule, contains three fields. Fields are separated by at least one blank space.

The first field is the rule number. The second field is the IF part of the rule. The IF part may be a question to the user, which is surrounded with double quote characters (''). Or the IF part may consist of one or more references to THEN rule part names. Questions to the user must be phrased so that they begin with ''IS'' and are answerable with a ''YES'' or a ''NO''. The references to the THEN rule part names can be surrounded in square brackets to denote negation. If multiple THEN rule part names are referenced in the IF part of one rule, they must be separated by semicolons (;). Multiple THEN rule references are regarded as containing a logical AND connector.

Finally, the third field of each rule, or the ''THEN rule part,'' contains the name to be applied to a positive condition for the rule. Some of the THEN rule part names must be followed by ''(GOAL)'' to denote that they represent terminal, or goal, states. Unlike the second field, the THEN rule part reference in the third field may not be surrounded by square brackets for negation. Only one reference may be in this third field.

Example: A 1 PROGRAM ES ''ES1''

OPERATION SUMMARY: The DRIVER Program

The tool kit program can be invoked directly, without building a menu, through use of the DRIVER program. The DRIVER program is invoked by keying ''DRIVER'' at the A> prompt. Once invoked, the program prompts the user for the required control information.

APPENDIX C

INTRODUCTION

This appendix lists the program code for the DSS Tool Kit. The code is written in the new ANSI STANDARD BASIC and follows the chapter-by-chapter development of program concepts and applications:

- The DTREE Program
- The DSSDTREE Library
- The LED Program
- The DSSLED Library
- The SED Program
- The DSSSED Library
- The MMENU Program
- The DSSMENU Library
- The DSSDBMS Library
- The DSSGRAPH Library
- The DSSSPREA Library
- The DSSES Library
- The DSSSUBS Library
- The DRIVER Program.

The following pages show the DSS Tool Kit control structure.

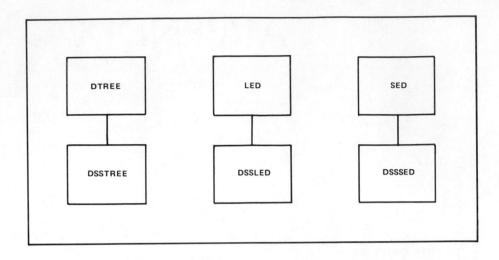

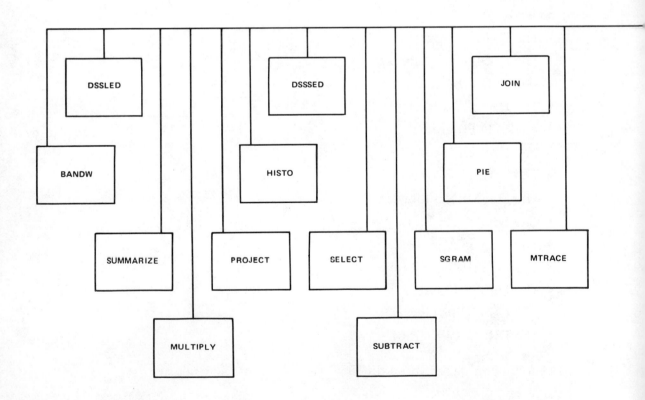

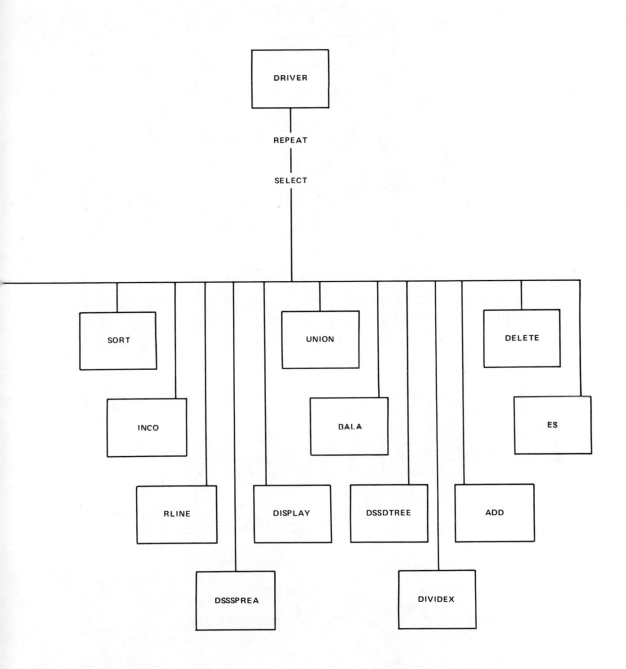

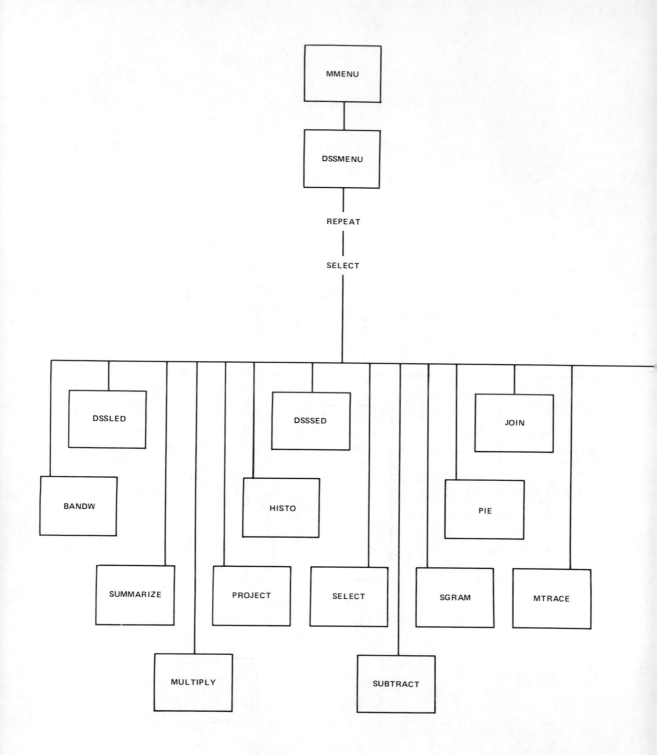

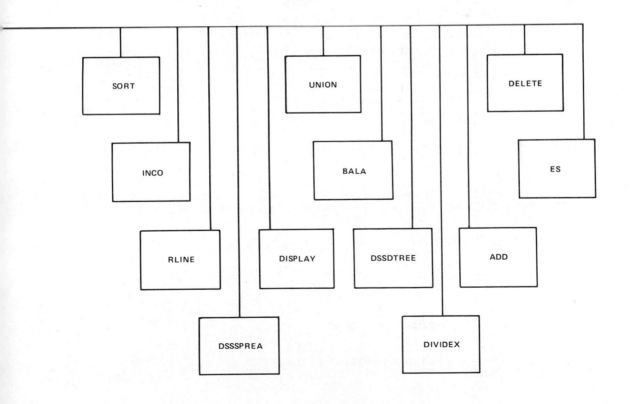

```
!!!!!!!!!!!!!!!!!!!!!!!!!!!!!!!!!!!!!!!!!!!!!!!!!!!!!!!!!!!!!!!!!!!!!!!!!!!!!!!!!!!
!                                                                               !
!  THE FOLLOWING CODE IS SUPPLIED SO THAT YOU MAY EXAMINE THE ALGORITHMS        !
!  AND PROGRAM DESIGNS EMPLOYED IN THE DSS TOOL KIT.                            !
!                                                                               !
!  THIS CODE IS WRITTEN IN THE NEW ANSI STANDARD BASIC.                         !
!                                                                               !
!  FOR A MACHINE-READABLE VERSION OF THIS CODE AND/OR AN EXECUTABLE VERSION,    !
!  CONTACT THE AUTHOR AT THE BELOW ADDRESS:                                     !
!                                                                               !
!                                                                               !
!                         WILLIAM LEIGH                                         !
!                         DEPARTMENT OF COMPUTER SCIENCE AND STATISTICS         !
!                         UNIVERSITY OF SOUTHERN MISSISSIPPI                    !
!                         SOUTHERN STATION BOX 5106                             !
!                         HATTIESBURG, MISSISSIPPI 39406                        !
!                                                                               !
!                                                                               !
!!!!!!!!!!!!!!!!!!!!!!!!!!!!!!!!!!!!!!!!!!!!!!!!!!!!!!!!!!!!!!!!!!!!!!!!!!!!!!!!!!!
```

THE DTREE PROGRAM

This program provides a direct interface to the decision-tree computation module.

```
!!!!!!!!!!!!!!!!!!!!!!!!!!!!!!!!!!!!!!!!!!!!!!!!!!!!!!!!!!!!!!!!!!!!!!!!!!!!!!!!!!!
!                                                                               !
!  THIS IS MAIN PROGRAM DTREE                                                   !
!                                                                               !
!  THIS IS A STANDALONE DRIVER PROGRAM FOR THE DECISION TREE PROGRAM            !
!      WHICH IS DSSDTREE                                                        !
!  SEE CHAPTER 2 FOR EXPLANATION OF THIS FUNCTION                               !
!                                                                               !
!!!!!!!!!!!!!!!!!!!!!!!!!!!!!!!!!!!!!!!!!!!!!!!!!!!!!!!!!!!!!!!!!!!!!!!!!!!!!!!!!!!

REM DTREE.TRU

REM THIS IS THE STANDALONE DRIVER PROGRAM FOR THE DSSTREE SUBROUTINE
REM    THIS PROGRAM IS USED TO INVOKE DSSDTREE OUTSIDE OF THE
REM        DSS TOOL KIT MENU FRAMEWORK

LIBRARY "DSSDTREE.TRU","DSSSUBS.TRU"

LET MAXLINES=40
LET LINELENGTH=80
LET LL=LINELENGTH

CLEAR
PRINT "        DTREE DRIVER PROGRAM"
PRINT

PRINT "HOW MANY ALTERNATIVES ARE TO BE CONSIDERED";
INPUT NUMALT
```

```
LET OUT$=STR$(NUMALT)&" "

FOR I=1 TO NUMALT

    PRINT

    PRINT "ALTERNATIVE # ";I
    PRINT "WHAT IS THE NAME OF THIS ALTERNATIVE ";
    INPUT ALTNAME$
    LET OUT$=OUT$&CHR$(34)&ALTNAME$&CHR$(34)&REPEAT$(" ",LL-LEN(ALTNAME$)-2)

    PRINT "HOW MANY CHANCE OUTCOMES ARE TO BE DEFINED ";
    INPUT ALTNUMCHANCE
    IF ALTNUMCHANCE>20 THEN LET ALTNUMCHANCE=20
    IF ALTNUMCHANCE<1 THEN LET ALTNUMCHANCE=1
    LET A$=STR$(ALTNUMCHANCE)
    LET OUT$=OUT$&A$&REPEAT$(" ",LL-LEN(A$))

    FOR J=1 TO ALTNUMCHANCE

        PRINT
        PRINT "ALTERNATIVE # ";I;"  CHANCE OUTCOME # ";J
        PRINT "WHAT IS THE NAME OF THIS CHANCE OUTCOME (20 CHARS OR LESS) "
        INPUT CHANCENAME$
        LET CHANCENAME$=CHR$(34)&CHANCENAME$&CHR$(34)
        LET CHANCENAME$=CHANCENAME$&REPEAT$(" ",20)
        LET CHANCENAME$=CHANCENAME$[1:20]
        LET C$=CHANCENAME$
        LET OUT$=OUT$&C$&REPEAT$(" ",LL-LEN(C$))

        PRINT "WHAT IS THE PROBABILITY OF THIS CHANCE OUTCOME (.1 TO 1.0) ";
        INPUT PROB
        IF PROB<.1 THEN LET PROB=.1
        IF PROB>1 THEN LET PROB=1
        LET P$=STR$(PROB)
        LET OUT$=OUT$&P$&REPEAT$(" ",LL-LEN(P$))

    PRINT "WHAT IS THE OUTCOME VALUE FOR THIS CHANCE OUTCOME (-9999 TO 9999)
";
        INPUT OUTC
        IF OUTC<-9999 THEN LET OUTC=-9999
        IF OUTC>9999 THEN LET OUTC=9999
        LET O$=STR$(OUTC)
        LET OUT$=OUT$&O$&REPEAT$(" ",LL-LEN(O$))

    NEXT J
NEXT I

LET OUT$=OUT$&REPEAT$(" ",MAXLINES*LINELENGTH)
LET OUT$=OUT$(1:MAXLINES*LINELENGTH)

CALL WRITELINES (OUT$,"DTREEX",MAXLINES,LINELENGTH)

CALL DSSDTREE("","DTREEX",MAXLINES,LINELENGTH)

END
```

THE DSSDTREE LIBRARY

This library contains the subroutine that computes decision trees.

```
!!!!!!!!!!!!!!!!!!!!!!!!!!!!!!!!!!!!!!!!!!!!!!!!!!!!!!!!!!!!!!!!!!!!!!!!!!!!!!!!
!                                                                            !
!  THIS IS THE EXTERNAL LIBRARY DSSDTREE                                     !
!                                                                            !
!      THIS CONTAINS THE DSSDTREE SUBROUTINE                                 !
!  SEE CHAPTER 2 FOR EXPLANATION OF THIS FUNCTION                            !
!                                                                            !
!!!!!!!!!!!!!!!!!!!!!!!!!!!!!!!!!!!!!!!!!!!!!!!!!!!!!!!!!!!!!!!!!!!!!!!!!!!!!!!!

EXTERNAL

REM   DSSDTREE
REM    DSS TOOL KIT DECISION TREE PROGRAM
REM  THIS PROGRAM IS A SUBROUTINE WHICH MAY BE INVOKED BY:
REM   A.  THE DSS MENU PROGRAM
REM   B.  AN INDEPENDENT DRIVER PROGRAM NAMED DTREE
REM   C.  THE DRIVER PROGRAM
```

The DSSDTREE Subroutine

This subroutine computes decision trees.

```
SUB DSSDTREE(SCHEMA$,FILENAME$,MAXLINES,LINELENGTH)

    CALL READLINES(LINE$,FILENAME$,MAXLINES,LINELENGTH)
    PRINT LINE$[1:800]

    LET LP=0
    LET LL=LINELENGTH
    DIM ALTNAME$(20)
    DIM ALTNUMCHANCE(20)
    DIM EVALUE(20)
    DIM CHANCENAME$(20,20)
    DIM CHANCEPROB(20,20)
    DIM CHANCEOUTCOME(20,20)

    CLEAR
    PRINT "        DTREE CALCULATION PROGRAM"
    PRINT

    WHEN ERROR IN

        CALL GETTOKEN(LINE$,LP,TOKEN$)
        CALL PROMPT(TOKEN$)
        LET NUMALT=VAL(TOKEN$)

        FOR I=1 TO NUMALT
```

```
        PRINT

        PRINT "ALTERNATIVE # ";I
        PRINT "WHAT IS THE NAME OF THIS ALTERNATIVE ";
        CALL GETTOKEN(LINE$,LP,TOKEN$)
        CALL PROMPT(TOKEN$)
        PRINT TOKEN$

        LET  ALTNAME$(I) =TOKEN$

        PRINT "HOW MANY CHANCE OUTCOMES ARE TO BE DEFINED ";

      CALL GETTOKEN(LINE$,LP,TOKEN$)
      CALL PROMPT(TOKEN$)
      PRINT TOKEN$

      LET ALTNUMCHANCE(I)=VAL(TOKEN$)
      IF ALTNUMCHANCE(I)>20 THEN LET ALTNUMCHANCE(I)=20
      IF ALTNUMCHANCE(I)<1 THEN LET ALTNUMCHANCE(I)=1

      FOR J=1 TO ALTNUMCHANCE(I)

          PRINT "ALTERNATIVE # ";I;"  CHANCE OUTCOME # ";J
      PRINT "WHAT IS THE NAME OF THIS CHANCE OUTCOME (20 CHARS OR LESS) "
          CALL GETTOKEN(LINE$,LP,TOKEN$)
          CALL PROMPT(TOKEN$)
          PRINT TOKEN$

          LET CHANCENAME$(I,J)=TOKEN$
          LET CHANCENAME$(I,J)=CHANCENAME$(I,J)&REPEAT$(" ",20)
          LET CHANCENAME$(I,J)=CHANCENAME$(I,J)[1:20]

      PRINT "WHAT IS THE PROBABILITY OF THIS CHANCE OUTCOME (.1 TO 1.0) ";
          CALL GETTOKEN(LINE$,LP,TOKEN$)
          CALL PROMPT(TOKEN$)
          PRINT TOKEN$

          LET PROB =VAL(TOKEN$)
          IF PROB<.1 THEN LET PROB=.1
          IF PROB>1 THEN LET PROB=1
          LET CHANCEPROB(I,J)=PROB

PRINT "WHAT IS THE OUTCOME VALUE FOR THIS CHANCE OUTCOME (-9999 TO 9999) ";
          CALL GETTOKEN(LINE$,LP,TOKEN$)
          CALL PROMPT(TOKEN$)
          PRINT TOKEN$
          LET OUTC  =VAL(TOKEN$)
          IF OUTC<-9999 THEN LET OUTC=-9999
          IF OUTC>9999 THEN LET OUTC=9999
          LET CHANCEOUTCOME(I,J)=OUTC

      NEXT J
   NEXT I

   PAUSE 5
```

```
REM NOW CALCULATE AND PRINT ANALYSIS
CLEAR

FOR I=1 TO NUMALT
    LET EVALUE(I)=0
    FOR J=1 TO ALTNUMCHANCE(I)
        LET EVALUE(I)=EVALUE(I)+CHANCEPROB(I,J)*CHANCEOUTCOME(I,J)
    NEXT J
PRINT "EXPECTED OUTCOME FOR ALTERNATIVE ";I;" ";ALTNAME$(I);" ";EVALUE(I)
    NEXT I

USE

    PRINT "ERROR READING THE DTREE FILE"

END WHEN

PRINT "PRESS ANY KEY TO CONTINUE "
GET KEY N

END SUB
```

THE LED PROGRAM

This program provides a direct interface to the line-oriented text editor.

```
!!!!!!!!!!!!!!!!!!!!!!!!!!!!!!!!!!!!!!!!!!!!!!!!!!!!!!!!!!!!!!!!!!!!!!!!!!!!!!!!!!!!!
!                                                                                !
!   THIS IS MAIN PROGRAM LED                                                     !
!                                                                                !
!   THIS IS A STANDALONE DRIVER PROGRAM FOR THE LINE EDITOR -- LED               !
!                                                                                !
!   SEE CHAPTER 3 FOR EXPLANATION OF THIS FUNCTION                               !
!                                                                                !
!!!!!!!!!!!!!!!!!!!!!!!!!!!!!!!!!!!!!!!!!!!!!!!!!!!!!!!!!!!!!!!!!!!!!!!!!!!!!!!!!!!!!

REM LED.TRU

REM THIS IS THE STANDALONE DRIVER PROGRAM FOR THE LED SUBROUTINE
REM    THIS PROGRAM IS USED TO INVOKE SED OUTSIDE OF THE
REM       DSS TOOL KIT MENU FRAMEWORK

LIBRARY "DSSLED.TRU","DSSSUBS.TRU"

LET MAXLINES=40
LET LINELENGTH=80

CLEAR
PRINT "        LED DRIVER PROGRAM"
PRINT
```

```
INPUT PROMPT "ENTER THE FILE YOU WANT TO WORK WITH) ":FILENAME$

CALL DSSLED("",FILENAME$,MAXLINES,LINELENGTH)

END
```

THE DSSLED LIBRARY

This library contains the subroutines that implement the line-oriented text editor.

```
!!!!!!!!!!!!!!!!!!!!!!!!!!!!!!!!!!!!!!!!!!!!!!!!!!!!!!!!!!!!!!!!!!!!!!!!!!!!!!!!!!
!                                                                              !
!    THIS IS EXTERNAL LIBRARY DSSLED.TRU                                       !
!                                                                              !
!    THIS LIBRARY CONTAINS THE DSSLED SUBROUTINES                              !
!    DSSLED IMPLEMENTS THE TOOL KIT LINE EDITOR FUNCTION.                      !
!                                                                              !
!    SEE CHAPTER 3 FOR EXPLANATION OF THIS FUNCTION                            !
!                                                                              !
!!!!!!!!!!!!!!!!!!!!!!!!!!!!!!!!!!!!!!!!!!!!!!!!!!!!!!!!!!!!!!!!!!!!!!!!!!!!!!!!!!

EXTERNAL
```

The DSSLED Subroutine

This subroutine implements a rudimentary, line editing function.

```
SUB DSSLED (XX$,FILENAME$,MAXLINES,LINELENGTH)

    REM DSSLED
    REM      DSS LINE EDITOR
    REM THIS PROGRAM IS A SUBROUTINE WHICH MAY BE INVOKED BY:
    REM    A.  THE DSS MENU PROGRAM
    REM    B.  AN INDEPENDENT DRIVER PROGRAM NAMED LED
    REM    C.  THE DRIVER PROGRAM

    PRINT "(LED -- DSS TOOLKIT LINE EDITOR)  ENTER H FOR HELP"

    SET CURSOR "ON"

    IF FILENAME$<>"" THEN
        CALL READLINES(LINE$,FILENAME$,MAXLINES,LINELENGTH)
        PRINT FILENAME$," IS SUCCESSFULLY READ IN OR CREATED"

    ELSE
        LET LINE$=REPEAT$(" ",MAXLINES*LINELENGTH)
    END IF
```

```
      LET A$=""

DO WHILE ((A$()"S" OR B$()""))
      LINE INPUT PROMPT "?":O$
      LET POSITION=1
      CALL GETTOKEN(O$,POSITION,TOKEN$)
      LET A$=UCASE$(TOKEN$)
      LET B$=""
      LET C$=""

      SELECT CASE A$

      CASE "GET","G"
            CALL GETTOKEN(O$,POSITION,TOKEN$)
            LET FILENAME$=TOKEN$
            CALL READLINES(LINE$,FILENAME$,MAXLINES,LINELENGTH)

      CASE "SAVE","S"
            CALL GETTOKEN(O$,POSITION,TOKEN$)
            LET B$=TOKEN$
            IF B$()"" THEN
                  LET FILENAME$=B$
            END IF
            CALL WRITELINES(LINE$,FILENAME$,MAXLINES,LINELENGTH)
            LET A$="S"

      CASE "DELETE","D"
            CALL GETTOKEN(O$,POSITION,TOKEN$)
            WHEN ERROR IN
                  LET J=INT(VAL(TOKEN$))
                  IF J=1 THEN
                     LET L=LINELENGTH
                     LET LINE$=LINE$[L+1:MAXLINES] & REPEAT$(" ",L)
                  END IF
                  IF J=MAXLINES THEN
                     LET L=LINELENGTH
                     LET M=MAXLINES
                     LET LINE$=LINE$[1:L*(M-1)] & REPEAT$(" ",L)
                  END IF
                  IF J>=2 AND J<=MAXLINES-1 THEN
                     LET L=LINELENGTH
                     LET M=MAXLINES
                     LET LINE$=LINE$[1:(J-1)*L] & LINE$[(J*L)+1:M*L]
                     LET LINE$=LINE$ & REPEAT$(" ",L)
                  END IF
                  IF J>MAXLINES THEN
                     PRINT "INVALID LINE NUMBER"
                  END IF
            USE
                  PRINT "INVALID LINE NUMBER"
            END WHEN

      CASE "HELP","H"
            PRINT "   AVAILABLE COMMANDS ARE:"
            PRINT "      GET FILENAME"
            PRINT "      SAVE FILENAME"
            PRINT "      DELETE LINE#"
```

```
            PRINT "      INSERT LINE#"
            PRINT "      REPLACE LINE#"
            PRINT "      NEW FILENAME"
            PRINT "      LIST LINE# OR LIST LINE# LINE#"
            PRINT "ENTER SAVE OR S WITH NO FILENAME TO SAVE AND END"
            PRINT

      CASE "INSERT","I"
            CALL GETTOKEN(O$,POSITION,TOKEN$)

            WHEN ERROR IN

                  LET B=ROUND(VAL(TOKEN$))

                  IF B>=1 AND B<=MAXLINES THEN
                     LINE INPUT PROMPT "":L$
                     LET L$=L$ & REPEAT$(" ",LINELENGTH)
                     LET L$=L$[1:LINELENGTH]
                  END IF

                  IF B=1 THEN
                     LET LINE$=L$ & LINE$
                     LET LINE$=LINE$[1:MAXLINES*LINELENGTH]
                  END IF

                        IF B=MAXLINES THEN
                  LET LINE$=LINE$[1:(MAXLINES-1)*LINELENGTH] & L$
                  END IF

                  IF B>1 AND B<MAXLINES THEN
                     LET D=(MAXLINES-1)*LINELENGTH
                     LET M$=LINE$
                     LET L=LINELENGTH
                     LET LINE$=M$[1:(B)*L]&L$&M$[(B)*L+1:D]
                  END IF
            USE
                  PRINT "INVALID LINE NUMBER"
            END WHEN


      CASE "REPLACE","R"
            CALL GETTOKEN(O$,POSITION,TOKEN$)

            WHEN ERROR IN
                  LET B=INT(VAL(TOKEN$))

                  IF B>=1 AND B<=MAXLINES THEN
                     LINE INPUT PROMPT "":L$
                     LET L$=L$ & REPEAT$(" ",LINELENGTH)
                     LET L$=L$[1:LINELENGTH]
                  END IF

                  IF B=1 THEN
                     LET L=LINELENGTH
                     LET LINE$=L$ & LINE$[L+1:MAXLINES*L]
                  END IF
```

```
        IF B=MAXLINES THEN
           LET LINE$=LINE$[1:(MAXLINES-1)*LINELENGTH] & L$
        END IF

           IF B>1 AND B<MAXLINES THEN
              LET D=(MAXLINES-1)*LINELENGTH
              LET L=LINELENGTH
              LET LINE$=LINE$[1:(B-1)*L]&L$&LINE$[B*L+1:D]

           END IF
        USE
           PRINT "INVALID LINE NUMBER"
        END WHEN


     CASE "NEW","N"
        CALL GETTOKEN(O$,POSITION,TOKEN$)
        LET LINE$=REPEAT$(" ",MAXLINES*LINELENGTH)
        IF TOKEN$<>"" THEN
           LET FILENAME$=TOKEN$

        END IF
        LET LINE$=REPEAT$(" ",MAXLINES*LINELENGTH)
        CALL WRITELINES (LINE$,FILENAME$,MAXLINES,LINELENGTH)


     CASE "LIST","L"
        CALL GETTOKEN (O$,POSITION,B$)
        CALL GETTOKEN (O$,POSITION,C$)
        WHEN ERROR IN

           IF LEN(B$)=0 THEN
              LET B$="1"
           END IF

           LET B=INT(VAL(B$))

           IF LEN(C$)=0 THEN
              LET C$="0"
           END IF

           LET C=INT(VAL(C$))

           IF C>MAXLINES THEN
              LET C=MAXLINES
           END IF

           IF C=0 THEN
              LET C=B
           END IF

           IF B>0 AND B<=MAXLINES THEN
              FOR J=B TO C
                    PRINT J;":";
                 LET L=LINELENGTH
```

```
                    PRINT LINE$[(J-1)*L+1:(J-1)*L+L]
               NEXT J
          END IF
      USE
          PRINT "INVALID LINE NUMBER"
      END WHEN

   CASE ELSE
       PRINT "NOT A VALID COMMAND"
       PRINT " TRY GET,SAVE,DELETE,INSERT,REPLACE,HELP,"
       PRINT "  NEW, OR LIST--USE SAVE TO SAVE FILE AND EXIT"
       PRINT

   END SELECT

 LOOP

END SUB
```

THE SED PROGRAM

This program provides a direct interface to the screen-oriented text editor.

```
!!!!!!!!!!!!!!!!!!!!!!!!!!!!!!!!!!!!!!!!!!!!!!!!!!!!!!!!!!!!!!!!!!!!!!!!!!!!!!!!!
!                                                                             !
!   THIS IS MAIN PROGRAM SED                                                  !
!                                                                             !
!   THIS IS A STANDALONE DRIVER PROGRAM FOR THE SCREEN EDITOR -- SED          !
!                                                                             !
!   SEE CHAPTER 3 FOR EXPLANATION OF THIS FUNCTION                            !
!                                                                             !
!!!!!!!!!!!!!!!!!!!!!!!!!!!!!!!!!!!!!!!!!!!!!!!!!!!!!!!!!!!!!!!!!!!!!!!!!!!!!!!!!

REM SED.TRU

REM THIS IS THE STANDALONE DRIVER PROGRAM FOR THE SED SUBROUTINE
REM    THIS PROGRAM IS USED TO INVOKE SED OUTSIDE OF THE
REM        DSS TOOL KIT MENU FRAMEWORK

LIBRARY "DSSSED.TRU","DSSSUBS.TRU"

LET MAXLINES=40
LET LINELENGTH=80

CLEAR
PRINT "        SED DRIVER PROGRAM"
PRINT
INPUT PROMPT "ENTER THE FILE YOU WANT TO WORK WITH> ":FILENAME$

CALL DSSSED("",FILENAME$,MAXLINES,LINELENGTH)

END
```

THE DSSSED LIBRARY

This library contains the subroutines that implement the screen-
oriented text editor.

```
!!!!!!!!!!!!!!!!!!!!!!!!!!!!!!!!!!!!!!!!!!!!!!!!!!!!!!!!!!!!!!!!!!!!!!!!!!!!!!!!!!
!                                                                              !
!  THIS IS EXTERNAL LIBRARY DSSSED.TRU                                         !
!                                                                              !
!  THIS LIBRARY CONTAINS THE DSSSED SUBROUTINES                                !
!  DSSLED IMPLEMENTS THE TOOL KIT SCREEN-ORIENTED EDITOR FUNCTION.             !
!                                                                              !
!  SEE CHAPTER 3 FOR EXPLANATION OF THIS FUNCTION                              !
!                                                                              !
!!!!!!!!!!!!!!!!!!!!!!!!!!!!!!!!!!!!!!!!!!!!!!!!!!!!!!!!!!!!!!!!!!!!!!!!!!!!!!!!!!

REM DSSSED.TRU

EXTERNAL
```

The DSSSED Subroutine

This subroutine implements a rudimentary, screen editing function.

```
SUB DSSSED (XX$,FILENAME$,MAXLINES,LINELENGTH)

REM DSSSED   TOOL KIT SCREEN EDITOR
REM THIS PROGRAM IS A SUBROUTINE WHICH MAY BE INVOKED BY:
REM  A.   THE MENU PROGRAM
REM  B.   AN INDEPENDENT DRIVER PROGRAM NAMED SED
REM  C.   THE DRIVER PROGRAM

REM FOR THIS PROGRAM (XX$)SCHEMA$ IS UNUSED.

SUB HELP

    CLEAR
    PRINT
    PRINT
    PRINT "  (SED -- DSS TOOL KIT SCREEN EDITOR)"
    PRINT
    PRINT "         H E L P   S C R E E N"
    PRINT
    PRINT "VALID COMMANDS ARE:"
    PRINT "  (ESC) TO END"
    PRINT "  (CTRL)S TO SAVE FILE"
    PRINT "  (CTRL)D OR PGDN TO SHOW NEXT SCREEN"
    PRINT "  (CTRL)U OR PGUP TO SHOW PREVIOUS SCREEN"
    PRINT "  (CTRL)H TO DISPLAY HELP SCREEN"
    PRINT "  (CTRL)N TO CREATE AND FILL NEW FILE WITH BLANKS"
```

```
    PRINT "  <CTRL>G TO GET A FILE"
    PRINT "  <CTRL>X OR DEL TO DELETE A CHARACTER"
    PRINT "  <CTRL>I OR INS TO TOGGLE INSERT MODE"
    PRINT "  <CTRL>+ TO INSERT A NEW BLANK LINE BEFORE THE CURRENT LINE"
    PRINT
    PRINT "PRESS ANY KEY TO CONTINUE..."
    GET KEY A
    CALL DISPLAYSCREEN

END SUB

SUB DISPLAYSCREEN
    CLEAR

    IF (CURSCREEN<1) THEN
        LET CURSCREEN=1
        LET CURROW=1
    END IF

    DO WHILE(CURSCREEN*20>MAXLINES)
        LET CURSCREEN=CURSCREEN-1
        LET CURROW=20
    LOOP

    FOR I=1 TO 20
        SET CURSOR I,1
        LET J=((CURSCREEN-1)*20)*LINELENGTH+1+(I-1)*LINELENGTH
        PRINT LINE$[J:J+LINELENGTH-1];
    NEXT I
    CALL STATUS

END SUB

SUB STATUS
    SET CURSOR 21,1
    PRINT REPEAT$("
",80);
    PRINT "FILE:";FILENAME$;"        INSERT IS: ";INSMODE$;
    PRINT "     SCREEN:";CURSCREEN;
    PRINT "     <CTRL>H FOR HELP"
    SET CURSOR CURROW,CURCOL
END SUB

SUB CHECKCURSOR

    IF CURCOL<1 THEN
        LET CURCOL=LINELENGTH
        LET CURROW=CURROW-1
    END IF

    IF CURCOL>LINELENGTH THEN
        LET CURCOL=1
        LET CURROW=CURROW+1
    END IF

    IF CURROW>20 THEN
        LET CURROW=1
```

```
                LET CURSCREEN=CURSCREEN+1
                CALL DISPLAYSCREEN
            END IF

            IF CURROW<1 THEN
                LET CURROW=20
                LET CURSCREEN=CURSCREEN-1
                CALL DISPLAYSCREEN
            END IF

    END SUB

    CLEAR

    IF FILENAME$()"" THEN
        CALL READLINES(LINE$,FILENAME$,MAXLINES,LINELENGTH)
        PRINT FILENAME$," IS SUCCESSFULLY READ IN OR CREATED"
        PAUSE 5
        LET LINE$=LINE$&REPEAT$(" ",MAXLINES*LINELENGTH)
        LET LINE$=LINE$(1:MAXLINES*LINELENGTH)
    ELSE
        LET LINE$=REPEAT$(" ",MAXLINES*LINELENGTH)
    END IF

    LET INSMODE$="OFF"
    LET CURROW=1
    LET CURCOL=1
    LET CURSCREEN=1
    LET QUIT=0

    CALL HELP

    DO WHILE (QUIT<> 1)

        GET KEY A
        SELECT CASE A

        CASE 32 TO 126

            PRINT CHR$(A);
            LET F=(CURSCREEN-1)*20*LINELENGTH+(CURROW-1)*LINELENGTH
            LET F=F+CURCOL
            IF INSMODE$="ON " THEN
                LET C=(CURROW-1)*LINELENGTH
                LET D=C+LINELENGTH
                LET LINE$[C:D]=LINE$[C:F-1]&CHR$(A)&LINE$[F:D-1]
                SET CURSOR CURROW,1
                PRINT LINE$[C+1:D];
                SET CURSOR CURROW,CURCOL
            ELSE
                LET LINE$[F:F]=CHR$(A)
            END IF
            LET CURCOL=CURCOL+1

        CASE 27                          !ESCAPE -- END IT
            LET QUIT=1
```

```
    CASE 9,338                    !CTRL I OR INS -- TOGGLE INSERT MODE
        IF INSMODE$="OFF" THEN
            LET INSMODE$="ON "
        ELSE
            LET INSMODE$="OFF"
        END IF
        CALL STATUS

    CASE 13                       !CARRIAGE RETURN
        LET CURROW=CURROW+1
        LET CURCOL=1

    CASE 24,339                   !CTRL X OR DELETE  -- DELETE CHARACTER
        LET C=(CURROW-1)*LINELENGTH
        LET D=C+LINELENGTH
        LET F=(CURSCREEN-1)*20*LINELENGTH+(CURROW-1)*LINELENGTH
        LET F=F+CURCOL
        LET LINE$[C:D]=LINE$[C:F-1]&LINE$[F+1:D]&" "
        SET CURSOR CURROW,1
        PRINT LINE$[C+1:D];
        SET CURSOR CURROW,CURCOL

    CASE 21,329                   !CTRL U OR PAGE UP
        LET CURSCREEN=CURSCREEN-1
        CALL DISPLAYSCREEN

    CASE 4,337                    !CTRL D OR PAGE DOWN
        LET CURSCREEN=CURSCREEN+1
        CALL DISPLAYSCREEN

    CASE 19                       !CTRL S -- SAVE FILE
        SET CURSOR 23,1
        INPUT PROMPT "SAVE -- ENTER FILE NAME > ": F$
        CALL WRITELINES(LINE$,FILENAME$,MAXLINES,LINELENGTH)
        CALL DISPLAYSCREEN

    CASE 8                        !CTRL H -- HELP
        CALL HELP

    CASE 7                        !CTRL G -- GET FILE
        SET CURSOR 23,1
        INPUT PROMPT "GET -- ENTER FILE NAME > ": FILENAME$
        CALL READLINES(LINE$,FILENAME$,MAXLINES,LINELENGTH)
        LET CURSCREEN=1
        LET CURROW=1
        LET CURCOL=1
        CALL DISPLAYSCREEN

    CASE 14                       !CTRL N -- BLANK AREA FOR NEW FILE
        SET CURSOR 23,1
        INPUT PROMPT "NEW -- ENTER FILE NAME > ": F$
        LET LINE$=REPEAT$(" ",MAXLINES*LINELENGTH)
        CALL WRITELINES (LINE$,FILENAME$,MAXLINES,LINELENGTH)
        LET CURSCREEN=1
        LET CURROW=1
        LET CURCOL=1
        CALL DISPLAYSCREEN
```

```
        CASE 328                        !UP CURSOR ARROW
            LET CURROW=CURROW-1

        CASE 336                        !DOWN CURSOR ARROW
            LET CURROW=CURROW+1

        CASE 333                        !RIGHT CURSOR ARROW
            LET CURCOL=CURCOL+1

        CASE 331                        !LEFT CURSOR ARROW
            LET CURCOL=CURCOL-1

        CASE 406                        !<CTRL>+ TO INSERT NEW BLANK LINE
            LET C=(CURROW-1)*LINELENGTH
            LET E=MAXLINES*LINELENGTH
            LET LINE$[C+1:E]=REPEAT$(" ",LINELENGTH)&LINE$[C+1:E-LINELENGTH]
            CALL DISPLAYSCREEN

        CASE ELSE

        END SELECT

        CALL CHECKCURSOR

        SET CURSOR CURROW,CURCOL

    LOOP

    CLEAR

END SUB
```

THE MMENU PROGRAM

This program implements the MENU interface for the DSS Tool Kit.

```
!!!!!!!!!!!!!!!!!!!!!!!!!!!!!!!!!!!!!!!!!!!!!!!!!!!!!!!!!!!!!!!!!!!!!!!!!!!!!!!!
!                                                                            !
!  THIS IS MMENU DRIVER PROGRAM FOR THE MENU FUNCTION                        !
!                                                                            !
!  SEE CHAPTER 3 FOR EXPLANATION OF THIS FUNCTION                            !
!                                                                            !
!!!!!!!!!!!!!!!!!!!!!!!!!!!!!!!!!!!!!!!!!!!!!!!!!!!!!!!!!!!!!!!!!!!!!!!!!!!!!!!!

REM MMENU.TRU

REM THIS IS THE MAIN DRIVER PROGRAM FOR THE DSS TOOL KIT
REM    THIS PROGRAM INVOKES DSSMENU.TRU
REM       AND INSTRUCTS IT TO USE THE "MENU" AND "SCHEMA" FILES

LIBRARY "DSSMENU.TRU"
```

```
LET MAXLINES=40
LET LINELENGTH=80

CLEAR

PRINT
PRINT
PRINT
PRINT "            D S S   T O O L   K I T"
PRINT
PRINT
PRINT
PRINT

PAUSE 2

CLEAR

CALL DSSMENU("MENU","SCHEMA",MAXLINES,LINELENGTH)

END
```

THE DSSMENU LIBRARY

This library contains the subroutines that implement the menu-oriented interface to DSS Tool Kit functions.

```
!!!!!!!!!!!!!!!!!!!!!!!!!!!!!!!!!!!!!!!!!!!!!!!!!!!!!!!!!!!!!!!!!!!!!!!!!!!!!!!!!!!
!                                                                              !
!  THIS IS EXTERNAL LIBRARY DSSMENU.TRU                                        !
!                                                                              !
!  MENU IS THE MAIN SUBROUTINE FOR THE TOOL KIT MENU FUNCTION                  !
!                                                                              !
!  SEE CHAPTER 3 FOR EXPLANATION OF THIS FUNCTION                              !
!                                                                              !
!!!!!!!!!!!!!!!!!!!!!!!!!!!!!!!!!!!!!!!!!!!!!!!!!!!!!!!!!!!!!!!!!!!!!!!!!!!!!!!!!!!

REM DSSMENU.TRU

EXTERNAL
```

The DSSMENU Subroutine

This subroutine implements the menu-oriented interface to the DSS Tool Kit functions.

```
SUB MENU(MENUNAME$,SCHEMANAME$,MAXLINES,LINELENGTH)
    LIBRARY "DSSSED.TRU","DSSLED.TRU","DSSDBMS.TRU","DSSSUBS.TRU"
    LIBRARY "DSSGRAPH.TRU","DSSES.TRU","DSSSPREA.TRU","DSSDTREE.TRU"
```

```
REM   DSSMENU
REM     DSS TOOL KIT MENU PROGRAM
REM
REM   THIS SUBROUTINE MAY BE CALLED BY:
REM      A DRIVER PROGRAM WHICH DETERMINES THE
REM         MENU AND SCHEMA FILES AND SETS
REM          THE MAXLINES AND LINELENGTH CONSTANTS
REM               THIS PROGRAM IS CALLED MMENU

DIM MENUPARSE(200)

REM MENUPARSE WILL CONTAIN AN ENTRY FOR EACH LINE IN THE MENUFILE$
REM THIS ENTRY TELLS HOW MANY TOKENS IN THAT LINE
REM NOTE THAT THE MAXLINES MUST BE LESS THAN 200


REM CURRENTMENU$ HOLDS THE IDENTIFIER FOR THE CURRENT MENU

REM HOW TO PARSE THE MENU FILE:

REM IF 0 TOKENS IN LINE THEN DISREGARD
REM IF ONLY 1 TOKEN IN THE LINE THEN SHOW IN EVERY MENU DISPLAY
REM IF ONLY 2 TOKENS IN THE LINE THEN IS MENU HEADER
REM IF THREE TOKENS IN THE LINE THEN IS SELECTION DESCRIPTION
REM IF FOUR OR FIVE TOKENS IN THE LINE THEN IS ACTUAL INSTRUCTIONS
REM      AND THIRD TOKEN MUST BE GOTO OR PROGRAM

SUB COUNTTOKENS

    FOR I=1 TO MAXLINES

        LET MENUPARSE(I)=0
        LET TOKEN$=""
        LET LL$=MENU$[(I-1)*LINELENGTH+1:I*LINELENGTH]
        LET J=1

        CALL GETTOKEN(LL$,J,TOKEN$)

        DO WHILE (TOKEN$()"")
           LET MENUPARSE(I)=MENUPARSE(I)+1
           CALL GETTOKEN(LL$,J,TOKEN$)
        LOOP

        IF MENUPARSE (I))5 THEN
           PRINT "ERROR TOO MANY TOKENS IN MENU LINE",I
        END IF

    NEXT I

END SUB

CLEAR

PRINT
PRINT "READING IN THE MENU FILE"
CALL READLINES (MENU$,MENUNAME$,MAXLINES,LINELENGTH)
PRINT "READING IN THE SCHEMA FILE"
```

```
CALL READLINES (SCHEMA$,SCHEMANAME$,MAXLINES,LINELENGTH)
PRINT "CHECKING THE MENU FILE"

CALL COUNTTOKENS
CALL COLUMN(1,COLUMN1$,MENU$,LINELENGTH,MAXLINES)
CALL COLUMN(2,COLUMN2$,MENU$,LINELENGTH,MAXLINES)
CALL COLUMN(3,COLUMN3$,MENU$,LINELENGTH,MAXLINES)
CALL COLUMN(4,COLUMN4$,MENU$,LINELENGTH,MAXLINES)
CALL COLUMN(5,COLUMN5$,MENU$,LINELENGTH,MAXLINES)

DO WHILE (TOKEN4$<>"END")

    CLEAR

    IF CURRENTMENU$="" THEN
       LET CURRENTMENU$="A"
    END IF

    REM NOW DISPLAY THE MENU
    REM AND ASK FOR SELECTION

    LET LASTCELL=0
    LET LASTPOS=0
    LET LC2=0
    LET LP2=0
    LET LC3=0
    LET LP3=0

    FOR I=1 TO MAXLINES

        IF MENUPARSE(I)=1 THEN
           CALL VECTORCELL (LASTCELL,LASTPOS,I,TOKEN1$,COLUMN1$)
           PRINT TOKEN1$
        END IF

        IF MENUPARSE(I)=2 OR MENUPARSE(I)=3 THEN
           CALL VECTORCELL (LASTCELL,LASTPOS,I,TOKEN1$,COLUMN1$)

           IF TOKEN1$=CURRENTMENU$ THEN
              CALL VECTORCELL(LC2,LP2,I,TOKEN2$,COLUMN2$)
              PRINT TOKEN2$;

              IF MENUPARSE(I)=3 THEN
                 CALL VECTORCELL(LC3,LP3,I,TOKEN3$,COLUMN3$)
                 PRINT " ",TOKEN3$;
              END IF

              PRINT

           END IF

        END IF

    NEXT I

    PRINT
```

```
LET ISAVE=0
LET I=1

INPUT PROMPT "ENTER YOUR SELECTION> ":ENTRY$

LET LASTCELL=0
LET LASTPOS=0
LET LC2=0
LET LP2=0

DO WHILE (ISAVE=0 AND I<=MAXLINES)

    IF MENUPARSE(I)=3 THEN

        CALL VECTORCELL (LASTCELL,LASTPOS,I,TOKEN1$,COLUMN1$)

        IF TOKEN1$=CURRENTMENU$ THEN

            CALL VECTORCELL (LC2,LP2,I,TOKEN2$,COLUMN2$)

            IF TOKEN2$=ENTRY$ THEN
                    LET ISAVE=I
            END IF

        END IF

    END IF

    LET I=I+1

LOOP

CLEAR

REM IF SELECTION INVALID THEN REDISPLAY THE MENU
REM IF SELECTION VALID THEN DO CALL TO APPROPRIATE SUBROUTINE
REM                         OR ADJUST CURRENTMENU$ FOR GOTO

IF ISAVE<>0 THEN

    DO WHILE (ENTRY$=TOKEN2$)

        LET LC3=0
        LET LP3=0
        LET LC4=0
        LET LP4=0
        LET LC5=0
        LET LP5=0

        IF MENUPARSE(ISAVE)>3 THEN
            CALL VECTORCELL (LC3,LP3,ISAVE,TOKEN3$,COLUMN3$)

            SELECT CASE TOKEN3$

            CASE "PROGRAM"
```

```
CALL VECTORCELL(LC4,LP4,ISAVE,TOKEN4$,COLUMN4$)
CLEAR
CALL VECTORCELL(LC5,LP5,ISAVE,TOKEN5$,COLUMN5$)
CALL PROMPT(TOKEN5$)

SELECT CASE TOKEN4$

CASE "SED"
     CALL DSSSED("",TOKEN5$,MAXLINES,LINELENGTH)

CASE "LED"
     CALL DSSLED("",TOKEN5$,MAXLINES,LINELENGTH)

CASE "JOIN"
     CALL JOIN(SCHEMA$,TOKEN5$,MAXLINES,LINELENGTH)

CASE "SORT"
     CALL SORT (SCHEMA$,TOKEN5$,MAXLINES,LINELENGTH)

CASE "UNION"
     CALL UNION (SCHEMA$,TOKEN5$,MAXLINES,LINELENGTH)

CASE "DELETE"
     CALL DELETE (SCHEMA$,TOKEN5$,MAXLINES,LINELENGTH)

CASE "PROJECT"
     CALL PROJECT (SCHEMA$,TOKEN5$,MAXLINES,LINELENGTH)

CASE "SELECT"
     CALL SELECT (SCHEMA$,TOKEN5$,MAXLINES,LINELENGTH)

CASE "SGRAM"
     CALL SGRAM (SCHEMA$,TOKEN5$,MAXLINES,LINELENGTH)

CASE "MTRACE"
     CALL MTRACE (SCHEMA$,TOKEN5$,MAXLINES,LINELENGTH)

CASE "RLINE"
     CALL RLINE (SCHEMA$,TOKEN5$,MAXLINES,LINELENGTH)

CASE "BANDW"
     CALL BANDW (SCHEMA$,TOKEN5$,MAXLINES,LINELENGTH)

CASE "HISTO"
     CALL HISTO (SCHEMA$,TOKEN5$,MAXLINES,LINELENGTH)

CASE "PIE"
     CALL PIE (SCHEMA$,TOKEN5$,MAXLINES,LINELENGTH)

CASE "INCO"
     CALL INCO (SCHEMA$,TOKEN5$,MAXLINES,LINELENGTH)

CASE "BALA"
     CALL BALA (SCHEMA$,TOKEN5$,MAXLINES,LINELENGTH)
```

```
              CASE "ES"
                   CALL ES (SCHEMA$,TOKEN5$,MAXLINES,LINELENGTH)

              CASE "DISPLAY"
                   CALL DISPLAY (SCHEMA$,TOKEN5$,MAXLINES,LINELENGTH)

              CASE "DTREE"
                   CALL DSSDTREE (SCHEMA$,TOKEN5$,MAXLINES,LINELENGTH)

              CASE "SPREAD"
                   CALL DSSSPREA (SCHEMA$,TOKEN5$,MAXLINES,LINELENGTH)

              CASE "ADD"
                   CALL ADD (SCHEMA$,TOKEN5$,MAXLINES,LINELENGTH)

              CASE "SUBTRACT"
                   CALL SUBTRACT (SCHEMA$,TOKEN5$,MAXLINES,LINELENGTH)

              CASE "MULTIPLY"
                   CALL MULTIPLY (SCHEMA$,TOKEN5$,MAXLINES,LINELENGTH)

              CASE "DIVIDE"
                   CALL DIVIDEX (SCHEMA$,TOKEN5$,MAXLINES,LINELENGTH)

              CASE "SUMMARIZE"
                   CALL SUMMARIZE (SCHEMA$,TOKEN5$,MAXLINES,LINELENGTH)

              CASE "END"
                   CLEAR
                   PRINT "ENDING DSS TOOL KIT MENU SESSION"
                   PAUSE 5

              CASE ELSE
                   PRINT "INVALID PROGRAM NAME"
                   PAUSE 5

              END SELECT

         CASE "GOTO"
              CALL VECTORCELL(LC4,LC5,ISAVE,CURRENTMENU$,COLUMN4$)
              LET ENTRY$=""

         CASE ELSE

              PRINT "INVALID OPERATOR IN MENU"
              PAUSE 5

         END SELECT

    END IF

    LET ISAVE=ISAVE+1
    CALL VECTORCELL(LC2,LP2,ISAVE,TOKEN2$,COLUMN2$)
```

```
        LOOP

     ELSE
        PRINT "INVALID SELECTION"
        PAUSE 5

     END IF

  LOOP

END SUB
```

THE DSSDBMS LIBRARY

This library contains the subroutines that implement the relational-
style database management facilities for DSS Tool Kit users.

```
!!!!!!!!!!!!!!!!!!!!!!!!!!!!!!!!!!!!!!!!!!!!!!!!!!!!!!!!!!!!!!!!!!!!!!!!!!!!!!!!!
!                                                                            !
!  THIS IS EXTERNAL LIBRARY DSSDBMS.TRU                                       !
!                                                                            !
!  THIS LIBRARY CONTAINS THE SUBROUTINES USED IN THE TOOL KIT                 !
!  RELATIONAL MODEL DATABASE MANAGEMENT SYSTEM                                !
!                                                                            !
!  SEE CHAPTER 4 FOR EXPLANATION OF THIS FUNCTION                             !
!                                                                            !
!!!!!!!!!!!!!!!!!!!!!!!!!!!!!!!!!!!!!!!!!!!!!!!!!!!!!!!!!!!!!!!!!!!!!!!!!!!!!!!!!

EXTERNAL

REM    LIBRARY DSSDBMS
REM       DSS TOOL KIT DATABASE MANAGEMENT SYSTEM

REM    THIS IS A SET OF SUBROUTINES WHICH MAY BE INVOKED BY:
REM       A.  THE DSS MENU PROGRAM
REM       B.  AN INDEPENDENT DRIVER PROGRAM NAMED DRIVER

REM    THE SCHEMA CONTAINS 3 COLUMNS:
REM       TABLE NAME, COLUMN NUMBER, COLUMN NAME
```

The COLSCHEMA Subroutine

This subroutine converts database schemas to individual columns of
information.

```
REM ***************************************************************
SUB COLSCHEMA (SCHEMA$,SCOL1$,SCOL2$,SCOL3$,MAXLINES,LINELENGTH)
```

```
REM THIS SUBROUTINE COLUMNIZES THE SCHEMA

    CALL COLUMN(1,SCOL1$,SCHEMA$,LINELENGTH,MAXLINES)
    CALL COLUMN(2,SCOL2$,SCHEMA$,LINELENGTH,MAXLINES)
    CALL COLUMN(3,SCOL3$,SCHEMA$,LINELENGTH,MAXLINES)


END SUB
```

The GETSCOLUMN Subroutine

This subroutine searches schemas for an instance of a table name and
attribute name. The subroutine returns the column number of the attribute and its data table name.

```
REM *************************************************************
SUB GETSCOLUMN (TNAME$,ANAME$,S1$,S2$,S3$,CNUMBER,MAXLINES)

    REM TNAME$ CONTAINS THE TABLE NAME
    REM ANAME$ CONTAINS THE ATTRIBUTE (COLUMN) NAME
    REM SCOL1$ THRU SCOL3$ CONTAIN THE 3 COLUMNS OF THE SCHEMA

    REM THE COLUMN NUMBER IS RETURNED IN CNUMBER

    REM SEARCH SCHEMA FOR FIRST INSTANCE OF TNAME$ AND ANAME$
    REM  RETURN THE COLUMN NUMBER FOR THIS IN CNUMBER

    REM IF ANAME$ IS AN INTEGER NUMBER THEN RETURN THE VALUE OF THAT
    REM  INTEGER IN CNUMBER    WITHOUT SEARCHING
    REM

    CALL DEDOUBQUOTES(TNAME$,T$)
    CALL DEDOUBQUOTES(ANAME$,A$)

    WHEN ERROR IN

        LET CNUMBER=VAL(A$)

    USE

        LET ENDIT=0
        LET LASTCELL=0
        LET LASTPOS=0
        LET LC2=0
        LET LP2=0
        LET COUNT=1
        LET CNUMBER=1

        DO WHILE (ENDIT=0 AND COUNT<MAXLINES+1)

            CALL VECTORCELL (LASTCELL,LASTPOS,COUNT,CELL$,S1$)
```

```
          IF CELL$=T$ THEN
              CALL VECTORCELL (LC2,LP2,COUNT,CELL$,S3$)

            IF CELL$=A$ THEN
                LET LC3=0
                LET LP3=0

                CALL VECTORCELL (LC3,LP3,COUNT,CELL$,S2$)

                WHEN ERROR IN
                    LET CNUMBER=VAL(CELL$)
                USE
                    LET CNUMBER=1
                    PRINT "ERROR FOUND IN COLUMN NUMBER IN SCHEMA"
                    PAUSE 5
                END WHEN

                LET ENDIT=1
            END IF

          END IF

          LET COUNT=COUNT+1

      LOOP

    END WHEN

END SUB
```

The JOIN Subroutine

This subroutine matches input rows from two data tables and produces a third, coordinated table.

```
REM *******************************************
SUB JOIN(SCHEMA$,PARM$,MAXLINES,LINELENGTH)

    CLEAR

    PRINT "PERFORMING JOIN DATABASE OPERATION"

    CALL COLSCHEMA(SCHEMA$,S1$,S2$,S3$,MAXLINES,LINELENGTH)

    CALL DEDOUBQUOTES(PARM$,PARM1$)
    LET PARM$=PARM1$

    CALL DEBLANK(PARM$,PARM1$)
    LET PARM$=PARM1$

    LET LASTPOS=0
```

```
        CALL GETTOKEN(PARM$,LASTPOS,TOKEN$)
        LET FILENAME1$=TOKEN$

        CALL GETTOKEN(PARM$,LASTPOS,TOKEN$)
        LET FILENAME2$=TOKEN$

        CALL GETTOKEN(PARM$,LASTPOS,TOKEN$)
        LET ARGUMENT$=TOKEN$

        CALL GETTOKEN(PARM$,LASTPOS,TOKEN$)
        LET OUTPUTFILENAME$=TOKEN$

        PRINT "READING IN DATA TABLES FOR JOIN"

        CALL READLINES (FILE1$,FILENAME1$,MAXLINES,LINELENGTH)
        CALL READLINES (FILE2$,FILENAME2$,MAXLINES,LINELENGTH)

        PRINT "PERFORMING JOIN"

        REM NOW BREAK OUT THE COLUMN NAMES FROM ARGUMENT$
        REM AND CHANGE THEM TO NUMBERS

        LET ARGUMENT$=ARGUMENT$&";"
        LET ASTOP=POS(ARGUMENT$,";")
        LET OLDASTOP=0
        LET NEWARGUMENT$=""
        LET DUPECOL$=""

        DO WHILE (ASTOP<>0)

           LET WORK$=ARGUMENT$[OLDASTOP+1:ASTOP-1]
           LET WHERECOLON=POS(WORK$,":")

           IF WHERECOLON=0 THEN

              CALL GETSCOLUMN (FILENAME1$,WORK$,S1$,S2$,S3$,CNUMBER,MAXLINES)
              LET WORK1$=STR$(CNUMBER)

              CALL GETSCOLUMN (FILENAME2$,WORK$,S1$,S2$,S3$,CNUMBER,MAXLINES)
              LET WORK2$=STR$(CNUMBER)
              LET WORK$=WORK1$&":"&WORK2$

           ELSE

              LET WORK1$=WORK$[1:WHERECOLON-1]
              CALL GETSCOLUMN (FILENAME1$,WORK1$,S1$,S2$,S3$,CNUMBER,MAXLINES)

              LET WORK1$=STR$(CNUMBER)
              LET WORK2$=WORK$[WHERECOLON+1:LEN(WORK$)]

              CALL GETSCOLUMN (FILENAME2$,WORK2$,S1$,S2$,S3$,CNUMBER,MAXLINES)
              LET WORK2$=STR$(CNUMBER)
              LET WORK$=WORK1$&":"&WORK2$

           END IF
```

```
      LET NEWARGUMENT$=NEWARGUMENT$&WORK$&";"
      LET OLDASTOP=ASTOP
      LET ASTOP=POS(ARGUMENT$,";",OLDASTOP+1)

   LOOP

   LET ARGUMENT$=NEWARGUMENT$

   REM DO THE JOIN BY PREPARING LISTS OF ORDERED PAIRS
   REM  OF THE INDICES OF MATCHING VALUES FROM EACH PAIR OF COLUMNS

   REM THEN PREPARE THE OUTPUT TABLE BY LOGICALLY COMBINING THESE LISTS:
   REM  LOOKING FOR MATCHING PAIRS FOR ALL SETS OF ATTRIBUTES INCLUDED
   REM  IN THE JOIN

   REM THEN GENERATING THE  OUTPUT ROWS FROM THE PAIRS REPRESENTED
   REM  IN THE JOIN

   REM THEN GENERATING THE  OUTPUT ROWS FROM THE PAIRS REPRESENTED
   REM  IN ALL OF THE LISTS

   LET ASTOP=POS(ARGUMENT$,";")
   LET OLDASTOP=0
   LET FINALLIST$=""
   LET DUPECOL$=""

DO WHILE (ASTOP()0)

   LET WORK$=ARGUMENT$[OLDASTOP+1:ASTOP-1]
   LET WHERECOLON=POS(WORK$,":")

   LET WORK1=VAL(WORK$[1:WHERECOLON-1])
   CALL COLUMN (WORK1,COL1$,FILE1$,LINELENGTH,MAXLINES)

   LET WORK2=VAL(WORK$[WHERECOLON+1:LEN(WORK$)])
   CALL COLUMN (WORK2,COL2$,FILE2$,LINELENGTH,MAXLINES)

   LET DUPECOL$=DUPECOL$&STR$(WORK2)&" "

   LET LC1=0
   LET LP1=0
   LET LIST$=""

   FOR I=1 TO MAXLINES

       CALL VECTORCELL(LC1,LP1,I,CELL1$,COL1$)

       IF CELL1$()"" THEN
          LET LC2=0
          LET LP2=0

         FOR J=1 TO MAXLINES

             CALL VECTORCELL(LC2,LP2,J,CELL2$,COL2$)

             IF CELL1$=CELL2$ THEN
```

```
                        LET LIST$=LIST$&" "&STR$(I)&":"&STR$(J)&" "
                END IF

        NEXT J

    END IF

NEXT I

IF FINALLIST$="" THEN
    LET FINALLIST$=LIST$
ELSE

    REM LOOK FOR MATCHES BETWEEN FINALLIST$ AND LIST$ AND CHANGE
    REM  FINALLIST$ ACCORDINGLY

    REM DUPECOL$ CONTAINS A LIST OF THE COLUMNS OF THE SECOND
    REM  DATA TABLE TO LEAVE OUT

    LET LC1=0
    LET LP1=0
    LET NEXT=1

    CALL VECTORCELL(LC1,LP1,NEXT,CELL$,FINALLIST$)


        DO WHILE (CELL$<>"")

            IF POS(LIST$," "&CELL$&" ")=0 THEN
                LET FINALLIST$[LP1-LEN(CELL$):LP1]=REPEAT$(" ",LEN(CELL$)+1)
            END IF

            LET NEXT=NEXT+1
            CALL VECTORCELL(LC1,LP1,NEXT,CELL$,FINALLIST$)

        LOOP

    END IF

    LET OLDASTOP=ASTOP
    LET ASTOP=POS(ARGUMENT$,";",OLDASTOP+1)

LOOP

REM NOW GENERATE THE OUTPUT DATA TABLE ACCORDING TO FINALLIST$
REM FIRST REMOVE THE DUPECOL$ COLUMNS FROM THE SECOND TABLE

LET LC1=0
LET LP1=0
LET NEXT=1

CALL VECTORCELL(LC1,LP1,NEXT,CELL$,DUPECOL$)

DO WHILE (CELL$<>"")

    FOR I=1 TO MAXLINES
```

```
          LET LCX=0
          LET LPX=0

          LET LLINE$=FILE2$[(I-1)*LINELENGTH+1:I*LINELENGTH]
          CALL VECTORCELL(LCX,LPX,VAL(CELL$),CELLX$,LLINE$)

          LET LLINE$[LPX-LEN(CELLX$):LPX]=REPEAT$("^",LEN(CELLX$))&" "
          LET FILE2$[(I-1)*LINELENGTH+1:I*LINELENGTH]=LLINE$

      NEXT I

      LET NEXT=NEXT+1
      CALL VECTORCELL(LC1,LP1,NEXT,CELL$,DUPECOL$)

   LOOP

   REM NOW BUILD THE OUTPUT TABLE
   REM DRIVE THE PROCESS WITH FINALLIST$

   LET NEXT=1
   LET LC1=0
   LET LP1=0


   CALL VECTORCELL (LC1,LP1,NEXT,CELL$,FINALLIST$)

   LET OUTPUTFILE$=""

   DO WHILE (CELL$<>"")

      REM NOW TAKE THE ROW FOR THE NUMBER TO THE LEFT OF THE COLON
      REM  FROM THE FIRST TABLE
      REM   AND CONCATENATE THE ROW FOR THE NUMBER TO THE RIGHT OF
      REM    THE COLON FROM THE SECOND TABLE

      REM THIS WILL BE ROW NEXT IN THE OUTPUTFILE$
      REM OUTPUTFILE$ IS TO BE 2 * LINELENGTH WIDE

      LET WHERECOLON=POS(CELL$,":")
      LET WORK1=VAL(CELL$[1:WHERECOLON-1])
      LET WORK2=VAL(CELL$[WHERECOLON+1:LEN(CELL$)])
      LET RECORD1$=FILE1$[(WORK1-1)*LINELENGTH+1:WORK1*LINELENGTH]
      LET RECORD2$=FILE2$[(WORK2-1)*LINELENGTH+1:WORK2*LINELENGTH]
      LET OUTPUTFILE$=OUTPUTFILE$&RECORD1$&RECORD2$

      LET NEXT=NEXT+1
      CALL VECTORCELL(LC1,LP1,NEXT,CELL$,FINALLIST$)

   LOOP

   CALL COMPRESSTABLE (OUTPUTFILE$,MAXLINES,2*LINELENGTH)

   LET OUTFILE$=""

   FOR I=1 TO MAXLINES

      LET LL=LINELENGTH
      LET OUTFILE$=OUTFILE$&OUTPUTFILE$[(I-1)*(2*LL)+1:I*(2*LL)-LL]
```

```
    NEXT I

    PRINT "WRITING THE OUTPUT TABLE RESULTING FROM THE JOIN"
    CALL WRITELINES(OUTFILE$,OUTPUTFILENAME$,MAXLINES,LINELENGTH)

END SUB
```

The SELECT Subroutine

This subroutine searches for designated records and inserts them into another data table.

```
REM **********************************************
SUB SELECT (SCHEMA$,PARM$,MAXLINES,LINELENGTH)

    DECLARE DEF CRUNCH$

    CLEAR

    PRINT "PERFORMING SELECT DATABASE OPERATION"

    CALL COLSCHEMA(SCHEMA$,S1$,S2$,S3$,MAXLINES,LINELENGTH)

    CALL DEDOUBQUOTES(PARM$,PARM1$)
    LET PARM$=PARM1$

    LET PARM$=UCASE$(PARM$)

    LET AFTER=0
    LET POSX=POS(PARM$,"<=",AFTER)

    DO WHILE (POSX<>0)
       LET PARM$[POSX:POSX+1]="[ "
       LET AFTER=POSX
       LET POSX=POS(PARM$,"<=",AFTER)
    LOOP

    LET AFTER=0
    LET POSX=POS(PARM$,">=",AFTER)

    DO WHILE (POSX<>0)
       LET PARM$[POSX:POSX+1]="] "
       LET AFTER = POSX
       LET POSX=POS(PARM$,">=",AFTER)
    LOOP

    LET AFTER=0
    LET POSX=POS(PARM$," AND ",AFTER)
    DO WHILE (POSX<>0)
       LET PARM$[POSX:POSX+4]=" &   "
       LET AFTER=POSX
       LET POSX=POS(PARM$," AND ",AFTER)
```

```
LOOP

LET AFTER=0
LET POSX=POS(PARM$," OR ",AFTER)

DO WHILE (POSX<>0)
    LET PARM$[POSX:POSX+3]=" | "
    LET AFTER=POSX
    LET POSX=POS(PARM$," OR ",AFTER)
LOOP


LET AFTER=0
LET POSX=POS(PARM$," <> ",AFTER)

DO WHILE (POSX<>0)
    LET PARM$[POSX:POSX+3]=" # "
    LET AFTER=POSX
    LET POSX=POS(PARM$," <> ",AFTER)
LOOP


CALL DEBLANK(PARM$,PARM1$)
LET PARM$=PARM1$

LET LASTPOS=0
CALL GETTOKEN(PARM$,LASTPOS,TOKEN$)
LET FILENAME1$=TOKEN$

CALL GETTOKEN(PARM$,LASTPOS,TOKEN$)
LET SEARCHARG$=TOKEN$

CALL GETTOKEN(PARM$,LASTPOS,TOKEN$)
LET OUTPUTFILENAME$=TOKEN$

PRINT "READING IN DATA TABLE FOR SELECT"

CALL READLINES (FILE1$,FILENAME1$,MAXLINES,LINELENGTH)
CALL COMPRESSTABLE (FILE1$,MAXLINES,LINELENGTH)

PRINT "PERFORMING SELECT"

REM NOW APPLY SEARCH ARGUMENT TO EACH COLUMN OF THE RELATION
REM   WORK FROM LEFT TO RIGHT IN SEARCHARG$

REM FIRST PUT BLANKS BETWEEN TOKENS IN SEARCHARG$

LET NEWSEARCHARG$=""
LET START=1
LET END=LEN(SEARCHARG$)

DO WHILE (START<=END)

   LET CHK$=SEARCHARG$[START:START]

   SELECT CASE CHK$

   CASE "[","]","(",")","&","|","=","#","<",">"
        LET NEWSEARCHARG$=NEWSEARCHARG$&" "&CHK$&" "
```

```
      CASE ELSE
          LET NEWSEARCHARG$=NEWSEARCHARG$&CHK$

    END SELECT

    LET START=START+1


    LOOP


    LET SEARCHARG$=NEWSEARCHARG$

    REM THEN REPLACE THE SINGLE QUOTES WITH DOUBLE QUOTES SO
    REM CAN USE GETTOKEN SUBROUTINE ON SEARCHARG$.
    LET AFTER=0
    LET POSX=POS(SEARCHARG$,"'",AFTER)

    DO WHILE (POSX<>0)
        LET PARM$[POSX:POSX]=CHR$(34)
        LET AFTER=POSX
        LET POSX=POS(SEARCHARG$,"'",AFTER)

    LOOP

    LET TRUTH$=""
    LET POINTER=1
    LET SEARCHARG$=SEARCHARG$&" \"

    LET L=LINELENGTH
    LET TRUTH$= CRUNCH$ (POINTER,SEARCHARG$,FILE1$,MAXLINES,L,S1$,S2$,S3$)

    REM NOW CREATE NEW RELATION
    REM   USING TRUTH VALUES IN TRUTH$

    LET J=1
    LET NEWTABLE$=REPEAT$(" ",LINELENGTH*MAXLINES)
    LET LL=LINELENGTH

    FOR I=1 TO LEN(TRUTH$)

        SELECT CASE TRUTH$[I:I]

        CASE "0"
            LET J=J+1
        CASE "1"
            LET NEWTABLE$[(J-1)*LL:J*LL]=FILE1$[(J-1)*LL:J*LL]
            LET J=J+1
        CASE ELSE

        END SELECT

    NEXT I

    LET NEWTABLE$=NEWTABLE$&REPEAT$(" ",LINELENGTH*MAXLINES)
    LET NEWTABLE$=NEWTABLE$[1:LINELENGTH*MAXLINES]

    CALL COMPRESSTABLE (NEWTABLE$,MAXLINES,LINELENGTH)
```

```
      PRINT "WRITING THE OUTPUT TABLE RESULTING FROM THE SELECT"
      CALL WRITELINES(NEWTABLE$,OUTPUTFILENAME$,MAXLINES,LINELENGTH)

END SUB
```

The CRUNCH Subroutine

This subroutine interprets the search criteria designated in the
SELECT database operation and then performs the operation.

```
REM *****************************************************************
DEF CRUNCH$ (POINTER,SEARCHARG$,FILE$,MAXLINES,LINELENGTH,S1$,S2$,S3$)

    DECLARE DEF MATCH$

    SUB COMBINETRUTH

        LET NEWRETAINEDTRUTH$=""

        FOR I=1 TO LEN(TRUTH$)

            IF TRUTH$[I:I]=" " THEN
                LET NEWRETAINEDTRUTH$=NEWRETAINEDTRUTH$&" "
            ELSE

                SELECT CASE LASTLINK$

                CASE "&"

                    IF TRUTH$[I:I]="1" AND RETAINEDTRUTH$[I:I]="1" THEN
                        LET NEWRETAINEDTRUTH$=NEWRETAINEDTRUTH$&"1"
                    ELSE
                        LET NEWRETAINEDTRUTH$=NEWRETAINEDTRUTH$&"0"
                    END IF

                CASE "¦"

                    IF TRUTH$[I:I]="1" OR RETAINEDTRUTH$[I:I]="1" THEN
                        LET NEWRETAINEDTRUTH$=NEWRETAINEDTRUTH$&"1"
                    ELSE
                        LET NEWRETAINEDTRUTH$=NEWRETAINEDTRUTH$&"0"
                    END IF

                END SELECT

            END IF

        NEXT I

        LET RETAINEDTRUTH$=NEWRETAINEDTRUTH$
```

```
             LET LASTLINK$=""

        END SUB

        LET RETAINEDTRUTH$=""
        LET LASTLINK$=""

        DO WHILE (1=1)

            CALL GETTOKEN(SEARCHARG$,POINTER,TOKEN$)

            SELECT CASE TOKEN$

            CASE "&","!"
                LET LASTLINK$=TOKEN$

            CASE ")","\"
                LET CRUNCH$=RETAINEDTRUTH$

                EXIT DEF


            CASE "("
    LET TRUTH$=CRUNCH$(POINTER,SEARCHARG$,FILE$,MAXLINES,LINELENGTH,S1$,S2$,S3$)
                IF RETAINEDTRUTH$<>"" THEN
                    CALL COMBINETRUTH
                ELSE
                    LET RETAINEDTRUTH$=TRUTH$
                END IF

            CASE ELSE
                REM MUST BE VALUE
                WHEN ERROR IN

                CALL GETSCOLUMN (FILENAME1$,TOKEN$,S1$,S2$,S3$,CNUMBER,MAXLINES)
                    CALL COLUMN (CNUMBER,COL$,FILE$,LINELENGTH,MAXLINES)
                    CALL GETTOKEN (SEARCHARG$,POINTER,OPERATOR$)
                    CALL GETTOKEN (SEARCHARG$,POINTER,SEARCHVALUE$)
                    CALL DEDOUBQUOTES(SEARCHVALUE$,X$)
                    LET SEARCHVALUE$=X$
                    LET TRUTH$= MATCH$(COL$,SEARCHVALUE$,OPERATOR$)

                    IF LASTLINK$<>"" THEN
                        CALL COMBINETRUTH
                    ELSE
                        LET RETAINEDTRUTH$=TRUTH$
                    END IF

                USE
                END WHEN

            END SELECT

        LOOP

    END DEF
```

```
DEF MATCH$ (COL$,PATTERN$,OPERATION$)

    DECLARE DEF MATCHX$

    LET HOLD$=""

    LET LASTPOS=0
    CALL GETTOKEN(COL$,LASTPOS,TOKEN$)
    CALL DEDOUBQUOTES (TOKEN$,TOKEN1$)
    LET TOKEN$=TOKEN1$

    DO WHILE (TOKEN$<>"")

        LET TRUTH$= MATCHX$(OPERATION$,TOKEN$,PATTERN$)

        LET HOLD$=HOLD$&" "&TRUTH$&" "

        CALL GETTOKEN(COL$,LASTPOS,TOKEN$)
        CALL DEDOUBQUOTES (TOKEN$,TOKEN1$)
        LET TOKEN$=TOKEN1$

    LOOP

    LET MATCH$=HOLD$

    EXIT DEF

END DEF

DEF MATCHX$(OPERATION$,TARGET$,PATTERN$)

    LET PATTERN$=PATTERN$&"\"
    LET PATPOSITION=1
    LET TARGETPOSITION=1
    LET SUBTARGET$=""

    SELECT CASE OPERATION$
    CASE "[","]","(",")"
        LET MODE=1
    CASE ELSE
        LET MODE=0
    END SELECT


    DO WHILE (1=1)

        SELECT CASE PATTERN$[PATPOSITION:PATPOSITION]

        CASE "*"

            IF MODE=1 THEN
                LET TARGETPOSITION=POS(TARGET$,SUBTARGET$,TARGETPOSITION)
                IF TARGETPOSITION=0 THEN

                IF OPERATION$="=" THEN
                    LET MATCHX$="0"
                ELSE
```

```
               LET MATCHX$="1"
           END IF

           EXIT DEF

      ELSE
         LET TARGETPOSITION=TARGETPOSITION+LEN(SUBTARGET$)
         LET SUBTARGET$=""
         LET MODE=0
      END IF

   ELSE
      LET MODE=1
      LET SUBTARGET$=""

   END IF


CASE "\"

   IF MODE=1 AND SUBTARGET$<>""  THEN

      IF OPERATION$="=" OR OPERATION$="#" THEN

         LET TARGETPOSITION=POS(TARGET$,SUBTARGET$,TARGETPOSITION)

         IF TARGETPOSITION=0 THEN
            IF OPERATION$="=" THEN
               LET MATCHX$="0"
            ELSE
               LET MATCHX$="1"
            END IF

            EXIT DEF

         END IF

      ELSE

         WHEN ERROR IN
              LET WORK1=VAL(SUBTARGET$)
              LET WORK2=VAL(TARGET$)

              SELECT CASE OPERATION$
              CASE "#"
                  IF WORK1<>WORK2 THEN
                     LET MATCHX$="1"
                  ELSE
                     LET MATCHX$="0"
                  END IF

              CASE ">"
                  IF WORK1>WORK2 THEN
                     LET MATCHX$="1"
                  ELSE
                     LET MATCHX$="0"
                  END IF
```

```
                        CASE "<"
                              IF WORK1<>WORK2 THEN
                                    LET MATCHX$="1"
                              ELSE
                                    LET MATCHX$="0"
                              END IF
                        END SELECT

              USE
                        LET WORK1$=SUBTARGET$
                        LET WORK2$=TARGET$

                        SELECT CASE OPERATION$
                        CASE "#"
                              IF WORK1$<>WORK2$ THEN
                                    LET MATCHX$="1"
                              ELSE
                                    LET MATCHX$="0"
                              END IF

                        CASE ">"
                              IF WORK1$>WORK2$ THEN
                                    LET MATCHX$="1"
                              ELSE
                                    LET MATCHX$="0"
                              END IF

                        CASE "<"
                              IF WORK1$<>WORK2$ THEN
                                    LET MATCHX$="1"
                              ELSE
                                    LET MATCHX$="0"
                              END IF
                        CASE ">="
                              IF WORK1$>=WORK2$ THEN
                                    LET MATCHX$="1"
                              ELSE
                                    LET MATCHX$="0"
                              END IF

                        CASE "<="
                              IF WORK1$<=WORK2$ THEN
                                    LET MATCHX$="1"
                              ELSE
                                    LET MATCHX$="0"
                              END IF

                        END SELECT

                                    END WHEN

                                    EXIT DEF

                              END IF

                        ELSE IF MODE=1 AND SUBTARGET$="" THEN
                              LET MATCHX$="1"
```

```
                    EXIT DEF

            END IF

            IF TARGETPOSITION=LEN(TARGET$)+1 THEN
                               LET MATCHX$="1"
                EXIT DEF
            ELSE
                LET MATCHX$="0"
                EXIT DEF
            END IF

      CASE ELSE
            LET AP=PATPOSITION

            IF MODE=1 THEN
                LET SUBTARGET$=SUBTARGET$&PATTERN$[AP:AP]

            ELSE
                IF PATTERN$[AP:AP]<>TARGET$[TARGETPOSITION:TARGETPOSITION] THEN
                    LET MATCHX$="0"
                    EXIT DEF
                ELSE
                    LET TARGETPOSITION=TARGETPOSITION+1
                END IF
            END IF

      END SELECT

      LET PATPOSITION=PATPOSITION+1

   LOOP

END DEF
```

The PROJECT Subroutine

This subroutine extracts specific columns from a data table and creates a new table.

```
REM **********************************************************

SUB PROJECT(SCHEMA$,PARM$,MAXLINES,LINELENGTH)

   CLEAR

   PRINT "PERFORMING PROJECT DATABASE OPERATION"

   CALL COLSCHEMA(SCHEMA$,S1$,S2$,S3$,MAXLINES,LINELENGTH)
```

```
      CALL DEDOUBQUOTES(PARM$,PARM1$)
      LET PARM$=PARM1$


      CALL DEBLANK(PARM$,PARM1$)
      LET PARM$=PARM1$


      LET LASTPOS=0
      CALL GETTOKEN(PARM$,LASTPOS,TOKEN$)
      LET FILENAME1$=TOKEN$


      CALL GETTOKEN(PARM$,LASTPOS,TOKEN$)
      LET ARGUMENT$=TOKEN$


      CALL GETTOKEN(PARM$,LASTPOS,TOKEN$)
      LET OUTPUTFILENAME$=TOKEN$


      PRINT "READING IN DATA TABLE FOR PROJECT"


      CALL READLINES (FILE1$,FILENAME1$,MAXLINES,LINELENGTH)


      PRINT "PERFORMING PROJECT"

 REM NOW BREAK OUT THE COLUMN NAMES FROM ARGUMENT$ AND CHANGE THEM TO NUMBERS

      LET ARGUMENT$=ARGUMENT$&";"
      LET ASTOP=POS(ARGUMENT$,";")
      LET OLDASTOP=0
      LET NT$=REPEAT$(" ",2*MAXLINES*LINELENGTH)

      DO WHILE (ASTOP<>0)

         LET WORK$=ARGUMENT$[OLDASTOP+1:ASTOP-1]

         CALL GETSCOLUMN (FILENAME1$,WORK$,S1$,S2$,S3$,CNUMBER,MAXLINES)

         REM NOW COMBINE THE COLUMN WITH NUMBER IN CNUMBER
         REM   WITH COLUMNS IN NEWTABLE$

         CALL COLUMN(CNUMBER,WORKCOL$,FILE1$,LINELENGTH,MAXLINES)

      LET LASTPOS=0
      CALL GETTOKEN(WORKCOL$,LASTPOS,CELL$)
      LET RN=1
      LET LL=LINELENGTH

      DO WHILE (CELL$<>"" AND CELL$<>CHR$(34)&CHR$(34))

         LET CELL$=CELL$&REPEAT$(" ",LINELENGTH-LEN(CELL$))

         LET NT$[(RN-1)*LL*2+LL+1:RN*LL*2]=CELL$

         CALL GETTOKEN(WORKCOL$,LASTPOS,CELL$)

         LET RN=RN+1
```

```
        LOOP

        CALL COMPRESSTABLE (NT$,MAXLINES,2*LINELENGTH)

        LET OLDASTOP=ASTOP
        LET ASTOP=POS(ARGUMENT$,";",OLDASTOP+1)

    LOOP

    LET OUTFILE$=""

    LET LL=LINELENGTH

    FOR I=1 TO MAXLINES

        LET OUTFILE$=OUTFILE$&NT$[(I-1)*(2*LL)+1:I*(2*LL)-LL]

    NEXT I

    PRINT "WRITING THE OUTPUT TABLE RESULTING FROM THE PROJECT"
    CALL WRITELINES(OUTFILE$,OUTPUTFILENAME$,MAXLINES,LINELENGTH)

END SUB
```

The DISPLAY Subroutine

This subroutine displays data tables.

```
REM ************************************************************
SUB DISPLAY(SCHEMA$,PARM$,MAXLINES,LINELENGTH)

    CLEAR

    PRINT "PERFORMING DISPLAY DATABASE OPERATION"

    CALL DEDOUBQUOTES(PARM$,PARM1$)
    LET PARM$=PARM1$

    CALL DEBLANK(PARM$,PARM1$)
    LET PARM$=PARM1$

    LET LASTPOS=0
    CALL GETTOKEN(PARM$,LASTPOS,TOKEN$)
    LET FILENAME1$=TOKEN$

    CALL GETTOKEN(PARM$,LASTPOS,TOKEN$)
    LET OPTION$=TOKEN$

    PRINT "READING IN DATA TABLE FOR DISPLAY"

    CALL READLINES (FILE1$,FILENAME1$,MAXLINES,LINELENGTH)
```

```
CLEAR

PRINT "DISPLAY OF DATA TABLE >";FILENAME1$
PRINT OPTION$
PRINT

IF OPTION$<>"" THEN
   OPEN #1: PRINTER
   PRINT #1: "DISPLAY OF DATA TABLE >";FILENAME1$
   PRINT #1: OPTION$
   PRINT #1
END IF

FOR I=1 TO MAXLINES

    LET LLINE$=FILE1$[(I-1)*LINELENGTH+1:I*LINELENGTH]
         IF LLINE$<>REPEAT$(" ",LINELENGTH) THEN

    LET LC1=0
    LET LP1=0
    LET NEXT=1

    CALL VECTORCELL(LC1,LP1,NEXT,CELL$,LLINE$)

    DO WHILE (CELL$<>"")

       IF LEN(CELL$)  <10 THEN
          LET CELL$=CELL$&REPEAT$(" ",10-LEN(CELL$))
       ELSE IF LEN(CELL$)<20 AND LEN(CELL$)>10 THEN
          LET CELL$=CELL$&REPEAT$(" ",20-LEN(CELL$))
       END IF

       PRINT CELL$&" ";

       IF OPTION$<>"" THEN
          PRINT #1: CELL$&" ";
       END IF

       LET NEXT=NEXT+1
       CALL VECTORCELL(LC1,LP1,NEXT,CELL$,LLINE$)

    LOOP

    PRINT

    IF OPTION$<>"" THEN
       PRINT #1
    END IF

    END IF

NEXT I

PRINT
CLOSE #1
PRINT "PRESS ANY KEY TO CONTINUE"
```

```
GET KEY A
CLEAR

END SUB
```

The ADD Subroutine

This subroutine performs column addition.

```
REM **********************************************************
SUB ADD (SCHEMA$,PARM$,MAXLINES,LINELENGTH)

 LET OP$="ADD"

 CALL ARITHMETIC(OP$,SCHEMA$,PARM$,MAXLINES,LINELENGTH)

END SUB
```

The SUBTRACT Subroutine

This subroutine performs column subtraction.

```
REM **********************************************************
SUB SUBTRACT (SCHEMA$,PARM$,MAXLINES,LINELENGTH)

 LET OP$="SUBTRACT"

 CALL ARITHMETIC(OP$,SCHEMA$,PARM$,MAXLINES,LINELENGTH)

END SUB
```

The MULTIPLY Subroutine

This subroutine performs column multiplication.

```
REM **********************************************************
SUB MULTIPLY (SCHEMA$,PARM$,MAXLINES,LINELENGTH)

 LET OP$="MULTIPLY"

 CALL ARITHMETIC(OP$,SCHEMA$,PARM$,MAXLINES,LINELENGTH)

END SUB
```

The DIVIDEX Subroutine

This subroutine performs column division.

```
REM **********************************************************
SUB DIVIDEX (SCHEMA$,PARM$,MAXLINES,LINELENGTH)

 LET OP$="DIVIDE"

 CALL ARITHMETIC(OP$,SCHEMA$,PARM$,MAXLINES,LINELENGTH)

END SUB
```

The ARITHMETIC Subroutine

This subroutine performs generalized column arithmetic.

```
REM **************************************************
SUB ARITHMETIC(OP$,SCHEMA$,PARM$,MAXLINES,LINELENGTH)

 CLEAR

 PRINT "PERFORMING ";OP$;" DATABASE OPERATION"

 CALL COLSCHEMA(SCHEMA$,S1$,S2$,S3$,MAXLINES,LINELENGTH)

 CALL DEDOUBQUOTES(PARM$,PARM1$)
 LET PARM$=PARM1$

 CALL DEBLANK(PARM$,PARM1$)
 LET PARM$=PARM1$

 LET LASTPOS=0
 CALL GETTOKEN(PARM$,LASTPOS,TOKEN$)
 LET FILENAME1$=TOKEN$

 CALL GETTOKEN(PARM$,LASTPOS,TOKEN$)
 LET FIRSTINDEX$=TOKEN$

 CALL GETTOKEN(PARM$,LASTPOS,TOKEN$)
 LET SECONDINDEX$=TOKEN$

 CALL GETTOKEN(PARM$,LASTPOS,TOKEN$)
 LET OUTPUTFILENAME$=TOKEN$

 PRINT "READING IN DATA TABLE FOR ";OP$

 CALL READLINES (FILE1$,FILENAME1$,MAXLINES,LINELENGTH)

 PRINT "PERFORMING ";OP$
```

```
CALL GETSCOLUMN (FILENAME1$,FIRSTINDEX$,S1$,S2$,S3$,FIRST,MAXLINES)
CALL GETSCOLUMN (FILENAME1$,SECONDINDEX$,S1$,S2$,S3$,SECOND,MAXLINES)

CALL COLUMN(FIRST,FIRSTCOL$,FILE1$,LINELENGTH,MAXLINES)
CALL COLUMN(SECOND,SECONDCOL$,FILE1$,LINELENGTH,MAXLINES)

LET LASTPOS1=0
LET LASTPOS2=0
LET RN=1
LET LL=LINELENGTH

CALL GETTOKEN(FIRSTCOL$,LASTPOS1,CELL1$)
CALL GETTOKEN(SECONDCOL$,LASTPOS2,CELL2$)

CALL DEDOUBQUOTES(CELL1$,WORK$)
LET CELL1$=WORK$
CALL DEDOUBQUOTES(CELL2$,WORK$)
LET CELL2$=WORK$

DO WHILE (CELL1$<>"" OR CELL2$<>"")

    WHEN ERROR IN
         LET CELL1=VAL(CELL1$)
         LET CELL2=VAL(CELL2$)
    USE
         LET CELL1=0
         LET CELL2=0
    END WHEN

    WHEN ERROR IN

         SELECT CASE OP$

         CASE "ADD"
               LET RESULT = CELL1+CELL2

         CASE "SUBTRACT"
               LET RESULT=CELL1-CELL2

         CASE "DIVIDE"
               LET RESULT=CELL1/CELL2

         CASE "MULTIPLY"
               LET RESULT=CELL1*CELL2

         CASE ELSE
               LET RESULT=0

         END SELECT

    USE
         LET RESULT=0
    END WHEN

    LET CELL$=STR$(RESULT)
    LET CELL$=CELL$&REPEAT$(" ",80-LEN(CELL$))
```

```
    LET NEWTABLE$[(RN-1)*LL*2+1:(RN-1)*2*LL-LL]=FILE1$[(RN-1)*LL+1:RN*LL]
    LET NEWTABLE$[(RN-1)*2*LL+LL+1:RN*2*LL]=CELL$

    CALL GETTOKEN(FIRSTCOL$,LASTPOS1,CELL1$)
    CALL GETTOKEN(SECONDCOL$,LASTPOS2,CELL2$)
    CALL DEDOUBQUOTES(CELL1$,WORK$)
    LET CELL1$=WORK$
    CALL DEDOUBQUOTES(CELL2$,WORK$)
    LET CELL2$=WORK$

    LET RN=RN+1

LOOP

CALL COMPRESSTABLE (NEWTABLE$,MAXLINES,2*LINELENGTH)

 LET OUTFILE$=""

 LET LL=LINELENGTH

 FOR I=1 TO MAXLINES

     LET OUTFILE$=OUTFILE$&NEWTABLE$[(I-1)*(2*LL)+1:I*(2*LL)-LL]

 NEXT I

 PRINT "WRITING THE OUTPUT TABLE RESULTING FROM THE ";OP$
 CALL WRITELINES(OUTFILE$,OUTPUTFILENAME$,MAXLINES,LINELENGTH)

END SUB
```

The SORT Subroutine

This subroutine sorts data tables.

```
REM *************************************************************

SUB SORT(SCHEMA$,PARM$,MAXLINES,LINELENGTH)

 CLEAR

 PRINT "PERFORMING SORT DATABASE OPERATION"

 CALL COLSCHEMA(SCHEMA$,S1$,S2$,S3$,MAXLINES,LINELENGTH)

 CALL DEDOUBQUOTES(PARM$,PARM1$)
 LET PARM$=PARM1$

 CALL DEBLANK(PARM$,PARM1$)
 LET PARM$=PARM1$

 LET LASTPOS=0
 CALL GETTOKEN(PARM$,LASTPOS,TOKEN$)
 LET FILENAME1$=TOKEN$
```

```
      CALL GETTOKEN(PARM$,LASTPOS,TOKEN$)
      LET ARGUMENT$=TOKEN$

      CALL GETTOKEN(PARM$,LASTPOS,TOKEN$)
      LET OUTPUTFILENAME$=TOKEN$

      PRINT "READING IN DATA TABLE FOR SORT"

      CALL READLINES (FILE1$,FILENAME1$,MAXLINES,LINELENGTH)
      CALL COMPRESSTABLE (FILE1$,MAXLINES,LINELENGTH)

      PRINT "PERFORMING SORT"

      REM NOW BREAK OUT THE COLUMN NAMES FROM ARGUMENT$
      REM AND CHANGE THEM TO NUMBERS

      LET ARGUMENT$=ARGUMENT$&";"
      LET ASTOP=POS(ARGUMENT$,";")
      LET OLDASTOP=0
      LET NT$=REPEAT$(" ",2*MAXLINES*LINELENGTH)

      DO WHILE (ASTOP()0)

         LET WORK$=ARGUMENT$[OLDASTOP+1:ASTOP-1]

         CALL GETSCOLUMN (FILENAME1$,WORK$,S1$,S2$,S3$,CNUMBER,MAXLINES)

         CALL COLUMN(CNUMBER,WORKCOL$,FILE1$,LINELENGTH,MAXLINES)

         LET LASTPOS=0
         CALL GETTOKEN(WORKCOL$,LASTPOS,CELL$)
         LET RN=1
         LET LL=LINELENGTH

         DO WHILE (CELL$()"" AND CELL$()CHR$(34)&CHR$(34))

            LET CELL$=CELL$&REPEAT$(" ",LINELENGTH-LEN(CELL$))

            LET NT$[(RN-1)*LL*2+LL+1:RN*LL*2]=CELL$

            CALL GETTOKEN(WORKCOL$,LASTPOS,CELL$)

            LET RN=RN+1

         LOOP

         CALL COMPRESSTABLE (NT$,MAXLINES,2*LINELENGTH)

         LET OLDASTOP=ASTOP
         LET ASTOP=POS(ARGUMENT$,";",OLDASTOP+1)

      LOOP

      LET OF$=""

      LET LL=LINELENGTH
      LET NUMROWS=0
```

```
FOR I=1 TO MAXLINES

    LET XX$=FILE1$[(I-1)*LL+1:I*LL]
    LET OF$=OF$&NT$[(I-1)*(2*LL)+1:I*(2*LL)-LL]&XX$
    IF XX$<>REPEAT$(" ",LINELENGTH) THEN
        LET NUMROWS=NUMROWS+1
    END IF

NEXT I

CALL SORTLIST(NUMROWS,2*LINELENGTH,OF$)

LET OF$=OF$&REPEAT$(" ",2*LINELENGTH*MAXLINES)
LET OF$=OF$[1:2*LINELENGTH*MAXLINES]

LET NEWOF$=""

FOR I=1 TO MAXLINES

    LET NEWOF$=NEWOF$&OF$[(I-1)*2*LL+LL+1:I*2*LL]

NEXT I

PRINT "WRITING THE OUTPUT TABLE RESULTING FROM THE SORT"
CALL WRITELINES(NEWOF$,OUTPUTFILENAME$,MAXLINES,LINELENGTH)

END SUB
```

The SORTLIST Subroutine

This subroutine is called by the SORT subroutine to perform the actual sorting of data.

```
REM ******************************************************
SUB SORTLIST(MAXLINES,LL,FILE$)

 FOR I=MAXLINES TO 2 STEP -1
    FOR J=1 TO I-1
        IF FILE$[(J-1)*LL+1:J*LL]>FILE$[J*LL+1:(J+1)*LL] THEN CALL SWAP
    NEXT J
 NEXT I

 SUB SWAP

    LET TEMP$=FILE$[(J-1)*LL+1:J*LL]
    LET FILE$[(J-1)*LL+1:J*LL]=FILE$[J*LL+1:(J+1)*LL]
    LET FILE$[J*LL+1:(J+1)*LL] = TEMP$

 END SUB

END SUB
```

The DELETE Subroutine

This subroutine deletes, or erases, data tables.

```
REM *******************************************************

SUB DELETE(SCHEMA$,PARM$,MAXLINES,LINELENGTH)

  CLEAR

  PRINT "PERFORMING DELETE DATABASE OPERATION"

  CALL DEDOUBQUOTES(PARM$,PARM1$)
  LET PARM$=PARM1$

  CALL DEBLANK(PARM$,PARM1$)
  LET PARM$=PARM1$

  LET LASTPOS=0
  CALL GETTOKEN(PARM$,LASTPOS,TOKEN$)
  LET FILENAME1$=TOKEN$

  WHEN ERROR IN
       UNSAVE FILENAME1$
  USE
  END WHEN

  CLEAR

END SUB
```

The UNION Subroutine

This subroutine concatenates two data tables.

```
REM *******************************************************
SUB UNION(SCHEMA$,PARM$,MAXLINES,LINELENGTH)

  CLEAR

  PRINT "PERFORMING UNION DATABASE OPERATION"

  CALL DEDOUBQUOTES(PARM$,PARM1$)
  LET PARM$=PARM1$

  CALL DEBLANK(PARM$,PARM1$)
  LET PARM$=PARM1$

  LET LASTPOS=0
  CALL GETTOKEN(PARM$,LASTPOS,TOKEN$)
  LET FILENAME1$=TOKEN$

  CALL GETTOKEN(PARM$,LASTPOS,TOKEN$)
  LET FILENAME2$=TOKEN$
```

```
     CALL GETTOKEN(PARM$,LASTPOS,TOKEN$)
     LET OUTPUTFILENAME$=TOKEN$

     PRINT "READING IN DATA TABLES FOR UNION"

     PRINT FILENAME1$,FILENAME2$

     CALL READLINES (FILE1$,FILENAME1$,MAXLINES,LINELENGTH)
     CALL READLINES (FILE2$,FILENAME2$,MAXLINES,LINELENGTH)

     LET OUTPUTFILE$=FILE1$&FILE2$

     CALL COMPRESSTABLE (OUTPUTFILE$,2*MAXLINES,LINELENGTH)

     LET OUTPUTFILE$=OUTPUTFILE$[1:MAXLINES*LINELENGTH]

     PRINT "WRITING THE OUTPUT TABLE RESULTING FROM THE UNION"
     CALL WRITELINES(OUTPUTFILE$,OUTPUTFILENAME$,MAXLINES,LINELENGTH)

     CLEAR

END SUB
```

The SUMMARIZE Subroutine

This subroutine causes the system to develop and report summary totals. The subroutine functions are similar to those of control break reports.

```
REM ************************************************************

SUB SUMMARIZE(SCHEMA$,PARM$,MAXLINES,LINELENGTH)

  CLEAR

  PRINT "PERFORMING SUMMARIZE DATABASE OPERATION"

  CALL COLSCHEMA(SCHEMA$,S1$,S2$,S3$,MAXLINES,LINELENGTH)

  CALL DEDOUBQUOTES(PARM$,PARM1$)
  LET PARM$=PARM1$

  CALL DEBLANK(PARM$,PARM1$)
  LET PARM$=PARM1$

  LET LASTPOS=0
  CALL GETTOKEN(PARM$,LASTPOS,TOKEN$)
  LET FILENAME1$=TOKEN$

  CALL GETTOKEN(PARM$,LASTPOS,TOKEN$)
  LET ARGUMENT$=TOKEN$

  CALL GETTOKEN(PARM$,LASTPOS,TOKEN$)
```

```
LET OUTPUTFILENAME$=TOKEN$

PRINT "READING IN DATA TABLE FOR SUMMARIZE"

CALL READLINES (FILE1$,FILENAME1$,MAXLINES,LINELENGTH)
CALL COMPRESSTABLE (FILE1$,MAXLINES,LINELENGTH)

PRINT "PERFORMING SUMMARIZE"

REM NOW BREAK OUT THE COLUMN NAMES FROM ARGUMENT$
REM AND CHANGE THEM TO NUMBERS

LET ARGUMENT$=ARGUMENT$&";"
LET ASTOP=POS(ARGUMENT$,";")
LET OLDASTOP=0
LET COLLIST$=""
LET NT$=REPEAT$(" ",2*MAXLINES*LINELENGTH)

DIM COLT(50)

FOR III=1 TO 50
    LET COLT(III)=0
NEXT III

DO WHILE (ASTOP()0)

   LET WORK$=ARGUMENT$[OLDASTOP+1:ASTOP-1]

   CALL GETSCOLUMN (FILENAME1$,WORK$,S1$,S2$,S3$,CNUMBER,MAXLINES)
   IF CNUMBER)0 AND CNUMBER(=50 THEN LET COLT(CNUMBER)=1
   CALL COLUMN(CNUMBER,WORKCOL$,FILE1$,LINELENGTH,MAXLINES)

   LET LASTPOS=0
   CALL GETTOKEN(WORKCOL$,LASTPOS,CELL$)
   LET RN=1
   LET LL=LINELENGTH

   DO WHILE (CELL$()"" AND CELL$()CHR$(34)&CHR$(34))

      LET CELL$=CELL$&REPEAT$(" ",LINELENGTH-LEN(CELL$))

      LET NT$[(RN-1)*LL*2+LL+1:RN*LL*2]=CELL$

      CALL GETTOKEN(WORKCOL$,LASTPOS,CELL$)

      LET RN=RN+1

   LOOP

   CALL COMPRESSTABLE (NT$,MAXLINES,2*LINELENGTH)

   LET OLDASTOP=ASTOP
   LET ASTOP=POS(ARGUMENT$,";",OLDASTOP+1)

LOOP
```

```
    LET OF$=""

    LET LL=LINELENGTH
    LET NUMROWS=0

    FOR I=1 TO MAXLINES

        LET XX$=FILE1$[(I-1)*LL+1:I*LL]
        LET OF$=OF$&NT$[(I-1)*(2*LL)+1:I*(2*LL)-LL]&XX$
        IF XX$<>REPEAT$(" ",LINELENGTH) THEN
            LET NUMROWS=NUMROWS+1
        END IF

    NEXT I

    CALL SORTLIST(NUMROWS,2*LINELENGTH,OF$)
    LET NEWOF$=""
    LET COUNT=0
    LET OREC$=""

    REM NOW MAKE THE SUMMARY RECORD AND APPEND THE COUNT
    LET OCON$=OF$[1:LL]

    FOR I=1 TO NUMROWS

        LET CON$=OF$[(I-1)*2*LL+1:I*2*LL-LL]
        IF CON$<>OCON$ THEN

            LET TOK2$=STR$(COUNT)
            CALL DEBLANK(TOK2$,TOK3$)
            LET OREC$=OREC$& " "&TOK3$
            LET OREC$=OREC$&REPEAT$(" ",LL)
            LET NEWOF$=NEWOF$&OREC$[1:LL]
            LET COUNT=0
            LET OREC$=""

            LET OCON$=CON$

        END IF

        LET REC$=OF$[(I-1)*2*LL+LL+1:I*2*LL]
        CALL COMB
        LET COUNT=COUNT+1

    NEXT I

    LET TOK2$=STR$(COUNT)
    CALL DEBLANK(TOK2$,TOK3$)
    LET OREC$=OREC$& " "&TOK3$
    LET OREC$=OREC$&REPEAT$(" ",LL)
    LET NEWOF$=NEWOF$&OREC$[1:LL]

    LET OF$=NEWOF$&REPEAT$(" ",LINELENGTH*MAXLINES)

    LET NEWOF$=NEWOF$[1:LINELENGTH*MAXLINES]
```

```
PRINT "WRITING THE OUTPUT TABLE RESULTING FROM THE SUMMARIZE"
CALL WRITELINES(NEWOF$,OUTPUTFILENAME$,MAXLINES,LINELENGTH)

SUB COMB

    REM OREC$ IS THE RECORD TO BE ADDED TO AND TO HAVE THE COUNT APPENDED TO
    REM REC$ IS THE NEW RECORD TO BE ADDED IN

    LET JM=0
    LET JN=0
    CALL GETTOKEN(OREC$,JM,TOK1$)
    CALL GETTOKEN(REC$,JN,TOK2$)
    LET NEWREC$=""
    LET COLN=1

    DO WHILE (TOK1$<>"" OR TOK2$<>"")

        IF TOK1$="" THEN LET TOK1$="0"

        IF COLT(COLN)=1 THEN
            LET NEWREC$=NEWREC$&" "&TOK2$
        ELSE

            WHEN ERROR IN

                    CALL DEDOUBQUOTES(TOK1$,TOK1X$)
                    CALL DEDOUBQUOTES(TOK2$,TOK2X$)

                    LET XX=VAL(TOK2X$)
                    LET YY=VAL(TOK1X$)
                    LET ZZ=XX+YY
                    LET TOK2$=STR$(ZZ)
                    CALL DEBLANK(TOK2$,TOK3$)
                    LET TOK2$=TOK3$

            USE
            END WHEN

            LET NEWREC$=NEWREC$&" "&TOK2$

        END IF

        CALL GETTOKEN(OREC$,JM,TOK1$)
        CALL GETTOKEN(REC$,JN,TOK2$)

        LET COLN=COLN+1

    LOOP

    LET OREC$=NEWREC$

END SUB

END SUB
```

THE DSSGRAPH LIBRARY

This library contains the subroutines that implement graphics and accounting models for the DSS Tool Kit.

```
!!!!!!!!!!!!!!!!!!!!!!!!!!!!!!!!!!!!!!!!!!!!!!!!!!!!!!!!!!!!!!!!!!!!!!!!!!!!!!!!
!                                                                            !
!   THIS IS EXTERNAL LIBRARY DSSGRAPH.TRU                                     !
!                                                                            !
!   THIS LIBRARY CONTAINS THE SUBROUTINES FOR THE GRAPHIC DISPLAYS           !
!   AND DESCRIPTIVE MODELS.                                                   !
!                                                                            !
!   SEE CHAPTER 5 FOR EXPLANATION OF THIS FUNCTION                            !
!                                                                            !
!!!!!!!!!!!!!!!!!!!!!!!!!!!!!!!!!!!!!!!!!!!!!!!!!!!!!!!!!!!!!!!!!!!!!!!!!!!!!!!!

EXTERNAL
```

The SGRAM Subroutine

This subroutine generates scattergraphs.

```
REM ********************************************************
SUB SGRAM(SCHEMA$,PARM$,MAXLINES,LINELENGTH)

    CLEAR

    PRINT "PERFORMING SGRAM (SCATTERGRAM) GRAPHICS OPERATION"

    CALL COLSCHEMA(SCHEMA$,S1$,S2$,S3$,MAXLINES,LINELENGTH)

    CALL DEDOUBQUOTES(PARM$,PARM1$)
    LET PARM$=PARM1$

    CALL DEBLANK(PARM$,PARM1$)
    LET PARM$=PARM1$

    LET LASTPOS=0
    CALL GETTOKEN(PARM$,LASTPOS,TOKEN$)
    LET FILENAME1$=TOKEN$

    CALL GETTOKEN(PARM$,LASTPOS,TOKEN$)
    LET XCOL$=TOKEN$

    CALL GETTOKEN(PARM$,LASTPOS,TOKEN$)
    LET YCOL$=TOKEN$

    PRINT "READING IN DATA TABLE FOR SGRAM"

    CALL READLINES (FILE1$,FILENAME1$,MAXLINES,LINELENGTH)
```

```
       CALL COMPRESSTABLE (FILE1$,MAXLINES,LINELENGTH)

       PRINT "PREPARING SCATTERGRAM"

       CALL GETSCOLUMN (FILENAME1$,XCOL$,S1$,S2$,S3$,XCOL,MAXLINES)
       CALL GETSCOLUMN (FILENAME1$,YCOL$,S1$,S2$,S3$,YCOL,MAXLINES)

       CALL COLUMN(XCOL,XCOLVALUES$,FILE1$,LINELENGTH,MAXLINES)
       CALL COLUMN(YCOL,YCOLVALUES$,FILE1$,LINELENGTH,MAXLINES)

       LET LPX=0
       LET LPY=0

       CALL GETTOKEN(XCOLVALUES$,LPX,CELL$)
       CALL DEDOUBQUOTES(CELL$,CELLX$)
       CALL GETTOKEN(YCOLVALUES$,LPYX,CELL$)
       CALL DEDOUBQUOTES(CELL$,CELLY$)

       DIM ARR(200,2)

       LET J=1

       DO WHILE (CELLX$()"" AND CELLY$()"")

       WHEN ERROR IN
            LET X=VAL(CELLX$)
       USE
            LET X=0
       END WHEN

       WHEN ERROR IN
            LET Y=VAL(CELLY$)
       USE
            LET Y=0
       END WHEN

       LET ARR(J,1)=X
       LET ARR(J,2)=Y
       LET J=J+1

       CALL GETTOKEN(XCOLVALUES$,LPX,CELL$)
       CALL DEDOUBQUOTES(CELL$,CELLX$)
       CALL GETTOKEN(YCOLVALUES$,LPYX,CELL$)
       CALL DEDOUBQUOTES(CELL$,CELLY$)

LOOP

CLEAR

REM PRINT AXES
REM FIRST FIND MAX AND MIN VALUES FOR EACH COORDINATE AXIS

LET XMAX=-999999
LET XMIN=999999
LET YMAX=-999999
LET YMIN=999999
```

```
FOR I=1 TO J-1

    IF ARR(I,1)>XMAX THEN
       LET XMAX=ARR(I,1)
    END IF

    IF ARR(I,1)<XMIN THEN
       LET XMIN=ARR(I,1)
    END IF

    IF ARR(I,2)>YMAX THEN
       LET YMAX=ARR(I,2)
    END IF

    IF ARR(I,2)<YMIN THEN
       LET YMIN=ARR(I,2)
    END IF

NEXT I

    OPEN #1: SCREEN 0, .49,0,.6
    SET WINDOW XMIN-1,XMAX+1,YMIN-1,YMAX+1
    BOX LINES XMIN-1,XMAX+1,YMIN-1,YMAX+1

    FOR I=1 TO J-1

        REM PLOT POINTS
        PLOT POINTS: ARR(I,1),ARR(I,2)

    NEXT I

    OPEN #2: SCREEN .5,1,0,1
    SET CURSOR 2,5

    PRINT "SCATTERGRAM"
    PRINT

    PRINT "X-AXIS DATA IS"
    PRINT "        ";XCOL$
    PRINT "Y-AXIS DATA IS"
    PRINT "        ";YCOL$
    PRINT

    PRINT "X-AXIS MIN IS ",XMIN
    PRINT "X-AXIS MAX IS ",XMAX
    PRINT
    PRINT "Y-AXIS MIN IS ",YMIN
    PRINT "Y-AXIS MAX IS ",YMAX
    PRINT

    PRINT "PRESS ANY KEY"
    PRINT "  TO CONTINUE>"

    GET KEY X
    CLOSE #1
    CLOSE #2
```

```
      WINDOW #0
      SET MODE "80"
END SUB
```

The MTRACE Subroutine

This subroutine generates median trace diagrams.

```
REM ***********************************************************

SUB MTRACE(SCHEMA$,PARM$,MAXLINES,LINELENGTH)

    CLEAR

    PRINT "PERFORMING MTRACE (MEDIAN TRACE) GRAPHICS OPERATION"

    CALL COLSCHEMA(SCHEMA$,S1$,S2$,S3$,MAXLINES,LINELENGTH)

    CALL DEDOUBQUOTES(PARM$,PARM1$)
    LET PARM$=PARM1$

    CALL DEBLANK(PARM$,PARM1$)
    LET PARM$=PARM1$

    LET LASTPOS=0
    CALL GETTOKEN(PARM$,LASTPOS,TOKEN$)
    LET FILENAME1$=TOKEN$

    CALL GETTOKEN(PARM$,LASTPOS,TOKEN$)
    LET XCOL$=TOKEN$

    CALL GETTOKEN(PARM$,LASTPOS,TOKEN$)
    LET YCOL$=TOKEN$

    PRINT "READING IN DATA TABLE FOR MTRACE"

    CALL READLINES (FILE1$,FILENAME1$,MAXLINES,LINELENGTH)
    CALL COMPRESSTABLE (FILE1$,MAXLINES,LINELENGTH)

    PRINT "PREPARING MEDIAN TRACE"

    CALL GETSCOLUMN (FILENAME1$,XCOL$,S1$,S2$,S3$,XCOL,MAXLINES)
    CALL GETSCOLUMN (FILENAME1$,YCOL$,S1$,S2$,S3$,YCOL,MAXLINES)

    CALL COLUMN(XCOL,XCOLVALUES$,FILE1$,LINELENGTH,MAXLINES)
    CALL COLUMN(YCOL,YCOLVALUES$,FILE1$,LINELENGTH,MAXLINES)

    LET LPX=0
    LET LPY=0

    CALL GETTOKEN(XCOLVALUES$,LPX,CELL$)
    CALL DEDOUBQUOTES(CELL$,CELLX$)
    CALL GETTOKEN(YCOLVALUES$,LPYX,CELL$)
```

```
CALL DEDOUBQUOTES(CELL$,CELLY$)

DIM ARR(200,2)

LET J=1

DO WHILE (CELLX$<>"" AND CELLY$<>"")

    WHEN ERROR IN
        LET X=VAL(CELLX$)
    USE
        LET X=0
    END WHEN

    WHEN ERROR IN
        LET Y=VAL(CELLY$)
    USE
        LET Y=0
    END WHEN

    LET ARR(J,1)=X
    LET ARR(J,2)=Y
    LET J=J+1

    CALYCOLVALUES$,LPYX,CELL$)
    CALL DEDOUBQUOTES(CELL$,CELLY$)

LOOP

CLEAR

REM FIRST FIND MAX AND MIN VALUES FOR EACH COORDINATE AXIS

LET XMAX=-999999
LET XMIN=999999
LET YMAX=-999999
LET YMIN=999999

LET NUMPOINTS=J-1

FOR I=1 TO NUMPOINTS

    IF ARR(I,1)>XMAX THEN
        LET XMAX=ARR(I,1)
    END IF

    IF ARR(I,1)<XMIN THEN
        LET XMIN=ARR(I,1)
    END IF

    IF ARR(I,2)>YMAX THEN
        LET YMAX=ARR(I,2)
    END IF

    IF ARR(I,2)<YMIN THEN
        LET YMIN=ARR(I,2)
    END IF
```

```
NEXT I

OPEN #1: SCREEN 0, .49,0,.6
SET WINDOW XMIN-1,XMAX+1,YMIN-1,YMAX+1
BOX LINES XMIN-1,XMAX+1,YMIN-1,YMAX+1

FOR I=1 TO NUMPOINTS

    REM PLOT POINTS
    PLOT POINTS: ARR(I,1),ARR(I,2)


NEXT I

IF NUMPOINTS>=6 THEN

    LET NUM1=1
    LET NUM2=J-1
    CALL SORTLIST

    LET SIXTH=INT((NUMPOINTS)/6)

    LET POINT=1
    FOR SECTOR=1 TO 5
        LET II=(SECTOR-1)*SIXTH+INT(SIXTH/2)+1
        LET X=ARR(II,1)
        LET NUM1=(SECTOR-1)*SIXTH+1
        LET NUM2=SECTOR*SIXTH
        FOR III=NUM1 TO NUM2
            LET ARR(III,1)=ARR(III,2)
        NEXT III

        CALL SORTLIST
        LET Y=ARR(II,1)

        PLOT X,Y;

    NEXT SECTOR

    LET II=(6-1)*SIXTH
    LET II=II+INT((NUMPOINTS-II)/2) +1
    LET X=ARR(II,1)
    LET NUM1=5*SIXTH+1
    LET NUM2=NUMPOINTS
    FOR III=NUM1 TO NUM2
        LET ARR(III,1)=ARR(III,2)
    NEXT III

    CALL SORTLIST
    LET Y=ARR(II,1)

    PLOT X,Y;

END IF

OPEN #2: SCREEN .5,1,0,1
```

```
    SET CURSOR 2,5
    PRINT "MEDIAN TRACE"
    PRINT


    IF NUMPOINTS<6 THEN
        PRINT "NEED AT LEAST 6 POINTS FOR MEDIAN TRACE"

    ELSE

        PRINT "X-AXIS DATA IS"
        PRINT "      ";XCOL$
        PRINT "Y-AXIS DATA IS"
        PRINT "      ";YCOL$
        PRINT


        PRINT "X-AXIS MIN IS ",XMIN
        PRINT "X-AXIS MAX IS ",XMAX
        PRINT
        PRINT "Y-AXIS MIN IS ",YMIN
        PRINT "Y-AXIS MAX IS ",YMAX
        PRINT

    END IF

    PRINT "PRESS ANY KEY"
    PRINT "  TO CONTINUE)"

    GET KEY X
    CLOSE #1
    CLOSE #2


    WINDOW #0
    SET MODE "80"

    SUB SORTLIST

        FOR I=NUM2 TO NUM1+1 STEP -1
            FOR J=NUM1 TO I-1
                IF ARR(J,1)>ARR(J+1,1) THEN
                    LET TEMP=ARR(J,1)
                    LET ARR(J,1)=ARR(J+1,1)
                    LET ARR(J+1,1)=TEMP
                    LET TEMP=ARR(J,2)
                    LET ARR(J,2)=ARR(J+1,2)
                    LET ARR(J+1,2)=TEMP

                END IF
            NEXT J
        NEXT I

    END SUB

END SUB
```

The RLINE Subroutine

This subroutine generates resistant line graphs.

```
REM *********************************************************
SUB RLINE(SCHEMA$,PARM$,MAXLINES,LINELENGTH)

    CLEAR

    PRINT "PERFORMING RLINE (RESISTANT LINE) GRAPHICS OPERATION"

    CALL COLSCHEMA(SCHEMA$,S1$,S2$,S3$,MAXLINES,LINELENGTH)

    CALL DEDOUBQUOTES(PARM$,PARM1$)
    LET PARM$=PARM1$

    CALL DEBLANK(PARM$,PARM1$)
    LET PARM$=PARM1$

    LET LASTPOS=0
    CALL GETTOKEN(PARM$,LASTPOS,TOKEN$)
    LET FILENAME1$=TOKEN$

    CALL GETTOKEN(PARM$,LASTPOS,TOKEN$)
    LET XCOL$=TOKEN$

    CALL GETTOKEN(PARM$,LASTPOS,TOKEN$)
    LET YCOL$=TOKEN$

    PRINT "READING IN DATA TABLE FOR RLINE"

    CALL READLINES (FILE1$,FILENAME1$,MAXLINES,LINELENGTH)
    CALL COMPRESSTABLE (FILE1$,MAXLINES,LINELENGTH)

    PRINT "PREPARING RESISTANT LINE"

    CALL GETSCOLUMN (FILENAME1$,XCOL$,S1$,S2$,S3$,XCOL,MAXLINES)
    CALL GETSCOLUMN (FILENAME1$,YCOL$,S1$,S2$,S3$,YCOL,MAXLINES)

    CALL COLUMN(XCOL,XCOLVALUES$,FILE1$,LINELENGTH,MAXLINES)
    CALL COLUMN(YCOL,YCOLVALUES$,FILE1$,LINELENGTH,MAXLINES)

    LET LPX=0
    LET LPY=0

    CALL GETTOKEN(XCOLVALUES$,LPX,CELL$)
    CALL DEDOUBQUOTES(CELL$,CELLX$)
    CALL GETTOKEN(YCOLVALUES$,LPYX,CELL$)
    CALL DEDOUBQUOTES(CELL$,CELLY$)

    DIM ARR(200,2)

    LET J=1

    DO WHILE (CELLX$<>"" AND CELLY$<>"")
```

```
      WHEN ERROR IN
            LET X=VAL(CELLX$)
      USE
            LET X=0
      END WHEN

      WHEN ERROR IN
            LET Y=VAL(CELLY$)
      USE
            LET Y=0
      END WHEN

      LET ARR(J,1)=X
      LET ARR(J,2)=Y
      LET J=J+1

      CALL GETTOKEN(XCOLVALUES$,LPX,CELL$)
      CALL DEDOUBQUOTES(CELL$,CELLX$)
      CALL GETTOKEN(YCOLVALUES$,LPYX,CELL$)
      CALL DEDOUBQUOTES(CELL$,CELLY$)

LOOP

CLEAR

REM FIRST FIND MAX AND MIN VALUES FOR EACH COORDINATE AXIS

LET XMAX=-999999
LET XMIN=999999
LET YMAX=-999999
LET YMIN=999999

LET NUMPOINTS=J-1

FOR I=1 TO NUMPOINTS

    IF ARR(I,1)>XMAX THEN
       LET XMAX=ARR(I,1)
    END IF

    IF ARR(I,1)<XMIN THEN
       LET XMIN=ARR(I,1)
    END IF

    IF ARR(I,2)>YMAX THEN
       LET YMAX=ARR(I,2)
    END IF

    IF ARR(I,2)<YMIN THEN
       LET YMIN=ARR(I,2)
    END IF

NEXT I

OPEN #1: SCREEN 0, .49,0,.6
SET WINDOW XMIN-1,XMAX+1,YMIN-1,YMAX+1
```

```
BOX LINES XMIN-1,XMAX+1,YMIN-1,YMAX+1

FOR I=1 TO NUMPOINTS

    REM PLOT POINTS
    PLOT POINTS: ARR(I,1),ARR(I,2)

NEXT I

IF NUMPOINTS>=6 THEN

    LET NUM1=1
    LET NUM2=NUMPOINTS
    CALL SORTLIST

    LET THIRD=INT((NUMPOINTS)/3)

    LET POINT=1
    LET II=(THIRD/2)+1
    LET X=ARR(II,1)
    LET NUM1=1
    LET NUM2=THIRD
    FOR III=NUM1 TO NUM2
        LET ARR(III,1)=ARR(III,2)
    NEXT III

    CALL SORTLIST
    LET Y=ARR(II,1)

    LET X1=X
    LET Y1=Y

    PLOT X,Y;

    LET II=2*THIRD
    LET II=II+INT((NUMPOINTS-II)/2)+1
    LET X=ARR(II,1)
    LET NUM1=2*THIRD+1
    LET NUM2=NUMPOINTS
    FOR III=NUM1 TO NUM2
        LET ARR(III,1)=ARR(III,2)
    NEXT III

    CALL SORTLIST
    LET Y=ARR(II,1)

    PLOT X,Y;

END IF

OPEN #2: SCREEN .5,1,0,1
SET CURSOR 2,5
PRINT "MEDIAN TRACE"
```

```
PRINT

IF NUMPOINTS<6 THEN
    PRINT "NEED AT LEAST 6 POINTS FOR MEDIAN TRACE"

ELSE

    PRINT "X-AXIS DATA IS"
    PRINT "      ";XCOL$
    PRINT "Y-AXIS DATA IS"
    PRINT "      ";YCOL$
    PRINT

    PRINT "X-AXIS MIN IS ",XMIN
    PRINT "X-AXIS MAX IS ",XMAX
    PRINT
    PRINT "Y-AXIS MIN IS ",YMIN
    PRINT "Y-AXIS MAX IS ",YMAX
    PRINT
    PRINT "SLOPE IS ",(Y-Y1)/(X-X1)
    PRINT "Y-INTERCEPT IS ",Y-((Y-Y1)/(X-X1))*X
    PRINT

END IF

PRINT "PRESS ANY KEY"
PRINT "  TO CONTINUE)"

GET KEY X
CLOSE #1
CLOSE #2

WINDOW #0
SET MODE "80"

SUB SORTLIST

    FOR I=NUM2 TO NUM1+1 STEP -1
        FOR J=NUM1 TO I-1
            IF ARR(J,1)>ARR(J+1,1) THEN
                LET TEMP=ARR(J,1)
                LET ARR(J,1)=ARR(J+1,1)
                LET ARR(J+1,1)=TEMP
                LET TEMP=ARR(J,2)
                LET ARR(J,2)=ARR(J+1,2)
                LET ARR(J+1,2)=TEMP

            END IF
        NEXT J
    NEXT I

END SUB

END SUB
```

The BANDW Subroutine

This subroutine calculates and generates box-and-whisker diagrams.

```
REM **************************************************************

SUB BANDW(SCHEMA$,PARM$,MAXLINES,LINELENGTH)

    CLEAR

    PRINT "PERFORMING BANDW (BOX-AND-WHISKER) GRAPHICS OPERATION"

    CALL COLSCHEMA(SCHEMA$,S1$,S2$,S3$,MAXLINES,LINELENGTH)

    CALL DEDOUBQUOTES(PARM$,PARM1$)
    LET PARM$=PARM1$

    CALL DEBLANK(PARM$,PARM1$)
    LET PARM$=PARM1$

    LET LASTPOS=0
    CALL GETTOKEN(PARM$,LASTPOS,TOKEN$)
    LET FILENAME1$=TOKEN$

    CALL GETTOKEN(PARM$,LASTPOS,TOKEN$)
    LET XCOL$=TOKEN$

    PRINT "READING IN DATA TABLE FOR BANDW"

    CALL READLINES (FILE1$,FILENAME1$,MAXLINES,LINELENGTH)
    CALL COMPRESSTABLE (FILE1$,MAXLINES,LINELENGTH)

    PRINT "PREPARING BOX-AND-WHISKER DIAGRAM"

    CALL GETSCOLUMN (FILENAME1$,XCOL$,S1$,S2$,S3$,XCOL,MAXLINES)

    CALL COLUMN(XCOL,XCOLVALUES$,FILE1$,LINELENGTH,MAXLINES)

    LET LPX=0

    CALL GETTOKEN(XCOLVALUES$,LPX,CELL$)
    CALL DEDOUBQUOTES(CELL$,CELLX$)

    DIM ARR(200)

    LET J=1

    DO WHILE (CELLX$()"")

        WHEN ERROR IN
            LET X=VAL(CELLX$)
        USE
            LET X=0
        END WHEN

        LET ARR(J)=X
        LET J=J+1
```

```
          CALL GETTOKEN(XCOLVALUES$,LPX,CELL$)
          CALL DEDOUBQUOTES(CELL$,CELLX$)

LOOP

CLEAR

LET XMAX=-999999
LET XMIN=999999

LET NUMPOINTS=J-1

FOR I=1 TO NUMPOINTS

     IF ARR(I)>XMAX THEN
        LET XMAX=ARR(I)
     END IF

     IF ARR(I)<XMIN THEN
        LET XMIN=ARR(I)
     END IF

NEXT I

OPEN #1: SCREEN 0, .49,0,.6
SET WINDOW XMIN-1,XMAX+1,0,10
BOX LINES XMIN-1,XMAX+1,0,10

IF NUMPOINTS>=6 THEN

     LET NUM1=1
     LET NUM2=NUMPOINTS
     CALL SORTLIST

     LET QTR=INT((NUMPOINTS)/4)

     LET POINT=1
     LET II=(QTR*2)+1
     LET MEDIAN=ARR(II)
     LET UPQTR=ARR(II+QTR)
     LET LOQTR=ARR(II-QTR)
     LET MIDSPREAD=UPQTR-LOQTR

     LET I=NUMPOINTS
     DO WHILE (ARR(I)>UPQTR+MIDSPREAD)
        LET I=I-1
     LOOP
     LET UPWHISKER=ARR(I)

     LET I=1
     DO WHILE (ARR(I)<LOQTR-MIDSPREAD)
        LET LOWHISKER=ARR(I)
        LET I=I+1
     LOOP
     LET LOWHISKER=ARR(I)
```

```
        REM NOW DRAW DIAGRAM

        FOR I=1 TO NUMPOINTS
            PLOT POINTS: ARR(I),5
        NEXT I

        BOX LINES LOQTR,MEDIAN,4,6
        BOX LINES MEDIAN,UPQTR,4,6

        PLOT LINES:UPQTR,5;UPWHISKER,5
        PLOT LINES:LOQTR,5;LOWHISKER,5

   END IF

   OPEN #2: SCREEN .5,1,0,1
   SET CURSOR 2,5
   PRINT "BOX-AND-WHISKER"
   PRINT

   IF NUMPOINTS<6 THEN
       PRINT "NEED AT LEAST 6 POINTS FOR MEDIAN TRACE"

   ELSE

       PRINT "MEDIAN IS ",MEDIAN
       PRINT "UPPER HINGE IS AT"
       PRINT "    ";UPQTR
       PRINT "LOWER HINGE IS AT"
       PRINT "    ";LOQTR
       PRINT "UPPER WHISKER IS AT"
       PRINT "    ";UPWHISKER
       PRINT "LOWER WHISKER IS AT"
       PRINT "    ";LOWHISKER
       PRINT

       PRINT "MIN IS ",XMIN
       PRINT "MAX IS ",XMAX
       PRINT

   END IF

   PRINT "PRESS ANY KEY"
   PRINT "  TO CONTINUE)"

   GET KEY X
   CLOSE #1
   CLOSE #2

   WINDOW #0
   SET MODE "80"

   SUB SORTLIST

       FOR I=NUM2 TO NUM1+1 STEP -1
           FOR J=NUM1 TO I-1
               IF ARR(J)>ARR(J+1) THEN
                   LET TEMP=ARR(J)
```

```
                    LET ARR(J)=ARR(J+1)
                    LET ARR(J+1)=TEMP

                END IF
            NEXT J
        NEXT I

    END SUB

END SUB
```

The HISTO Subroutine ·

This subroutine produces histograms.

```
REM ***********************************************************

SUB HISTO(SCHEMA$,PARM$,MAXLINES,LINELENGTH)

    CLEAR

    PRINT "PERFORMING HISTO (HISTOGRAM) GRAPHICS OPERATION"

    CALL COLSCHEMA(SCHEMA$,S1$,S2$,S3$,MAXLINES,LINELENGTH)

    CALL DEDOUBQUOTES(PARM$,PARM1$)
    LET PARM$=PARM1$

    CALL DEBLANK(PARM$,PARM1$)
    LET PARM$=PARM1$

    LET LASTPOS=0
    CALL GETTOKEN(PARM$,LASTPOS,TOKEN$)
    LET FILENAME1$=TOKEN$

    CALL GETTOKEN(PARM$,LASTPOS,TOKEN$)
    LET XCOL$=TOKEN$

    CALL GETTOKEN(PARM$,LASTPOS,TOKEN$)
    LET YCOL$=TOKEN$

    PRINT "READING IN DATA TABLE FOR HISTO"

    CALL READLINES (FILE1$,FILENAME1$,MAXLINES,LINELENGTH)
    CALL COMPRESSTABLE (FILE1$,MAXLINES,LINELENGTH)

    PRINT "PREPARING HISTOGRAM"

    CALL GETSCOLUMN (FILENAME1$,XCOL$,S1$,S2$,S3$,XCOL,MAXLINES)
    CALL GETSCOLUMN (FILENAME1$,YCOL$,S1$,S2$,S3$,YCOL,MAXLINES)

    CALL COLUMN(XCOL,XCOLVALUES$,FILE1$,LINELENGTH,MAXLINES)
    CALL COLUMN(YCOL,YCOLVALUES$,FILE1$,LINELENGTH,MAXLINES)
```

```
LET LPX=0
LET LPY=0

CALL GETTOKEN(XCOLVALUES$,LPX,CELL$)
CALL DEDOUBQUOTES(CELL$,CELLX$)
CALL GETTOKEN(YCOLVALUES$,LPYX,CELL$)
CALL DEDOUBQUOTES(CELL$,CELLY$)

DIM ARR(200,2)

LET J=1

DO WHILE (CELLX$<>"" AND CELLY$<>"")

    WHEN ERROR IN
        LET X=VAL(CELLX$)
    USE
        LET X=0
    END WHEN

    WHEN ERROR IN
        LET Y=VAL(CELLY$)
    USE
        LET Y=0
    END WHEN

    LET ARR(J,1)=X
    LET ARR(J,2)=Y
    LET J=J+1

    CALL GETTOKEN(XCOLVALUES$,LPX,CELL$)
    CALL DEDOUBQUOTES(CELL$,CELLX$)
    CALL GETTOKEN(YCOLVALUES$,LPYX,CELL$)
    CALL DEDOUBQUOTES(CELL$,CELLY$)

LOOP

CLEAR

REM FIRST FIND MAX AND MIN VALUES FOR EACH COORDINATE AXIS

LET XMAX=-999999
LET XMIN=999999
LET YMAX=-999999
LET YMIN=999999

LET NUMPOINTS=J-1

FOR I=1 TO NUMPOINTS

    IF ARR(I,1)>XMAX THEN
        LET XMAX=ARR(I,1)
    END IF

    IF ARR(I,1)<XMIN THEN
        LET XMIN=ARR(I,1)
    END IF
```

```
        IF ARR(I,2))YMAX THEN
            LET YMAX=ARR(I,2)
        END IF

        IF ARR(I,2)(YMIN THEN
            LET YMIN=ARR(I,2)
        END IF

    NEXT I

    OPEN #1: SCREEN 0, .49,0,.6
    SET WINDOW XMIN-1,XMAX+1,YMIN-1,YMAX+1
    BOX LINES XMIN-1,XMAX+1,YMIN-1,YMAX+1

    FOR I=1 TO NUMPOINTS

        PLOT LINES: ARR(I,1),YMIN;ARR(I,1),ARR(I,2)

    NEXT I

    OPEN #2: SCREEN .5,1,0,1
    SET CURSOR 2,5
    PRINT "HISTOGRAM"
    PRINT

    PRINT "X-AXIS DATA IS"
    PRINT "     ";XCOL$
    PRINT "Y-AXIS DATA IS"
    PRINT "     ";YCOL$
    PRINT

    PRINT "X-AXIS MIN IS ",XMIN
    PRINT "X-AXIS MAX IS ",XMAX
    PRINT
    PRINT "Y-AXIS MIN IS ",YMIN
    PRINT "Y-AXIS MAX IS ",YMAX
    PRINT

    PRINT "PRESS ANY KEY"
    PRINT "  TO CONTINUE)"

    GET KEY X
    CLOSE #1
    CLOSE #2

    WINDOW #0
    SET MODE "80"

SUB SORTLIST

    FOR I=NUM2 TO NUM1+1 STEP -1
        FOR J=NUM1 TO I-1
            IF ARR(J,1))ARR(J+1,1) THEN
                LET TEMP=ARR(J,1)
                LET ARR(J,1)=ARR(J+1,1)
                LET ARR(J+1,1)=TEMP
                LET TEMP=ARR(J,2)
```

```
                LET ARR(J,2)=ARR(J+1,2)
                LET ARR(J+1,2)=TEMP

            END IF
        NEXT J
    NEXT I

    END SUB

END SUB
```

The PIE Subroutine

This subroutine generates pie charts.

```
REM ***********************************************************

SUB PIE(SCHEMA$,PARM$,MAXLINES,LINELENGTH)

    OPTION ANGLE DEGREES

    CLEAR

    PRINT "PERFORMING PIE (PIE CHART) GRAPHICS OPERATION"

    CALL COLSCHEMA(SCHEMA$,S1$,S2$,S3$,MAXLINES,LINELENGTH)

    CALL DEDOUBQUOTES(PARM$,PARM1$)
    LET PARM$=PARM1$

    CALL DEBLANK(PARM$,PARM1$)
    LET PARM$=PARM1$

    LET LASTPOS=0
    CALL GETTOKEN(PARM$,LASTPOS,TOKEN$)
    LET FILENAME1$=TOKEN$

    CALL GETTOKEN(PARM$,LASTPOS,TOKEN$)
    LET XCOL$=TOKEN$

    CALL GETTOKEN(PARM$,LASTPOS,TOKEN$)
    LET YCOL$=TOKEN$

    PRINT "READING IN DATA TABLE FOR PIE"

    CALL READLINES (FILE1$,FILENAME1$,MAXLINES,LINELENGTH)
    CALL COMPRESSTABLE (FILE1$,MAXLINES,LINELENGTH)

    PRINT "PREPARING PIE CHART"

    CALL GETSCOLUMN (FILENAME1$,XCOL$,S1$,S2$,S3$,XCOL,MAXLINES)
    CALL GETSCOLUMN (FILENAME1$,YCOL$,S1$,S2$,S3$,YCOL,MAXLINES)
```

```
CALL COLUMN(XCOL,XCOLVALUES$,FILE1$,LINELENGTH,MAXLINES)
CALL COLUMN(YCOL,YCOLVALUES$,FILE1$,LINELENGTH,MAXLINES)

LET LPY=0

CALL GETTOKEN(YCOLVALUES$,LPYX,CELL$)
CALL DEDOUBQUOTES(CELL$,CELLY$)

DIM ARR(200)

LET J=1

DO WHILE (CELLY$()"")

    WHEN ERROR IN
        LET Y=VAL(CELLY$)
    USE
        LET Y=0
    END WHEN

    LET ARR(J)=Y
    LET J=J+1

    CALL GETTOKEN(YCOLVALUES$,LPYX,CELL$)
    CALL DEDOUBQUOTES(CELL$,CELLY$)

LOOP

CLEAR

REM FIRST FIND MAX AND MIN VALUES FOR EACH COORDINATE AXIS

LET YMAX=-999999
LET YMIN=999999

LET NUMPOINTS=J-1
LET TOTAL=0

FOR I=1 TO NUMPOINTS

    LET TOTAL=TOTAL+ARR(I)

    IF ARR(I)>YMAX THEN
        LET YMAX=ARR(I)
    END IF

    IF ARR(I)<YMIN THEN
        LET YMIN=ARR(I)
    END IF

NEXT I

OPEN #1: SCREEN 0, .49,0,.6

SET WINDOW -1.1,+1.1,-1.1,+1.1
LET WHERE =0
```

```
FOR I=1 TO NUMPOINTS

    LET PROPO=(ARR(I)/TOTAL)*360

    IF I=NUMPOINTS THEN
       LET END=360
    ELSE
       LET END=PROPO+WHERE
    END IF

    FOR J=WHERE TO END
        PLOT SIN(J),COS(J);
    NEXT J

    PLOT LINES: 0,0;SIN(J),COS(J)

    LET WHERE=WHERE+PROPO
NEXT I

OPEN #2: SCREEN .5,1,0,1
SET CURSOR 1,5
PRINT "PIE CHART"
PRINT

PRINT "FIRST COL DATA IS"
PRINT "     ";XCOL$
PRINT "SECOND COL DATA IS"
PRINT "     ";YCOL$

PRINT "Y-AXIS MIN IS ",YMIN
PRINT "Y-AXIS MAX IS ",YMAX
PRINT "TOTAL OF Y-DATA IS "
PRINT "     ";TOTAL
PRINT "SLICES DENOTE (IN "
PRINT "  CLOCKWISE ORDER):"

LET LPX=0
IF NUMPOINTS>8 THEN
   LET NUMPOINTS=8
END IF

FOR J=1 TO NUMPOINTS
    CALL GETTOKEN(XCOLVALUES$,LPX,CELL$)
    CALL DEDOUBQUOTES(CELL$,CELLX$)
    PRINT CELLX$
NEXT J

PRINT "ANY KEY TO CONTINUE"

GET KEY X
CLOSE #1
CLOSE #2

WINDOW #0
SET MODE "80"

END SUB
```

The INCO Subroutine

This subroutine computes, formats, and prints income statements.

```
REM ***********************************************************

SUB INCO(SCHEMA$,PARM$,MAXLINES,LINELENGTH)

    CLEAR

    CALL DEDOUBQUOTES(PARM$,PARM1$)
    LET PARM$=PARM1$

    CALL DEBLANK(PARM$,PARM1$)
    LET PARM$=PARM1$

    LET LASTPOS=0
    CALL GETTOKEN(PARM$,LASTPOS,TOKEN$)
    LET FILENAME1$=TOKEN$

    PRINT "READING IN DATA TABLE FOR INCO"

    CALL READLINES (FILE1$,FILENAME1$,MAXLINES,LINELENGTH)
    CALL COMPRESSTABLE (FILE1$,MAXLINES,LINELENGTH)

    PRINT "PREPARING INCOME STATEMENT"

    CALL COLUMN(1,XCOLVALUES$,FILE1$,LINELENGTH,MAXLINES)
    CALL COLUMN(2,YCOLVALUES$,FILE1$,LINELENGTH,MAXLINES)
    CALL COLUMN(3,ZCOLVALUES$,FILE1$,LINELENGTH,MAXLINES)

    LET LPY=0

    CALL GETTOKEN(YCOLVALUES$,LPYX,CELL$)
    CALL DEDOUBQUOTES(CELL$,CELLY$)

    DIM ARR(200)

    LET J=1

    DO WHILE (CELLY$()"")

        WHEN ERROR IN
            LET Y=VAL(CELLY$)
        USE
            LET Y=0
        END WHEN

        LET ARR(J)=Y
        LET J=J+1

        CALL GETTOKEN(YCOLVALUES$,LPYX,CELL$)
        CALL DEDOUBQUOTES(CELL$,CELLY$)

    LOOP
```

```
CLEAR
LET NUMPOINTS=J-1

PRINT "                INCOME STATEMENT"
PRINT " INCOME"

LET TOTALI=0
LET LPX=0
LET LPZ=0

FOR J=1 TO NUMPOINTS

    CALL GETTOKEN(XCOLVALUES$,LPX,CELL$)
    CALL DEDOUBQUOTES(CELL$,CELLX$)
    CALL GETTOKEN(ZCOLVALUES$,LPZ,CELL$)
    CALL DEDOUBQUOTES(CELL$,CELLZ$)


    IF CELLX$="IN" THEN
       LET CELLZ$=CELLZ$&REPEAT$(" ",30)
       LET CELLZ$=CELLZ$[1:30]
       PRINT "         ";CELLZ$;
       PRINT USING "--------#":ARR(J)
       LET TOTALI=TOTALI+ARR(J)
    END IF

NEXT J

PRINT REPEAT$(" ",40);
PRINT "----------"

PRINT REPEAT$(" ",40);
PRINT USING "--------#":TOTALI

PRINT " EXPENSE"

LET TOTALE=0
LET LPX=0
LET LPZ=0

FOR J=1 TO NUMPOINTS

    CALL GETTOKEN(XCOLVALUES$,LPX,CELL$)
    CALL DEDOUBQUOTES(CELL$,CELLX$)
    CALL GETTOKEN(ZCOLVALUES$,LPZ,CELL$)
    CALL DEDOUBQUOTES(CELL$,CELLZ$)

    IF CELLX$="EX" THEN
       LET CELLZ$=CELLZ$&REPEAT$(" ",30)
       LET CELLZ$=CELLZ$[1:30]
       PRINT "         ";CELLZ$;
       PRINT USING "--------#":ARR(J)
       LET TOTALE=TOTALE+ARR(J)
    END IF
```

```
      NEXT J

      PRINT REPEAT$(" ",40);
      PRINT "----------"

      PRINT REPEAT$(" ",40);
      PRINT USING "---------#":TOTALE

      PRINT
      PRINT " PROFIT OR LOSS                        ";
      PRINT USING "---------#":TOTALI - TOTALE

      PRINT "ANY KEY TO CONTINUE"

      GET KEY X

END SUB
```

The BALA Subroutine

This subroutine computes, formats, and prints balance sheets.

```
REM ***********************************************************

SUB BALA(SCHEMA$,PARM$,MAXLINES,LINELENGTH)

      CLEAR

      CALL DEDOUBQUOTES(PARM$,PARM1$)
      LET PARM$=PARM1$

      CALL DEBLANK(PARM$,PARM1$)
      LET PARM$=PARM1$

      LET LASTPOS=0
      CALL GETTOKEN(PARM$,LASTPOS,TOKEN$)
      LET FILENAME1$=TOKEN$

      PRINT "READING IN DATA TABLE FOR BALA"

      CALL READLINES (FILE1$,FILENAME1$,MAXLINES,LINELENGTH)
      CALL COMPRESSTABLE (FILE1$,MAXLINES,LINELENGTH)

      PRINT "PREPARING BALANCE SHEET"
```

```
CALL COLUMN(1,XCOLVALUES$,FILE1$,LINELENGTH,MAXLINES)
CALL COLUMN(2,YCOLVALUES$,FILE1$,LINELENGTH,MAXLINES)
CALL COLUMN(3,ZCOLVALUES$,FILE1$,LINELENGTH,MAXLINES)

LET LPY=0

CALL GETTOKEN(YCOLVALUES$,LPYX,CELL$)
CALL DEDOUBQUOTES(CELL$,CELLY$)

DIM ARR(200)

LET J=1

DO WHILE (CELLY$()"")

   WHEN ERROR IN
        LET Y=VAL(CELLY$)
   USE
        LET Y=0
   END WHEN

   LET ARR(J)=Y
   LET J=J+1

    CALL GETTOKEN(YCOLVALUES$,LPYX,CELL$)
    CALL DEDOUBQUOTES(CELL$,CELLY$)

LOOP

CLEAR
LET NUMPOINTS=J-1

PRINT "              BALANCE SHEET"
PRINT " ASSETS - CURRENT"

LET TOTALA=0
LET LPX=0
LET LPZ=0

FOR J=1 TO NUMPOINTS

    CALL GETTOKEN(XCOLVALUES$,LPX,CELL$)
    CALL DEDOUBQUOTES(CELL$,CELLX$)
    CALL GETTOKEN(ZCOLVALUES$,LPZ,CELL$)
    CALL DEDOUBQUOTES(CELL$,CELLZ$)

    IF CELLX$="AC" THEN
        LET CELLZ$=CELLZ$&REPEAT$(" ",30)
        LET CELLZ$=CELLZ$[1:30]
        PRINT "        ";CELLZ$;
        PRINT USING "---------#";ARR(J)
        LET TOTALA=TOTALA+ARR(J)
    END IF
```

```
NEXT J

PRINT " ASSETS - LONG-TERM"

LET LPX=0
LET LPZ=0

FOR J=1 TO NUMPOINTS

    CALL GETTOKEN(XCOLVALUES$,LPX,CELL$)
    CALL DEDOUBQUOTES(CELL$,CELLX$)
    CALL GETTOKEN(ZCOLVALUES$,LPZ,CELL$)
    CALL DEDOUBQUOTES(CELL$,CELLZ$)

    IF CELLX$="AL" THEN
       LET CELLZ$=CELLZ$&REPEAT$(" ",30)
       LET CELLZ$=CELLZ$[1:30]
       PRINT "           ";CELLZ$;
       PRINT USING "---------#";ARR(J)
       LET TOTALA=TOTALA+ARR(J)
    END IF

NEXT J

PRINT REPEAT$(" ",40);
PRINT "----------"

PRINT "TOTAL ASSETS         ";REPEAT$(" ",20);
PRINT USING "---------#";TOTALA
LET TOTALASSETS=TOTALA

PRINT " LIABILITIES - CURRENT"

LET TOTALA=0
LET LPX=0
LET LPZ=0

FOR J=1 TO NUMPOINTS

    CALL GETTOKEN(XCOLVALUES$,LPX,CELL$)
    CALL DEDOUBQUOTES(CELL$,CELLX$)
    CALL GETTOKEN(ZCOLVALUES$,LPZ,CELL$)
    CALL DEDOUBQUOTES(CELL$,CELLZ$)

    IF CELLX$="LC" THEN
       LET CELLZ$=CELLZ$&REPEAT$(" ",30)
       LET CELLZ$=CELLZ$[1:30]
       PRINT "           ";CELLZ$;
       PRINT USING "---------#";ARR(J)
       LET TOTALA=TOTALA+ARR(J)
    END IF

NEXT J
```

```
      PRINT " LIABILITIES - LONG-TERM"

      LET LPX=0
      LET LPZ=0

      FOR J=1 TO NUMPOINTS

          CALL GETTOKEN(XCOLVALUES$,LPX,CELL$)
          CALL DEDOUBQUOTES(CELL$,CELLX$)
          CALL GETTOKEN(ZCOLVALUES$,LPZ,CELL$)
          CALL DEDOUBQUOTES(CELL$,CELLZ$)

          IF CELLX$="LL" THEN
             LET CELLZ$=CELLZ$&REPEAT$(" ",30)
             LET CELLZ$=CELLZ$[1:30]
             PRINT "           ";CELLZ$;
             PRINT USING "--------#":ARR(J)
             LET TOTALA=TOTALA+ARR(J)
          END IF

      NEXT J

      PRINT " EQUITY"

      LET LPX=0
      LET LPZ=0

      FOR J=1 TO NUMPOINTS

          CALL GETTOKEN(XCOLVALUES$,LPX,CELL$)
          CALL DEDOUBQUOTES(CELL$,CELLX$)
          CALL GETTOKEN(ZCOLVALUES$,LPZ,CELL$)
          CALL DEDOUBQUOTES(CELL$,CELLZ$)

          IF CELLX$="EQ" THEN
             LET CELLZ$=CELLZ$&REPEAT$(" ",30)
             LET CELLZ$=CELLZ$[1:30]
             PRINT "           ";CELLZ$;
             PRINT USING "---------#":ARR(J)
             LET TOTALA=TOTALA+ARR(J)
          END IF

      NEXT J

      PRINT "         ";"NET WORTH";REPEAT$(" ",21);
      PRINT USING "---------#":TOTALASSETS-TOTALA
      PRINT REPEAT$(" ",40);
      PRINT "----------"

      PRINT "TOTAL LIABILITIES AND EQUITY  ";REPEAT$(" ",10);
      PRINT USING "---------#":TOTALASSETS

      PRINT "ANY KEY TO CONTINUE"

      GET KEY X

END SUB
```

THE DSSSPREA LIBRARY

This library contains the subroutines that implement spreadsheet capabilities for the DSS Tool Kit.

```
!!!!!!!!!!!!!!!!!!!!!!!!!!!!!!!!!!!!!!!!!!!!!!!!!!!!!!!!!!!!!!!!!!!!!!!!!!!!!!!!!!!!!
!                                                                                 !
!  THIS IS EXTERNAL LIBRARY DSSSPREA.TRU                                          !
!                                                                                 !
!  THIS LIBRARY CONTAINS THE SUBROUTINES FOR THE SPREAD SHEET OPERATOR.           !
!  DSSSPREA IS THE MAIN SUBROUTINE.                                               !
!  EVALUATE IS THE SUBROUTINE WHICH EVALUATES A SINGLE CELL.                      !
!                                                                                 !
!  SEE CHAPTER 5 FOR EXPLANATION OF THIS FUNCTION                                 !
!                                                                                 !
!!!!!!!!!!!!!!!!!!!!!!!!!!!!!!!!!!!!!!!!!!!!!!!!!!!!!!!!!!!!!!!!!!!!!!!!!!!!!!!!!!!!!

EXTERNAL
```

The DSSSPREA Subroutine

This subroutine formats, calculates, and displays spreadsheets from user-supplied models, or templates.

```
SUB DSSSPREA(SCHEMA$,NEWTOKEN$,MAXLINES,LINELENGTH)

    REM DSSSPREA
    REM    DSS TOOL KIT SPREAD SHEET PROGRAM
    REM THIS PROGRAM IS A SUBPROGRAM WHICH IS INVOKED BY:
    REM    A. THE DSS MENU PROGRAM
    REM    B. AN INDEPENDENT DRIVER NAMED DRIVER

    CALL DEDOUBQUOTES(NEWTOKEN$,FILENAME1$)

    CLEAR
    PRINT "DSS TOOL KIT SPREAD SHEET OPERATOR"
    PRINT "EXECUTING SPREAD SHEET FILE NAMED ",FILENAME1$
    PRINT

    CALL READLINES (FILE1$,FILENAME1$,MAXLINES,LINELENGTH)
    LET FILE1$=UCASE$(FILE1$)
    LET CELLLENGTH=16

    REM FIRST DISPLAY THE ORIGINAL UN-EVALUATED SPREAD SHEET.
    CLEAR
    FOR I=1 TO 24
        PRINT FILE1$[(I-1)*LINELENGTH+1:I*LINELENGTH]
    NEXT I

    LET WORKCELLS$=""
```

```
    FOR J=1 TO 5

        FOR I=1 TO MAXLINES

            LET BEGIN = (I-1)*LINELENGTH+(J-1)*CELLLENGTH+1
            LET RESULT$=""
            LET CELL$=FILE1$[BEGIN:BEGIN+CELLLENGTH-1]

          CALL EVALUATE(RESULT$,CELL$,CELLLENGTH,FILE1$,LINELENGTH,WORKCELLS$)

            LET FILE1$[BEGIN:BEGIN+CELLLENGTH-1]=RESULT$

            IF I<=24 THEN
                SET CURSOR I,(J-1)*CELLLENGTH+1
                REM DISPLAY THE CELL

                WHEN ERROR IN
                    LET NUMBER=VAL(RESULT$)
                    PRINT USING "-############.##":NUMBER;
                USE
                    PRINT RESULT$;
                END WHEN

            END IF

        NEXT I

    NEXT J

    REM BLANK OUT THE AUXILIARY CELLS
    LET LP=0
    CALL GETTOKEN(WORKCELLS$,LP,TOKEN$)

    DO WHILE (TOKEN$<>"")
        LET I=VAL(TOKEN$)
        CALL GETTOKEN(WORKCELLS$,LP,TOKEN$)
        LET J=VAL(TOKEN$)

        IF I<=24 THEN
            SET CURSOR I,(J-1)*CELLLENGTH+1
            PRINT REPEAT$(" ",CELLLENGTH)
        END IF

        CALL GETTOKEN(WORKCELLS$,LP,TOKEN$)

    LOOP

    SET CURSOR 24,50
    PRINT "PRESS ANY KEY TO CONTINUE"
    GET KEY N

END SUB

SUB EVALUATE(RESULT$,CELL$,CELLLENGTH,FILE$,LINELENGTH,WORKCELLS$)

    DECLARE DEF OP
```

```
CALL PROMPT(CELL$)

FOR I=1 TO LEN(CELL$)
    LET CHK$=CELL$[I:I]

    SELECT CASE CHK$
    CASE "[","]","A","B","C","D","E","F","G","H","I","J"
    CASE "K","L","M","N","O","P","Q","R","S","T","U","V"
    CASE "W","X","Y","Z","0","1","2","3","4","5","6","7"
    CASE "8","9",".","*","/","+","-","{","}"," "
    CASE ELSE
        LET CELL$[I:I]=" "
    END SELECT

NEXT I

IF CELL$[1:LEN(CELL$)]=REPEAT$(" ",LEN(CELL$)) THEN
    LET RESULT$=REPEAT$(" ",CELLLENGTH)
    EXIT SUB
END IF


IF CELL$[1:1]="{" THEN

LET CELL$=CELL$[2:LEN(CELL$)]
LET WORK=POS(CELL$,"}")
LET CELL$=CELL$[1:WORK-1]
CALL DEBLANK (CELL$,CELL1$)
LET CELL$=CELL1$

REM CHECK FOR THE "+" AND "-" OPERATORS WHEN UNARY
REM CONVERT TO A LIST OF TOKENS

LET I=2

DO WHILE (I<LEN(CELL$))

   LET CHAR$=CELL$[I:I]
   LET OPERATOR=OP(CHAR$)

   IF OPERATOR=1 THEN
      LET CELL$=CELL$[1:I-1]&","&CELL$[I:I]&","&CELL$[I+1:LEN(CELL$)]
      LET CHAR1$=CELL$[I+3:I+3]
      LET I=I+2
      IF CHAR1$="-" OR CHAR1$="+" THEN
         LET I=I+1
      END IF
   END IF

   LET I=I+1

LOOP

REM NOW REPEAT READING TOKENS LEFT TO RIGHT--
REM    IF CAN CONVERT TO NUMBER DO SO
REM    IF CANNOT THEN CHECK TO SEE IF OPERATOR--
REM       IF YES THEN EXECUTE OPERATION
REM    ELSE MUST BE A CELL REFERENCE--2 TYPES: AUXILIARY AND NOT
```

```
REM      MAKE A LIST OF AUX CELLS SO CAN BLANK OUT LATER
REM       USE EVALUATE$ AGAIN ON AUXILIARY CELLS

LET LP=0
CALL GETTOKEN(CELL$,LP,TOKEN$)
LET LASTOP$=""
LET ACCUM=0
LET NUMBER=0

DO WHILE (TOKEN$()"")

   IF OP(TOKEN$)=1 THEN
      LET LASTOP$=TOKEN$
   ELSE

      WHEN ERROR IN
            LET NUMBER=VAL(TOKEN$)
      USE
            SELECT CASE TOKEN$[1:1]

      CASE "A","B","C","D","E"

            CALL GETFROMCELL

            WHEN ERROR IN
                  LET NUMBER=VAL(WORK$)
            USE
                  LET NUMBER=1
            END WHEN

       CASE "["
            LET TOKEN$=TOKEN$[2:LEN(TOKEN$)-1]

            CALL GETFROMCELL

            LET WORKCELLS$=WORKCELLS$&" "&STR$(ROWNUM)
            LET WORKCELLS$=WORKCELLS$&" "&STR$(COLNUM)

            WHEN ERROR IN
                  LET NUMBER=VAL(WORK$)
            USE
                  LET WORK1$=""

CALL EVALUATE(WORK1$,WORK$,CELLLENGTH,FILE$,LINELENGTH,WORKCELLS$)

                  LET NUMBER=VAL(WORK1$)
            END WHEN

      CASE ELSE
            LET NUMBER=1

      END SELECT

   END WHEN

   SELECT CASE LASTOP$
```

```
        CASE ""
              LET ACCUM=NUMBER
        CASE "+"
              LET ACCUM=ACCUM+NUMBER
        CASE "-"
              LET ACCUM=ACCUM-NUMBER
        CASE "/"
              LET ACCUM=ACCUM/NUMBER
        CASE "*"
              LET ACCUM=ACCUM*NUMBER
        CASE ELSE

        END SELECT

    END IF

    CALL GETTOKEN(CELL$,LP,TOKEN$)

       LOOP

       LET CELL$=STR$(ACCUM)

    END IF

    LET CELL$=CELL$&REPEAT$(" ",CELLLENGTH)
    LET CELL$=CELL$[1:CELLLENGTH]

    LET RESULTS$= CELL$

    SUB GETFROMCELL

        SELECT CASE TOKEN$[1:1]
        CASE "A"
              LET COLNUM=1
        CASE "B"
              LET COLNUM=2
        CASE "C"
              LET COLNUM=3
        CASE "D"
              LET COLNUM=4
        CASE "E"
              LET COLNUM=5
        END SELECT

        LET TOKEN$=TOKEN$[2:LEN(TOKEN$)]

        WHEN ERROR IN
              LET ROWNUM=VAL(TOKEN$)
        USE
              LET ROWNUM=1
        END WHEN

        LET FIRST=(ROWNUM-1)*LINELENGTH+(COLNUM-1)*CELLLENGTH+1
        LET WORK$=FILE$[FIRST:FIRST+CELLLENGTH-1]

    END SUB

END SUB
```

```
DEF OP (CHAR$)

    SELECT CASE CHAR$

    CASE "/","*","+","-"
        LET OP=1
    CASE ELSE
        LET OP=0

    END SELECT

    EXIT DEF

END DEF
```

THE DSSES LIBRARY

This library contains the subroutines that implement the Expert System.

```
!!!!!!!!!!!!!!!!!!!!!!!!!!!!!!!!!!!!!!!!!!!!!!!!!!!!!!!!!!!!!!!!!!!!!!!!!!!!!!!!
!                                                                            !
!   THIS IS EXTERNAL LIBRARY DSSES.TRU                                       !
!                                                                            !
!   THIS LIBRARY CONTAINS TWO SUBROUTINES: ES AND PROVE$                     !
!   ES IS THE MAIN SUBROUTINE FOR THE TOOL KIT EDITOR ES                     !
!   PROVE$ IS THE RECURSIVE SUBROUTINE WHICH DOES A                          !
!      BACKWARD CHAIN TO PROVE THE GOALS AND SUBGOALS                        !
!      INVOLVED IN EXECUTING THE RULE BASE.                                  !
!                                                                            !
!   SEE CHAPTER 6 FOR EXPLANATION OF THIS FUNCTION.                          !
!                                                                            !
!!!!!!!!!!!!!!!!!!!!!!!!!!!!!!!!!!!!!!!!!!!!!!!!!!!!!!!!!!!!!!!!!!!!!!!!!!!!!!!!

EXTERNAL
```

The ES Subroutine

This subroutine performs expert system inferencing and user consultation. Expert system functions are guided by the rule base.

```
SUB ES(SCHEMA$,NEWTOKEN$,MAXLINES,LINELENGTH)

    REM     DSS TOOL KIT EXPERT SYSTEM
    REM   THIS PROGRAM IS A SUBROUTINE WHICH MAY BE INVOKED BY:
    REM   A.   THE DSS MENU PROGRAM
    REM   B.   AN INDEPENDENT DRIVER PROGRAM NAMED DRIVER

    DECLARE DEF PROVE$
```

```
CALL DEDOUBQUOTES(NEWTOKEN$,FILENAME1$)

CALL READLINES (FILE1$,FILENAME1$,MAXLINES,LINELENGTH)
LET FILE1$=UCASE$(FILE1$)

CLEAR
PRINT "DSS TOOL KIT EXPERT SYSTEM"
PRINT "EXECUTING ES FILE NAMED ",FILENAME1$
PRINT

LET FILE2$=""
FOR I=1 TO MAXLINES
 IF FILE1$[(I-1)*LINELENGTH+1:I*LINELENGTH]<>REPEAT$(" ",LINELENGTH) THEN
       LET FILE2$=FILE2$&FILE1$[(I-1)*LINELENGTH+1:I*LINELENGTH]
    END IF
NEXT I

LET FILE1$=FILE2$&REPEAT$(" ",MAXLINES*LINELENGTH)
LET FILE1$=FILE1$[1:MAXLINES*LINELENGTH]

LET FOUND =POS(FILE1$,";")

DO WHILE (FOUND<>0)

   LET FILE1$[FOUND:FOUND]=" "
   LET FOUND =POS(FILE1$,";",FOUND)

LOOP

LET GOALS$=REPEAT$(" ",MAXLINES*LINELENGTH)

LET RULE=1
LET ROW$=FILE1$[(RULE-1)*LINELENGTH+1:RULE*LINELENGTH]

DO WHILE (ROW$<>REPEAT$(" ",LINELENGTH))

   LET LP=0
   CALL GETTOKEN(ROW$,LP,TOKEN$)

   LET OLDTOKEN$=""

   DO WHILE (TOKEN$<>"")

      LET OLDTOKEN$=TOKEN$
      LET OLDLP=LP

      CALL GETTOKEN(ROW$,LP,TOKEN$)

   LOOP

   LET BEGINIT=(RULE-1)*LINELENGTH+OLDLP-LEN(OLDTOKEN$)
   LET LENGTHOFIT=LINELENGTH-OLDLP+LEN(OLDTOKEN$)+1
   LET FILE1$[BEGINIT:RULE*LINELENGTH]=REPEAT$(" ",LENGTHOFIT)
   CALL DEDOUBQUOTES(OLDTOKEN$,TOKENOLD$)
   LET OLDTOKEN$=TOKENOLD$
   LET L=LINELENGTH
   LET GOALS$[(RULE-1)*L+1:RULE*L]=OLDTOKEN$&REPEAT$(" ",L-LEN(OLDTOKEN$))
```

```
         LET RULE=RULE+1
         LET ROW$=FILE1$[(RULE-1)*LINELENGTH+1:RULE*LINELENGTH]

      LOOP

      LET NUMRULES=RULE-1

      FOR I=1 TO NUMRULES

         LET GOAL$=GOALS$[(I-1)*LINELENGTH+1:I*LINELENGTH]
         LET GOAL=POS(GOAL$,"(GOAL)")

         IF GOAL<>0 THEN

            LET GOALNUMBER=I
            LET TOPROVE$=FILE1$[(I-1)*LINELENGTH+1:I*LINELENGTH]

            LET FILE1$=FILE1$[1:NUMRULES*LINELENGTH]
            LET GOALS$=GOALS$[1:NUMRULES*LINELENGTH]

            LET G=GOALNUMBER
            LET L=LINELENGTH
            LET N=NUMRULES
            LET TRUE$=PROVE$(TOPROVE$,G,GOALS$,FILE1$,NUMRULES,L,N)
            LET FILE1$=TRUE$[2:LINELENGTH*NUMRULES+1]
            LET TRUE$=TRUE$[1:1]

            IF TRUE$="Y" THEN
               PRINT "INDICATES ---> ",GOAL$[1:50]
            END IF

         END IF

      NEXT I

      PRINT
      PRINT "PRESS ANY KEY TO CONTINUE>"
      GET KEY N

END SUB


DEF PROVE$  (TOPROVE$,GOALNUMBER,GOALS$,FILE$,NUMRULES,LINELENGTH,MAXLINES)

   REM FILE$ IS THE LEFT HAND SIDE OR Y/N IF GOAL PROVED
   REM GOALS$ IS THE RIGHT HAND SIDES
   REM TOPROVE$ IS THE LIST OF GOALS TO BE PROVED AS AN AND
   REM NUMRULES IS THE TOTAL NUMBER OF LINES

   REM WORK LEFT TO RIGHT IN TOPROVE$
   REM DISCARD THE FIRST TOKEN IN FILE$ AS IT IS THE RULE NUMBER

   LET TRUTH$="Y"
   LET LPX=0

   CALL GETTOKEN(TOPROVE$,LPX,TOKEN$)
   CALL GETTOKEN(TOPROVE$,LPX,TOKEN$)
```

```
DO WHILE (TOKEN$<>"" AND TRUTH$<>"N")

    LET NEGATESW=0

    IF TOKEN$[1:1]=CHR$(34) THEN
        PRINT "IS ",TOKEN$
        LET ANS$=""

        DO WHILE (ANS$<>"Y" AND ANS$<>"N")

            PRINT "ANSWER Y OR N>";
            INPUT ANS$
            LET ANS$=UCASE$(ANS$)

        LOOP

        IF ANS$="Y" THEN
            LET TRUTH$="Y"
        ELSE
            LET TRUTH$="N"
        END IF

    ELSE

        REM NOW PROCESS CASE OF NOT QUERY-THE-USER

        IF TOKEN$[1:1]="C" THEN
            LET NEGATESW=1
            LET TOKEN$=TOKEN$[2:LEN(TOKEN$)-1]
        ELSE
            LET NEGATESW=0
        END IF

        LET TOKEN$=TOKEN$&REPEAT$(" ",LINELENGTH-LEN(TOKEN$))
        LET J=1
        LET TOKEN1$=GOALS$[(J-1)*LINELENGTH+1:J*LINELENGTH]

        DO WHILE (TOKEN$<>TOKEN1$ AND J<NUMRULES)
            LET J=J+1
            LET TOKEN1$=GOALS$[(J-1)*LINELENGTH+1:J*LINELENGTH]
        LOOP

        LET VALUE$= FILE$[(J-1)*LINELENGTH+1:(J-1)*LINELENGTH+3]

        SELECT CASE VALUE$

        CASE "%Y%"

                IF NEGATESW=0 THEN
                    LET TRUTH$="Y"
                                        ELSE
                    LET TRUTH$="N"
                END IF

        CASE "%N%"

                IF NEGATESW=0 THEN
```

```
                        LET TRUTH$="N"
                ELSE
                        LET TRUTH$="Y"
                END IF

            CASE ELSE

                LET TOPROVE1$=FILE$[(J-1)*LINELENGTH+1:J*LINELENGTH]
                LET L=LINELENGTH
                LET N=NUMRULES
                LET TRUE$=PROVE$(TOPROVE1$,J,GOALS$,FILE$,N,L,MAXLINES)
                LET FILE$=TRUE$[2:LINELENGTH*MAXLINES+1]
                LET TRUE$=TRUE$[1:1]

                IF TRUE$="Y" THEN
                    IF NEGATESW=0 THEN
                        LET TRUTH$="Y"
                                    ELSE
                        LET TRUTH$="N"
                    END IF

                ELSE

                    IF NEGATESW=0 THEN
                        LET TRUTH$="N"
                                    ELSE
                        LET TRUTH$="Y"
                    END IF

                END IF

            END SELECT

        END IF

        CALL GETTOKEN(TOPROVE$,LPX,TOKEN$)

    LOOP

    LET I=GOALNUMBER

    IF TRUTH$="Y" THEN
        LET L=LINELENGTH
        LET FILE$[(I-1)*L+1:I*L]="%Y%"&REPEAT$(" ",L-3)
    ELSE
        LET L=LINELENGTH
        LET FILE$[(I-1)*L+1:I*L]="%N%"&REPEAT$(" ",L-3)
    END IF

    LET PROVE$=TRUTH$&FILE$

    EXIT DEF

END DEF
```

THE DSSSUBS LIBRARY

This library contains the utility subroutines common to the programs and libraries in the DSS Tool Kit.

```
!!!!!!!!!!!!!!!!!!!!!!!!!!!!!!!!!!!!!!!!!!!!!!!!!!!!!!!!!!!!!!!!!!!!!!!!!!!!!!!!!!!!
!                                                                              !
!  THIS IS EXTERNAL LIBRARY DSSSUBS.TRU                                        !
!                                                                              !
!  THIS LIBRARY CONTAINS THE SUBROUTINES USED IN COMMON BY ALL OF THE          !
!     OTHER TOOL KIT PROGRAMS                                                  !
!                                                                              !
!!!!!!!!!!!!!!!!!!!!!!!!!!!!!!!!!!!!!!!!!!!!!!!!!!!!!!!!!!!!!!!!!!!!!!!!!!!!!!!!!!!!

EXTERNAL
```

The SETTOKEN Subroutine

This subroutine is used by all other program modules for acquiring tokens, such as table cell values from strings.

```
SUB GETTOKEN( L$,P,TOKEN$)

    REM SUB TO SEPARATE THE NEXT TOKEN FROM A STRING
    REM IF TOKEN SURROUNDED BY DOUBLE QUOTES THEN
    REM      DOUBLE QUOTES RETURNED AROUND THE TOKEN
    REM BLANK OR COMMA IS THE DELIMITER BETWEEN TOKENS

    LET L=LEN(L$)
    LET TOKEN$=""

    IF P<=0 THEN
       LET P=1
    END IF

    DO WHILE ((L$[P:P]=" " OR L$[P:P]=",") AND P<L)
       LET P=P+1
    LOOP

    DO WHILE (L$[P:P]<>" " AND L$[P:P]<>"," AND L$[P:P]<>CHR$(34) AND P<=L)
       LET TOKEN$=TOKEN$ & L$[P:P]
       LET P=P+1
    LOOP

    IF L$[P:P]=CHR$(34) THEN
       LET P=P+1

       DO WHILE (L$[P:P]<>CHR$(34) AND P<=L)
          LET TOKEN$=TOKEN$ & L$[P:P]
          LET P=P + 1
       LOOP

       LET TOKEN$=CHR$(34)&TOKEN$&CHR$(34)
```

```
        LET P=P+1

    END IF

    LET TOKEN$=UCASE$(TOKEN$)

END SUB
```

The READLINES Subroutine

This subroutine is used by other program modules for reading data
tables and other data files, such as menu files, spreadsheet templates,
and expert system rules.

```
REM *********************************************
SUB READLINES (LINE$,FILENAME$,MAXLINES,LINELENGTH)

    REM SUB TO READ A FILE INTO LINE$ STRING

    LET LINE$=REPEAT$(" ",MAXLINES*LINELENGTH)
    LET FILENAME$=UCASE$(FILENAME$)

    IF FILENAME$<>"" AND LEN(FILENAME$)<=6 THEN

        WHEN ERROR IN

            OPEN #1: NAME FILENAME$, ACCESS INPUT, ORGANIZATION TEXT

        USE
            PRINT "FILE NAMED DOES NOT EXIST"
            PRINT "CREATING NEW FILE NAMED ";FILENAME$

            CALL WRITELINES (LINE$,FILENAME$,MAXLINES,LINELENGTH)

            CLOSE #1

        END WHEN

        WHEN ERROR IN

            FOR I=0 TO MAXLINES-1
                LINE INPUT #1:X$
                LET LINE$[I*LINELENGTH+1:I*LINELENGTH+LINELENGTH]=X$
            NEXT I

        USE
            LET LINE$=LINE$&REPEAT$(" ",MAXLINES*LINELENGTH)
            LET LINE$=LINE$[1:MAXLINES*LINELENGTH]

        END WHEN

        CLOSE #1

    ELSE
```

```
        PRINT "INVALID FILE NAME"

    END IF

    LET LINE$=UCASE$(LINE$)

END SUB
```

The WRITELINES Subroutine

This subroutine writes data tables and edited files to disk storage devices.

```
REM ********************************************
SUB WRITELINES (LINE$,FILENAME$,MAXLINES,LINELENGTH)

    LET LINE$=LINE$ & REPEAT$(" ",MAXLINES*LINELENGTH)
    LET LINE$=LINE$[1:MAXLINES*LINELENGTH]

    OPEN #1: NAME FILENAME$,ACCESS OUTPUT,ORGANIZATION TEXT,CREATE NEWOLD

    ERASE #1

    LET I=0
    LET QUIT=0

    DO WHILE (I<=MAXLINES AND QUIT<>1)

        LET X$=LINE$[(I*LINELENGTH)+1:(I*LINELENGTH)+LINELENGTH]
        PRINT #1: X$
        LET I=I+1
        LET ML=MAXLINES*LINELENGTH -(I*LINELENGTH)

        IF LINE$[(I*LINELENGTH)+1:MAXLINES*LINELENGTH]=REPEAT$(" ",ML) THEN
            LET QUIT=1
        END IF

    LOOP

    CLOSE #1

END SUB
```

The COLUMN Subroutine

This subroutine separates a column from a data table.

```
REM ********************************************
SUB COLUMN(ICOL,COLUMN$,LINE$,LINELENGTH,MAXLINES)

    REM RETURNS IN COLUMN$ THE COLth COLUMN FROM LINE$ IN THE FORM OF A VECTOR$
    REM HAS "" AROUND ALL TOKENS AND SEPARATES TOKENS WITH BLANKS
```

```
    IF ICOL<1 THEN
        LET ICOL=1
    END IF

    LET COLUMN$=""

    FOR I=1 TO MAXLINES

        LET LL=(I-1)*LINELENGTH
        LET L$=LINE$[LL+1:LL+LINELENGTH]

        CALL VECTORCELL(0,0,ICOL,CELL$,L$)

        LET CELL$=CHR$(34)&CELL$&CHR$(34)
        LET COLUMN$=COLUMN$&CELL$&" "

    NEXT I

END SUB
```

The VECTORCELL Subroutine

This subroutine acquires tokens from a string, as specified in command parameters.

```
REM *******************************************
SUB VECTORCELL (LASTCELL,LASTPOS,ICELL,CELL$,VECTOR$)

    REM RETURNS IN CELL$ THE CELLth TOKEN FROM VECTOR$
    REM REMOVES THE """ FROM TOKENS IF THEY ARE PRESENT

    FOR I=LASTCELL+1 TO ICELL

        CALL GETTOKEN(VECTOR$,LASTPOS,TOKEN$)

    NEXT I

    LET CELL$=TOKEN$

    CALL DEDOUBQUOTES(CELL$,CELL$)

    LET LASTCELL=ICELL
END SUB
```

The DEDOUBQUOTES Subroutine

This subroutine removes double-quote delimiters from strings.

```
REM *******************************************
SUB DEDOUBQUOTES(IN$,OUTX$)
```

```
REM REMOVES THE """ FROM TOKENS IF THEY ARE PRESENT

LET OUT$=IN$
LET L=LEN(IN$)

IF OUT$[1:1]=CHR$(34) THEN
    LET OUT$=OUT$[2:L]
    LET L=L-1
END IF

IF OUT$[L:L]=CHR$(34) THEN
    LET OUT$=OUT$[1:L-1]
END IF

LET OUTX$=OUT$

END SUB
```

The DEBLANK Subroutine

This subroutine removes blank characters from strings.

```
REM *********************************************
SUB DEBLANK(S$,S9$)

    REM REMOVES BLANKS FROM S$ EXCEPT THOSE SURROUNDED BY ?,OR '.

    LET ILEN=LEN(S$)
    LET S1$=""
    LET LEVEL=0
    LET IS1=1

    FOR I=1 TO ILEN

        IF S$[I:I]=CHR$(34) OR S$[I:I]="'"  AND LEVEL=0 THEN
            LET LEVEL=LEVEL+1

        ELSEIF S$[I:I]=CHR$(34) OR S$[I:I]="'" AND LEVEL>0  THEN
            LET LEVEL=LEVEL-1

        END IF

        IF LEVEL>0 THEN
            LET S1$[IS1:IS1]=S$[I:I]
            LET IS1=IS1+1

        ELSEIF S$[I:I]<>" " THEN
            LET S1$[IS1:IS1]=S$[I:I]
            LET IS1=IS1+1

        END IF

    NEXT I
```

```
        LET S9$=S1$

END SUB
```

The PROMPT Subroutine

This subroutine prompts the user to input data and information in
menu command lines and in spreadsheet templates. Recall that question marks are used to surround prompts in menu commands or
spreadsheet cells. The presence of double question marks causes the
PROMPT subroutine to be called.

```
REM *******************************************
SUB PROMPT (TOKEN$)

    REM THIS SUB SCANS A STRING FOR THE PRESENCE OF ?.
    REM  IF ?'s FOUND SURROUNDING A TOKEN, THEN THE
    REM  IF TOKEN IS DISPLAYED AS A PROMPT TO THE USER AND
    REM  THE REPLY USED TO REPLACE THE PROMPT IN THE INPUT STRING

    LET PLACE =POS(TOKEN$,"?")

    DO WHILE (PLACE()0)

       LET PLACE2=POS(TOKEN$,"?",PLACE+1)

       IF PLACE2=0 THEN
          LET PLACE2=LEN(TOKEN$)+1
          LET TOKEN$=TOKEN$&"?"
       END IF

       SET CURSOR 24,30
       PRINT TOKEN$[PLACE+1:PLACE2-1];
       INPUT ANS$
       SET CURSOR 24,30
       PRINT REPEAT$(" ",50);
       LET TOKEN$=TOKEN$[1:PLACE-1]&ANS$&TOKEN$[PLACE2+1:LEN(TOKEN$)]
       LET PLACE=POS(TOKEN$,"?")

    LOOP

END SUB
```

The COMPRESSTABLE Subroutine

This subroutine removes blank spaces from data tables, decreasing the amount of storage space required to hold tables.

```
REM ********************************************
SUB COMPRESSTABLE (FILE$,MAXLINES,LINELENGTH)

    LET FILE2$=REPEAT$(" ",MAXLINES*LINELENGTH)

    LET J=1

    FOR I=1 TO MAXLINES

        LET LLINE$=FILE$[(I-1)*LINELENGTH+1:I*LINELENGTH]

        IF LLINE$<>REPEAT$(" ",80) THEN

            LET LC1=0
            LET LP1=0
            LET NEXT=1
            LET XLINE$=""

            CALL VECTORCELL(LC1,LP1,NEXT,CELL$,LLINE$)

            DO WHILE (CELL$<>"")

                IF CELL$[1:1]<>"^" THEN
                    LET CELL$=CHR$(34)&CELL$&CHR$(34)
                    LET XLINE$=XLINE$&CELL$&" "
                END IF

                LET NEXT=NEXT+1
                CALL VECTORCELL(LC1,LP1,NEXT,CELL$,LLINE$)

            LOOP

            LET XLINE$=XLINE$&REPEAT$(" ",LINELENGTH)
            LET XLINE$=XLINE$[1:LINELENGTH]
            LET FILE2$[(J-1)*LINELENGTH+1:J*LINELENGTH]=XLINE$
            LET J=J+1

        END IF

    NEXT I

    LET FILE$=FILE2$

END SUB
```

THE DRIVER PROGRAM

This program provides access to DSS Tool Kit subroutines without use
of the MENU interface.

```
!!!!!!!!!!!!!!!!!!!!!!!!!!!!!!!!!!!!!!!!!!!!!!!!!!!!!!!!!!!!!!!!!!!!!!!!!!!!!!!!
!                                                                            !
!   THIS IS THE DRIVER PROGRAM                                               !
!                                                                            !
!                                                                            !
!!!!!!!!!!!!!!!!!!!!!!!!!!!!!!!!!!!!!!!!!!!!!!!!!!!!!!!!!!!!!!!!!!!!!!!!!!!!!!!!

REM DRIVER.TRU

REM THIS IS THE STANDALONE DRIVER PROGRAM FOR THE DSS TOOL KIT SUBROUTINES
REM   THIS PROGRAM IS USED TO INVOKE INDIVIDUAL SUBROUTINES OUTSIDE OF THE
REM      DSS TOOL KIT MENU FRAMEWORK

LIBRARY "DSSLED.TRU","DSSDBMS.TRU","DSSSUBS.TRU","DSSSED.TRU"
LIBRARY "DSSGRAPH.TRU","DSSES.TRU","DSSSPREA.TRU","DSSDTREE.TRU"

LET MAXLINES=40
LET LINELENGTH=80

SUB MAINPROMPT

    CLEAR
    PRINT "         DSS TOOL KIT DRIVER PROGRAM"
    PRINT
    PRINT "AVAILABLE PROGRAMS ARE:"
    PRINT "   SED,LED,DTREE,PROJECT,SELECT,JOIN,DELETE,"
    PRINT "   SORT,UNION,ES,SPREAD,SGRAM,MTRACE,RLINE,"
    PRINT "   BANDW,INCO,BALA,HISTO,PIE,DISPLAY,ADD,"
    PRINT "   SUBTRACT,MULTIPLY,DIVIDE,SUMMARIZE,"
    PRINT "      OR END"
    PRINT
    PRINT "WHICH PROGRAM DO YOU WANT>";

    INPUT SELECTION$
    LET SELECTION$=UCASE$(SELECTION$)

END SUB

CLEAR

PRINT "READING IN THE SCHEMA FILE"
CALL READLINES (SCHEMA$,"SCHEMA",MAXLINES,LINELENGTH)

PRINT
CALL MAINPROMPT

DO WHILE (SELECTION$<>"END")

   PRINT "ENTER YOUR CONTROL STRING BETWEEN DOUBLE QUOTES "
   INPUT PROMPT ">>":TOKEN$
```

```
     LET TOKEN$=UCASE$(TOKEN$)
     CALL PROMPT(TOKEN$)
     CALL DEDOUBQUOTES(TOKEN$,NEWTOKEN$)

     CLEAR

     SELECT CASE SELECTION$

     CASE "SED"
          CALL DSSSED (SCHEMA$,NEWTOKEN$,MAXLINES,LINELENGTH)

     CASE "SORT"
          CALL SORT (SCHEMA$,NEWTOKEN$,MAXLINES,LINELENGTH)

     CASE "UNION"
          CALL UNION (SCHEMA$,NEWTOKEN$,MAXLINES,LINELENGTH)

     CASE "DELETE"
          CALL DELETE (SCHEMA$,NEWTOKEN$,MAXLINES,LINELENGTH)

     CASE "PROJECT"
          CALL PROJECT (SCHEMA$,NEWTOKEN$,MAXLINES,LINELENGTH)

     CASE "JOIN"
          CALL JOIN (SCHEMA$,NEWTOKEN$,MAXLINES,LINELENGTH)

     CASE "SELECT"
          CALL SELECT (SCHEMA$,NEWTOKEN$,MAXLINES,LINELENGTH)

     CASE "SGRAM"
          CALL SGRAM (SCHEMA$,NEWTOKEN$,MAXLINES,LINELENGTH)

     CASE "MTRACE"
          CALL MTRACE (SCHEMA$,NEWTOKEN$,MAXLINES,LINELENGTH)

     CASE "RLINE"
          CALL RLINE (SCHEMA$,NEWTOKEN$,MAXLINES,LINELENGTH)

     CASE "BANDW"
          CALL BANDW (SCHEMA$,NEWTOKEN$,MAXLINES,LINELENGTH)

     CASE "HISTO"
          CALL HISTO (SCHEMA$,NEWTOKEN$,MAXLINES,LINELENGTH)

     CASE "PIE"
          CALL PIE (SCHEMA$,NEWTOKEN$,MAXLINES,LINELENGTH)

     CASE "INCO"
          CALL INCO (SCHEMA$,NEWTOKEN$,MAXLINES,LINELENGTH)

     CASE "BALA"
          CALL BALA (SCHEMA$,NEWTOKEN$,MAXLINES,LINELENGTH)

     CASE "ES"
          CALL ES (SCHEMA$,NEWTOKEN$,MAXLINES,LINELENGTH)
```

```
      CASE "DISPLAY"
          CALL DISPLAY (SCHEMA$,NEWTOKEN$,MAXLINES,LINELENGTH)

      CASE "DTREE"
          CALL DSSDTREE (SCHEMA$,NEWTOKEN$,MAXLINES,LINELENGTH)

      CASE "LED"
          CALL DSSLED (SCHEMA$,NEWTOKEN$,MAXLINES,LINELENGTH)

      CASE "SPREAD"
          CALL DSSSPREA (SCHEMA$,NEWTOKEN$,MAXLINES,LINELENGTH)

      CASE "ADD"
          CALL ADD (SCHEMA$,NEWTOKEN$,MAXLINES,LINELENGTH)

      CASE "SUBTRACT"
          CALL SUBTRACT (SCHEMA$,NEWTOKEN$,MAXLINES,LINELENGTH)

      CASE "MULTIPLY"
          CALL MULTIPLY (SCHEMA$,NEWTOKEN$,MAXLINES,LINELENGTH)

      CASE "DIVIDE"
          CALL DIVIDEX (SCHEMA$,NEWTOKEN$,MAXLINES,LINELENGTH)

      CASE "SUMMARIZE"
          CALL SUMMARIZE (SCHEMA$,NEWTOKEN$,MAXLINES,LINELENGTH)

      CASE ELSE
          PRINT "NO SUCH PROGRAM"
          PAUSE 3

      END SELECT

      CALL MAINPROMPT

  LOOP

  END
```

APPENDIX D

INTRODUCTION

This appendix contains a bibliography of selected references that is designed to help students interested in Decision Support and Expert Systems to identify sources of information in this fast-changing field.

BIBLIOGRAPHY

Ackoff, Russell L. "Management Misinformation Systems." *Management Science* (December, 1967), pp. 147–156.

Alter, Steven. *Decision Support Systems: Current Practice and Continuing Challenges.* Reading: Addison-Wesley Publishing Company, 1980.

Ariv, Gad, and Michael J. Ginzberg. "DSS Design: A Systemic View of Decision Support." *Communications of the ACM* (Volume 28, Number 10, October, 1985), pp. 1045–1052.

Barnard, Chester I. *The Functions of the Executive.* Cambridge: Harvard University Press, 1968.

Bennett, John L. (ed.). *Building Decision Support Systems.* Reading: Addison-Wesley Publishing Company, 1983.

Bolt, Richard A. *The Human Interface.* London: Wadsworth, Inc., 1984.

Bonczek, Robert H., Clyde W. Holsapple, and Andrew B. Whinston. *Foundations of Decision Support Systems.* New York: Academic Press, Inc., 1981.

Clocksin, W. F., and C. S. Mellish. *Programming in PROLOG.* New York: Springer-Verlag, 1981.

Davis, Randal, Bruce Buchanan, and Edward Shortliffe. ''Production Rules as a Representation for a Knowledge-Based Consultation Program.'' *Artificial Intelligence* (Volume 8, 1977), pp. 15–45.

Dearden, John. ''MIS is a Mirage.'' *Harvard Business Review* (January–February, 1972), pp. 90–99.

Flavin, Matt. *Fundamental Concepts of Information Modelling.* New York: Yourdon Press, 1981.

Gerrity, T. P., Jr., ''The Design of Man-Machine Decision Systems: An Applicaton to Portfolio Management,'' *Sloan Management Review,* Vol. 112, No. 2 (Winter, 1971), pp. 59–75.

Hartwig, Frederick, and Brian E. Dearing. *Exploratory Data Analysis.* Beverly Hills: Sage Publications, 1979.

Hayes, John R. *The Complete Problem Solver.* Philadelphia: The Franklin Institute Press, 1981.

Hayes-Roth, Frederick, Donald A. Waterman, and Douglas B. Lenat. *Building Expert Systems.* Reading: Addison-Wesley Publishing Company, 1983.

Hoaglin, David C., Frederick Mosteller, and John W. Tukey. *Understanding Robust and Exploratory Data Analysis.* New York: John Wiley and Sons, 1983.

Jackson, Barbara Bund. *Computer Models in Management.* Homewood: Richard D. Irwin, Inc., 1979.

Jenkins, A. Milton. *MIS Design Variables and Decision Making Performance.* Ann Arbor: UMI Research Press, 1983.

Keen, Peter G. W. '' 'Interactive' Computer Systems for Managers: A Modest Proposal.'' *Sloan Management Review* (Fall, 1976), pp. 1–17.

Keen, Peter G. W., and Michael S. Scott Morton. *Decision Support Systems: An Organizational Perspective.* Reading: Addison-Wesley Publishing Company, 1978.

Kleijnen, Jack P. C. *Computers and Profits: Quantifying Financial Benefits of Information.* Reading: Addison-Wesley Publishing Company, 1980.

Mason, Richard O., and E. Burton Swanson. *Measurement for Management Decision.* Reading: Addison-Wesley Publishing Company, 1981.

McCorduck, Pamela. *Machines Who Think.* San Francisco: W. H. Freeman and Company, 1979.

Merrett, T. H. *Relational Information Systems.* Reston: Reston Publishing Co., 1984.

Michie, Donald (ed.). *Introductory Readings in Expert Systems.* New York: Gordon and Breach Science Publishers, Inc., 1982.

Nolan, Richard L. "Managing the Crises in Data Processing." *Harvard Business Review* (March–April, 1979), pp. 115–126.

Odiorne, George S. *Management Decisions by Objectives.* Englewood Cliffs: Prentice-Hall, Inc., 1969.

O'Shea, Tim, and Marc Eisenstadt (eds.). *Artificial Intelligence.* New York: Harper and Row, Publishers, 1984.

Polya, G. *How to Solve It.* Garden City: Doubleday and Company, 1957.

Raiffa, Howard. *Decision Analysis.* Reading: Addison-Wesley Publishing Company, 1970.

Reimann, Bernard C., and Allen D. Warren. "User-Oriented Criteria for the Selection of DSS Software." *Communications of the ACM* (Volume 28, Number 2, Feburary, 1985), pp. 166–179.

Rockart, John F. "Chief Executives Define Their Own Data Needs." *Harvard Business Review* (March–April, 1979), pp. 81–93.

Rubinstein, Moshe F. *Patterns of Problem Solving.* Englewood Cliffs: Prentice-Hall, Inc., 1975.

Simon, H. A. *The Science of the Artificial.* Cambridge: Massachusetts Institute of Technology Press, 1981.

Simon, H. A. *The New Science of Management.* New York: Harper and Row, Publishers, 1960.

Sprague, Ralph H., Jr., and Eric D. Carlson. *Building Effective Decision Support Systems.* Englewood Cliffs: Prentice-Hall, Inc., 1982.

Thierauf, Robert J. *Decision Support Systems for Effective Planning and Control.* Englewood Cliffs: Prentice-Hall, Inc., 1982.

Weizenbaum, Joseph. *Computer Power and Human Reason.* San Francisco: W. H. Freeman and Company, 1976.

Wickelgren, Wayne A. *How to Solve Problems.* San Francisco: W. H. Freeman and Company, 1974.

Wiederhold, Gio. *Database Design.* New York: McGraw-Hill, 1983.

Witten, Ian H. *Communicating with Microcomputers.* New York: Academic Press, Inc., 1980.

GLOSSARY

A

ad hoc For a particular purpose or application. A model concerned only with a selected purpose and application.

adaptive design A method for designing a new system by enhancing and expanding upon the capabilities of an existing system.

analytic model A data model built around mathematical equations representing the behavior of an entity.

APL (A Programming Language) A high-level programming language, particularly well suited for mathematical modeling.

arithmetic operator A command or symbol that designates a mathematical function, such as the plus, minus, division, and multiplication signs.

attribute A column of data items within a relation of a relational database.

B

balance sheet equation A formula for determining equity, or the difference between assets and liabilities.

bar chart A graphic image in which varying data values are represented as lines or bars of different lengths.

bivariate Consisting of two variables or dimensions.

black box A simplistic method of viewing a procedure, program, or module as an entity in terms of results produced. Under black-box analysis, inputs and outputs are studied as a means of deducing the processing that took place.

bottom line A term for profit, used because of the location of profit values on financial statements.

box-and-whisker diagram A method for presenting distributions of statistical data. A single column of data values onto which median and low and high hinge values are plotted.

brainstorming A structured method for generating ideas from multiple contributions through a series of give-and-take meetings.

bulletin board Communications software that accepts and stores messages that can be accessed by any caller linked into the host system.

C

catastrophic outcome In decision making, an outcome that holds serious, undesirable consequences for an organization; a result that decision makers strive to avoid.

cells Positions within a relation or table, located at the intersections of columns and rows.

column arithmetic Mathematical operations applied to one or more columns within a relation, and in which the results can be displayed within a separate column.

command-driven A characteristic of an operation in which user input is required in an acceptable form and format before execution. A type of system that uses specified-format commands.

communications program A combination of hardware and software features that establish communication between two or more computers.

computer conference A computer communication technique by which multiple participants are linked for simultaneous information exchange.

concatenate To connect in a series. To append one value or statement to another as is done when two or more fields from the same record are treated as a single entity.

consultation A dialog consisting of specific questions about a problem and recommendations for solution. Also refers to this type of dialog between a user and a knowledge system.

control variable A predetermined value that establishes a condition to be met before an action is taken.

cooperative A quality of being easy to work with. In DSS context, a system designed to display "help" messages to users as assistance is needed.

critical path The longest series of related tasks needed to complete a project.

current assets Cash or other assets that are readily convertible to cash.

D

data dependencies Relationships among data items in a database, defined according to the way data items must be used within specific applications.

data dictionary A structured listing in which data entities in a database are defined according to name, meaning, and format.

data element *See* data entity.

data entity A basic unit of data that describes a person, place, thing, concept, or event. The most primitive unit of data that has meaning to a system.

data item *See* data entity.

data model Data used to represent an organization or operation. A logical system for representing a collection of data and data relationships.

data processing (DP) system A set of procedures for handling related business transactions, such as payroll, accounts receivable, and others. Also called application processing.

data reduction The process of giving meaning to large volumes of data by reducing volumes of entries through summary or selection methods.

database A collection of data organized so that each element can be identified and accessed individually or can support processing based on structures and relationships among items.

database management system (DBMS) A series of programs that comprise a system for creating, accessing, managing, and altering a database.

debugging The process of locating and correcting errors in the logic or syntax of a source program.

decision A determination to take action to deal with a specific problem. A step in the problem-solving process.

decision simulator A capability of DSS that allows managers to preview the outcomes of decision alternatives before committing to a decision. Also called ''what if . . . ?'' analysis.

decision support system (DSS) A set of computer-based tools used by managers to assist in evaluation and selection of quantifiable decision alternatives.

decision table A two-dimensional table that supports decision making by listing possible conditions and corresponding ''yes'' or ''no'' responses or actions.

declarative A characteristic of a programming language that establishes a knowledge base to support its data manipulation operations.

Delphi process A method of generating decision alternatives by which suggestions are collected and evaluated, with the process being repeated until a solution is reached. The name is taken from the Delphic Oracle in ancient Greece.

descriptive model   A presentation of collected data values that represents an entity under study or subject to management.

descriptive modeling   A category of modeling encompassing the techniques of data modeling, analytic modeling, and graphic display.

desktop metaphor   A characteristic of dialog managers based on icons of items commonly found on a desk or in an office.

dialog management   Techniques for interfacing between nontechnical users and hierarchical software.

dialog manager   Software routine for interfacing between users and data management or model management packages.

download   A transfer of data from mainframe to microcomputer or from central to satellite terminal in a computer network.

DSS generator   A user facility within a DSS assembled from generic, general-purpose components that allows the user to combine standard functions to meet specific needs, and to incorporate the new, composite function as a special-purpose system. *See also* generating.

E

editor   A software utility for entering and capturing text.

electronic mail   A computerized message-distribution system in which users are assigned memory addresses for accumulation of items awaiting delivery. Messages are delivered to terminals of addresses upon presentation of qualifying passwords. An electronic mail system is similar to a bulletin board, except that messages are directed to addresses rather than being posted for general access.

end user programming   *See* fourth-generation techniques.

exception reporting   *See* management by exception.

exogenous variables   Variables in the decision-making process that originate from the outside world. DSS users cannot control the accuracy or reliability of exogenous variables.

expected value   A weighted average used to select decision alternatives, based on possible outcome values and their probabilities.

expert decision support system   An expert system that incorporates a knowledge subsystem.

expert system   An application package characterized by its capability to recommend solutions to problems and to trace and identify the logic applied in reaching recommendations.

extrapolate To project or extend into the future or a previously unknown area.

extreme point The value(s) defined by a mathematical model as the optimal solution to a linear program.

F

feasible region The region, representing a range of values, that encompasses all possible solution values of a problem.

financial model A type of mathematical model in which an organization is represented by data on assets, liabilities, and equity.

financial modeling A technique for presenting financial data using a special set of commands and output displays that resemble spreadsheets.

formal model A DSS model characterized by established theoretical principles and proven mathematical structures.

fourth generation A characteristic of systems that use an interface by which nontechnical users can communicate with and control the system.

fourth-generation techniques Systems development methods by which nontechnical users are able to construct a system using macro commands and modular building blocks.

G

general-purpose language based A type of DSS that runs within the environment of an interactive, general-purpose programming language, such as APL or BASIC.

generating The act of originating, as in a DSS. *See also* DSS generator.

generic component system A DSS constructed as a framework, or "tool kit," of general information processing and presentation functions.

graphic display A set of data represented in pictorial form. Modeling techniques for representing quantitative information as pictorial presentations.

graphics output Outputs that present quantitative data in pictorial form. A computer capability for displaying pictorial outputs.

H

heuristics Non-quantifiable problem-solving techniques. Judgmental selection of decision alternatives.

hierarchical Having to do with multiple levels, or structured, master-to-subordinate relationships.

hinges   First- and third-quarter points in a data array which define the mid-spread group of values.

histogram   A graphic method of comparing items by presenting their values as lines or bars of varying length. Also called a bar chart.

I

icon   A pictorial representation of an entity.

icon-based   A specialized menu system that uses pictures representing processing options and a pointing mechanism as a basis for user selection.

iconic   Bearing a physical resemblance to an entity.

implicit schema   A schema that is purposefully inaccessible to users due to its obvious, or transparent, nature.

income statement   A document or model incorporating data on revenue, expense, and profit or loss to represent the financial condition of a person or organization.

inference engine   *See* logic machine.

integer program (IP)   A type of mathematical program in which decision variables may be integers, which include negative numbers, zero, and non-whole numbers.

interactive   A characteristic of computer systems in which the system prompts users for required inputs and responds to user requests.

interpolate   To insert. To estimate an unknown value or values that lie within a range established by known values.

K

keyboard macro   A software tool by which a user can prerecord a sequence of commands and initiate them automatically through use of a function key.

knowledge base   Production rules for a specific problem situation or application within a DSS.

knowledge system   A type of expert system that performs judgmental selection based on formal, systematic logic.

L

life cycle   A management structure for monitoring and controlling systems development, typically divided into phases concluded by status reports and management reviews.

line editor A software utility for entering or changing text one line at a time, with total content assembled by the computer.

linear program (LP) A type of mathematical model in which all formulas are linear equations.

logic machine A computer capable of combining data and systematic logic to produce new data, or conclusions.

long-term assets Items that have value to an organization, but that are not converted readily into cash.

M

macro Characterized by having comparatively little detail. An overview-type model.

macro instruction A macro command that initiates multiple processing operations from a single statement.

major Utmost in importance or degree. In a sorting operation, the primary field(s) to which the sort routine is applied.

management by exception A method under which managers rely on information reporting systems to identify and deliver status information about situations that represent "exceptions" from normal operating expectations. Managers concentrate upon exception situations rather than having to spend time on business areas performing to normal expectations.

management information system (MIS) A set of procedures for giving additional meaning to data, by either summary or selection, to support managerial control functions.

management science The study of guidance and planning for organizations based on quantitative, mathematically oriented principles and methods.

manufacturing requirements planning A method for generating production operating plans on the basis of sales estimates.

mathematical program A formal model in which objectives and constraints are represented by mathematical formulas.

mathematical programming Techniques for establishing a data model of an entity by defining its objectives and constraints with mathematical equations.

maxmax A theory of selecting decision alternatives based on assuming the best possible outcome.

median Middle point. In an array of data, the point at which there is an equal number of values to either side.

median trace A method for presenting nonlinear trend patterns. A median trace uses multiple key points to diagram a curved-line illustration of a trend.

menu generator A user facility interface that enables a user to select from software components to compose menus and submenus that control processing.

menu specifications Machine code instructions to a dialog manager to implement menu selections.

menu-driven A characteristic of software routines in which processing is controlled by user selections from lists of processing options called menus and submenus.

metamodel A model that represents, or "models," another model.

micro Highly detailed. A specifics-oriented model.

midspread The range of values that lies between the upper and lower hinges of a box-and-whisker diagram. The value determined by subtracting the lower hinge value from the upper hinge value.

minmax A conservative method for selecting decision alternatives. Best and worst cases are determined for each alternative, and assuming the worst, the least undesirable possible outcome is selected.

minor Inferior in importance or degree. Secondary fields used within a sorting routine to determine sequencing.

model A representation of an actual person, place, thing, event, or idea. In management science, a set of mathematical formulas that represent the behavior of an entity.

modeling errors Conditions within accounting practices that prevent the reflection of reality within models.

modeling system A type of DSS in which a host modeling language determines the environment and features of the system.

mouse A cursor moving device, often used with icon-based dialog managers.

MUMPS A programming language with excellent data management and report generating capabilities.

N

natural language Language used in communication with computers that resembles closely the normal language of the user's industry or profession. A type of interface that uses natural language.

navigation The use and optimization of access paths to conduct inquiries within a database.

nonlinear Of or resembling shapes that cannot be defined by a line.

normalization The process of improving a data model by eliminating duplicate data items, identifying dependencies, and improving table structures.

O

optimizing model A modeling technique for establishing optimum performance criteria and determining the conditions and/or actions that will most closely realize these criteria.

P

painting a screen An operation by which a user designs the layout of a record display on a terminal screen.

parameter A value representing a physical property that determines behavior or characteristics. A numeric limit to a range of values.

pie chart A graphic method for comparing a whole entity with the size or magnitude of its parts.

portfolio A collection of securities held by an investor.

Portfolio Management System (PMS) A decision support system (DSS) designed to aid in the management of securities investments.

predictive model A model that anticipates future conditions on the basis of historic data.

prescriptive model A data model that projects outcomes of decision alternatives and recommends courses of action based on assumptions about future conditions.

primitive Basic or fundamental. A low-level data representation or program function.

problem A condition or situation that requires change or adjustment to conform to established standards or to restore satisfactory conditions.

procedural Based on a step-by-step methodology.

production rule A statement that initiates an output when a quantitative condition is sensed or a defined event occurs. A type of system that incorporates such statements.

profitability model A modeling equation for determining profitability as the difference between income and expense.

pro forma Literally, for the future. Refers to financial statements used to project income, expenses, and profits for designated future periods.

project management A process for controlling and administering the tasks of computer systems development. A type of computer program that assists in these activities.

PROLOG (PROgramming in LOGic) A declarative programming language that establishes a knowledge base, then manipulates its elements to respond to queries.

prompt A computer display or output that requests user input.

prototyping A developmental technique by which a functional test model is designed and tested, then enhanced and implemented or discarded and redesigned.

Q

QBE Query by example. A functionally oriented database query language. This is an IBM product.

query language A set of commands for accessing and retrieving specific data items or combinations of data items from a database.

R

real-time A response, or turnaround, that occurs within the normal time framework of the application being supported. Reference to a computer system that accepts inputs and delivers outputs with a degree of immediacy, usually a half second to a few seconds.

record A group of data elements that constitute a description of a particular entity.

regression Backward movement. In statistical analysis, techniques for computing formulas to describe a condition by beginning with the condition and deriving formulas from it.

relation A collection of data represented within a table consisting of defined rows and columns of data items.

relational algebra The command structures used in accessing a relational database.

resistant line A graphic technique by which a trend line is superimposed over scattergram-type diagrams and extended beyond existing entries to project future results and patterns.

S

satisficing model A modeling technique defined by quantified constraints and resulting "least-worst" solutions that fall within the constraints.

scattergram A graphic device in which data are represented as points on a two-dimensional grid.

schema A set of data within a database that identifies the content and structure of the database.

screen editor A software utility that allows the text of an entire document, or screen, to be entered, reviewed, and altered prior to processing or compiling.

semi-structured A condition of a problem-solving situation in which a significant portion of the elements involved are partially known or unknown; thus, selection of decision alternatives is not effectively supported by previous experience or existing standards.

shell program A type of software package with an integration capability created by surrounding the operating system and resident application programs with a superimposed "shell" of menus and other command structures.

SIMSCRIPT A programming language for creating mathematical models of an entity and useful in simulating operational behavior of the entity.

simulation model A descriptive model that simulates the actual operation of a system in response to "what if . . . ?" questions.

smart modem A hardware/software package computer communication package that uses a built-in microprocessor to support the services provided.

special-purpose system A system designed and configured to do a specific job, such as a DSS tailored to the decision-making requirements of a particular management area.

speech recognition A capability of computers to recognize and interpret spoken commands.

spreadsheet A presentation of numerical data within a table of columns and rows. A type of software package for generating and presenting spreadsheets.

standalone A characteristic of programs or systems that operate independently, without external support.

statistical analysis A data management capability for reducing masses of data, particularly numeric data, and presenting them in a meaningful form.

statistical model A descriptive model concerned with quantifiable relationships, such as mathematical probabilities, among its data items.

steady state A condition achieved by a simulation model representing typical behavior of the actual system.

subjective judgments An educated guess. An estimation or assumption based upon experience and intuition rather than certainties and probabilities.

support To assist or help. In DSS terminology, the act of aiding the decision-making and problem-solving activities of managers by improving the quality and usefulness of information.

T

technology transfer   A process for generating decision alternatives by researching new technologies or problem solutions developed in other areas.

teleconference   *See* computer conference.

template   A blank form designed by a user to enter and store data to support a specific application.

time series   Data entered and required in their sequence of occurrence.

tool kit   A reference within this text to a set of generic software modules from which decision support systems or modules can be assembled readily.

transparent   Easily detected or seen through. In DSS terminology, describes implicit schemas.

truth table   *See* decision table.

tuple   A row of data items within a relation of a relational database; roughly the equivalent of a data record.

U

univariate   Consisting of one variable or dimension.

upload   An operation in which data or programs are transfered from microcomputer to mainframe.

user facility   An interface between users and multi-level software sets for assembling DSS or other systems.

user friendly   A term qualifying the relative ease with which a nontechnical user can relate to a software package or computer system.

V

view   A selective subset of an overall database from the viewpoint of, or need to be met by, a specific user or application.

W

whisker   In a box-and-whisker diagram, a value derived by adding or subtracting the median value to or from the upper or lower hinges. Values that exceed the whiskers on such diagrams are considered to be exception items.

windowing   A software capability for accommodating multiple programs by partitioning main memory to accommodate them. A separate frame, or window, is displayed on the terminal screen for each program in memory.

INDEX

Page numbers in *italics* refer to figures in the text.

443

Jewel

famous Collectors

STEFANO PAPI and ALEXANDRA RHODES

HARRY N. ABRAMS, INC., PUBLISHERS

This book is dedicated to our mothers   A.R.   S.P.

Library of Congress Cataloging-in-Publication Data

Papi, Stefano.
    Famous jewelry collectors / by Stefano Papi
    and Alexandra Rhodes.
        p.   cm.
    Includes bibliographical references and index.
    ISBN 0–8109–3341–1
    1. Jewelry—Collectors and collecting—
Biography. I. Rhodes, Alexandra. II. Title.
NK7397.P36 1999
739.27'092'2—dc21   99–18038
[B]

Copyright © 1999 Thames & Hudson Ltd, London

Published in 1999 by Harry N. Abrams, Incorporated,
New York

Printed and bound in Singapore

Harry N. Abrams, Inc.
100 Fifth Avenue
New York, N.Y. 10011
www.abramsbooks.com

Contents

Preface

An object of beauty and desire, a jewel also provides a perfect reflection of the personality, lifestyle and tastes of the owner. Jewelry auctions are not a 20th-century phenomenon, but over the past few decades we have seen a wealth of the world's most fabulous jewels, once owned by some of the most notable personalities of the century, pass through the salerooms. These jewels were once in the possession of royalty, aristocracy, high society and stars of the screen. In each instance, whether it was one piece or a whole collection, the designated jewelry gives us a fascinating insight into the life and times of the owner as well as the opportunity to see some of the finest gemstones and the most stunning jewels ever created during the last three centuries.

The world of the stars has been well represented with jewels from many of the Hollywood greats, all of whom had glittering careers as well as magnificent jewelry. Ava Gardner, once described by United Artists' publicity department as 'the world's most beautiful animal', had a marvellous collection of suitably glamorous jewels. The majority were created for her by Van Cleef & Arpels or William Ruser. Both on and off the screen jewelry was one of Paulette Goddard's greatest passions and she wore contemporary as well as antique pieces with great style. In the main her jewels were bold and beautiful, very much in keeping with her own personality and image. Among the many other Hollywood queens whose equally spectacular jewelry collections were sold at auction were Merle Oberon, Mary Pickford and Joan Crawford.

The early years of the 20th century were conceivably the most glamorous of all for the society hostess and the woman of means. These people were extremely rich and powerful, leading hectic social lives which required the appropriate designer dresses as well as designer jewels. Mona Bismarck, Barbara Hutton and Daisy Fellowes were such women. However, they all collected jewels not as a required accessory, but because jewels had an irresistible attraction for them. As they could all afford to buy the best and had great style, their collections were memorable. Other notable personalities on the social scene whose collections were sold were Helena Rubinstein, Lydia, Lady Deterding and Ganna Walska, all of whom lived highly glamorous lifestyles with suitably impressive jewels.

The other name which is inevitable in this world of high society is the Duchess of Windsor, but her jewelry collection was incomparable, truly unique. In their own right these were some of the most important and sensational examples of the 20th-century jeweler's art, but they were also jewels which had been chosen by a king to give to the woman for whom he abdicated his throne.

From the jewelry collections of royalty and aristocracy there are some wonderful examples of historical importance combined with excellent design. The Thurn und Taxis collection, for instance, contained some of the most sumptuous and creative jewels of the 18th and 19th centuries. Jewels from the estate of King Umberto II of Italy and those of Princess Mary, the Princess Royal, were equally impressive. Other wonderful collections had belonged to Cornelia, Countess of Craven and Gladys Marie, Dowager Duchess of Marlborough.

In combination, these represent some of the finest and most extravagant jewels ever created and give us a fascinating insight into the personalities and worlds of their equally intriguing owners.

STEFANO PAPI ALEXANDRA RHODES

Merle Oberon

erle Oberon had an unusual exotic beauty and a ladylike British elegance that secured her a sparkling Hollywood career. The high point of that career was her portrayal of Cathy in *Wuthering Heights* with Laurence Olivier, but she played a good many more roles that kept her in the upper brackets of film-making. Her early success, starting in several of Alexander Korda's splendid British pictures, gave her the opportunity to indulge in her taste for beautiful objects and being the recipient of them.

For various reasons, including racial prejudice, her parentage and place of birth were always falsified, initially by her press agents, and then by Merle herself. She was in fact the daughter of a Eurasian mother and an English father. Estelle Merle O'Brien Thompson was born in February 1911 in Bombay, where her father was employed in the railways. In 1914 patriotism led him to the battle-fields of France, where he was to die, not in battle but of pneumonia. In 1917 Merle and her mother moved to Calcutta, where a place was found for Merle in a rather prestigious school as the daughter of a man who had been 'killed in action'. It was here that she was first to experience the feeling of shame for her dark-skinned mother, a feeling that would remain with her all her life.

By 1927 she was working as a telephonist and, with her stunning looks, was never short of an eligible beau to partner her to the dance hall or the movies. She had developed a great passion for the cinema and when given the chance to go to France and meet Rex Ingram, the famous film director, she naturally leapt at it. The invitation had been offered by one of her admirers, Col. Ben Finney, an ex-actor, whose apparent generosity had ulterior motives. After being captivated by Merle, he had by chance met her mother, and this immediately decided him to end the relationship. He was leaving for France and his invitation was given rather out of embarrassment than generosity, as he had no intention of meeting her there should she in fact go.

Merle was ecstatic and in 1929 sailed for Europe with her mother, who continued on to England while Merle remained in France to pursue her dream of a career in films. Though there was no sign of Finney, she did contrive to meet Ingram, who gave her a role as an extra in a film called *The Three Passions*. When she went on to London, she found jobs as a dance hostess in well-known and reputable establishments. Eventually she acquired the much-coveted job of a hostess at the Café de Paris, which catered to high society, and indeed royalty. It was one of the favourite haunts of the Prince of Wales and his circle. Though the rules for a hostess were extremely strict, she thoroughly enjoyed her view of this dazzling life where she had the opportunity to meet people who could be influential to her future. During the day she was hard at work at Elstree Studios, where she was given several small parts.

Merle Oberon photographed by Horst in 1942 wearing the three flowerhead clips by Cartier, London, which had originally formed part of a hair ornament. These clips were a wedding present from Alexander Korda on the occasion of their marriage in 1939. *Horst/Vogue*

In 1931, the prominent producer Alexander Korda returned to England after a stint in Hollywood. Merle appeared in minor roles in a few of his films, but he had already noticed her talent and unusual beauty and in 1933 gave her the part which was to change her life. Her brief role as Anne Boleyn in *The Private Life of Henry VIII*, with Charles Laughton cast as the King, was a critical and financial success.

In 1934 Merle was briefly engaged to Joseph Schenk, a powerful Hollywood figure who was reputed to have showered her with jewels and the promise of roles in pictures. When the engagement was broken off, she returned the expensive diamond engagement ring he had given her, and Schenk honoured his promise of a role for her in a Hollywood production. Later that year she arrived in the film centre of the world and in 1935 she starred with Maurice Chevalier in *Folies Bergere*. That same year the acutely business-minded Alexander Korda made an agreement with Samuel Goldwyn to share part of her contract, and over the next few years she played some of her finest and most memorable movie characters on both sides of the Atlantic.

It was also the period when she acquired one of her most treasured jewels and one which she wore frequently, both on and off the screen. The antique emerald and diamond necklace is in a design of festoons and clusters fringed by emerald and diamond drops. The detachable central motif can also be worn as a brooch. This style of necklace is typical of the 1860s. According to legend it had been presented by Napoleon III to Baroness Haussmann, whose husband had planned the redevelopment of Paris during the Second Empire. At a later date, two of the emerald and diamond drops had been converted to a pair of earrings. In the 1938 film *The Divorce of Lady X*, with Laurence Olivier, Merle wore it to great effect.

During this period she worked and played hard, her name often linked with prominent names of the film world. However, it was apparent over the years that the feelings she and Korda had for each other and the interests they shared were not part of the business contract. In August 1939 they were married in Antibes. Despite plans for a grand wedding it ended up as a small ceremony. The witnesses were an old friend, Henri Guenot, and Maître Suzanne Blum, who was Merle's French lawyer and was to become the Duchess of Windsor's later. As a wedding present, Korda bought Merle three superb diamond brooches from Cartier, London, in June 1939. Each in the form of a rose in full bloom, a pair and one larger, they were set throughout with diamonds, the largest with the diamond pistils mounted *en tremblant*. They had originally been part of a head ornament, but when Merle wore them as clips on her dress or attached to a ribbon around her neck, they were sensational. In the sale of her collection, they were unfortunately sold consecutively as two separate lots.

What happened to the original head ornament is unknown, but on Princess Elizabeth's marriage to Prince Philip of Greece in 1947 she was given an identical set of diamond clips, mounted in a tiara, by the Nizam of Hyderabad and Berar, which had also been created by Cartier.

(Opposite) An antique emerald and diamond necklace, and Merle Oberon wearing the jewel in 1938. At a later date she removed two of the emerald and diamond drops, which she then had converted into earrings. She also wore the central cluster and drop as a brooch in the film *Of Love and Desire* in which she starred in 1963. *The Kobal Collection; Christie's, New York*

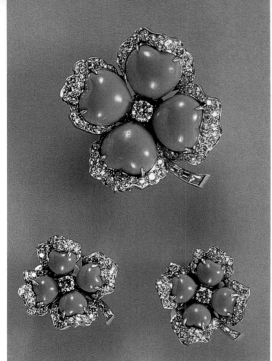

In this photograph of Merle Oberon during the shooting of the movie *Hotel* in 1967, she is wearing her turquoise and diamond parure in its original 1950s form; in the 1970s she had it and the pendent earrings re-designed (opposite) by Van Cleef & Arpels, using the turquoise and diamond clusters from the original necklace. Van Cleef & Arpels also used the pear-shaped turquoise drop to create a jewel that she could wear either as a pendant hanging from the centre of the necklace or as a brooch (above). In *Of Love and Desire* she wore the four-leaf clover brooch and matching pair of earrings (top). *Christie's, New York; The Kobal Collection*

As Queen Elizabeth II, she later had the diamonds in the tiara unmounted to form a new ruby and diamond tiara. However, she kept the three clips, which she still often wears.

In November 1939, possibly with Christmas in mind, Korda bought, again from Cartier in London, an incomparable emerald bead and diamond necklace. This sumptuous jewel is designed as a fringe of 29 graduated emerald drops, capped by diamonds, and on a collar of diamond set rondels linked by a platinum chain. Indian in inspiration, it matched Merle's exotic looks.

In the auction of her collection, another beautiful pair of jewels designed by Cartier were sold individually. The two diamond clips, both designed as flowerheads, one set with ruby pistils and the other with diamond pistils, were created in the late 1930s. They were designed to be worn together or separately as clips, or could be attached to a diamond strap bracelet to form an impressive clasp. Merle wore this bracelet, as well as the three rose clips, in the film *Till We Meet Again* (1940). Another jewel which was sold in two separate lots was the superb sapphire and diamond floral brooch by Cartier, London. The detachable flowerhead clip was set with a large oval sapphire centre and the petals pavé-set with diamonds. The diamond stem was sold separately, with no mention of the fact that it could be attached to the flowerhead clip. Merle wore the two together on many occasions and also wore the flowerhead clip either on a velvet band as a choker centre or on a platinum bangle which Cartier had also furnished. It is apparent from her collection that Merle not only loved Cartier jewels, but also the versatility which they often provided. Another pair of Cartier diamond flowerhead clips were designed with a detachable chain of baguette and fancy-cut diamonds. Simply by having the chain attached, the jewel became a stylish garment clasp.

From the same period, but unsigned, were a pair of diamond feather scroll clips and a pair of ruby, blue and yellow sapphire ornaments of flowerhead and foliate design. The latter are most probably the clips which could be converted into a necklace centre, which she is pictured wearing on the set of *A Night in Paradise* in 1945.

The Kordas had made London their home, but upon the outbreak of war they returned to Hollywood. Korda had two reasons for this move: it would enable him to finish filming *The Thief of Baghdad*, but more important, he could carry out the vital secret work he had agreed to do for British Intelligence. This activity meant that over the next few years, with his frequent trips to New York and Europe, he often left Merle alone. She busied herself with films and working for the British war effort, both in the USA and in Britain. The Kordas' assistance to the cause did not go unrecognized: on 22 September 1942 Merle accompanied Alexander to Buckingham Palace where he was knighted by King George VI for his services to the Crown.

Merle Oberon in the early 1940s wearing ruby and diamond flowerhead clips created by Cartier, London, 1939, pinned to her dress, and original archive photographs showing them from various angles mounted as the centrepiece of a diamond bracelet. *Cartier Ltd. London; The Kobal Collection*

(Opposite) With her husband Alexander Korda in 1941 attending a Russian Medical Aid Relief Concert in Los Angeles, Oberon is wearing her Cartier ruby and diamond flowerhead clips as a bracelet centre. *UPI/CORBIS*

Her splendid Cartier jewels from this period are a fitting tribute to the success she was enjoying in her acting career and her happy early years with Korda. Unfortunately their time apart had strained their marriage and in 1943 they separated. Within a few years they obtained a Mexican divorce and Merle promptly married Lucien Ballard, a successful Hollywood cameraman. By the time this relationship too had ended in divorce in 1949 Merle was already deeply committed to Count Giorgio Cini. By all accounts theirs was a whirlwind romance which resulted in several gifts of jewelry. Tragi-

cally, the Count, while he was still trying to persuade his aristocratic and disapproving parents to accept Merle as his bride, was killed in a plane crash.

Merle was devastated but threw herself back into work and starred in several films over the next few years. In 1956 she became involved with Bruno Pagliai, a powerful and extremely wealthy businessman in Mexico, and a year later they were married in Rome. Although wealthy in her own right, she had nothing compared to Pagliai, who pro-vided her with luxury and security. They adopted two Italian children, Bruno and Francesca, and Merle rarely made any films. She devoted herself to a full and glittering round of social events, friendships with princes and presi-dents, and indulged in her appetite for fine clothes and jewelry. Her dresses were designed by Luis Estevez, with a view to showing off her jewels.

It was in the late '50s and '60s that she acquired and indeed altered many of her jewels. The diamond clasp of the impressive two-row emerald bead necklace was originally the clasp of her pearl and diamond bracelet. To match this necklace she acquired a pair of emerald and diamond earclips from David Webb and a cabochon emerald and diamond ring from Harry Winston. It is evident that she was extremely fond of emeralds. One of the finest in her collection was a step-cut stone, mounted as a brooch, at the centre of a foliate diamond border, in the style of Van Cleef & Arpels.

Pearls were still highly fashionable at this time and she had a pair of natural pearl earrings which were surmounted by circular-cut diamonds; she wore these with a single-row cultured pearl necklace. The stylish bombé cluster clasp of the necklace was originally a ring.

At this period in her life Merle spent a great deal of time in Italy, espe-cially Rome, where she liked nothing better than to indulge herself in the fashionable shops in the via Condotti. From Bulgari she acquired a striking diamond brooch, the central step-cut stone weighing over 15cts, and an extremely elegant floral brooch set with rubies and diamonds, the flowerheads mounted *en tremblant*. This style of brooch was in vogue, and Bulgari created some fine inter-pretations of it. They also created for Merle a smart evening bag in an unusual design of stylized acorns, the gold clasp set with turquoise and diamonds, which she used on many occasions.

In 1966 she starred in the film version of Arthur Hailey's popular novel *Hotel*, in which her role was that of a glamorous duchess who wore fabulous jewels. The director, aware of her own wonderful collection of jewelry, persuaded Merle to wear them for the production, with the proviso that the studio would cover the large insurance bill. Both the film and studio publicity portraits show her wearing a stunning turquoise and diamond parure. The necklace was designed as a fringe of oval turquoise and diamond clusters with a large pear-shaped turquoise drop at the centre, and the pendent earrings were of similar design.

The turquoise and diamond necklace, brooch and earrings which were included in the sale of her jewels were almost certainly a re-working of the original parure by Van Cleef & Arpels in the early 1970s. Her collection also contained a quatrefoil brooch and matching earrings and a bracelet, each set with turquoise and diamonds and dating from a similar period. Van Cleef & Arpels were also the creators of her pink coral and diamond necklace, which could be converted into a choker and bracelet. The large pear-shaped cluster pendant could be worn as a brooch.

Merle also had a small but fine collection of rubies. This included a ruby bead five-row necklace and a sumptuous ruby and diamond necklace by David Webb, slightly reminiscent in style of the one created by Van Cleef & Arpels for the Duchess of Windsor. David Webb also created her ruby and diamond ring, set at the centre with a lozenge-shaped ruby weighing approximately 12cts. She also had two ruby and diamond pendants, each centred by two oval rubies of over 13cts each, framed by diamonds, that she could hang from diamond surmounts as earrings. These surmounts could also be used to support other drops, including two important cabochon emeralds, weighing together over 70cts, with diamond caps and drop-shaped cultured pearls capped by marquise-shaped diamonds. However, by far the most important drops were designed as cascades of pear-shaped and brilliant-cut diamonds; the largest pear-shaped stone could be detached and worn singly as a drop. She would often wear these with her sensational diamond necklace of flowerhead cluster design set with diamonds of similar shape to the earrings. She also wore this jewel as a head ornament entwined in her coiffure, as seen at the Ballo Romantico in New York in December 1965 and at the opening of the film *Hotel*. An important diamond bracelet also accompanied this necklace, which was of simple but classical design. The single row of pear and cushion-shaped diamonds weighed over 40cts.

Merle's final divorce and last marriage took place in 1975. With Robert Wolders, an actor of less than half her age, she spent four happily married years, which ended with her death in 1979. The sale of her collection of jewels took place in New York on 22 April 1980. The 38 pieces represented not only her stylish lifestyle and some memorable occasions in her successful career, but also the work of many of the finest jewelers of her time.

(Opposite) The legendary emerald and diamond necklace by Cartier, London, 1938, which Oberon is shown wearing in the late 1960s.
Christie's, New York; UPI /CORBIS

A spectacular group of Merle Oberon's jewels by Cartier, including ruby and diamond flowerhead clips, 1939; three diamond flowerhead brooches, 1939; and a sapphire and diamond five-petalled flower brooch, designed in 1940 to be worn with the diamond stem (which was sold separately in the sale of her jewels) or as the centrepiece of a yellow gold rigid bangle

(Opposite) Merle Oberon leaving her London hotel for Ascot in June 1950, wearing the sapphire and diamond flower brooch by Cartier and the diamond ring which she later converted to become the clasp of her pearl necklace. *Christie's, New York; Hulton Getty*

18

Mary Pickford

'America's Sweetheart' was her popular name when she was the top star of the early silent Hollywood years. Her pictures made more money than any others and she earned more money than any other actor in the business. She was a universal personality, an adored icon whose every activity was considered newsworthy. She stood for ringleted innocence in an innocent America. And yet, according to her birth certificate, she was born in Toronto, Canada, in 1892 and her name was Gladys Louise Smith. Making her first stage appearance at the age of six, she went on to become not only a wildly adulated star but also a very astute business woman.

After she changed her name, her face became one of the most recognizable in the USA and Europe, as well as in many other faraway corners of the world where people could watch the flickering images of the silent screen. She starred in hundreds of these films, sometimes producing two a week. Long golden curls and a child's face were her usual trademarks; well into her adult life she was still playing these parts.

As with many of her fellow actors, her childhood was something of a hand-to-mouth existence, her father having died when she was only five. But by her early teens she was well able to support her widowed mother and her two siblings, both of whom often appeared with her later in films or on the stage. Mary's stage debut in 1898 took place at the Princess Theatre in Toronto. For the next few years she went on tour, spending much of her time in boarding houses with her family. On one occasion they shared rooms with Lillian Gish.

Although poor, Mary had a relatively happy childhood, adored and vehemently protected by her mother. In 1907 she and her mother moved to New York and Mary's break came that year when she appeared in a play on Broadway, *The Warrens of Virginia*, directed by the powerful David Belasco, for which she received excellent reviews. It toured for two seasons; after it closed in 1909, she made her first appearance in the movies with the Biograph Studios in Brooklyn.

Professionally, the screen did not have the cachet of the theatre but it paid an exceptionally good salary. In 1911, much to her mother's disapproval, Mary married fellow actor Owen Moore, a man of no great acting ability but a great liking for the bottle. It was almost a spur-of-the-moment decision which was almost as quickly regretted by Mary.

By 1917 she had an apartment in New York where she lived with her mother. That year she earned just over half a million dollars for her work in the movies. Her future seemed favourable, and by now she was in love with the man who was to play a great part in her life. The only obstacle was that both of them were still married. Two years later Mary applied for a divorce from Owen, which became final in 1920.

Mary Pickford at the peak of her career in *Dorothy Vernon of Haddon Hall*, 1924. *CORBIS*

Mary Pickford with Buddy Rogers attending the Academy Awards in 1941. She is wearing a Trabert & Hoeffer, Inc.- Mauboussin diamond bangle with a fancy yellow diamond, and a diamond necklace of ribbon bow design with matching earrings which were probably by the same jewelers. Over a decade later she is shown blowing out the candles on her birthday cake to celebrate her sixtieth birthday in 1953. She is with Joe Woodruff, State Director of Saving Bonds. Once again she is wearing her much-favoured necklace and earrings. *CORBIS; UPI/CORBIS*

(Opposite) A diamond ribbon bow necklace and matching earrings, together with a diamond double clip brooch made by Trabert & Hoeffer, Inc.-Mauboussin. *Christie's, New York*

Douglas Fairbanks, the man in question, also secured a divorce from his wife who agreed not to name Mary in the proceedings in exchange for a large settlement. Free to marry, their only worry was the possible reaction of their loyal fans to the marriage of two divorcees. But they did not hesitate for long and on 28 March 1920 they became Mr and Mrs Douglas Fairbanks.

Their honeymoon was spent in Europe, where the famous couple were feted like royalty. Crowds had to be controlled by the police in nearly every major city they visited. As a wedding present Fairbanks had bought a property in Benedict Canyon in Beverly Hills. Wallace Neff, who was engaged to redesign the existing building, created a magnificent Tudor-style mansion which was renamed 'Pickfair' and became the setting for many of Hollywood's most glittering social events. In Hollywood terms, their life together was a great success and for more than a decade they held court at Pickfair. Both of them were still involved in the movie business, and in 1929 they made their first talkies. Many actors lived in dread that their voices would not match up to their screen images, but both Mary and Douglas passed the test with no problems. Indeed, for Mary's first speaking role in *Coquette*, she won an Academy Award for Best Actress.

They were deeply involved in their film distribution company, United Artists, which they had founded in 1919 with their great friends Charlie Chaplin and the film director D.W. Griffiths. In 1933 Mary starred in what was to be her last movie, *Secrets*. It made a loss and Mary knew her box office appeal was waning – as was the success of her marriage.

Slowly the feted couple had drifted apart. Douglas was spending more and more time abroad and Mary stayed at home and pursued her business deals. From all accounts they still loved each other but the honeymoon period was long over and they both sought new interests. Finally, the divorce suit which Mary had filed in 1933 became final in 1936. That same year Douglas married Lady Sylvia Ashley and the following year Mary married the band leader and actor, Buddy Rogers, with whom she had appeared in her last silent movie, *My Best Girl*, in 1927.

Life at Pickfair continued with its same stylish hospitality now that Buddy was in the role of

host. Despite her close involvement in film production and distribution, Mary still had a yearning for the children she could never have. In the early 1940s, when Mary was in her fifties, they adopted a girl and a boy. Mary produced her very last film in 1949 but retained her interest in United Artists. The next years were spent watching her business affairs and supporting charity and fund-raising events. By the early 1970s her health was failing; she had a much-publicized drink problem and she became a virtual recluse. Buddy had proved a devoted and supportive husband and was at her bedside when she died in May 1979.

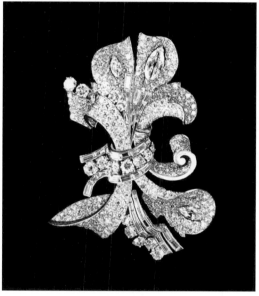

Throughout her life Mary had loved beautiful objects and her jewelry collection represented some of the style and beauty to which she aspired. In June 1980 pieces from her collection were sold in New York. There were 35 lots, several of which included a variety of jewels. These lots, although not of any great intrinsic value, contained pieces with personalized inscriptions or monograms. The majority, however, were important examples of some of the most talented designers mainly of the 1920s-1940s era, with only a few examples from the '60s.

Mary's collection was as diverse as it was beautiful. It included very delicate items, such as an elegant pearl and diamond *sautoir* dating from around 1915. It was designed as two 40-inch strands of natural pearls fringed by two pearl tassels with diamond caps. As she was often photographed wearing this necklace, both on and off the stage, it was obviously one of her favourite jewels during that early period.

Highly representative of the early 1920s style was a delightful carved crystal intaglio and diamond brooch of oval form. The centre was set with a crystal intaglio, the carving representing a classical female figure with arms outstretched to a bird, mounted within an onyx and diamond border.

From the mid-1920s she had acquired a sapphire bead bracelet, the beads alternating with diamond set rondels, and a sapphire and diamond line bracelet. During this same period it became fashionable to wear a multitude of charms, draped from the arms, which were often extremely personal symbols serving as mementoes of special events. Mary had several of these which were mounted on a white and yellow gold link bracelet of a slightly earlier date. Mainly set in platinum, with some in white gold, they depicted skiers and ice skaters, fashionable sports of the period, as well as a man, a lantern and a telephone. They were set with sapphires and diamonds and decorated with enamel, three of them by Cartier. Like many of her affluent contemporaries, Mary collected jewels by Cartier. During the late '20s she acquired one of their gold powder compacts which was decorated with black enamel lotus flowers and leaves as well as her monogram.

Other creations from Cartier included a small gold pendant watch which she received in the late 1930s, after her marriage to Buddy Rogers, and it bore the monogram MR. There were also a very stylish pair of sapphire and diamond clips from the mid-1930s, typical of the art deco style. These were mitre-shaped, each set with a calibré-cut and a large cushion-shaped sapphire, and baguette and brilliant-cut diamonds.

Mary's favourite jewelers were undoubtedly Trabert & Hoeffer, Inc.-Mauboussin, one of the leading American design teams. Trabert & Hoeffer, Inc., had enjoyed a success in New York in the late 1920s, specializing in designing modern jewelry and buying Estate jewels. In 1929 the Paris jewelers Mauboussin opened a shop in New York, an unpropitious move, for within a matter of weeks the Stock Exchange had crashed and Mauboussin's future looked hopeless. Trabert & Hoeffer made a deal to take on the Mauboussin name and inventory; not only were the French firm's losses kept to a minimum, but under the new title of Trabert & Hoeffer, Inc.-Mauboussin the business went from strength to strength. They opened several branches throughout the USA and in 1934 they established a shop in Los Angeles where they soon had Hollywood stars as their clients. The partnership lasted until the 1950s.

A diamond bangle by Trabert & Hoeffer, Inc.-Mauboussin, 1930s, set at the centre with a step-cut fancy yellow diamond of over 27.00cts; a pair of sapphire and diamond clips by Cartier, 1920s; a sapphire and diamond bracelet, 1930s; and a sapphire and diamond ring. *Christie's, New York*

Of the many jewels Mary was known to have acquired from only a few were included in the sale. From archive material it is evident that she was not averse to trading in her out-dated jewels for more fashionable pieces. However, the jewels which were in the sale were some of the company's finest creations. There was an outstanding bangle and matching pair of earrings set with cabochon emeralds and diamonds. During this period cabochon gemstones were considered the height of fashion – especially popular with Hollywood stars such as Marlene Dietrich and Joan Crawford – and the larger they were the more obvious their statement of success and wealth.

Trabert & Hoeffer Inc.-Maubousson created many wonderful jewels using such stones, and several were named after their place of origin. In the late 1930s Mary reportedly bought from them 'The Star of Bombay', a cabochon sapphire thought to weigh 60cts which was mounted between baguette and brilliant-cut diamond scrolled shoulders as a ring. In their advertisements for this stone they had described it as 'In all the world the only one'; but in the sale catalogue this jewel appeared without its name or that of its makers. The star sapphire, now stated to weigh approximately 58.04cts, was not even illustrated.

Among the diamond jewels Mary probably acquired from them she appears to have had firm favourites which she wore on many occasions. Both were in the form of stylized ribbon bows. One was a double clip brooch, the scrolled ribbon bow set with baguette and brilliant-cut diamonds, enhanced with three larger marquise-shaped diamonds. The other was a dramatic necklace, the

front designed as a tasseled ribbon bow set with variously cut diamonds and detachable so as to be worn as a brooch. .

The most important jewel by Trabert & Hoeffer, Inc.-Mauboussin in this sale was a diamond bangle. It was of stylized sunburst and flowerhead design set with baguette and brilliant-cut diamonds, with a step-cut yellow diamond of approximately 27.74cts mounted at the centre, on a white gold and diamond link band. This jewel has recently reappeared at auction, but with the yellow diamond removed and replaced by an emerald.

Other important jewels in the 1980 sale included an impressive sapphire and diamond bracelet, the centre set with a cabochon sapphire weighing approximately 73.62cts. This was mounted within a border of baguette and brilliant-cut diamonds and the tapered sides were set with similarly shaped diamonds and a row of calibré-cut sapphires. She used to wear this with her 'Star of Bombay' ring or with a cushion-shaped sapphire of 24.88cts set between baguette diamonds as an equally attractive ring.pair of earrings and a ring.

Mary Pickford achieved unrivalled success in her profession, which gave her the financial security to enjoy a lavish lifestyle and acquire the usual trappings of wealth which she admired. Her upbringing had ensured her prudence where matters of finance were concerned; she could have existed without jewelry, but she adored and loved wearing it – and she could afford it.

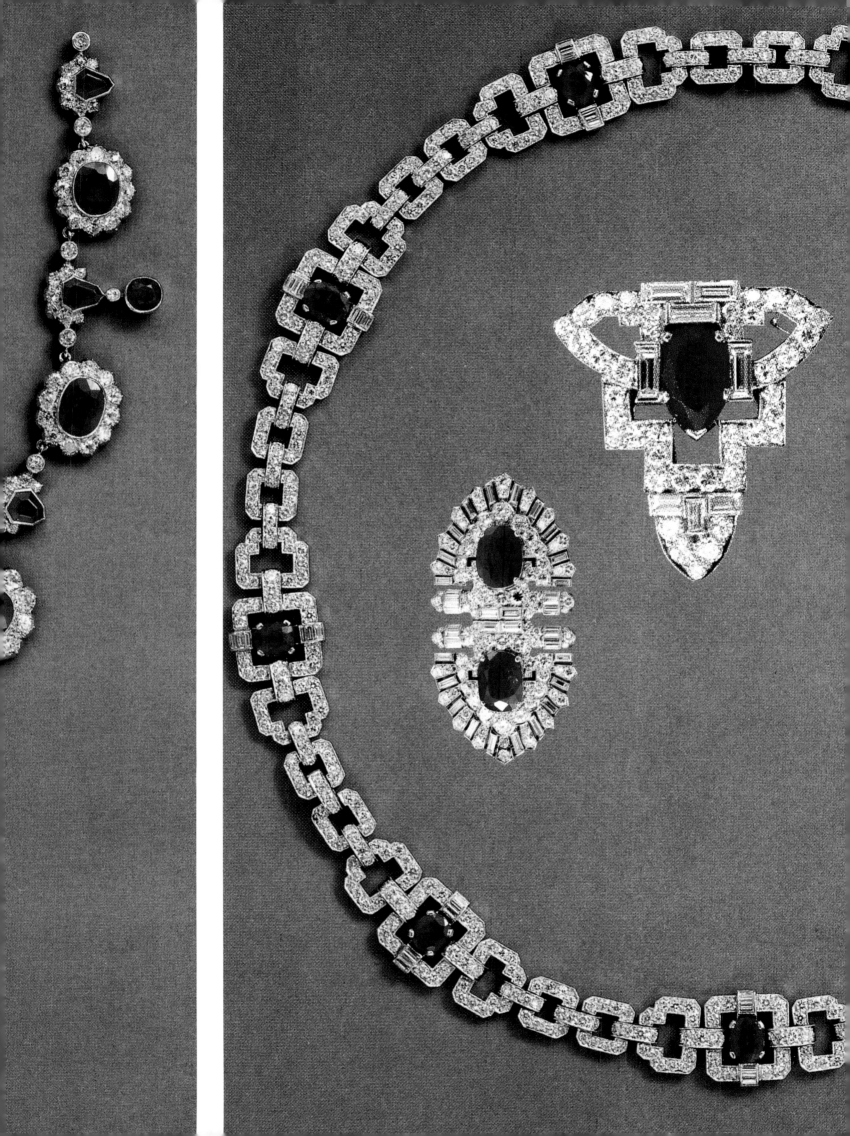

Paulette Goddard

The screen actress Paulette Goddard is quoted as having said, 'Oscar Wilde and Goddard say that any woman who tells her age tells anything.' Certainly in her case it was to the point: her date of birth has always been subject to much discussion. The most widely accepted version is that she was born on 3 June 1911, named Pauline Marion Levy, and brought up by her mother in humble surroundings. Though her mother is supposed to have been poor, there was evidently enough money to provide Pauline with acting, singing and dancing lessons. After a short career in modelling, she appeared at the age of 14 in her first Ziegfeld revue, under her newly adopted name of Paulette Goddard.

In 1927 she married a Mr E. James, who was not only much older than she but also well-to-do; two years later she left him with a divorce settlement of $100,000. By 1931 she had made her first movie and entered the world of Hollywood society, where the following year she met her future mentor and husband, Charlie Chaplin. He was captivated by her beauty and her understated charm and intelligence. Although over 20 years her senior, he chose her not only to share his life but also to star in his next film, *Modern Times*.

The actual date of their marriage was another closely guarded secret, but it is thought that the wedding took place in 1936, the same year that *Modern Times* was released. They spent some time in the Far East and it was noted that glittering bangles of rubies and diamonds were acquired on what is assumed to have been their honeymoon trip. She was an avid collector of jewelry, which she claimed never to have bought but always received as gifts from her many admirers. She was well known for the cigar box full of jewels which she would carry around the studio wardrobe departments and delightedly reveal its contents to the young workers.

In the costume drama *Kitty* she ignored historical accuracy and wore her beautiful diamond necklace, probably made in the 1940s. The deep diamond fringe was centred with an emerald-cut diamond, rumoured to be her engagement ring from Chaplin. Again, at the opening of the winter season of La Scala, Milan, in 1958, she flouted normal conventions when she wore a delicate 19th-century diamond ribbon and floral necklace festooned below her diamond fringed necklace.

Among her large collection of jewels, many had been given to celebrate important occasions in her life and career, and some were suitably inscribed. After her attempts to get the part of Scarlett O'Hara in *Gone with the Wind* were thwarted, Chaplin gave her a gold, cabochon emerald and diamond bangle by Trabert & Hoeffer Inc.-Mauboussin. It is a wonderfully bold cluster of flowerheads and she was often photographed wearing it. The bangle was accompanied by a pair of cabochon emerald and diamond earclips of similar floral design. The 'flower style' was much in vogue in the USA

Paulette Goddard in a Horst photograph of 1942. She is wearing her diamond fringe necklace as a bracelet. *Horst/Vogue*

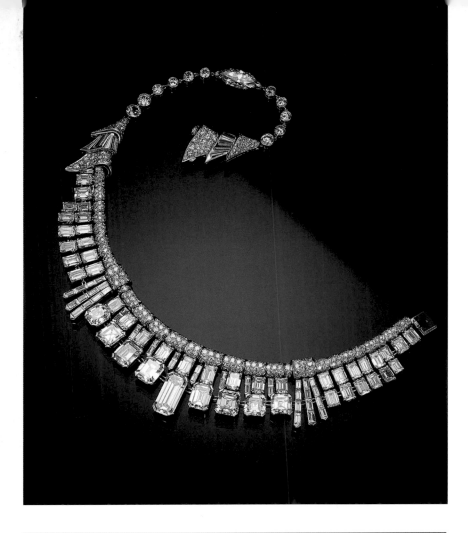

Paulette Goddard's important diamond fringe necklace, c. 1940 and a diamond tiara/necklace of floral and ribbon design, dating from the late 19th century.
Sotheby's New York

(Opposite) A group of Paulette Goddard's stylish jewels from the 1940s, including the gold, emerald and diamond bangle with matching earclips by Trabert & Hoeffer, Inc.-Mauboussin, that she received from Charlie Chaplin when she narrowly missed winning the role of Scarlett O'Hara in *Gone with the Wind*; a gold, platinum, enamel, diamond and coloured stone bangle set with nearly thirty platinum charms of various design, one appropriately in the form of a 'tramp' referring to Chaplin's famous film character; a pair of platinum, gold and diamond domed earclips by Van Cleef & Arpels; a gold, cabochon emerald and synthetic ruby ring and a gold, ruby and diamond cluster ring.
Sotheby's New York

Erich Maria Remarque and his wife, Paulette Goddard, arriving at La Scala, Milan, for the opening performance of the 1958 winter season. She is wearing her diamond fringe necklace together with her antique diamond necklace and her diamond bombé earrings.
Hulton Getty

during this period and her bangle and earclips are reputed to have been inspired by a Van Cleef & Arpels flowerspray brooch worn by the Duchess of Windsor. A similar bangle appeared in the collection of Mary Pickford.

During her marriage to Chaplin, Paulette became one of the most sought-after actresses in Hollywood and also one of the most admired for her pert charm and beauty. She had a short-lived relationship with George Gershwin, who was besotted by her. Their affair ended well before his untimely death in 1937.

In 1940 her portrait was painted by Diego Rivera and she had several sittings with Cecil Beaton. In that year she also appeared again in one of her husband's masterpieces, *The Great Dictator*, but it was also the year when she moved out of the Chaplin mansion. Two years later they had a divorce in Mexico. Her years with Chaplin had been exciting and educational, but often difficult. He had personally coached her for her acting roles, but his strict sense of direction often carried over into their domestic life.

During the 1940s she married and divorced fellow actor Burgess Meredith and her career continued on its successful path. She made well over twenty movies. She even survived the suspicions of the House Un-American Activities Committee in its search for Communist agents in Hollywood. Her riposte to the accusation that she was or had been a member of the Communist Party was that whoever made such a scurrilous statement would be hit 'with my diamond bracelets'.

In the next decade she made fewer films but her marriage to the popular German novelist Erich Maria Remarque in 1958 was to open a new chapter in her life. They had a very happy marriage which lasted until his death in 1970. For once Paulette had found someone whom she was almost prepared to put before her career, and in 1965 she played in her last film.

Throughout her life, Paulette had not only amassed a wonderful array of jewels but had also collected other works of art, particularly some important Impressionist paintings. In 1979 she sold part of this collection, which included works by Cézanne, Monet and Degas, but she retained a number of other paintings, as well as her important collection of pre-Columbian art. To attend the auction, Paulette wore a fantastic brooch of enamelled red lips embellished with diamonds, which had been designed for her by Salvador Dalí.

There were frequent rumours that she might sell her collection of jewels, but it was not until April 1990 that a large part of this appeared at auction. She was now living in Switzerland although actively still supporting a scholarship programme at New York University's Tisch School of Art to assist young talented artists. The same month as the sale she died, and the following October jewels from her estate were auctioned. Again, her will provided further substantial bequests for New York University.

In both auctions, the pieces offered for sale consisted mainly of pieces dating from the 1940s, among them the bangle and earrings by Trabert & Hoeffer, Inc.-Mauboussin given to her by Chaplin. Among her other colourful jewels were a delightful pair of gold, yellow and blue sapphire and ruby flower-head earclips by Van Cleef & Arpels with a matching pair of clips and a ring. Also from Van Cleef & Arpels were a pair of diamond earrings of domed form set with bands of brilliant-cut diamonds, and a gold and diamond snowflake brooch as well as a diamond hair clip to add the finishing touch to her attire.

A more unusual bangle was covered in gem-set charms that she had collected over many years and of which several held highly sentimental memories. Originally she had them set on the cover of a powder compact but never hanging from a bracelet as convention would require. From Cartier, dating from this same period, was a charming brooch designed as a carved coral hand, decorated with a diamond bracelet and holding a gold and diamond flower. There were also three large rings, typical of the '40s, set with a cabochon emerald, a cabochon star sapphire and a bombé cluster of rubies respectively.

Along with her two large diamond necklaces she had a *rivière* of coloured diamonds, the brilliant-cut stones varying from shades of yellow to a brown, and a very elegant crossover ring of similar colours accompanied this necklace. A spectacular necklace was created for her by Van Cleef & Arpels in New York in the '60s; it was set with a graduated row of large cabochon rubies within diamond borders, alternating with cabochon ruby and diamond flower-heads. The necklace was detachable in several places so it was also possible for her to wear it as a shorter necklace and a bracelet. This jewel was complemented by a matching ring set with a cabochon ruby of 48.00cts within a diamond border. It is possible that the cabochon ruby and diamond earclips which she bought from Bulgari during the same period were also acquired to wear with the necklace and ring.

The only other necklace included in the sale of her collection was a complete contrast in style. Dating from the late 19th century, the gold chain was hung with a graduated fringe of alternating steatite and faience scarab beetles and capped by gold lotus blossom motifs; there was a pair of pendent earrings *en suite*.

The first auction included several stylish dress sets which she had acquired from jewelers such as Van Cleef & Arpels and David Webb and given to her husband Erich Maria Remarque.

Paulette Goddard's jewels were a fitting statement of the distinctive style of this successful Hollywood star, who was also a woman of beauty and intelligence. Many were gifts from the men who were so enthralled by her and, as she once said, 'I don't accept flowers. I take nothing perishable.'

(Overleaf) A group of Paulette Goddard's jewels, including a diamond necklace set with fancy coloured diamonds of various shades of yellow and brown; a diamond crossover ring set with a fancy yellow and a brown diamond; a diamond solitaire ring mounted by Van Cleef & Arpels; a star sapphire and diamond ring ; and a pair of yellow and blue sapphire and ruby clips, a pair of earclips and a ring ensuite, by Van Cleef & Arpels. *Sotheby's New York*

(Right) A cabochon ruby and diamond necklace/bracelet combination dating from the late 1960s by Van Cleef & Arpels; and Goddard wearing her yellow and blue sapphire and ruby clips and earclips together as clips and her fancy yellow and brown diamond crossover ring. *Sotheby's, New York; The Kobal Collection*

Ava Gardner

The screen 'goddess' Ava Gardner had an overpowering magnetism which extended from her films to real life. She was a woman of great beauty and sensuality which, together with her vibrant Southern charms and warmth, captivated her audiences both on and off the screen. The youngest of seven children, Ava Lavinia Gardner was born on Christmas Eve, 1922, on a tobacco farm in Boon Hill, North Carolina. Her father, a sharecropper, was soon to suffer the effects of the Depression. In 1929 the subsequent fall in the price of tobacco lost him both his livelihood and his tenant farm, and was to cause a family split. Jonas Gardner found work in a sawmill in the neighbouring town of Smithfield and Ava and her mother moved to a house in Virginia where they scraped an income by taking in boarders. The three eldest daughters, Bappie (Beatrice), Elsie May and Inez, were already married and her other sister, Myra, left to live with her brother Jack at their uncle's home in Winston-Salem. Her other brother Raymond had died in infancy.

The Gardners' separation was caused not by lack of love but by sheer hardship and the struggle for survival. A severe bout of illness the following year left Jonas bedridden and he joined his wife and Ava in Newport, where he died within a year. Once again Ava and her mother moved to another town. Throughout her childhood Ava's education suffered through constant moves but she was determined to gain secretarial qualifications. When she was 18 she succeeded in attaining the necessary speeds to find her gainful employment and, more importantly, a salary. In her autobiography she remarked of these years, 'When you are poor, dirt poor, and there is no way of concealing it, life is hell.'

Although she might have made a sensational secretary, the world would have been deprived of one of its greatest stars had it not been for photographs taken by her brother-in-law Larry Tarr. Married to her sister Bappie, he was a professional photographer living and working in New York. During the summer of 1940 Bappie persuaded her mother to let Ava visit them in New York, where she could give her rather shy sister a taste of city life. Ava adored it. During her stay, Larry took several photographs of her, one of which he placed in his studio window, where it was spotted by a Metro Goldwyn Mayer talent scout who had copies forwarded to the studio in California. Impressed by what they saw, the Hollywood executives arranged for a screen test in New York. The director in charge quickly realized that to give her any chance, the test would have to be without sound: Ava's deep Southern drawl was almost impossible for them to understand. The excited reply came from George Sydney, the director who watched the test in Hollywood: 'Tell New York to ship her out! She's a good piece of merchandise.'

Ava left for Hollywood, with Bappie as her companion, still rather sceptical about the whole situation. A further screen test was arranged in Hollywood, but this time with sound. On this occasion it was

Ava Gardner photographed in Spanish costume by Hoynigen-Huene. *The Kobal Collection*

A group of Ava Gardner's jewels, including her superb emerald and diamond ring; a pair of diamond pendent earrings with interchangeable pendent drops (namely a pair of emerald and diamonds, a pair of cultured pearls with diamond caps, a pair of pear-shaped diamonds); and a sapphire and diamond ring, the 8.75cts sapphire of Kashmir origin. All these jewels are by Van Cleef & Arpels and date from the 1960s.
Sotheby's, New York and London

(Opposite) Another selection of her jewels dating from the 1960s and 1970s which includes a diamond brooch by Tiffany & Co. designed as the word 'Love' and a pair of turquoise and diamond pendent earrings. All the other jewels are by Van Cleef & Arpels: a pair of gold and diamond foliate earrings and a bombé ring *en suite*; a yellow sapphire and diamond ring; a cultured pearl and diamond cluster ring; and a gem-set brooch designed as an Angel seated on a cloud. This brooch was inscribed to Ava and was possibly given to her by William Ruser, who was famous for making similar jewels.
Sotheby's, London

the studio head Louis B. Mayer himself who exclaimed, 'She can't act, she can't talk, she's terrific.' In 1941 she signed a seven-year contract with MGM, at an initial salary of $50 a week.

Between 1941 and 1945 Ava's appearances on screen were either as an extra or in very minor featured roles. But even in those few minutes on screen she could mesmerize her audiences, and fan letters flooded in. Although she found the lack of substantial parts highly frustrating it did give her the time to concentrate on her acting and elocution lessons and to endeavour to perfect both her dialogue delivery and a 'suitable' accent. It also gave her the chance to enter and enjoy the Hollywood life. Before long her most ardent admirer and escort was one of the big Hollywood stars, Mickey Rooney. Theirs was a whirlwind romance and despite objections from MGM that it was not good for his career to marry an 'unknown', Mickey proposed to Ava on her 19th birthday. They were married in January 1942.

On the screen Ava was to have all the success she could wish for, but in marriage this was never to be. Her first marriage ended in divorce in May 1943. Two further marriages – to the big band leader and clarinetist Artie Shaw and Frank Sinatra – ended in failure. Mickey Rooney had taught her a great deal about acting and Artie Shaw instilled in her a love for literature, music and paintings. They both remained firm friends with her and it was often to them that she turned in times of trouble.

Her first leading role came in 1945, when she was loaned out to United Artists to star with George Raft in *Whistle Stop*. Film critics viewed this as a second-rate thriller but noted Ava's magnetic charms. In 1946 she was again on loan, but this time to Universal Pictures for the screen adaptation of Ernest Hemingway's story *The Killers* and this proved to be a huge financial success as well as a personal success for Ava. Over the next 35 years she was to star in well over that number of films.

In 1951 she married Sinatra; this was perhaps her most tempestuous relationship and the one that left the greatest impact on her life. At the time they married Ava was a box-office sensation and Sinatra was in turmoil in both his career and private life. Several of the films she shot during this period were set on location in Africa, Italy or Spain, which she viewed either as a respite from her turbulent life with Frank or as a dreadful separation – depending on their relationship at the time. Occasionally he was able to join her, but again the success of the visit could never be assured.

During these years Ava seemed especially captivated by the charms of Spain where she enjoyed life, more often than not, in the company of a handsome young matador, Luis Miguel Dominguin. The thrill of fiestas and flamenco dancing suited her temperament perfectly; she once said she felt 'emotionally close to Spain.' Knowing her marriage was over, she left the USA in December 1955 and acquired a house in La Moraleja, a suburb near Madrid. By 1957 her divorce from Sinatra was final.

A gold and diamond flower brooch dating from the 1960s by Van Cleef & Arpels. *Sotheby's, New York*

(Opposite) Ava Gardner at a nightclub wearing her turquoise and diamond pendent earrings and her diamond cluster ring by Van Cleef & Arpels. *Hulton Getty*

(Overleaf two pages) This group of Ava Gardner's jewels, all dating from the 1950s and 1960s, includes the stylish diamond ring made by special order by Van Cleef & Arpels for her and believed to have been set with the 6.35cts step-cut diamond that had originally been mounted as her engagement ring from Mickey Rooney; a gold and diamond bracelet and a stunning cultured pearl and diamond bracelet both by Van Cleef & Arpels. The cultured pearl and diamond ring and the pair of cultured pearl and diamond earclips are by Ruser. On the second page is another group of Gardner's jewels, including a four-row cultured pearl bracelet dating from the 1960s, by Ruser, the clasp set with diamonds and cabochon jades; a jade and diamond ring by Van Cleef & Arpels, 1965, which was made as a special order for her; a pair of jade and diamond cluster earrings, 1960s; a pair of jade and diamond earring drops which could be worn with her Van Cleef & Arpels diamond cluster earrings; and an emerald and diamond flowerhead clip also by Van Cleef & Arpels, 1964. *Sotheby's, New York; Sotheby's, London*

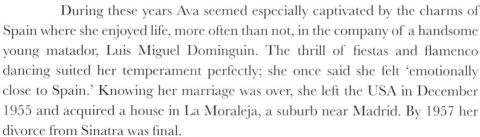

In the early '60s she moved into an apartment in the centre of Madrid as she felt the 'damn place had life!' But by 1968 her mood had changed and she went to London because she said, the 'British leave you alone.'

In 1989 she decided to sell part of her jewelry collection in New York and after her death several more pieces were sold in London. Ava's jewelry collection was extremely classic and stylish in content, dating mainly from the 1960s. Despite her exotic beauty, her jewels were always highly discreet in style. The finest piece in the whole collection was the emerald and diamond ring by Van Cleef & Arpels. The almost flawless step-cut emerald of 7.46cts, with its fantastic saturated vibrant green colour, so typical of 'old mine' Colombian emeralds, was mounted as a ring in New York in 1961. The stone was set within a petalled border of brilliant-cut diamonds, a fashionable design of that period. On Ava's nineteenth birthday Mickey Rooney arranged a party at Romanoff's, where he announced their engagement and presented her with a diamond ring. It is possible that the step-cut stone, weighing 6.35cts, from this ring is the same one that Ava later had remounted by Van Cleef & Arpels as a special order.

Indeed Van Cleef & Arpels were the makers of nearly all her important jewels. These included an elegant set of diamond earrings of floral cluster design with interchangeable pendants. She could use either pear-shaped diamond drops, jadeite drops or important emerald and diamond drops or cultured pearls capped by diamonds. In the thriller *The Cassandra Crossing* she wore these earrings with the pearl drops as well as nearly all her other important jewels.

Ava mentioned in her memoirs that she returned a superb Kashmir sapphire ring to Howard Hughes in the late '50s. In her collection was a cushion-shaped Kashmir sapphire and diamond cluster ring, a special order from Van Cleef & Arpels in the 1960s. Again from the same jewelers was a very attractive diamond flexible bracelet created in the early '60s and two diamond flowerhead brooches from the same period. The centre of one of the brooches was set with emeralds.

Like many of her generation, Ava also loved pearls. For her marriage to Frank Sinatra in 1951 she chose to wear a double-row pearl necklace and matching pearl and diamond earrings. In her collection there was a beautiful cultured pearl and diamond bracelet by Van Cleef & Arpels, New York, and a cultured pearl bracelet by Ruser with an attractive clasp set with jadeite and diamonds and a pair of cultured pearl earclips and a ring, all set with diamonds. There was a Mississippi pearl and diamond brooch designed as an angel seated on a cloud with ruby hearts. It was not only signed Van Cleef & Arpels, but also bore the inscription: 'To Ava our Angel, our hearts are at your feet, DR xxxxxx VCA xxxxx BR'. The initials BR are most probably those of William Ruser, who was known to her as Bill. In 1947 he and his wife had opened a shop in Los Angeles where they became extremely popular with the film world of the 1950s.

In comparison with many of Ava's Hollywood contemporaries, her collection of jewels was small, but it consisted of some of the finest and most stylish jewels of the period, qualities which could be equally well attributed to the star herself.

Joan Crawford

When she arrived in Hollywood in 1925, Metro Goldwyn Mayer recorded a rather uninspiring profile of their new actress: 'plain, with light brown hair, and weighing 145 pounds'. But by 1937 *Life* magazine had given her the title of 'First Queen of the Movies'. Joan Crawford's career in the movie business was phenomenal and due in great part to her sheer determination to succeed and, above all, to survive. Her life story was a scriptwriter's dream: rags to riches, sex and scandal – but always a star in the eyes of her adoring fans. She appeared in over eighty films and over a dozen television shows, and appeared with many of the great stars of her times. Her career was without doubt one of the most successful and longest in Hollywood history, starting with her first role in the silent film *Pretty Ladies* in 1925 and ending forgettably with *Trog* in 1970. Her private life by no means matched this success and from the outset she had to fight all the way.

When Lucille Fay LeSeuer was born in Texas on 23 March 1904 disaster had already struck the family: her father had left and one sister had died. Impoverished and desperate, her mother moved with her two remaining children to Lawton, Oklahoma. Fortunately she soon met and married Henry Cassin, the owner of the Opera House as well as an open-air theatre. These were the humble venues that inspired young Lucille to become a star. Her aspirations to become a dancer were thwarted at the beginning by a bad accident; despite doctors' predictions that she would always walk with a limp, she persevered and by 1923 was working as a dancer in Detroit. The settings for her new career were unglamorous strip-joints and bars but it was a beginning, and by 1924 she had moved on to a chorus line in Detroit. It has been suggested that at this time she married a musician from the pit orchestra, whom she divorced in the late 1920s, but this has never been satisfactorily substantiated.

In 1924, however, she had the good fortune to meet Marcus Loew who had just acquired MGM. Depite two rather discouraging screen tests, by January 1925 she had arrived in Hollywood with a six-months contract and her name was soon changed to Joan Crawford. That year she appeared in four films. In 1929 she married Douglas Fairbanks Jr and gained Mary Pickford, only ten years her senior, as a step-mother. From Douglas she received a wedding ring and a diamond anklet engraved 'To my darling wife' and a gold cigarette box and lighter. That same year she appeared in her first talkie and her voice was pronounced 'alluring'. Her success in the movies seemed sealed and she now revelled in the Hollywood lifestyle and the trappings that it offered. Her glamorous looks were the perfect canvas for designer clothes and designer jewels.

Paradoxically, Crawford's private life appeared to be a succession of failures. After her divorce from Fairbanks Jr in 1933 she married two other actors, Franchot Tone in 1935, whom she divorced within four years, and Phillip Terry in 1942. Both were not destined to last and when she

Joan Crawford in the late 1930s wearing her aquamarine and diamond parure by E.M.Tompkins. *The Kobal Collection*

(Overleaf two pages) The Tompkins aquamarine and diamond parure, on page 48, comprising a necklace, a brooch and a bracelet. This was one of her favourite parures and in the sale of her jewels it was purchased by Andy Warhol. In the 1939 photograph she is again wearing the parure, with the clip placed in her turban. The other parure, of gold and citrine, is by Raymond Yard and includes a necklace with a detachable pendant, a bangle, a ring and a pair of earrings. *Sotheby's, New York; The Kobal Collection*

divorced Terry in 1946 she swore she would never marry again. During this period of instability she had adopted a boy and a girl and later on she managed to adopt two more girls. It would appear from all accounts that her failure as wife was matched by her utter misunderstanding of motherhood.

By 1955 she was married yet again, this time to Alfred Steele, the President of the Pepsi-Cola Company. This marriage to a non-actor was to prove a success and they spent four happy years together until his sudden death in 1959. When she had married Steele he was exceedingly rich but by the time of his death his fortune was gone, as was hers. They had spent nearly half a million dollars on their apartment which had turned out to be a loan from Pepsi-Cola. Never one to give up, Joan not only took a position on the board of Pepsi-Cola but pursued her acting career with a vengeance. By 1962, aged 58, she was back in the limelight with the highly successful movie *What Ever Happened to Baby Jane*, in which she co-starred with Bette Davis. A few other less successful films followed until her final appearance in 1970. Three years later Pepsi-Cola pensioned her off, which was a severe blow to her as it meant the loss of fringe benefits, such as an invaluable expense account. She seemed to withdraw at that time from any social life and to concentrate her interests on Christian Science, a discipline that persuaded her to abstain from the alcohol which had taken such a heavy toll on her life and, eventually, her looks. She died at home in May 1977, more than twenty years after her glittering star had begun to flicker.

The jewelry collection which was sold at auction after her death was a tribute both to her own style and to American jewelers, for nearly all the pieces were their creations. However, it was only a part of her original collection, as she had dispersed a large number of pieces a few years before her death. Interestingly, the jewels which she had kept were not of the greatest commercial value but must be considered among her favourites, those she most enjoyed wearing – a fact to which many contemporary photographs bear witness. There were also many which held fond memories for her of former triumphs and former loves.

The majority of these jewels were from the 1930s through the '50s when the style was bold, with large stones and big parures proving the height of fashion. Raymond C. Yard was the creator of her gold and citrine parure which comprised a necklace with a detachable clip, a cuff bangle, earclips and a ring, all set with citrines of huge proportions. Yard had established his own business in the early 1920s, having started his career in jewelry at an early age at the jewelers Marcus, and became one of America's most highly regarded jewelers. He is most noted for his great attention to quality and his preference for using large and important stones in his jewelry. Raymond Yard was instrumental in persuading his friend, the highly regarded gem dealer Raphael Esmerian, to move from Paris to New York, thus giving Yard access to a constant supply of fine gemstones, which was of benefit to the two friends and astute businessmen.

Although it was not included in the sale, Crawford was known to have bought in 1938 a spectacular star sapphire and diamond bracelet from Yard which was designed in three panels, each set at the centre with a cabochon star sapphire. The three stones weighed respectively 73.12cts, 63.61cts and 57.65cts and she would wear this bracelet with other star sapphire and diamond jewels. These included a pendant, a ring and a pair of earrings, which did appear in the sale. In the '30s Crawford made many purchases from Yard, among them a very stylish diamond plaque bracelet which appeared at auction in New York in 1997.

Another parure was by William Ruser, who had opened his firm on Rodeo Drive in Beverly Hills in the late 1940s. This was mounted with amethysts, the necklace of a very bold assymetrical design comprising a row of large amethysts, with a matching bracelet, earrings and a ring. Ruser was noted for his sculptural jewels, which often took the form of birds and flowers, sometimes of a rather whimsical nature, and usually set with Mississippi pearls. They proved fashionable with the film set. Crawford had a gold, pearl and sapphire brooch designed as a girl with a mirror, the back engraved 'Monday's child is fair of face', with a lapel pin and a pair of earrings *en suite*, as well as Ruser's version of a gold, pearl and sapphire poodle mounted as a brooch, together with another matching brooch and earrings. He also created for her a spectacular parure of Mississippi and baroque pearls set with diamonds. This suite had a brooch which was in the style of early 20th-century Tiffany jewels, with Mississippi pearls forming the petals of a splendid flowerhead. Her favourite parure, however, was probably the aquamarine and diamond suite of French manufacture, by E.H.Tompkins, which she was often photographed wearing both on and off the screen during this period. This parure was later acquired by Andy Warhol and was included in the sale of his 'Collection of Jewelry and Watches' in 1988.

Joan Crawford in her Hollywood apartment, hoiding up a copy of her autobiography which was published in 1962. She is wearing her pearl and diamond parure by Ruser.
Hulton Getty

Memories of successes both in Crawford's career and in her private life were inscribed on several jewels. 'Joan Crawford, Mildred Pierce, 1945' was engraved on a gold charm designed as the Oscar award in honour of her Oscar-winning role. Other generous and grateful inscriptions on charms were from producers and fellow actors. There were also tributes from the press and the Variety Club. Her birthsign, Aries, was celebrated by a set of gold jewels, comprising a brooch, a ring and a pair of earrings, each designed as a ram – the work of the Hollywood jewelers Joseff.

Her husbands, especially Alfred Steele, gave her many jewels with affectionate messages, one of the simplest on a gold cigarette lighter by Ruser: 'Joan, I love you, Alfred'. Among the gifts which she received from two of her less successful marriages were a gold lipstick case containing a watch inscribed 'Joan, love Franchot' and a ruby and diamond floral wristwatch, the back engraved 'Dearest Wife Joan, Every second says I love you, Phillip, 21st July 1943'. Unfortunately for both Franchot Tone and Phillip Terry, the choice of jewel for their words was not a good omen as their blissful times with Joan ran out rapidly. When it became Alfred Steele's prerogative to present his wife with a watch, he chose one of a more substantial nature. The platinum and diamond watch bracelet he bought for her was created by Ruser at his most flamboyant. The small circular dial nestled within clusters of variously cut diamond flowerheads on a bracelet of similarly cut stones. The inscription read 'To my love, Xmas 1958, Alfred'. Within the collection of jewels that Joan had kept were many jewelled dress sets, cufflinks and tie clips, several by Cartier and Ruser, and bearing the monogram A.N.S. Obviously she was loath to part with these reminders of Steele.

In 1938 *Harpers Bazaar* had shown a sensational set of three ruby and diamond clips of foliate scroll design by the jeweler Paul Flato. Having started his career in the 1920s, by the '30s Flato was highly successful in New York as both a jeweler and as an accepted and welcome member of the social set. Not only were his jewels stylish but he was popular for his engaging personality and sense of humour, qualities which served him well with the Hollywood crowd when he opened a branch in Los Angeles in 1938. This set of clips was designed for Flato by Fulco di Verdura, one of his chief designers, and acquired by Crawford, who would wear them clipped to the neck of her dress with stunning effect. Some years later she acquired a *rivière* of baguette diamonds, highly elegant when worn on its own; but as it was sometimes not sufficiently extravagant for her, she would attach these Flato jewels or another large diamond clip to create a dazzling ensemble. Although she sold the ruby and diamond clips before her death, she kept the matching pair of earrings. In 1939 Fulco di Verdura gave up designing for Flato and set up his own company. While Verdura's business flourished, Paul Flato's began to fail financially and he was forced to cease trading in the early 1940s.

Dating from the late '50s were a dramatic pair of diamond earrings in the Crawford collection. They were designed as a scrolled cluster of baguette, marquise-shaped and brilliant-cut diamonds, each holding a detachable tasseled drop of baguette diamonds. Other fine jewels in her collection included a natural black pearl and diamond necklace with a matching bracelet which she would wear with a dyed black cultured pearl ring and earrings.

At her memorial service in Hollywood in 1977, the director George Cukor gave an address in which he pronounced that Joan Crawford was 'the perfect image of the movie star, and, as such, largely the creation of her own, indomitable will.' Her jewelry collection, although depleted of its more important pieces prior to her death, was equally representative of her star-quality and the great panache with which she created her life.

(Opposite) Joan Crawford in the early 1960s in St. Mark's Square, Venice, where she is admiring the exquisite locally made lace. She is wearing her baroque and Mississippi pearl and diamond parure by Ruser.
Hulton Getty

The baroque and Mississippi pearl and diamond necklace and the diamond bracelet watch, also by Ruser, which were given to her by her husband, Alfred Steele, for Christmas 1958. The diamond tassel earrings also date from the 1950s.
Christie's, New York

Renata Tebaldi

Voce d'angelo, the voice of an angel, was the epithet the legendary Italian conductor Arturo Toscanini used to baptize soprano Renata Tebaldi on the occasion of her debut in what was the most exciting musical event of the immediate post-war period. The date was 11 May 1946 and the setting La Scala opera house in Milan where, after its wartime bomb damage had been repaired, an inaugural concert was conducted by the great maestro and transmitted all over the world by radio. But who was this young soprano who started her spectacular career that night?

Renata Tebaldi was born on 1 February 1922 in Pesaro, Italy, where she lived for the first three years of her life. Her parents then parted and she moved with her mother to the northern town of Langhirano, her mother's birthplace. Her childhood seemed doomed not only by her parents' unhappy marriage but also by her own ill health. At an early age she contracted polio, which caused five long years of suffering and was cured only by painful treatment that miraculously left her physically unscathed. Having endured such circumstances it was entirely due to her mother's love and dedication that Renata felt both stability and happiness in what otherwise had been a difficult childhood.

By the age of ten she already had a passion for the piano, and her grandfather organized lessons for her. When her studies at school were about to finish she had to decide on her future career. Facing several options, she chose the most difficult, the piano. This meant rising at 5 in the morning and travelling two hours on the train from Langhirano to the Conservatory in Parma.

Her piano teacher heard her sing for the first time when she was 17 and sensed an extraordinary talent. An audition was arranged in the Conservatory, where she was immediately placed in the advanced group taught by Ettore Campogalliani, one of the most sought-after vocal teachers of the time. He later described Tebaldi as a 'scrupulously perceptive student and animated by an immense passion for music.'

In 1940 she met the soprano Carmen Melis, who immediately recognized the young singer's potential, and this meeting was to prove a turning point in her career. Thanks to the help of Carmen Melis, she obtained her first major operatic role, that of Helen of Troy in Boito's *Mephistopheles*. This took place in 1944 in Rovigo with a quite exceptional cast, which included Tancredi Pasero, Onelia Fineschi and Francesco Albanese, conducted by Giuseppe del Campo.

From that moment successes accumulated at an extraordinary rate. In 1945 Tebaldi sang *La Bohème*, *Amico Fritz* and *Andrea Chenier* in Parma and made her debut at the Verdi Theatre in Trieste in *Otello*. The following year proved another turning point with the famous audition with Toscanini that was to open the gilded doors of international fame to her.

Renata Tebaldi on the cruise liner *'Andrea Doria'* on her way to New York in 1955. She is wearing jewels that she was later to have remounted. *Renata Tebaldi*

(Overleaf two pages) A diamond sunflower brooch together with the diamond tassel pendent earrings and matching brooch and one of Tebaldi's diamond bracelets. In the photograph by Scavullo in the late 1960s she is wearing a step-cut diamond bracelet and diamond tassel earrings. Also shown are Tebaldi's stylish gold and diamond flowerhead brooch with a matching bombé ring and a pair of earrings. *Sotheby's, Milan; Renata Tebaldi; Sotheby's, Milan*

There has never been a sweeter or more beautiful voice than Tebaldi's. Equally pure in every part of the range, it has been described by discriminating critics as the finest voice of all dramatic opera sopranos. An artist of great sensitivity and modesty, consecrated by universal success, Renata Tebaldi undoubtedly ranks among the greatest singers of our times. The noted American critic Harold C. Schonberg compared her with the painting Primavera; Botticelli, he wrote, 'would have rushed for his brushes'. He also stated that 'she started at the top and remained there.'

By the late 1940s her operatic success was already legendary. During this period La Scala repeatedly invited Tebaldi to sing the role of *Aida*, but she hesitated until her mentor Toscanini finally persuaded her. She remembers vividly the day when she went to his home in via Durini with the score. 'I know why you are hesitating,' he said. 'You're worrying about the *recitativi* and "*Ritorna vincitor*". You feel more at home in the second and third acts…' This was exactly how she felt about the role. 'It's an opera for you,' he continued. 'Aida is not a fiery, passionate woman. She's a gentle person. Until now this role has never been interpreted as Verdi wrote it. Everyone insists on expressing dramatic intensity by agitated and loud singing. What is needed is nostalgia, expression and diction! Aida is not a heroic role, it's a human one. If you understand this, you'll sing the role of Aida as it should be sung.'

In 1950 La Scala added *Aida* to its roster for her and she thrilled her audiences with seven performances. Three further appearances were scheduled, but other engagements in Lisbon forced her to cancel. This situation resulted in Maria Callas's debut at this famous theatre. This event marked the beginning of the rivalry between the two great divas and their loyal fans, often referred to as Tebaldists and Callasites, which was in reality mainly a creation of the media but which produced an exciting period in opera history.

In 1955, after many approaches by the opera house, Tebaldi had finally accepted a contract with the Metropolitan in New York and made her debut in the role of Desdemona. Her impact on American opera fans was immediate: they adored her and affectionately named her 'Miss Sold Out' as she always sang to full houses. After seeing her in *La Bohème*, Elsa Maxwell, the famous party-giver, wrote, 'Last week an angel descended from heaven and landed on the stage of the Metropolitan with a golden harp in her throat rather then her hand. This angel, of course, was the great Tebaldi.'

The acclaim continued: during a performance of *Tosca*, Tebaldi's '*Vissi d'arte*' evoked such enthusiastic applause that the conductor, Dimitri Mitropoulos, had to stop the orchestra, take a seat and wait ten minutes before the ovation came to an end and the performance could resume. In 1958, her world-wide fame was acknowledged by *Time* magazine, which devoted its cover to her.

Ground-breaking performances and international honours defined the following decades. On 23 May 1976 she gave a benefit recital at La Scala, the proceeds of which went to help the victims of the devastating earthquake that had occurred in the Friuli region of Italy. After this she decided to withdraw from the world of public performances and it was by pure chance that this last appearance

at La Scala was held on exactly the same date as her debut in Rovigo. Although a great part of her career was spent in the United States she is still known affectionately to her Italian following as 'la nostra Tebaldi'.

Although Tebaldi was one of the great prima donnas, her temperament is far removed from that which the term usually suggests. The beautiful Renata Tebaldi epitomizes serenity and a discreet charm which, in her retirement, still endear her to her peers and fans just as they did at the peak of her career. In Paris in the late 1950s Marlyse Schaeffer, a reporter for *France Soir*, visited Tebaldi in her dressing room after a performance of *Aida* and wrote with great enthusiasm of her 'alabaster skin, the gentle light from within, the captivating dimples, all reflected her serenity. We were seeing someone completely at peace with herself.'

Since she was a child Tebaldi had a passion for jewelry. She remembers that when she used to go into the countryside with her grandfather, she collected sunflower seeds and put them in his pocket. On returning home, she would immediately rush for a needle and thread to style the seeds into necklaces and bracelets which she wore with great pride and joy. As an adult, she still took enormous pleasure in jewels and the collection she created reflects her great love for jewelry as an object of beauty and perfection; pieces were acquired for those reasons alone and never as status symbols.

The elegant group of jewels, which were included in her collection auctioned in 1998, dated from the late 1950s through to the '70s. Of the jewels that she had acquired earlier in her career, very few pieces survived. She had nearly all her gold jewels from this period melted down so that it could be used to create new pieces. Certain exceptions included a cocktail ring designed as a cluster of foliage, set with cabochon emeralds, rubies and sapphires and brilliant-cut diamonds, and a matching pair of clips dating from the early '50s. She subsequently had the clips redesigned as a flower spray brooch in the early '60s. Another piece that survived was the gold and Florentine mosaic necklace that she wore on stage for her debut in 1947 as Violetta in *La Traviata*. Also from the '40s she had an important diamond bib necklace that she wore for several concerts in those years. In the '60s this jewel was broken up and the numerous diamonds were used to create new jewels, most of which were created for her by the Milanese jeweler Merzaghi. Whenever and wherever she saw a design which appealed to her she would send her loyal maid, Ernestina Viganó (who was also a skilled miniaturist), to sketch the jewel and then send the design to the jeweler to be realized. Examples include a fine turquoise parure, the earrings of which were inspired by the

(Opposite below) Tebaldi dressed for her role as *Tosca* for the cover of *Time* magazine in November 1958; and the dramatic gold, cabochon sapphire, ruby, emerald and brilliant-cut diamond ring she wore for many of her performances of *Tosca*. *Renata Tebaldi; Sotheby's, Milan*

(Opposite above) Two of Tebaldi's highly impressive rings, one a diamond which can be converted into a pendant and the other an emerald and diamond. She often wore these large jewels on stage. *Sotheby's, Milan*

(Below) A pair of turquoise and diamond pendent earrings which were part of a parure comprising a brooch, a bracelet and a ring. (Above) Tebaldi photographed by Saez in 1962 as *Adriana Lecouvreur* at the Teatro Coliseo Alba in Bilbao. She is wearing costume jewelry created for her in this role, including the earrings which she had copied later in turquoise and diamonds. *Sotheby's, Milan; Renata Tebaldi*

(Overleaf two pages) A collection of Renata Tebaldi's sapphire and diamond jewels, including flowerhead cluster earrings by Van Cleef & Arpels, and the ring and brooch which she had designed to wear with the earrings; a diamond brooch, which she also used to wear as a pendant on a diamond *rivière* necklace; an elegant diamond crossover ring; and her important diamond bracelet. In the 1973 photograph by Christian Steiner, she is wearing the sapphire and diamond flowerhead earrings and the sapphire and diamond brooch. *Sotheby's, Milan; Renata Tebaldi*

costume jewelry created for her starring role in *Adriana Lecouvreur* and a splendid sapphire and diamond brooch designed to accompany the splendid flowerhead earrings by Van Cleef & Arpels. The most stylish and important jewel she designed was the crossover ring set with two oval diamonds of 'D' colour between baguette diamond shoulders. She also acquired from Merzaghi the elegant diamond line bracelet set with a tapered row of step-cut diamonds connected by trefoils of marquise-shaped and brilliant-cut diamonds. Another equally chic diamond bracelet, which they created for her, was designed as arched bands of baguette diamonds alternating with cross motifs pavé-set with brilliant-cut diamonds. In both these jewels the quality of the diamonds was exceptionally high.

Tebaldi's collection also included pieces she had bought on the spur of the moment. Among them is the diamond garland necklace, dating from the '50s, that she discovered in a Fifth Avenue shop window. It was also in New York, although it was manufactured in France, that she acquired the delightful ruby and diamond brooch. Designed as a realistic rose, it happened to catch her eye, and in studio portraits she was often photographed wearing it. There was also a beautiful brooch in diamond and emeralds that she acquired in Barcelona, perhaps as a keepsake after one of her performances there in *Tosca*.

Another charming jewel that she acquired in New York in the '60s is the diamond sunflower brooch that is depicted as a half-open flower. After it had been worn at numerous concerts, Tebaldi's Milan jewelers added more petals to create a flower in full bloom. During this period brooches were highly fashionable and she had several examples in her collection, the majority chosen to compliment her other jewels. A particularly striking example is the yellow gold and diamond stylized flowerhead brooch that she had created to match an equally stylish bombé ring and a pair of earrings. Her collection also included a very dramatic pair of diamond chandelier earrings with six cascading drops of baguette and brilliant-cut diamonds. To accompany these jewels she used some of the diamonds originally mounted in her bib necklace to create an impressive chandelier brooch with a floral and ribbon bow surmount; they matched to perfection and she wore them at many glittering occasions.

Her collection included many other stylish jewels and in every instance the emphasis was on the quality of both the gems and the design, whether it was a simple gold and diamond chain bracelet or an elaborate diamond brooch.

Intimately connected with the career of one of the twentieth century's most acclaimed opera artists, this collection of jewelry, in its beauty and purity of colours, formed the perfect compliment to the talent of Renata Tebaldi, *voce d'angelo*.

Tebaldi's ruby and diamond brooch designed as a rose, and a gold, ruby and diamond stylized flowerhead brooch. She is wearing the rose brooch in the 1967 photograph by Bruno of Hollywood (opposite). *Sotheby's, Milan; Renata Tebaldi*

Cornelia, Countess of Craven

Cornelia Martin was born in New York on 22 September 1876, the daughter of Bradley and Cornelia Martin, both prominent members of the so-called 'Four Hundred', the cream of New York society. Bradley Martin was a member of the Bar and had been on active military service during the Civil War. His wife was the daughter of Isaac Sherman, a highly successful businessman who had made a large fortune in lumber and barrel staves. On his death in 1881 Sherman left his entire estate of $6 million to his only daughter. That same year the Martins leased the estate of Balmacaan in Scotland, a beautiful property of some 63,000 acres, 19 miles of which bordered Loch Ness. The large ivy-clad mansion was ideal for entertaining the many guests who were invited during the shooting season. The *New York Times* reported that in one season Mr Martin and his guests killed '70 deer, 2,080 pheasants and 1,200 grouse which was the best bag in the country for the year.' During August, Mrs Martin would arrive for the grouse shooting and to entertain during the rest of the shooting season, her house parties sometimes numbering up to seventy. They now divided their time between Scotland, New York and their newly acquired house in London.

The Martins' home in New York was at 22 West 20th Street, next door to Cornelia's parents' house. After her father's death the two houses were converted into one extremely large townhouse where they could entertain even more extravagantly.

Their daughter, Cornelia, had just finished school when she became engaged to William George Robert, 4th Earl of Craven. Lord Craven, 24 years old, had a fine estate and an equally impressive and long family history but an insufficiency of funds. The marriage was welcomed by both families as it assured the Martins of a position in fashionable British society and the $75,000-a-year allowance which Bradley Martin settled on his daughter was quite acceptable to the Cravens.

This was a time when even the American press was discussing eligible British aristocrats and their waning fortunes. The marriage of Consuelo Vanderbilt to the 9th Duke of Marlborough in 1895 prompted a memorable caption under photographs of all of England's eligible Dukes in the *New York World* which read, 'Attention, American heiresses, what will you bid?'

The marriage, which took place in New York on 18 April 1893, was a great society occasion. The Martins were not only lavish with the wedding but also with their presents. Their main gift to the young couple was a house in London, next door to their own in Chesterfield Gardens. The newly married Cravens returned to England where they spent most of their time between their main country estate, Hampstead Marshall, near Newbury, and the London house. Cornelia, charming and intelligent as well as attractive and elegant, was readily accepted into British society. On 31 July 1897 their only child, William

Cornelia, Countess of Craven, wearing her three strings of pearls as one single rope and her pearl and diamond earrings.
Lady Teresa Craven

George Bradley Craven, was born. Cornelia's main disappointment was that her pregnancy had prevented her from attending an amazing ball which her parents organized in New York.

In 1883 Alva Vanderbilt's fancy dress ball, at the cost of over $250,000, had been hailed by both the city press and her guests as a triumph and the most important and lavish social event ever to be held in New York. It had also gained the Vanderbilts a much-desired place in society; and as part of the same set the Bradley Martins had been present at this spectacle. In the early 1890s the USA was gripped by strikes and civil unrest, mainly caused by a severe depression in the economy, which did not improve during the decade. In 1897 the Martins hit on the idea of giving a grand ball, to be held at such short notice that the guests would be unable to acquire their costumes anywhere other than in New York. The thought may have stemmed from memories of the much-publicized Vanderbilt event but its intent was also to benefit the poor and unemployed as it would, according to Mrs Martin, 'give an impetus to trade that nothing else will.'

Over 1,000 guests were invited to their spectacular ball which was to be held at the Waldorf, the ballroom decorated to look like a state room in Versailles. The directive was that the guests should wear costumes from the 16th, 17th or 18th centuries as if they were attending the French royal court. On the night of the ball, Bradley Martin, dressed as Louis XV, and his wife as Mary, Queen of Scots, greeted their guests in the 'throne room'. Her dress was of dark velvet over a white petticoat, the bodice embroidered with gold and decorated with pearls and gemstones. The costume was highly elaborate, but it was the jewels she wore which were staggering. In 1887 Bradley Martin had acquired several pieces from the sale of the French crown jewels. The two ruby and diamond bracelets which had come from the Duchesse d'Angoulême's parure were worn around her neck as a choker. These bracelets had formed part of the magnificent parure created for the Duchesse by Menière in 1816, using the designs of his nephew, Evrard Bapst. The parure used many of the rubies and diamonds from one which had originally belonged to Empress Marie-Louise of France. Mr Martin bought the gems from Tiffany & Co. which had acquired them in the famous Paris sale. There was also a wonderful tiara belonging to the same parure which again Mr Martin managed to acquire. The original buyer at the Paris sale was a Mr Hass, but in 1890 Mr Martin bought it from Carrington & Co. Curiously, however, Mrs Bradley Martin chose to wear another magnificent diamond tiara that her husband had bought in Paris in 1889 for over £6,000. This may well bear out the

Mary 'Minnie' Paget, The American wife of Sir Arthur Paget, dressed as Cleopatra for the spectacular Devonshire Ball held in London 1897. For this event the Martins lent her some of their wonderful jewels to embellish her exotic costume. These were the sapphire and diamond flower brooch, the large diamond *rivière* necklace and the clasp of the Great Girdle, originally from the French Crown Jewels.
The National Portrait Gallery

(Opposite below) The same sapphire and diamond flowerspray brooch. The flowerhead is detachable and could be worn separately.
(Opposite above) An important sapphire and diamond twin heart brooch which could also be worn as a bangle. *Sotheby's, London*

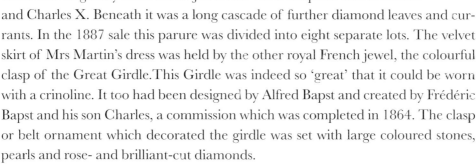

theory that the Martins had already given the ruby and diamond tiara to their daughter as a wedding present.

Further down Mrs Martin's sensational costume, two other jewels from the French crown jewels were in evidence. The bodice-front jewel from the currant-leaf parure was attached to her bodice. This came from one of the most sensational parures in the royal collection and had been designed by Alfred Bapst in 1855 for the Empress Eugénie. The bodice-front jewel or stomacher was designed as a trefoil of diamond leaves with a 20.03cts-diamond currant at the centre. This stone had originally been set in jewels for both Empress Marie-Louise and Charles X. Beneath it was a long cascade of further diamond leaves and currants. In the 1887 sale this parure was divided into eight separate lots. The velvet skirt of Mrs Martin's dress was held by the other royal French jewel, the colourful clasp of the Great Girdle. This Girdle was indeed so 'great' that it could be worn with a crinoline. It too had been designed by Alfred Bapst and created by Frédéric Bapst and his son Charles, a commission which was completed in 1864. The clasp or belt ornament which decorated the girdle was set with large coloured stones, pearls and rose- and brilliant-cut diamonds.

As if these royal jewels were insufficient, she also wore several other 19th-century jewels. A large diamond *rivière* was hung across her waist and three further diamond *rivières* were nonchalantly draped from the top of her bodice to her waist. An enormous diamond sunburst brooch was clasped to her breast and beneath her choker she wore a wonderful ruby and diamond cluster necklace; pinned to her shoulder was a splendid ruby and diamond cruciform pendant. The latter two jewels were originally believed also to have been part of the French crown jewels but recent research has more or less disproved this theory.

The cost of the ball was put at $369,200 and although hailed as a most glamorous occasion by the guests, it received strong criticism from both press and public at large who saw it as a great and unnecessary display of wealth and extravagance during such times of hardship. This was of course not the reaction that the Martins had expected: it also prompted a visit from the income tax collectors, who reassessed their wealth and doubled their property tax. The couple decided it was time to leave America for good.

Back at their home in London and at their estate in Scotland, they resumed their ostentatious entertaining. The Cravens were their guests on many occasions, although much of their time was spent at their country seats or in London. Bradley Martin died of pneumonia in 1913 and seven years later his wife also died. The marriage of their daughter had assured them of a standing in British society and their wealth had given them the power to enjoy it. Their fortune had also been of great benefit to the Craven family.

On 10 July 1921, when only 52 years old, Lord Craven accidentally drowned after falling overboard from his yacht. By all accounts Cornelia was a sensible and stalwart woman who tried to keep the fortune that she had brought to the Craven family intact. She survived to the age

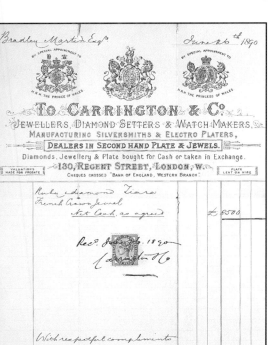

of 84. From the contents of her will, in which she made sure that her two Pekingese, Teddy Tail and Winkie, were suitably taken care of, it was clear that, despite the decline in the Craven family fortunes, her magnificent collection of jewels and many wonderful works of art were still in her possession. She specified that certain paintings were to be given to Queen Elizabeth II as well as to the Trustees of the National Gallery, London.

On 30 November 1961, the same year she died, a 'Casket of Magnificent Jewels' was sold by order of her executors. This was truly a treasure box of jewelry. It included not only the ruby and diamond tiara and pair of bracelets from the French crown jewels, together with the diamond tiara, the ruby and diamond necklace, the ruby and diamond cruciform pendant, the diamond sunburst brooch and one of the diamond *rivières* that her mother had worn at the famous ball, but other equally fabulous jewels.

An elegant pair of diamond earrings, designed as two large pear-shaped diamond drops mounted within double row borders of cushion-shaped diamonds and with cluster surmounts, had, according to family tradition, formerly been the property of Mrs Fitzherbert (1756-1837). In 1905 a sealed package deposited in Coutts Bank in 1833 was opened by Royal permission. This was found to contain the marriage certificate and other conclusive evidence of Mrs Fitzherbert's morganatic marriage to George IV when he was Prince of Wales. It is thought that these earrings had been given by Mrs Fitzherbert to her niece Charlotte Georgina Harriet Smythe, who married George Augustus Craven, second son of the first Earl of Craven, in 1833. Charlotte herself had been described by the Duke of Orleans as 'the prettiest girl in England'.

In Lady Craven's will she curiously refers to Mrs Fitzherbert's earrings as having been the property of her mother and being 'large flat Brazilian diamonds'. Later in her will she refers to her 'long diamond earrings reputed to have belonged to Maria Theresa of Austria'. Indeed, the collection included a pair of important diamond earrings, dating from the 18th century, each set with a large flattish oval-shaped stone, the mounts with

The bill of sale for the ruby and diamond tiara which had been purchased during the 1887 Paris auction of the French Crown Jewels by a Mr. Hass for 160,000F (£6,344). In 1890 it was bought by Mr. Bradley Martin, from Carrington & Co., for the sum of £8500. *Private Collection*

A pair of diamond pendent earrings, which were catalogued as being 'by family tradition' formerly the property of George IV's mistress, Mrs. Fitzherbert, and a pair of diamond single stone earrings. *Sotheby's, London*

foliate decoration. Undoubtedly both have fascinating provenances and are equally attractive.

Another stunning jewel which she had inherited from her mother was a large sapphire and diamond lotus flower dating from the 19th century. The detachable flowerhead, which can be worn separately, is set with a cushion-shaped sapphire and the petals, leaves and stem are set with diamonds. Her mother had also given her a large marquise-shaped diamond. In the early part of the 20th century she mounted it as a brooch, to which she added a detachable pearl and diamond drop.

Many of the other important jewels in this collection also dated from the 19th century. There was a sapphire and diamond paired-heart brooch which could also be worn as a bracelet centre, as well as a sapphire and diamond lavallière pendant. Other highlights of her jewels included two important ruby and diamond hinged bangles and three diamond bow brooches, one of which is an exquisite stomacher pierced and decorated with floral motifs. The 176 lots also included jewels by Cartier, Tiffany and Fabergé, among the most attractive of them being a pair of cabochon emerald and diamond pendent earrings and an elegant diamond *sautoir*, both created by Cartier in the 1920s. It goes without saying that there were also the natural pearl necklaces, earrings and a ring, a vital part of every lady's jewelry collection during that period.

Lady Craven's casket proved to contain not only fabulous jewels but also pieces of historical importance. The collection had been created both by her wealthy American parents and the inheritance of her husband, but also represented her own desire to be surrounded by beauty. This was an aim she managed to achieve throughout her life.

Gladys, Duchess of Marlborough

A year after she died at the age of 97, an almost forgotten, vanished figure, 'A Casket of Highly Important Jewels' that had been the property of Gladys Marie, Dowager Duchess of Marlborough, came to auction on 5 July 1978. It was surprising to learn that this isolated, aged woman who once inspired writers like Marcel Proust, who wrote after their first meeting in 1907: 'I never saw a girl with such beauty, such magnificent intelligence, such goodness and charm.' Those who knew her in her youth agreed with Proust that she was extraordinarily attractive, and for years she was pursued by many of the most eligible bachelors in Europe. But it was not until her fortieth year that she finally married the 9th Duke of Marlborough.

Gladys was born in Paris in 1881, the progeny of two well-established and extremely wealthy American families, the Deacons and the Baldwins. Her parents, Edward and Florence Deacon, were part of the fashionable American set who made their base in Europe and thrived on the high social lifestyle on both sides of the Atlantic. Gladys was the eldest of four sisters and grew to be the most beautiful and most intelligent of them all. From her mother she had inherited not only her striking looks but also her deep passion for the arts. Her early years were spent in the company of the best of European and American society and the elite of the artistic world.

The Deacons' marriage was not a great success, but on one subject they were in total agreement: the security and happiness of their children. In this, however, they failed, for the charmed childhood of the four girls came to an abrupt end when their father was found guilty of 'unlawfully wounding but without intent to cause death'.

The victim of this action was a Frenchman, Emile Abeille, whom Deacon had suspected for years of having a relationship with his wife. His suspicions proved well-founded and Abeille was shot while hiding in Florence's boudoir. This affair caused a great scandal and, despite Deacon's being pardoned and released from prison by the French President after pressure from the American Legation, the family was torn apart and the Deacons were divorced. Somewhat astonishingly, Mr Deacon was awarded custody of the three elder girls, with the result that Gladys spent the next three years in the USA under his supervision. It was evident that she was not happy with this arrangement and in 1896, after a number of legal wrangles, she was able to rejoin her mother in France.

During her years in the USA Gladys, like most girls in her social circle, had followed the reports of Consuelo Vanderbilt's engagement to the Duke of Marlborough in 1895, and two years later she and her mother had occasion to meet the Duke in London. Captivated by Gladys, he promptly invited her to his home, Blenheim Palace. The American-born

Gladys Deacon in her wedding dress, seated in the Paris garden of her cousin, Eugene Higgins, on 25 June 1921, the day of her marriage to the 9th Duke of Marlborough. She is wearing the navette-shaped diamond engagement ring shown above. *Private collection; Christie's, London*

Gladys, Duchess of Marlborough, as sketched by Cecil Beaton for *Vogue* in July 1927, wearing her pearl and diamond tiara, in the form of a *kokoshnik*, from the Russian Crown Jewels. *Vogue, Condé Nast Publications*

Duchess was also enchanted by Gladys and a firm friendship between them developed, which was to last for many years.

The next few years were for Gladys a period of learning. She spent her time on the Continent mastering new languages and increasing her already wide knowledge of literature and the arts. Her father died in 1901, after a series of mental illnesses, and this entitled her to receive her own income from the Deacon Trust. That year she spent six months at Blenheim, where she attracted another ardent admirer. Crown Prince William of Prussia was a fellow guest; during his brief stay he became so infatuated with Gladys that he presented her with a ring given to him by his mother. Gladys responded by giving him her bracelet. The Crown Prince returned to Germany love-sick and ringless. This was soon noticed by the Kaiser who insisted that the ring be returned immediately. Gladys reluctantly agreed, and in return received back her bracelet. As the Kaiser would never permit his son to marry a commoner, the romance was suppressed but evidently not forgotten. Years later the Crown Prince made reference to the 'charming American' he had wished to marry.

Despite the excitement of her visits to Blenheim, Gladys could not ignore the fact that the Marlboroughs' marriage was far from blissful. Divorce was discussed, though they were both reluctant to cause any scandal. In 1907 a legal separation was arranged, but it was almost fourteen years before their divorce took place. During this period Gladys spent a good deal of time travelling, especially to Rome where her mother was living in the beautiful Villa Farnese in Caprarola. It was probably during one of these visits that she acquired a gold bracelet by Castellani, in classical style, inscribed with the motto '*Fides Probitas Forma Pvdicitia*'. Revivalist jewels by the Castellani family were still fashionable at the beginning of the 20th century.

(Above) Gladys Deacon's black and white pearl and diamond pendant in the garland style, which was so fashionable at the beginning of the century. She chose to wear this jewel for her portrait by Boldini (opposite) that was commissioned by the Duke of Marlborough in 1916. *Christie's, London*

It was in Rome that she developed an almost obsessive passion for the classical forms and features which she saw in the many statues. As a slave to beauty she decided that her nose did not have the desired classical straightness of line, and in 1903 she had taken the drastic decision to have paraffin wax injected into the bridge of her nose. At first this painful process achieved her aim, but in later life it was to cause problems and mar her beauty. It was an action that illustrates her determination to find perfection at all costs.

By 1911 it was evident that she and Marlborough had become more than friends. In 1916, he commissioned Boldini to paint a portrait of her which captured some of her extraordinary allure. In the portrait she is wearing an elegant pearl and diamond pendant, typical of the 'garland' style so popular at the beginning of the 20th century. What is striking is the contrast between this simple jewel and the opulent ones she came to wear as the Duchess of Marlborough. In May 1921, when the divorce decree became absolute and the Duke was free to marry Gladys, she realized that to accept his proposal would not only entail leaving behind her carefree lifestyle, but might also ruin their happy relationship. Such doubts, however, were short-lived and on 24 June 1921 they were married in a civil ceremony at the British Consulate in Paris. The religious

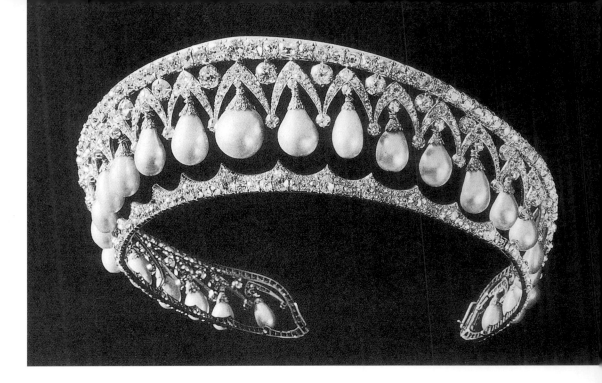

(Right) The Imperial pearl and diamond tiara. Set with twenty-five pearls of exceptional size hanging from a diamond frame, it was reminiscent of an exaggerated halo. It can be clearly seen (below left) in an original photograph of a section of some of the magnificent jewels of the Treasure which were exhibited in the offices of the Moscow National-Meta -Fund while the cataloguing took place in 1922. The receipt from Holmes & Co. dated 12 May 1927 shows that the price of the tiara was £3500. *Fersman Catalogue; Private collection*

ceremony was held the following day at the home of her cousin Eugene Higgins. Gladys wore a wonderful dress of gold and silver, designed in her favourite classical style, and on her left hand was a sparkling diamond ring. The navette-shaped diamond, weighing over 12cts, was mounted between diamond shoulders. This was her engagement ring from the Duke and the first major jewel she received as the Duchess of Marlborough. 'We are both awfully poor,' was the Duke's response when asked by the press about the wedding present, but he went on to remark, 'What will the miners think, reading about wedding presents, jewellery costing £50,000?...say I gave the bride a motor-car.'

When they returned to Blenheim in July, Gladys assumed her new role and tried for the next two decades to come to terms with the change in her style of life. As the wife of a divorced man, she often found social acceptance denied her, and even after her presentation at Court in 1923, she sometimes found her situation difficult. A requirement of her new position was to accompany her husband

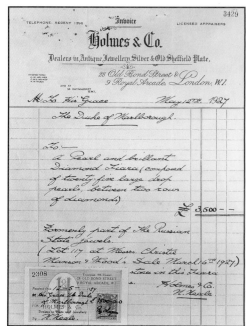

to State ceremonies, such as the Opening of Parliament, and society weddings and balls. For these she had to be suitably attired, and during the 1920s and early '30s she acquired some truly sensational jewels.

An historic auction was held in London in 1927 of 'An important assemblage of magnificent jewellery, mostly dating from the 18th century, which formed part of the Russian State Jewels and which have been purchased by a Syndicate in this country. They are now sold in order to close the partnership account.' The Russian treasure was originally catalogued in 1922, each individual piece being photographed, measured and weighed, and given a new inventory number by the mineralogist A.E. Fersman, assisted by S.N. Troinitzky, the Director of the Hermitage National Museum, and A.N. Benois, the well-known art critic and painter.

As the jewels of the treasure were not all of the same class, it was decided to divide them into three distinct categories. The first, by far the most important, included all the jewels of great value and historic fame; the second, specimens of minor interest; and the third, all fashion jewels. At the time of the auction, the treasure comprised only the first of these categories, including a beautiful pearl and diamond tiara, described at length by the Russians in their original catalogue as being 'from the Private Apartments of H.I.M. Maria-Feodorovna'.

Unfortunately, it was not illustrated in the auction catalogue, but was simply described as a 'pearl and brilliant tiara with 25 large drop pearls', with no statement of its Imperial provenance. The jewel was bought by Holmes & Co. and two months later the Duke of Marlborough acquired it for £3,500. Gladys now had a most exquisite and historically important head ornament, suitable for any grand occasion. Indeed on 13 November 1932 she organized a most spectacular 'Coming of Age Party' to celebrate the Duke's 60th birthday – although it was discovered after the invitations had been sent that the Duke

was actually to be 59. It was decided that the party should go ahead and it proved to be one of the most glittering occasions ever held at Blenheim. Amidst all the fabulous jewels adorning the invited aristocracy, Gladys looked resplendent in a classical gown embroidered in turquoise blue and her regal tiara worn across her forehead.

Two years later, she was involved in a court case regarding an unpaid account, and in a letter to her solicitors, dated 17 March, she

The 1926 version of the amethyst and diamond *sautoir* by Cartier, London, with the turquoise and diamond clasp, and the 1928 version with the two panels from the diamond bracelet which had been created by Chaumet in 1925, as illustrated below. *Cartier Ltd.; Christie's, London*

(Opposite) The 'Belt Ornament' from the 1978 auction, which was indeed the amethyst and diamond chains from the original Cartier *sautoir*. The amethyst, turquoise and diamond pendant is also by Cartier. Designed as a vase of flowers on a cord necklet, decorated with onyx beads and diamond rondel terminals, this jewel is representative of the Art Deco jewels of the early 1920s. *Sotheby's, St. Moritz; Christie's, London*

makes a revealing statement. 'The Duke has not only a great love of display, pomp and circumstance but a love for jewels and I did see for myself that although I had never cared for wearing jewels having no personal vanity about my appearance other duchesses wore tiaras etc and on several occasions I was the only one not wearing one. Well so he chose a very pretty one and contributed £500 towards it and I paid the rest which was a large sum.'

In the 1978 auction after her death, the description of the tiara still made no mention of its Imperial Russian origins; nor was one of her major commissions from Cartier recognized. Lot 80 was described as an 'important amethyst and diamond belt ornament'. The long chains of amethyst and diamonds were originally part of a sumptuous *sautoir* first ordered by Gladys in 1926 from Cartier, London. During this period Cartier was creating wonderful interpretations of this extremely fashionable jewel. The first design of this *sautoir* was a long chain of oval amethysts connected by links of baton-shaped amethysts and diamonds, and the clasp was designed as an open circle set with calibré-cut-turquoises and diamonds, connected by an amethyst-set fob attachment. From Cartier's records it is clear that the Marlboroughs supplied the 34 larger amethysts and four diamonds, previously set in a brooch. The turquoises and the

baton-shaped amethysts, together with a further nearly 20cts of diamonds were supplied by Cartier at a cost of £360. The clasp of this *sautoir* was sold as a brooch.

In 1928 Gladys had the *sautoir* altered yet again, this time adding two panels of diamonds to connect the festooned rows of amethysts and diamonds. The diamond panels came from a diamond bracelet which could be divided into three separate sections. It had been created in 1925 for the sum of £800 by the French jewelers J. Chaumet, late Morel & Co., at their New Bond Street establishment. They used five diamonds from one of Gladys's bar brooches and supplied the remaining 359 stones and detachable fittings for conversion as three brooches. This bracelet was included in the 1978 sale and it is somewhat sad to think that merely by detaching the two diamond panels from the bracelet and connecting them with the amethyst chain, the sensational original Cartier creation could have been re-formed.

The jewel made its last appearance at auction in St Moritz in 1989 when again, although described as 'spectacular', it had been split into two lots and neither its provenance nor its creators were mentioned. In all its many forms, the *sautoir* was an exciting Cartier jewel.

In the spring of 1928 Cartier carried out two further commissions for Gladys. They were both brooches designed as foliate scroll clusters, for which she supplied nearly half the diamonds. The centre of the larger was fitted to hold either an emerald or an cat's eye chrysoberyl which she possessed, the latter

having been bought by the Duke in 1927. The original central stone in the other slightly smaller brooch is unknown. Again Gladys must have had them altered at a later date, and in the 1978 catalogue they appear as one ornament formed by two brooch/pendants connected by a loop. The central stones had been replaced by green pastes and the important unmounted chrysoberyl cat's eye, weighing around 82cts, was sold separately.

During the same period, Gladys commissioned Holmes & Co. to buy a diamond bangle at auction on her behalf. The sale took place on 21 March 1928 and the jewel was acquired for £1,950, on top of which she paid Holmes & Co. £100. The central cushion-shaped diamond, weighing 48cts, was surrounded by a border of diamonds, the back designed as a five-row hinged gold band. The style of this jewel is typical of the late 19th century. In the same letter of 1934 to her solicitors, Gladys mentions that the 'Duke then saw a huge diamond in a sale and telling me he conceived it an incredible bargain induced me to buy it. This wretched stone's payment was the origin of the frightful tangle I got into later financially.' In the sale of her jewels it was catalogued as a 'highly important diamond bangle forming brooch pendant'.

Also included in her collection were two very stylish rings, both mounted in gold and dating from her period as Duchess. One was a cabochon emerald mounted between calibré-cut sapphire shoulders and the other a cushion-shaped sapphire, weighing over 12cts, and set between calibré-cut emerald shoulders. The sapphire was described as superb and was believed to be of Kashmir origin. Another important jewel from her collection was a diamond *rivière*. The necklace was set with 14 diamonds, weighing in total over 130cts, connected by knife-wires; the largest central stone weighed approximately 21.66cts. It appears probable that this jewel was acquired at Chaumet's in the mid-'20s. A letter from R.G. Astley for Chaumet, dated 2 June 1927, acknowledges that the necklace has been left in their safekeeping, together with the bracelet which they had made for her in 1925, and confirms the weight of the centre stone.

During her years at Blenheim, Gladys continued to attract new friends from the literary and the artistic worlds, such as Lytton Strachey, Siegfried Sassoon, Evelyn Waugh, Edith Sitwell and Harold Nicolson. When the occasion required, she was the perfect hostess for visitors to the Palace, but she still missed her carefree younger years. By 1933 the marriage was finally over and even friendship seemed impossible once the Duke began to say that Gladys's mind was unbalanced. In 1934 he died, still officially married to her, but Consuelo took her place at Blenheim as the mother of the 10th Duke.

(Left) A diamond *rivière* necklace and a diamond bangle, of which the detachable central cluster was set with a cushion-shaped diamond weighing 48.00cts. It could also be worn as a brooch or a pendant. *Christie's, London*

(Above) A receipt from J. Chaumet stating the exact weights of the fourteen diamonds in the necklace. The London branch of the famous French jewelers had opened in New Bond Street in 1905 where it was patronized by the British aristocracy and society as well as wealthy foreign visitors. By the early 1920s, Gladys, as the new Duchess of Marlborough, numbered among their illustrious clientele. *Private collection*

To the world at large Gladys seemed to have disappeared, and her remaining years might well have remained a mystery but for the intrepid and painstaking investigations of the excellent biographer, Hugo Vickers. He had become fascinated by this woman after reading a reference to her in the diaries of 'Chips' Channon and he finally tracked her down to a hospital in Northampton. He made numerous visits to her and during their conversations her fascinating story unfolded.

After leaving Blenheim she had taken the name of 'Mrs Spencer' (the Marlborough family name) and spent over twenty years living on a farm in Chalcombe near Banbury. To her fellow villagers she appeared to be a rather eccentric, reclusive old lady, usually dressed in scruffy clothes, and the large portrait which dominated the dining room seemed somewhat incongruous. This was the exquisite painting of her elegant mother which Boldini had finished in 1906.

In 1962, Gladys was forcibly taken away from Chalcombe and spent her remaining days in St Andrews Hospital which cared for private psychiatric patients. In October 1977, this legendary figure of beauty and intelligence died in obscurity.

A group of the Duchess of Marlborough's jewels, including an Art Deco silk cordette and diamond bracelet, by Cartier; an unmounted chrysoberyl cat's eye; a sapphire and diamond ring; the turquoise and diamond brooch that had originally been the clasp from the 1926 version of the amethyst and diamond *sautoir* created by Cartier, London; and a gold, enamel, sapphire drop and agate cameo pendant, the cameo of Flora believed to be of 16th-century origin.

(Above and opposite) Two original Cartier, London, designs for the Duchess's jewels. On this page is one of the two brooches they created for her in 1928, and the design opposite incorporates the three panels from her Chaumet diamond bracelet. This 1929 version would have enabled the Duchess to wear the panels with either a moonstone or a blue bead necklace. *Private collection; Sotheby's, London*

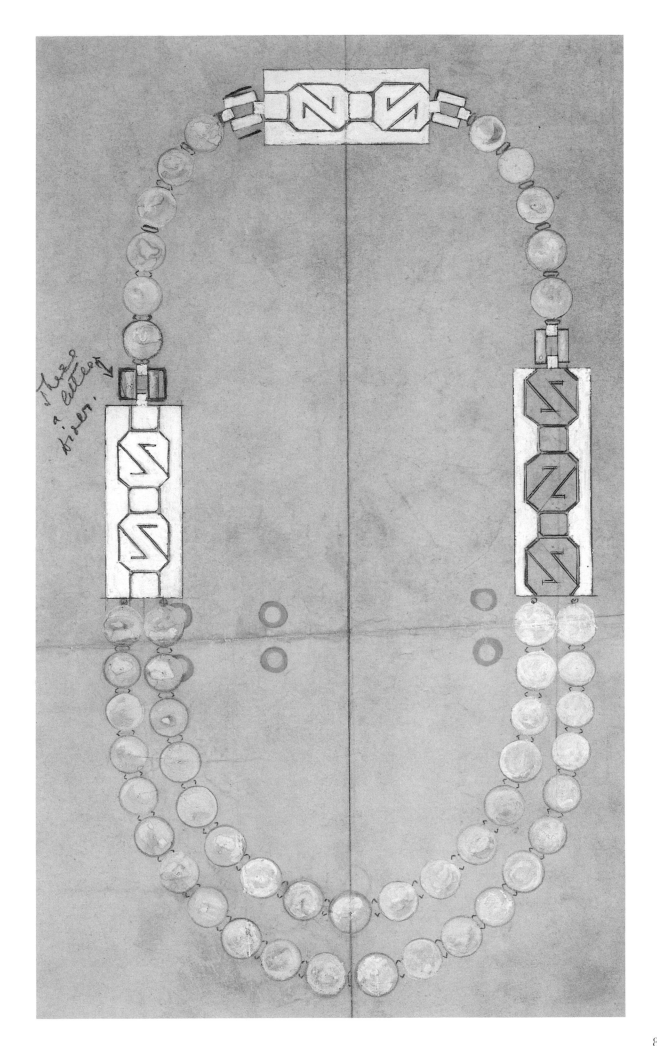

King Umberto II of Italy

On 15 May 1985 a small but unique group of jewels was offered at auction, under the provenance of His Majesty the late King Umberto II of Italy. Born on 15 September 1904 in the Castle of Racconigi, he was the son of Elena of Montenegro and Victor Emmanuel III of Italy, and as heir to the throne he was given the title of Prince of Piemonte. He grew up to be considered one of the most handsome and elegant Princes in the whole of Europe and was known as the Prince 'Charmant'. On 8 January 1930, in the Capella Palatina in the Royal Palace of the Quirinale in Rome, he was married to Princess Maria José, the daughter of Albert, King of Belgium.

Throughout his life Umberto II had a great passion for history and every form of art, which included jewelry. He loved his own family collection of royal jewels not only for their historical importance but also for their beauty. In accordance with his artistic nature, however, he could not resist altering some of the pieces. They were unmounted and re-set many times, but always by the best jewelers in Italy. In 1968 he had a beautiful pearl and diamond tiara designed by the Roman jeweler Petochi on the basis of his own ideas, and set with stones removed from other royal jewels. Petochi was the court jeweler and his son remembers his father visiting the King abroad with a wax model of the tiara to show the different phases of its construction and to seek the King's advice on the final version. The tiara was stunning and was presented to his daughter, Princess Maria Gabriella, on the occasion of her wedding. She wore it to the famous 'Proust' Ball at the Château de Ferrières hosted by the Baron and Baroness Guy de Rothschild in 1972.

Some of the jewels that were offered in the 1985 auction had belonged to Umberto's grandmother, Queen Margherita, the consort of Umberto I. She was the epitome of elegance and regalness for the Italian people who knew her affectionately as 'The Queen of Pearls', in

Queen Margherita as a young bride wearing the Mellerio tiara she had received as a wedding gift from her father-in-law, King Victor Emmanuel II. *Umberto II Foundation, Lausanne*

(Right) Princess Maria Gabriella of Savoy photographed by Cecil Beaton at the Proust Ball at the Château de Ferrière. She is wearing the tiara designed for her by her father, King Umberto II, using gemstones from other Royal jewels. *Princess Maria Gabriella of Savoy*

(Below) A model in plaster of Paris of the pearl and diamond tiara used by the jeweler to show King Umberto II the various phases during its making. *Petochi, Rome*

The Royal emerald, pearl and diamond necklace in its original form. The central cluster was set with the step-cut emerald of 47.76cts that was sold separately at auction in 1985 as a brooch. The necklace was originally accompanied by a stomacher that mirrored the design of its central part, with the exception that the surmount was set with a cushion-shaped emerald rather than a step-cut stone. In the 1985 sale the two pear-shaped drops from the necklace and the stomacher were set together as a brooch/pendant, one drop supporting the other. *Umberto II Foundation, Lausanne; Sotheby's, Geneva*

Queen Margherita in court dress wearing her magnificent Royal necklace together with the Stuart emerald brooch (see p, 89). *Umberto II Foundation, Lausanne*

The Mellerio stand at the 1867 Paris Exhibition. Clearly displayed on the left-hand side is the tiara King Victor Emmanuel II gave to his niece and future daughter-in-law, Margherita, as a wedding present. *Mellerio dits Meller*

(Opposite) The Mellerio diamond flowerhead and laurel leaf tiara, and (below) Queen Maria José is shown wearing the jewel at a reception she and the King attended on the occasion of the wedding of the Prince of Asturias and Princess Sophia of Greece and Denmark. *Sotheby's, Geneva; Princess Maria Gabriella of Savoy*

recognition of her love of jewelry, particularly the pearls which she wore on most occasions, often several rows at one time. Her husband was known to have given her a string for each year of their marriage. Indeed, it is therefore highly appropriate that her name signifies 'pearl' in Latin. Both prior to and after the 1985 sale, other superb jewels that she had received during her husband's reign and loved to wear have been offered at auction.

Margherita was born on 20 November 1851 at Palazzo Chiablese in Turin, the daughter of Ferdinand of Savoy, the Duke of Genova, and of Elizabeth of Saxony, the daughter of King John of Saxony. She was chosen by her uncle, Victor Emmanuel II of Savoy, to marry his cousin, Umberto, who was the heir to the throne of Italy. In 1868, in a white silk wedding dress embroidered in silver with daisies and sprays of flowers, and wearing the magnificent pearl necklace that once belonged to Queen Maria Adelaide of Savoy and two diamond stars on her head, Margherita was married to Umberto in the Renaissance Cathedral of San Giovanni in Turin. As is customary, Margherita had received some superb wedding presents which included jewels. When it was auctioned in 1985 the true historical importance of a beautiful tiara of diamond laurel leaves, so typical of the mid-19th-century craftsmanship, was unknown. In a photograph taken in 1867 of the stand of the Paris jeweler Mellerio at the Paris Universal Exhibition of that year, a tiara identical to the one auctioned in 1985 is exhibited by the side of the pearl tiara bought by Queen Isabella II of Spain, which is worn today by Queen Sophia.

Further research into the archives of the Umberto II and Maria José of Savoy Foundation in Geneva, and thanks to the help of their daughter, Princess Maria Gabriella of Savoy, it was revealed to be that same tiara. A list of personal jewelry that had belonged to Queen Margherita, drafted by a lady-in-waiting, contains a very detailed description of the tiara, and Queen Margherita herself added a handwritten note stating that the tiara had been purchased from the Paris jeweler Mellerio and was her wedding present from King Victor Emmanuel II.

Many official portraits of Margherita show her wearing this tiara from her youth until only a few months prior to her death at Bordighera in 1926. She was obviously especially attached to it, as is borne out by a photograph of her

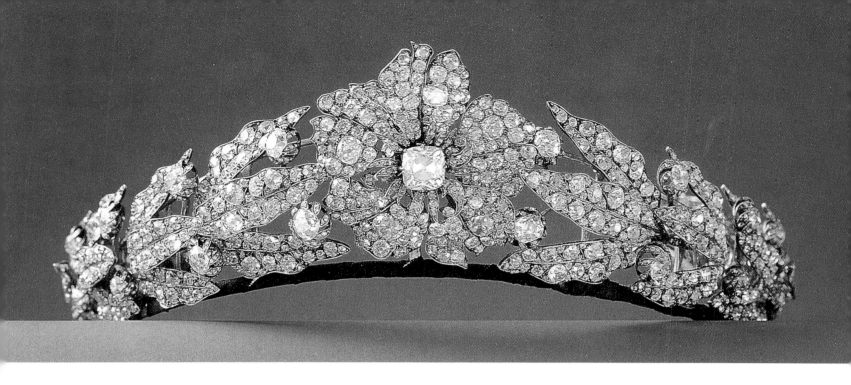

attending the wedding of her favourite granddaughter, Princess Mafalda, to Prince Philip of Hesse in 1925.

In 1878, upon the death of his father, Umberto became King of Italy and as her father-in-law had been a widower throughout his reign this made Margherita Italy's first Queen. Under her reign the Court enjoyed a period of splendour. She was admired not only for her style and bearing but also for her patronage of the arts and her dedication to the support of charities. She managed to be present at most of the important occasions, such as exhibitions, the opening of new state buildings, in particular hospitals, and cultural events. The Italians came to love and trust her and eventually the monarchy for which she stood.

When the poet and avid republican Josué Carducci (a Nobel Prize winner in 1906) met Queen Margherita in Bologna in 1878, he was totally won over by her. In deference to her, he too became converted to the monarchy. In a photograph that the Queen gave and inscribed to him in 1890, she is portrayed wearing the superb royal emerald necklace and the 'Stuart Emerald' brooch. The necklace had been part of the dowry of Elizabeth of Saxony when she married and she in turn gave it to her daughter Margherita.

This jewel was designed as six emerald and diamond clusters, connected by three rows of pearls. It had an emerald and diamond drop at the centre, with a matching stomacher brooch/pendant. After Umberto II died in 1983, the clusters and drops were divided among his children. In the 1985 auction, one of the clusters from the necklace was sold as a brooch, set with the splendid step-cut emerald of over 47.76cts. The emerald was Colombian and therefore the marvellous saturated green so typical of stones from that country.

When this jewel reappeared at auction in 1996, the two drops, each set with a

pear-shaped emerald of around 20cts, one originally hanging from the necklace and the other from the stomacher, were mounted together as a pendant.

In Geneva in 1971, bearing the provenance of 'The Italian Royal Family', the beautiful pearl and diamond brooch set with the 'Stuart Emerald' was auctioned. This emerald was presented by Cardinal Henry Stuart to Prince Charles Felix of Savoy on the announcement of the Prince's marriage to Princess Maria Cristina of Bourbon in 1807. The Cardinal was the last of the Royal House of Stuart and was known by the 'Legitimists' as Henry IX, King of England, Scotland and Ireland.

At the end of 1878, Treves of Milan published the first edition of *Margherita*, a fashion magazine for women, named after the Queen as a tribute to her sense of style. From the point of view of a historian of fashion it was an important publication, as it documented the Queen's own personal taste. As has already been mentioned, she was famous for her vast collection of pearl jewelry. In 1996 an important pair of pearl and diamond earrings came up for auction bearing her provenance. The beauty and quality of the large drop pearls was indeed a fitting tribute to her love of these gems. A bold and cosmopolitan woman, she had an adventurous spirit; in 1881, on being advised against crossing the dangerously stormy seas by the captain of the battleship *Roma*, she is said to have responded '*Sempre Avanti Savoya*' (Savoy always forward), a theatrical utterance which became a family motto.

Sensitive to technical developments, she was perhaps the first royal female who seriously took to the motor car. She became famous for her travels abroad, accompanied only by her driver, a mechanic and a lady-in-waiting; a rifle was attached under the roof of the car to deal with any unforeseen danger.

In the 1985 sale of the estate there was an important diamond *rivière* of substantial size. This jewel, together with another *rivière* that appeared at auction in 1996, was originally combined to form a sumptuous two-row necklace that had been created in the 1930s by Petochi, commissioned by the future king Umberto II for his bride. Also in the later sale were a pair of diamond clips designed as Savoy knots made by the Genoa jewelers Chiappe in the 1930s.

Although only relatively few jewels from the original collection of the Royal House of Savoy have come to auction they have mainly been exceptional jewels and important in terms of their unique and often romantic provenance.

(Above) An official portrait of Crown Princess Maria José of Piemonte, later to become Queen of Italy, in court dress and wearing one of the two Savoy knot clips on the shoulder of her sash. *Prince Dimitri of Yugoslavia*

(Below) Queen Margherita's pearl and diamond pendent earrings. *Christie's, Geneva*

(Above) One of the two diamond *rivière* necklaces that were created in the 1930s by the Roman jewelers Petochi by order of the future King Umberto II for his bride. The two *rivières* were set with diamonds from Queen Margherita's collection. *Sotheby's, New York*

These diamond clips by Chiappe, designed as Savoy knots, were a wedding gift for Queen Maria José. The earrings she is wearing on p. 88 were also by Chiappe. *Sotheby's, New York*

The pearl and diamond brooch set with the Stuart emerald. *Christie's, Geneva*

89

The Princess Royal,
Countess of Harewood

When a third child, a girl, was born to the Duke and Duchess of York on 25 April 1897, her great-grandmother Queen Victoria sent a brief telegram to the Yorks: 'All happiness to you and my little Diamond Jubilee baby.' A visit soon followed and the Queen even suggested that the child be named 'Diamond' in memory of the Jubilee she had recently celebrated. Her whim was diplomatically ignored and a few weeks later the infant was christened Victoria Alexandra Alice Mary; it was the last name by which she was known out of deference to her mother.

Princess Mary had a thorough education during her early years; she not only read the classics, spoke French and sang and played the piano beautifully, but she also became an excellent equestrian and gymnast. She built up a strong rapport with all her four brothers, but it was with the elder two, Princes Edward and Albert, that there was a particularly strong bond.

In 1910 the coronation of her parents took place, and it was the first time that she had been required to wear State robes. Over her white dress she wore purple velvet trimmed with ermine with a long train, and around her neck she wore three ropes of magnificent pearls. Her coronet sat rather precariously on top of her abundant golden curls, for which her family nickname was 'Goldilocks'.

This event also marked a pronounced change in her life, for she now took on her new role as the only daughter of the King and Queen. By all accounts the young Princess was an extremely intelligent and gifted child with a tendency to shyness, but one of her main attributes was noted in later years by her elder son, Lord Harewood, as an 'extraordinary sweetness of nature'. Her teenage years were often spent in the company of her mother, from whom she inherited a love of beautiful objects and the arts. She eagerly visited art exhibitions and acquired an informed knowledge of the great masters. Other keen interests included gardening and needlework, in both of which she became extremely accomplished.

In 1917 the Princess was required to make her first official solo public appearance, deputizing for her mother. This was the first of many such occasions and although she never quite overcame her shyness, she soon managed to charm the variety of people to whom she was presented with her kindness and her genuine interest in them.

In that time of war she took to visiting the wounded in hospital and helping in the canteens for both the sick and factory workers and generally ministering to her war-weary people. In his biography of the Princess, Evelyn Graham

An official portrait by Vandyk of Princess Mary, Countess of Harewood, taken in June 1922. She is wearing some of her historically important jewels, including Queen Victoria's sapphire and diamond necklace and a Russian sapphire and diamond necklace/corsage ornament. *National Portrait Gallery*

A 19th-century sapphire and diamond necklace of quatrefoil cluster design which had belonged to Queen Victoria, as it appeared at auction without the pendant. As for the sapphire and diamond brooch, the Princess Royal could also wear it as the centrepiece in her diamond diadem of scroll and palmette design. *Christie's, London*

(Below) An emerald and diamond brooch set with three step-cut emeralds within borders of variously cut diamonds. The three clusters were detachable. *Christie's, London*

(Opposite) An emerald and diamond necklace, the five clusters of which were originally mounted as a lavallière. *Christie's, London*

notes that 'there is no doubt that these years left their mark upon the Princess, and gave to her whole nature a tinge of seriousness which she has never entirely lost.'

In 1918 she celebrated her twenty-first birthday and was at last allowed to embark on the career which she had set her heart on. During that summer she started her training at the Hospital for Sick Children in Great Ormond Street as a Voluntary Aid Detachment 'probationer'. In 1920 she became President of the Girl Guides, another great interest in her life.

On 22 November 1921, it was announced from Buckingham Palace that she was engaged to marry 'Viscount Lascelles, D.S.O., eldest son of the Earl of Harewood'. The couple were ideally suited, sharing many interests, including a great love of the arts and a passion for riding, especially hunting. Lord Lascelles was fifteen years older than the Princess, but she was mature for her age and it was evidently a genuine love-match. Harewood House was Lord Lascelles's country seat in Yorkshire and his London residence was Chesterfield House. Together with his family's wealth, he had inherited from his great-uncle, Lord Clanricarde, a large fortune and a marvellous art collection. Upon her marriage, the Princess received the Clanricarde diamonds which had been kept in a London bank vault for over a century. According to legend, it had been prophesied over two hundred years previously that these diamonds would be worn by a King's daughter.

The wedding presents included many jewels. The Princess had often hunted with the West Norfolk Foxhounds, and they presented her with a sapphire and diamond brooch, the crystal centre engraved with a fox. The Citizens of London gave her a diamond pendant and chain. The pendant was set with a pear-shaped diamond within a border of smaller diamonds 'of the first water' and was hung from a chain of large single stones connected by smaller diamonds, measuring 34 inches.

The city of Edinburgh sent her a replica of the Queen Mary Brooch which is named after Mary Queen of Scots. Together with a silver cheese tray, her faithful Girl Guides sent her a 'Tenderfoot Badge' set with rubies and diamonds, which could be worn as a brooch. One her most beautiful presents was an emerald and diamond tiara which was bought with funds raised by 50,000 members of the Voluntary Aid Detachment.

The wedding took place on 28 February 1922 at Westminster Abbey. entwined with silver trelliswork. As the wife of Lord Lascelles, Princess Mary now thrived on making both Goldsborough Hall on the Harewood estate and Chesterfield House homes of both great comfort and great style. The couple thoroughly enjoyed collecting new treasures as well as resiting the Earl's already vast collection. With the birth of her two sons, her previous experience with children was invaluable. She was now able to pursue the outdoor activities she loved, namely gardening and hunting, while still taking an active part in the social scene. Although the majority of their time was spent in Yorkshire, the Lascelles still visited their London residence as frequently as required. By 1930, following the

(Opposite above) A diamond *rivière* necklace. *Christie's, London*

An illustration from the catalogue of an exhibition of Russian art that was held in London in 1935, showing the sapphire and diamond necklace which had been lent by the Princess Royal and which had originally belonged to Grand Duke Mikhail Mikhailovich. Also shown is the impressive sapphire and diamond tiara created by Cartier, Paris, in 1909 by order of Grand Duchess Vladimir of Russia. In the 1935 exhibition it was lent by Queen Marie of Roumania who had acquired it from her sister, the Grand Duchess Victoria Melita, daughter-in-law of the Grand Duchess Vladimir. *John Stuart*

The antique Russian sapphire and diamond necklace/corsage ornament. *Christie's, London*

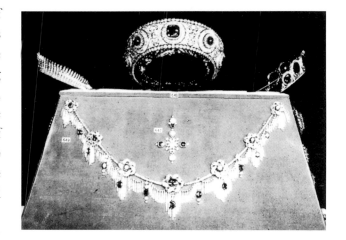

death of the 5th Earl the previous year, they had moved into Harewood House. In January 1932 Princess Mary was declared the Princess Royal of Great Britain. In 1947 Viscount Lascelles died and the Princess Royal continued to live at Harewood until she died in 1965.

There were three separate auctions of the Princess Royal's jewelry, the first in 1960 and the others, after her death, in 1966 and 1970. Between the three sales 174 lots, from small sentimental pieces to important historical jewels, were dispersed. In the first sale two lots were sold under her name, one a lovely pair of late 18th-century diamond feather brooches and the other a diamond pendent watch. However, in the same sale, under the provenance of her son, the Earl of Harewood, some major pieces from her collection were included. Probably the most interesting and historically important was the magnificent 19th-century *devant de corsage* of Russian origin. This jewel was composed of seven graduated sapphire and diamond clusters of scrolled ribbon design, which could be detached and worn as brooches, each supporting a deep fringe of diamonds with a sapphire centre, and connected by fringed swag motifs. This piece was lent by the Princess Royal for an exhibition of Russian art which was held in London in 1935 and was catalogued as having been formerly the property of the Grand Duke Mikhail Mikhailovich (1861-1929). The Grand Duke was the nephew of Alexander III and brother-in-law of the Tsar's daughter, Grand Duchess Xenia. Due to his royal birth he had to obtain the permission of the Tsar to marry. The Tsar gave his approval to the girl in question but in the meantime the Grand Duke Mikhail met and fell in love with an entirely different one: Countess Sophia Meremberg, one of Pushkin's granddaughters, and later known as Countess Torby. In 1891, after they married secretly, the furious Tsar exiled them and they moved to England, never to return to Russia. During the early 20th century many Russian émigrés were dispersing their jewelry collections and Queen Mary was a great buyer of these jewels. It is probable that she bought this *devant de corsage* from the Grand Duke and gave it to her daughter.

Two official portraits of the
Princess Royal. At left, in 1936,
she is wearing one of her
diamond *rivière* necklaces, the
emerald and diamond lavallière
which was later re-mounted as a
cluster necklace, the emerald and
diamond triple cluster brooch,
and an emerald and diamond
bracelet. In 1963 (right), she is
wearing the so-called tiara 'russe'
together with her two diamond
rivière necklaces and her diamond
stomacher. In several of the
official portraits taken during the
early years of her marriage, she is
wearing the diamond stomacher
as a pendant suspended from a
long diamond *rivière* necklace.
The National Portrait Gallery;
Private collection

In the same sale there was an important diamond *rivière* and a magnificent emerald and diamond necklace, the front with five emerald and diamond clusters connected by a double row of diamonds. The clusters in this necklace were originally part of a negligé pendant, as can been seen in a studio portrait of the Princess Royal taken in 1936, in which she is also wearing the *rivière* as well as an emerald and diamond bracelet and an emerald and diamond brooch, which were also included in this sale.

A year after her death a major part of her collection was sold at auction. The majority of the jewels were small, sentimental pieces, many reflecting her love of the countryside and country pursuits. Bejeweled snowdrops, pansies, foliage, ladybirds, swallows and squirrels, to name but a few, formed brooches and pins, as indeed did several horseshoe motifs. The sapphire, crystal and diamond 'running fox' brooch that she had received as a wedding present was also included. Her abiding interest in the Girl Guides movement (she had been the supreme 'Brown Owl') may account for the many owl jewels in her collection; they included a delightful cabochon emerald and rose diamond brooch by Cartier.

Towards the end of the sale came the important jewels. There was an early 20th-century sapphire and diamond brooch of negligé design, the triangular surmount set with a larger oval diamond within a border of cushion-shaped diamonds. The two sapphire briolette pendants were supported by sapphire and diamond cluster motifs and tapered links, and it was an extremely elegant jewel. There was an emerald and diamond brooch/pendant, dating from the early 20th century, in a shield-shaped design of looped scroll- and- bud motifs set with brilliant-cut diamonds and a step-cut emerald, supporting a pear-shaped emerald and diamond drop. This was indeed the centrepiece of the tiara that she had received as a wedding gift from the V.A.D.

As well as an important diamond *rivière* of 38 brilliant-cut stones, there was a beautiful diamond tiara, very similar to the King George III fringed tiara in the Royal Collection. This stylish form of tiara 'russe', which could also be worn as a necklace, was very fashionable during the 19th century and is still a royal favourite today.

The third memorable sale, held in October 1970, included several highly personal pieces, including a very fine diamond- set star of the Dame Grand Cross of the Order of the British Empire and two well-made regimental brooches, one of the Royal Scots, and the other from the Royal Corps of Signals. From the Art Deco period, and also the period of her early marriage, there were several diamond brooches, one by Cartier, as well as bracelets in rubies, sapphires and diamonds.

There were also some delightful antique jewels, such as a highly sentimental diamond necklet, composed of five diamond and rose diamond star clusters, alternating with lozenge and crescent motifs. This was the same necklet that her mother, Queen Mary, wore for her coming-out ball, along with the requisite Prince of Wales feathers. This, together with a diamond bracelet of foliate motifs with a star centre, dated from the early 19th century.

There was a lovely diamond and pearl brooch which she wore on her wedding day and the attractive pearl and diamond tassel which she probably received as a present from her aunt Princess Victoria. One of her wedding presents, the diamond pendant and necklace she received from the City of London, was also in the sale.

One of the most beautiful jewels that was offered had belonged to Queen Victoria. It was designed as a graduated row of sapphire and diamond clusters, originally supporting a sapphire pendant. The Princess Royal had lent both this necklace

A photograph of the young Princess May of Teck, the future Queen Mary, in her coming-out gown and feathers, wearing the diamond necklace with the pearl and diamond brooch/pendant attached. *Suzy Menkes*

A pearl and diamond tassel, which the Princess Royal in seen wearing with a pearl necklace in the early years of her marriage. She is with her dog 'Happy'. *Christie's, London; Hulton Getty*

(Below) An important diadem of scroll, palmette and cluster design. The three large clusters were detachable and the Princess Royal could replace them with her sapphire and diamond cluster brooch and two sapphire and diamond cluster motifs from her necklace/corsage ornament. *Christie's, London*

and her diamond pendant and necklace for an exhibition of antique and contemporary jewels held in London in 1953.

In all there were three diamond tiaras in this collection. The most delicate dated from about 1920 and had a large butterfly as the central design, the tapered sides pierced with flowerhead, foliate and scroll motifs. Another was designed as a row of scroll motifs surmounted by a single row of larger cushion-shaped stones, dating from the 19th century. The most impressive and important of these three was a diadem in a sumptuous design of scroll, palmette and cluster motifs, created in the late 19th century. She wore this tiara for many State occasions and official functions. The three larger clusters could be detached, and she often substituted the central cluster with the large sapphire and diamond brooch.

The jewels which have been sold from the collection of the Princess Royal are historically important in their own right as well as fitting to their royal status: several of the jewels had been worn by at least two Queens of England. However, some of the less important jewels gave a wonderful insight into the life and loves of a very private but much admired Princess.

(Opposite) Queen Alexandra seated between two of her daughters, Princess Louise and Princess Victoria. Princess Victoria is wearing the pearl and diamond tassel and pearl necklace that she gave to her niece, the Princess Royal, probably as a wedding present. *Hulton Getty*

The Princes
von Thurn und Taxis

In November 1992, two years after the death of Johannes, 11th Prince von Thurn und Taxis, an amazing selection of the family jewelry collection came up for sale. As the Prince's premature death left a young widow and a nine-year-old heir, a reorganization of the family affairs became a necessity. Princess Gloria, the widow, instructed the sale of various items of silver, objets de vertu and jewelry which represented only a small part of the family's extensive collections, and the auction was held in Geneva. A year later, an additional sale took place at Schloss St Emmeram, the family residence in Regensburg. This enormous auction was held over a period of ten consecutive days and included many items from the castle, as well as wine from the cellars and a few more jewels. It was the 1992 sale, however, which comprised over 150 pieces of jewelry, including some of the most sumptuous and creative jewels of the 18th and 19th centuries. In many cases the exceptional size of these dazzling jewels was extraordinary.

The prominence and wealth of the house of Thurn und Taxis had their beginnings in the late 15th century with Francisco de Tasso (Franz von Taxis), one of four brothers from Bergamo in Northern Italy who ran an official postal service covering the dominions of the expanding Holy Roman Empire. By far the most enterprising of the four brothers, Francisco left Italy for Brussels and, after extending his Imperial postal operations to incorporate services to the French King and the Spanish Court, eventually became Master General of the Posts to the Holy Roman Empire. The horn of the Taxis courier became the familiar symbol of a postal system which spread throughout Europe.

In 1608 Francisco's grandson Leonhard (1521-1612) was given the title of Count of the Empire. Upon authorization in 1650 by Philip VI of Spain and Emperor Ferdinand II, the family began to use the title of Thurn und Taxis. They continued to receive more exalted titles and by the late 18th century were living in splendour and high style. In 1775 Carl Anselm, 4th Prince von Thurn und Taxis (1733-1805), became a Knight of the Order of the Golden Fleece. The Order had been founded in Bruges by Philip the Good, Duke of Burgundy, in commem-oration of his marriage in 1429 to the Infanta Isabelle, daughter of Kind John I of Portugal. Jason and the Argonauts are the legendary inspiration for the design of the Order and their courageous exploits were meant as heroic examples to the chosen Knights.

In the Thurn und Taxis jewelry collection there were nine pieces which had originally formed integral parts of the neck badges of the Austrian Order of the Golden Fleece and which would have been worn by Prince Carl Anselm. In all but one case, however, they had been

Princess Margarete von Thurn und Taxis in court dress wearing her emerald and diamond jewels. The stomacher and choker, together with her string of pearls, were included in the 1992 auction. *Fürstliches Zentralarchiv, Regensburg*

A rare gold and diamond 18th-century pendant badge from a jewel of the Austrian Order of the Golden Fleece.

(Below) The yellow gold and diamond jewel of the Austrian Order of the Golden Fleece, c. 1800, is the neck badge in its complete form. The Golden Fleece is supported by a middle section of radiating flames with a large cluster surmount.

(Above and opposite) In 1775 Prince Carl Anselm became a Knight of the Order of the Golden Fleece and several of these jewels were made especially for him. This dazzling collection of jewels were all originally integral sections of the Neck Badge of the Austrian Order of the Golden Fleece. They date from the last quarter of the 18th century to the early part of the 19th. At a later date the Golden Fleeces were removed and the jewels were converted to brooches. The examples here are set with various gems, including garnet, topaz, citrine, amethyst, green beryl and diamonds. *Sotheby's, Geneva*

adapted at a later date to form brooches, a pendant and a bracelet. The jeweled Order which had remained unaltered was highly impressive and dated from around 1800. The flames, the fleece and the cluster surmount were set throughout with diamonds, with a large cushion-shaped diamond of yellow tint set at the centre. Among the earlier and most skilfully executed pieces in this group of Orders was a rare gold and diamond pendant badge made during the second half of the 18th Century. This piece was so exquisitely chased and carved that it could almost have been the fabled golden fleece itself. Another example from a similar date was an impressive amethyst and diamond brooch in the form of the middle and upper section of the neck badge of the Austrian Order. The radiating diamond set flames are centred by a cushion-shaped amethyst and support a large detachable amethyst and diamond drop. This jewel, according to the Thurn und Taxis archives, had indeed been made for Carl Anselm soon after he was made a Knight of the Order.

In the 19th century, male members of the family married into European royal houses; the two wives who had perhaps the greatest influence on the jewelry collection were Helene, Duchess in Bavaria, the elder sister of Empress Elisabeth of Austria, who married prince Maximilian Anton von Thurn und Taxis in 1858; and Margarete, Archduchess of Austria and Princess of Hungary and Bohemia, who married Prince Albert VIII of Thurn und Taxis in 1890.

On her marriage, Helene was given as a wedding present from Queen Elise of Prussia a set of three glorious opal and diamond brooches. Made in the 1850s, each was in the design of foliate scrolls and berries; worn as shoulder brooches, they were the height of fashion at that time. Mounted in silver and gold, they could also be combined to form a single corsage ornament.

When Margarete married Prince Albert, the second son of Maximilian, he gave her among his wedding presents two of the most important jewels to be added to the already impressive family collection. The first was a stunning pearl and diamond *devant de corsage*, of French origin and dating from the 1850s, set with three large pearls within foliate scroll borders of diamonds and supporting five large pear-shaped pearl drops.

The other gift was justifiably catalogued at the time of the sale as 'Fine and Historically Important' and was perhaps the most desirable jewel in the collection. It had been part of the French Crown Jewels and was known as the Empress Eugénie tiara. Created in 1853 by Gabriel Lemonnier using precious stones and pearls from the French State Treasury, it was commissioned by Napoleon III for his bride Eugénie Maria de Montijo de Guzmán, Comtesse de Teba. This

In this 1855 portrait of Empress Eugénie of France by Franz Xaver Winterhalter, she is wearing the pearl and diamond tiara which entered the Thurn und Taxis collection towards the end of the 19th century. *Musée de Versailles*

(Opposite) Princess Margarete von Thurn und Taxis wearing the French pearl and diamond *devant de corsage*, the Empress Eugénie tiara and several of her pearl necklaces. *Fürstliches Zentralarchiv, Regensburg*

Marie Regina 1899.

The Empress Eugénie tiara, by Gabriel Lemonnier, 1853, and the pearl and diamond mid-19th-century *devant de corsage* that Prince Albert von Thurn und Taxis gave to Princess Margarete as a wedding present in 1889. *Sotheby's, Geneva*

(Opposite) This diamond girdle with a detachable bow brooch, c. 1890, is a magnificent jewel of extraordinary size and intricate workmanship. *Sotheby's, Geneva*

Prince Johannes and Princess Gloria von Thurn und Taxis on their wedding day in Regensburg in 1980. Princess Gloria is wearing the Empress Eugénie tiara and the pearl and diamond *devant de corsage*. *Fürstliches Zentralarchiv, Regensburg*

jewel combines history, superb design, exceptional pearls and skilled craftsmanship. In 1887, when the republican French government decided to sell the Crown Jewels, the tiara was erroneously dated 1820 and attributed to Bapst, substantiating the false legend that it had once belonged to Marie Antoinette. It may have been this false attribution that convinced Prince Albert that it was indeed the perfect wedding present for his Austrian bride. (Having been bought by the Friends of the Louvre, it is now housed in that museum.)

Princess Margarete is often portrayed wearing the tiara along with many other jewels from the collection. One which was undoubtedly a great favourite with her was the very simple but sentimental baroque pearl and gem-set acrostic pendant, often worn together with several rows of pearls. The single large baroque pearl is in the shape of the Madonna and Child and the first letter of each of the various gemstones by which it is surrounded spells out the words: MARIA MATER DEI.

Another impressive jewel which was probably made for her was a diamond girdle and bow brooch. Again it is the sheer size and opulence of the piece that first strike the eye. Created around 1890 when such ornaments were in fashion, the girdle is a wide band decorated with diamond flowers and scrolled foliage which supports a detachable ribbon bow of lace-like appearance.

According to an account, written by one of their descendants, of the courtly life led by Prince Albert and Princess Margarete, much of their time was filled with the pursuit of country sports, attending to their religious and material duties and appearing at social gatherings, at which the women were always expected to show off their jewels. The selection of their jewels from the 19th century was extensive and covered nearly every style and period. The variety of gemstones used was also phenomenal, but it was the diamond jewels which were the most astounding.

Apart from the superb pieces already mentioned there were other equally impressive diamond jewels. These included three tiaras. The 'Empire Diadem' was in a design of palmettes and foliate scroll motifs set with pear- and cushion-shaped stones, typical of the 1820s, and had belonged to Princess Therese von Thurn und Taxis (1773-1839). A wonderful crescent of paired volutes and foliage capped by detachable pear-shaped cluster drops, set with cushion-shaped diamonds, was named the 'Kleines Diadem'; this too had belonged to Therese and was of a similar date to the 'Empire Diadem'. The third, known as the 'Fuchsien Diadem' and dating from around 1845, was a great tribute to naturalism. The sprays of fuchsias and eglantines were set throughout with rose and cushion-shaped diamonds.

There were also a number of 19th-century diamond necklaces, many of which are seen in portraits of Princess Margarete. Among the most impressive was one designed as four *rivières* of cushion-shaped stones, graduated in size from the front and on a large diamond clasp, and another designed as a '*collier de chien*' with a matching pair of bracelets which were set respectively with nine and seven rows of diamonds.

The Thurn und Taxis desire to collect fine jewelry did not come to an end with the turn of the century; indeed, some of the finest pieces were added by the Princes in the 20th century. After Prince Johannes von Thurn und Taxis married the beautiful Mariae Gloria Countess von Schönburg-Glauchau, whose aristocratic roots dated back to the 12th century, they enjoyed a glamorous social lifestyle for a number of years. Although the family jewelry collection was already extensive, Prince Johannes bought many more splendid jewels for his wife to wear, some of them with equally important historical provenances. In 1982, for example, he acquired an emerald and diamond corsage ornament from a sale in Geneva. This impressive jewel dated from the 1830s and had been owned by Elizabeth (1815-85), Princess Karl of Hesse, of the Prussian royal family and first cousin to the King. Her husband was brother and heir to the Grand Duke of Hesse-Darmstadt, and their son Ludwig (later the Grand Duke Ludwig IV of Hesse and the Rhine) had married Princess Alice, Queen Victoria's second daughter, in 1862. Thus there were family connections which Prince Johannes must have found as captivating as the brooch. In the same sale he bought for Princess Gloria a pair of ruby and diamond pendent earrings which had once belonged to his ancestor Princess Margarete von Thurn und Taxis. The catalogue noted that 'by tradition' these jewels had been given by King Louis Philippe (1773-1850) to his youngest daughter Princess Clementine d'Orléans, who was the grandmother of Princess Margarete.

Prince Johannes was known to be particularly fascinated by India and its ancient culture. In April 1980, a month before their marriage, he bought at an auction in New York a particularly spectacular Guluband made in Rajastan in the late 18th or early 19th century. The Guluband, or bridal necklace, was set with rose diamonds, pearls and emerald bead drops and decorated on both the front and the back with enamel.

He also recognized his wife's love of contemporary art when he bought her 20th-century jewels. Among the most important was a sapphire and diamond bracelet by Cartier, dating from the mid-'30s, which he bought at auction in Geneva in 1984. The centre was set with five step-cut sapphires between two rows of baguette diamonds, the tapered sides set with similarly cut diamonds. There were other jewels of the period, which included a gold, pearl and diamond bracelet by David Webb, purchased at auction, and a gold and gem-set parure by Lalaounis.

The Thurn und Taxis collection had been built up over many years, indeed centuries, and was a tribute to the family's sense of style and desire for quality. Piece by piece, it traced not only the family's own remarkable history, but that of other European royal houses.

An emerald and diamond stomacher brooch/pendant, c. 1860. The central cluster could be detached to form a smaller brooch or clasp. *Sotheby's, Geneva*

An impressive 19th-century diamond necklace, designed as four *rivières* of cushion-shaped stones graduated in size from the centre. *Sotheby's, Geneva*

(Below) A baroque pearl and gem-set acrostic pendant, 19th century, the border set with coloured stones, the first letter of each forming the words: MARIA MATER DEI. *Sotheby's, Geneva*

(Opposite) A diamond corsage ornament, c. 1830, of flowerhead and foliate design. All the drops were detachable and the lateral scrolls detached to form a smaller brooch. (Below) An early 19th-century diamond necklace designed as three chains of rectangular, lozenge-shaped and oval linking respectively, set throughout with cushion-shaped stones, the centre designed as a large sunburst motif. From the extra links visible on the larger cluster motifs and clasp it is evident that the necklace has been subject to alterations but in its present form is a truly magnificent jewel. *Sotheby's, Geneva; Private collection*

The Duchess of Windsor

It is difficult to compare the Duchess of Windsor's jewelry collection with any other. The eventual sale of the collection was unique: not only were these jewels that had been chosen by a King to give to the woman he loved and gave up his throne for, but they also included, in their own right, some of the most important examples of the art and creativity of 20th-century jewelers.

Throughout the Prince of Wales's courtship of Wallis Warfield Simpson and during their married life as well, they shared a passion for jewelry, commissioning a series of fabulous creations from some of the finest jewelers of the time. Before she died in 1986, the Duchess of Windsor left instructions that her collection of jewelry was to be sold after her death and all the proceeds to be donated to the Pasteur Institute in Paris, as a token of her gratitude to the people of France for all the kindness they had shown her and her husband.

'The Jewels of the Duchess of Windsor' were offered for auction in Geneva in April 1987, giving the world a fascinating insight into the life and style of the Windsors. For the social and the jewelry historian, the sale proved irresistible, as many of the pieces bore inscriptions which were usually dated and often of a rather intimate nature. For the jewelry connoisseur it was manna, for the jewels represented some of the finest designs of the greatest 20th-century jewelers, with a strong emphasis on work of the 1930s and '40s. For the public in general, it was a rare chance to see the jewels which had been worn by a woman who had been so notorious in her relations with King Edward VII.

To his people the Prince of Wales had been the epitome of a Prince Charming, surrounded by historic and important works of art which instilled in him a taste for beautiful objects, and in particular jewelry. Many of the pieces he commissioned for Wallis were based on his own ideas, and he spent many pleasurable hours with the designers, offering his suggestions. It was then up to her to have a suitable dress designed to complement the jewel. The uniting of two such stylish people with similar tastes resulted in distinctive collections, not only of jewelry but also of furniture and works of art.

Though Bessie Wallis Warfield's birth date is subject to some debate, it is generally agreed as 19 June 1896. Because of her father's death when he was only 26, her mother was to rely heavily on her brother-in-law Solomon Warfield and her own sister Bessie Merriman for financial support. Aunt Bessie continued this support for Wallis throughout her life.

When Wallis met Edward for the first time in January 1931 she was already into her second marriage; her first, to an American naval aviator, Earl Winfield Spencer, had ended in divorce in 1927; in November 1928 in London, she married Ernest Simpson. She loved the capital's

The Duchess of Windsor photographed by Cecil Beaton at the Château de Candé, France, during the Christmas period of 1936. She is wearing her invisibly set ruby and diamond clip designed as two *'feuilles de noux'* and her ruby and diamond bracelet, both made by Van Cleef & Arpels in 1936. She is also wearing her emerald engagement ring and her diamond cross bracelet by Cartier. The ruby and diamond earrings which she is wearing are in their original form. *Sotheby's, London (Cecil Beaton Archive)*

(Overleaf two pages) Some major pieces from the Duchess of Windsor's collection, including several of her 'Great Cat' jewels by Cartier, Paris; the 'McLean' diamond ring; the ruby and diamond necklace, bracelet and clip by Van Cleef & Arpels; and the emerald, ruby and diamond heart-shaped brooch by Cartier made to commemorate the Windsors' twentieth wedding anniversary. *Sotheby's, Geneva*

social lifestyle with its glamorous social occasions and became a popular hostess, admired for her sense of style and elegance. By the end of 1931, she had not only been presented at Court but had also met the Prince of Wales, who wrote later that this meeting was 'destined to change the whole course of my life.'

The earliest dated inscription was found on a necklet of twelve charms. A cushion-shaped plaque decorated with a red enamel figure 3 was dated on the reverse: 9/4/34 march 12th 1934 14/5/34. It has not been possible to match these dates to particular occasions, but the other charms on the necklet record weekends at Fort Belvedere in Windsor, holidays together, often with Aunt Bessie and other friends, and events mentioned in letters and diaries. The necklet was a simple but highly personal piece, and when the original estimate of SF2,000-3,000 was surpassed at the 1987 sale by a bid of SF198,000, it became obvious that buyers were willing to pay a high price for what they regarded as a piece of history.

The next significant dates are to be found on a gold Latin cross pendant that Wallis gave to the Prince on ?5.11.34 and on a similar platinum Latin cross pendant given to Wallis which is inscribed and dated: 'WE are too [sic] 25.XI-34.' It was catalogued as 'a punning allusion to Mrs Simpson and the Prince of Wales, (WE) feelings for one another; WE (Wallis and Edward) are also in love, and We two are in love'. Another possible meaning was ascribed to the fact that the Prince's brother, the Duke of Kent, was to be married a few days later, on 29 November 1934, to Princess Marina of Greece.

The platinum Latin cross pendant was one of nine other similar crosses, the others all gem-set, which were attached to a diamond bracelet made by Cartier in 1935. Each had interesting and sometimes amusing inscriptions. There was one commemorating her appendicitis operation in 1944; another, inscribed 'God save the King for Wallis 16.VII.36', was a reminder of the day an Irish journalist attempted to shoot the King. There was also a cross inscribed for the marriage; Wallis is seen wearing it in the wedding portraits taken by Cecil Beaton. Again it was a jewel of great personal significance as well as enormous charm.

The gifts continued during the courtship with an impressive emerald and diamond bracelet, which Edward gave her for Christmas 1935. She gave him in return a gold cigarette case by Cartier, which was engraved with a map focussing on Europe and North Africa with routes applied in enamel to show their various holidays together and a gemstone set at the various meaningful locations. One of the trips was aboard Daisy Fellowes's yacht, the *Sister Anne*, which she had generously lent them for cruising. Christmas 1935 was distressing for them both: they were unable to spend time together because of the gravity of George V's illness. On 20 January 1936 the King died and Edward's life changed.

Wallis and Ernest Simpson spent the weekend of 27 March at Fort Belvedere with Edward and some other guests. Edward was finding it difficult to carry out his new royal duties and ensure that he spent as much time as he wished with Wallis. For each of them it was a time of great uncertainty. His present at this time was given with a message of both love and reassurance. It was an impressive ruby and diamond bracelet by Van Cleef & Arpels, created by one of their best Paris designers, René-Sim Lacaze: a simple design but extremely elegant and set with vibrant Burmese rubies. The clasp was inscribed, 'Hold Tight 27.III.36'. It was also around this time that the King informed Ernest Simpson that he wished him to seek a divorce from Wallis.

On an earlier gift from Wallis to Edward in 1935 she had used the same phrase, 'Hold Tight', and on this diamond dress suite she had also added the date of her birthday to the cufflinks. This had obviously proved an excellent reminder, as on her fortieth birthday on 19 June 1936 she received from him a splendid necklace of Burmese rubies and diamonds by Van Cleef & Arpels. This original design can be seen in contemporary photographs of the Duchess and in the firm's archives, but when it came to auction it was in a completely different style. She was a woman who not only kept up with fashion but virtually led it. The original design of her necklace was soon outdated, and in 1939 Lacaze was commissioned to redesign the jewel. The creation he produced was stunning: the rubies and diamonds were mounted as an *entrelac-de-ruban* collar supporting a detachable tassel, a few stones were added and the result was a masterpiece of the jeweler's craft. Wallis wore it with a matching pair of earrings which had also been updated from their original 1936 design; indeed, when they appeared in the auction they had been altered yet again. In 1965 Cartier had remounted them as stylized flowerhead clusters.

During that summer there was incessant discussion regarding their future together. The die was cast on 27 October, when her divorce proceedings were heard in Ipswich. This date was also the one they chose for their engagement and the King gave his future bride an exquisite ring to celebrate the occasion. An exceptionally fine Colombian emerald of 19.77cts was bought from Cartier and mounted in a plain platinum shank with the inscription: 'We are ours now 27.X.36', a simple but bold statement. According to an entry in Marie Belloc Lowndes's diary, the emerald had been acquired by Cartier in Baghdad, but was originally double the size. Cartier decided that the market for such a gem was limited and had it cut into two stones. One was bought by an American millionaire and the other by the King. However, it is also possible that this stone came from the magnificent emerald and diamond *sautoir* once owned by Nancy Leeds of which some of the emeralds had come from the Sultan of Turkey; whatever its origins, the stone was superb. Once again, Wallis had the stone remounted to keep abreast of changing fashions and the ring as auctioned was in a 1958

A studio portrait of the Duchess of Windsor by Dorothy Wilding in 1950. She is wearing her emerald bead and diamond necklace/tiara by Cartier, Paris, as a head ornament, as well as several of her other important jewels: her emerald engagement ring by Cartier, the emerald and diamond bracelet (French, 1935) which was inscribed and dated: W-25.XII.35-D, and the diamond bracelet as it was before being remounted by Cartier in the 1960s. *The National Portrait Gallery*

An emerald bead and diamond necklace that was made for stock by Cartier, Paris, in 1949. The Duchess's was made the same year with her own emeralds, the diamond supplied by Cartier. Hers was mounted with a special fitting which enabled her to wear it also as a diadem. *Cartier Ltd (Paris)*

A gold, turquoise, amethyst and diamond bib necklace, by Cartier, Paris, 1947, the front of lattice design set with step-cut amethysts, brilliant-cut diamonds and turquoises, and with a larger heart-shaped amethyst at the centre. The back was of gold 'Prince of Wales' linking. She also had a matching pair of earrings, a brooch, a bracelet and a ring. *Sotheby's, Geneva*

An emerald and rose diamond necklace which was sold to the Windsors by Harry Winston in 1956. It was possible to adapt and wear this exotic Indian necklace in three different ways: as one single row as illustrated here; divided and worn as a two-row choker (see photograph p.127 above middle); or as a bib necklace, the two rows connected at the back by two chains of gold 'Prince of Wales' linking. In 1957 she had a pair of gold, emerald bead and rose diamond earrings of Indian inspiration mounted by Cartier to wear with this necklace, and these were sold in the 1987 auction. *Christie's, New York*

(Opposite) A spectacular sapphire and diamond necklace by Cartier, Paris, c.1940. The front is designed as nine articulated flowerhead clusters set with cabochon sapphires and circular-cut diamonds and supporting a fringe of diamond dart-shaped motifs, the back designed as two chains of sapphire beads. At a later date she had a pair of sapphire bead and diamond creole earrings made by Cartier to match this necklace. *Sotheby's, Geneva*

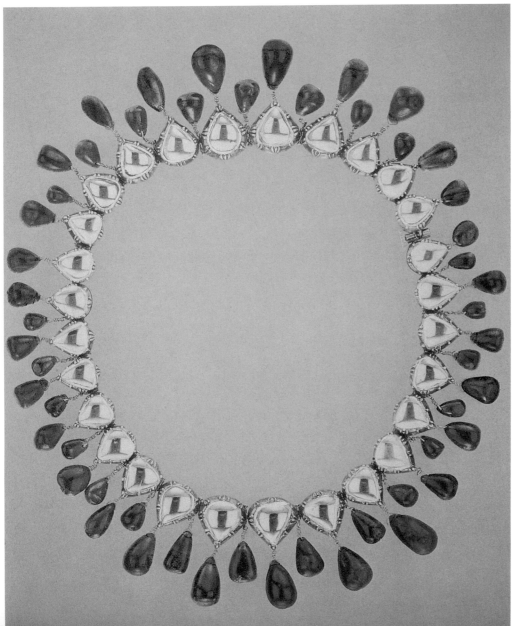

diamond setting by Cartier, Paris. She did, however, keep the original setting with its significant inscription.

By December the British public finally became aware of the Wallis-Edward liaison, and after months of meetings with his advisers and Government officials, the King delivered his abdication speech on 10 December. Wallis had already left England to stay with friends in France. Edward soon followed, but because of the sensitivity of the situation he headed for Austria, where he was the guest of Baron Eugène de Rothschild and his American wife Kitty at Schloss Enzesfeld. Once again Edward and Wallis had to spend Christmas apart, and Edward sent Wallis another jewel by Lacaze in the form of a ruby and diamond clip designed as two *feuilles de houx* (holly leaves). The stones were 'invisibly set', a new technique for which Van Cleef & Arpels are now famous. This is one of the best-known examples: the stones are held by small grooves on their pavilions and, as all this work is at the back of the jewel, no metal can be seen from the front.

There were several other sentimental gifts during these enforced months of separation, culminating in the magnificent sapphire and diamond *jar-retière* bracelet by Van Cleef & Arpels, which Lacaze designed to celebrate the finalizing of their marriage contract according to French law on 18 May 1937. The bracelet was designed as a band of baguette and circular-cut diamonds with a large central clasp of stylized bow shape invisibly set with cushion-shaped sapphires. The wedding took place on 3 June at the Château de Candé in France.

The following year the now Duke of Windsor gave his bride a spectacular ruby and diamond hinged penannular bangle by Cartier, Paris, inscribed: 'For our first anniversary of June third'. The two large terminals were set with cushion-shaped Burmese rubies in raised collets which were pavé-set all over with brilliant-cut diamonds. These terminals had originally been set as the centre of a necklace forming a crossover clasp. The same concept was used in a wonderful double-leaf necklace that she wore on many occasions, often together with the ruby bangle.

Twenty years later the Duke asked Cartier to make a delightful heart-shaped brooch applied with the initials W.E. to mark their anniversary.

Throughout their married life, the couple continued to amass an extremely interesting collection of jewel among them an array of 'great cats' jewels inspired by Jeanne Toussaint, who had worked with Cartier since 1915. She was nicknamed 'The Panther' by her close companion Louis Cartier because of her passion for all animals, and in particular panthers, whose skins adorned the floors of her apartment. She worked closely with Cartier's designer Peter Lemarchand and together they created the 'great cat menagerie'. The Windsors acquired their first panther clip in 1948. A realistic gold panther decorated with black enamel and crouched on a large cabochon emerald, it was Cartier's first fully three-dimensional cat jewel.

In 1946 the Windsors had returned to England for a private visit and were staying with Lord Dudley at Ednam Lodge in Berkshire, where a burglar stole all the jewels Wallis had brought with her. There has always been a certain amount of controversy as to the extent of her loss but from all accounts it was small, for the bulk of her collection had remained in France. The panther clip was their first commission from Cartier after this unhappy event. For nearly two decades the Windsors continued to purchase these magnificent cats. In 1949 they acquired a sapphire and diamond clip designed as a panther seated on a large cabochon sapphire, and in 1952 an onyx and diamond panther bracelet, though the matching clip was not bought until 1966. As with many of these jewels, not only was the cat's body completely flexible but its neck was mounted in such a fashion that the angle of the head could be altered at whim. An onyx and fancy yellow diamond tiger bracelet was acquired in 1956 and the matching clip in 1959. Her cat acquisition in 1954 was somewhat more unusual as it was a pair of lorgnettes designed as a tiger with a raised paw. In every case the design and workmanship were exquisite, giving these jungle cats power and beauty along with a strong feeling of movement.

Jeanne Toussaint was also responsible for the splendid flamingo clip the Duchess bought in 1940. From Cartier's archives it is evident that to make this jewel she had several of her own pieces unmounted so that the stones could be re-used in this clip.

In 1945 Cartier designed a gold and gem-set bib necklace, again remounting many of the Duchess's unused jewels. Indian in inspiration, this necklace looked particularly attractive on the Duchess's petite frame. One especially noteworthy example, again of Indian inspiration, was designed as two rows of ruby beads fastened by a gold clasp encrusted with diamonds, emeralds and rubies. The two long gold chains

Two brooches by Cartier, Paris, dating
from the 1930s. One is a 20 pesos
gold coin surrounded and surmounted
by emeralds, rubies and diamonds
and the other is a medallion of the
Virgin set with diamonds. The
Duchess is photographed by Cecil
Beaton wearing these brooches as
well as her Mabe pearl and diamond
earclips created by Verdura in the
1950s. *Sotheby's, Geneva; Sotheby's,
London (Cecil Beaton Archive)*

A pair of fancy yellow diamond
earclips mounted by Cartier, Paris, in
1968. The pear-shaped stones
weighed 8.13cts and 8.01cts
respectively and the two larger
brilliant-cut diamonds weighed
5.17cts and 5.18cts. These stones
had originally been purchased from
Harry Winston mounted as pendent
earrings to match the two fancy yellow
diamond lapel clips which he had sold
to the Windsors in 1948. *Sotheby's,
Geneva*

that hung over her shoulders supported two large spheres set with cabochon emeralds and ruby beads. When this jewel was later altered by Cartier, the clasp and the spheres became an elegant brooch and the ruby beads were fashioned into dramatic creole earrings. The brooch did not appear in the 1987 auction, but six years later it was sold in New York as the property of 'a member of a European Royal House'.

The only jewel the Duke is known to have received from his mother, Queen Mary, was a single row necklace of twenty-eight pearls. They were remounted by Cartier, Paris, and the Duchess often chose to wear them with the large pearl and diamond pendant acquired from Cartier in 1950. Among her other pearl jewels were an attractive pair of pearl and diamond earrings made by Van Cleef & Arpels in 1957 and bought by the Windsors the next year. They were set with a large black and a large white pearl, each within borders of diamonds. The Windsors also patronized designers such as Suzanne Belperron, Verdura, Seaman Schepps and David Webb. The latter created for her his own version of the 'jungle jewels'. These came in the form of delightful gem-set frogs decorated with enamel and set with diamonds and cabochon rubies. He also cleverly mounted the shells of Cuban tree snails (which the Duchess had collected on her travels) as earclips – as did the French jewelers Darde & Fils.

Harry Winston played an important part in adding some fine gemstones to the Windsors' collection. The pair of fancy yellow diamonds which he sold to them in 1948 were superb. They weighed 40.81cts and 52.13cts, were well-matched pear-shaped stones, and were mounted as lapel clips. He probably also supplied them with the two pear-shaped and the two brilliant-cut yellow diamonds that Cartier remounted for the Duchess as earrings in 1968.

In 1953 he acquired ftrom the Maharajah of Baroda a pair of cabochon emerald and diamond anklets from which he created a necklace. This was sold to the Windsors in 1956 with unfortunate consequences. The Duchess wore the necklace at a ball in Paris in 1957 which was also attended by the Maharani of Baroda. The necklace caused a stir and when asked for ·her opinion of the jewel, the Marahani, though agreeing on its beauty, added 'those emeralds used to be one of my anklets'.

This did not amuse the Duchess who seldom wore it again; in 1960 she exchanged it for another jewel with the proviso that Harry Winston would not sell the anklet to anyone who might have known about her brief ownership of it. The jewel that she now acquired was a very fine 48.95cts pear-shaped emerald, which had once belonged to King Alfonso XIII of Spain, mounted with diamonds as a pendant.

(Overleaf, p. 128) A 1939 Cecil Beaton photograph of the Duchess of Windsor, in which she is wearing her sapphire and diamond 'Contract' bracelet, her emerald engagement ring, a diamond head ornament, diamond earrings and an emerald and diamond brooch. This brooch is set with five pear-shaped emeralds in a stylized flowerhead design. It is probable that this brooch together with the double leaf diamond necklace, were unmounted in 1960 by Cartier to create her magnificent emerald necklace. *Sotheby's, London (Cecil Beaton Archive)*

The emerald and diamond engagement ring by Cartier, an emerald and diamond bracelet (French, 1935), and a diamond brooch by Harry Winston, New York. *Sotheby's, Geneva*

The emerald and diamond necklace mounted by Cartier, Paris, 1960, together with the emerald and diamond pendant created in the same year by Harry Winston. This pendant is set with a 48.95cts emerald that had once belonged to King Alfonso XIII of Spain. *Sotheby's, Geneva*

The Duchess of Windsor arriving at the Grand Bal held at the 'Galerie de l'Orangerie de Versailles' in June 1953. She is wearing the gold, turquoise, amethyst and diamond bib necklace by Cartier, Paris, and matching earclips and ring. Her dress was created by Dior to match these jewels. *Roger Viollet*

At the British Fashion Gala in Biarritz in 1959, the Duchess is wearing the emerald and rose diamond Indian necklace as a double-row choker, together with her Cartier emerald bead and rose diamond earclips. *Sygma-Keystone*

The Duchess of Windsor with the Baron de Chabrol, photographed by Cecil Beaton. She is wearing the pearl necklace which the Duke inherited from Queen Mary, the fancy yellow diamond pendent earrings by Harry Winston before they were remounted by Cartier, Paris, in 1968, and a pair of fancy yellow diamond lapel clips, also by Harry Winston, New York. *Sotheby's, London (Cecil Beaton Archive)*

The Duke and Duchess of Windsor in December 1955 dancing at the Lido, the Champs-Elysée cabaret in Paris. The Duchess is wearing her Van Cleef & Arpels invisibly set ruby and diamond foliate earclips, her sapphire, ruby and diamond hinged bangle designed as a peacock's feather by Cartier, Paris, 1946, her ruby bead, emerald and diamond tasselled necklace of Indian inspiration by Cartier, and her pearl necklace. Her evening gown is of brocaded silk, the pale celadon ground woven with gold, silver, blue, scarlet and purple flowers and scrolls. This stunning dress was included in the auction of the Windsors' private collections which took place in New York in 1998. *Hulton Getty*

The 'McLean' diamond was probably Harry Winston's star contribution to the Windsors' collection. It was a cushion-shaped stone weighing 31.26cts and of the finest 'D' colour, from the old Golconda mines in India. It had been owned previously by Evelyn Walsh McLean, the celebrated Washington hostess and avid jewelry collector. She owned the fabulous blue diamond known as the 'Hope', as well as two other important diamonds called the 'Star of the East' and the 'Star of the South'. Such was her love of jewelry that in her autobiography she wrote, 'when I neglect to wear jewels, astute members of my family call in the doctors because it's a sign I'm becoming ill.' Harry Winston bought her jewelry collection in 1949, two years after her death, and in May 1950 the 'McLean' diamond was sold to the Windsors.

The total the Windsor jewels fetched at their auction was just over $31,000,000. The auctioneer, Nicholas Rayner, said at the time of the sale, 'The three elements of history, quality and design make the collection altogether unique.' It is remarkable and encouraging that these criteria achieved such phenomenal results, which are enabling the Pasteur Institute to carry out vital medical research into AIDS and cancer.

Countess Mona Bismarck

The collection of Mona Bismarck showed her love of diamonds, pearls, rubies and emeralds, as well as her devotion to the luxurious pursuits of life. Unlike many of her famous contemporaries, Mona had not come from a background of wealth or high social standing, but she did have both the beauty and the intelligence which enabled her to acquire them.

Born Mona Travis Strader in Louisville, Kentucky, in 1897, she had been twice married and divorced by the age of 27. The first marriage, to a wealthy businessman, Henry Schlesinger, prompted a move to Milwaukee, and she gave birth to a son, Robert. The second marriage, which ended in 1924, was to another extremely rich businessman, James Irving Bush.

After these two failures at marriage, Mona moved to New York, where she revelled in the world of high society. She soon met Harrison Williams, a leading industrialist who was thought to be one of the richest men in America, and in 1926 they were married. Mona was in her element in the sphere of fashionable glamour and wealth that she now inhabited. She was generally regarded as one of the most elegant and beautiful women of her times. The Williamses had grand residences in various locations in the USA as well as in Europe, all exquisitely furnished: Goyas and Bouchers graced their walls, the rooms were filled with priceless furniture, tasteful objets d'art were strewn on all available surfaces, and the gardens and flowers were glorious, especially at their villa on the island of Capri. They were a celebrated and much admired couple, whose circle included many of the best-known personalities from the worlds of politics, the arts and society. Mona was famous for her matchless sense of style and fashion, and she was a much sought-after subject for many of the most prominent photographers of the period, especially her great friend Cecil Beaton. His studio portraits of her were classical and inspired, often showing her dressed in creations by her favourite couturier, Cristobal Balenciaga. Informal photographs were equally revealing, reflecting her vivacious and animated character. Beaton once described her as 'one of the few outstanding beauties of the thirties... who represented the epitome of all that taste and luxury can bring to flower.'

After many years of illness, Harrison Williams died in 1953. A few years later Mona married Comte Edouard Bismarck, grandson of the Grand Chancellor, and Paris became their home. After his death in 1970, she married yet again and for the last time. Her marriage to Umberto de Martini ended after eight years in 1979. Mona died at the age of 86 in 1983, having enjoyed a long life full of glamour, style and the best that money could buy.

The auction of her jewels took place in Geneva on 13 May 1986, and although it included only 41 lots, a small proportion of her original collection, most of her major pieces were being offered. Like many of her contemporaries, she wore jewels that were constantly redesigned to keep up with the fashions of the time. In the numerous photographic portraits

Mrs Harrison Williams (later Countess Mona Bismarck), photographed by Cecil Beaton wearing her 19th-century enamel, pearl and diamond serpent necklace (p. 141).
Prince Henry of Hesse

Mona's two-row pearl necklace, together with matching pearl and diamond earrings, by Petochi. *Sotheby's, Geneva*

(Below) A jade and diamond bracelet dating from the early 1930s. The five rows of jade beads are connected at intervals by diamond rondels and on a large diamond clasp set with a jade carved in the form of a finger-citron with a small spider. *Sotheby's, Geneva*

(Opposite) An elegant carved emerald and diamond negligé brooch by Cartier, Paris, and an emerald and diamond bracelet. The two carved emerald drops from the brooch were originally mounted as clips and the central carved emerald rectangular plaque from the bracelet was formerly set as a ring. Mona Bismarck had these stones remounted to their present forms in the 1960s. The cabochon emerald and diamond earclips were created in the late '40s by Cartier, Paris. *Sotheby's, Geneva*

A stylish jade, onyx and ruby Art Deco brooch/pendant by Cartier, Paris. *Sotheby's, Geneva*

of her taken in the 1920s and '30s, especially those by Cecil Beaton, her beauty is enhanced by the stylish period jewels she is seen wearing; yet in the whole collection only a few Art Deco pieces survived. There was a chic brooch/pendant by Cartier in jade, onyx and rubies, reminiscent of the Oriental styles popular at that period. The circular centre was set with two carved jade leaves decorated with diamonds and mounted within a border of onyx, and the mitre-shaped sides were set with cabochon rubies. Another jewel which exuded Eastern flavour was her jade and diamond bracelet. Composed of five rows of jade beads, connected at intervals by diamond rondels, the diamond clasp was set at the centre with a jade plaque carved in the form of a finger-citron with a small spider. The Art Deco period, noted for its bold colour combinations, especially black- and- white, and its geometric designs is perfectly illustrated by her diamond and black bead bracelet.

A photograph of Mona published in 1938 shows her wearing emerald and diamond jewels dating from the 1920s: their style was soon outdated and she decided to have these jewels redesigned. The first to be altered was an emerald and diamond bangle. The central carved emerald and diamond flowerhead motif became the clasp of a bracelet strung with seven rows of natural pearls. In the 1960s the two carved emeralds, formerly set in two clips, were remounted as the drops for an extremely elegant brooch by Cartier, Paris. These pear-shaped emeralds, carved with flowerheads and foliage, were capped by diamonds and suspended from a ribbon bow of baguette and brilliant-cut diamonds.

In the same photograph Mona is wearing a large emerald ring, carved with motifs similar to those on the emerald drops. Again in the late 1960s she had this rectangular emerald remounted and set at the centre of a bracelet. It was mounted between two leaves pavé-set with diamonds and bordered by green enamel, and the back was composed of two rows of emeralds beads connected by diamond rondels, originally sections of another 1920s jewel.

Although Mona's jewelry collection reflected an apparent willingness to conform to the fashions of the day, it also showed that she had her own individual sense of style that surpassed all vagaries of fashion. Many of the most important jewels in this collection either originated in the 19th century or were created for her in that style. A stunning example was the diamond festoon necklace designed as a simple *rivière* of variously shaped old cut diamonds supporting detachable garlands and drops which were all mounted in silver collets backed by gold. This jewel, dating from the 19th century, had been subject to some later alterations, such as the addition of two diamond briolette drops and a

(Above) A pearl, carved emerald and diamond bracelet. The carved emerald and diamond flowerhead clasp was originally the centrepiece of a stylish bangle, as can be seen in the 1938 photograph of Mona Bismarck taken by Cecil Beaton for *Vogue* (opposite). Once again, this was one of the jewels that she had altered at a later date. In the photograph she is also wearing the carved emerald ring and the carved emerald drops in their original form as clips. *Sotheby's, Geneva; Vogue, The Condé Nast Publications Ltd*

(Left) A gold and diamond 'gourd' brooch designed as a sculptured matte-finish gold gourd with a diamond stem. This brooch is identical to one of the pair worn by Mona Bismarck when photographed for *Vogue* in 1936. These brooches are highly reminiscent of the style of René Boivin. In the same studio portrait she is also wearing her carved emerald ring and her jade and diamond bracelet. *Christie's, New York; Vogue, The Condé Nast Publications Ltd*

A magnificent diamond festoon necklace; a diamond *rivière* necklace by Cartier, Paris, together with diamond solitaire earclips and matching diamond bracelet; and an exquisite ruby and diamond necklace of foliate and cluster design. Each necklace shows Mona Bismarck's penchant for adding a stylish drop at the back. *Sotheby's, Geneva*

(Opposite) A pair of ruby and diamond bracelets by Petochi, together with a ruby and diamond cluster ring and earrings that Mona Bismarck would wear together with her ruby and diamond necklace. *Sotheby's, Geneva*

four-stone pendant hanging from the clasp, an embellishment that she added to most of her necklaces. The grandeur and exquisite design of the necklace greatly appealed to Mona, and elements of this style were mirrored in the important necklace created for her by Cartier in the 1940s. The *rivière* of 24 circular-cut diamonds was embellished with two briolette diamond drops hanging from the clasp. The stones were graduated in size from the front, the largest weighing approximately 16.45cts and the smallest over 2cts. This necklace was complemented by a matching bracelet and earclips, the centre of the bracelet set with an even larger stone of over 18cts, and the whole parure was mounted in platinum and yellow gold. Cartier also created another splendid diamond bracelet for Mona based on 19th-century designs. The centre was set with a large marquise-shaped diamond of nearly 9.00cts within an oval border of cushion-shaped stones and connected to two graduated rows of similarly shaped stones.

Another beautiful example of her period jewelry was a ruby and diamond necklace in a design of foliate and cluster motifs. In the 1950s the jeweler Petochi of Rome created a pair of bracelets from rubies and old cut diamonds in 19th-century style which could be worn with the necklace. Over the years she acquired a ruby and diamond cluster ring, earrings and an impressive brooch, set with a step-cut ruby of 36.36cts, to complete the ensemble.

The important emerald and diamond necklace and cluster earclips by Cartier also recreated the stylish designs of the previous century. Cartier provided her with a five-row pearl bracelet, the diamond clasp centred by a step-cut emerald and a stunning pair of diamond earrings set with two large pear-shaped cabochon emeralds. However, the finest emerald in her collection was another step-cut stone, weighing approximately 10cts, which was mounted within a double-row border of diamonds as a ring.

Mona Bismarck was famous for her pearls and for her love of them. 'By day,' wrote Diana Vreeland, 'I never saw her without her enormous pearls gleaming on her immaculate skin.' There were several pearl jewels in her collection, the most magnificent of which was a two-row necklace. Strung with 37 and 33 pearls, the two rows were graduated in size from 7.7mm to 15mm and on a diamond clasp. For natural pearls their size, their lustre and their colour were superb. They were matched by a pair of 17.25mm pearl and diamond earclips by Petochi. Another important pearl necklace was composed of a single row of 27 pearls, graduated from 13.8mm to 10.8mm. Mona had also bought an elegant pair of button pearl and diamond cluster earclips by Chantecler, the noted jewelers from Capri. Each of the pearls, approximately 16mm in diameter, was mounted within a border of cushion-shaped diamonds. From Cartier she acquired a two-row pearl bracelet, the clasp set with two brilliant-cut diamonds, entwined by a looped border of cushion-shaped diamonds. Mona's choice of these jewels set with cushion-shaped diamonds, often termed 'old-cut', rather than modern brilliant-cuts, provides further evidence of her preference for older styles and her individuality of taste. Her other pearl jewels, all embellished with diamonds, included a stylish hat pin from the 1920s, a chandelier brooch and a pendant set with a spectacular button pearl of 19.20mm.

There were many other equally desirable jewels in this collection including two very elegant turquoise and diamond necklaces, one designed as a *résille* and the other, decorated with twisted gold wire and floral motifs, designed by Mauboussin. Sensational is a word which could justifiably describe the serpent necklace which she wore coiled around her neck. Dating from the late 19th century, the reptile is realistically enamelled and its diamond head is capped by a pearl. However, the highlight of the sale was the diamond ring by Cartier set with a step-cut stone of the finest colour, 'D', and weighing 31.77cts. This one jewel encapsulates her desire for perfection and beauty.

Mona Bismarck's jewels were as beautiful and as memorable as the lady herself, classic and timeless. As Cecil Beaton once wrote, 'her houses, her furniture, her jewelry, her way of life were little short of a tour de force.'

(Opposite) Mona Bismarck with the Duke and Duchess of Windsor at the Lido nightclub in Paris in December 1962. She is wearing her turquoise necklace *résille* and a black tulle dress embroidered in turquoise, created by Balenciaga to match the necklace. The Duchess of Windsor is wearing her emerald and diamond pendant by Harry Winston suspended from Queen Mary's pearl necklace. *The Mona Bismarck Foundation*

(Below) Mona Bismarck photographed by Cecil Beaton in 1958 in the Hotel Lambert. She is wearing her emerald and diamond cluster necklace together with the matching emerald and diamond earclips by Cartier, Paris. She is also wearing her emerald and diamond ring and her jade and diamond bracelet. Her purple lace dress is by her favourite designer, Balenciaga. *Sotheby's, London (Cecil Beaton Archive)*

The diamond cluster necklace
and matching earrings by Cartier,
Paris, seen in the photograph on
the preceding p.. Also, her very
fine emerald and diamond ring, a
step-cut diamond ring by Cartier,
Paris, the exquisite turquoise and
diamond necklace *résille*, and her
antique enamel, pearl and
diamond serpent necklace.
Sotheby's, Geneva

Lydia, Lady Deterding

The former owner of a 'Casket of Magnificent Jewels' that was offered for auction in 1980 was the late Lydia, Lady Deterding, who was herself as intriguing as some of the historically important pieces that were being sold. A portrait by Philip de Lazslo, which appeared at the front of the catalogue, depicted an elegant lady with an enigmatic smile; in the absence of any biography, this was the only slender clue to her personality and lifestyle. Far more was known about her former husband, the Dutchman Sir Henri Deterding, whose highly successful career in the oil industry is well documented. He was instrumental in the merger of Royal Dutch Petroleum and Shell Transport and Trading in 1907, and under his astute leadership the Group enjoyed fabulous growth. In 1936, at the age of seventy, Deterding resigned from the Group, recognized as one of the most imposing entrepreneurial figures of the 20th century. As for his former wife, Lydia, the owner of the jewelry collection, she posed a mystery.

In conformity with the habits of her generation, Lydia always kept the exact date of her birth a closely guarded secret, even from her immediate family. It is know that she was born in Tashkent during the late 19th century and that she was the daughter of an academic, Paul Koudoyaroff. Her Russian origins were not suppressed during her lifetime and may have instilled in her a strong appreciation of beautiful objects, especially jewels. At the age of sixteen she married a Russian diplomat, General Bagratouni, who was more than thirty years older than she. The first few years of their marriage were spent in St Petersburg where they mixed in grand social circles. This was a time of pomp and glamour in Imperial Russia and was bound to have nurtured Lydia's enthusiasm for social gatherings of the highest order. Though she rarely talked about the past, Lydia once divulged to one of her daughters the fact that she had encountered various members of the Russian Imperial family in St Petersburg, as well as the mysterious Rasputin, whom she found 'terrifying'.

The couple soon left Russia for Paris, where her husband was appointed as an attaché, and before long he was posted to London. It was here that she met Henri Deterding, again a much older man. By 1924, they were both free to marry, both for the second time. They spent their married life in great style and comfort at Buckhurst Park in Ascot, amid glorious grounds. Because of Deterding's wealth and his constant anxiety lest his daughters be kidnapped for ransom, the family was surrounded by high security; but the gardens were so large and beautiful that the two girls never felt unduly restricted. Indeed, they grew up in a happy and loving environment and adored 'Mama', whom one daughter affectionately recalls as not being the 'perfect Mother in the true sense of the word', but as being an 'extraordinary person'.

Lady Deterding could never have been called a great beauty, but she had a magnetic personality and charm, and there was an alluring sparkle in her eyes that de Lazslo's portrait seems to have captured. She

Sir Henri and Lady Deterding dressed for Court Presentation in the late 1920s. She is wearing the emerald and diamond necklace set with the 'Polar Star'.
Private collection

143

A studio portrait by Dorothy Wilding in which Lady Deterding is wearing the Empress Maria Feodorovna pearl and diamond pendant together with her pearl drop earrings. These she later had remounted by Cartier. The pair of carved emerald, ruby and diamond 'Tutti Frutti' clips were made by Cartier, Paris, in the 1920s. *Private collection*

The 'Polar Star' diamond mounted as a ring by Boucheron. *Christie's, Geneva*

(Opposite) In this portrait of Empress Maria Feodorovna of Russia by Henrick Von Angeli, c. 1870, the Empress is wearing the pearl and diamond pendant which was included later in the Deterding sale. *The Hermitage, Moscow; Christie's, Geneva*

(Left) A portrait by Philip de Laszlo, 1922, of Princess Anastasia of Greece, formerly Mrs Nancy Leeds. She is wearing an emerald and diamond *sautoir* and tiara, both by Cartier, New York. The parure was created by Pierre Cartier in 1921 remounting stones from a necklace and an epaulette. After her death in 1926 the *sautoir* was repurchased by Cartier and the emerald pendant remounted by Cartier in London as a necklace with the 'Polar Star' for Lady Deterding. The largest step-cut emerald, together with several others, were remounted in a necklace which was sold to the Maharajah of Nawangar. It is intriguing that the first emerald in the chain on the front left-hand side is exactly the same size and shape as the emerald mounted in the Duchess of Windsor's engagement ring. *Cartier Ltd*

(Opposite above) The necklace belonging to Princess Anastasia of Greece, and the emerald and diamond necklace with the 'Polar Star' as it was designed for Lady Deterding by Cartier, London, in 1926. *Christie's; Cartier Ltd, London*

(Below) Lady Deterding attending an official reception at the British Embassy in Paris in 1938. She is wearing the 'Polar Star' necklace but on this occasion with the step-cut emerald and pear-shaped drops positioned as they had been in the original *sautoir*. *Private collection*

Boucheron as an extremely impressive ring. She did not, however, discard or sell the diamond necklace which had once held the 'Polar Star'. It was to provide the setting for yet another sensational Russian gem. Bought after the Revolution by Lady Deterding, possibly using Cartier as the intermediary, this was the famous 'Azra Pearl'. This pear-shaped black pearl was part of a diamond ornament, also set with a black button pearl, which was suspended from a necklace of 110 perfectly matched pearls. Until 1783, the Azra was among the Russian Crown Jewels. The Empress Catherine II gave it to one of her famous favourites, Prince Potemkin, who bequeathed it to his niece Princess Tatiana Youssoupoff and it had remained in that family since then. It was exhibited in London in 1935, together with the much-admired 'Pellegrina' pearl and a pair of pearl earrings which also belonged to the Youssoupoff family. Cartier dismantled the original pearl necklace and reset the black pearl and diamond pendant in a diamond necklace. Lady Deterding was unfortunate enough to lose the Azra pearl 'somewhere in Paris', and it was therefore only the necklace with the black button pearl and diamond pendant, but without this romantic pearl, which was included in the 1980 sale.

Besides their great beauty and historical importance, another factor which may well have strengthened Lady Deterding's determination to possess these jewels was her acquaintance with the Youssoupoff family from her years in Russia, and she may have seen this as a mutually agreeable means of helping them financially once they had left their homeland.

Few pieces in the Deterding collection remained in their original form. These included a ruby and diamond bracelet, typical of the Art Deco period, set with four rows of cushion-shaped rubies and with diamond clasps. It was a Cartier creation. All the other jewels sold dated from the late 1930s onwards and confirmed that Lydia never lost her appetite for beautiful jewelry. Again designed and made by her favourite jewelers, Cartier, was a superb ruby and diamond parure, which included a necklace with five detachable palmette motifs that could be worn also as clips. The matching earrings and bangle were of similar design and were all created in 1938.

Lydia would often visit Cartier either to exchange pieces or to have them redesigned. It is evident that the majority of her acquisitions came from Cartier. It was from them that she bought a very elegant canary yellow and white diamond rose brooch, a turquoise and diamond parure, a 47.00cts sapphire which was mounted as the centre of a striking diamond flowerhead brooch, and

(Opposite below) A photograph from the catalogue of the exhibition of Russian art held in London in 1935, showing the pearl necklace set with the black button pearl and the black 'Azra' pearl with the 'Pellegrina' pearl, and (above) the black button pearl and diamond necklace as it appeared in the 1980 auction. It was now devoid of the famous 'Azra' pearl and mounted on the Cartier diamond necklace which was originally created for the 'Polar Star' and emerald pendant. *John Stuart; Sotheby's, London*

(This page) A turquoise and diamond necklace and earrings from a parure which also included a bracelet. This was created by Cartier in the late 1960s. In the photograph of Lady Deterding attending a reception at the Cercle Interallié in Paris in 1973, she is wearing this parure. *Christie's, Geneva; Private collection*

other equally attractive coloured stone and diamond jewels. In the late 1920s she added one of their most sensational jewels to the collection: a pair of carved emerald, ruby and diamond 'Tutti Frutti' clips. Each mitre-shaped clip was set with a large carved emerald leaf within borders of baguette- and brilliant-cut diamonds and ruby beads. She also obtained several of their stylish gold and diamond compacts and cigarette cases to complete her outfits, as well as splendid evening bags decorated with gemstones and colourful enamels.

During the late 1930s chalcedony, stained a mauvish blue reminiscent of lavendar jade, became extremely fashionable, as is illustrated by the wonderful parure Suzanne Belperron created for the Duchess of Windsor. Lydia Deterding had a stylish necklace of large stained chalcedony beads which were connected by a gold clasp set with pink tourmaline and emerald beads and supported gold pod motifs. To match this jewel Cartier created a pair of pendent earrings, further embellished with rubies and diamonds.

The collection as a whole, consisting of pieces with important provenance as well as a highly personal selection of the best of modern jewelry, bespoke an owner confident of her own taste with a high regard for quality as well as beauty. The mysterious Lydia, Lady Deterding, can be best read from her jewels.

A pair of pearl and diamond pendent earrings. The pearl drops had been remounted by Cartier in the 1950s. *Christie's, Geneva*

A diamond necklace and a brooch, designed as a pair of swallows dating from the late 1920s. Both jewels were created by Cartier. *Private collection*

(Opposite) A three-row pearl necklace with a sapphire clasp photographed over a portrait of Lady Deterding by A. Vidal Quadras, 1969, in which she is wearing this necklace together with her pearl and diamond pendent earrings by Cartier. *Private collection*

A gold and rose diamond Indian necklace, together with a pair of gold and rose diamond earrings which were created by Cartier at a later date to match the necklace. These are photographed over a studio portrait of Lady Deterding by Dorothy Wilding taken in the 1930s. She is wearing the necklace, a fashion which was very much in vogue during this period. *Private collection*

A. Vidal-Quadras '64

Daisy Fellowes

Daisy Fellowes is acknowledged as having been one of the 20th century's most stylish and glamorous women, words which could equally well describe her jewelry collection. Named Marguerite Severine Philippine, but always known as 'Daisy', she was born in Paris in 1890 into a world of wealth and nobility, of American and French extraction; her mother, Isabelle Blanche Singer, was a daughter of the sewing machine magnate Isaac Singer, and her father was the fourth Duc Decazes et de Glucksbierg. Due to the untimely death of her mother in 1894, Daisy was brought up in France by her mother's sister, Winnaretta Singer, the wife of the Prince de Polignac. Surprisingly, certain accounts of her childhood, which report an open contempt for her appearance, a refusal to wash or even comb her hair, seem a direct contradiction to her future role as one of the world's best-dressed women.

At 20, she was married to Prince Jean de Broglie and had three daughters, Emeline, Isabelle and Jacqueline. It was during the first years of this marriage that Daisy commissioned her portrait from a well-known society painter. The portrait had a remarkable affect on her: she hated what she saw and from that moment decided to create a new Daisy, far removed from the plain and uninteresting person she saw staring back at her from the canvas. According to her grandson, Comte de La Moussaye, she particularly disliked the line of her nose, which she immediately had reshaped, horrifyingly without the aid of an anaesthetic. She then bought a whole new wardrobe of clothes and changed her hairdresser. Perhaps more significantly, having the intelligence to recognize the great importance in life of a good knowledge of literature and the arts and her own lack of this social advantage, she immersed herself in books and visited museums and art galleries. In 1918 de Broglie died of influenza in a military hospital in Algiers.

Through her own efforts, Daisy had achieved a remarkable transformation and she was now regarded as one of the most elegant and fascinating women in Europe. It was therefore hardly surprising that her period of widowhood was short-lived: in August 1919 she married the Hon. Reginald Fellowes. He was the second son of the 2nd Baron de Ramsey; and through his mother, Lady Rosamond Spencer-Churchill, he was first cousin to the 9th Duke of Marlborough. Throughout their marriage Daisy was devoted to Reginald. He died in 1953, having been ill and wheelchair-bound for several years, and Daisy was always an attentive and caring wife.

Daisy Fellowes photographed by Cecil Beaton in 1937. Among the wonderful jewels she is wearing is the 'Tutti Frutti' necklace by Cartier, Paris, as it was originally created for her in 1936. She is also wearing two diamond bracelets by Cartier. *Sotheby's, London (Cecil Beaton Archives)*

(Above) Daisy Fellowes on her wedding day in August 1919. *Private collection*

(Overleaf two pages) The coloured gemstone and diamond 'Tutti Frutti' necklace after it had been redesigned for Daisy Fellowes's daughter, the Comtesse de Casteja, in 1963. The carved emerald and diamond buds, now mounted as pendent earrings, had originally been the tassel drops of a bead necklace created by Cartier in 1945 for Daisy Fellowes. This Cartier archive photograph shows the original carved tassel drops above a drawing for a bead necklace and bears a great similarity to the one they then created for the Duchess of Windsor in 1949. The pair of bracelets set with various cabochon gemstones were worn by Daisy Fellowes with her Cartier 'Tutti Frutti' necklace, as she did at the famous Beistegui masked ball in Venice in 1951. *Sotheby's, Geneva; Cartier Ltd; Private collection*

From the 1920s onwards, she was one of the uncrowned queens of the social scene and a leader of fashion. Noted as a great hostess, a sportswoman and an author, she was also an individualist with a pronounced sense of humour. In the account James Pope-Hennessy wrote of her for American *Vogue* in 1964, he commented that in her 'career she could rely on four major assets: very great beauty, a subtle, exquisite and barbed sense of humour, an inborn taste for dress, and a considerable fortune.' Her hair was usually sleeked back, whether short or long, and her look was of elegant classicism, with no fuss or frills. She will be remembered as the beauty who wore black, not white, when presented at Court; conveniently she found some obscure French cousin who had recently died as a valid reason for this unconventional attire. In *The Glass of Fashion* Cecil Beaton, one of her long-standing friends, writes that she had a 'way of handling a situation with aplomb.'

The Felloweses spent their married life flitting between homes in various fashionable locations, including a house in Paris and Les Zoraides, their villa at Cap Martin on the Riviera, where, amidst the orange groves and cypress trees and on the lake, with Daisy's three daughters and their own daughter, Rosamund, they spent idyllic days, enjoying beautiful views over the sea to Monte Carlo.

They also had a gracious home in Berkshire, Donnington Grove, where Daisy kept a flock of black sheep and entertained her friends. Another marvellous home was the Fellowes yacht, the *Sister Anne*, which was the venue for many of their lavish parties. It was also lent to the Prince of Wales in 1935 for a memorable cruise with Mrs Simpson and in 1944 to their nephew, Winston Churchill, to oversee the D-Day landings in Normandy.

Daisy had a passion for fine jewels; indeed, her collection was famous enough for press reporters and fashion magazines to keep watch to see with which new jewel the stylish Mrs Fellowes would next stun the world. However, only tantalizing few of her jewels have ever been sold at auction and it is to contemporary photographs and articles and to archive material and the generous help of her relations that one must turn to gain a better knowledge of her amazing collection.

Daisy Fellowes was known to patronize many of the leading jewelers of her time, such as Cartier, Van Cleef & Arpels and Boivin. The incredibly long list of jewels which she acquired from Cartier confirms her image as a remarkably stylish lady, one of the world's best dressed. One of her most memorable acquisitions from that house was the 17.47cts light rose-pink diamond, known as the '*Tête de Belier*', or Ram's Head. This unusual stone, cut in the shape of a flattened octahedron, had been purchased by Cartier in 1927 from Prince Youssoupoff of Russia. This fabled diamond was thought to have been given by Catherine the Great to one of her favourites, Potemkin, who in turn gave it to his niece, Princess Tatiana Youssoupoff, who was also the recipient of the 'Azra' pearl and had acquired the 'Polar Star'. Elsa Schiaparelli, the fashion designer, decided to commemorate the new addition to Daisy Fellowes's collection by creating for her the

(Opposite) Another Cecil Beaton photograph of Daisy Fellowes (1930). She is wearing the '*Tête de Belier*', or 'Ram's Head', a light rose pink diamond of 17.47cts, mounted as a ring by Cartier, Paris, and a diamond clip pinned to her hat. She is also wearing two very long necklaces, designed as *torsades* of beads. Beaton also sketched her at the time of this sitting, as illustrated in his book *The Glass of Fashion*. Sotheby's, London (Cecil Beaton Archive)

Daisy Fellowes as featured in *The Tatler* in January 1935 under the title of 'The Quintessence of Chic. Studies of the Hon. Mrs. Reginald Fellowes'. Here she is wearing the pair of emerald and ruby bead and diamond cuff bracelets of Indian inspiration by Van Cleef & Arpels, 1920s (overleaf p. 161). *The Illustrated London News Picture Library*

'shocking pink' which would complement the colour of the stone. In 1939 the diamond was stolen and has not reappeared since – one of the abiding mysteries of jewelry lore.

In 1921 Daisy Fellowes bought a very chic Cartier bracelet, typical of the Art Deco style. Entered in their stock books on 3 December, it was sold to her just over a week later. Based on a design by Charles Jacqueau and made by Renault for Cartier, Paris, the centre was a loop pavé-set with an oval cabochon emerald within a border of brilliant-cut diamonds and four small cabochon emeralds. This was connected to the sides by two carved onyx hoops linked to a three-row pearl tapered bracelet by two smaller diamond and cabochon emerald sections. Some years later Daisy had the onyx hoops removed and replaced with coral, and this is how it appeared when sold at auction in 1987 and later in 1989. Daisy's liking for the vibrant salmon pink of coral, more often than not combined with the rich green of emeralds enhanced by diamonds, is also evident in a coral flowerhead brooch. The carved coral petals are decorated with small pear-shaped emeralds and circular-cut diamonds, and two are tipped by diamonds and form the stamen. This too was sold in the 1987 sale and had been created by Cartier in the 1950s. Daisy had bought many more coral jewels from Cartier, including two bracelets and a brooch with coral cylinders, which she commissioned from their Paris branch in 1932.

In May 1991 a world record price was achieved for any Cartier jewel sold at auction. Previously owned by Daisy Fellowes, acknowledged as one of Cartier's biggest buyers of their jewels in the Indian style, this piece is perhaps their most masterful interpretation of a jewel of that genre. However, the necklace had been subject to many alterations over the years and the final version was completed in 1963 for her daughter, the Comtesse de Casteja.

In June 1928 Daisy bought a necklace from Cartier which was designed as a string of emerald and sapphire beads supporting a fringe of thirteen oval sapphire briolettes, capped by foliate platinum mounts set with brilliant-cut diamonds and with baguette diamond stems. A year later she acquired a bracelet of carved emerald buds decorated with diamond husks and ruby and turquoise bead tips, with carved ruby leaves and with two larger sapphires of 50.80cts and 42.45cts, carved as bud motifs. In 1936 she decided to up-date both the necklace and the bracelet, along with another unidentified bracelet, and commissioned Cartier in Paris to design a new jewel.

Lavabre created her sensational 'Collier Hindou' and the transformation was a triumph. Apart from the small turquoise beads, all the stones were re-used and nearly 250 extra stones were supplied by Cartier. The necklace was a graduated fringe of carved ruby, sapphire and emerald buds and foliage, the carved emerald buds forming a ruff, and the sapphire briolettes forming the fringe. The central section, which was also a detachable clip,

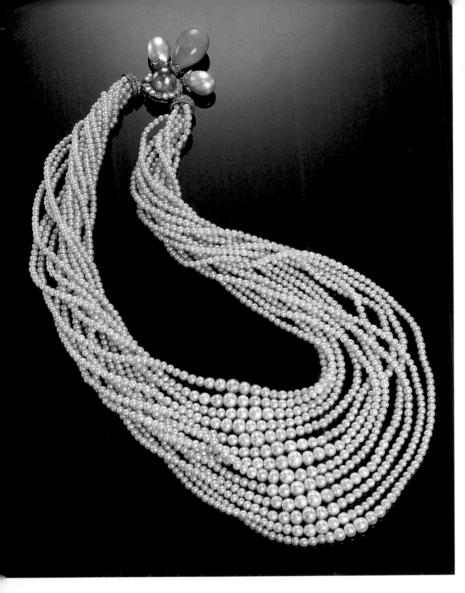

(Left) Daisy Fellowes's pearl necklace. The thirteen rows of graduated pearls are mounted on a grey and white pearl and pink coral clasp by Cartier, Paris. *Private collection*

(Below left) One of the Cartier diamond bracelets that Daisy Fellowes is wearing in Cecil Beaton's 1937 studio portrait (p. 154). *Private collection*

Daisy Fellowes's ruby bead and diamond fringe bracelet and her emerald bead and diamond fringe bracelet, both by Van Cleef & Arpels and dating from the 1920s. *Sotheby's, Geneva*

was set with the two larger sapphire bud motifs. The necklace was fastened at the back by silk cords: this is a typically Indian method of fastening which is still in use today as it gives the wearer complete flexibility to alter the length of the necklace, and hence the overall effect of the jewel. Daisy wore this necklace at the famous Beistegui masked ball in Venice in 1951 and it is often suggested that this was the only occasion when she ever wore it. However, photographs by Cecil Beaton published by *Vogue* in January 1937 reveal the necklace being worn to great effect. In 1963 her daughter decided to alter the necklace and once again Cartier's expertise was sought. The silk cords were removed and the centre was redesigned: the two large carved sapphire buds became the clasp and the carved rubies and some of the emeralds were removed to the sides.

When this necklace was sold in 1991 it was accompanied by a pair of pendent earrings. Each earring was designed as a large emerald bead drop carved with floral motifs and with a diamond tip, capped by a calix motif set with diamonds and suspended from a flowerhead cluster surmount, set with a diamond studded emerald bead within a border of diamonds. These carved emerald drops and the calix motifs had been created by Cartier in 1945 as the tassel drops for a gold chain necklace, the original drawing showing the tasseled chain attached to a two-row bead necklace.

Daisy ordered another carved coloured stone and diamond 'Tutti Frutti' necklace from Cartier which she acquired in May 1931. The dramatic fringe of carved flowerheads, foliage and buds was decorated with diamonds and was surmounted by Indian flowerhead clusters beneath a row of beads. Again, the fastener was cord, but this time gold wire cord, the slide set with calibré-cut rubies and the looped tassels decorated with a diamond band. This same gold fastener with its gem-set decorations was again re-used for various ruby bead necklaces; the final version of six rows, connected to the cord fastener by diamond calix motifs, was purchased by her in July 1939.

In many photographs Daisy Fellowes is seen wearing pearls which she obviously loved, particularly in the form of bracelets and necklaces. In the 1930s she had thirteen graduated rows of natural pearls mounted on a pearl and diamond clasp by Cartier. The clasp was set with a grey pearl within a border of diamonds and had a pink coral drop between two pear-shaped pearl drops, capped by diamonds. The position of the clasp was such that it was worn at the nape of the neck, an elegant style which was eminently fashionable at that period. In June 1938 she added one of Cartier's necklace/tiaras to her collection, the choice of the daisies design being of course particularly appropriate. The three detachable flowerheads were set with diamonds and could also be worn as clips. Another stunning necklace she

bought in the 1930s was composed of diamonds supporting a fringe of emerald drops. A more unusual acquisition during this period was a bracelet made of panther skin which was set at the centre with a gemstone.

In the 1940s her many purchases from Cartier included an exquisite sapphire, emerald and diamond brooch designed as an iris made in their London workshop. The petals were set with cushion-shaped sapphires and brilliant-cut diamonds, the emerald stem entwined with baguette diamonds. Like many of her contemporaries, Daisy admired the great cat jewels inspired by Jeanne Toussaint and created by Cartier. In the 1950s she commissioned apanther brooch in sapphires and diamonds, modelled on the pendant part of the Order of the Golden Fleece. Toussaint substituted a highly realistic hanging leopard decorated with a band of diamonds for the Golden Fleece.

Early in 1962 Daisy bought one of the most stunning chimera bangles, again based on ideas by Jeanne Toussaint for Cartier. These were originally produced in coral in 1922 and then in diamonds in 1929. Toussaint instigated a new series in 1954, transforming the earlier, almost terrifying creatures into rather more docile and appealing animals. Daisy's bangle was carved from coral, the terminals forming two dolphin heads, and the piece was decorated throughout with variously cut diamonds and emeralds.

Daisy Fellowes also patronized Van Cleef & Arpels and two of her most attractive acquisitions were made by them in the 1920s. These were two bracelets of very similar design, in the 'Indian style', and as Daisy always preferred a bracelet on each wrist, they looked spectacular when worn together. Each was designed as a wide band of baguette, marquise-shaped and brilliant-cut diamonds set at intervals with larger step-cut diamonds, and one was fringed with ruby drops and the other with emerald drops.

Her choice of jewels from the talented designers at Boivin revealed in particular her great admiration for their spectacular brooches. Based in Paris, the house of Boivin was founded by René Boivin in the late 19th century and upon his death in 1917 the business was carried on by his equally gifted wife, Jeanne, the eldest sister of the couturier Paul Poiret. Mme Boivin, herself a highly innovative designer and an astute business woman, engaged several aspiring young designers, such as Suzanne Belperron and Juliette Moutard, as well as her own daughter, Germaine, and the company went from strength to strength, admired for their imaginative sculptural style. Very few of their creations were signed as Mme Boivin felt that a beautiful jewel did not require a signature, and that its addition would be 'pure affectation'. Signatures were added only if the client insisted.

Daisy Fellowes became one of their most important clients, sometimes acquiring several jewels at one time: Boivin's records show that in March 1939 she ordered 'an orchid, a daffodil ring, a chameleon, a pair of earrings, a daisy, an arrow and two tourmaline

(Opposite) In this Cecil Beaton photograph, Daisy Fellowes has pinned on her dress the wonderful ruby and diamond orchid brooch by Boivin that she had ordered in 1939. She is also wearing a pair of diamond bracelets. *Sotheby's, London (Cecil Beaton Archives)*

(Above) With the Marchese Strozzi at a Gala evening at the Monte Carlo Sporting Club in 1937. She is wearing her spectacular butterfly brooch, probably by Boivin. *The Illustrated London News Picture Library*

leaves.' Apart from the chameleon brooch, every other design was a new creation from Boivin. In 1991 one especially dramatic example from Daisy's collection came up for auction. It was impressive not only for its design but also for its size: designed as the wing of a pigeon, it was almost 13 cms in width. Pavé-set with cabochon sapphires and baguette and circular-cut diamonds, it had a distinct feeling of movement which only a truly skilled craftsman can achieve and was created by Boivin in 1938. Comte de La Moussaye recounts that some of these sapphires were acquired by Daisy in Ceylon during one of her voyages aboard the *Sister Anne* and that she spent many hours on the sun-drenched deck of the boat musing as to what jewel the stones should embellish.

Another of her wonderful brooches, although again unsigned, bears all the hallmarks of these creative jewelers. The design is that of a huge butterfly, its upper wings set with citrines of various cut and size and the lower wings pavé-set with emeralds and diamonds, the body decorated with blue enamel and set with a cabochon ruby, the head with a step-cut emerald and the antennae with two pear-shaped emeralds. There was also another stylish sapphire and diamond 'pineapple' brooch which did bear Boivin's makers marks. The large briolette sapphire was close-set at the centre of a gold scrolled border, surrounded by diamonds and surmounted by a diamond foliate motif.

Among the other Boivin jewels in her collection was a large grey enamel and diamond 'whelk' brooch and a ruby and diamond orchid brooch. She also had a pair of highly colourful bracelets set with a variety of cabochon gemstones (again unsigned but evocative of the Boivin style) which she wore at the Beistegui ball with her Cartier 'Collier Hindou'.

Her collection was further enhanced by jewels by the talented Jean Schlumberger. A piece of particular note was a gem-set clip from the late 1940s designed as a plum. The jewel was set with a large cabochon amethyst in the shape of a plum, the carved peridot leaf set with cabochon rubies and brilliant-cut diamonds and surmounted by a frond of turquoise.

When Daisy Fellowes died in Paris in December 1962, Graham Sutherland was completing her portrait. Remembering her extraordinary reaction to her first portrait and its consequences, Daisy surely would not have been unpleased with this canvas when it was finally finished. Although it depicted her in her seventies, according to James Pope-Hennessy it still contained 'a sense of her disciplined serenity, an inkling of her grand allure.' She had indeed fashioned herself, as she had wished, into a 'living work of art'.

A sapphire and rose and cushion shaped diamond bracelet, 1930s. *Private collection*

(Opposite) An original drawing of Daisy Fellowes by Cecil Beaton. *Private collection*

The gold and gem-set butterfly brooch she is wearing on p. 163. *Private collection*

A gold, sapphire and diamond 'Pineapple' brooch by Boivin. *Private collection*

A magnificent sapphire, emerald and diamond brooch designed as an iris by Cartier, London, c. 1940. *Private collection*

From Cecil

Ganna Walska

When Ganna Walska's jewelry collection came up for auction in New York in 1971 the press described the collection as 'exotic and wonderfully designed' and including 'many fine gem-stones and a selection of Indian jewelry'. The sale total of $916,000 for 146 lots was a world sensation in the midst of a recession and at least double what had been expected. However, this sale took place at a time when jewelry cataloguing was brief and little emphasis was placed on researching the origins of the pieces; therefore, the remarkable and true importance of this collection was not apparent. Discovering the origins of these jewels has been as intriguing as uncovering the true history of their owner.

Dedicating it to 'all those who are seeking their place in the sun', Ganna Walska published her autobiography *Always Room at the Top* in 1943. In the opening chapter she professes that her main reason for writing her memoirs was that her 'secretive nature desired a confidant'. Secretive is certainly an apt word, as in the first few chapters she refers vaguely to her youth being spent in Poland and Russia and states that she travelled to the USA in her late teens. Her whole life story seems dotted with discrepancies. But what she herself is perfectly clear about is that her name was fictitious. Requiring a stage name for her chosen career as an opera singer, she tells us that like all Poles she loved dancing, especially the waltz, 'So suddenly I said "Waltz, Valse, Walska...!"' And so as Ganna Walska she became a celebrated, though somewhat unsuccessful, opera and concert singer in both America and Europe during the 1920s through to the 1940s, and led an interesting and extravagant life.

Accounts of her origins vary. According to one operatic biography she was born in Belleville, Arkansas, in 1885. Another reputable, and possibly more accurate publication reports that she was born on 20 June 1892 in Poland. Ganna maintains that she was educated in Warsaw and that by the age of 17 she was married to Baron Arcadie d'Eingorne and living in St Petersburg. Shortly after their marriage, her husband contracted tuberculosis and in the hope of finding a cure they spent three years in a Swiss clinic where he died. Facts which cannot be disputed are that by 1915 she was in New York, beautiful and with a consuming desire to be a great singer.

Her singing career started out with a series of concerts and on 18 February 1918 she made her debut in a recital of Caruso's at the Biltimore Morning Musicals, singing an aria from *Pagliacci* and a duet from *The Pearl Fishers* with the famous tenor himself. Two years later she was signed up to sing with the Chicago Opera Company in their 1921 season.

Ganna Walska photographed by Baron de Meyer in the 1920s. She is wearing the emerald and diamond necklace created by Cartier, Paris, in 1923 and a matching pair of emerald and diamond pendent earrings. Other jewels are her emerald and diamond clasp worn as a bracelet centre and her heart-shaped diamond ring. *From Richard R. Smith,' Always at the Top', New York 1943*

(Above) A caricature of Ganna Walska wearing her emerald and diamond pendent earrings. *From Richard R. Smith, op. cit.*

She had also met the man who would play such an important role in her life, Harold McCormick, the millionaire son of the Chicago Reaper King, himself the chairman of the International Harvester Company, and, of obvious importance to Ganna, an 'angel' for the Chicago Opera Company. During this period she had also embarked on the next of her many marriages, on this occasion to a Dr Joseph Fraenkel, a neurologist many years her senior. Indeed in 1936 the United Press Association reported that she was 'estimated to have married fortunes totalling $125,000,000 in her marital ventures with four wealthy men. She likewise was believed to have spent one-twelfth of this sum in attempting to further her great ambition to become an opera star.' What proportion she was to spend on her jewelry collection was not revealed but it must have been quite extensive.

The earliest existing photographs of Ganna Walska show her wearing simple pearl jewels. It is not until the early 1920s that her great passion for wearing and acquiring spectacular jewels was fulfilled. Her time with Dr Fraenkel was brief: he died within a few years of their marriage. Shortly after his death friends persuaded her to join them on a trip to Paris. During the long voyage across the Atlantic she met Harold McCormick again, and he introduced her to a fellow passenger, Alexander Smith Cochran. Cochran seems to have been immediately smitten by the ravishing Ganna; even before the voyage was completed he had proposed to her. Despite the fact that Alec Cochran had already 'forcibly placed a perfect oriental pearl ring' on her finger saying that 'if by January you still do not want to marry me, send back this ring. I will understand that Harold McCormick is too much on your mind', Ganna was still hesitant to accept his offer of marriage. Only after many protestations she finally agreed, kept the ring, and their wedding took place in Paris in September 1920.

Alec Cochran was reputed to be the richest bachelor in the world and his wedding present to her was 'to go with Carte blanche to Cartier and choose anything' she desired. Her choice has never been revealed but it may well have been the fantastic yellow diamond pear-shaped briolette weighing 95cts which was sold in 1971. How this gem was originally mounted is unknown, possibly as a drop for one of those long *sautoirs* which were so fasionable at that period, but by the time it was auctioned it was capped by five small marquise diamonds and mounted with a simple tonguepiece fitting by which it could be attached to a suitable necklace as a pendant. A few days after their marriage the Cochrans returned to America.

Ganna was determined to pursue her career in opera and initially Alec agreed to her wishes. Soon after their arrival in the USA, however, his attitude changed and he made it impossible for her to continue with her commitments to the Chicago Opera Company. Their relationship inevitably started to go badly wrong. That Christmas, when they were in their New York house, Alec was continuously asking Ganna what she wanted as a present and she would emphatically reply that she did not want anything.

Some of the highlights of Ganna Walska's jewelry collection: an emerald and diamond clasp, c. 1900, set with a 20.00cts step-cut emerald; a 21.15cts heart-shaped diamond ring; a pair of natural pearl and diamond pendent earrings (the diamond settings originally supported ruby drops and the tops were cabochon rubies. In their original form they had been a Cartier creation but in the sale the rubies were mounted together with diamonds in a far less dramatic style); a natural black pearl and diamond ring; a ruby and carved diamond butterfly brooch by Boucheron, c. 1894; a sapphire and diamond ring, the step-cut stone weighing approximately 39.00cts; another sapphire and diamond ring, the cabochon stone weighing approximately 44.00cts; and a fancy yellow diamond briolette of 95.00cts mounted as a pendant. This pendant and the heart-shaped diamond ring were purchased in the sale of her jewels by Van Cleef & Arpels and were then named the 'Walska Briolette' and the 'Walska Heart'. *Sotheby's, New York (Parke Bernet)*

Throughout her life Ganna was highly interested in fashion, although she was not always ready to follow its dictates. She had her own sense of style, which often preceded the current vogues. A few weeks prior to Christmas she had visited Cartier in New York and decided to try on several bracelets to verify whether she 'would care to follow the trend of fashion', sometimes referred to somewhat unkindly as 'service stripes'. Ganna decided that she did not want to cover the 'natural beauty' of her wrists with the 'artificial beauty' of precious stones. Alec Cochran had spotted his wife at Cartier and had returned there a few days later as he had 'almost half an hour to waste before luncheon' and if he bought the bracelets in question for Ganna 'it would kill a few minutes' of his time. He had then unceremoniously thrust the package containing the jewels on her desk, ensuring that Ganna would be enraged by the manner in which the gift was both chosen and given. She could not even bring herself to thank him.

Two weeks later the couple returned to Paris, but immediately after their arrival Alec left for England to indulge his passion for hunting. Despite a reunion later at their new home in Rue de Lubeck, the relationship gradually deteriorated; Ganna bitterly resented his hindering her singing career and Alec became increasingly suspicious of her affections. They were divorced in July 1922 and within fourteen days she was married in Salzburg to Harold McCormick, who had also recently been divorced from the famous heiress Edith Rockefeller. Ganna's latest marriage was greeted by the French press with the suggestion that she had started a new fashion, 'two weeks of mourning after the final divorce decree!'

McCormick now set about trying to advance his wife's career while showering her with the wonderful jewels which she adored. Sadly for Ganna, even

his enormous wealth could not assure her of success on the opera stage, and she received many negative reviews for her performances, but it could buy her the most incredible jewels. In 1923, she acquired two fabulous necklaces from Cartier in Paris which rank among the greatest pieces ever created by these jewelers. One was a sapphire and emerald necklace designed as a row of sapphire beads connected by sections of smaller emerald beads, from which hung a spectacular Mogul engraved emerald of 256.60cts, carved with flowers and foliage, suspended from an engraved sapphire oval bead of 39.14cts. The first of Cartier's many alterations to the necklace (which Cartier historian Hans Nadelhoffer refers to as 'chameleon-like') was undertaken in 1927.

(Opposite) Ganna Walska in fancy dress, wearing her emerald, sapphire and diamond necklace by Cartier, Paris, in its 1927 form. *From Richard R. Smith, op. cit.*

(Below left to right) Between the time it was first created in 1923 and its final version in 1929, the wonderful Cartier emerald, sapphire and diamond necklace underwent several alterations. These original Cartier, Paris, archive photographs show four different versions dating from 1927 to 1929. The 1927 version can also be worn without the briolette sapphire on the side and replaced by a chain of emerald beads *Cartier Ltd (Paris)*

(Above) The 'Russian' sapphire in its original diamond mount as a brooch by Fabergé. *Private collection*

The vastly altered necklace as it appeared in the 1971 auction. *Sotheby's, New York (Parke Bernet)*

The sapphire became a vase embellished with a diamond rim and handles which was surmounted by a 33.58cts emerald engraved with leaves (the *giardinetto* motif was highly fashionable at this period as was the combination of green and blue). This was then connected to the emerald and sapphire beads by two pear-shaped motifs pavé-set with onyx points and diamonds. The next transformation was the addition of an important 197.75cts rectangular-shaped facetted 'Russian' sapphire. In the catalogue of *Russia's Treasure of Diamonds and Precious Stones* printed in Moscow in 1926 under the general supervision of Professor A.E. Fersman, member of the Academy of Science of Russia, this sapphire is mentioned in the fourth and last part of the catalogue as number 161. Described as 'two beautiful brooches/fermoirs decorated with ancient sapphires from Ceylon', this sapphire mounted within a border of diamonds is detailed as a 'large sapphire of flat Hindu cutting... the setting is modern by Fabergé.' As this brooch was not included in the famous sale of treasures from the Russian State Jewels held in London in 1927, exactly how it was acquired by Cartier is unknown but in their archives it is simply referred to as the sapphire '*historique*' from the Russian Tsars. In Ganna's necklace this sapphire was capped by diamonds and incorporated into the side of the necklace between the sapphire and emerald beads. Not many months later the 'Russian' sapphire became the pendant drop connected by an emerald rondel. After all these interesting alterations to satisfy Ganna's quest for perfection, in the final version in 1929 the smaller

carved emerald and sapphire were removed and the 'Russian' sapphire surmounted the magnificent Mogul emerald drop. This was one of the jewels she wore at the famous society wedding of Barbara Hutton to Prince Mdivani in Paris in 1933.

When the necklace appeared in the sale it was yet again in an entirely different style, dating from the 1940s. The 'Russian' sapphire was the centre of the necklace, the sides composed of thirty sapphire beads from the original necklace which were now divided by diamond set spacers and the back was designed as a chain of diamonds on a sapphire bead clasp. The Mogul emerald was sold separately as a pendant and the emerald rondel had become the centre of a sapphire, emerald and diamond pendant. In 1992 the 'Russian' sapphire appeared once again in a saleroom in Geneva. On this occasion it was the centre of a contemporary emerald bead torsade, supporting an emerald briolette drop.

The other marvellous necklace which she bought from Cartier in 1923 was set with emeralds and diamonds. The front was elegantly fringed by a pendant of seven drop-shaped emerald beads weighing 167.54cts in total, capped by diamonds and connected by lunette-shaped diamonds and two pear-shaped diamond scroll motifs. This was connected to a two-row emerald bead neckchain by a row of cabochon emeralds, the whole chain interspersed at intervals by variously cut diamonds. Again this necklace was obviously subject to many alterations and by the time of her sale it had been totally dismounted. The only jewel remaining as a reminder of the former creation was a spectacular brooch which was set with all the baguette and fancy-shaped diamonds together with the scroll motifs formerly in the necklace.

In 1929 Ganna was one of several society ladies to add a Cartier chimera bangle to her collection of jewels. This bangle, designed by Charles Jacqueau, was set with two coral serpent's heads carved by the lapidary Dalvy, and decorated with carved sapphire leaves and cabochon sapphires and with diamond eyes and teeth. Held between their jaws were two large fluted emerald beads of 48.43cts and the back was decorated with blue and green enamel. The bracelet was made for Cartier in 1928 for stock by Lavabre, and Ganna bought it the following July. In the 1971 sale it was described as an 'Indian Tawiz Arm Amulet'. Indeed, much of the inspiration was eastern and the carved heads represented Makara, the mythical Indian sea-serpent. The previous lot in her sale was similarly described but was also a European interpretation of these exotic jewels. This sensational bangle, made by Van Cleef & Arpels in the late 1920s, was set with carved coral chimera heads decorated with sapphires and diamonds and holding jade beads between their jaws. The back of the bangle was decorated with green, blue and white enamel.

These two bangles are superb examples of Art Deco jewelry which used a dramatic combination of colours, materials and sybolism. The Van Cleef & Arpels piece was sold again in 1988 in New York. Another bangle in Ganna Walska's collection of a similar period was a version in onyx, carved emerald and diamond, almostly certainly by Cartier. The hinged mount of platinum and onyx was decorated with brilliant-cut diamonds and the terminals set with two large carved emerald beads.

Also in the late '20s she bought a wonderful coral and onyx fuchsia necklace from Cartier which was originally designed for stock in 1925. The catalogue of her collection refers to a carved coral, carved emerald, onyx and pearl pendant necklace which would appear from the description to be the fuchsia jewel of which the original drawings are still in existence. Unfortunately there is no photographic evidence in the catalogue to confirm or deny this theory. In the sale several other coral jewels of a similar date and Art Deco influence, some signed by Cartier, were in evidence. These included a small group of hair ornaments and hatpins, possibly the most interesting of which was in the form of a Japanese pagoda set with lapis lazuli, diamonds, a cabochon sapphire and a carved jade. This design and combination of materials was typical of Cartier's oriental style of the late 1920s. There were also coral necklaces, some carved and some matched with jade, coral bracelets and a stylish coral, diamond and black enamel ring.

In 1929 Ganna bought a most unusual Cartier jewel, which in the 1971 catalogue was described simply as a 'crystal and diamond bracelet'. The style of bracelets in the 1920s was of flat strap form, from which this was a complete departure. Of tubular form, it was composed of a flexible row of carved crystal demi-lune discs strung together on wire, the sides of each crystal set with brilliant-cut diamonds. The back was set with several platinum bars to strenghten the form of the jewel. Ganna's bracelet was the first which Cartier created in this style. The following year they made two further versions, one of which was sold to the actress Gloria Swanson and the second to Madame Coty.

In 1929 Ganna also acquired from Cartier a wonderful amethyst and diamond *sautoir* designed as a long rope of larger step-cut amethysts, alternating with pairs of smaller rectangular amethysts and with a large clasp of pear and similarly shaped stones bordered by diamonds. *Sautoirs* were still highly fashionable at this period, but by 1936 Ganna needed an up-dated version. Cartier remounted most of the stones from this jewel, and added a few, and it became a stylish fringed necklace and a pair of bracelets.

For the first few years of their marriage Harold is said to have spent a fortune attempting to promote her operatic career, but according to the critics she did not have the talent to succeed. Despite her husband's advice to relinquish her ambitions, Ganna travelled throughout America

and Europe pursuing her quest. By 1929 she had left Chicago for Paris, agreeing to a separation from Harold. Once back in France she bought the Château of Galluis, halfway between Paris and Chartres, where she entertained the rich and famous to extravagant galas. She also spent time at the Théâtre des Champs Elysées, which she reportedly received as a present from Harold, and where she organized various operatic events.

In 1931, the year when Harold McCormick finally divorced her on the grounds of desertion, she made several important purchases from Cartier. In the early autumn she bought a wonderful carved ruby and diamond necklace designed as two rows of ruby beads with baguette diamond spacers; the front supported a fringe of fourteen rubies carved in the form of leaves and decorated with baguette and brilliant-cut diamonds. Of Indian inspiration, this necklace was one of the highly popular 'Tutti Frutti' jewels in the Cartier repertoire. The same month she purchased from them an extraordinary belt composed of fifteen carved jade circular plaques, each set with a cabochon ruby and with two larger carved jade and ruby plaques mounted as the clasp. The belt measured over 28 inches and there were two extra links to increase the size. The belt was accompanied by a pair of matching bracelets set with jade beads and jade and ruby plaques, one embellished with diamonds. Ganna had admitted to 'liking big jewels and fortunate enough to get them of any existing size and color, twenty years before the actual fashion for big gems I designed for myself huge necklaces, bracelets and rings, and to make them I got the biggest stones I could find on the market, the largest generous Nature created.' These jewels were in fact stock designs from Cartier and not designed by Ganna but they certainly were big.

That November, Cartier had added to their stock a diamond necklace of Indian inspiration set with ten large triangular-shaped rose diamonds. Each stone was set within a border of brilliant-cut diamonds with the largest six hanging as a fringe at the front; they were connected by baguette diamonds and on a back chain of marquise-shaped stones and smaller rose and brilliant-cut diamond clusters. Whether or not Ganna bought it that year is unclear, but in the 1971 sale it was presented in a completely altered style. There were still the ten larger rose diamonds in their brilliant-cut diamond borders but they were now mounted as a fringe of five two-stone pendants supported by a chain of brilliant-cut diamonds, and it was now accompanied by a clip and a pair of pendent earrings set with similar stones.

Though Ganna Walska bought an enormous amount of jewels from Cartier between the 1920s and '40s, in her sale only a small percentage of them were acknowledged as Cartier creations or from their stock. Indeed Van Cleef &

Arpels received no mention at all even though she was one of their important patrons. The Paris firm of Chaumet is also known to have sold her several jewels including a sapphire of 67.34cts in 1926. Surprisingly, the only piece in her sale recognized as being by Chaumet was a gold, ruby, emerald and diamond pendant necklace of typical 1940s style. The front was of gold scrolled openwork stylized buckle design set with two large carved rubies and two pear-shaped and oval rubies, cylindrical shaped emeralds and decorated with rose- and brilliant-cut diamonds on a necklace of flexible 'gas-pipe' linking. Again, this had been subject to alterations and it was sold with a pendant mount which originally held the two carved rubies. Since the 1971 sale the necklace has once again been unmounted and the two carved rubies, one depicting a dove and the other an angel, are now reunited as a pendant.

The cover of her catalogue illustrated a ruby and diamond butterfly brooch, the description noting that the body was set with a ruby of approximately 3.50cts and a pear-shaped diamond, and that the four diamond wings were carved and mounted *en tremblant*. What it failed to mention was that this remarkable jewel was created by Boucheron around 1894 and that the diamond wings were carved by C. Bordinckx, Frédéric Boucheron's well-known diamond cutter. Towards the end of the 19th century Bordinckx was already famous for his skilfully carved and excuted diamond jewels, and the realistic veins on this butterfly's wings are a testament to his talent.

(Opposite) A diamond necklace by Cartier, 1931, set with ten large rose diamonds, and (below) the necklace as it appeared in the 1971 auction. By then it was a far less elaborate fringe necklace. Cartier Ltd; Sotheby's, New York (Parke Bernet)

There were also jewels by Seaman Schepps, the talented New York jeweler who created many fine sculptural pieces from the 1930s onwards and counted the likes of Coco Chanel and the Duchess of Windsor among his clients. Ganna acquired from him several jewels, including two large brooches, each designed as a sunburst motif of looped goldwork decorated with brilliant-cut diamonds, one set at the centre with a cabochon emerald and the other with a baroque pearl, both probably dating from the 1940s. Among her other purchases was a gold and citrine bracelet together with a matching ring and a gold and cabochon ruby bangle, which was included in the sale with a gold oval frame decorated with twenty-six baroque pearls in which it had originally been mounted.

A dramatic group of gold, sapphire, ruby and emerald jewels, dating from the late 1930s, is reminiscent of those sported by the Duchess of Windsor. The large butterfly clip of ribbed textured gold is set with cabochon stones and is together with a pair of bangles and a two-stone ring. Their style is so distinctive that they are almost certainly the creations of either Belperron or Boivin, as is a carved chalcedony bracelet set with a star sapphire of approximately 125cts. It would also seem unlikely that a jewelry devotee such as Ganna would have omitted these two great French designers from her patronage.

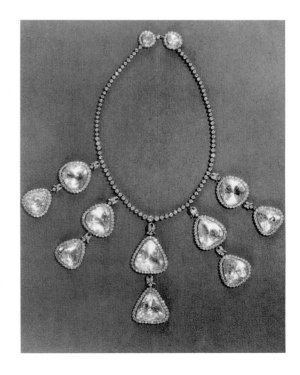

Her reference to time spent in St Petersburg during her first marriage may be substantiated by two jewels by Fabergé. They were both made in St Petersburg by one of Fabergé's workmasters, Hendrik Wigstrom, around 1900. Both were forms of vanity cases, one of simple rectangular design decorated with blue guilloché enamel, the sides and thumbpiece set with rose and cushion-shaped diamonds and inscribed on the top 'Ganna'. The interior contained the usual compartments for powder, rouge and lipstick. The other jewel came in a more ingenious form, that of a parasol handle and vanity case combined. Again decorated with grey guilloché enamel and set with rose diamonds, the hinged top opened to reveal a mirror and compartments for powder and lipstick. It is unknown whether Ganna received these as gifts while in St Petersburg, if indeed she was there, or if they were bought as a reminder of her youth.

Ganna's collection was also remarkable for its extensive array of traditional Indian jewels, the majority of which she most certainly purchased from Cartier, whose archives since the 1870s had recorded Indian jewels included in their stock. By the early years of the 20th century Indian maharajahs were eager to have their jewels remounted in Europe, while fashionable Europeans were craving Indian jewels with their colourful enamel decoration and carved gemstones. These Indian jewels were also an important source of inspiration for European jewelers of the Art Deco period – especially Cartier, as can be seen by Ganna's collection. In 1911 Jacques Cartier made his first trip to India and was quick to capitalize on both the important selling as well as buying opportunities which this vast country offered. Hans Nadelhoffer noted that by the 1930s 'trendsetters like the Hon. Mrs Fellowes, Mrs Drexel Biddle, Ganna Walska and Mrs Harrison Williams spread the Indian fashion, which soon even the Duchess of Windsor was to take up.' Ganna's collection of over thirty Indian jewels included many bracelets, earrings and necklaces, one of the most spectacular examples being a suite of 19th century jewelry from South India. The parure comprised a necklace, a bracelet and a pair of earrings set with rubies, emeralds and diamonds, and would have been worn by a traditional Indian dancer.

By the mid-'30s Ganna had finally bowed to public opinion and reluctantly gave up her dream of becoming a great opera diva. She decided to spend most of her time at her château in France, where she continued to entertain the rich and famous and was easily persuaded to give impromptu recitals. Her attention now turned to mystics and gurus, much of her time occupied in searching for her true self and the 'meaning of life'. There are reports that she made a fifth and final marriage to a Grindell Matthews in the late 1930s.

In due course she returned to America and the sale of her jewels took place in New York in April 1971 when by all accounts she was nearing her eightieth year, if not well into her eighties. One can merely speculate on the reasons why she decided to part with all her remarkable jewels but this sale did assure Ganna that even if she was not to be immortalized as a wonderful opera singer, she would surely be remembered as a one of the 20th century's greacollectors of jewels.

(Below) Two 19th century carved rubies mounted as a pendant, embellished with a baroque pearl. In the 1940s Chaumet used these two rubies to make a necklace. This jewel, which was in the 1971 auction, was also set with two large briolette rubies and baton-shaped emeralds linked by diamond scroll motifs and on a chain of gold gas-pipe linking. *Private collection; Sotheby's, New York (Parke Bernet)*

(Right) A carved Mogul emerald drop, weighing 256.00cts, originally from the Cartier sapphire, emerald and diamond necklace she bought in 1923. The emerald, ruby and rose diamond necklace is South Indian, probably from Madras, and dates from the 19th century. This style of Indian necklace was usually worn by traditional dancers. *Sotheby's, New York (Parke Bernet)*

An enamel, carved coral, sapphire, jade and diamond Chimera bangle, by Van Cleef & Arpels, late 1920s. *Christie's, New York*

Barbara Hutton

When Barbara Hutton died in 1979, she reportedly left very little money in her estate, but when her will was probated it revealed that she had retained many of her most important jewels. Among her bequests were mentioned the fabulous 'Pasha' diamond, a spectacular suite of rubies and diamonds, and various pearl and diamond pieces. As there has never been an entire auction of her jewels and only a few of her most famous pieces have appeared in the sales rooms since 1985, it is tantalizing to try to discover the full extent of her collection.

Barbara Woolworth Hutton was born in New York City on 14 November 1912, the daughter of Edna and Franklyn Hutton and the granddaughter of Frank Winfield Woolworth, founder of the phenomenally successful chain of retail stores bearing his name. At the age of four, she was to discover the body of her mother who, it was reported in the press, had died of complications caused by a chronic ear ailment. There was no mention of Franklyn Hutton's womanizing or of the police reports that an empty vial of poison was found in Edna's bathroom. Frank Woolworth had been aware of his daughter's unhappiness and had attempted to persuade her to start divorce proceedings as well as to stop his son-in-law's philandering. Whatever the circumstances of her death, it was not made the subject of further investigation.

Until his death in 1919, Barbara Hutton was cared for by her grandfather; after that, her life became even more unsettled as she was moved from one relative to another, her father always ready with material but not emotional support. This disorganized start to her life obviously had a strong impact on her as an adult. The only stable aspect of her life appears to have been the vast fortune she inherited from her grandparents and her mother: before she was in her teens, she had well over $28 million in trust, and this was to be nearly doubled by the time she came of age. She partied, travelled, and lived a life of excessive excitement and self-indulgence, but even after seven marriages, she was still the 'poor little rich girl' of Noël Coward's 1920s song, never finding the contentment she craved. By the end of her life, her wealth was seriously eroded and she became a virtual recluse.

Her debut, or coming-out party, was held in December 1930, the first year of the Depression, at a cost of some $60,000. It took place in three venues: the first was a tea party at the home of her aunt and uncle, Marjorie (formerly Marjorie Merriweather Post) and Edward Hutton. The second setting was the Central Park Casino, where 500 guests dined and danced; and the final event was a ball at the Ritz-Carlton Hotel on Madison Avenue. As orchestras played and the scent of thousands of flowers filled the air,

A studio portrait of Barbara Hutton by Horst, New York, 1939. She is wearing the 'Pasha' diamond ring, her famous 'Marie Antoinette' pearl necklace and her bracelet of large pear-shaped diamonds. *Private collection*

Barbara Hutton and Prince Alexis Mdivani being married at the Russian Cathedral of St Alexander Nevsky in Paris, June 1933. She is wearing the tortoiseshell and diamond Balinese tiara that she commissioned from Cartier, Paris. *UPI/CORBIS*

A two-row golden cultured pearl necklace with an opal and diamond clasp, by Cartier, which Hutton would often wear with her fabulous ruby and diamond tiara. *Christie's, London*

(Below) An emerald and diamond bracelet by Cartier, 1935. It was commissioned by Count Henrik Haugwitz Hardenberg-Reventlow using the family emeralds and given to Barbara Hutton shortly after her marriage to his brother. *Christie's, Geneva*

(Opposite) Barbara Hutton's historically important necklace of pearls that had formerly been worn by Queen Marie Antoinette of France. Bought from Cartier, Paris, this jewel was given to Barbara Hutton by her father as a wedding present on the occasion of her marriage to Prince Alexis Mdivani in 1933. *Sotheby's, Geneva*

Barbara Hutton officially entered the world of society. The following year she was taken to England and, as one of the most recent American debutantes, was presented to King George V and Queen Mary at Buckingham Palace.

Her first marriage was to a prince, the Russian aristocrat Alexis Mdivani. The wedding took place in Paris over a period of three days. A civil ceremony was held on 20 June 1933, and the religious ceremony two days later at the Russian Orthodox Cathedral of St Alexander Nevsky in the rue Daru. For the first, she wore a pale grey outfit by Chanel to compliment her black pearl engagement ring, created by Cartier; and for the church ceremony she chose ivory satin and lace. She commissioned Cartier to design a somewhat unusual tiara which was reminiscent of those she had seen and admired during a recent trip to Bali. It was made of tortoiseshell decorated with delicate diamond trefoil motifs, a design which was echoed in the lace veil which it held.

The wedding was hailed as a glorious success and it was attended by hundreds of guests, among them Daisy Fellowes, resplendent in two large cuff bracelets of Indian inspiration by Cartier, and the opera singer and socialite Ganna Walska, who wore her sapphire and emerald jewels, again by Cartier. The presents received by the bride included several exquisite pieces of jewelry, the most impressive from her father. Bought from Cartier, it was a necklace of 53 pearls that had been worn by Marie Antoinette. This jewel, which the press described as 'one of the rarest strands of pearls ever sold by Cartier', became one of her most cherished possessions; she wore it in daytime or at night, and had it shortened or lengthened according to the vagaries of fashion. When it was sold in 1992, it comprised 40 pearls, but according to Cartier's records the pearls had been restrung and altered many times for their valued client.

Grand Duchess Vladimir of Russia dressed for a fancy dress ball. Among the spectacular jewels she is wearing is the 100.00cts hexagonal emerald which formed the central cluster of her emerald and diamond necklace. This amazing stone is used here as the centre of a hair ornament, the border of which is her tiara/necklace 'Russe'. *From George Frederick Kunz and Charles Hugh Stevenson,* The Book of the Pearl, *London 1908.*

Grand Duchess Vladimir's emerald and diamond necklace in its original antique Russian setting. As the emerald and diamond drops and clusters were all detachable, the Grand Duchess wore them in a variety of forms. *Cartier Ltd*

In 1923 Cartier, New York, redesigned the necklace for Edith Rockefeller McCormick. The step-cut emeralds were mounted in a long *sautoir* of diamond set links, a style of necklace extremely fashionable during that period. *Cartier Ltd*

By 1936 Grand Duchess Vladimir's necklace had been acquired by Barbara Hutton and she commissioned Cartier in London to create a ring, a pair of earrings and a necklace from these extraordinary gems. The large hexagonal emerald became the central drop of this necklace. *Cartier Ltd*

(Right) The last version of the emerald and diamond necklace was created for Barbara Hutton in Paris in 1947 by one of Cartier's great designers, Lucien Lachassagne. The seven largest emeralds were remounted together in yellow gold as the fringe of an exotic diamond neckace/tiara of Indian inspiration.

(Below) At a reception with the actor Joseph Cotten in the palace of Count Volpi di Misurata in Venice in the early 1950s, she is wearing the Vladimir emeralds as a necklace together with the 'Pasha' diamond ring. *Cartier Ltd; Count Volpi di Misurata*

(Overleaf two pages) In this Cecil Beaton photograph taken in Tangier in the early 1960s, Hutton is wearing the Vladimir emeralds as a tiara together with a pair of emerald and diamond pendent earrings, two diamond bracelets, her wonderful pearl necklace and the 'Pasha' diamond ring. *Sotheby's, London (Cecil Beaton Archive)*

A jade bead necklace by Cartier, c. 1930. Mounted on a ruby and diamond clasp, this jewel is believed to have been a gift from Hutton's father. The jade, ruby and diamond ring was created by Cartier in 1934 to match the necklace. *Christie's; Cartier Ltd*

This extravagant wedding present was the beginning of Barbara's passion for pearls. One of her social secretaries, Mona Eldridge, recalls not only those famous white pearls but also a necklace of extraordinary golden pearls and an equally remarkable row of black pearls. In London in 1988 an important golden cultured pearl necklace was auctioned with the provenance of the Princess Nina Mdivani.

The white pearl necklace was sold as 'the property of a member of a European Noble Family, formerly from the collection of Barbara Hutton'. It had not been Franklyn Hutton's first purchase for his daughter at Cartier. In the summer of 1929 he persuaded his reluctant daughter to accompany him on a trip to Europe by offering her a jewel of her choice. The story is told that when they called in at Cartier in New York, trays of wonderful rubies were brought out for her to inspect. Once she had made her choice the salesman beamed but her father

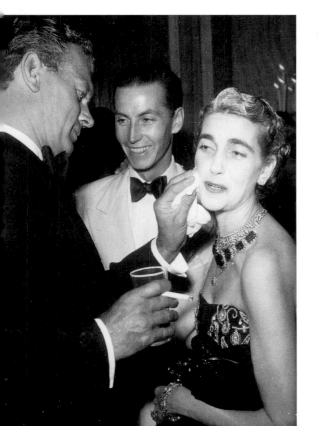

was less ecstatic: the ring she had chosen was the finest ruby in Cartier's stock and cost her father $50,000, over ten times the figure he had envisaged spending, but it reassured him of her impeccable taste in jewels. Barbara Hutton became a lavish admirer of Cartier's jewels, and made many purchases from them.

Both friends and jewelers noted that Barbara not only loved her jewels and gems but knew a great deal about them. She was also known to be so fascinated by them that she would spend many hours holding, studying and admiring each piece, not as an object of commercial value but as a beautiful combination of nature's and man's creation.

By 1935 her first marriage ended in divorce, 24 hours after which she married the Prussian-born Danish Count Haugwitz-Reventlow, and as the Countess Haugwitz-Reventlow she made one of her most famous

acquisitions from Cartier: the Romanov emeralds, once in the possession of the Grand Duchess Vladimir.

Early in the century, they had been bought by the Chicago tycoon Harold McCormick for his first wife, who was John D. Rockefeller's daughter Edith. They had been mounted for her as a *sautoir*. After her death the stones were unmounted and sold by the executors of her will to Cartier for $480,000. It had reportedly cost Barbara Hutton over $1,000,000 to acquire them.

Initially, she commissioned Cartier in London to create a ring, a pair of earrings and a necklace with the largest emerald, weighing 100cts, set at the centre. In 1947, by now the wife of Prince Troubetzkoy, she had Lucien Lachassagne of Cartier design for her a wonderful necklace/tiara in Oriental style, using the same emeralds. In 1965 she sold the jewel to Van Cleef & Arpels, who subsequently remounted all the stones into several jewels and had the largest emerald re-cut to 89.47cts.

It was from Bulgari that Barbara bought the famous 40cts 'Pasha' diamond which, at the time it had been acquired by the Viceroy of Egypt, Ibrahim Pasha, was believed to be the finest stone in the Egyptian treasury. It remained there until Ismail Pasha was deposed in 1863, when he took it out of the country and sold it to an Englishman. Its whereabouts were unknown for many years until Bulgari bought it from King Farouk. Unhappy with its slightly octagonal form, Barbara had it re-cut at Cartier to a weight of 38.19cts and mounted as a dazzling ring. Upon her death, according to reports, it was removed from her finger by her 'house manager', Bill Robertson, who placed it along with the contents of three jewelry cases in a brown paper bag, which was taken to a bank in Bermuda to await the dispersal of her bequests.

In Geneva in 1971 an important emerald-and-diamond bracelet was auctioned with the provenance: 'The late Count Henrik Haugwitz Hardenberg-Reventlow'. Shortly after Barbara's marriage to the Count, she had travelled with him and her playboy cousin Jimmy Donahue to his family home in Denmark, the Castle Hardenberg, to meet the rest of his family. Sadly, their arrival coincided with the news of Alexis Mdivani's fatal motor accident, which plunged Barbara into a state of depression during most of the visit. Her spirits were lifted by the dinner party that her brother-in-law Henrik was hosting for neighbouring gentry and European diplomats. After the feast he presented her with an impressive bracelet, recently set with the family emeralds. She was thrilled. 'It's the first time I've ever really been

(Top) One of Barbara Hutton's fine carved jadeite bangles, and (above) in Paris in June 1951 to attend a party given by Elsa Maxwell, she is wearing her magnificent ruby and diamond necklace and a pair of earrings *en suite*. The rubies set in the necklace/tiara were originally mounted in her *fin de siècle* necklace *résille* (p. 188). *Sotheby's, Hong Kong; Associated Press Photo*

given a present I didn't have to pay for myself.' It has been suggested that Henrik had this bracelet made at Tiffany's, New York, but it is more probable that this is the jewel which he commissioned from Cartier in London on 31 May 1935 and for which he supplied the emeralds.

After she divorced his brother, Henrik wrote requesting the return of the emerald bracelet in a somewhat curt manner: 'The emeralds are family stones and since you are no longer in the family I think they should be returned.' Although she was shocked by this letter, it is probable that she complied with his request.

Barbara Hutton was also a lover of the stylish 'Great Cat' jewels, exquisite creations inspired by Cartier's director of *haute joaillerie*, Jeanne Toussaint, working closely with the designer Peter Lemarchand. She chose three of the finest examples from the cat menagerie: a bracelet, a brooch and a pair of earrings, dated 1962, 1957 and 1961 respectively. Designed as tigers, the brooch and the earrings echo the bold curve of the Golden Fleece, the pelts being set with carved onyx and yellow diamond stripes.

Barbara was enamoured of jade, having been introduced to it when young by the owner of the San Francisco shop Gump's, which specialized in Oriental objects. Although the majority of her vast collection was ornamental, she did have some amazing jade jewels. It is believed that both her father and her first husband gave her jade necklaces. In 1988 a highly important jade bead necklace was auctioned in Geneva for the estate of Princess Nina Mdivani. It was designed as a row of 27 large jade beads on a ruby and diamond clasp, and was described in the catalogue as 'one of the most splendid jade necklaces (of the jadeite variety) for size and colour to have been offered on the international market.'

Early in our research we had located a photograph of Barbara arriving with Prince Mdivani at the Metropolitan Opera House in New York in 1933, in which she appears to be wearing this very necklace. In 1994 a jade necklace was included in another auction in Hong Kong, and this time it was identified as one that had belonged to Barbara. Indeed, the same photograph was used as confirmation of what we had suspected.

This was an unhappy, restless woman, married seven times (including the actor Cary Grant), who had a luxurious lifestyle, with residences in many locations, not least an exotic palace in Morocco. Her final years, following the death in a plane crash of her only child, Lance Reventlow, were spent in ill health, and she died in her suite at the Beverly Wilshire Hotel in Los Angeles in May 1979 at the age of 66. During her lifetime she had amassed a remarkable collection of jewelry, rich in both fine gemstones and stylish designs, which represented not only her wealth but also her appreciation of beauty.

(Left) Princess Mdivani arriving at the Metropolitan Opera House, New York, in 1933, wearing her jade bead necklace. *(Above)* Her passion for the Orient is evident in this photograph taken in 1966 where she is dressed in a Japanese-style kimono. She is also wearing a pair of her fine carved jadeite bangles.
Sygma London-Keystone; Associated Press Photo London

(Overleaf two pages) Barbara Hutton looking somewhat less than festive at a birthday party given to her by her husband Prince Mdivani at the Paris Ritz, 1934. She is wearing her ruby and diamond necklace in its original form. *UPI/CORBIS*

Barbara Hutton's yellow diamond and onyx 'Great Cat' jewels by Cartier, Paris. The tiger earrings were made in 1961, the brooch in 1957 and the bracelet in 1962.
Sotheby's, Geneva

Helena Rubinstein

By the time of her death in April 1965 at the age of 94, Helena Rubinstein, through sheer hard work and enterprise, had built up an enormously successful empire in the world of beauty and cosmetics. Though she was only 4'10" tall, she possessed incredible stamina and an astute mind for business, attributes which enabled her not only to survive but to thrive in a world not accustomed to the career woman. Alongside this powerful business acumen she also had a passion for art and objects of beauty. Through the success of her company she was able to indulge her acquisitive nature and created extraordinarily diverse and interesting collections, which included jewelry.

The eldest of eight sisters, her only brother having died in infancy, Helena was born in Cracow, Poland, in 1870. Throughout her life her family were of enormous importance to her and the very strong bonding between the sisters was to ensure the success of many of her enterprises. Her strong will and sense of adventure emerged when she was young. Her father persuaded her to attend medical school, which was not altogether to her liking; she was fascinated by the laboratory work but loathed the practical side which involved dealing with the blood and gore. Marriage was perceived by her father to be solution to her problem and he selected a 35-year-old rich widower as a suitable candidate. Helena, who would have none of this, convinced herself that she was in love with a young medical student who conveniently proposed. As her enraged father refused to permit this match, Helena saw that she would have to find another means of escape.

Her mother's brother, Louis, had emigrated to Australia after the death of his wife. His daughter, Eva, had lived with the Rubinsteins until her early teens when she left to join her father. Eva and Helena corresponded regularly and the descriptions of Australian life encouraged Helena to believe that her salvation lay in that land of opportunities rather than in Poland. Uncle Louis agreed to accommodate her, and at the age of 18 she embarked on the three-month journey which was to change her life. In her luggage she unwittingly carried the key to her future: twelve pots of face cream made by a Dr Jacob Lykusky.

Her mother had always instilled in her daughters the need to maintain a perfect complexion and had introduced them to Dr Lykusky's cream. The Hungarian chemist had supplied Mrs Rubinstein with his concoction for many years and they had become firm friends. The ingredients of this cream were always a closely guarded secret but their effect seemed highly successful.

The Australian climate was extremely harsh on the complexion and Helena generously gave pots of the cream to friends who found the results amazing. Soon her mother was sending her regular supplies. This

Helena Rubinstein photographed by Cecil Beaton wearing one of her spectacular necklaces of multi-coloured pearls. *Sotheby's, London (Cecil Beaton Archives)*

(Overleaf two pages) Helena Rubinstein's ruby, emerald and chrysoprase four-row bead necklace decorated with diamond rondels and on a cabochon emerald and diamond clasp. Also her ruby ring, the cabochon ruby mounted in platinum, within a border of calibré-cut rubies. In another Cecil Beaton photograph, she is wearing her ruby bead and diamond ring, her ruby bead necklace and other ruby jewels. *Christie's, New York; Sotheby's, London (Cecil Beaton Archive)*

fueled ideas in Helena's active mind, and within a few years she had opened the first beauty salon in Australia. These three rooms in Melbourne were the start of her eventual empire. Before long Lykusky joined her and their days, and often nights, were spent experimenting on new creams to combat the ravages of time and the unkindly climate. The popularity of the salon was such that she could soon afford to move to a larger building and recruit the aid of her sister Ceska, who had been studying chemistry in Berlin. Her clientele included the best of Melbourne society and she was thrilled when Dame Nellie Melba, the great opera diva, gave her patronage.

With the salon now in the safe hands of Ceska it was possible for Helena to pursue her own studies and research. She spent an extremely informative year in Europe where she visited the most highly regarded skin specialists and doctors to learn and discuss all she could about skin and dietary requirements. She was determined to be a true expert in her profession from the very start.

Soon after she returned to Australia, Edward Titus, an American newspaper man of Polish extraction, who had known her sisters in Cracow, fell in love with her and asked her to marry him. Still at the start of her career, Helena was undecided and left for London in 1907 without having given any commitment. Titus pursued her to London and this time his proposal was accepted. Their registry office wedding was followed by a honeymoon in Nice and their first disagreement. Helena felt that Titus was being rather too attentive to another woman and after a heated row she left alone on the next train to Paris – but not before purchasing a rather expensive pearl necklace. This was an indulgence that she would allow herself on every occasion when she had a serious confrontation and which she called her 'quarrel' jewelry. She said, 'Some women buy hats, but I am more extravagant in anger, as I am in most things.'

Back in London, she opened a salon in Grafton Street and was soon enjoying a colourful social life, mainly with artistic and literary groups. One of her great friends at this time was Baroness d'Erlanger, and through Margot Asquith she met with a more exalted circle of London society. She now enlisted her sister Manka to help with the London salon, and as soon as she felt confident that Manka was in full control of the business she departed for Paris. Here she opened a salon in the Rue St Honoré. In

(Above) Helena Rubinstein in 1936 wearing several jewels, including her antique pearl and diamond pendant and the important emerald and diamond ring, the emerald weighing approximately 35.00cts.

(Below) The antique pearl and diamond pendant mounted in gold and silver and set with three larger baroque pearls and a pearl and diamond brooch/pendant. The latter is a combination of a 19th century diamond cluster and a baroque pearl drop mounted together with baguette diamonds in the 1920s. *Collection Helena Rubinstein Foundation; Parke-Bernet Galleries Inc.- Sotheby's*

(Opposite) A pair of brushed platinum and diamond bangles, 1940s, probably by Boivin. *Christie's, New York*

1909 her son Roy was born and her sister Pauline was called upon to run the Paris enterprise.

Returned to London, Helena spent a great deal of her time at home, especially after the birth of her second son Horace in 1912. Despite her love of the business, these days of family life were very dear to her. In 1914 she and Titus and the boys moved to Paris and entered into Parisian artistic circles. Helena's collecting began with a vengeance: the likes of Picasso and Braque now graced her walls. After the declaration of war the family managed to stay on in Paris until the beginning of 1915. They decided then that, as Titus and their two sons had American citizenship, it would be prudent to move to the USA for the duration of the war.

Towards the end of 1915 Helena opened her first salon in New York but she was already aware that one outlet was insufficient. 'It was wartime, and American women, with all their new responsibilities, were becoming more aware of themselves.' Once again she enlisted the help of Manka. By 1917 there were salons in Boston, San Francisco and Philadelphia; these were soon followed by Washington, Chicago and Toronto. Her products were also being sold through high-class department stores where they trained their employees to be beauty consultants.

After the war was over, Helena bought property in Paris to increase the size of the business and also built an apartment house in the Boulevard Raspail. Edward Titus was pursuing a career in publishing which was proving a success and the guests at their dinner table consisted mainly of writers and artists. Helena was able to pursue once again her passion for collecting and benefitted by being acquainted with many of the artists themselves. Matisse, Modigliani, Chagall, Braque and Dufy all entered her home and she either bought their works or listened to their advice.

During this period she appeared to be spending more time with her business empire than with her husband. The result was that she and Edward were eventually divorced. In 1935, she met Prince Archil Gourielli-Tchkonia, a Georgian living in Paris, and married him in 1938.

The outbreak of another world war forced her and her Prince to leave Paris for New York. Here her apartment, where she entertained lavishly, was the setting for a startling array of art: Renoirs, Picassos, a Toulouse-Lautrec, two Modiglianis, Matisse, Braque and Chagall, to name but a few, plus a substantial collection of African art. After the war, she also filled her Paris and London apartments with a wealth of art objects.

Her passion for art was almost matched by her passion for clothes and jewelry. She enjoyed spending her free time in Paris either selecting exquisite gowns from designers such as Poiret and Chanel, who were also her friends, or looking for ideas to have copied in the U.S.A. by her own dressmaker. In her later years one of her favoured modes of attire was a bowler hat which she sported in a variety of materials.

In 1956 Archil unexpectedly died of a heart attack and her son Horace died a few years later. Well into her eighties, Helena threw herself into her work even more relentlessly and undertook exhausting travel schedules to promote the company. She could be a hard taskmaster and somewhat irascible, but by the time of her death she had built success upon success. She had also created an extraordinary collection of paintings, works of art, furniture and jewelry. Her will stipulated that all these 'belongings', apart from a few specific bequests, were to be auctioned.

Her jewelry collection was proof that, as she herself quite rightly once stated, 'a woman's choice of jewels reveals much about her personality. If I had been a tall, statuesque woman, I would probably have chosen tiny, delicate pieces. But since I am small and favor simple, even severely cut clothes, I feel they need the contrast of large colourful stones. My hair, too, is worn simply, but I bring to it the dramatic effect of necklaces and long earrings.'

Towards the end of her life, all her jewels were kept in a filing cabinet, labelled alphabetically, and from contemporary photographs of this 'casket' it is evident that the collection was vast. The jewelry auctioned in 1965 was obviously just a small part of this collection but it was a true reflection of her diverse choice in jewels and was justly described as unique. The entire collection was based on Helena's own highly individual taste and not governed by the dictates of fashion. The majority of the 187 pieces had been chosen by her for their theatrical and colourful effect rather than for the quality of the gems or workmanship. She said, 'I like large, beautifully coloured stones, and I am not concerned about their value.'

Indeed her jewels were mainly so big and so colourful that she seldom encountered any problems with customs officers on her frequent travels. She

(Below) One of Helena Rubinstein's 'filing cabinet' jewelry boxes, the drawers opened to reveal some of the contents. She was reported to have had ten such cabinets. *Vogue-Condé Nast Publications Inc.*

Rubinstein's sapphire and diamond hand ornament made by Ecalle c.1935, from the design by Anna Semenoff, together with a diamond ring, set with a cushion-shaped diamond of approximately 21.50cts, and an emerald and diamond ring, set with an emerald of nearly 35.00cts. *Parke-Bernet Inc. - Sotheby's*

usually informed them that it was all costume jewelry and they always believed her.

Helena's collection of necklaces was perhaps the most spectacular. She had several large necklaces of coloured stone beads. One extravagant example created in the 1930s consisted of four rows of large emerald and ruby beads connected by diamond rondels and on a large cabochon emerald and diamond clasp. The others included simple strings of emeralds, rubies or sapphires and more elaborate versions mixed with baroque pearls. Two other very stylish necklaces also came from the late Art Deco period when the motifs were still rather formal and geometric. One was a yellow and blue sapphire and diamond necklace, the front designed as three tapered detachable clips. The other, an emerald and diamond necklace, was one of her most important jewels. Quite classic in design, it was set with ten large cabochon emeralds, the largest as a drop at the centre, connected by baguette and brilliant-cut diamonds. As was the case with most of her necklaces, she had a matching pair of earrings.

Among the many photographs taken of Helena wearing her jewels, one poses an enigma. She is seen in her New York apartment in the early '60s wearing a striking necklace set with cabochon stones in Indian style. Intriguingly, this necklace is identical to the one that the Duchess of Windsor had acquired from Harry Winston and then returned to him after the embarrassing incident when the Maharani of Baroda remarked that it had been her anklet. According to Laurence S. Krashes in his book on Harry Winston, the emerald and diamond necklace was then sold to a socialite from Dallas. The necklace reappeared at auction in New York in 1981.

Like many other jewelry collectors, she had a passion for pearls. One of her favourite necklaces was made of seven graduated rows of pearls mounted on a beautiful diamond Art Deco rectangular clasp, the centre stone weighing over 2cts. This much-loved jewel she chose to wear for her portrait by Graham Sutherland. In the sale were several other natural and cultured pearl necklaces in a variety of sizes and colours. She also had many pairs of pearl earrings and pearl bracelets, often mixed with other stones.

Particularly astonishing in the collection of a woman of such small stature was the size of the rings, some of them almost barbaric in dimension. 'One ring is never enough,' she would say, 'but two will tell the world you mean business.' Together with the sheer size of her rings, their selection was enormous. One was set with a carved cabochon ruby of over 115cts which was surrounded by 165 diamonds. Many other rings were equally opulent and set with stones of substantial sizes. They included a cushion-shaped sapphire weighing 70cts, a square step-cut yellow diamond weighing over 50cts, an emerald weighing over 35cts and a cushion-shaped diamond of over 20cts mounted in a gold petalled border. Another striking ruby

(Above) In her New York apartment, wearing her rose diamond and emerald drop necklace as two rows. *Bettmann*

(Overleaf two pages) Helena Rubinstein discussing with Graham Sutherland the colour of the Balenciaga dress which she wore for his portrait of her. She is wearing one of her pearl necklaces and other striking jewels, including her emerald and diamond ring.
(Right) The portrait by Sutherland, 1957. When she first saw the completed canvas, Rubinstein thought 'it was an incredibly bold, domineering interpretation of what I had never imagined I looked like.' Later, when it was shown at the Tate Gallery in London she admitted it was a 'masterpiece'. *Collection Helena Rubinstein Foundation*

197

and diamond ring was set at the centre with a brilliant-cut diamond, weighing around 10cts, bordered by ruby beads and diamonds; there was a matching pair of earrings. She chose to wear this ring with a multi-strand ruby necklace for a portrait taken by Cecil Beaton in the room in her New York apartment which he had recently decorated for her.

Perhaps her most unusual jewel was the sapphire and diamond hand ornament. It took the form of a platinum starfish decorated with diamonds and set at the centre with an oval faceted sapphire weighing nearly 85cts. When worn, the piece covers the entire back of the hand and stretches from the wrist to the fingers. This piece was signed: '*Executé par Ecalle d'après la maquette d'Anna Semenoff*'. Born in France in 1888, Anna Semenoff, the daughter of Russian émigrés, became a highly talented sculptor and painter and part of the Parisian artistic elite of the '20s and '30s. To commemorate her marriage to the Marquis Bossard de La Fresnaye in 1935 she designed a highly unusual sapphire and diamond ring. Charles Ecalle was a very avant-garde jeweler in the Rue Faubourg St Honoré and she commissioned him to create her ring. The starfish hand ornament was also a result of their collaboration, which the Marquise de La Fresnaye sold to Helena in 1945.

Although the main part of Rubinstein's collection was from the '30s and '40s, she also had an interesting selection dating from the 19th century. An unusual example was a pearl and diamond brooch pendant set with three large baroque pearls decorated with diamonds. The design incorporated ribbon bows and flowerheads as well as a coiled serpent and was possibly a successful combination of two late 19th-century jewels. Dating from the second half of the 19th century was adiamond brooch, mounted *en tremblant* in gold and silver, and designed as a spray of wheat. She also had an impressive diamond floral spray brooch with each of the five flowerheads mounted *en tremblant*, so typical of the 1890s.

Among her antique jewels was a pair of earrings set with amethysts and diamonds in Girandole style, reminiscent of the 18th century. Another stylish pair was set with diamonds in a design of ribbons and garlands, again harking back to the previous century. The most elaborate of these was a necklace which was a combination of early 19th-century chains of topaz and diamonds in closed settings, cleverly adapted over a century later to form one piece.

Shortly before she died, Helena completed her autobiography and her own words provide a perfect description of her jewelry collection and her reasons for forming it: 'Although I no longer need the added courage that handsome jewelry once gave me (it was not easy being a hard-working woman in a man's world many years ago), I am aware that the wearing of exotic jewelry has become associated in many people's minds with the "image" of Helena Rubinstein, a mark of my identity, so to speak. And since I shall always love beautiful things, I feel I might as well enjoy wearing those I have.'

Helena Rubinstein's sapphire and diamond necklace, 1930s, set with yellow and pale blue sapphires and diamonds. The central three sections detach to form clips. The yellow gold and sapphire ring is set with a cushion-shaped stone of approximately 70.00cts. *Parke-Bernet Inc.- Sotheby's*

Acknowledgments

Our greatest thanks go to the following: The Umberto II Foundation, especially H.R.H. Princess Maria Gabriella of Savoy, for her most generous help and enthusiasm for our project and for providing invaluable information and material; Lilla Rowcliffe, the daughter of Lydia, Lady Deterding, whose fascinating accounts of her mother's life brought the chapter to life; Renata Tebaldi for sharing her memories with us; Hugo Vickers for his great generosity in providing invaluable information and material relating to Gladys, Duchess of Marlborough and the Princess Royal, Countess of Harewood; Richard Jay Hutto for all the invaluable information he so generously gave us relating to Cornelia, Countess of Craven; Elizabeth Wickham for her understanding of how we envisaged the book and for being so enjoyable to work with; and special thanks to our editor, Stanley Baron, for his endless support and encouragement with this project and his excellent advice.

We would also like to thank the many others, including colleagues and friends, for all their help in providing information, photographic material, archival material and advice for our project. In particular we would like to thank the following:

Michel Ailgia, Cartier S.A., Paris; Peter Batkin, Sotheby's, London; Don Franco Victor de Baux, Sotheby's, London; Tally Belsinger, Christie's, New York; Dorothy Bosomworth, Cartier Ltd, London: Judith Clarke, Sygma; Moya Cocoran, Cartier Ltd, London; Lydia Cresswell-Jones, Sotheby's, London: Lady Teresa Craven; Claudine Delcambre, Cartier Joaillerie S.A., Geneva; H.R.H. Prince Dimitri of Yugoslavia, Sotheby's, New York; Monica Dunham, The Mona Bismarck Foundation, Paris; Johannes Ernst, Sotheby's, Frankfurt; Dr Roger Evans, The British Library, London; Prof. Michele Falzone del Barbaro; Giorgio Fiori, F. Chiappe, Genova; Jeremy Flax; Angela Folino, Christie's, New York; Joe Freidman, Sotheby's, London; Philippe Garner, Sotheby's, London; The Earl of Harewood, K.B.E.; Elaine Hart, *The Illustrated London News*; H.H. Prince Henry of Hesse; Anne Holbach, Cartier Ltd., New York; Betty Jais, Cartier S.A., Paris; Kathy Kermian, Christie's, New York; The Kobal Collection; Gabriella Mantegani, Sotheby's, Paris; Brendan Lynch; Stephanie Mellerio, Mellerio dits Meller, Paris; Suzy Menkes; Angela Minshall, Hulton Getty Collection Ltd.; Amoury de la Moussaye; Count de la Moussaye; Eric Nussbaum, Cartier Joaillerie S.A., Geneva; Isabelle Pardo; Terence Pepper, The National Portrait Gallery, London; Giuseppe Petochi, Petochi, Rome; Julia Richardson, Sotheby's, London; Raymond Sancroft-Baker, Christie's, Geneva; Elda Scotti Ferrario; Heinrich Graf von Spreti, Sotheby's, Munich; Amanda Stucklin, Sotheby's, London; John Stuart; Mario Tavella, Sotheby's, London; Mrs Judy Taubman; Simon Teakle, Christie's, New York; Helen Tricker; Daniele Turian, Sotheby's, Geneva; Baron Robert Vaes, Sotheby's, London; Natalie Vianello-Chiodo, Christie's, Geneva; Ernestina Vigano; Valerie Vlasaty, Sotheby's, New York; and Wayne Williams, Sotheby's, London

Bibliography

BALFOUR, IAN *Famous Diamonds*, London 1987

BEATON, C. *The Glass of Fashion*, London 1954

BLOCH, M. *The Duchess of Windsor*, London 1996

— *Wallis & Edward Letters 1931 –1937*, London 1986

—*The Reign & Abdication of Edward VII*, London 1990

BRACILINI, R. *Queen Margherita*, Milan 1983

BURY, S. *Jewellery 1789-1910, The International Era*, Woodbridge 1991

CAILLES, F. *Rene Boivin Jeweller*, London 1994

CASANOVA, C. *Renata Tebaldi The Voice of an Angel*, Dallas 1995

COLOGNI, F. and NUSSBAUM, E. *Platinum by Cartier. Triumphs of the Jewelers' Art*, New York, 1996

CULME, J. and RAYNER, N. *The Jewels of the Duchess of Windsor*, London 1987

ELDRIDGE, M. *In Search of a Prince, My Life with Barbara Hutton*, London 1988

EYMAN, S. *Mary Pickford, America's Sweetheart*, New York 1990

FIELDING, D. *The Face of the Sphinx, A Portrait of Gladys Deacon, Duchess of Marlborough*. London 1978

FLAMINI, R. *Ava, A Biography*, London 1984

GARDNER, A. *Ava, My Story*, New York 1990

GASPARRI ROSSOTTO, A.M. *La Tebaldi*, Milan 1989

GATTI, C. *Il Teatro alla Scala nella storia e neil'arte, 1778-1958*, Milan 1958

GRAHAM, E. *Princess Mary, Viscountess Lascelles*, London 1930

HAREWOOD, The Earl of *The Tongs and the Bones, The Memoirs of Lord Harewood*, London 1981

HERNDON, B. *Mary Pickford and Douglas Fairbanks*, New York 1977

HEYMANN, C.D. *Poor Little Rich Girl, The Life and Legend of Barbara Hutton*, London, 1985

HIGHAM, C. *The Duchess of Windsor, The Secret Life*, New York 1988

HIGHAM, C. and MOSELEY, R. *Princess Merle, The Romantic Life of Merle Oberon*, Toronto 1983

HINKS, P. *Nineteenth Century Jewellery*, London 1975

HOUGH, R. *Born Royal. The Lives and Loves of the Young Windsors (1894-1937)*, London 1988

HUGHES, G. *Modern Jewellery*, London 1963

JENNING, D. *Barbara Hutton, A Candid Biography of the Richest Woman in the World*, London/New York 1968

KRASHES, L.S. *Harry Winston, The Ultimate Jeweler*, New York 1993

KUNZ, G.F. and STEVENSON, C.H. *The Book of the Pearl*, London 1908

LONGFORD, E. *The Royal House of Windsor*, London 1974

MENKES, S. *The Royal Jewels*, London 1985

—*The Windsor Style*, London 1987

MOREL, B. *The French Crown Jewels*, Antwerp 1988

MORELLA, J and EPSTEIN, E.Z. *Pauleite. The Adventurous Life of Paulette Goddard*, New York,1985

NADELHOFFER, H. *Cartier. Jewelers Extraordinary*, London/New York 1984

NERET, G. *Boucheron, Four Generations of a World Renowned Jeweller*, Paris 1988

O'HIGGENS, P. *Madame. An Intimate Biography of Helena Rubinstein*, New York 1971

PATCH, S.S. *Blue Mystery The Story of the Hope Diamond*, Washington, D.C., 1976

PEPPER, T. *Dorothy Wilding. The Pursuit of Perfection*, London 1991

PETACCO, A. *Regina. La vita e i segreti di Maria Jose*, Milan 1997

PRODDOW, P. and HEALEY, D. *American Jewelry, Glamour and Tradition*, New York 1987

—*Hollywood Jewels*, New York 1992

RAULET, S. *Van Cleef & Arpels*, Paris 1986

RUBIN, N. *American Empress. The Life and Times of Marjorie Merriweather Post*, New York 1995

RUBINSTEIN, H. *My Life for Beauty*, London 1965

RUDOE, J. *Cartier 1900-1939*, London/New York 1997

SCARISBRICK, D. *Chaumet, Master Jewellers since 1780*, Paris 1995

SNOWMAN, K., et al. *The Master Jewelers*, London/New York 1990

SPERONI, G. *Umberto II. Il Dramma Segreto dell'Ultimo Re*, Milan 1992

TEBBEL, J. *An American Dynasty*, New York 1947

TWINING, Lord *A History of the Crown Jewels of Europe*, London 1960

VANDERBILT II, A. *Fortune's Children, The Fall of the House of Vanderbilt*, London 1990

VEVER, H. *La Bijouterie française au XIXe siècle*, Paris 1908

VICKERS, H. *Gladys Duchess of Marlborough*, London 1979

—*Cecil Beaton. The Authorized Biography*, London 1985

—*The Private World of the Duke and Duchess of Windsor*, London 1995

WALKER, A. *Joan Crawford, The Ultimate Star*, London/New York 1983

WALSKA, G. *Always Room at the Top*, New York 1943

WAYNE, J.E. *Crawford's Men*, New York 1988

—*Ava's Men, The Private Life of Ava Gardner*, London 1990

WINDSOR, H.R.H. The Duke of, K. G., *A King's Story. The Memoirs of H.R.H. The Duke of Windsor*, London/New York 1951

YOUSSOUPOFF, F. *Avant L'Exil, 1887-1919*, Paris 1952

OTHER PUBLICATIONS

The New York Times, February 6, 1913; *The New York Times*, December 15, 1920;
Catalogue of the Exhibition of Russian Art, 4 June to 13 July 1935, London;
Cartier. Splendeurs de la Joaillerie (Exhibition Catalogue), Lausanne 1996;
Roma Capitale 1970-1971. I Piaceri ed I Giorni: La Moda (Exhibition Catalogue) Rome 1983;
Russia's Treasure of Diamond and Precious Stones (catalogue), under the general supervision of Prof. A.E. Fersman, Moscow 1925

Sources of Illustrations

Bettmann Archives
Cecil Beaton Photographs, Courtesy of Cecil Beaton archives, Sotheby's, London
Christie's, New York
Christie's, Geneva
Christie's, London
Christie's, Hong Kong
Collection, Helena Rubinstein Foundation
Lady Teresa Craven
H.R.H. Prince Dimitri of Yugoslavia
Fürstliches Zentralarchiv, Regensburg
H.R.H. Maria Gabriella of Savoy
H.H. Prince Henry of Hesse
The Hermitage, St Petersburg
Hulton Getty
The Illustrated London News
The Kobal Collection
Mellerio dits Meller
Suzy Menkes
The Mona Bismarck Foundation
Count de la Moussaye
The National Portrait Gallery
Petochi, Rome
Private Collection (Photographed by Clarissa Bruce, London)
Private Collection (Photographed by John Quinn, London)
Private Collection (Photographed by Marc Kuchen, Art Image Studio, Geneva)
Private Collection (Photographed by Otello Bellamio, Milan)
Roger-Viollet, Paris
Sotheby's, New York
Sotheby's Parke Bernet, New York
Sotheby's, Geneva
Sotheby's, London
Sotheby's, Hong Kong
Sotheby's, Milan
John Stuart
Renata Tebaldi
The Umberto II Foundation, Lausanne
Hugo Vickers
Vogue, Conde Nast
Count Giovanni Volpi di Misurata

Index

B&T
4/00